Entity Framework 4 in Action

D1467470

Entity Framework 4
in Action

STEFANO MOSTARDA
MARCO DE SANCTIS
DANIELE BOCHICCHIO

MANNING

Shelter Island

For online information and ordering of this and other Manning books, please visit
www.manning.com. The publisher offers discounts on this book when ordered in quantity.
For more information, please contact

> Special Sales Department
> Manning Publications Co.
> 20 Baldwin Road
> PO Box 261
> Shelter Island, NY 11964
> Email: orders@manning.com

©2011 by Manning Publications Co. All rights reserved.

No part of this publication may be reproduced, stored in a retrieval system, or transmitted, in
any form or by means electronic, mechanical, photocopying, or otherwise, without prior written
permission of the publisher.

Many of the designations used by manufacturers and sellers to distinguish their products are
claimed as trademarks. Where those designations appear in the book, and Manning
Publications was aware of a trademark claim, the designations have been printed in initial caps
or all caps.

⊗ Recognizing the importance of preserving what has been written, it is Manning's policy to have
the books we publish printed on acid-free paper, and we exert our best efforts to that end.
Recognizing also our responsibility to conserve the resources of our planet, Manning books
are printed on paper that is at least 15 percent recycled and processed without the use of
elemental chlorine.

Manning Publications Co.
20 Baldwin Road
PO Box 261
Shelter Island, NY 11964

Development editor: Sebastian Stirling
Copyeditor: Andy Carroll
Typesetter: Dottie Marsico
Cover designer: Marija Tudor

ISBN 978-1-935182-18-4
Printed in the United States of America
1 2 3 4 5 6 7 8 9 10 – MAL – 16 15 14 13 12 11

brief contents

v

contents

foreword

I spend a lot of my time here at Microsoft thinking about complexity—and asking myself lots of questions. My guess is that you do the same.

When we design code, we ask ourselves questions such as these: Can I make this code more readable? Can I write this loop with fewer lines? Can I factor out behavior into a separate class? Can I architect this system so that it is more cohesive?

When we design user interfaces, we ask similar questions: Are we asking the user to make too many decisions? Did we lay out this UI in the clearest possible way? Can we make error states clearer and easier to avoid?

When we design systems, we ask other questions: How many concepts must the user learn? Do those concepts map to things the user knows and cares about? Does everything hang together in a clear, sensible, consistent way?

I think about these things a lot. But first I'd like to answer another question that I often get asked: Just how complicated is the Entity Framework? The answer is, that it depends on what you want to do with it.

To see how simple the Entity Framework is, let's spend five minutes making it jump through a simple set of hoops. You'll need Visual Studio 2010 (the Express editions will work) and SQL Server (again, the Express editions will work just fine). In SQL Server, create a database called "EntityFrameworkIsSimple."

1 Launch Visual Studio 2010.
2 From the View menu, select Server Explorer.
3 In Server Explorer, add a new connection to your EntityFrameworkIsSimple database.

4 Create a new Console Application project, and call it EntityFrameworkIsSimple.

5 Right-click the project and select Add > New Item. In the Add New Item dialog box, select ADO.NET Entity Data Model.

6 Click Add.

7 In the Entity Data Model Wizard that comes up, select Empty Model and click Finish.

8 The entity designer will appear. Right-click in it and select Add > Entity.

9 In the Add Entity dialog box, set the entity name to Person. This will automatically make the entity set People. (The set is the name of the collection to which you'll add new instances of the Person class.)

10 Click OK.

11 A new entity will appear. Right-click on the Properties bar inside of it and select Add > Scalar Property. (Or just click on the Insert key.)

12 Rename the new property to FirstName.

13 Do this again, creating a new property called LastName.

14 Add another entity and call it Book.

15 To this new entity, add a property called Title.

16 Right-click the "Person" text in the Person entity and select Add > Association.

17 In the Add Association dialog box, change the Multiplicity on the Person end to `* (Many)`, and change the Navigation Property value at right, from `Person` to `Authors`.

18 Click OK.

19 At this point, your model should look like this:

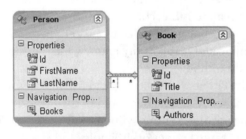

20 Now, right-click on an empty area of the designer and select Generate Database from Model.

21 In the Generate Database Wizard that comes up, provide a connection to your database. Because we've added a connection to the database at the beginning of this walkthrough, it should show up in the drop-down list of available connections.

22 Click Next.

23 The DDL for a database to hold your model shows up. Click Finish.

24 In the T-SQL editor that comes up, right-click and select Execute SQL. Provide your local database information when asked to connect.

That's it! We've got a model. We've got code. We've got a database. We've even got a connection string in App.Config that the designer creates and maintains for you.

Let's take this model for a test drive. Let's name the model:

1 In the designer, right-click in an empty area of the canvas and select Properties.

2 In the Properties window, find the property called Entity Container Name and change its value to `SimpleModel`.

3 In Program.cs, enter the following code into the body of the `Main` function:

```
//Create and write our sample data
using (var context = new SimpleModel()) {
  var person1 = new Person() { FirstName = "Stefano", LastName="Mostarda" };
  var person2 = new Person() { FirstName = "Marco", LastName="De Sanctis" };
  var person3 = new Person() { FirstName = "Daniele", LastName="Bochicchio" };
  var book = new Book() { Title = "Microsoft Entity Framework In Action"};
  book.Authors.Add(person1);
  book.Authors.Add(person2);
  book.Authors.Add(person3);
  context.People.AddObject(person1);
  context.People.AddObject(person2);
  context.People.AddObject(person3);
  context.Books.AddObject(book);
  context.SaveChanges();
}
//Query our sample data
using (var context = new SimpleModel()) {
  var book = context.Books.Include("Authors").First();
  Console.Out.WriteLine("The authors '{0}' are:", book.Title);
  foreach(Person author in book.Authors) {
    Console.Out.WriteLine(" - {0} {1}", author.FirstName, author.LastName);
  }
}
Console.Read();
```

4 Compile and run this code. You should see the following output:

```
The authors 'Microsoft Entity Framework in Action' are:
 - Stefano Mostarda
 - Marco De Sanctis
 - Daniele Bochicchio
```

As you can see, we've created a system that issues queries and updates three different tables. And not a single `join` statement in sight!

Of course, in the real world, we have many other concerns: How do we bind these types to UI elements? How do we send and update them across distributed application tiers? How do we handle concurrency, dynamic querying, and stored procedures? While the Entity Framework may be simple to get started with, the real world is not simple, and the Entity Framework has a host of features for dealing with real-world situations.

Including an example like this may not be standard for a foreword to a book, but I did so to show how easy getting started with Entity Framework is and also to show you where this book comes in. *Entity Framework 4 in Action* will take you from handling transactions to understanding how to deal with performance problems and using ESQL to writing dynamic queries. And it will answer all of your questions along the way—even ones you did not know you had!

I look forward to seeing what you will do with the Entity Framework and to hearing what you want us to work on next. The authors are as excited as I am to show you what is in store in the future!

NOAM BEN-AMI
PROGRAM MANAGER
ENTITY FRAMEWORK TEAM, MICROSOFT

preface

Yatta, we did it! We wrote a book about Entity Framework! It's not our first book, but it's the first one written in English and distributed worldwide. It was a great challenge, but having the opportunity to spread the word about Entity Framework made it worth the effort. Entity Framework is a great tool that speeds up the development of data access code and that can save you days and days of coding. We know coding is our job, but wouldn't you prefer to be more productive while writing less and better code?

Entity Framework is a great O/RM tool that's integrated into the .NET Framework, meaning not only is it free, it's also maintained and improved in each .NET Framework release. The result is that it's a great platform today, and tomorrow it will be an outstanding one that will likely rule over all other O/RM platforms.

When we started planning this book, we had a clear idea in mind: we didn't want to create a reference book; we wanted to create a practical one. We wanted you to read about real-world problems and learn real-world solutions. That's why we developed an example and improved on it throughout the book, avoiding common pitfalls and solving problems that you'd face on the job.

This is a book that we felt was missing among those that are available. You won't find a detailed description of all classes and properties here, but you'll learn the best way to use them and how to combine features to get the most out of Entity Framework. We'd love to hear what you think about the book—you can reach us online at the various addresses listed in the "About this book" section on page xxiv.

It took a long time to write this book, but now that it's in your hands we can stop spending endless nights in front of our monitors and finally sit down and spend more time with our families.

Now it's your turn. Enjoy the read, get your hands dirty, and have fun.

acknowledgments

We can't begin to count all the individuals who contributed to this book, each one helping to improve the final product. All of them deserve a warm thank-you. While we can't name everyone here, we would like to offer special thanks to the following individuals who were particularly helpful:

Sebastian Stirling, our developmental editor at Manning—Sebastian worked with us from the beginning and masterfully transformed a bunch of words and images into an appealing book. Thank you.

Elisa Flasko, Program Manager of the Entity Framework team at Microsoft—Elisa provided valuable information and routed our questions to the right person when she didn't have the answers. Without her, this book wouldn't be so thorough. Thank you.

Noam Ben-Ami, Program Manager of the Entity Framework team at Microsoft—Noam pointed us to the right solutions to many problems, and was especially helpful when we were writing chapter 13. He also wrote the foreword to our book. Thank you.

Alessandro Gallo, an ASP Insider, consultant, and lead author of Manning's *ASP.NET Ajax in Action*—Alessandro didn't contribute to the content of this book, but he was the spark that started everything. Thank you.

Many individuals at Manning worked hard to make this book possible. First of all, special thanks to Michael Stephens and Marjan Bace for believing in us. Others who contributed are Karen Tegtmeyer, Mary Piergies, Maureen Spencer, Andy Carroll, Dottie Marsico, Tiffany Taylor, Susan Harkins, Janet Vail, and Cynthia Kane.

Our reviewers deserve special mention—their suggestions were invaluable. We thank Jonas Bandi, David Barkol, Timothy Binkley-Jones, Margriet Bruggeman, Nikander Bruggeman, Gustavo Cavalcanti, Dave Corun, Freedom Dumlao, Rob Eisenberg, Marc Gravell, Berndt Hamboeck, Jason Jung, Lester Lobo, Darren Neimke,

Braj Panda, Christian Siegers, Andrew Seimer, Alex Thissen, Dennis van der Stelt, and Frank Wang. We'd also like to thank Deepak Vohra, our technical proofreader, for the outstanding job he did reviewing the final manuscript during production.

Last, but not least, thank you, dear reader, for your trust in our book. We hope that it will help you in your everyday job and will encourage you to fall in love with the world of O/RMs.

In addition to the people we've already mentioned, there are others who are important in our lives. Even if they didn't contribute to the book, they contributed to keeping us on track during the writing process. We acknowledge them below.

STEFANO MOSTARDA

I'd like to thank my wife Sara for her support and patience, as well as my family (yes, the book is finally done!). Special thanks to my closest friends (in alphabetical order): Federico, Gabriele, Gianni, and Riccardo. Of course, I can't help mentioning Filippo, who already bought a copy of the book. And a big thank-you to William and Annalisa for their friendship and invaluable support.

My last words are for Marco and Daniele: thank you, guys!

MARCO DE SANCTIS

My thanks to Stefano and Daniele. It was a privilege to work with such smart and funny guys. And thanks to the whole ASPItalia.com team. I'm proud to be a part of it.

Special thanks to my family, and to Barbara, for their support and their patience. You have all my love.

DANIELE BOCHICCHIO

I would like to thank my wife Noemi for her support and patience, and for giving me our beautiful sons, Alessio and Matteo. A big thank-you to my parents for letting me play with computers when I was a kid, and to my family for supporting me.

A special thank-you to Stefano for the opportunity to help with this book. And thanks to both Stefano and Marco for sharing their passion for Entity Framework. You guys rock!

about this book

Entity Framework is the Microsoft-recommended tool to read and persist data inside a relational database. With this software, Microsoft has entered the O/RM market with a reliable product that significantly eases data access development.

This book will take you from the apprentice to the master level in the Entity Framework technology. You can think of this book as a guided tour through Entity Framework features and best practices. When you have finished reading *Entity Framework 4 in Action*, you'll be able to confidently design, develop, and deliver applications that rely on Entity Framework to persist business data.

WHO SHOULD READ THIS BOOK?

This book was written for all Entity Framework developers, whether you develop small home applications or the largest enterprise systems. Everything from home DVD library applications to e-commerce solutions that interact with many heterogeneous systems and store lots of information can benefit from Entity Framework, and this book will show you how.

ROADMAP

This book will walk you through the creation of an application from scratch, and will show you how to keep improving it with various Entity Framework features. This Entity Framework tour will cover all of Framework's features over the course of nineteen chapters, grouped in four parts.

In part 1 we introduce the basics of the O/RM pattern and show you the fundamentals of Entity Framework as we create the foundation for an application.

Chapter 1 provides a high-level overview of the O/RM pattern and of the Entity Framework components. By the end of this chapter, you'll understand why O/RM tools are so useful and how Entity Framework accomplishes its tasks.

Chapter 2 shows how you can create an application from scratch and how to persist objects in the database. First, you'll learn two ways of designing an application using Entity Framework. Then, after the application is created, you'll learn how to read, manipulate, and persist data. By the end of this chapter, you'll have a clear understanding of the advantages of adopting Entity Framework.

In part 2 of the book, we discuss the main building blocks of Entity Framework in detail: mapping, querying, and persistence.

Chapter 3 covers the basics of querying. Here you'll learn about the main component that enables Entity Framework to work with objects. You'll also discover how Entity Framework enables you to write queries against your model that will successfully hit the database.

Chapter 4 focuses on querying with LINQ to Entities. In this chapter, you'll learn how to filter, group, project, and join data using the main query language of Entity Framework. By the end of this chapter, you'll be able to perform any type of query.

Chapter 5 discusses mapping between entities in the model and the database. Here you'll learn how to accomplish this visually with the designer, but you'll also learn how to manually modify the mapping file. By the end of this chapter, you'll have a full knowledge of the mapping mechanism in Entity Framework.

Chapter 6 tours the entity lifecycle. You'll learn how Entity Framework treats entities, what state an entity can be in, how to modify the state, and how state affects an entity's persistence. By the end of the chapter, you'll be able to write code that prepares your objects for persistence into the database.

Chapter 7 discusses persisting objects into the database. In chapter 6 you learned how to prepare entities for persistence; here you'll learn how to actually save them. This subject has many intricacies and pitfalls, especially where related entities are involved. This chapter focuses on these potential problems so that you can understand and avoid them. By the end of the chapter, you'll be able to persist any entity in any way you need.

Chapter 8 covers Entity Framework's concurrency and transaction features. In the first part of the chapter, you'll be introduced to the concept of concurrency and what problems it solves when data is saved to the database. Then you'll learn how Entity Framework lets you easily manage concurrency. Finally, you'll learn how Entity Framework manages transactions to persist multiple entities, and how you can extend a transaction's lifetime to execute custom commands.

Part 3 of the book will show you how to take advantage of Entity Framework's most advanced features.

Chapter 9 introduces Entity SQL. Entity SQL is Entity Framework's other querying language, and it's still the most powerful (although less appealing than LINQ to Entities).

In this chapter, we'll take the LINQ to Entities examples from chapter 4 and rewrite them in Entity SQL. You can see them side by side and choose the approach that is easier for you. By the end of this chapter, you'll have a full knowledge of all the querying techniques Entity Framework offers.

Chapter 10 covers stored procedures. Here you'll learn how to have Entity Framework call stored procedures to query and update entities instead of having it generate SQL for you. By the end of this chapter, you'll be able to create your own set of stored procedures and have Entity Framework invoke them, so that your DBA is happy.

Chapter 11 discusses views and functions embedded in mapping. You'll see how to create internal views that can be queried easily, and how to create functions that can be reused when querying with both LINQ to Entities and Entity SQL. By the end of this chapter, you'll be able to write queries that are easy to maintain and reusable.

Chapter 12 discusses how to retrieve mapping information. Chapter 5 explains how to map your model classes to database tables and views; in this chapter you'll learn how to retrieve this mapping information. You'll also see some real-world examples that will demonstrate why this technique is valuable. After finishing this chapter, you'll be able to write powerful generic code that takes data from mapping files.

Chapter 13 covers code generation. Here you'll discover how Entity Framework is integrated with Visual Studio, and how this integration lets you create code and even generate database scripts starting with mapping information. You'll also discover how to customize the Entity Framework designer inside Visual Studio. After you've finished this chapter, you'll be able to fully customize the designer, adding behaviors that simplify development.

In part 4 of the book, we'll show you how to best use Entity Framework with different types of applications: Windows, web, and web services applications.

Chapter 14 discusses application design. You'll learn about the classic three-layer pattern and then go on to the Domain Model pattern. Finally, you'll read about the famous Repository pattern, and learn why it's a great choice for many applications. By the end of this chapter, you'll be able to create a well-designed and layered application.

Chapter 15 explains how to integrate Entity Framework into ASP.NET applications. In this chapter, you'll read about ASP.NET controls and about best practices for handling objects. This will enable you to create web applications using the correct patterns.

Chapter 16 discusses how to create web service applications. Here you'll learn about specific features dedicated to the web service environment and how and when to use them instead of resorting to other techniques. By the end of this chapter, you'll have a strong understanding of web services and Entity Framework integration.

Chapter 17 explains how to integrate Entity Framework into Windows applications. Here you'll discover how to let your model classes implement a specific interface so that they are integrated with the data-binding capabilities of Windows Form and WPF applications. By the end of this chapter, you'll be able to face everyday problems involving these types of applications.

Chapter 18 covers testing. Here you'll learn how to test the code that accesses the database and your repositories, and how to create batteries of tests to reveal if your modifications have broken something.

Chapter 19 discusses performance. You'll learn how Entity Framework performance compares to performance in the classic ADO.NET approach. You'll also learn some tricks and tips to improve performance in various situations. By the end of the chapter, you'll be able to boost the performance of your data access code to the edge.

Appendix A introduces LINQ. LINQ to Entities is the most popular querying language for Entity Framework. It's a dialect of LINQ, so to better understand it you should have a good knowledge of LINQ. That's what this appendix offers.

Appendix B presents some good Entity Framework tips. You won't learn about new features here, but you'll learn how to merge existing features to produce powerful behaviors. This is your ultimate resource in understanding how much power Entity Framework hands you.

CODE CONVENTIONS

All source code in listings or set off from the text is in a `fixed-width font like` this to separate it from ordinary text. The .NET code is provided in both C# and Visual Basic so that you should be comfortable with it, whatever your development language. For longer lines of code that won't fit on the page, a code-continuation character (➡) is used to indicate lines that are broken on the page but shouldn't be broken in the code. Code annotations accompany many of the listings, highlighting important concepts. In some cases, numbered bullets link to explanations that follow the listing.

SOURCE CODE DOWNLOADS

All the examples in this book can be downloaded from http://www.entityframeworkinaction.com/download.aspx or from the publisher's website at www.manning.com/EntityFramework4inAction. The code comes in both VB and C# versions.

The code comes with a Visual Studio 2010 solution file so you only need Visual Studio 2010 to run the examples. We did not try to open the solution file with Visual Studio Express 2010 (that is the free version), but it's likely to work.

AUTHOR ONLINE

The purchase of *Entity Framework 4 in Action* includes free access to a private forum run by Manning Publications where you can make comments about the book, ask technical questions, and receive help from the authors and other users. You can access and subscribe to the forum at http://www.manning.com/EntityFramework4inAction. This page provides information on how to get on the forum once you're registered, what kind of help is available, and the rules of conduct in the forum.

Manning's commitment to our readers is to provide a venue where a meaningful dialogue between individual readers and between readers and the authors can take place. It isn't a commitment to any specific amount of participation on the part of the authors, whose contributions to the book's forum remain voluntary (and unpaid). We suggest you try asking the authors some challenging questions, lest their interest stray! The Author Online forum and the archives of previous discussions will be accessible from the publisher's website as long as the book is in print.

In addition to the Author Online forum available on Manning's website, you may also contact us about this book, or anything else, through one of the following avenues:

Stefano's blog—http://blogs.5dlabs.it/author/mostarda.aspx
Daniele's blog—http://blogs.5dlabs.it/author/bochicchio.aspx
Marco's blog—http://blogs.aspitalia.com/cradle

All comments sent to these blogs are moderated. We post most of the comments, but if you include your email address or phone number, we won't post the comment out of respect for your privacy.

ABOUT THE AUTHORS

STEFANO MOSTARDA is a Microsoft MVP in the Data Platform category. He's a software architect mainly focused on web applications, and is a cofounder of 5DLabs.it, a consulting agency specializing in ASP.NET, Silverlight, Windows Phone 7, and the .NET Framework. Stefano is a professional speaker at many Italian conferences on Microsoft technologies and he's a well-known author. He has written many books for the Italian market and is a coauthor of Manning's *ASP.NET 4.0 in Practice*. He's one of the leaders of the ASPItalia.com Network and a content manager of the LINQNItalia.com website dedicated to LINQ and Entity Framework. You can read his technical deliriums both on his blog and on Twitter at http://twitter.com/sm15455/.

MARCO DE SANCTIS has been designing and developing enterprise applications in distributed scenarios for the last seven years. He started developing with ASP.NET as soon as it came out, and since then has become an application architect. Through the years he specialized in building distributed services, widening his knowledge to encompass technologies like Workflow Foundation, Windows Communication Foundation, LINQ, and ADO.NET Entity Framework. Today he works as a senior software engineer for major Italian companies in the IT market. In his spare time, he's a content manager at ASPItalia.com and has recently been named a Microsoft Most Valuable Professional in ASP.NET. You can read his thoughts on twitter at http://twitter.com/crad77.

DANIELE BOCHICCHIO is a cofounder of 5DLabs.it, a consulting agency specializing in ASP.NET, Silverlight, Windows Phone 7, and the .NET Framework. He has worked on a lot of cool projects with many different technologies. Daniele is a well-known professional speaker and author, and you can find him at developer-focused events worldwide. He has written several books, both in Italian and English, including *ASP.NET 4.0 in Practice*, published by Manning. He is also the network manager of the ASPItalia.com Network, the largest Italian .NET Framework community. Daniele's personal website is located at http://www.bochicchio.com/ and he shares his thoughts in 140 chars or less at http://twitter.com/dbochicchio/.

about the cover illustration

The figure on the cover of *Entity Framework 4.0 in Action* is captioned "Limonaro," or a vendor of lemons. The illustration is taken from a collection of *Italian Fine Arts, Prints, and Photographs* that includes hand-colored drawings of Italian regional dress costumes from the nineteenth century. Wearing a white linen shirt, blue breeches, and a wide-brimmed straw hat, and carrying a basket of lemons in one hand and a jug of lemonade in the other, the itinerant limonaro was a welcome figure in the streets of Italian towns and villages, especially in the hot summer weather.

The diversity of the drawings in the collection speaks vividly of the uniqueness and individuality of the world's towns and provinces just 200 years ago. Isolated from each other, people spoke different dialects and languages. In the streets or in the countryside, it was easy to identify where they lived and what their trade or station in life was just by what they were wearing.

Dress codes have changed since then and the diversity by region, so rich at the time, has faded away. It is now often hard to tell the inhabitant of one continent from another. Perhaps, trying to view it optimistically, we have traded a cultural and visual diversity for a more varied personal life. Or a more varied and interesting intellectual and technical life.

We at Manning celebrate the inventiveness, the initiative, and the fun of the computer business with book covers based on the rich diversity of regional life of two centuries ago brought back to life by the pictures from collections such as this one.

Part 1

Redefining your
data-access strategy

Welcome to *Entity Framework 4 in Action*. Entity Framework is the O/RM tool that Microsoft introduced with .NET Framework 3.5 Service Pack 1 and has now updated to version 4.0. This book will enable you to use Entity Framework 4.0 to quickly build data-centric applications in a robust and model-driven way. If you're an Entity Framework novice, you'll learn how to create an application from scratch and build it correctly. If you're an experienced Entity Framework developer, you'll find lots of in-depth coverage that will improve your knowledge of this powerful tool.

The book is divided into four parts, and part 1 dives right into the fundamentals of Entity Framework. In chapter 1, you'll discover what an O/RM tool is, and when and why it should be used. You'll then learn about the modules that make up the Entity Framework architecture and how they interact with each other and with you.

Chapter 2 will show you how to build an application from scratch using Entity Framework. Here you'll be introduced to the example application we'll use throughout the book, and you'll learn how to create its model and automatically generate code. In the last section, you'll get an overview of how to read data from and persist data to a database.

Data access reloaded: Entity Framework

1

This chapter covers

- `DataSet` and classic ADO.NET approach
- Object model approach
- Object/relational mismatch
- Entity Framework as a solution

When you design an application, you have to decide how to access and represent data. This decision is likely the most important one you'll make in terms of application performance and ease of development and maintainability. In every project we've worked on, the persistence mechanism was a relational database. Despite some attempts to introduce object databases, the relational database is still, and will be for many years, the main persistence mechanism.

Nowadays, relational databases offer all the features you need to persist and retrieve data. You have tables to maintain data, views to logically organize them so that they're easier to consume, stored procedures to abstract the application from the database structure and improve performance, foreign keys to relate records in different tables, security checks to avoid unauthorized access to sensitive data, the

3

ability to transparently encrypt and decrypt data, and so on. There's a lot more under the surface, but these features are ones most useful to developers.

When you must store data *persistently*, relational databases are your best option. On the other hand, when you must *temporarily* represent data in an application, objects are the best way to go. Features like inheritance, encapsulation, and method overriding allow a better coding style that simplifies development compared with the legacy DataSet approach.

Before we delve into the details of Entity Framework, we'll take the first three sections of this chapter to discuss how moving from the DataSet approach to the object-based approach eases development, and how this different way of working leads to the adoption of an object/relational mapping (O/RM) tool like Entity Framework.

When you opt for using objects, keep in mind that there are differences between the relational and object-oriented paradigms, and the role of Entity Framework is to deal with them. It lets the developer focus on the business problems and ignore, to a certain extent, the persistence side. Such object/relational differences are hard to overcome. In section 1.4, you'll discover that there is a lot of work involved in accommodating them. Then, the last sections of the chapter will show how Entity Framework comes to our aid in solving the mismatch between the paradigms and offering a convenient way of accessing data.

By the end of this chapter, you'll have a good understanding of what an O/RM tool is, what it's used for, and why you should always think about using one when creating an application that works with a database.

1.1 Getting started with data access

Data in tables is stored as a list of rows, and every row is made of columns. This efficient tabular format has driven how developers represent data in applications for many years. Classic ASP and VB6 developers use recordsets to retrieve data from databases—the *recordset* is a generic container that organizes the data retrieved in the same way it's physically stored: in rows and columns. When .NET made its appearance, developers had a brand new object to maintain in-memory data: the *dataset*. Although this control is completely different from the recordset we used before the .NET age, it has similar purposes and, more important, has data organized in the same manner: in rows and columns.

Although this representation is efficient in some scenarios, it lacks a lot of features like type safety, performance, and manageability. We'll discuss this in more detail when we talk about datasets in the next section.

In the Java world, a structure like the dataset has always existed, but its use is now discouraged except for the simplest applications. In the .NET world, we're facing the beginning of this trend too. You may be wondering, "If I don't use general-purpose containers, what do I use to represent data?" The answer is easy: *objects*.

Objects are superior to datasets in every situation because they don't suffer from the limitations that general-purpose structures do. They offer type safety, autocompletion in Visual Studio, compile-time checking, better performance, and more. We'll talk more about objects in section 1.2.

The benefits you gain from using objects come at a cost, resulting from the differences between the object-oriented paradigm and the relational model used by databases. There are three notable differences:

- *Relationships*—In a tabular structure, you use foreign keys on columns; with classes, you use references to other classes.
- *Equality*—In a database, the data always distinguishes one row from another, whereas in the object world you may have two objects of the same type with the same data that are still different.
- *Inheritance*—The use of inheritance is common in object-oriented languages, but in the database world it isn't supported.

This just touches the surface of a problem known as the *object/relational mismatch*, which will be covered in section 1.4.

In this big picture, O/RM takes care of *object persistence*. The O/RM tool sits between the application code and the database and takes care of retrieving data and transforming it into objects efficiently, tracks objects' changes, and reflects them to the database. This ensures that you don't have to write almost 80 percent of the data-access code (that's a rough estimate based on our experience).

1.2 Developing applications using database-like structures

Over the last decade, we have been developing applications using VB6, Classic ASP, Delphi, and .NET, and all of these technologies use external components or objects to access databases and maintain data internally. Both tasks are similar in each language, but they're especially similar for internal data representation: data is organized in structures built on the concept of rows and columns. The result is that applications manage data the same way it's organized in the database.

Why do different vendors offer developers the same programming model? The answer is simple: developers are accustomed to tabular representation, and they don't need to learn anything else to be productive. Furthermore, these generic structures can contain any data as long as it can be represented in rows and columns. Potentially, even data coming from XML files, web services, or rest calls can be organized this way.

As a result, vendors have developed a subset of objects that can represent any information without us having to write a single line of code. These objects are called *data containers*.

1.2.1 Using datasets and data readers as data containers

At the beginning of our .NET experience, many of us used *datasets* and *data readers*. With a few lines of code, we had an object that could be bound to any data-driven control and that, in case of the data reader, provided impressive performance. By using a data adapter in combination with a dataset, we had a fully featured framework for reading and updating data. We had never been so productive. Visual Studio played its

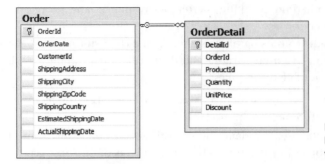

Figure 1.1 The Order table has a related OrderDetail table that contains its details.

role, too. Its wizards and tight integration with these objects gave us the feeling that everything could be created by dragging and dropping and writing a few lines of code.

Let's look at an example. Suppose you have a database with Order and Order-Detail tables (as shown in figure 1.1), and you have to create a simple web page where all orders are shown.

The first step is creating a connection to the database. Then, you need to create an adapter and finally execute the query, pouring data into a data table that you bind to a list control. These steps are shown in the following listing.

Listing 1.1   Displaying a list of orders

C#
```csharp
using (SqlConnection conn = new SqlConnection(connString))
{
  using (SqlDataAdapter da = new SqlDataAdapter("Select * from order",
    conn))
  {
    DataTable dt = new DataTable();
    da.Fill(dt);
    ListView1.DataSource = dt;
    ListView1.DataBind();
  }
}
```

VB
```vb
Using conn As New SqlConnection(connString)
  Using da As New SqlDataAdapter("Select * from order", conn)
    Dim dt As New DataTable()
    da.Fill(dt)
    ListView1.DataSource = dt
    ListView1.DataBind()
  End Using
End Using
```

By doing a bit of refactoring, you get the connection and the adapter in a single method call, so the amount of code is further reduced. That's all you need to do to display the orders.

After playing with the prototype, your customer changes the specifications and wants to see the details under each order in the list. The solution becomes more challenging, because you can choose different approaches:

- *Retrieve data from the Order table and then query the details for each order.* This approach is by far the easiest to code. By intercepting when an order is bound to the `ListView`, you can query its details and show them.
- *Retrieve data joining the Order and OrderDetail tables.* The result is a Cartesian product of the join between the tables, and it contains as many rows as are in the OrderDetail table. This means the resultset can't be passed to a control as is, but must be processed locally first.
- *Retrieve all orders and all details in two distinct queries.* This is by far the best approach, because it performs only two queries against the database. You can bind orders to a control, intercept when each order is bound, and filter the in-memory details to show only those related to the current order.

Whichever path you choose, there is an important point to consider: *you're bound to the database structure.* Your code is determined by the database structure and the way you retrieve data; each choice leads to different code, and changing tactics would be painful.

Let's move on. Your customer now needs a page to display data about a single order so it can be printed. The page must contain labels for the order data and a `ListView` for the details. Supposing you retrieve the data in two distinct commands, the code would look like this.

Listing 1.2   Displaying data for a single order

C#
```csharp
using (SqlConnection conn = new SqlConnection(connString))
{
  using (SqlCommand cm = new SqlCommand("Select * from order
➥ where orderid = 1", conn))
  {
    conn.Open();
    using (SqlDataReader rd = cm.ExecuteReader())
    {
      rd.Read();
      date.Text = ((DateTime)rd["OrderDate"]).ToString();
      shippingAddress.Text = rd["ShippingAddress"].ToString();
      shippingCity.Text = rd["ShippingCity"].ToString();
    }
    using (SqlDataReader rd = cm.ExecuteReader())
    {
      details.DataSource = rd;
      details.DataBind();
    }
  }
}
```

VB
```vb
Using conn As New SqlConnection(connString)
  Using cm As New SqlCommand("Select * from order
➥     where orderid = 1", conn)
    conn.Open()
    Using rd As SqlDataReader = cm.ExecuteReader()
```

```
      rd.Read()
      [date].Text = DirectCast(rd("OrderDate"), DateTime).ToString()
      shippingAddress.Text = rd("ShippingAddress").ToString()
      shippingCity.Text = rd("ShippingCity").ToString()
    End Using
    Using rd As SqlDataReader = cm.ExecuteReader()
      details.DataSource = rd
      details.DataBind()
    End Using
  End Using
End Using
```

The way you access data is completely unsafe and generic. On the one hand, you have great flexibility, because you can easily write generic code to implement functions that are unaware of the table field names and rely on configuration. On the other hand, you lose *type safety*. You identify a field specifying its name using a string; if the name isn't correct, you get an exception only at runtime.

You lose control not only on field names, but even on datatypes. Data readers and data tables (which are the items that contain data in a dataset) return column values as `Object` types (the .NET base type), so you need to cast them to the correct type (or invoke the `ToString` method as well). This is an example of the object/relational mismatch we mentioned before.

Now that you've seen the big picture of the generic data-container world, let's investigate its limitations and look at why this approach is gradually being discontinued in enterprise applications.

1.2.2   *The strong coupling problem*

In the previous example, you were asked to determine the best way to display orders and details in a grid. What you need is a list of orders, where every order has a list of details associated with it.

Data readers and data tables don't allow you to transparently retrieve data without affecting the user interface code. This means your application is strongly coupled to the database structure, and any change to that structure requires your code to do some heavy lifting. This is likely the most important reason why the use of these objects is discouraged. Even if you have the same data in memory, how it's retrieved affects how it's internally represented. This is clearly a fetching problem, and it's something that should be handled in the data-access code, and not in the user interface.

In many projects we have worked on, the database serves just one application, so the data is organized so the code can consume it easily. This isn't always the case. Sometimes applications are built on top of an existing database, and nothing can be modified because other applications are using the database. In such situations, you're even more coupled to the database and its data organization, which might be extremely different from how you would expect. For instance, orders might be stored in one table and shipping addresses in another. The data access code could reduce the impact, but the fetching problem would remain.

And what happens when the name of a column changes? This happens frequently when an application is under development. The result is that interface code needs to be adapted to reflect this change; your code is very fragile because a search and replace is the only way to achieve this goal. You can mitigate the problem by modifying the SQL and adding an alias to maintain the old name in the resultset, but this causes more confusion and soon turns into a new problem.

1.2.3 *The loose typing problem*

To retrieve the value of a column stored in a data reader or a data table, you usually refer to it using a constant string. Code that uses a data table typically looks something like this:

C#
```
object shippingAddress = orders.Rows[0]["ShippingAddress"];
```

VB
```
Dim shippingAddress As Object = orders.Rows(0)("ShippingAddress")
```

The variable `shippingAddress` is of type `System.Object`, so it can contain potentially any type of data. You may know it contains a string value, but to use it like a string, you have to explicitly perform a casting or conversion operation:

C#
```
string shippingAddress = (string)orders.Rows[0]["ShippingAddress"];
string shippingAddress = orders.Rows[0]["ShippingAddress"].ToString();
```

VB
```
Dim shippingAddress As String = _
  DirectCast(orders.Rows(0)("ShippingAddress"), String)
Dim shippingAddress As String = _
  orders.Rows(0)("ShippingAddress").ToString()
```

Casting and converting cost, both in terms of performance and memory usage, because casting from a value type to a reference type and vice versa causes boxing and unboxing to occur. In some cases, conversion can require the use of the `IConvertible` interface, which causes an internal cast.

Data readers have an advantage over data tables. They offer typed methods to access fields without needing explicit casts. Such methods accept an integer parameter that stands for the index of the column in the row. Data readers also have a method that returns the index of a column, given its name, but its use tends to clutter the code and is subject to typing errors:

C#
```
string address = rd.GetString(rd.GetOrdinal("ShippingAddress"));
string address = rd.GetString(rd.GetOrdinal("ShipingAdres")); //exception
```

VB
```
Dim address As String = _
  rd.GetString(rd.GetOrdinal("ShippingAddress"))
Dim address As String = _
  rd.GetString(rd.GetOrdinal("ShipingAdres")) 'exception
```

The problem resulting from column name changes, discussed in the previous section, involves even the loss of control at compile time. It's not desirable to discover at runtime that a column name has changed or that you have mistyped a column name. Compilers can't help avoid such problems because they have no knowledge of what the name of the column is.

1.2.4 *The performance problem*

`DataSet` is likely one of the most complex structures in the .NET class library. It contains one or more `DataTable` instances, and each of these has a list of `DataRow` objects made of a set of `DataColumn`objects. A `DataTable` can have a primary key consisting of one or more columns and can declare that certain columns have a foreign key relationship with columns in another `DataTable`. Columns support versioning, meaning that if you change the value, both the old and the new value are stored in the column to perform concurrency checks. To send updates to the database, you have to use a `DbDataAdapter` class (or, more precisely, one of its derived classes), which is yet another object.

Although these features are often completely useless and are ignored by developers, `DataSet` internally creates an empty collection of these objects. This might be a negligible waste of resources for a standalone application, but in a multiuser environment with thousands of requests, like a web application, this becomes unacceptable. It's useless to optimize database performance, tweaking indexes, modifying SQL, adding hints, and so on, if you waste resources creating structures you don't need.

In contrast, `DataReader` is built for different scenarios. A `DataTable` downloads all data read from the database into memory, but often you don't need all the data in memory and could instead fetch it record by record from the database. Another situation is in data updates; you often need to read data but don't need to update it. In such cases, some features, like row versioning, are useless. `DataReader` is the best choice in such situations, because it retrieves data in a read-only (faster) way. Although it boosts performance, `DataReader` can still suffer from the casting and conversion problems of `DataSet`, but this loss of time is less than the gain you get from its use.

All of these problems may seem overwhelming, but many applications out there benefit from the use of database-like structures. Even more will be developed in the future using these objects without problems. Nonetheless, in enterprise-class projects, where the code base is large and you need more control and flexibility, you can leverage the power of object-oriented programming and use classes to organize your data.

1.3 *Using classes to organize data*

We're living in the object-oriented era. Procedural languages still exist, but they're restricted to particular environments. For instance, COBOL is still required for applications that run on mainframe architectures.

Using classes is a natural choice for most applications today. Classes are the foundation of object-oriented programming. They easily represent data, perform actions, publish events, and so on. From a data organization point of view, classes express data through methods and properties (which, in the end, are special methods).

By using classes, you can choose your internal representation of data without worrying about how it's persisted—you need to know nothing about the storage mechanism. It could be a database, a web service, an XML file, or something else. Representing data without having any knowledge of the storage mechanism is referred to as *persistence ignorance,* and the classes used in this scenario are called *POCOs* (plain old CLR objects).

The use of classes offers several benefits that are particularly important in enterprise applications:

- *Strong typing*—You no longer need to cast or convert every column in a row to get its value in the correct type (or, at least, you don't have to do it in the interface code).
- *Compile-time checking*—Classes expose properties to access data; they don't use a generic method or indexer. If you incorrectly enter the name of a property, you immediately get a compilation error. You no longer need to run the application to find typos.
- *Ease of development*—Editors like Visual Studio offer IntelliSense to speed up development. IntelliSense offers the developer hints about the properties, events, and methods exposed by a class. But if you use `DataSet`, editors can't help you in any way, because columns are retrieved using strings, which aren't subject to IntelliSense.
- *Storage-agnostic interface*—You don't have to shape classes to accommodate the structure of the database, which gives you maximum flexibility. Classes have their own structure, and although it's often similar to that of the table they're related to, it doesn't need to be. You no longer have to worry about database organization and data retrieval, because you code against classes. Data-retrieval details are delegated to a specific part of the application, and the interface code always remains the same.

To get a look at these concepts in practice, let's refactor the example from the previous section.

1.3.1 Using classes to represent data

Let's start from scratch again. The customer wants to display orders in a grid. The first step is to create an `Order` class to contain order data, as shown in figure 1.2.

The `Order` class has the same structure as the related database table. The only obvious difference here is that you have .NET types (`String`, `Int32`, `DateTime`) instead of database types (int, varchar, date).

Figure 1.2
The `Order` class contains data from the Order table.

The second step is to create a class with a method that reads data from the database and transforms it into objects, as in the following listing. The container class is often in a separate assembly, known as *data layer*.

Listing 1.3   Creating a list of orders

C#

```csharp
public List<Order> GetOrders()
{
  using (SqlConnection conn = new SqlConnection(connString))
  {
    using (SqlCommand comm = new SqlCommand("select * from orders", conn))
    {
      conn.Open();
      using(SqlDataReader r = comm.ExecuteReader())
      {
        List<Order> orders = new List<Order>();
        while (rd.Read())
        {
          orders.Add(
            new Order
            {
              CustomerCode = (string)rd["CustomerCode"],
              OrderDate = (DateTime)rd["OrderDate"],
              OrderCode = (string)rd["OrderCode"],
              ShippingAddress = (string)rd["ShippingAddress"],
              ShippingCity = (string)rd["ShippingCity"],
              ShippingZipCode = (string)rd["ShippingZipCode"],
              ShippingCountry = (string)rd["ShippingCountry"]
            }
          );
        }
        return orders;
      }
    }
  }
}

...

ListView1.DataSource = new OrderManager().GetOrders();
ListView1.DataBind();
```

VB

```vb
Public Function GetOrders() As List(Of Order)
  Using conn As New SqlConnection(connString)
    Using comm As New SqlCommand("select * from orders", conn)
      conn.Open()
      Using r As SqlDataReader = comm.ExecuteReader()
        Dim orders As New List(Of Order)()
        While rd.Read()
          orders.Add(New Order() With {
            .CustomerCode = DirectCast(rd("CustomerCode"), String),
            .OrderDate = DirectCast(rd("OrderDate"), DateTime),
            .OrderCode = DirectCast(rd("OrderCode"), String),
```

```
                .ShippingAddress = DirectCast(rd("ShippingAddress"), String),
                .ShippingCity = DirectCast(rd("ShippingCity"), String),
                .ShippingZipCode = DirectCast(rd("ShippingZipCode"), String),
                .ShippingCountry = DirectCast(rd("ShippingCountry"), String)
            })
        End While
        Return orders
      End Using
    End Using
  End Using
End Function

...

ListView1.DataSource = New OrderManager().GetOrders()
ListView1.DataBind()
```

"What a huge amount of code!" That's often people's first reaction to the code in listing 1.3. And they're right; that's a lot of code, particularly if you compare it with listing 1.1, which uses a dataset. If your application has to show simple data like this, the dataset approach is more desirable. But when things get complex, classes help a lot more.

Let's take a look at the next required feature: displaying a single order in a form. After the order is retrieved, displaying its properties using classes is far more straightforward:

C#
```
shippingAddress.Text = order.ShippingAddress;
shippingCity.Text = order.ShippingCity;
```

VB
```
shippingAddress.Text = order.ShippingAddress
shippingCity.Text = order.ShippingCity
```

The final step is showing the orders and related details in a grid. Doing this requires in-depth knowledge because it introduces the concept of *models*. You can't represent orders and details in a single class—you have to use two separate classes the same way you do with tables. In the next section, we'll discuss this technique.

1.3.2 *From a single class to the object model*

You have now seen how to develop a single standalone class and how to instantiate it using data from a database, but the real power comes when you create more classes and begin to link them to each other (for instance, when you create an OrderDetail class that contains data from the OrderDetail table).

In a database, the relationship between an order and its detail lines is described using a foreign key constraint between the OrderId column in the Order table and the OrderId column in the OrderDetail table. From a database design point of view, this is the correct approach.

In the object-oriented world, you have to follow another path. There's no point in creating an OrderDetail class and giving it an OrderId property. The best solution is to take advantage of a peculiar feature of classes: they can have properties whose type is a user-defined class. This means the `Order` class can hold a reference to a list of `OrderDetail` objects, and the `OrderDetail` class can have a reference to `Order`.

When you create these relationships, you're beginning to create an *object model*. An object model is a set of classes related to each other that describe the data consumed by an application.

The real power of the object model emerges when you need to show orders and their related details in a single grid. In section 1.2.1, there was a fetching problem with a spectrum of solutions. Every one was different, but what's worse is that every one required a different coding style on the interface.

Using classes, your interface code is completely isolated from fetching problems because it no longer cares about the database. A specific part of the application will fetch data and return objects. This is where the storage-agnostic interface feature of using classes comes into play.

The Object Model and Domain Model patterns

The *Object Model* and *Domain Model* patterns are often considered to refer to the same thing. They may initially look exactly the same, because both carry data extracted from storage. But after digging a bit, you'll find that they have differences: the object model contains only the data, whereas the domain model contains data and exposes behavior.

The `Order` class that we've been looking at is a perfect expression of an object model. It has properties that hold data and nothing more. You could add a computed property that reports the full address by combining the values of other properties, but this would be a helper method. It wouldn't add any behavior to the class.

If you want to move on from an object model to a domain model, you have to add behavior to the class. To better understand the concept of behavior, suppose you need to know if an order exceeds the allowed total amount. With an object model, you have to build a method on another class. In this method, you call the database to retrieve the maximum amount allowed, and then compare it with the amount of the order. If you opt for a domain model, on the other hand, you can add an `IsCorrect` method to the `Order` class and perform the check there. This way you're adding behavior and expressiveness to the `Order` class.

Creating and maintaining a domain model isn't at all easy. It forces the software architect to make choices about the design of the application. In particular, classes must be responsible for their own validation and must always be in a valid state. (For instance, an order must always have a related customer.) These checks may contribute to code bloating in the classes; so, to avoid confusion, you may have to create other classes that are responsible for validation, and keep those classes in the domain model.

The details of the Object Model and Domain Model patterns are beyond the scope of this book and won't be covered, but plenty of books focus on this subject and all its implications. We recommend *Domain Driven Design* by Eric Evans (Addison-Wesley Professional, 2004). We'll discuss the Domain Model pattern and Entity Framework in chapter 14.

The example we've looked at so far is oversimplified. You'll have noticed that the `Order` class has a `CustomerId` property and the `OrderDetail` class has a `ProductId` property. In a complete design, you'd have `Customer` and `Product` classes too. Likely, a customer has a list of applicable discounts based on some condition, and a product belongs to one or more categories. Creating a strong object model requires a high degree of knowledge, discipline, and a good amount of practice.

At first sight, it may seem that a one-to-one mapping between classes and database tables is enough. Going deeper, though, the object-oriented paradigm has much more expressiveness and a different set of features compared with the database structure. Inheritance, many-to-many-relationships, and logical groups of data are all features that influence how you design a model. More importantly, such features create a mismatch between the relational representation and the model; in literature, this problem is known as the *object/relational mismatch,* and it's discussed in the next section.

1.4   Delving deep into object/relational differences

Understanding the differences between the object-oriented and relational worlds is important, because they affect the way you design an object or domain model and the database.

The mismatch can be broken down into different parts relating to datatypes, associations, granularity, inheritance, and identity, and in the following sections we'll look at them in turn. To better illustrate this mismatch, we'll make use of the example introduced in previous sections.

1.4.1   The datatype mismatch

The *datatype mismatch* refers to the different data representations and constraints that are used in the object and relational worlds. When you add a column to a table in a database, you have to decide what datatype to assign to it. Any modern database supports `char`, `varchar`, `int`, `decimal`, `date`, and so on. When it comes to classes, the situation is different. Database `int` and `bigint` types fit naturally into .NET `Int32` and `Int64` types, but other database types don't have an exact match in .NET.

In the database, when you know that the value of a column has a maximum length, you set this constraint into the column to enforce the business rule. This is particularly desirable when the database serves several applications, and yours isn't the only one that updates data. In .NET, `varchar` doesn't exist. The nearest type to `varchar` is `String`, but it doesn't support any declarative limitations on its length (it can contain 2 GB of data). If you want to check that the value of the `String` isn't longer than expected, you have to implement this check in the setter of the property, or call a check method before sending the data back to the database.

Another example of this mismatch involves binary data. Every database accepts binary data, but the column that contains the data doesn't know anything about what the data represents. It might be a text or PDF file, an image, and so on. In .NET, you could represent such a column using an `Object`, but it would be nonsense, because you know perfectly well what kind of data you have stored in the binary column. If the value is a file, you can use a `Stream` property, whereas the `Image` type is your best choice for images.

One last example of the datatype difference emerges when you use dates. Depending on the database vendor and version, you have lots of datatypes you can use to store a date. For instance, until version 2005 of SQL Server, you had `DateTime` and `Small-DateTime`. SQL Server 2008 has introduced two more datatypes: `Date` and `Time`. As you can imagine, the first contains only a date and the second only a time. In .NET, you have only a `DateTime` class that represents both date and time. Handling this mismatch isn't difficult, but it requires a bit of discipline when instantiating the object from database data and vice versa.

As you can see, the datatype mismatch is trivial and doesn't cause developers to lose sleep at night. But it does exist, and it's something you must take care of.

The second difference, which already emerged in section 1.2, is the association between classes. Databases use foreign keys to represent relationships, whereas object-oriented applications use references to other objects. In the next section, we'll go deeper into this subject.

1.4.2   *The association mismatch*

When talking about associations, the biggest mismatch between the relational and object worlds is how relationships are maintained. Database tables are related using a mechanism that is different from the one used by classes. Let's examine how the cardinality of relationships is handled in both worlds.

ONE-TO-ONE RELATIONSHIPS

The Order table contains all the data about orders. But suppose the application needs to be improved, and an additional column has to be added to the Order table. This may initially seem like a minor improvement, because adding a column isn't too dangerous. But it's more serious than that. There may be lots of applications that rely on that table, and you don't want to risk introducing bugs. The alternative is to create a new table that has OrderId as the primary key and contains the new columns.

On the database side, that's a reasonable tradeoff, but repeating such a design in the object model would be nonsense. The best way to go is to add properties to the `Order` class, as shown in figure 1.3.

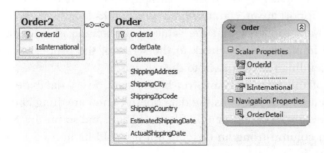

Figure 1.3 The Order2 table contains columns for the new data and is related to the Order table. In the object model, there's no new class—just a new property on the `Order` class.

The method that interacts with the database will handle the differences between the two schemas. Such a method isn't complicated at all; it performs a join between the two tables and updates data in both to handle the mismatch:

```
Select a.*, b.* from Orders a join Order2 on (a.orderid = b.orderid)
```

This association difference leads to the granularity mismatch, which will be discussed later in this section.

ONE-TO-MANY RELATIONSHIPS

You've already seen a one-to-many relationship when we linked details to an order. In a database, the table that represent the "many" side of the relationship contains the primary key of the master table. For example, the OrderDetail table contains an OrderId column that links the detail to its order. In database jargon, this column is called a *foreign key*.

By nature, database associations are unique and bidirectional. By *unique*, we mean that you have to define the relationship only on one side (the OrderDetail side); you don't need to define anything in the Order table. *Bidirectional* means that even if you modify only one side, you have automatically related the master record to its details and a detail to its master. This is possible because SQL allows you to perform joins between tables to get the order related to a detail and all details related to an order.

In the object-oriented world, such automatism doesn't exist because everything must be explicitly declared. The OrderDetail class contains a reference to the order via its Order property, and this behavior is similar to the database. The real difference is that you also need to modify the Order class, adding a property (OrderDetails) that

contains a list of OrderDetail objects that represent the details of the order. In figure 1.4, you can see this relationship.

So far, you have handled orders and their details. Now, let's move on to handle products and their suppliers. A product can be bought from more than one supplier, and a single supplier can sell many products. This leads to a many-to-many association.

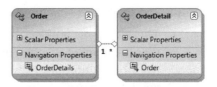

Figure 1.4   The relationship between Order and OrderDetail in the object model is expressed with properties.

MANY-TO-MANY RELATIONSHIPS

The many-to-many relationship represents an association where each of the endpoints has a multiple relationship with the other. This means there's no master-detail relationship between tables—both of them are at the same level.

For example, if you have Product and Supplier tables, you can't express the relationship between them simply by creating a foreign key in one of the tables. The only way to link them is to not link them at all. Instead, you create a middle table, known as a *link table*, that contains the primary key of both tables. The Product and Supplier tables contain only their own data, whereas the link table contains the relationship between them. This way, the two main tables aren't directly connected, but rely on a third one that has foreign keys.

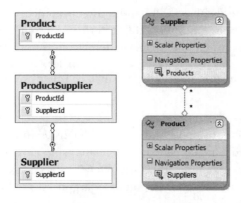

Figure 1.5   In the database, the Product and Supplier tables are related via the ProductSupplier table. In the model, the `Product` and `Supplier` classes are directly related using properties.

In an object model, the concept of a link table doesn't exist because the relationship is represented as a list of references to the other class on both sides. Because you have Product and Supplier tables in the database, you create `Product` and `Supplier` classes in the model. In the `Product` class, you add a `Suppliers` property that contains a list of `Supplier` objects representing those who sell the product. Similarly, in the `Supplier` class you add a `Products` property that contains a list of `Product` objects that represent the products sold by the supplier. Figure 1.5 shows such associations.

Like one-to-one relationships, many-to-many relationships are one of the causes of the granularity problem that appears in the object model. The other cause of the granularity problem is covered in the next section.

1.4.3   *The granularity mismatch*

The *granularity* problem refers to the difference in the number of classes compared with the number of tables in the database. You've already seen that depending on the types of relationships, you might end up with fewer classes than tables. Now we're going to explore another cause for the granularity mismatch: value types.

Let's get back to our example. The Order table has a shipping address that's split into four columns: address, city, zip code, and country. Suppose you need to handle another address, say the billing address, and you decide to add four more columns to the Order table, so it looks like the one shown in figure 1.6.

The `Order` class already has four properties for the shipping address, so adding further properties won't be a problem. But although it works smoothly, these new properties let the class grow, making it harder to understand. What's more, customers and suppliers have an address, the product store has an address, and maybe other classes have addresses too. Classes are reusable, so wouldn't it be good to create an `AddressInfo` class and reuse it across the entire model?

Figure 1.6   An excerpt of the new Order table with the new billing address field

With a bit of refactoring, you can modify the `Order` class to remove the address-related properties and add two more: `ShippingAddress` and `BillingAddress`. The code after refactoring looks like this.

Listing 1.4   The `AddressInfo` and `Order` classes

C#
```
public class AddressInfo
{
  public string Address { get; set; }
  public string City { get; set; }
  public string ZipCode { get; set; }
  public string Country { get; set; }
}

public class Order
{
  public Address ShippingAddress { get; set; }
  public Address BillingAddress { get; set; }
}
```

VB
```
Public Class AddressInfo
  Public Property Address() As String
  Public Property City() As String
  Public Property ZipCode() As String
  Public Property Country() As String
End Class

Public Class Order
  Public Property ShippingAddress() As Address
  Public Property BillingAddress() As Address
End Class
```

As you see, the code after the refactoring is easy to understand.

Avoiding overnormalization

We have seen solutions where the database has been *overnormalized*. The addresses were moved into a different table with its own identity, and foreign keys were used to link the customer table to the address. From a purist database designer point of view, this approach *might* be correct, but in practice it doesn't perform as well as if the columns were stored in the customer table. It's very likely that you'll need address information each time you retrieve an order, so every access will require a join with the address table.

This design might or might not have optimized the overall database design, but from a developer's perspective it was a painful choice. This design affected the design of the object model too. The `AddressInfo` class was originally a mere container of data, but it was turned into an entity that has its own correspondence with a database table. The consequences were a higher number of lines of code to maintain the new database table, and slower performance because SQL commands increased (updating a customer meant updating its personal data and address). Forewarned is forearmed.

Another cause of the different levels of granularity is the inheritance feature of OOP. In a model, it's common to create a base class and let other classes inherit from it. In relational databases, though, the concept of inheritance doesn't exist, so you have to use some workaround to handle such scenarios, as we'll see next.

1.4.4 *The inheritance mismatch*

The inheritance mismatch refers to the impossibility of representing inheritance graphs in a database. Let's go back to the example to see why this difference represents a problem.

Let's refine the object model to add the `Customer` class, and we'll let it and the `Supplier` class inherit from `Company`. It's highly likely that these entities share columns, such as address, VAT number, name, and so on, so using inheritance is the most natural way to design such classes. Figure 1.7 shows these classes.

Figure 1.7 The `Supplier` and `Customer` classes inherit from `Company`.

In a relational database, you can't simply declare a Customer table and say that it inherits from another table. That isn't how relational organization works. You can create a single table that contains both customer and supplier data, or create one for each type. Whatever your decision is, there will be a mismatch between database and model.

In the model, you have a `Product` class. A store can sell different types of products such as shoes, shirts, golf equipment, swimming equipment, and so on. All these products share some basic types of data, like price and color, and they'll also have other information that's specific to each product.

Even in this case, inheritance comes to your aid. To reflect this situation, you write a `Product` class, and then you create a class for each specific product. The biggest problem emerges when you design the `OrderDetail` class. In that class, you'll need a property indicating what product the detail refers to; this property is of type `Product` even if at runtime the concrete instance of the object might be of type `Shoes`, `Shirts`, or any type that inherits from `Product`. Figure 1.8 shows this inheritance hierarchy in the model.

This type of association is referred to as *polymorphic*, and it's absolutely impossible to natively represent in a database. Furthermore, to retrieve the product related to an order detail, you need a polymorphic query, which isn't supported in a database.

Fortunately, after years of experience, developers have found a way to use a combination of database design, SQL statements, and code to simulate the effect of a polymorphic query. This means that you can write a query and get instances of objects of

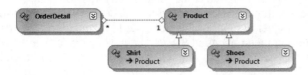

Figure 1.8 `Shirt` and `Shoes` inherit from `Product`, which is referenced by `OrderDetail`.

the correct type based on the data in the OrderDetail table. Naturally, you don't just need polymorphic queries; you need polymorphic inserts, updates, and deletes too. Indeed, the code that interacts with the database has to both retrieve and update data, so you need to solve both sides of the mismatch.

The last difference we'll talk about is identity. Databases and objects have different concepts of equality. Databases base identity on the primary key column, whereas objects use a pointer comparison.

1.4.5 *The identity mismatch*

The identity mismatch refers to the different ways that objects and databases determine equality.

The identity of a row in a table is represented by the value of its primary key columns. As a result, you have to pay attention when choosing a primary key for a table. Sometimes you may want to use a *natural key*, such as a product code, but this choice can introduce troubles instead of simplifying things.

For example, suppose you need to change a product code because you entered an incorrect one. The product code is a foreign key column in the OrderDetail table, so you have to update it too. The problem is that you can't update the product code column in the OrderDetail table, because if you change it to a value that doesn't yet exist in the Product table, you'll receive an error. On the other hand, you can't change the value in the Product table because it would violate the foreign key constraint. Lots of steps are necessary to solve this problem; what seems to be a simple update turns out to be a nightmare.

That's likely the most annoying problem, but there's another reason to avoid the use of natural keys. A product code might be a relatively long string, and almost all databases are optimized for storing and searching integer values, so the most effective primary key is a *surrogate key* that's a meaningless value to the business. By using a surrogate key, you leave the burden of creating it to the database, and you can concentrate on the data. The use of surrogate keys allows you to change data in any column in the table without affecting any other table; you don't have to perform a complicated series of steps to change the product code.

> **NOTE** We have opted for an integer key, but GUID keys are good too. In many scenarios, GUIDs are a better choice than integers. There's no absolute rule about this; it must be considered on a case-by-case basis.

So far, we can state that an object is the object-oriented representation of a table row, and that the primary key property is what links the object to the row. The problem is that if you compare two different objects of the same type, they turn out to be different even if they contain the same data.

Why are objects with the same data different? Because, by default, two variables that point to different objects representing the same row of a table are different. If the two variables point to the same instance, then they are equal. This is called *equality by reference*.

An approach that changes this default behavior is certainly more desirable. If two different objects contain the same data, their comparison should return *true*. In .NET, such equality can be achieved by overriding the `Equals` and `GetHashCode` methods, and stating the equality rules in these methods. The most natural way to represent equality is to compare properties that represent the primary key on the table, but there are complex cases where this approach can't be followed.

1.4.6   *Handling the mismatches*

Now that you've seen all of the differences between the relational and object worlds, you'll have an idea of what writing code that accesses the database in object-model–based applications involves. We haven't talked about the techniques for handling the mismatches, but you may easily guess that a flexible system requires a lot of lines of code. Naturally, if you focus on solving the problems for an individual application, the solution is simpler; but if you want to create something reusable, complexity increases.

In our experience, one of the most difficult features to implement is polymorphic queries. You need to accommodate the design of the database to create (sometimes very complex) ad hoc SQL queries and to write a huge amount of code to correctly transform the data extracted by the query into objects.

Relationships come at a cost too. As stated before, it's easy to write code that retrieves the orders. If you need to retrieve orders and details, it requires a bit more work, but nothing too difficult. Whichever path you choose, you'll have to write a lot of code to handle fetching features. Even if this code isn't too complicated to write, you still have to write it.

Fortunately, the datatype and granularity mismatches are trivial to solve. Handling the datatype differences just requires a bit of discipline to check that database constraints aren't violated when data is sent back for updates. The granularity problem is even simpler to handle and doesn't need particular attention.

Sometimes the way you shape classes can't be represented in a database, or it results in a poor database design. Even if databases and models represent the same data, the way they're organized can be so different that some compromise is required.

In our experience, designing an application so it works as well as it can often involves bending and twisting both database and object model (mainly the latter) so that they *might* look tricky in places. Someone looking at them could say that the application isn't well designed. These are words often spoken by purists of one of the two models who only consider their side. Always remember: the *best* design is the one that accommodates *both* models without losing too much of their benefits.

As you can see, an application that uses a model has many intricacies when dealing with a database. The next question is who has to deal with this complexity. The answer is that if you're crazy, you can reinvent the wheel on your own. Otherwise, you can adopt an O/RM tool. More precisely, you can use Entity Framework.

1.5   *Letting Entity Framework ease your life*

The key to delivering an application that's maintainable and easy to evolve is to separate the concerns into different logical layers and sometimes into different physical layers (tiers). You can gain many benefits from adopting such a technique.

First of all, there is the *separation of concerns*. Each layer has its own responsibilities: the interface layer is responsible for the GUI; the business layer maintains business rules and coordinates the communication between the GUI and the data layer; and the data layer is responsible for the interaction with the database.

After the interface between the layers is defined, they can evolve independently, allowing *parallel development*, which always speeds things up.

Another great advantage of using different logical layers is the ease of *maintaining and deploying* the application. If you need to change how you access the database, you only have to modify the data layer. When deploying the new packages, you deploy only the modified assemblies, leaving the others untouched.

Obviously, the data layer is the one affected by the adoption of an O/RM tool. In a well-designed application, the GUI and the business layer don't need to know that an O/RM tool is in use. It's completely buried in the data-layer code.

Let's move on and look at what an O/RM tool can do for us.

1.5.1   *What is O/RM?*

O/RM is an acronym that stands for *object/relational mapping*. In a nutshell, an O/RM framework is used to persist model objects in a relational database and retrieve them. It uses metadata information to interface with the database. This way, your data-layer code knows nothing about the database structure; the O/RM tool becomes middleware that completely hides the complexity.

The heart of O/RM is the mapping—the mapping technique is what binds the object and relational worlds. By mapping, you express how a class and its properties are related to one or more tables in the database. This information is used by the O/RM tool's engine to dynamically build SQL code that retrieves data and transforms it into objects. Similarly, by tracking changes to objects' properties, it can use mapping data to send updates back to the database. The mapping information is generally expressed as an XML file. As an alternative, some O/RM tools use attributes on the classes and their properties to maintain mapping data.

An O/RM tool is a complex piece of software that saves the developer from the burden of managing the interaction with the database. It handles the collision between object and relational worlds, it transforms query data into objects, it tracks updates to objects to reflect changes in the database, and a lot more. The idea of coding these features manually is absurd when you have a tool that does it for you.

There are plenty of O/RM tools on the market, both free and commercial. So far, NHibernate has been the most powerful and stable one. The stability was inherited from its parent (NHibernate is the .NET port of Hibernate, which is an O/RM tool written in Java, available since 2001), and the fact that it's an open source project has encouraged its adoption. Now, its leadership is being threatened by the new version of Entity Framework.

In the next section, we'll look at why Entity Framework is a valid alternative.

1.5.2 The benefits of using Entity Framework

"Why should I adopt an O/RM tool, and more specifically Entity Framework? What benefits will I gain from its use? Is it a stable technology? Why should I add another complex framework to my application?"

These are the most common questions we're asked by people who approach this technology for the first time. If you've read the whole chapter so far, you should be convinced that O/RM technology is worth a chance (if you have a model in your application). To get the complete answers to the preceding questions, you'll have to read at least the first two parts of this book. But here are some quick answers, in case you can't wait:

- *Productivity*—In our experience, persistence code that doesn't rely on an O/RM tool can take up to 35 percent of the entire application code. The use of an O/RM tool can cut that percentage down to 5 percent in some edge cases, and to 15–20 percent in a normal situation. The API that Entity Framework introduces make the developer's life easier than ever. In spite of its limitations, the designer integrated into Visual Studio dramatically simplifies the mapping process.
- *Maintainability*—The fewer lines of code you have, the fewer lines of code you have to maintain. This is particularly true in the long run, when refactoring comes into play and a smaller code base is easier to inspect. Furthermore, the ability of an O/RM tool to bridge the gap between the object and relational models opens interesting scenarios. You can refactor the database structure or model definition without affecting the application code, and only changing the mapping. If you think about the code needed to manually handle persistence and to refactor a database or classes, you'll immediately understand that maintainability increases if you adopt an O/RM tool.
- *Performance*—This is one of the most-discussed subjects relating to O/RM. The complexity of O/RM introduces an obvious slowdown in performance. In most cases, though, this is an acceptable trade-off because the slowdown is almost irrelevant. We have seen only *one* edge case where the performance decrease was unbearable.

The preceding features are shared by all O/RM tools available. Now let's look at the benefits that Entity Framework adds to your development phase.

- *It's included in the .NET Framework.*   Microsoft fully supports Entity Framework and guarantees bug fixes, documentation, and improvements at a pace its competitors can't keep up with. Often, customers choose Entity Framework instead of NHibernate because Entity Framework's presence in the .NET Framework reassures them about the overall quality of the project. What's more, because the .NET Framework is free, Entity Framework is free as well.

- *It's integrated into Visual Studio.* When you install Visual Studio 2010, you have wizards and a designer to manage the mapping phase visually, without worrying about the implementation details. As you'll see throughout the rest of the book, Visual Studio allows you to reverse-engineer existing databases to automatically create object model classes and mapping files and keep them updated when the database design changes. It allows even the reverse process: creating the object model and then creating the database to persist it. Should you make any modifications to the object model, you can immediately re-create the database.

- *The current version solves most of the problems of the past.* Microsoft has listened attentively to community feedback. Since the release of Entity Framework v1.0, Microsoft has engaged a board of experts, including Jimmy Nilsson, Eric Evans, Martin Fowler, and others, to make Entity Framework a great competitor. The first release of Entity Framework was struck by a vote of no confidence on the web, but the current version solves all of the problems raised at that time.

  Although its version number is 4.0, this is the *second* version of Entity Framework. In the past, Microsoft has confused developers with version numbers. The company shipped .NET Framework 3.0, which was not a new version but a set of classes including WCF, WPF, and WF; but the CLR was still at version 2.0. When .NET Framework 3.5 shipped, the CLR was again version 2.0. Old assemblies remained in version 2.0, whereas those shipped in version 3.0 and the new ones were upgraded to version 3.5. This versioning policy introduced so much confusion that with .NET Framework 4.0, Microsoft realigned everything to version 4.0. This is why we have Entity Framework 4.0 instead of 2.0.

- *It's independent from the type of database you use.* The persistence layer uses the Entity Framework API to interact with the database. Entity Framework is responsible for translating method calls to SQL statements that are understood by the database. But even if all modern databases support standard SQL, lots of features differ between vendors. Sometimes there are subtle differences even between different versions of the same product. SQL Server 2005 introduced a huge number of improvements, and a good O/RM tool has to generate optimized SQL for both SQL Server 2005/2008 and SQL Server 7/2000 platforms. Entity Framework guarantees that the correct SQL code is (almost) always generated, and it relieves the developer of checking which database is in use at every command.

  This helps a lot, but it doesn't mean you can forget about SQL code—you always have to check the SQL code produced by Entity Framework to be sure it respects your performance prerequisites.

- *It uses LINQ as a query language.* You can express your queries using LINQ, and Entity Framework will take care of translating your LINQ query into SQL code. This means you can write queries with IntelliSense, strong typing, and compile-time checking! At the moment, no other O/RM tool on the market (apart from the ghost of the LINQ to SQL project) allows that.

- *Entity Framework is recommended for data access by Microsoft.*   Microsoft clearly states that the future of data access for the .NET platform is Entity Framework. This is why the company is working so hard to make Entity Framework so powerful. Microsoft is also working on other products to make them rely on Entity Framework for accessing the database.

An O/RM tool is useful, but it isn't going to save your life. There are many cases where its use isn't feasible. In the next section, we'll delve into this subject.

1.5.3   When isn't O/RM needed?

In the last couple of years, the thrust toward O/RM has dramatically increased. Now, many developers think that an O/RM tool is the silver-bullet solution to all problems, and they tend to use it in every project. Sometimes its use isn't the right choice.

Despite the huge improvement in productivity it offers, O/RM is just a framework. It's something you have to study and test in several situations, and it takes time to correctly use it. In projects with a limited budget or where the delivery date is relatively soon, time is something you don't have, and you'll have to resort to hand-coding the data access layer.

The type of application you're developing is another thing you have to take into account when choosing whether to adopt an O/RM tool. If you're developing a web application that's mainly focused on displaying data, an O/RM tool may be a waste, because you get the best out of it when you have to both retrieve and persist objects. Even if it gives great flexibility in retrieving data, you may not need it if you know exactly what the fetching level is. For instance, applications that generate statistical reports won't get any benefit from O/RM. They probably wouldn't benefit from a model either.

If your application must perform bulk inserts, O/RM isn't what you need. Databases have internal features that allow bulk inserts, so you're better off relying on those features.

In short, you should always plan ahead before adopting an O/RM tool. This isn't news; in our field, everything must be planned for in advance.

So far, you've seen that working with objects improves application stability and makes them easier to maintain. You've also learned that there is a mismatch between data organized in objects and data organized in relational databases, and that this mismatch can easily be handled by O/RM tools like Entity Framework. In the next section, we'll look at the components Entity Framework is made up of, and how those components interact with each other to solve data-access problems.

1.6   How Entity Framework performs data access

Entity Framework is a complex piece of software. Its overall architecture consists of several components, each fulfilling a specific task. Figure 1.9 illustrates Entity Framework's key components and gives an idea of where each fits in.

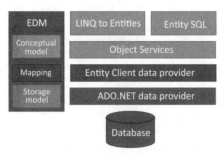

Figure 1.9 The overall architecture of Entity Framework: The query languages lie on top of Object Services, which relies on Entity Client to interact with the database. Entity Client uses the standard ADO.NET providers to physically communicate with the database. The EDM is a layer that's referenced by all the others and is used by them to obtain metadata about classes.

The *Entity Data Model* (EDM) is the layer where the mapping between the classes and the database is expressed. This component consists of the three mapping files shown in figure 1.9.

LINQ to Entities and *Entity SQL* are the languages used to write queries against the object model. Entity SQL was the first language to be developed, because when Entity Framework first appeared, LINQ was still in a prototype phase and a dedicated language for querying was necessary. During development, LINQ reached stability, so the team decided to include a LINQ dialect for Entity Framework. That's why we now have two query languages in Entity Framework.

The *Object Services* layer is the gateway to accessing data from the database and sending it back. As a result, this component is the most important for developers. Object Services is responsible for *materialization*—the process of transforming the data obtained from the Entity Client data provider, which has a tabular structure, into objects. Another important part of this layer is the `ObjectStateManager` object, or *state manager,* which tracks any changes made to the objects.

The *Entity Client data provider,* which we'll refer to as the *Entity Client* from now on, is responsible for communication with the ADO.NET data providers, which in turn communicate with the database. The main task of this layer is to convert Entity SQL and LINQ to Entities queries into SQL statements that are understood by the underlying database. Furthermore, it converts the results of queries from database tabular structure into a model tabular structure that's then passed to Object Services.

Now that you have a general idea of what the parts of the software do, let's discuss them in greater detail, starting with the EDM.

1.6.1 The Entity Data Model

The EDM is the link between the model and the database. Here you describe the database and the model structure and how to map them. The great thing about the EDM is that it decouples your application from the underlying store. Database and model can have completely different structures, but they're always related by the EDM.

The EDM consists of three XML files, each with a precise task. These files are summarized in table 1.1.

At runtime, these files are parsed and their data is stored in classes that can be queried to obtain metadata about the classes, the database, and their mapping. The main

Table 1.1   The mapping files of the EDM

Filename	Description	Alternative name	Extension
Conceptual model	Describes the model classes and their relationships	Conceptual schema, conceptual side	CSDL
Storage model	Describes the database tables, views, and stored procedures, and their keys and relationships	Storage schema, storage side	SSDL
Mapping model	Maps the conceptual and storage models	Mapping schema, mapping side	MSL

application that uses the data in these classes is Entity Framework itself. When it materializes objects from a query, it asks the EDM for metadata. We'll discuss mapping in detail in chapter 12.

> **NOTE**   One of the most despised features of Entity Framework is the extreme verbosity of the EDM. Creating the classes and describing them in the model is a useless duplication. The same objection is made against the storage model, because the engine could analyze the database structure and retrieve the schema on its own. If it did, the only task the user would need to do is create the mapping file, as is the case in other frameworks. There are several reasons why the team included all the files in the EDM; the main reasons are for performance and maximum decoupling from the physical structures.

THE CONCEPTUAL MODEL

The conceptual model is where you describe the model classes. This file is split into two main sections: the first is a container that lists all the entities and the relationships that are managed by Entity Framework, and the second contains a detailed description of their structure.

One important peculiarity of this file is that it can be separated into several files. This may become helpful when your model gets too large and the performance of the Visual Studio designer becomes unacceptable. We'll return to this subject in chapter 19, which is dedicated to performance.

THE STORAGE MODEL

The storage model is the equivalent of the conceptual model, but it describes the database organization. Not only is this file conceptually similar to the previous one, but it also uses the same XML nodes. Unlike the conceptual model, it isn't possible to split this model into several physical files.

The first section of this file lists all the tables, views, stored procedures, and foreign keys that are affected. The second section describes the items listed in the first node. Regarding tables and views, the columns and primary keys are described. When it comes to stored procedures, input and output parameters are described. The description of a foreign key contains information about the table involved, the cardinality, and the delete and update rules.

THE MAPPING MODEL

The mapping file is completely different. Its job isn't to describe something but to compensate for the differences that exist between the two previous models. This is where the real magic of mapping happens: you map a class to one or multiple tables, map one table to one or multiple classes, define inheritance mapping, and map stored procedures for both updates and object retrieval.

There is only one important node in this file: it associates the class to a table and can be repeated more than once to ensure that a class can be mapped against multiple tables, and vice versa.

Like the storage description file and unlike the conceptual file, the mapping file can't be split into multiple files.

THE VISUAL STUDIO MAPPING FILE

As you'll see in the next section, Visual Studio has a wizard that automatically generates the mapping information from the database, and a designer that allows you to modify the mappings visually, without worrying about the underlying files.

To easily integrate the mapping requirements and the designer in Visual Studio, there is a new file with the EDMX extension. The EDMX file merges the three EDM files into one, adding designer-required information. The Entity Framework designer team invented the EDMX file to allow visual modifications to be made to object model classes and their mappings against the database, whereas the EDM is the real mapping layer. At compile time, the EDMX file is split up, and the three mapping files are generated.

In terms of the object/relational mismatch, the mapping layer is where all the problems enumerated in section 1.4 are resolved. But mapping only provides metadata to solve the problem—the code lies in the Object Services and Entity Client layers. In the next section, we'll discuss the former.

1.6.2　*Object Services*

Object Services is the layer responsible for managing objects in Entity Framework. Entity Framework is mostly interested in handling the mismatch between database and objects, so there are lots of tasks to be performed against objects.

The first key feature of Object Services is that it exposes the API to generate the objects that queries are written against. Fortunately, the Visual Studio wizard helps a lot in generating the code necessary to write queries, so you only have to worry about the query and not about the plumbing.

When a query is executed, the Object Services layer translates it into a command tree that's then passed on to the underlying Entity Client. The process is slightly different depending on which query technology you use. If you use LINQ to Entities, the LINQ provider generates an expression tree that's then parsed and transformed in the command tree. If the query was developed using Entity SQL, Object Services parses the string and generates another command tree. This process is known as *query transformation*.

CompanyId	Name	ShippingAddress				BillingAddress			
		Address	City	Country	ShippingZipCode	Address	City	Country	BillingZipCode
1	First Company	7th Avenue	New York	USA	98765	7th Avenue	New York	USA	98765
		Address	City	Country	ShippingZipCode	Address	City	Country	BillingZipCode
2	Second Company	5th Avenue	Los Angeles	USA	34243	5th Avenue	Los Angeles	USA	34243

Figure 1.10   How data is received by the Object Services layer

When the query against the database has been executed and the underlying layer has reorganized the data using the mapping, Object Services is responsible for creating objects using the input structure. The input data is organized as rows and columns, but in a conceptual-model way and not in a database manner. This means each row represents an object, and if it has a property that references another class, the column contains the overall row for the class. Figure 1.10 illustrates how the data is organized.

Due to this organization of data, the process of creating objects is fairly simple. This process is *object materialization.*

When the objects are ready to be consumed, the context comes into play. By *context* we mean the lifetime of the communication between the application and Entity Framework. It's established using a well-known class (ObjectContext, or *context*), and it's active as long as the class is referenced in the code or it isn't disposed of. The context class is used from the beginning because this class creates the entry point for querying the object model.

After the objects are materialized, they're automatically added to the context memory, but this behavior can be overridden for performance reasons. During the materialization process, if the object that's going to be created already exists in the context memory, it's skipped by the engine, and a reference to the in-memory object is returned to the code executing the query. This means the context acts as a sort of local cache.

The objects that are attached to the context are automatically tracked by the state manager component. This mechanism ensures that any modifications made to objects are correctly managed and recorded in the database. To do this, the state manager stores the original data of every object that's loaded so it can compare them and perform an optimized update. This component gives you many options to customize its behavior.

Finally, the Object Services layer coordinates the updates to the data store, querying the state manager for modifications, and it controls the creation of the plumbing code needed to execute the commands.

Each of the preceding steps will be discussed in detail in chapters 4, 6, 7, and 8. But now that you know how objects are handled, it's time to investigate the layer that interacts with the database.

1.6.3   *Entity Client data provider*

The Entity Client is responsible for communicating with the database. To simplify its architecture, this layer isn't physically connected to the database, but relies on the well-known ADO.NET data-provider infrastructure.

Whereas Object Services manages objects using the conceptual model of the EDM, the Entity Client uses all the EDM files. It needs the mapping and storage model files to convert the command tree into SQL commands to execute against the database. It then needs the conceptual model file to convert the tabular database results into conceptual shaped data, as shown in figure 1.9, which is later moved into objects by Object Services.

At this point, you should have a clear understanding of how the system handles queries, uses them to hit the database, and converts the resulting data to objects. In particular situations, where maximum performance is required, you may query this layer directly, ignoring Object Services. The great boost in performance is obtained not only by jumping one layer in the chain, but also by avoiding the materialization process, which is the slowest task of query execution. For obvious reasons, LINQ to Entities can't be used when you directly query Entity Client, because LINQ manipulates objects, and this layer knows nothing about them. Entity SQL is the only language you can use in such a scenario.

Let's now move on to the first querying option: LINQ to Entities.

1.6.4   *LINQ to Entities*

LINQ to Entities is the LINQ dialect that enables typed queries against the model. Thanks to the LINQ syntax, you can write a typed query against the model and have an object returned with compile-time checking.

Even though LINQ to Entities operates on objects, it must still be translated into the SQL that's finally launched against the database. Many of the LINQ methods or overloads can't be represented in SQL. For instance, the `ElementAt` method isn't supported but is still syntactically valid. A call to this method won't cause a compile-time error but will produce a `NotSupportedException` at runtime. Similarly, the overload of the `Where` method that accepts an integer as the second parameter can't be translated to SQL, so its use causes only a runtime exception. Apart from unsupported methods, you'll encounter other cases where the compile-time checking isn't enough, but they're pretty rare and are well documented in MSDN.

> **NOTE**   It's important to emphasize that LINQ to Entities isn't Entity Framework. Many developers tend to see LINQ to Entities as a technology opposed to LINQ to SQL, but that's a mistake. LINQ to SQL is a full-featured O/RM tool that shipped with .NET Framework 3.5, whereas LINQ to Entities is only a query language inside Entity Framework. LINQ to Entities is the main querying language in Entity Framework, but Entity SQL is still a great tool to have in your toolbox.

1.6.5   *Entity SQL*

Entity SQL is the second way of querying the object model. Like LINQ to Entities queries, Entity SQL queries are always expressed against the model. The difference is that Entity SQL is string-based, so it may be preferable in some scenarios.

Entity SQL is one of the most complicated languages we have ever met. When the Entity Framework team had to create a query language for Entity Framework (before LINQ was available), they wanted to create a language that was easy for developers to understand and opted for a SQL-like syntax (which is why it was called Entity SQL). As Entity Framework evolved, and more and more features were added, the spectrum of query capabilities widened, and new functions in the language were required. It currently includes over 150 functions and has maintained only a little compatibility with the original SQL syntax.

Although it's complex, Entity SQL is ahead of LINQ to Entities in some situations. First, it's string-based, so it's easier to create queries at runtime based on conditions. Second, Entity SQL is the only language that can be used to retrieve data at low level, directly using the Entity Client. Finally, there are functions that can't be invoked using LINQ to Entities but can using Entity SQL. You'll learn more about that in chapter 9.

1.7   *Summary*

In this chapter, you've seen what O/RM is, what problems it solves, and how it fits into application design.

You've learned the basics of data access using ready-to-use structures like datasets and data readers, and why they're used in some environments and discouraged in others. In scenarios where tabular structures aren't applicable, an object/domain model is the obvious replacement, because the use of classes lets you take advantage of the power of object-oriented programming.

Naturally, the introduction of a domain model carries a new set of problems with it, due to the many differences that exist between object and relational representations of data. Handling such differences is sometimes easy for small to medium-sized business applications, but it may result in overwhelming code as the applications grow.

This is where O/RM tools like Entity Framework come into play. As you've seen, O/RM tools make database-interaction code easier to develop and maintain. Although O/RM tools aren't the silver bullet for any application, a wide spectrum of applications can benefit from the adoption of O/RM.

Finally, you've learned about the core components of Entity Framework and how they interact to solve the object/relational mismatches.

You haven't seen Entity Framework in action yet, but in the next chapter we'll start tackling its complexity and learning how to work with it.

Getting started
with Entity Framework

2

This chapter covers

- Introducing the book's example application
- Database-first and model-first design
- Introducing the Visual Studio Entity Framework designer
- An overview of Entity Framework's capabilities

Now that you have a good idea of what Entity Framework is and why it might be useful, it's time to start digging into it. In this chapter, we won't go deep into the technology; what we're going to look at is how to create an application from scratch and how to perform basic tasks, so you'll get a feel for the power of Entity Framework. The walkthrough in this chapter will also help you get started creating any kind of application you'll need to write on the job.

This chapter has three main parts. First, we'll look at the example that runs through this book in terms of both the model and the database, and we'll explain why we took certain approaches. Then we'll look at how to use the designer to create the classes (the *entities*) and have it automatically generate the code. At the end of the chapter, the code will finally make its appearance. You'll learn how to create a basic application that reads data and updates it in the database.

By the end of this chapter, you'll be able to create an application from the ground up and perform basic operations on data. You'll discover why in chapter 1 we said that *productivity* is one of the winning points of Entity Framework.

2.1 *Introducing the OrderIT example*

Many books have a running example, and this one is no exception. We'll use a classic order application called *OrderIT* that manages products, orders, customers, and so on. Here's the list of the requirements:

- *OrderIT must store data about customers.* Each customer has a name, billing address, and shipping address. The address isn't plain text but consists of four separate pieces of data: street, city, ZIP code, and country. What's more, customers can access a web service to place or update orders, so they'll need a username and password to access the web service.
- *OrderIT must store data about suppliers.* Each supplier has a name, an International Bank Account Number (IBAN), and payment terms (the number of days the customer has to pay the invoice).
- *OrderIT must store data about products.* The system must be able to sell any product, from shoes to T-shirts, from a computer mouse to a table-tennis paddle, and so on. The application must be ready to accept new types of products with a minimal effort and with no impact on the previous products and related orders.
- *OrderIT must track the number of items currently in stock.* Every time an item is sold or bought, the inventory quantity must be updated. The user must also be able to add new items to the current quantity.
- *OrderIT must be able to store whatever products are sold by the suppliers.* A single supplier can sell many products, and a single product can be bought from many suppliers.
- *OrderIT must manage any incoming orders from customers.* Every order must store data about the customer who made it and give that customer the option to use a shipping address different from the one held in the database. A customer can buy many products at once, so an order can contain multiple details.
- *OrderIT must calculate the applicable discount.* The policy for discounts states that if the customer buys more than five of the same product, there is a discount of 10 percent for each subsequent item. Should the discount be applicable, the order must contain two details: the first contains data about the first five items with no discount, and the other contains data about the additional items and the related discount.
- *OrderIT must allow the user to change the price of items easily and quickly.* Sometimes the user needs to change the price of one product, and other times prices need to be updated based on some characteristic (such as the type of product or the brand).
- *OrderIT must allow the customer to retrieve and modify account details and orders.* OrderIT exposes a web service that customers can use to place, modify, or delete orders. Customers can modify their own account details too.

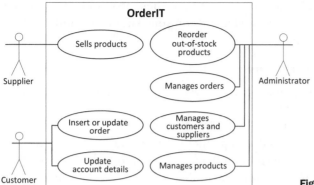

Figure 2.1 OrderIT use cases

Figure 2.1 illustrates the OrderIT use cases based on the preceding requirements.

OrderIT supports only a subset of the features that a real-world order-management application should. But even providing only these features will require you to use most of Entity Framework's features. It's important to note that some of the requirements can be handled using an object/relational mapping (O/RM) tool, but you'll have a better experience, both in terms of simplicity of development and runtime performance, if you hand-craft SQL and execute it against the database. As you build up the example, we'll explain when and why handmade SQL is better than using Entity Framework.

Now that you know *what* to do, let's explore *how* to do it. We'll start with the design of the model and the database, so that you'll have a well-established context to work in.

2.2 Designing the OrderIT model and database

Lots of things have changed since we started developing applications in early 1990s. For instance, languages have evolved, object-oriented environments have overcome procedural ones, web services have appeared, and workflow frameworks have been introduced. During this period, only one thing hasn't changed: relational databases.

Due to their stability, databases are familiar to most developers, and designing a good one is relatively simple for them. Designing a good object model may be simple too, but sometimes it requires strong discipline and lots of experience, especially when you take a domain-driven design (DDD) approach to building your application.

In small organizations, it's likely that a small group of developers creates the architecture, designs the components, and creates the database and the object model. In bigger firms, you likely have a DBA who takes care of the database and developers who design the other components.

In the smaller organizations, developers tend to design the object model considering its needs and ignoring the needs of the database. The business the object model represents is the heart of the application, and it comes first. This is referred to as *top-down design*.

In larger organizations, DBAs tend to put data organization first. This means that data could be stored in a different way from how it's represented in the application. This is referred to as *bottom-up design*.

Both bottom-up and top-down design have their pros and cons, so there isn't a firm rule to follow. Which you use depends on your knowledge and needs. Let's look at each technique in detail.

2.2.1   *Bottom-up vs. top-down design*

When you start designing an application, you have to decide what to create first: the database or the object model.

Putting the database first assumes that strong data organization is a central requirement. Data is organized independently from the way the application model may need it. Likely the application model will be bent to accommodate the design of the database. This is the bottom-up technique, and it's the most-used approach for two reasons: first, data is the core of any application; and second, model-oriented design is a relatively new technique in the Microsoft stack, so the idea of designing the model before the database isn't widespread yet. Also, as mentioned previously, DBAs often have a great decisional power, especially in big companies where a huge amount of data is persisted, and DBAs always consider the database first.

Bottom-up design guarantees the best performance and storage optimization. If the DBA works well, you'll likely interact with the database only though stored procedures, keeping the underlying database structure hidden. On the other hand, this approach means that data is organized according to database needs, which means it could be fragmented and difficult for the application to use. That's why a new approach has emerged over the years.

Designing the model before the database places more importance on the business. This is the top-down approach, where data is first organized in the model, and later the database comes in. Even in this case, when it comes to accommodating differences between the object model and the database, the object model is twisted more than the database; but you lose little expressiveness compared to the bottom-up approach, where the object model isn't considered at all.

The main advantage of the top-down approach is that the application can shape its model almost independently from how the database persists the data. The con is that sometimes this doesn't produce the best database organization, and performance may be hurt. This is why we suggest you always follow this rule: "*Never* forget completely about the database."

The database is a vital part of the application—you can't treat it like a mere storage mechanism. That would be like creating a Ferrari with the engine of a Smart. The model and database should be designed to work together seamlessly so you can make the most out of them. Top-down design puts more emphasis on the model and the business it represents than on data organization, but if it hurts database performance too much, it *must* be abandoned in favor of a bottom-up approach.

We think the top-down approach is the best one. The benefits you gain are enormous and, with a bit of practice, the database performance screams too. Even though the bottom-up approach is still more widespread, top-down design is increasing in popularity because of the benefits it offers.

The Entity Framework designer allows you to adopt both paths. You can visually create model classes and then let the designer generate the mapping information and the database script for you (a top-down, model-first approach), or you can import the database and let the designer generate classes that map one-to-one with the tables (a bottom-up, database-first approach). Later, in section 2.3, you'll see how to use both techniques to realize a model.

The first two steps in creating an application are designing entities and tables. In the next sections, we'll look at creating them, starting with the customers and suppliers.

2.2.2 *Customers and suppliers*

OrderIT's requirements state that customers and suppliers have only the name property in common, but in a real-world scenario they might have contact information, addresses, and so on. Creating a base class that holds common properties and a set of specialized ones for each concrete entity is the best way to represent data. More precisely, you can create a base *abstract* class named Company, and then the Customer and Supplier classes can inherit from Company.

Customers have shipping and billing addresses. Orders have shipping addresses, and in the future even suppliers might have an address. This makes the address a good candidate being created as a *complex type*. You can create an AddressInfo complex type and reuse it across entities.

> **NOTE** *Complex type* is the Entity Framework term for what is known as a *value object* elsewhere. Because they're exactly the same thing and this book is about Entity Framework, we'll use the *complex type* term.

When it comes to designing the database, you have to find a way to persist inheritance information. This is a typical feature of object-oriented programming, but it has no counterpart in relational databases. There are three possible approaches:

- *Table per concrete type* (TPC)—Create two separated tables, one for customers and one for suppliers.

  This solution is appealing. Unfortunately, it complicates mapping, especially when associations between entities come into play. What's worse, although this approach is supported in the EDM, it's not supported by the designer. Although TPC is a good solution, we generally disregard this option because of its limitations and the lack of support in the designer.

- *Table per type* (TPT)—Create one Company table that contains all data shared by customers and suppliers, and one table for each concrete entity: Supplier and Customer. The additional tables contains only data specific for the entity. In the end, there is a one-to-one correspondence between entities and the tables.

  This solution is fine, but it's overkill here. The most noticeable drawback is that to retrieve a customer or a supplier, you need to perform a join. You optimize storage, but performance could degrade. Nevertheless, this solution would be ideal in other situations.

- *Table per hierarchy* (TPH)—Create one table that contains all customer and supplier information, with a flag column to identify what entity type the row belongs to.

  This is by far the best approach. It performs well, because you don't need joins to retrieve customers and suppliers, and the storage is only slightly compromised.

  Unfortunately, because a row contains columns for both customer and supplier data, you can't enforce `null` constraints. For instance, in a row that holds a customer, the IBAN column isn't set, and the same happens for the shipping address column in supplier rows. This means that both columns must accept `null` values, although this isn't allowed by the business rules. Another problem arises with associations. An order *must* be related to a customer and not to a supplier. There is no way to enforce such a business rule unless you resort to database-specific features like triggers.

  Entity Framework handles all these problems; but if other applications write data to this table, you're obliged to enforce constraints on the database too.

In this scenario, it's best to use TPH. You can create a Company table, putting in it the columns needed for customers and suppliers. Furthermore, you can add a Type column, which is the *discriminator* specifying whether the row belongs to a supplier or a customer. The primary key column is CompanyId, and it's an *identity* column, meaning the database automatically generates its value using a sequential integer. Figure 2.2 shows the database table and the structure of the model classes.

Now that you've designed the first piece, it's time to move on to the second requirement: the products. Most of the considerations we made for the customer and supplier are valid in this situation too. There are little differences, but you'll find that creating the model and mapping it in this scenario is quite easy, now that you have learned the basics.

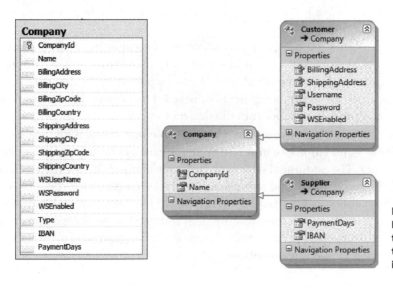

Figure 2.2   On the left is the Company table; on the right is the model with its inheritance hierarchy.

2.2.3   *Products*

The big difference between the customers and suppliers compared with the products is that there are a finite number of customers and suppliers, whereas the number of products might potentially be infinite, and each one has its own information. You could have a shirt, shoes, gloves, socks, and whatever else the human imagination can create.

From the model point of view, this isn't a big problem because inheritance is born to handle such circumstances. You can create a Product base class that contains data shared among all entities (the price, the brand, and the number of items in stock). Then, you can create a new class for each product you need to sell. These classes will inherit from Product and add item-specific information.

From the database perspective, placing data about each product in a single table, as you did for the customer and supplier, will make it grow too much, potentially overcoming modern database limitations on the number of columns. The optimal approach is to create a single table that contains shared information, and a specialized table for each product. The TPT approach is exactly what you need.

> **NOTE**   The drawback with TPT is that as products grow in number, so do the tables in the database. Depending on your workload, this may be unacceptable, and you might need to revert to a TPH strategy. Decide cautiously whether to opt for TPH or TPT. There's also a third completely different approach: using metadata. Instead of using a column to maintain a single piece of data about a product, you can use it to store an XML fragment containing all the product information. At runtime, you can re-create the classes from this XML. This approach is fine, but for the purposes of this book, following the TPT approach is equally good.

You can create a Product table that contains shared information about all products (you can think of it as a base table) and then create a table for each product, containing only specific data about for that product. For this example, you can create Shirt and Shoe tables.

The primary key for all these tables will be the ProductId column. The one in the Product table is an identity column, and the others aren't. To correctly relate the records, the primary key in the Product table must match the ones in the child tables. For instance, if a shirt has a record in the Product table with ID 1, there must be a record in the Shirt table with the same ID. The type of the product is detected by the join between tables, so a discriminator column isn't needed. Figure 2.3 shows the structure of the table and model classes.

One of the requirements for OrderIT states that you must keep track of the products sold by each supplier. Because a product can be bought by more than one supplier, and a supplier sells multiple products, you have a many-to-many relationship.

Modeling this kind of relationship is simple. You add a Suppliers property, of type ICollection<Supplier>, to the Product class, and then add a Products property, of type ICollection<Product>, to the Supplier class. That's all there is to it.

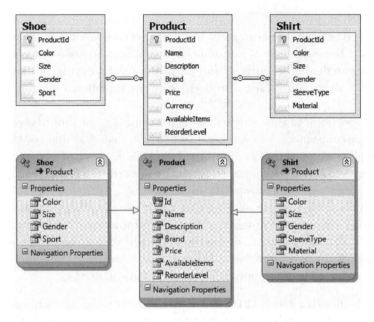

Figure 2.3   Mapping between the product tables and entities. Each class has its own mapped table (TPT).

Designing the database is slightly more difficult. You can't add a foreign key to the child table because there isn't a child table. In fact, there aren't any parent-child relationship here; the tables are at the same level.

The only way to link them is to add a third table (a *link table*), say ProductSupplier, which contains the IDs of both supplier and product, which together compose the primary key. This table resolves the problem of the many-to-many scenario, but it does create a granularity problem, because there are now three database tables and two model classes, as shown in figure 2.4. Don't worry, Entity Framework will handle the mismatch.

The last requirement to analyze concerns orders and their details. From an entity point of view, this is the simplest scenario. What makes it interesting is the high level of relationships between the involved entities. An order must have a customer and at least one detail, which in turn must be linked to a product. Let's look at how you can represent all of these associations.

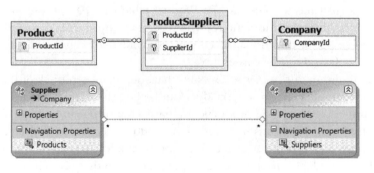

Figure 2.4
The relationship between suppliers and products is held in a link table in the database; there's a direct relationship in the model.

2.2.4 Orders

The order and details example is likely the most abused in the world. This isn't a limitation but a strength, because its simplicity will help you understand the scenario better. There's only one reasonable way to handle such data, and it's easy to apply.

In the model, you generate a class named `Order` and another one named `Order-Detail`. The first carries order information and the second its details. Because the user can select a different shipping address from the one stored in customer account, you have to add a `ShippingAddress` property to the order.

Regarding relationships, navigating from an order to its details is a must, so you need to add an `OrderDetails` *navigation* property to the `Order` class. The same way, moving from a detail to its order can be useful, so you add an inverse navigation property called `Order` to the `OrderDetail` class. An order must have a customer, so you need a `Customer` navigation property for the `Order` class. We said before that navigating from a customer to its orders isn't useful, so you leave the `Customer` class untouched. Finally, each order detail carries a product, so a `Product` navigation property is required in the `OrderDetail` class (the property type should be of type `Product` because it can contain any product). On the opposite side, navigating from a product to the order details is useless, so there should be no navigation property.

> **NOTE** In Entity Framework terminology, properties that express an association are called *navigation properties*. Navigation properties point to instances of other classes in the object model. They enable you to navigate inside the model, moving from one class to another. For instance, you can start from an order and navigate to its products, passing through the details.

In the database, you can create a table for the orders and another one for the details. The primary keys are identity columns, as in the Product and Company tables. The Order table will contain information about the address, as the class does.

When it comes to maintaining the relationships between tables, you'll have to add some foreign keys:

- *CustomerId column in the Order table*—To link the order and its customer
- *OrderId column in the OrderDetail table*—To link the order and its details
- *ProductId column in the OrderDetail table*—To link the order detail and its product

In a perfect world, such foreign keys shouldn't be part of the object model. Consider the customer-order relationship. The `Order` class references the `Customer` class via the `Customer` property. The `Customer` class has the `CompanyId` property, which carries the primary key, so it's pointless having the `CustomerId` property in the `Order` class. But in Entity Framework, it's not always like that.

One of the most painful characteristics of Entity Framework v1.0 is its extreme complexity when dealing with relationships. In v4.0, the limitations are still there, but using the new foreign-keys feature makes life much easier. In addition to adding the

`Customer` navigation property to the `Order` class, you need to add the `CustomerId` foreign key property to the `Order` class and map it in a certain way, and you're finished. This relationship is clearly visible in figure 2.5.

When you maintain relationships using only the navigation property, you use what's called *independent association*. When you add foreign-key properties, you use *foreign-key associations*. This terminology has been coined by the Entity Framework team, so it's standard.

Foreign-key associations aren't very useful when retrieving entities. But when it comes to updating data in a database, they

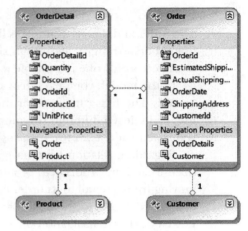

Figure 2.5   The `Order` and `OrderDetail` classes have their corresponding tables.

make things easy. In chapter 7, we'll dig deeper into this subject, and you'll discover why using foreign-key associations is a good practice.

The model is now coming to life. The entities and the related tables in the database are designed; now you need to create them. You'll see how to do that in the next section.

2.3   *Structuring the application*

Before creating the entities, you must do something more important: create the application structure inside Visual Studio. We'll keep the overall design pretty simple because we're focusing on Entity Framework's capabilities, not on how it suits a real-world architecture. That subject is covered in chapter 14, which is dedicated to application design and domain-driven design.

The following sections will walk you through the steps involved in creating the structure of the application, creating a new Entity Framework model, mapping it to the database, and generating the code. We'll start with the assemblies.

2.3.1   *Creating the assemblies*

The design is made of just one core assembly containing the model, the mapping information, and the generated code. Later, you'll create a set of client applications that use it. The client can be an ASP.NET application, a console application, a Windows Presentation Foundation (WPF) application, and so on. For this example, you'll use a Windows Form, but in later chapters we'll show you how get the best out of Entity Framework with other technologies.

To create the core assemblies, follow these steps:

1   In Visual Studio, create an empty solution named `OrderIT`.
2   Add a new Class Library project named `OrderIT.Model`.

3 Delete the `Class1` file.

4 Add a new Windows Form application named `OrderIT.WinGUI`.

5 Rename the `Form1` file to `Main`.

6 In the `OrderIT.WinGUI` project, add a reference to `OrderIT.Model`.

At the end of the process, the Solution Explorer will look like figure 2.6.

Figure 2.6   The design of OrderIT

That's it. Now that the plumbing is ready, you'll introduce Entity Framework into the application.

2.3.2 Designing entities using the database-first approach

The entity-creation process can be broken into two phases. Initially, you create entities and complex types, and map them against the database. Then, you create the navigation properties in the entities and instruct Entity Framework about the foreign keys in the related tables.

Earlier, we said that you can create entities and complex types and then let the designer generate mapping information and the database script. What we didn't say is that this process suffers from some limitations:

- The SQL script only generates tables, primary keys, and foreign keys. Every optimization to improve storage or performance capabilities must be made manually.
- Every time you modify classes and regenerate the script, it contains SQL statements that drop all existing objects and re-create them from scratch. All hand-crafted changes and data are lost.
- The designer creates a table for each class. At first this might seem fine, but when you have an inheritance hierarchy, it's persisted using TPT. Sometimes that's what you want, as in the product scenario, but other times you'll need TPH, as in the customer and supplier scenario.

The designer is fully extensible, meaning that you can create your own extensions to overcome such limitations, but it's not simple. Fortunately, the Entity Framework team has created a toolkit that provides designer extensibility features. This is great for two reasons:

- It solves the third problem in the previous list.
- It gives you great guidance for building your own extensions. If you download and study its code, you'll learn a lot about the part of the designer that enables database-generation extensibility.

> **NOTE** The toolkit isn't in the RTM but it is available as a free separate download. Look for the Entity Designer Database Generation Power Pack in the Microsoft Visual Studio Gallery (http://visualstudiogallery .msdn.microsoft.com/en-us/). We'll introduce it in chapter 13.

Getting back to entity creation, there are many ways to do this, but this is likely the best method:

1 Create the database using your favorite tool. (This task isn't related to Entity Framework, but the following steps require a database.)
2 Import the database into the designer so that it automatically generates classes.
3 Delete, re-create from scratch, and map entities that are completely different from the database (such as the `Customer` and `Supplier` classes).
4 Modify entities that have small differences from what the designer has generated (for instance, modify the `Order` class to refactor the shipping address properties into the `AddressInfo` complex type).

This approach offers the best tradeoff. The fact that you import the database into the designer before creating the classes doesn't mean you're putting the database first—it's only a technical way to ease your use of the designer. Furthermore, because the designer is aware of the database structure, you can map the entities as soon as you create them, eliminating the need to regenerate the database each time the model is modified.

> **NOTE** It would be wonderful if we could design classes using our favorite tools, generate their code, add them to Visual Studio, and then make the designer aware of that code. Unfortunately, this isn't currently possible. As an alternative, the Entity Framework team is working on a new feature called *code first*. With this feature, you can generate classes and then map them against the database with code, which is a great alternative to mapping via the designer. This feature isn't in the Entity Framework RTM, but it's in the Entity Framework Feature CTP, which means that as we write this, it's not ready yet.

Let's walk through how you can enable Entity Framework in the project. As you saw in the previous list, the first step is creating the database, but that's not an Entity Framework–related task. You can easily create the database using a tool like SQL Server Management Studio. The subsequent steps are discussed in the following sections.

IMPORTING THE DATABASE

Follow these steps to import the database (the pages of the wizard used in these steps are visible in figure 2.7):

1 In the `OrderIT.Model` assembly, add a new item; and from the wizard, select ADO.NET Entity Data Model. In the Name box, type `Model.edmx`. Click Next.
2 On the Choose Model Contents page, select Generate from Database, and click Next.
3 On the Choose Your Data Connection page, select the database from those available or create a new one on the fly that points to OrderIT. Leave the connection string name text box untouched, and click Next.

4   On the Choose Your Database Objects page, select all tables, and select the Include Foreign Key Columns in the Model check box to propagate foreign keys in the model. Leave the Pluralize or Singularize Generated Object Names check box unchecked, and click Finish.

The check box you left unchecked in step 4 is extremely interesting. It allows you to singularize the class name when a table has a plural name, and vice versa. This might look like a silly detail, but when you have to import many tables, you can save lots of time by letting the wizard generate the correct names. Microsoft implemented this feature in response to user feedback.

At this point, you have an entity for each table (the one exception being the ProductSupplier table, which doesn't require a counterpart in the object model). What you need to do now is to modify entities to match the design from section 2.2. To do that, you have to make small changes to entities that are similar enough to the database tables that they were generated nearly correctly (such as the order- and

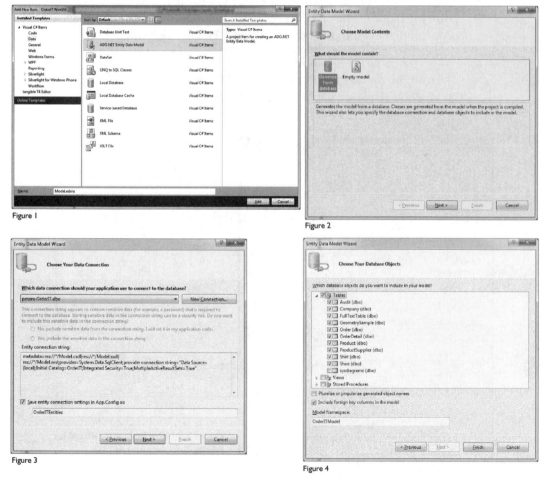

Figure 1

Figure 2

Figure 3

Figure 4

Figure 2.7   The wizard for importing the database

product-related entities), and re-create entities from scratch where they differ a lot
from the database structure (such as the company-related entities).

We'll start with the last task—creating entities from scratch—because it will cover
many Entity Framework features. You'll see how to create new entities from scratch
and map them against the database; you'll discover how to handle inheritance in the
designer, and you'll learn how to create complex types.

CREATING ENTITIES FROM SCRATCH

There's a lot to do in creating entities from scratch. Follow these steps:

1 Delete the `Company` entity. A prompt asks if you want to delete database information along with the entity. Click No, so that the entity is deleted but the database
   information remains in the EDMX file.
2 Right-click in the designer, and select Add > Entity.
3 A new wizard opens, and it asks for the Entity Name, an optional Base Type, and
   the Entity Set name, as shown in figure 2.8. In the Entity Name field, enter
   `Company`; leave the Base Type combo box untouched. In the Entity Set field, pluralize the name of the entity: `Companies`. In the second part of the form, set the
   property that maps to the key of the table. Finally, click OK.

> **TIP** The entity set is important, and for clarity we recommend that you
> set it to the plural of the entity name. At the end of this chapter, you'll
> get a sneak peek at what the entity set is used for, and you'll understand
> why we suggest this.

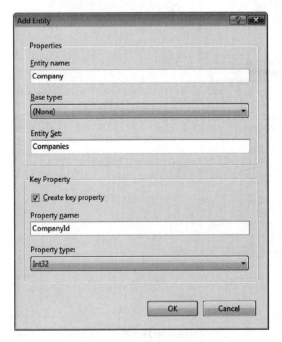

Figure 2.8 The Add Entity wizard for
adding the `Company` entity

4 A box representing the Company entity is shown in the designer. Right-click it, and select Properties. In the Properties window, set Abstract to true.

5 Right-click the entity, and select Add > Scalar Property.

6 A new text box is added to the properties section of the entity; type Name, and press Enter. Doing so adds the Name property to the Company class.

7 Right-click the Name property you just added, and select Properties. In the Properties window, set Max Length to 50 (it must match the length of the mapped column in the database).

That creates the Company entity.

Before creating the Customer entity, let's create AddressInfo so you can reuse it in Customer:

1 Right-click in a blank section of the designer, and select Add > Complex Type.

2 The Model Browser window opens and the new complex type is highlighted. Right-click the highlighted node, select Rename, and then change the name to AddressInfo.

3 Right-click the complex type, and select Add > Scalar Property > String.

4 The new property is added and highlighted. Right-click it, select Rename, and change the name to Address.

5 Right-click the property again, select Properties, and change Max Length to 30.

- Repeat steps 3 through 5 with the appropriate types and values to add the City, Country, and ZipCode properties (see figure 2.9).

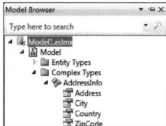

Figure 2.9 The AddressInfo complex type in the Model Browser window

Now that you have the Company and AddressInfo types, you're ready to create the Customer:

1 Right-click in a blank section of the designer, and select Add > Entity.

2 In the wizard, enter Customer in the Entity Name text box, and select Company as the base type. The Entity Set field and Key Property section are disabled because those settings are taken from Company. Click OK.

3 Right-click the entity, and select Add > Complex Property.

4 In the text box, type BillingAddress, and press Enter.

5 Right-click the BillingAddress property, and select Properties.

6 In the Properties window, set the Type property to AddressInfo.

7 Repeat steps 3 to 6 for the ShippingAddress property.

That creates the Customer entity. You can now repeat these steps to create the Supplier entity.

Now that the entities have been created, they must be mapped to the database. Let's look at how this process works:

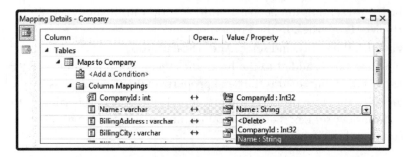

Figure 2.10   Mapping the Company entity

1 Right-click the Company entity and select Table Mapping.
2 In the Mapping Details window (shown in figure 2.10), select the Company table. The left column shows all the table columns, and the right column shows the mapped properties. When a property name matches the column name, the mapping is automatically performed. If the names don't match, you have to map them manually by clicking the right column and selecting the appropriate property for that database column.
3 Right-click the Customer entity, and select Table Mapping.
4 In the Mapping Details window, select the Company table. In the right column of the BillingAddress row, select the BillingAddress.Address property. This way, you can map all the simple properties in a complex type.
5 Repeat step 4 for each column in the Customer entity.
6 Click the Add a Condition] row, and select the Type column from the drop-down list.
7 On the right (for the value/property), enter the value C. This condition states that when the Type column (the discriminator) has the value C, the row is for a customer. The window looks like figure 2.11.
8 In the designer, right-click the Supplier entity, and select Table Mapping.

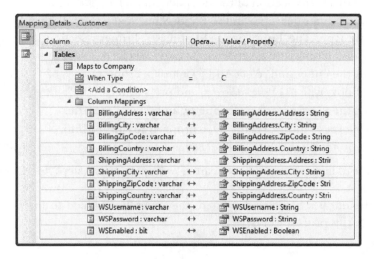

Figure 2.11   Mapping the Customer entity

9 In the right column for the IBAN field, open the drop-down list and select the IBAN property. Repeat this step for PaymentDays.

10 Click the Add a Condition row, and select the Type column from the drop-down list.

11 On the right, enter the value S. This condition states that when the Type column (the discriminator) has the value S, the row is for a supplier.

That's all. You now know how to create an entity, how to handle inheritance, and how to map entities persisted using the TPH inheritance strategy. That's a lot of stuff.

The next step is modifying the Order and OrderDetail classes so they match the design you created before. It turns out to be pretty easy.

MODIFYING ENTITIES THAT ARE SIMILAR TO DATABASE TABLES

The Order class doesn't need much work. You have to delete the address-related properties, add a complex property of AddressInfo type, and map the inner properties to the Order table. When it comes to the OrderDetail entity, it's even easier: you have to do absolutely *nothing*. The class is created exactly as you designed it. Easy as pie, isn't it?

The product-related classes are almost fine as they are. The problem is that the wizard that generates entities knows nothing about inheritance, so it maps Shoe and Shirt as if they were related to Product, and that's not what you need. The solution is fairly simple:

1 Right-click the association between Product and Shirt, and select Delete. The association is removed.

2 Repeat step 1 for the association between Product and Shoe.

3 Right-click the Product entity, and select Add > Inheritance.

4 The designer opens a dialog box where you can specify the base entity and the derived entity. Set Product as the base entity (already set by the designer), and set Shirt as the derived entity, as in figure 2.12.

5 Repeat steps 3 and 4 for the inheritance between Product and Shoe.

6 Delete the ProductId property from Shirt (it's inherited from Product).

7 Select the Shirt entity, open the Mapping Details window, and map the ProductId column to the ProductId inherited property.

8 Repeat steps 6 and 7 for the Shoe entity.

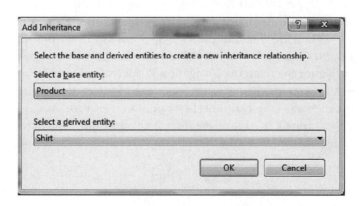

Figure 2.12 The dialog box for creating inheritance between existing entities

By performing these simple steps, you've mapped a TPT hierarchy. It's pretty easy.

You must make a little tweak to the `AvailableItems` property. Its value must not be handled by Entity Framework because it would create concurrency problems. In chapter 6, we'll discuss this subject in depth, and you'll understand the reasons for this choice.

The best way to accomplish this task is to make the property effectively read-only and set it using a stored procedure or custom SQL command. Unfortunately, changing the setter visibility to `protected` won't accomplish this, because Entity Framework will still try to persist the property. The only way to make it really read-only is to set its `StoreGeneratedPattern` property to `Computed` in both the conceptual schema and the storage one.

Making this change on the conceptual side is easy because it can be done in the Properties window. Modifying the value in the storage schema requires you to manually modify the EDM. I won't show you how to do it here—you'll learn about it in chapter 5, which is dedicated to mapping.

At this point, you're only missing the relationships between entities. Setting this up involves several steps. Adding navigation properties and foreign keys (if needed) is just part of the game; you also need to instruct Entity Framework what columns in the database act as foreign keys so it can retrieve related data correctly.

2.3.3 *Designing relationships*

Creating a relationship is a two-step job. First you create the navigation properties, and then you map the columns that establish the relationship in the database. For instance, you create a `Customer` navigation property in the `Order` entity, and then you map it to the `CustomerId` column in the `Order` table. This is what the SQL-generation engine needs to create the correct SQL joins when performing data retrieval (for instance, when you need to retrieve the customer for an order).

Here's how to create such relationships.

1 Right-click the `Customer` entity, and select Add > Association.

2 In the left End box of the dialog box, leave Customer selected in the Entity drop-down list, select 1 (One) in the Multiplicity drop-down list, and uncheck the Navigation Property check box. This ensures that the navigation property from `Customer` to `Order` isn't created (that is exactly what you want).

3 In the right End box in the dialog box, select Order in the Entity drop-down list, and select * (Many) in the Multiplicity drop-down list. Leave the Navigation Property check box selected, and leave Customer in the text box below. This instructs the designer to create the Navigation Property `Customer` in `Order`.

4 Deselect the Add Foreign Key Properties to the 'Order' Entity check box, because you already have the CustomerId column in the `Order` entity (it's been imported by the wizard). If you're creating a relationship from scratch, you should select this check box so the relationship is created and mapped at the same time.

Figure 2.13 Creating the association between `Customer` **and** `Order`

5 The completed dialog box is shown in figure 2.13. Click OK to add the association and the navigation properties.

6 A line representing the link between the entities is added to the designer. Double-click it.

7 In the Referential Constraint dialog box that's displayed, select Customer from the Principal drop-down list. This represents the master entity in the relationship.

8 In the grid below, the designer shows the principal entity's key properties (`CompanyId` in this case). Select the `CustomerId` property of the `Order` entity as the foreign key. This indicates that the other side of the relationship (`Order`) is linked to the master primary key via the `CustomerId` property. Figure 2.14 shows what the dialog box looks like at this point. Click OK to map the association.

9 Right-click the association link, and select Properties. Set the `End1 on Delete` property to `Cascade`. This specifies that when a customer is deleted, the deletion must propagate to its orders.

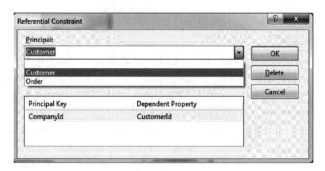

Figure 2.14 Mapping the association between `Customer` **and** `Order`

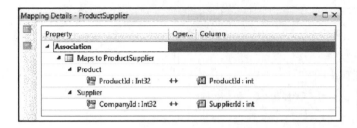

**Figure 2.15
Mapping the many-to-many
association between
Product and Supplier**

This process applies only to one-to-* associations. In many-to-many scenarios, there is
no master-detail relationship, so foreign keys can't be used in the model. This means
the relationship must use an independent association.

> **NOTE**   You can use foreign-key associations in many-to-many relation-
> ships, but that implies creating an entity that maps to the link table in the
> database. It's the solution adopted by LINQ to SQL, but it's a poor design,
> and we strongly discourage this practice.

Let's look at how you can map a many-to-many relationship:

1 Create an association between the Product and Supplier entities.
2 Right-click the link between the entities, and select Table Mapping.
3 In the Mapping Details window, map the association to the ProductSupplier
   table.
4 ProductId is automatically mapped by its name. Select the SupplierId column
   for the supplier side, as shown in figure 2.15.

This was the only way to map associations in v1.0, and it's possible to map any association using this mechanism. For instance, to map the association between a customer
and its orders, you'd select the Order table and then map the CustomerId column as
the foreign key.

> **NOTE**   An association can't be mapped using both techniques. You must
> choose between using foreign keys (recommended) and independent
> associations.

The model is now designed, but there are still questions to be answered. Where is the
code for the designed classes? How can you customize the generated code? How can
you access the database? That's all covered in the next section.

2.3.4   *Organizing the generated code*

By default, the designer generates a file and places all the code into it. The file is
named after the designer file with a .vb or .cs extension, depending on the language.
For instance, a model.edmx designer file creates a model.edmx.vb or model.edmx.cs
file. In the Solution Explorer window, this file is nested in the designer file.

   If you examine the code, you'll see that it's a mess. All the classes are in a single
file, and there are plenty of attributes on classes and properties, as well as lots of
partial methods. What's worse, classes inherit from EntityObject, and relationships

between classes are expressed using properties of type `EntityCollection<T>` and `EntityReference<T>`. This is how Entity Framework v1.0 code must be organized.

Entity Framework v4.0 maintains this behavior only for compatibility purposes. Sometimes, keeping code like this may be fine—many successful projects are based on v1.0. But sometimes you'll need more flexibility, and this can be achieved only by using the plain old CLR object (POCO) approach, which frees you from any persistence mechanism.

Fortunately, the code-generation process is completely customizable. In Visual Studio 2008, Microsoft introduced a text-template processor, and the designer uses it to create the classes' code. In fact, the code that's generated by default comes from a template file.

> **NOTE**   If you want to look at the default file, it's in a zip file named AdoNet-EntityDataModelT4CodeGenCSharp.zip located in %ProgramFiles%\ Microsoft Visual Studio 10.0\Common7\IDE\ItemTemplatesCache\CSharp\ Code\1033\.

You could create a custom template that solves the problem of generating messy code, like the one required by v1.0. It could create useful methods for each class, split classes into separate files, create POCO classes, and so on. But writing a template isn't always an easy task, as you'll discover in chapter 13.

Fortunately, the Entity Framework team has released a template that already solves most of these problems. This template isn't included in the RTM, but it's available as a separate download. You can download and automatically install it through the Extension Manager window in Visual Studio by following these steps:

1   Select Tools > Extension Manager.
2   In the Extension Manager window, select the Online Gallery tab on the left, and then type POCO in the top-right text box. Press Enter. The window will look like figure 2.16.
3   If the extension has already been installed, it has a green checkmark beside it in the middle column of the window. Otherwise, the Download button is shown. Click the Download button to automatically download and install the extension.

When it's installed, the extension adds a new template item in the wizard. Here's how you can use it to better organize your code:

1   Right-click the designer, and select Add Code Generation Item.
2   Select the ADO.NET POCO Entity Generator item, type `Entities.tt` in the Name text box, and click OK. Two new files are added to the project: Entities.tt and Entities.Context.tt.
3   Right-click both files, and select Run Custom Tool. Doing so triggers the code generation.
4   Click the model.edmx file, and in the Properties window set Code Generation Strategy to None to disable default code generation.

Figure 2.16   The Extension Manager window shows downloadable POCO templates as well as those that are already installed on the machine.

At this point, you have code and mapping information ready to be used. The code generated by the Entities.Context.tt template even contains a class that uses the Object Services features, enabling access to the database. All of this has been done by using the designer, without writing a single line of code. That's *productivity*.

There's more than that. By customizing the available templates, you can create an *n*-layered or a domain-driven design application. This means that with small changes, you can create both simple and robust applications.

As we've mentioned, in Entity Framework terminology, the bottom-up approach is called the *database-first approach* and the top-down approach is called *model-first*. Database-first is the approach used in the past few sections; but for completeness, let's look at how to use the model-first approach, where you design the classes and then let the designer generate the database script.

2.3.5   *The model-first approach in the designer*

When you opt for the model-first approach, you don't have a database to map entities against. This means you create the entities, and then the mapping is automatically handled by the designer. How does it work?

When you've finished designing the entities, right-click the designer and select Generate Database Script from Model. A wizard appears, asking for the connection string. After you enter it, the wizard returns the script. Just launch the SQL script on the database, and you're ready to go.

What's great about this technique is that while generating the database script, the designer generates the mapping and storage information too. More precisely, the designer generates the Store Schema Definition Language (SSDL) and the Mapping

Specification Language (MSL) sections of the EDMX and finally the database script (using the generated SSDL).

This behavior can be overridden so that you can modify the way the mapping is generated and adapt the script to serve other databases than SQL Server. Accomplishing this is hard because many steps are involved and, more important, a workflow activity must be written. Don't worry, we'll talk about this in chapter 13.

We consider the model-first approach to be useless as it is now. Until it's modified to update the database structure instead of re-creating it from scratch, we'll keep recommending the database-first approach. (OK, you could create a designer extension to accomplish the task of updating, instead of re-creating the database, but doing so wouldn't be simple.)

Now that all the plumbing is ready, you can put everything into action. In the next section, we'll take a quick tour of the main features of Entity Framework. If you're new to O/RM, you'll be surprised to see how little code is required for most operations, and how simple it is. If you're already accustomed to using an O/RM tool, you'll be pleased to see that querying with LINQ to Entities is far more effective than using any other approach.

2.4 A sneak peek at the code

In this "Hello World" example, you're going to learn how to accomplish the most basic tasks, like querying the database and persisting modifications made to entities. At the end of this section, you'll understand how much data-access code Entity Framework lets you eliminate.

Perhaps the most interesting aspect of Entity Framework is its query capabilities, because it engages the power of LINQ to simplify data retrieval. Let's start with querying.

2.4.1 Querying the database

Suppose you want to create a form that shows all orders in a grid. This is easy because you only have to create an instance of the context class (more on this in the next chapter), use its properties to access the orders, and bind them to the grid.

Listing 2.1 Displaying orders in a grid

C#
```
using (OrderITEntities ctx = new OrderITEntities())
{
  grd.DataSource = ctx.Orders;
}
```

VB
```
Using ctx As New OrderITEntities()
  grd.DataSource = ctx.Orders
End Using
```

OrderITEntities is the class that lets you interact with the database. It's the Object Services layer's main class (the context class). The Orders property is the entity set. Roughly speaking, you can think of the entity set as the equivalent of a database table. Naturally, records aren't physically loaded into the entity set; it's only used for querying purposes.

Now, let's create a more complex query that shows only the orders placed in the current month. If you're familiar with the LINQ syntax, you'll have no problem understanding the following listing. For brevity, only the query is shown here.

Listing 2.2   Displaying orders placed in the current month

C#
```
from o in ctx.Orders
where o.OrderDate.Year == DateTime.Now.Year &&
      o.OrderDate.Month == DateTime.Now.Month
select o;
```

VB
```
From d In ctx.Orders
Where d.OrderDate.Year = DateTime.Now.Year AndAlso
      d.OrderDate.Month = DateTime.Now.Month
Select d
```

When users select an order, they need to see it in a detailed form. The form needs only a single instance and not a list. This can be achieved by using the LINQ First method. Here it's used to retrieve the order with ID 1.

Listing 2.3   Retrieving a single order

C#
```
Order order = (from o in ctx.Orders.Include("OrderDetails")
               where o.OrderId == 1
               select o).First();
```

VB
```
Dim order = (From o In ctx.Orders.Include("OrderDetails") _
             Where o.OrderId = 1 _
             Select o).First()
```

Notice the use of the Include method. It retrieves the details along with the order. The string argument represents the navigation property that must be loaded.

You've now seen the main data-retrieval features of Entity Framework. But in a real-world application, it's likely that the user will not only view data, but also update it. We'll look at that next.

2.4.2   *Updating objects and reflecting changes into storage*

Entity Framework gracefully manages any modifications made to objects so they're correctly reflected in the database. You can apply three types of modifications: inserts, updates, and deletes. Let's look at them one by one.

INSERTS

Suppose you have to create a form where the user can insert, edit, delete, and display an order. When the user inserts an order, you create an `Order` object and as many `OrderDetail` instances as there are details. Next, you instantiate the context that manages and coordinates the updates to the database. Finally, you invoke the `AddObject` method to notify the `Orders` entity set that the order must be inserted into the database. `AddObject` doesn't communicate with the database; it only notifies the context about the persistence operation. The real operation on the database is triggered when the `SaveChanges` method is invoked.

All these steps are put into action in the following listing.

Listing 2.4   Inserting a new order

C#
```
Order o = new Order { ... };
o.OrderDetail.Add(new OrderDetail { ... });
o.OrderDetail.Add(new OrderDetail { ... });
o.OrderDetail.Add(new OrderDetail { ... });
using (OrderITEntities ctx = new OrderITEntities())
{
  ctx.Orders.AddObject(o);                              ❶ Adds order
  ctx.SaveChanges();                                       to context
}
```

VB
```
Dim o As New Order With { ... }
o.OrderDetails.Add(New OrderDetail With { ... })
o.OrderDetaila.Add(New OrderDetail With { ... })
o.OrderDetails.Add(New OrderDetail With { ... })
Using ctx As New OrderITEntities()                      ❶ Adds order
  ctx.Orders.AddObject(o)                                  to context
  ctx.SaveChanges()
End Using
```

The process of creating the `Order` and `OrderDetail` entities is a common practice; the real power shines in the last two lines of code. The code creates an order and three details, but the context is notified only about the order ❶. When the `SaveChanges` method is invoked, the context scans the `Order` object and all of its properties, including those referencing other objects. Because the order is linked to a list of details, the context recognizes that the entire object graph must be persisted. This feature is called *persistence by reachability*.

In this scenario, the persistence of the object graph requires four inserts in the database. They must be executed in a transactional context to ensure that everything works in an all-or-nothing way. In listing 2.4, there is no trace of a transaction, nor of any other database-related code. The missing plumbing is boxed inside the `SaveChanges` method, leaving you only the burden of invoking it.

If you compare listing 2.4 with the code necessary to create this feature manually, you'll understand how much Entity Framework can help in reducing and simplifying the data-access layer of your applications, making it more robust and less error prone.

UPDATES

If you find that persisting new objects into the database is pretty simple, you'll be surprised to discover that propagating the modifications made to objects into the data store is even easier. Suppose the page used for displaying an order is also used for modifying existing orders. After the user has finished modifying the data, your code must update the database.

You have two possible ways to perform the updates:

- Re-create the objects and add them to the context, indicating that they must be updated (the *disconnected* approach).
- Query the database again to retrieve the objects, and then modify them (the *connected* approach).

The disconnected approach is used most in scenarios where the context in which you retrieve data is different from the context you use to modify it (such as a web application or a web service). The connected approach is used most in scenarios where the context is a long-running concept (a Windows Form or Windows Presentation Foundation based application). The following code uses the connected approach. Later, in chapter 7, we'll go deeper into both techniques.

> **Listing 2.5 Updating an existing order**

C#

```
var order = (from o in ctx.Orders
             where o.OrderId == 1
             select o).First();
order.ShippingDate = DateTime.Now.Today;
order.OrderDetails.Add(new OrderDetail { ... });
ctx.SaveChanges();
```

VB

```
Dim order = (From o In ctx.Orders
             Where o.OrderId = 1
             Select o).First()
order.ShippingDate = DateTime.Now.Today
order.OrderDetails.Add(New OrderDetail With { ... })
ctx.SaveChanges()
```

The first query is necessary to load the order from the database into the context. The properties of the order and its details are modified with user-entered data. After the properties have been changed, there's no need to notify the context about modifications because it keeps track of any modifications made to loaded objects and their references. When the SaveChanges method is invoked, the context determines which objects and properties have been modified and prepares the statements to be executed against the database.

Because the context knows what has been modified, the SQL generated for updates is highly optimized—it contains only the changed columns. If you think about how much code and time you would spend implementing such a feature, you'll understand that this process of updating data is extremely powerful.

DELETES

Deleting an object is likely the simplest task. You need an object with its key properties set to the ID of the record to be deleted, and then you notify the context that such an object must be removed from the table in the database.

You can choose freely between the disconnected and the connected methods. Unless you're worried about concurrency, we recommend using the disconnected approach as your default choice. We'll look at both options.

In the disconnected case, you create an `Order` object and set the property corresponding to the key of the table to the ID of the record you want to delete. Then, you create the context, attach the order to it (with the `Attach` method), and use `DeleteObject` to notify the context that the row in the table related to the order must be deleted. Finally, the `SaveChanges` method issues the `DELETE` statement from the database.

> **Listing 2.6 Deleting an existing order in a disconnected way**

C#
```csharp
Order order = new Order { OrderId = 1 };
ctx.Orders.Attach(order);
ctx.Orders.DeleteObject(order);
ctx.SaveChanges();
```

VB
```vb
Dim order = New Order With { .OrderId = 1 }
ctx.Orders.Attach(order)
ctx.Orders.DeleteObject(order)
ctx.SaveChanges()
```

In some situations, you'll have the object, because you've already loaded it (from a query, for instance). Re-creating a new instance is completely useless in this case. You can pass the instance you already have directly to the `DeleteObject` method without having to attach it to the context. This is the classic connected scenario.

> **Listing 2.7 Deleting an existing order in a connected way**

C#
```csharp
Order order = (from o in ctx.Order
               where o.OrderId == 1
               select o).First();
ctx.Orders.DeleteObject(order);
ctx.SaveChanges();
```

VB
```vb
Dim order = (From o In ctx.Order
             Where o.OrderId = 1
             Select o).First
ctx.Orders.DeleteObject(order)
ctx.SaveChanges()
```

As you'd expect, the details are automatically deleted because of the database's delete-cascade constraint. To ensure that Entity Framework correctly checks the relationships, the cascade constraint is enforced in the EDM too.

You've now seen how little code you have to write to persist an object graph. It doesn't make any difference whether you have to insert, update, or delete data, because the basic idea is always the same: build or retrieve the object, modify its properties, and send it back to Entity Framework to persist the modifications.

2.5   Summary

You've now seen all the basics needed to start up a new project. In this first part of the book, you've learned what an O/RM tool is, you've seen where it stands in terms of application design, and you've even taken a sneak peek at how it speeds up development.

What you've seen so far isn't just for demo purposes. The design of this chapter's application is surely oversimplified, but it's still effective in many scenarios that have little complexity. Furthermore, the choice of importing the database and later modifying the classes isn't taken from documentation: it's the result of experience in developing several projects.

At this point, you're just beginning your discovery of Entity Framework. You have a solid background of what necessities it covers, but you need to get your hands dirty and explore all of its features. It's time to go deeper into the three main building blocks of Entity Framework: mapping databases and classes, querying databases, and persisting modifications made to objects. By the end of the next part of the book, you'll be able to design and develop real-world applications using Entity Framework.

The first subject we'll face in the next chapter is querying. Get ready for the show.

Part 2

Getting started

Entity Framework is Microsoft's answer to the O/RM needs in data-driven applications. In part 1 of this book, you learned which scenarios Entity Framework addresses and how it works internally to accomplish its tasks. In this part of the book, you'll use the components you've already seen to develop an application that covers all possible requests.

To fully cover data access, an application must be able to retrieve data, transform the data into objects, track any data modification, and persist the data to the database. All this must be done in a transactional and concurrency-safe way.

Chapter 3 introduces the basics of querying, covering the components that play a role in this function. Chapter 4 tours the LINQ to Entities dialect and demonstrates how all the tasks you can accomplish in SQL can be carried out with this new language. Chapter 5 shows how mapping works in Entity Framework. You'll learn how to use the designer to design classes and how designer actions are reflected in the EDM.

Chapter 6 discusses the entity lifecycle. Here you'll learn how Entity Framework manages the entities it retrieves from the database and the entities you attach to the context. You'll discover how an entity can change its state and how that affects the way it's persisted.

Chapter 7 uses the features explained in chapter 6 and examines how modifications made to entities are persisted to the database. Here you'll learn how to persist simple entities as well as complex ones. Finally, chapter 8 explains how to deal with transactions and how to avoid concurrency problems, which are a common concern in many applications.

Querying the object model: the basics

This chapter covers

- Entity Framework querying techniques
- Capturing the generated SQL
- Insights into the Entity Framework query engine
- Common query pitfalls

In the first part of this book, you gained a strong understanding of where Entity Framework stands and how it can be integrated into your application. Now it's time to start digging deep into the technology to understand the most important thing: *how* you use it.

In this chapter, you'll learn about the most basic feature in Entity Framework: querying. In particular, you'll learn how the Object Services layer enables you to query the database and which other components collaborate with it. What's more, you'll learn how to inspect the SQL generated by Entity Framework so that you can decide whether to use it or to handcraft a custom SQL command. By the end of this chapter, you'll understand how querying works under the covers and the theory behind it.

3.1   One engine, many querying methods

In chapter 2, you saw a couple of LINQ to Entities queries, but those just scratched the surface of the Entity Framework querying system. There is more than one method for querying the model, and more than one structure that can be used to execute queries.

These are the possible ways of querying with Entity Framework:

- *LINQ to Entities through Object Services*—You write LINQ to Entities queries, and the Object Services layer is responsible for handling the returned entities' lifecycles.
- *Query builder methods and Entity SQL through Object Services*—You use query builder methods to create Entity SQL queries. The Object Services layer is then responsible for handling the returned entities' lifecycles.
- *Entity SQL through Object Services*—You write the full Entity SQL query on your own, without resorting to query builder methods, and then submit it through Object Services, which takes care of the entities' lifecycles.
- *Entity SQL through Entity Client*—You bypass the Object Services layer and retrieve the data not as objects, but as a conceptual shaped set of `DbDataRecord` instances.

This chapter and the next focus on Object Services and LINQ to Entities, so we'll only cover the first option here. The other methods are covered in chapter 9, which is dedicated to Entity SQL and Entity Client.

3.2   The query engine entry point: Object Services

In chapter 1, you learned that the Object Services layer's task is managing objects' lifecycles from retrieval to persistence. The main class of the Object Services layer is `ObjectContext`. As you saw in chapter 2, it's the most useful class for your code because it provides the *only* entry point for executing LINQ to Entities queries.

One of the features of the Visual Studio designer is that, along with generating entities, it generates another class that inherits from `ObjectContext` and that has a set property for each object model class (with some exceptions). This property represents the *entity set*. You can think about the entity set as a database table—it doesn't actually contain data, but the entity set is what you write queries against. Later, in section 3.2.4, you'll see how a query written against the entity set is turned into SQL and returns the data. For the moment, though, let's focus on entity sets.

The property representing an entity set is of type `ObjectSet<T>`. The generic parameter corresponds to the type of the class that the entity set exposes. In OrderIT, the property that enables order retrieval is `Orders`; its type is `ObjectSet<Order>`, and it has the following definition.

> **Listing 3.1   The `Orders` property definition in the context class**

C#
```
public partial class OrderITEntities : ObjectContext
{
  public ObjectSet<Order> Orders
```

```
  {
    get
    {
      return _orders  ??
        (_orders = CreateObjectSet<Order>("Orders"));
    }
  }
  private ObjectSet<Order> _orders;
}
```

VB
```
Public Partial Class OrderITEntities
  Inherits ObjectContext
  Public ReadOnly Property Orders() As ObjectSet(Of Order)
    Get
      If _orders Is Nothing Then
        _orders = CreateObjectSet(Of Order)("Orders")
      End If
      Return _orders,
    End Get
  End Property
  Private _orders As ObjectSet(Of Order)
End Class
```

ObjectSet<T> inherits from ObjectQuery<T>, which was the class used in Entity Framework v1.0. ObjectSet<T> adds some convenient methods while maintaining compatibility with the past.

The ObjectContext class isn't abstract. The only reason the wizard generates a specialized class that inherits from ObjectContext is to automatically generate the entity-set properties plus some helper methods. The generated class is perfect as is, and you should always use it.

If there is a case where you can't use it, you can instantiate the ObjectContext class directly and pass the connection string name (more about connection strings in section 3.2.1). After that, you can use the CreateObjectSet<T> method, passing the entity set name as a parameter (more about this in chapter 4), to create the Object-Set<T> instance. You can see such code in the following snippet:

C#
```
using (ObjectContext ctx = new ObjectContext("name=ConnStringName"))
{
  var os = ctx.CreateObjectSet<Order>("Orders");
}
```

VB
```
Using ctx As new ObjectContext("name=ConnStringName")
  Dim os = ctx.CreateObjectSet(Of Order)("Orders")
End Using
```

As you can see, manually creating an ObjectSet<T> instance isn't difficult at all. But we still haven't encountered a situation where this is necessary—the wizard-generated file has always worked well for us.

NOTE `ObjectContext` implements the `IDisposable` interface. We strongly recommend adopting the *Using* pattern to ensure that all resources are correctly released. For brevity's sake, we won't show the context-instantiation code in subsequent snippets; `ctx` will be the standard name of the variable representing it.

When you instantiate the designer-generated context class, you don't need to pass the connection string name to the constructor, whereas you have to pass it when working directly with `ObjectContext`. The designer knows what the connection string name is (you passed it in the designer wizard that created the object model and the context class, as you saw in chapter 2); and when the template generates the context-class code, it creates a constructor that invokes the base constructor, passing the connection string name. The context-class constructor is visible in the following snippet:

C#
```
public class OrderITEntities
{
    public OrderITEntities() : base("name=ConnStringName") { }
}
```

VB
```
Public Class OrderITEntities
    Public Sub New()
        MyBase.New("name=ConnStringName")
    End Sub
End Class
```

The template generates other constructors that accept the connection string, including an `EntityConnection` object (the connection to the Entity Client). This way, you can change the connection string programmatically when needed.

Under the covers, Object Services takes care of lots of tasks:

- Manages connection strings
- Transforms LINQ to Entities queries into an internal representation understood by Entity Client
- Transforms database query results into objects
- Ensures that only one object exists for each row in the database (no duplicates)
- Enables capturing the SQL code issued against the database
- Enables database script creation and the creation and dropping of databases

We'll look at these features in the following subsections. Let's start at ground level and look at the connection string.

3.2.1   Setting up the connection string

As you've seen, the connection string name is mandatory for the `ObjectContext` class. How you pass the connection string is slightly different in the Entity Framework compared to how you do it with other ADO.NET frameworks. In Entity Framework, you have to apply the (case-insensitive) prefix `Name=` to the connection string:

```
Name=ConnStringName
```

This isn't the only difference from what you're likely to be used to. The connection string itself is quite odd. This is how the connection string for OrderIT appears in the connectionString section of the configuration file.

Listing 3.2 A connection string example

```
<add
  name="ConnStringName"
  connectionString="
    metadata=res://*/Model.csdl| res://*/Model.ssdl|res://*/Model.msl;
    provider=System.Data.SqlClient;
    provider connection string='
      Data Source=.\sqlexpress;
      database=EFInactionOrders;
      Integrated Security=True;
      MultipleActiveResultSets=True
    '
  "
  providerName="System.Data.EntityClient"
/>
```

The structure is always the same, but the data is organized in an unusual way. The attribute name represents the name of the connection string, and it's the one used when passing the connection string name to the context constructor. So far, so good.

The connectionString attribute is very different from what you're used to seeing, and it probably looks a bit muddled. You *must* understand how it's made, because you'll have to modify it when changing databases (when moving from development to production servers, for instance). It's split into three subsections:

- metadata—In this part, you specify where the three mapping files are located, separating the locations with pipe (|) characters. If the files are stored as plain text on the disk, you specify the path. If the files are stored as resources in the assembly, the res://*/filename convention is used.
- provider—Here you specify the ADO.NET invariant provider name for the database, as if you were populating the providerName attribute of the connection-String node.
- provider connection string—This represents the real connection string to the database. If you need to include a double-quote (") character, you must use its escaped format (") to avoid collision with XML format.

Finally, the providerName attribute contains the System.Data.EntityClient string, which is the invariant Entity Framework provider name.

Setting up the connection is an important task. Fortunately, it's handled by the designer, so you only have to touch it when you change databases. If you need to build it at runtime, you can use the EntityConnectionStringBuilder class.

CREATING CONNECTION STRINGS IN CODE

Usually the connection string can be put in the configuration file and read by the application. In some scenarios, though, you may need to change the connection string at runtime. We've encountered this situation a couple of times.

In the first case, each attribute of the connection string was returned by a service. This isn't the world's best architecture, but sometimes you have to live with it.

In the second case, the application was built to deal with two different versions of SQL Server (2005 and 2008). This meant having two different SSDL files, so the correct one had to be chosen at runtime based on the database version. There were two solutions:

- Creating the connection string by manually concatenating strings
- Building the connection string at runtime using `EntityConnectionString-Builder`

Needless to say, the second option was the better choice and is the one we'll discuss

The `EntityConnectionStringBuilder` class inherits from the ADO.NET base class `DbConnectionStringBuilder`, and it's responsible for building a connection string starting from a set of parameters and for parsing a given connection string into single parameters. Its properties are described in table 3.1.

Table 3.1　Properties of the `EntityConnectionStringBuilder` class

Property	Description
`Metadata`	Corresponds to the metadata section in the connection string.
`Provider`	Corresponds to the provider section in the connection string.
`ProviderConnectionString`	Corresponds to the provider connection string section in the connection string.
`ConnectionString`	The connection string in Entity Framework format. When you set it, the previous properties are automatically populated. When you modify one of the preceding properties, the connection string is automatically updated to reflect the changes.

In the first case we outlined, where the connection string was returned by a service, you can use `DbConnectionStringBuilder` class's ability to generate a connection string from a single parameter. You can receive the `Metadata`, `Provider`, and `Provider-ConnectionString` parameters from the web service and use them to set up the connection string and pass it to the context constructor, as shown here.

Listing 3.3　Building a connection string

C#
```
var connStringData = proxy.GetConnectionStringData();
var builder = new EntityConnectionStringBuilder();
builder.Provider = connStringData.Provider;
builder.Metadata = connStringData.Metadata;
```

```
builder.ProviderConnectionString = connStringData.ProviderConnectionString;
using (var ctx = new OrderITEntities(builder.ConnectionString))
{
    ...
}
```

VB

```
Dim connStringData = proxy.GetConnectionStringData()
Dim builder = new EntityConnectionStringBuilder()
builder.Provider = connStringData.Provider
builder.Metadata = connStringData.Metadata
builder.ProviderConnectionString = connStringData.ProviderConnectionString
Using ctx = New OrderITEntities(builder.ConnectionString)
    ...
End Using
```

The important thing is that the data must not contain the section name. For instance, the `provider` parameter *must* contain the value `System.Data.SqlClient`, and not `Provider=System.Data.SqlClient`. The `Provider=` string is automatically handled by the `EntityConnectionStringBuilder` class.

In the second case, where we built the connection string at runtime, we only needed to change part of the connection string: the SSDL location. In this case, you can put the connection string in the configuration file, putting a placeholder `{0}` in the SSDL location. Once you know the database version, you can replace the placeholder with the correct SSDL path. This could be done with a simple `String.Format`, but the `EntityConnectionStringBuilder` has the ability to parse a connection string and populate the related properties.

The following solution first loads the connection string and then uses the `String.Format` statement on the `Metadata` property only.

Listing 3.4 Modifying an existing connection string

C#

```
var builder = new EntityConnectionStringBuilder();
builder.ConnectionString = connString;
builder.Metadata = String.Format(builder.Metadata, "res://*/Model.ssdl");
using (var ctx = new OrderITEntities(builder.ConnectionString))
{
    ...
}
```

VB

```
Dim builder = New EntityConnectionStringBuilder()
builder.ConnectionString = connString
builder.Metadata = String.Format(builder.Metadata, "res://*/Model.ssdl")
Using ctx = New OrderITEntities(builder.ConnectionString)
    ...
End Using
```

The connection string is only the first part of the game. We mentioned in chapter 1 that one of the key features of Entity Framework is that it lets you write queries against the object model and not against the database. In the next section, we'll focus on this and look at what happens under the covers.

Figure 3.1   Queries written against classes are transformed into SQL.

3.2.2   *Writing queries against classes*

Because the database is completely abstracted by the EDM, you can write queries against the classes, completely ignoring the underlying database organization. Entity Framework uses mapping information to translate those queries into SQL. This work-flow is explained in figure 3.1.

The abstraction between classes and the database isn't too difficult to grasp. If a property is named differently from the column of the table it's mapped to, you still use the property name in your query—this is obvious because you query against the class. With LINQ to Entities, you probably won't type the wrong name because Visual Studio's IntelliSense will give you hints about the correct name. What's more, the compiler will throw an error if you type the incorrect property name.

Other situations can lead to differences between the database and the object model. Customers and suppliers have their own classes, but there is only one table containing their data. Once again, you write your queries against these entities, and not against the Company table.

Furthermore, we've grouped address information into a complex type. When writing queries, they're accessed like a part of a type, whereas in the database they're plain columns.

At first, these differences might deceive you, especially if you're experienced with the relational model. But after a bit of practice, you'll see that writing queries this way is more intuitive and productive than writing SQL. Classes represent your business scenario more meaningfully than the relational model, with the result that writing a query against classes is more *business oriented* (and more natural) than writing SQL. What's more, the intricacies of the relationships between classes are handled by Entity Framework, so you don't need to care how the data is physically related.

Now that you understand how a query against the model is different from a query against the database, we can touch on another important subject. How is a LINQ to Entities query processed by the Object Services layer, and why does it become SQL instead of triggering an in-memory search against the entity set?

3.2.3   *LINQ to Entities queries vs. standard LINQ queries*

LINQ is an open platform that can be customized to execute queries against *any* data source (a plethora of providers on the web can retrieve data from web services and databases like Oracle and MySQL, NHibernate, and so on). The important caveat is that the entry point for querying is a list implementing the IEnumerable<T> interface.

ObjectSet<T> implements IEnumerable and another interface that's required to customize LINQ: IQueryable<T>. This interface holds a reference to an object that implements the IQueryProvider interface, and that object overrides the base LINQ

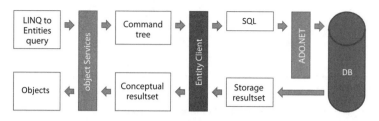

Figure 3.2   How a LINQ to Entities query passes through different layers and becomes a set of objects

implementation. Instead of triggering a local search, it analyzes the query and starts the SQL-generation process.

Now you know why queries written against `ObjectSet<T>` are evaluated differently than queries against other data sources. But that just explains how the query translation process starts, and *why* a LINQ to Entities query becomes SQL. In the next section, you'll discover *how* a query gets translated into SQL, you'll learn how it's executed, and you'll see that data is returned as a set of objects.

3.2.4   *Retrieving data from the database*

When you execute a query, the LINQ provider hosted by the entity set parses the query and creates a *command tree*. Because you're writing the query against classes, the command tree represents the query conceptually.

Object Services passes the command tree to the Entity Client, which, with the aid of mapping and the storage files, transforms it into a native SQL command. After that, the Entity Client uses the ADO.NET provider specified in the `provider` section of the `connectionString` attribute to launch the SQL against the database and obtain the result. The query result is then shaped in a tabular way that reflects the object model structure, as you saw in section 1.6.

Finally, the data is returned to the Object Services layer, which instantiates (or *materializes*) the objects. Figure 3.2 illustrates this process.

After scalar, complex, and reference properties are filled in, and before collection properties are dealt with, the context triggers the `ObjectMaterialized` event. This event accepts the entity that's being materialized and allows you to perform some logic before the object is returned to the application. The following listing shows how you can use this event.

> **Listing 3.5   Attaching a handler to the `ObjectMaterialized` event**

C#
```
public OrderITEntities()
{
  ctx.ObjectMaterialized +=
    new ObjectMaterializedEventHandler(ctx_ObjectMaterialized);
}

void ctx_ObjectMaterialized(object sender, ObjectMaterializedEventArgs e)
{
  var o = entity as Order;
```

```
  //any logic
}
```

VB
```
Public Sub New()
  AddHandler ctx.ObjectMaterialized, AddressOf ctx_ObjectMaterialized
End Sub

Private Sub ctx_ObjectMaterialized(ByVal sender As Object,
  ByVal e As ObjectMaterializedEventArgs)
  Dim o = TryCast(entity, Order)
  'any logic
End Sub
```

As you can see, subscribing to the `ObjectMaterialized` event is like subscribing to any other event in the .NET Framework class library.

There's an important caveat that you must keep in mind about the materialization step: the context implements the *Identity Map* pattern.

3.2.5   *Understanding Identity Map in the context*

The context holds references for all the entities it reads from the database and identifies them by their key properties. Before the context materializes a new entity, it checks whether one with the same key and of the same type already exists. If it does exist, the context returns the in-memory entity, discarding data from the database.

This pattern is named *Identity Map*, and it's vital for application consistency. Without the Identity Map, if you read an order, someone else updated it, and you read it again, you'd have two instances with different data representing the same order. Which one would be correct? Which one should you update? Should the OrderIT user know about it? The answers would depend on the situation, so you should never let this happen.

Keeping references to entities and checking whether there's already one in the context during materialization are heavy burdens for the context. Fortunately, this behavior isn't needed by all applications. Consider a web page that displays orders in a grid. After the orders are read from the context, they won't be touched in any way, so there's no point in storing references to the objects. Skipping this step makes the context lighter, because it doesn't memorize objects, and faster, because the Identity Map check doesn't happen.

> **NOTE**   In chapter 19, you'll see how tweaking applications in ways like this can dramatically improve performance.

More broadly speaking, you can choose the way the context treats entities after each query. This choice is made at the *query* level and not at the *context* level, meaning that the same context can use objects in one way for some queries and in another way for other queries.

More specifically, the context has four ways of managing entities returned by a query. You can set any of the following values for the `MergeOption` property:

- `AppendOnly`—If the entity is already in the context, it's discarded, and the context one is returned. If the entity isn't in the context, it's added. (This is the default behavior.)
- `NoTracking`—The entity isn't stored by the context.
- `OverwriteChanges`—If the entity is in the context, it's overwritten with values from the database and then is returned. If the entity isn't in the context, it's added.
- `PreserveChanges`—If the entity is in the context, properties modified by the user remain untouched, and the others are updated using database values. If the entity isn't in the context, it's added.

In our experience, the `AppendOnly` and `NoTracking` options have covered all our needs. We have never needed to use the other options. Nonetheless, never forget that they exist—one day you could need them.

> **NOTE** A context can't hold more than one object of the same type with the same key. For instance, it can't hold two orders or customers with the same key. In chapter 6, you'll learn that such operations cause exceptions. Also note that if a retrieved entity is tracked by a context, and a query retrieves it again, the `ObjectMaterialized` event isn't raised because the context entity is returned—there's no materialization process.

As mentioned in the previous list, `AppendOnly` is the default behavior, but you can override it by setting the `MergeOption` property of the entity set. This property is an enum of `MergeOption` type (defined in the `System.Data.Objects` namespace) whose possible values are in the previous list. Here's how you can set tracking behavior.

Listing 3.6 Setting tracking options

C#
```
var companies = ctx.Companies.ToList();
ctx.Orders.MergeOption = MergeOption.NoTracking;
var orders = ctx.Orders.ToList();
```

VB
```
Dim companies = ctx.Companies.ToList()
ctx.Orders.MergeOption = MergeOption.NoTracking
Dim orders = ctx.Orders.ToList()
```

Objects in the `companies` list are stored by the context because tracking is enabled by default. Objects in the `orders` list aren't tracked because the `Orders` entity set has been configured for no tracking.

So far, you've only had a brief description of the querying options. We'll cover more intricacies in chapter 6, which is dedicated to persistence.

The entity-set properties hide a nasty trap when dealing with tracking. They expose an `ObjectSet<T>` instance, but the way the instance is created affects the way you have to set tracking.

CREATEOBJECTSET<T> AND TRACKING

The default code generator and the POCO generator create code that instantiates an entity set lazily when it's first accessed. After the instance is created, it's reused for the entire context lifecycle. The result is that when you configure the tracking option, it remains the same for all queries issued against that entity set, unless you change it.

We have seen projects where, instead of reusing the same instance, a new one is created each time the entity set property is accessed. In this case, setting the tracking option has no effect. The `ObjectSet<T>` instance on which you set the option is different from the one returned when you later access the entity-set property. The result is that the context follows the default behavior.

To overcome this problem, you can assign the entity-set property to a local variable and then work directly with it, as shown here:

C#

```
var set = ctx.Companies;
set.MergeOption = MergeOption.NoTracking;
var companies = set.ToList();
```

VB

```
Dim set = ctx.Companies
set.MergeOption = MergeOption.NoTracking
Dim companies = set.ToList()
```

Setting the `MergeOption` property of the entity set isn't the only way to configure tracking. You can also use the `Execute` method.

EXECUTE AND TRACKING

The `Execute` method allows you to perform a query and set tracking in a single call. Keep in mind that, in this case, the value passed to the method overrides the entity set configuration.

Listing 3.7   Setting tracking via the `Execute` method

C#

```
ctx.Companies.MergeOption = MergeOption.NoTracking;
var companies = ctx.Companies.Execute(MergeOption.AppendOnly);
```

VB

```
ctx.Companies.MergeOption = MergeOption.NoTracking
Dim companies = ctx.Companies.Execute(MergeOption.AppendOnly)
```

Tracking is a key feature of Entity Framework. You'll find other APIs in this O/RM tool that are affected by tracking, and we'll discuss them in chapters 6 and 10. Now it's time to move on and discover how the Object Services layer interacts with the Entity Client.

3.2.6 Understanding interaction between Object Services and Entity Client

The `ObjectContext` class keeps an instance of the `EntityConnection` class. Just as the context is your entry point to Object Services, the connection is the entry point to the Entity Client. This instance isn't intended only for internal use—it's publicly exposed via the `Connection` property of the context. The context even has a constructor that accepts a connection.

The context handles this connection for you. It instantiates a new one if one has not been generated yet, opening it before executing a query and closing it when the query has been executed. When it persists objects, it opens the connection, starts the transaction, and commits or rolls back the transaction depending on whether an exception occurs.

Because you can access the connection through the context, you can manipulate it at will. Suppose that within the scope of a context, you must execute five queries. Opening and closing the connection each time isn't the best way to go. It isn't particularly expensive if the ADO.NET provider is configured for connection pooling (which is the default for SQL Server), but it can surely be optimized.

What you can do is manually handle the lifetime of the connection. When you manually open the connection, the context stops handling it, leaving it open and turning over to you the burden of physically closing it. This means you can open the connection, execute the five queries, and then close the connection within a single open-query-close cycle.

> **NOTE**   Even if you don't close the connection, it will be disposed of automatically when the context is disposed of. This is why we recommend the Using pattern.

You can further customize the interaction between the context and the connection by creating an instance of the connection and passing it to one of the context constructors. This way, the context ignores the connection lifecycle, leaving you in charge of its complete management.

This holds true during context disposal too. If the connection isn't generated by the context, it isn't disposed of. What's bad about this is that if you forget to close or dispose of the connection, it remains open until the garbage collector clears everything. Don't make this mistake.

In chapter 9, we'll go deeper inside the Entity Client and the `EntityConnection` class. Right now, though, it's time to take a look at the SQL generated by the Entity Client.

3.2.7   Capturing the generated SQL

Even if Entity Framework generates the SQL code, you can't assume the code is fine as is. You must *always* make sure that the generated statements perform well and don't require too many database resources to execute. Sometimes the generated query will be too heavy or complex, and you can get better performance by using a stored procedure or handcrafting the SQL.

The easiest way to inspect the SQL is to use the profiler tool that's included among the client-management tools that ship with most modern databases. With this tool, you can monitor all the statements executed against the database and then analyze the ones that need refinement or complete replacement.

Usually, this monitoring requires high-level permissions on the database, and sometimes you won't have such power. Fortunately, the Object Services layer comes to your aid with the `ObjectSet<T>` class's `ToTraceString` method. Here's how you can use it:

C#
```
var result = ctx.Orders.Where(o => o.Date.Year == DateTime.Now.Year);
var SQL = (result as ObjectQuery).ToTraceString();
```

VB
```
Dim result = ctx.Orders.Where(Function(o) o.Date.Year = DateTime.Now.Year)
Dim SQL = TryCast(result, ObjectQuery).ToTraceString()
```

Notice that this code doesn't cast to `ObjectQuery<T>` but to `ObjectQuery`. `Object-Query<T>` inherits from `ObjectQuery`, which is where the `ToTraceString` method is implemented.

All the steps in query processing should now be clear to you. But there is still one thing to know about the object creation done by the Object Services layer. We said that Object Services materializes the entities using the conceptual resultset coming from the Entity Client. What we didn't say is that the materialized entities may not be your model entities.

3.2.8   *Understanding which entities are returned by a query*

When you query for an order, you expect the returned entity to be of type `OrderIT.Model.Order`. This is pretty normal. You ask for an order, and you get an order. So you'll be surprised that, by default, the returned entity is of type `OrderIT.Model.Order_XXX`, where X is a number.

If you're accustomed to other O/RM tools, such as NHibernate, you'll be aware of what needs this technique satisfies. But if you're new to O/RM, you're probably trying to figure out the reason for this. What is this class? Who defined it? Why are you getting this class instead of the one you defined?

The answers are simple. The new class is a runtime-generated *proxy*. A proxy is a class that inherits from the one you expect and injects code in your properties to transparently add behavior to your class. Because the proxy is generated at runtime, nobody defined it. If you open the assembly with Reflector, you'll see that there is no definition of such a class.

> **NOTE**   Reflector is a tool that lets you browse a .NET assembly and discover its classes and their code. It's free, and you can download it from www.red-gate.com/products/reflector/.

Using reflection and runtime code emittance, Entity Framework generates a class that inherits from your type, injects custom code into properties, and then instantiates the class. The last question is probably the most interesting: Why?

The reason for this process is to provide features like lazy loading, object tracking, and others, without requiring you to write a single line of code. For instance, Entity

Framework 1.0 compliant classes had to inherit from a base class or implement interfaces, and write custom code in each property to interact with the object-tracking system. Thanks to the proxy technique, such plumbing is no longer required, because the necessary code is created dynamically by the proxy. Figure 3.3 shows a simplification of the code inside a proxy.

Making a POCO class extensible requires that you not seal it. To enable object tracking by the proxy, *all* properties must be virtual. If you need to enable lazy loading (more on this in the next chapter), even navigation properties must be virtual.

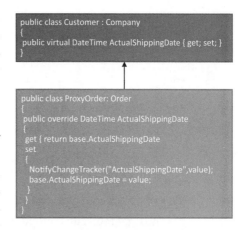

Figure 3.3　The proxy class (bottom) inherits from the object model class (top) and overrides properties.

> **NOTE**　You can turn off proxy creation and let the Object Services layer return the plain instance. Setting the `ContextOptions.ProxyCreation-Enabled` property to `false` disables this feature. By default, its value is `true`. A typical scenario where proxies are a problem is with web services, because a method that returns a proxy might run into serialization issues. Using a plain instance and not a proxy makes your class less powerful from an Entity Framework perspective, but it's still a fully functional class and you can still use it without any problem.

3.2.9　*When is a query executed?*

Generally speaking, LINQ queries are executed when the application code processes data (for instance, using a `foreach` or a `for`) or when certain methods are invoked (`ToList`, `ToArray`, `First`, `Single`, and so on).

Each time a LINQ to Entities query is executed, Entity Framework goes to the database and retrieves data. When it transforms data from record to object, it scans the in-memory objects to see if one is already there. If it is, the context returns the in-memory object, discarding the record. If it isn't, the context materializes the record into an object, puts it in memory, and returns it.

Let's look at an example. Suppose you have to iterate over the result of a query twice, as follows.

Listing 3.8　Iterating twice over query results, causing double query execution

C#

```
var result = LINQToEntitiesQuery;
foreach(var o in result)
{
    ...
}
```

```
foreach(var o in result)
{
  ...
}
```

VB

```
Dim result = LINQToEntitiesQuery
For Each o in result
  ...
Next

For Each o in result
  ...
Next
```

Each time the foreach (or For Each) statement is executed, a round trip to the database is triggered. The context doesn't care whether you have executed the same query before.

If the query is more complex than simply retrieving all orders, or if lots of data is returned, the double execution represents a serious problem for performance. The easy workaround is to force execution the first time and then download the objects in memory. Later, the in-memory collection is looped, so no round trip to the database is necessary. Here's the code for this useful technique.

Listing 3.9   Iterating twice over query results, causing single query execution

C#
```
var orders = LINQToEntitiesQuery.ToList();
foreach(var o in orders)
{
  ...
}

foreach(var o in orders)
{
  ...
}
```
Query execution

Collection iteration

VB
```
Dim orders = LINQToEntitiesQuery.ToList()
For Each o in orders
  ...
Next

For Each o in orders
  ...
Next
```
Query execution

Collection iteration

This approach must be followed not only for queries that return a list of objects, but for queries that return a single object too. Entity Framework makes no distinction between queries that return an object and queries that return a collection.

You can override the Identity Map behavior of the context so it doesn't keep objects in memory, but that wouldn't affect the double-execution problem.

The last thing to point out about the context is that it can re-create the database starting from the EDM.

3.2.10 *Managing the database from the context*

The `ObjectContext` class has four interesting methods that let you work with the database structure:

- `CreateDatabase`—Creates the database using the connection string and the information in the SSDL
- `CreateDatabaseScript`—Generates the database-creation script using the information in the SSDL
- `DatabaseExists`—Verifies that the database specified in the connection string exists
- `DeleteDatabase`—Deletes the database specified in the connection string

> **NOTE** This may seem a subject outside the scope of this chapter, but you can't query a database if it doesn't exist.

These methods are useful when you create an application and don't create an installation package. When the application starts, you can use `DatabaseExists` and `CreateDatabase` to create the database if it doesn't exist.

Apart from this situation, these methods aren't particularly important. Nonetheless, they're another string in your bow. Maybe one day you'll need them.

3.3 *Summary*

In this chapter, you have learned the basics of querying. Although you haven't seen much code in action, everything you've read in this chapter will benefit you in the real world.

For instance, you'll often have to modify the connection string, so having its structure clear in your mind is useful because it's complex. Similarly, when you're debugging an application, being able to inspect the SQL that's generated is important, because Entity Framework doesn't always generate friendly SQL.

Last, but not least, you have learned that a query is always executed against the database unless its result is downloaded in the client memory. This is an essential point, because often it's the cause of inadvertent query execution. We've often seen projects where the developers were not aware of this caveat, and the performance of their applications suffered.

Now that we've covered the fundamentals, it's time to write real queries.

Querying
with LINQ to Entities

This chapter covers

- Filtering with LINQ to Entities
- Projecting with LINQ to Entities
- Sorting and grouping with LINQ to Entities
- Executing handcrafted SQL code
- Choosing the fetching strategy

One of the most important features of Entity Framework is the LINQ to Entities query *dialect*. LINQ to Entities is a specialized version of LINQ that operates on Entity Framework models. LINQ to Entities isn't a LINQ to SQL competitor—it's the Entity Framework's main query language, whereas LINQ to SQL is a full-featured O/RM that shipped with the .NET Framework v3.5.

In this chapter, we'll begin by looking at how to filter data. Then we'll cover projecting, grouping, sorting, joining, and querying within inheritance hierarchies. With this approach, you'll gradually learn how LINQ to Entities works and understand how to obtain the same data you would get using native SQL queries. We'll assume that you're already familiar with LINQ. If you haven't seen it yet, you can read appendix A to learn the basics.

> ### What is the future of LINQ to SQL?
> It's no secret that LINQ to SQL is included in the .NET Framework v4.0 for compatibility reasons. Microsoft has clearly stated that Entity Framework is the recommended technology for data access. In the future, the Entity Framework will be developed and tightly integrated with other technologies, whereas LINQ to SQL will only be maintained and little evolved.

After LINQ to Entities has been discussed, we'll talk about other Object Services features, such as how you can integrate functions in LINQ to Entities, execute SQL queries, and choose a fetching strategy.

From this point on, you'll develop queries using LINQ *query syntax*. If you're familiar with LINQ, you'll already know what query syntax is; if you're not familiar with LINQ, you can learn more in appendix A, and we strongly recommend that you read it before continuing with this chapter. We'll resort to combining extension methods and lambda expressions when query syntax can't be used. We'll generally use query syntax because it's more intuitive, but that doesn't mean that it's recommended over its counterpart. The compiler produces the same IL code for both techniques.

In chapter 2, you created the OrderIT structure, and you'll reuse that to create the examples in this chapter.

4.1 Filtering data

Suppose you have a user who acts as the beta tester of OrderIT, and that user's first requirement is searching for orders by their shipping city. You can add the filtering capability by using the LINQ Where method. Where has an exact match in query syntax: where for C# and Where for VB. This clause is shown in action in the following code, which retrieves all orders shipped to New York:

C#
```
from o in ctx.Orders
where o.ShippingAddress.City == "New York"
select o;
```

VB
```
From o In ctx.Orders
Where o.ShippingAddress.City = "New York"
```

Filtering based on a single value is trivial. But sometimes you might need to search all orders placed in either New York or Seattle. That's a simple matter of slightly modifying the where clause to add the second city:

C#
```
o.ShippingAddress.City == "New York" || o.ShippingAddress.City == "Seattle"
```

VB
```
o.ShippingAddress.City = "New York" Or o.ShippingAddress.City = "Seattle"
```

Suppose the beta-testing user now wants to be able to enter multiple arbitrary shipping cities. Because you don't know in advance how many cities the user is going to search for, the filter becomes dynamic.

LINQ has the `Contains` method, which is perfect for this situation. Surprisingly, LINQ to Entities didn't support such a method in version 1.0. Fortunately, Entity Framework 4.0 has added this feature.

The first step in issuing a query that searches for multiple cities is creating a list of the cities. Later, in the `Where` clause, you can use the `Contains` method on this list, passing the field that must be searched. This is put into action in the following code, which retrieves all orders shipped to a dynamic list of cities:

C#
```
var cities = new[] { "New York", "Seattle" };

from o in ctx.Orders
where cities.Contains(o.ShippingAddress.City)
select o;
```

VB
```
Dim cities as New Array("New York, "Seattle")

From o In ctx.Orders
Where cities.Contains(o.ShippingAddress.City)
```

It's simple to filter data when the query involves only one entity (`Order` in this case), but real-world queries are more complex than that. In our experience, 95% of the queries in a project involve more than one entity. Fortunately, LINQ to Entities makes querying across associations between entities easier than ever.

4.1.1   *Filtering data based on associations*

When a query involves more than one entity, you have to navigate your model using navigation properties. In SQL, this *conceptual* navigation is represented using joins between tables, and it isn't always a simple task. Fortunately, because the mapping specifies the shapes of the model and the database and their associations, Entity Framework has enough information to transform the conceptual navigation across entities in SQL joins between the mapped tables without your having to specify anything.

The association cardinality makes a difference in how you do the filtering. There are two main situations. If your association refers to a single entity (one-to-one, such as a detail to its order), you work with a single entity—that's easy to do. If your association refers to a list of entities (one-to-many or many-to-many, such as an order to its details), the filter is based on an aggregation or subfilter applied to the associated list. That's a little more complicated.

Let's start with the simpler of the two situations.

FILTERING WITH A SINGLE ASSOCIATION

As we mentioned before, when you create a query that involves two entities with a one-to-one association, filtering data is trivial. Because the main class has a property that points to the associated class, you can easily perform a search on that property by navigating to it. The following code searches for orders placed by customers whose billing city is New York:

C#

```
from order in ctx.Orders
where order.Customer.BillingAddress.City == "New York"
select order;
```

VB

```
From order In ctx.Orders _
Where order.Customer.BillingAddress.City = "New York"
```

In this query, the mismatch between the relational model and the OOP model shines. First, even if two entities are involved (Order and Customer), only the Orders entity set is used. Second, you don't care how the relationship between Order and Customer is maintained in the database; you simply navigate your model, leaving to Entity Framework the burden of creating joins between tables while generating the SQL code. Finally, the Order table contains a plain BillingCity column, but in the model it's refactored into the AddressInfo complex type, which is the type of the Billing-Address property.

Here you can see the SQL code generated by Entity Framework.

Listing 4.1 SQL generated by the previous query

```
SELECT
[Extent1].[OrderId] AS [OrderId],
[Extent1].[OrderDate] AS [OrderDate],
[Extent1].[EstimatedShippingDate] AS [EstimatedShippingDate],
[Extent1].[ActualShippingDate] AS [ActualShippingDate],
[Extent1].[ShippingAddress] AS [ShippingAddress],
[Extent1].[ShippingCity] AS [ShippingCity],
[Extent1].[ShippingZipCode] AS [ShippingZipCode],
[Extent1].[ShippingCountry] AS [ShippingCountry],
[Extent1].[CustomerId] AS [CustomerId],
[Extent1].[Version] AS [Version]
FROM  [dbo].[Order] AS [Extent1]
INNER JOIN [dbo].[Company] AS [Extent2]        Creates join
  ON ([Extent2].[Type] = 'C')                  between tables
  AND ([Extent1].[CustomerId] = [Extent2].[CompanyId])
WHERE 'New York' = [Extent2].[BillingCity]
```

This SQL is close to what you would have written manually. The SQL Server team has closely collaborated with the Entity Framework developers to make the generated SQL as performant as possible. The SQL generated by Entity Framework isn't always the best, due to the generic nature of the SQL generator, but most of the time you can live with it.

Working with a single association is pretty straightforward, isn't it? Collection associations are harder to manage. Although LINQ to Entities generally simplifies the task of querying, this type of association is a little tricky.

FILTERING WITH COLLECTION ASSOCIATIONS

What's complex in this type of association is that the filter must be expressed on an aggregation of the associated list, and not directly on a property, as for single associations. But what seems difficult to understand using words turns out to be simple using an example.

Suppose the user wants to retrieve orders where a specific product is sold. You have to aggregate the details of each order, returning a Boolean that indicates whether at least one product is of the specified brand. This result is achieved using the Any method. It's a method that belongs to the *set* family, and it accepts a lambda stating the condition that needs to be satisfied at least once.

The following code puts this theory in action by retrieving all orders that included products of brand MyBrand:

C#
```
from order in ctx.Orders
where order.OrderDetails.Any(d => d.Product.Brand == "MyBrand")
select order;
```

VB
```
From order In ctx.Orders
Where order.OrderDetails.Any(Function(d) d.Product.Brand = "MyBrand")
```

Now, suppose the user wants to retrieve orders where no item is discounted. LINQ to Entities has another set method that deserves your attention: All. It allows you to specify a condition and ensure that all the items in the queried collection satisfy it. In this case, the condition is that the Discount property of each detail is 0:

C#
```
from order in ctx.Orders
where order.OrderDetails.All(d => d.Discount == 0)
select order;
```

VB
```
From order In ctx.Orders
Where order.OrderDetails.All(Function(d) d.Discount = 0)
```

Crafting the SQL code to perform this query isn't easy, but LINQ to Entities makes it simple and straightforward.

Filters can be applied even on data calculated on associations. Suppose the user wants to be able to search orders where the total discount exceeds a certain amount—in this case, five dollars. By using Sum to perform the calculation, the query becomes easy:

C#
```
from order in ctx.Orders
where order.OrderDetails.Sum(d => d.Discount * d.Quantity) > 5
select order;
```

VB
```
From order In ctx.Orders
Where order.OrderDetails.Sum(Function(d) d.Discount * d.Quantity) > 5
```

Sum belongs to the family of *aggregation* methods. It sums the result returned by the input lambda expression. The expression might be a simple field or an arithmetic expression, as in the preceding code.

You know you can chain LINQ methods—that's what makes LINQ one of the most powerful features of the entire .NET Framework. With a bit of method-chaining practice, you can write queries that involve set methods and aggregation methods to solve particular problems. The following listing enables the user to search for orders where more than one product has been sold.

> **Listing 4.2 Retrieving all orders that have sold more than one product**

C#
```
from order in ctx.Orders
where order.OrderDetails
  .Select(d => d.Product.ProductId)
  .Distinct()
  .Count() > 1
select order;
```

VB
```
From order In ctx.Orders _
Where order.OrderDetails.
  Select(Function(d) d.Product.ProductId).
  Distinct().
  Count() > 1
```

Let's examine this query to understand what's been done. The first method that's applied to the details list is Select. This is a *projection* method used to set the output of a query (more on this subject later in this chapter). In this case, you're extracting only the ProductId property, so the method gives back a list of integers. Next, you use the Distinct method to remove any duplicate ProductIds (remember that a product can appear twice in an order due to the discount policy). Finally, you use the Count method to count the occurrences and see if there is more than one. Figure 4.1 shows the workflow of this process.

You'd probably expect Entity Framework to generate GROUPBY and HAVING SQL clauses to execute such a query, but that doesn't happen because the SQL generator is configured to nest queries instead of using the preceding SQL clauses. This isn't always the best approach, but it's a good trade-off between SQL performance on the database and simplicity of the SQL generation code.

> **NOTE** Potentially, you can chain any method in your query. The drawback is that as chaining becomes more complex, so does the generated SQL, and it consequently performs more poorly. Don't make the capital sin of ignoring the SQL. The risks are too high. (We have seen cases where entire systems crash because of bad SQL queries.)

Figure 4.1 The chained methods filter data and count how many products are sold.

Often, the filter you'll have to apply isn't based on *what* data you have to retrieve but on *how much* data must be returned. A typical example is when a web application displays paged data in a grid. Let's see how you can apply this type of filter.

4.1.2   Paging results

One of the easiest ways to filter data is to return only the first *n* occurrences. Each database has its own syntax for performing this task. LINQ to Entities lets you declare one method and leave to the SQL generator the burden of generating the correct SQL. This is another wonderful example of the power of Entity Framework.

The ability to extract only the first *n* occurrences is useful when the beta-testing user asks for a little dashboard in the main form of the application. They want to see the last 15 orders placed by their customers so they can quickly start handling them.

The method that enables such a filter is Take. This method accepts an integer that specifies the number of objects to be retrieved. VB supports this method in the query syntax, but in C# you have to use the extension method:

C#
```
(from order in ctx.Orders
 orderby order.OrderDate
 select order).Take(15);
```

VB
```
From order In ctx.Orders
Order By order.OrderDate
Take(15)
```

The user's business is growing. In spite of the filters already enabled, each time the user searches for orders, they get so many records that it slows down the web page's performance and consequently its usability. Furthermore, dealing with hundreds of orders on a single page isn't user-friendly. The user needs the orders paged in a grid.

LINQ to Entities offers a method that, used in conjunction with Take, makes the paging operations easier than ever: Skip. This method lets you ignore the first *n* records. To enable paging, you use Skip to jump the first *n* records and then Take to retrieve only the next *n* after the ones skipped. The following code snippet skips the first 10 records and takes the next 10, which means it retrieves the second page of a grid where each page contains 10 records. As it does for the Skip method, VB supports Take in query syntax, whereas in C# you have to use the extension method:

C#
```
(from o in ctx.Orders
 orderby o.OrderId
 select o).Skip(10).Take(10);
```

VB
```
From o In ctx.Orders
Order By o.OrderId
Skip (10)
Take (10)
```

It's mandatory to invoke `orderby` for C#, or `Order By` for VB, before `Take` and `Skip` because it decides the order of the data before paging. If you don't do that, you'll get a runtime exception. You'll learn more about sorting in section 4.4.

So far, the queries we've looked at return a list of entities. But often you need only a single entity. The next section shows how to accomplish such a task.

4.1.3 Retrieving one entity

After the user has selected an order, you need to display a form where the user can see the details and even modify some of them. In the OrderIT model, you need to find the order given its ID.

LINQ queries return an `IEnumerable<T>` even if only one object is retrieved. When you know in advance that you're going to get a single object, it's more convenient to return it directly instead of dealing with the list. The `First` and `Single` methods allow you to do this.

Listing 4.3 Retrieving an order given its ID using `First`

C#
```
(from order in ctx.Orders
 where order.OrderId == 1
 select order).First();

(from order in ctx.Orders
 where order.OrderId == 1
 select order).Single();
```

VB
```
(From order In ctx.Orders
 Where order.OrderId = 1).First()

(From order In ctx.Orders
 Where order.OrderId = 1).Single()
```

The result of these queries is an `Order` object. The `First` method is translated into a `TOP 1` clause in SQL. (`TOP` is valid for SQL Server; providers for other databases will generate the appropriate equivalent statement.)

If the query doesn't return a record, the `First` method generates an `Invalid-OperationException` with the error message "Sequence contains no elements." You can include the query in a try-catch block, but handling exceptions is an expensive task for the runtime. The best option is to use the `FirstOrDefault` method, which has the same behavior as `First` with the noticeable difference that if no record is returned, it returns the default value of the searched object. Because `Order` is a reference type, `FirstOrDefault` returns `null` if no object is retrieved by the query.

You can achieve the same goal using `Single`. The subtle difference between `First` and `Single` is that the latter enforces the rule that the database query must return only one record. To ensure such a constraint, the `Single` method issues a `TOP 2` SQL clause. If two records are returned, it throws an exception. If zero records are returned, it throws an exception unless you use `SingleOrDefault`, which has the same behavior as `FirstOrDefault`.

We recommend using `First` instead of `Single` for three reasons:

- When you know that you're retrieving one object, it's pointless to issue a `Top 2` in the database.
- `Single` is slightly slower that `First`.
- Checking that only one record exists for the input parameters should be the responsibility of the database's update phase and not the querying phase.

> **NOTE** Because the result of a query that uses `First` or `Single` isn't an `IEnumerable<T>` instance but the object you were searching, you can't cast it to `ObjectQuery` and retrieve the SQL code generated. In this case, profiling the database is the only available path.

LINQ to Entities isn't the only way to retrieve a single entity. You can also do it via the `ObjectContext` class's methods.

USING CONTEXT METHODS

The `ObjectContext` class allows you to retrieve a single entity with the `GetObject-ByKey` and `TryGetObjectByKey` methods.

The question you may be asking is: "Why do I need specific methods to get an object by its key when I already have LINQ to Entities?" The answer is that these methods behave differently. Before going to the database, they check whether an object with that given key is already in the context memory (recall the Identity Map pattern we talked about in section 3.2.5). If the object does exist in the context memory, they immediately return the in-memory object, skipping the database round trip. If not, they go to the database and retrieve the object, following the same path as LINQ to Entities queries.

`GetObjectByKey` gets an `EntityKey` object as an argument representing the key of the entity to be retrieved, and it returns the instance of the entity. If the object isn't found either in memory or in the database, `GetObjectByKey` throws an exception.

`TryGetObjectByKey` gets an `EntityKey` object and an `out` parameter for C#, or `ByRef` for VB, representing the entity that's returned. If the entity is found, the method returns `true` and the entity parameter contains the entity; otherwise, it returns `false` and the entity parameter remains `null`. Here's an example that uses these methods.

Listing 4.4 Retrieving an entity by its key using context methods

C#
```
var key = new EntityKey("OrderITEntities.Orders", "OrderId", 1);
var entity = ctx.GetObjectByKey(key);

Object entity;
var found = ctx.TryGetObjectByKey(key, entity);
```

VB

```
Dim key = new EntityKey("OrderITEntities.Orders", "OrderId", 1)
Dim entity = ctx.GetObjectByKey(key)

Dim entity As Object = Nothing
Dim found = ctx.TryGetObjectByKey(key, entity)
```

Unless you're sure the object exists, use the `TryGetObjectByKey` method because it avoids exceptions, increasing performance.

So far, we've looked at creating *static* queries. Now the user needs to filter data by more optional parameters. This means you have to create the query at runtime. Generating the SQL string at runtime is pretty straightforward, because you simply have to concatenate strings. With LINQ to Entities, the situation is different.

4.1.4 *Creating queries dynamically*

Because the user wants to search orders by many parameters, you need to retrieve whichever parameters are entered by the user and create the query dynamically. Once again, LINQ to Entities keeps it simple, much as with plain SQL. First, you create an instance of the `ObjectQuery<T>` class. Then, you iterate over the filters and determine whether a filter needs to be applied. If a filter must be applied to the query, you concatenate a new LINQ method to the `ObjectQuery<T>` instance, reassigning the result to the same instance. At the end of the process, you'll have a dynamic query like this.

Listing 4.5   Applying filters dynamically

C#

```
var date = DateTime.Today;
string city = null;

var result = ctx.Orders.AsQueryable();

if (date != DateTime.MinValue)
  result = result.Where(o => o.OrderDate < date);

if (String.IsNullOrEmpty(city))
  result = result.Where(o => o.ShippingAddress.City == city);
```

VB

```
Dim searchDate = DateTime.Today
Dim city As String = Nothing

Dim result = ctx.Orders.AsQueryable()

If searchDate <> DateTime.MinValue Then
    result = result.Where(Function(o) o.OrderDate < searchDate)
End If

If String.IsNullOrEmpty(city) Then
    result = result.Where(Function(o) o.ShippingAddress.City = city)
End If
```

Because the query isn't executed until data is requested, you can concatenate as many methods as you need. Naturally, this technique applies to all LINQ to Entities methods, but it's likely that you'll use it only when applying filters.

So far, all the queries you've created return full entities. If you think in database terminology, it's similar to writing a SELECT * FROM statement. In our experience, you usually don't need all the data exposed by an entity, but rather only a small subset. In the next section, we'll discuss how to retrieve only the desired data.

4.2   *Projecting results*

Our insatiable user is getting more demanding. So far, the user has been shown the grid with all properties related to each order. That's no longer acceptable, because there's too much data cluttering up the page. The user wants to see only order date and shipping address information. Extracting all the data for each order is a waste of resources, in this case, because you only need only some of the data. What you need is a projection of the order.

Projecting is the process of shaping the output result so it's different from the entity that's being queried. The object containing the order date and the shipping address information is a projection of the Order entity. You already had a sneak peek at projecting in listing 4.2 with the Select method.

> **NOTE**   *Projection* isn't an Entity Framework or LINQ to Entities term. It's a general concept for the shaping of a result. For instance, in SQL a query like SELECT companyid, name FROM company is considered a projection.

A projection can contain properties coming from a single entity as well as entities referenced by navigation properties. Properties may be used to calculate new values that later are projected in the final result. The only limit to the possibilities of projections is your imagination (and business needs).

LINQ to Entities has one method for projecting: Select. Let's start with a simple query that returns the ID, the order date, and the shipping address of all orders:

C#
```
var result = from o in ctx.Orders
             select new { o.OrderId, o.OrderDate, o.ShippingAddress };
```

VB
```
Dim result = From o In ctx.Orders
             Select New With { o.OrderId, o.OrderDate, o.ShippingAddress }
```

The Select clause is where you specify the shape of the output objects. It accepts the list of properties that represent the projected object to be created. Notice how anonymous types and type inferences shine in this query. The output result is a list of anonymous objects because the output type is created only at compile time. What's more, you resort to the var keyword for C#, or Dim for VB, to declare the result variable.

What you're doing here is creating an anonymous object for each record retrieved from the database and placing it in a collection. The names of the properties are automatically inferred by the compiler, using the names of the original properties. In this case, the object will have the properties OrderId, OrderDate, and ShippingAddress.

Despite the fact that the result is a list of anonymous types, Visual Studio is still able to offer autocompletion for the properties, and the compiler can still check that the query is correct.

The user isn't happy yet. Now they want to see the address information in a single column of the grid, because they need to cut and paste it easily. Yes, this requirement should be handled by the interface code, but for the sake of this demonstration, let's see how you can handle this requirement using LINQ to Entities.

You can group several properties into a new property or even into a new nested anonymous type. The first option is what we need in this situation.

Listing 4.6 Grouping the shipping address information into a single property

C#

```
from o in ctx.Orders
select new {
  o.OrderId,
  o.OrderDate,
  ShippingAddress = String.Format("{0}-{1}-{2}-{3}",
    o.ShippingAddress.Address,
    o.ShippingAddress.City,
    o.ShippingAddress.ZipCode
    o.ShippingAddress.Country)
};
```

VB

```
From o In ctx.Orders
Select New With {
  o.OrderId,
  o.OrderDate,
  .ShippingAddress = String.Format("{0}-{1}-{2}-{3}",
    o.ShippingAddress.Address,
    o.ShippingAddress.City,
    o.ShippingAddress.ZipCode
    o.ShippingAddress.Country)
}
```

This listing is slightly different from the first query in this section because the name of the property that combines all address-related properties (`ShippingAddress`) can't be inferred automatically by the compiler due to its composed nature. Putting the name of the property before the expression allows you to assign an arbitrary name to the property. All properties names can be modified this way.

As we said previously, you can create an anonymous type inside another anonymous type. For instance, in the following listing you retrieve only the ID, the date, and the address and city of both billing and shipping addresses.

Listing 4.7 Nesting anonymous types to group properties

C#

```
from o in ctx.Orders
select new {                              ◁─── Anonymous type
  o.OrderId,
  o.OrderDate,
  Shipping = new
  {                                            Nested
                                               anonymous
    o.ShippingAddress.City,                    type
    o.ShippingAddress.Address
  }
};
```

VB

```
From o In ctx.Orders
Select New With {                    ⟵── Anonymous type
  o.OrderId,
  o.OrderDate,
  .Shipping = New With
  {                                            Nested
    o.ShippingAddress.City,                    anonymous
    o.ShippingAddress.Address                  type
  }
}
```

Like filtering, projections can involve more than one entity, because associated entities can participate in projections too. In the next section, we'll look at how this feature works.

4.2.1   *Projecting with associations*

So far, you've learned that associations are important not only for model expressiveness, but even for Entity Framework, which uses them to simplify searches through
LINQ to Entities. It's not surprising that associations can participate in the projection
mechanism too. There are almost no differences between projecting an association
collection or a single association. In both cases, the syntax is similar to what you have
seen already.

PROJECTING WITH A SINGLE ASSOCIATION

The user's next requirement is to add customer information to the columns shown in
the grid. The power of the `Select` method makes this easy.

Projecting with single associations is easy because of its one-to-one nature. The
associated class is an extension of the main class you're querying, so creating a new
object with the necessary properties from both classes is natural. As you can see, the
following code retrieves projected orders and their customers:

C#

```
from o in ctx.Orders
select new { o.OrderId, o.OrderDate, o.ShippingAddress, o.Customer };
```

VB

```
From o In ctx.Orders
Select New With { o.OrderId, o.OrderDate, o.Customer }
```

Retrieving the full customer isn't necessary, though, because all the user needs to see
is the name. The following solution flattens the objects with associations into a single
object with the necessary data.

> **Listing 4.8   Retrieving orders and customer information in a single object**

C#

```
from o in ctx.Orders
select new
{
  o.OrderId,
  o.OrderDate,
```

```
    o.ShippingAddress,
    o.Customer.Name
};
```

VB
```
From o In ctx.Orders
Select New With
{
    o.OrderId,
    o.OrderDate,
    o.Customer.CompanyId,
    o.ShippingAddress,
    o.Customer.Name
}
```

In the real world, working with anonymous types can be painful. They can't be exposed to the outer layers unless you expose them as an `Object` instance. In our experience, this isn't practical, so you have to find another way to make the data available.

One option is to iterate over the returned objects and then instantiate the entities, filling in only the properties extracted by the query; but this is a waste of code and runtime performance.

The most natural fix for this problem would be to use object initializers to create an instance of a model entity, initializing only the properties you need. Unfortunately, that's not allowed by Entity Framework, because only full instances of the model entities can be created with LINQ to Entities (in section 4.2.2, we'll discuss this caveat).

The alternative that we strongly recommend is to create a data transfer object (DTO) and fill it with the projected data directly in the query, as shown here.

Listing 4.9 Retrieving orders and customer information in a DTO

C#
```
public class OrderDTO
{
    public int Id { get; set; }
    public DateTime OrderDate { get; set; }
    public AddressInfo ShippingAddress { get; set; }
    public string CustomerName { get; set; }
}
```
Declares DTO

```
from o in ctx.Orders
select new OrderDTO
{
    Id = o.OrderId,
    OrderDate = o.OrderDate,
    ShippingAddress = o.ShippingAddress,
    CustomerName = o.Customer.Name
};
```
Sets DTO properties

VB
```
Public Class OrderDTO
    Public Property Id() As Int32
    Public Property OrderDate() As DateTime
    Public Property ShippingAddress() As AddressInfo
    Public Property CustomerName() As String
End Class
```
Declares DTO

```
From o In ctx.Orders
Select New OrderDTO With
{
  .Id = o.OrderId,
  .OrderDate = o.OrderDate,
  .ShippingAddress = o.ShippingAddress,
  .CustomerName = o.Customer.Name
}
```

**Sets DTO
properties**

The code is pretty simple. You define a new DTO class and then fill it instead of creating an anonymous type.

Now let's take a look at how projecting with collection associations works.

PROJECTING WITH COLLECTION ASSOCIATIONS

The user again changes their specifications. Now the grid must also list the details for each order.

This is a new challenge. Now you aren't working with a single related entity but with a collection. Fortunately, the following snippet is all you need to fulfill the task:

C#
```
from o in ctx.Orders
select new { o.OrderId, o.OrderDate, o.ShippingAddress, o.OrderDetails };
```

VB
```
From o In ctx.Orders
Select New With { o.OrderId, o.ShippingAddress, o.OrderDetails }
```

The result is an anonymous type with a scalar property (`OrderId`), a complex property (`ShippingAddress`), and a third property that contains order details.

Naturally, the user doesn't need the full order detail properties—only a subset of them. This means you have to perform a nested projection to retrieve only the desired properties from each detail. This may sound difficult, but it turns out to be pretty easy.

Listing 4.10 Retrieving projected orders and their projected details

C#
```
from o in ctx.Orders
select new
{
  o.OrderId,
  o.OrderDate,
  o.ShippingAddress,
  Details = from d in o.OrderDetails
            select new
            {
                d.OrderDetailId, d.Product.ProductId, d.Quantity
            }
};
```

VB
```
From o In ctx.Orders
Select New With
{
  o.OrderId,
```

```
        o.OrderDate,
        o.ShippingAddress,
        .Details = From d In o.OrderDetails
                   Select New With
                   {
                       d.OrderDetailId, d.Product.ProductId, d.Quantity
                   }
}
```

On seeing the new version, the user decides that displaying all the details along with
the containing order makes the grid unreadable. Now the user wants to see only the
order total instead of all its details. This means the returned type can be a flat structure again, because you no longer have a collection property. Let's look at how you
can retrieve a single column from the collection property.

Listing 4.11 Retrieving projected orders and their total

C#
```
from o in ctx.Orders
select new
{
  o.OrderId,
  o.OrderDate,
  o.ShippingAddress,
  Total = o.OrderDetails.Sum(
           d => d.Quantity * (d.UnitPrice - d.Discount))
};
```

VB
```
From o In ctx.Orders
Select New With
{
  o.OrderId,
  o.ShippingAddress,
  .Total = o.OrderDetails.Sum(Function(d)
             d.Quantity * (d.UnitPrice - d.Discount))
}
```

As you can see, projecting with collection associations isn't very challenging. With a bit
of practice, you can easily manage the methods you need. What's even more interesting
is that the association can be queried too. In listing 4.11, you use the Sum method to calculate the total amount of each order, but you could also filter the details or sort them.

4.2.2 *Projections and object tracking*

When working with projected objects, you have to keep a couple of points in mind
regarding the object-tracking mechanism you first saw in chapter 1 (and which we'll
return to in chapter 6):

- *Object Services doesn't allow you to create model entities filling only some
  properties.* You can't use object initializers in a projection to set the properties
  of a model entity. Although it's syntactically correct, the engine will throw a
  NotSupportedException at runtime with the message, "The entity or complex

type 'EntityType' cannot be constructed in a LINQ to Entities query." This happens because object tracking only tracks objects whose type implements the `IEntityWithChangeTracker` interface (automatically implemented by the proxy). If they aren't fully loaded, it can't correctly monitor changes and send them back to the database. That means this code is *not* valid:

C#
```
.Select(o => new Order { OrderId = o.OrderId });
```

VB
```
.Select(Function(o) New Order With { .OrderId = o.OrderId })
```

The alternative is to use DTOs.

- *Object Services doesn't track anonymous entities.* Because the object tracker only tracks objects whose type implements `IEntityWithChangeTracker`, anonymous types are ignored.

You should now have a clear understanding of the two main query building blocks: filtering and projecting. Another feature that's often required is *grouping*. In the next section, we'll look at how you can use the power of LINQ to Entities to perform such tasks.

4.3   *Grouping data*

LINQ to Entities allows you to group data and create even projections with shaped data, as you've seen in previous examples. A model offers a first level of grouping for free. You often have to group orders based on the customer who placed them, and the domain model represents this grouping naturally, because every `Customer` object contains a list of its orders. When we talk about grouping, we're referring to a different level, where you use a simple property as the key for a grouping.

LINQ to Entities allows you to group data by using either query syntax or query methods. In VB, the syntax is `Group By ... Into Group`, where the ellipsis in the middle contains the name of the grouping property. In C#, the query syntax uses the `group ... by ...` clause, where the first ellipsis is filled with the name of the variable declared in the `from` clause, and the second is filled with the grouping property. For example, suppose you had to return all orders grouped by shipping city. You could write the following query:

C#
```
from c in ctx.Orders
group c by c.ShippingAddress.City;
```

VB
```
From c In ctx.Orders
Group By c.ShippingAddress.City Into Group
```

The result type is a bit complex, because it's an object of type `IEnumerable<IGrouping<string, Order>>`. `IGrouping` is a special class with a key property—the shipping address value in this case—and a value property, which is an `IEnumerable<T>` holding

⊟ ⬤ result	{System.Data.Objects.ObjectQuery<System.Linq.IGrouping<string,CH03.Order>}
⊞ ⬤ base	{System.Data.Objects.ObjectQuery<System.Linq.IGrouping<string,CH03.Order>}
🔧 Name	"It"
⊞ ⬤ Non-Public members	
⊟ ⬤ Results View	Expanding the Results View will enumerate the IEnumerable
⊞ ⬤ [0]	{System.Data.Objects.ELinq.InitializerMetadata.Grouping<string,CH03.Order>}
⊞ ⬤ [1]	{System.Data.Objects.ELinq.InitializerMetadata.Grouping<string,CH03.Order>}
⊞ ⬤ [2]	{System.Data.Objects.ELinq.InitializerMetadata.Grouping<string,CH03.Order>}
⊟ ⬤ [3]	{System.Data.Objects.ELinq.InitializerMetadata.Grouping<string,CH03.Order>}
🔧 Key	"Miami"
⊟ ⬤ Results View	Expanding the Results View will enumerate the IEnumerable
⊞ ⬤ [0]	{CH03.Order}
⊞ ⬤ [1]	{CH03.Order}
⊞ ⬤ [4]	{System.Data.Objects.ELinq.InitializerMetadata.Grouping<string,CH03.Order>}
⊞ ⬤ [5]	{System.Data.Objects.ELinq.InitializerMetadata.Grouping<string,CH03.Order>}
⊞ ⬤ [6]	{System.Data.Objects.ELinq.InitializerMetadata.Grouping<string,CH03.Order>}

Figure 4.2   The structure returned by a grouping query

all the objects that correspond to the key. For instance, if the key property value is
Miami, the value property contains the order shipped to that city. Figure 4.2 summarizes the structure.

Iterating over this result requires a loop of all the keys and a nested loop that iterates over the values associated with the keys.

Listing 4.12   Iterating over the results of a grouping query

C#
```
foreach (var key in result)
{
  Console.WriteLine(key.Key);
  foreach (var item in key)
    Console.WriteLine(item.OrderId);
}
```

VB
```
For Each key In result
  Console.WriteLine(key.City)
  For Each item In key.Group
    Console.WriteLine(item.OrderId)
  Next
Next
```

By default, C# assigns the name Key to the key property, whereas VB uses the grouping property name. You can't override this behavior, but by giving a name to the group and using projection, you can name the key and the value properties in any way you prefer. Naming the group requires different coding styles across languages.

In VB, there's no need to use the Select clause, because everything can be managed in the Group By clause. After this clause, you add the new name of the key property, followed by the equals (=) symbol and the grouping property. After the Into keyword, you put the name of the property that contains the entities that correspond to the key, followed by the = Group string.

In C#, you need to modify the group by clause, adding the keyword into after the grouping key and stating the name of the group after that. Later, you have to add a select clause where you create a new anonymous type. It must contain the property for the key, with a different name if necessary, and the property that contains the entities that correspond to the key. This can be renamed if you want; otherwise it will take the name of the group.

Because the projection changes the way data is returned by the query, you have to adapt the iteration code to reflect this change. Here's how all this theory works in practice.

Listing 4.13   Changing the names of grouped data

C#

```
var result = from c in ctx.Orders
             group c by c.ShippingAddress.City into oGroup
             select new { CityName = oGroup.Key, Items = oGroup };

foreach (var key in result)
{
  Console.WriteLine(key.CityName);
  foreach (var item in key.Items)
    Console.WriteLine(item.OrderId);
}
```

VB

```
Dim result = From c In ctx.Orders
             Group By CityName = c.ShippingAddress.City Into Items = Group

For Each key In result
  Console.WriteLine(key.CityName)
  For Each item In key.Items
    Console.WriteLine(item.OrderId)
  Next
Next
```

We've mentioned the grouping key, but we didn't explain what a key can be. So far, you've used a single property, but that's only one of the possibilities. Often, you'll need to group data by multiple properties. For instance, you might want to group orders by shipping city and ZIP code, to better organize the shipments. Even in this case, there are differences between languages. In VB, you can insert a city and ZIP code separated by a comma, whereas in C# you have to use anonymous types to specify an object as a key and put the city and ZIP code into it. This is shown in the following listing.

Listing 4.14   Using multiple properties for grouping

C#

```
var result = from o in ctx.Orders
             group o by new
             {
                 o.ShippingAddress.City, o.ShippingAddress.ZipCode
```

```
                  };
foreach (var key in result)
{
  Console.WriteLine(key.Key.City + "-" + key.Key.ZipCode);
  foreach (var item in key)
    Console.WriteLine(item.OrderId);
}
```

VB

```
Dim result = From o In ctx.Orders
             Group By o.ShippingAddress.City, o.ShippingAddress.ZipCode
             Into Group

For Each key In result
  Console.WriteLine(key.City & "-" & key.ZipCode)
  For Each item In key.Group
    Console.WriteLine(item.OrderId)
  Next
Next
```

Just as the key can be customized to reflect your needs, the grouped data can be projected to save resources. You can invoke the `Select` method on the value list inside the `Select` method on the grouping, like this.

Listing 4.15 Projecting the grouped data

C#

```
from o in ctx.Orders
group o by o.ShippingAddress.City into g
select new
{
  g.Key,
  Items = g.Select(og => new { og.OrderId, og.OrderDate })
};
```

VB

```
From o In ctx.Orders
Group By o.ShippingAddress.City Into g = Group
Select New With
{
  City,
  .items = g.Select(Function(og) New With { og.OrderId, og.OrderDate })
}
```

The power of projection allows the grouped data to contain information from associated entities, too. We won't show you how to do this because it's similar to what you saw in the section 4.2.

LINQ to Entities allows you to filter data even after it's been grouped. That's our next topic.

4.3.1   Filtering aggregated data

Filtering on aggregated data is the equivalent of using the HAVING clause in SQL. For example, you may want to search for orders grouped by city, where the total number of orders is higher than a given number. This can be achieved easily by using LINQ methods belonging to the *aggregate* family.

Listing 4.16   Grouping orders only for cities that have more than two orders

C#
```
from o in ctx.Orders
group o by o.ShippingAddress.City into g
where g.Count() > 2
select g;
```

VB
```
From o In ctx.Orders
Group By o.ShippingAddress.City Into g = Group
Where g.Count() > 2
```

The where clause after the grouping affects only the grouped data. If you need to filter data before it's grouped, you have to invoke the where before the grouping. Depending on where you place the where clause, the variables in the query can go out of scope. Let's modify the example in listing 4.16. If you were to place the where before the group by clause, the o variable would be in scope, but the g variable wouldn't be in scope because it's not declared yet. In contrast, if you placed the where clause after the group by clause, the variable o would be out of scope and couldn't be referenced, whereas g would be in scope and could be used.

Now that you're a master of filtering, projecting, and grouping, you're ready to into another feature of LINQ to Entities: sorting. It's one of the easiest tasks enabled by LINQ to Entities. The situation is a bit more complicated when associations are involved, but you should be comfortable enough with them now.

4.4   Sorting

Our beta-testing user is back with requests for lots of new features. The first relates to the order in which results are shown. The user wants data to be sorted by the shipping city and ZIP code.

You'll be delighted to know that LINQ has an extension method that enables sorting by one or multiple properties; and it's no surprise that LINQ to Entities provides its own implementation of this method, which translates into an ORDER BY SQL statement.

Query syntax has the orderby clause in C# and Order By in VB. These clauses accepts the (comma-separated) properties on which the sorting operation is based. By default, the data is sorted in ascending order, but you can override this by adding the keyword descending for C# or Descending for VB after the sorting property. If you have multiple properties that need to be in descending order, you'll have to add the keyword after each of them. As in SQL, although the ascending sorting order happens by default, you can still specify it using the keyword ascending for C# or Ascending for VB. Here's an example.

Listing 4.17 Sorting with single and multiple properties

C#

```
from o in ctx.Orders
orderby o.ShippingAddress.City
select o;

from o in ctx.Orders
orderby o.ShippingAddress.City, o.ShippingAddress.ZipCode descending
select o;
```

VB

```
From o In ctx.Orders
Order By o.ShippingAddress.City

From o In ctx.Orders
Order By o.ShippingAddress.City, o.ShippingAddress.ZipCode Descending
```

There's little to discuss about sorting in a single class. It gets more interesting when you need to sort data by a property of an associated class.

4.4.1 Sorting with associations

The user now wants to show the most valuable orders at the top of the grid. In this case, the sorting is based on an aggregated value instead of a simple field.

Fortunately, this solution isn't complicated. You already know all the basics.

Listing 4.18 Sorting by an aggregated value of association

C#

```
from o in ctx.Orders
orderby o.OrderDetails.Sum(
  d => d.Quantity * (d.UnitPrice - d.Discount))
select new
{
  o.OrderId,
  o.OrderDate,
  o.ShippingAddress,
  Total = o.OrderDetails.Sum(
    d => d.Quantity * (d.UnitPrice - d.Discount))
};
```

VB

```
From o In ctx.Orders
Order By o.OrderDetails.Sum(
  Function(d) d.Quantity * (d.UnitPrice - d.Discount)
)
Select New With
{
  o.OrderId,
  o.OrderDate,
  o.ShippingAddress,
  .Total = o.OrderDetails.Sum(Function(d)
    d.Quantity * (d.UnitPrice - d.Discount))
}
```

The result of this query is an IOrderedQueryable<T> object. Because IOrdered-Queryable<T> implements IEnumerable<T>, it can be iterated using a foreach statement, a data-binding operation, or another enumeration mechanism.

Associated data can be ordered too. The only way to perform such an operation is to use projections and create a property in the anonymous type that holds sorted data. For instance, you might want to retrieve orders and their details, sorted by quantity, to bind them to a grid.

Listing 4.19   Retrieving projected orders and details ordered by quantity

C#
```
from o in ctx.Orders
select new
{
  o.OrderId,
  o.ShippingAddress.City,
  Details = o.OrderDetails.OrderBy(d => d.Quantity)
};
```

VB
```
From o in ctx.Orders
Select New With
{
  o.OrderId,
  o.ShippingAddress.City,
  .Details = o.OrderDetails.OrderBy(Function(d) d.Quantity)
}
```

When it comes to single associations, the solution is even simpler, because no aggregation must be performed—you can use an external property as if it were a property of the queried class. That's what the next snippet shows, retrieving orders sorted by the city of their customer:

C#
```
from o in ctx.Orders
orderby o.Customer.ShippingAddress.City
select o;
```

VB
```
From o in ctx.Orders
Order By o.Customer.ShippingAddress.City
```

We mentioned that the SQL generator uses mapping information to handle joins between tables when associated entities are involved in a query. There are situations when foreign keys aren't enough to join tables, and other columns must be used. In this situation, you have to handle joins manually, overriding the default behavior. In the next section, we'll cover this topic.

4.5   *Joining data*

When you write queries that span multiple associated tables, these joins are automatically handled by the SQL generator, and you don't have to worry about them. But there are situations where a relationship between properties exists, but it can't be represented using foreign keys. In such cases, you can use the `join` clause.

We have never found a situation where we had to resort to a join. The navigable nature of the model and the query capabilities of LINQ to Entities make joins almost useless.

> **NOTE** In his blog, a program manager on the Entity SQL team affirmed the following: "A well defined query against a well defined entity data model doesn't need JOIN. Navigation properties in combination with nesting sub-queries should be used instead. These latter constructs represent task requirements much more closely than JOIN does. That makes it easier to build and maintain correct Entity SQL queries." This statement was intended for Entity SQL, but it's valid for LINQ to Entities as well. You can find Zlatko Michailov's original post, "Entity SQL Tip #1," at http://mng.bz/4k7j.

Let's look at a practical example showing how unimportant manual joins are. Assume you have to find orders where the shipping city is the same as the city set in the customer profile. In the SQL world, you would join the Order and Company tables using the CompanyId and ShippingCity columns. In the LINQ to Entities world, the approach remains the same because when you're manually joining objects, the SQL generator *ignores* the relationships between classes. You can write queries like these.

Listing 4.20 Writing queries that use joins

C#
```
from o in ctx.Orders                                      ❶ Join by single
join c in ctx.Companies                                      property
    on o.ShippingAddress.City equals c.ShippingAddress.City
select o;

from o in ctx.Orders                                      ❷ Join by multiple
join c in ctx.Companies.OfType<Customer>()                   properties
    on new { o.ShippingAddress.City, o.Customer.CompanyId }
    equals new { c.ShippingAddress.City, c.CompanyId }
select o;
```

VB
```
From o In ctx.Orders                                      ❶ Join by single
Join c In ctx.Companies.OfType(Of Customer)                  property
    On o.ShippingAddress.City Equals c.ShippingAddress.City
Select o

From o In ctx.Orders                                      ❷ Join by multiple
Join c In ctx.Companies.OfType(Of Customer)                  properties
    On New With { o.ShippingAddress.City, o.Customer.CompanyId }
    Equals New With { c. ShippingAddress.City, c.CompanyId }
Select o
```

In the preceding listing, you see that there's little difference between joins that involve a single property ❶ and those that involve more ❷. In the first case, you put property names where required, and in the second you have to create an anonymous type and put all join properties into it.

> **NOTE** The preceding code uses the `OfType<T>` method. It is a LINQ method that in this example is required to ensure that the orders are joined with customers only. You'll learn more about this method in the next section.

The queries in listing 4.20 work correctly, but the join can be easily avoided by using a where clause. This requires you to write less code and consequently keeps it simple and readable:

C#
```
from o in ctx.Orders
where o.Customer.ShippingAddress.City == o.ShippingAddress.City
select o;
```

VB
```
From o in ctx.Orders
Where o.Customer.ShippingAddress.City = o.ShippingAddress.City
```

We aren't saying that joins must never be used, but a well-designed model only requires them to be applied in particular cases that must always be evaluated.

The example in listing 4.20 returns orders only if the customer data corresponds to filters expressed in the join clause. In particular cases, though, you may need to return orders even if the customer data doesn't correspond to filters expressed in the join clause. To achieve this result using SQL, you use an OUTER JOIN, but in LINQ to Entities you have to resort to a *group join* like the one in the following listing.

Listing 4.21 Performing a group join to simulate SQL OUTER JOIN clause

C#
```
from o in ctx.Orders
join c in ctx.Companies.OfType<Customer>()
  on new { o.ShippingAddress.City, o.Customer.CompanyId }
  equals new { c.ShippingAddress.City, c.CompanyId }
  into g
from item in g.DefaultIfEmpty()
select o;
```

VB
```
From o In ctx.Orders
Group Join c In ctx.Companies.OfType(Of Customer)()
  On New With _
    {.City = o.ShippingAddress.City, .CustomerId = o.Customer.CompanyId} _
  Equals New With _
    {.City = c.ShippingAddress.City, .CustomerId = c.CompanyId} _
  Into g = Group
From item In g.DefaultIfEmpty()
Select o
```

Real-world models use inheritance, and OrderIT is no exception. The customer/supplier and product scenarios rely heavily on this feature. Querying with inheritance is full of intricacies, but once again LINQ to Entities comes to the rescue. It's not always easy, but when you have learned how to avoid the pitfalls, you'll be ready to jump this hurdle.

4.6 Querying with inheritance

Inheritance introduces the concept of the *polymorphic query*. This type of query considers the inheritance hierarchy and returns objects that might be of different types but that inherit from the same base class.

Suppose you want to retrieve all products. What you receive from a polymorphic query is a list of Product objects, but the concrete types are Shirt or Shoe because the engine instantiates the correct type automatically. Not only do you get the correct type automatically, but you can even apply filters based upon the type. For instance, you can retrieve only shoes or only shirts.

Our beloved beta-testing user is finally happy about the way OrderIT shows orders. Now the user wants to concentrate on products. At first, they want to see all the products in a single page. This is trivial:

C#
```
from p in ctx.Products
select p;
```

VB
```
From p In ctx.Products
```

The result of this snippet is a list of Product objects, but the real types are one of its concrete inherited classes. This is clearly visible in figure 4.3.

((ObjectQuery<Product>)p).ToList() Count = 7	
⊞ ● [0]	{System.Data.Entity.DynamicProxies.Shoe_0B958C50253BA260AB71F577FBD0530096AC812ABEBF8A4AEC855B5AFC2BAE7F}
⊞ ● [1]	{System.Data.Entity.DynamicProxies.Shirt_D09AFDE8A41B9CE12DDEFE86F78C656536D9A75E82EBE989E96C225B690753CE}
⊞ ● [2]	{System.Data.Entity.DynamicProxies.Shoe_0B958C50253BA260AB71F577FBD0530096AC812ABEBF8A4AEC855B5AFC2BAE7F}
⊞ ● [3]	{System.Data.Entity.DynamicProxies.Shirt_D09AFDE8A41B9CE12DDEFE86F78C656536D9A75E82EBE989E96C225B690753CE}
⊞ ● [4]	{System.Data.Entity.DynamicProxies.Shirt_D09AFDE8A41B9CE12DDEFE86F78C656536D9A75E82EBE989E96C225B690753CE}
⊞ ● [5]	{System.Data.Entity.DynamicProxies.Shirt_D09AFDE8A41B9CE12DDEFE86F78C656536D9A75E82EBE989E96C225B690753CE}
⊞ ● [6]	{System.Data.Entity.DynamicProxies.Shirt_D09AFDE8A41B9CE12DDEFE86F78C656536D9A75E82EBE989E96C225B690753CE}
⊞ ● Raw View	

Figure 4.3 Seven products: five of type Shirt and two of type Shoe

Next, the user wants to apply a filter based on the type of product. LINQ offers two ways of specifying a type: the type equality operator (is for C#; TypeOf for VB) and the OfType<T> method. There is an important difference between these approaches. The equality operator performs a filtering operation, whereas the OfType<T> method not only filters, but also casts the result to the searched-for type. The following listing makes it clear.

Listing 4.22 Filtering products by type

C#
```
IEnumerable<Product> products = from p in ctx.Products
                                where p is Shoe
                                select p;
```

```
IEnumerable<Shoe> shoes = from p in ctx.Products.OfType<Shoe>()
                         select p;
```

VB

```
Dim products As IEnumerable(Of Product) = From p in ctx.Products
                                          Where TypeOf p is Shoe

Dim shoes As IEnumerable(Of Shoe) = From p in ctx.Products.
                                    OfType(Of Shoe)()
```

Due to this subtle difference, choosing between the methods isn't a matter of personal taste. Suppose you have several product types, and you need to find only shoes and shirts.

In this case, using OfType<T> is possible, but it's complicated because you have to merge two queries that retrieve different objects. Before merging the results, you have to cast their inner objects to the Product base class. In contrast, the equality operator doesn't alter the final result, so you don't need to do any extra work after the filter.

In other scenarios, you may want to search only for products of a specific type. In this case, using the OfType<T> method is the best way to go.

Filtering on properties of the base class can be done the same way. The user now wants to filter on data of an inherited type. For example, the user needs all shoes whose Sport property contains Basket. This is another scenario where OfType<T> works like a charm. Because OfType<T> casts the data, the where method (which is put after the OfType<T> method in the query) already knows that the output type is Shoe, so the search is pretty simple:

C#

```
from p in ctx.Products.OfType<Shoe>()
where p.Sport == "Basket" select p;
```

VB

```
From p In ctx.Products.OfType(Of Shoe)()
Where p.Sport = "Basket
```

But what if you want to find all "basket" shoes but have them returned as a list of Product objects? In this case, the preceding code doesn't work because it returns a list of Shoe objects.

You have two solutions: use the LINQ Cast<T> method, which casts the items back to Product, or cast the object in the Where clause to the desired type and apply the filter. With the second option, you can't use *explicit* casting—that would cause a runtime exception. You have to resort to a soft-casting operator like as for C# and TryCast for VB.

Listing 4.23   Filtering products by type and data, and returning them as base types

C#

```
from p in ctx.Products
where (p as Shoe).Sport == "Basket"
select p;
```

 1 Scans all products

```
(from p in ctx.Products.OfType<Shoe>()
 where p.Sport == "Basket" select p)
.Cast<Product>();
```
❷ Scans only shoes

VB
```
From p In ctx.Products
Where TryCast(p, Shoe).Sport = "Basket"
```
❶ Scans all products

```
(From p In ctx.Products.OfType(Of Shoe)()
 Where p.Sport = "Basket").
Cast(Of Product)
```
❷ Scans only shoes

In the first option ❶, the desired type is `Product`, so all products are scanned and only the "basket" shoes are returned. The same path is followed by the generated SQL: it scans all Product, Shoe, and Shirt tables and uses a `select case` SQL clause to identify whether a row is about a shoe or a shirt, wasting lots of resources because you don't need to fetch data from the Shirt table. (The `select case` syntax is valid for SQL only; other databases will use a different syntax.)

In the second option ❷, because it's immediately stated that the desired type is `Shoe`, the generated SQL uses only the Product and Shoe tables, optimizing the performance of the query. Unless you have a *strong* motivation to use the casting in the `where`, always prefer the `OfType<T>` method.

There is another performance caveat to keep in mind when querying hierarchies persisted via table per type (TPT). Consider the following query:

C#
```
from p in ctx.Products
select p.Name;
```

VB
```
From p In ctx.Products
Select p.Name
```

The only column involved is Name, which is in the Product table. What you'd probably expect is that the generated SQL only queries that table. Well, it's not like that. The SQL performs an outer join with all tables involved in the hierarchy (Shirt and Shoe), even if doing so is completely useless. This is the sort of case where a stored procedure is the best way to go.

So far, you've used standard LINQ methods. They're powerful, but they don't cover all the querying possibilities. LINQ to Entities allows you to potentially apply any CLR method, but the SQL translation engine doesn't understand everything. What's more, you might have a database function or custom functions that would be useful in LINQ to Entities queries, but there's no way to use these functions. This is where the new Entity Framework 4.0 *functions* feature comes into play.

4.7 *Using functions*

Functions are a convenient way to extend the capabilities of LINQ to Entities queries. Four types of functions can be applied:

- *Canonical functions*—A set of predefined functions that expose functionalities not natively available in LINQ to Entities
- *Database functions*—A set of predefined SQL Server–only functions
- *Model defined functions*—User-defined Entity SQL functions stored in the EDM
- *Custom database functions*—User-defined database functions that can be used in queries

In this section, we'll only cover the canonical and SQL database functions because they can be used easily. The other two options deserve more explanation and require a deeper knowledge of Entity Framework. They will be discussed in chapter 11.

4.7.1   Canonical functions

Canonical functions are utility methods that *express* an operation on the database. For instance, there are functions that perform math algorithms, date comparisons, and so on. In Entity Framework v1.0, canonical functions could only be executed in Entity SQL queries, but now they've been wrapped in conveniently marked CLR methods that can be invoked by LINQ to Entities. This change has widened LINQ to Entities' capabilities by reusing existing features.

Let's look at an example. Our user has decided they want a list of orders that have taken more than five days to ship. This is pretty easy using a LINQ query:

C#
```
from o in ctx.Orders
where o.OrderDate.AddDays(5) < o.ActualShippingDate
select o;
```

VB
```
From o In ctx.Orders
Where o.OrderDate.AddDays(5) < o.ActualShippingDate
```

The query compiles, but at runtime you get an exception because the translation engine isn't able to translate the AddDays method into the appropriate SQL.

Canonical functions cover this hole by introducing the DiffDays method, which accepts the two dates as arguments and returns the number of days difference between them. This method, and all others that are part of the canonical function family, is exposed via the EntityFunctions class in the namespace System.Data. Objects, as shown here:

C#
```
from o in ctx.Orders
where EntityFunctions.DiffDays(o.OrderDate, o.ActualShippingDate) > 5
select o;
```

VB
```
From o In ctx.Orders
Where EntityFunctions.DiffDays(o.OrderDate, o.ActualShippingDate) > 5
```

Another example where canonical functions help is with mathematical functions. Rounding off a number, rounding to the next upper or lower integer, and elevating a number to the *n*th power are all operations that can be performed using the methods in the `System.Math` class. Like the `DateTime` methods, the `Math` methods aren't supported by the SQL translation engine, which raises an exception at run-time. The alternative is using the methods `Pow`, `Round`, `Ceiling`, and `Floor` in the `EntityFunctions` class.

Such functions can obviously be invoked anywhere in a query, and not only in a `where` clause. For instance, you can use the `Abs` function to extract the absolute value of a number in the `select` clause.

Canonical functions are Entity SQL database-agnostic functions. But in many cases, tying your code to a specific database isn't a problem, because you know you'll never change. Should this be the case, you can invoke database-specific functions to make the best use of a platform.

4.7.2 *Database functions*

Each database has its own set of functions. Some of them are common across different RDBMSs like `ABS`, `LTrim`, `RTrim`, and can be invoked via LINQ to Entities or entity functions. Other functions are peculiar to each database or have different signatures.

Fortunately, you can invoke these sorts of functions too. Entity Framework ships with a bunch of SQL Server–specific functions exposed by the `SqlFunctions` class under the namespace `System.Data.Objects.SqlClient`. `Checksum`, `CharIndex`, `Cos`, `GetDate`, and `Rand` are examples of available functions.

Apart from the fact that the canonical and database functions belong to different classes, there's no difference between using these two types of functions. They're invoked as static methods and can be invoked in all sections of a query. The following code demonstrates this by using a database function to display orders that took more than five days to ship:

C#
```
from o in ctx.Orders
where SqlFunctions.DateDiff("d", o.OrderDate, o.ActualShippingDate) > 5
select o;
```

VB
```
From o In ctx.Orders
Where SqlFunctions.DateDiff("d", o.OrderDate, o.ActualShippingDate) > 5
```

> **NOTE** You can write your own custom functions and reuse them in queries. This will be covered in chapter 11.

By using database functions, you tie your code to a specific database (SQL Server in this example). That isn't always a good idea, because if you ever have to change databases, you'll have to change your code. But if you know you won't ever change the database that the application uses, you can use database functions without any problems. Always consider carefully whether you should use these functions or not.

Using database-specific functions is one of the two ways you can tie your code to a database platform. The other option is embedding SQL queries in the code. Even if SQL is a standard language, queries often rely on database specific features, so you end up tying your code to a specific database.

4.8   *Executing handmade queries*

There are several reasons you could decide to manually write a query. Perhaps the SQL generated by the Entity Framework is too slow, or it takes too many resources to execute. Another case may be when you have to dynamically generate a query that is so complex that creating the SQL code is easier than using LINQ to Entities.

In such situations, you can create an SQL command on your own and use the `ObjectContext` class's `ExecuteStoreQuery<T>` method. It allows you to issue an arbitrary query and map the result to a class. Its usage is shown here:

C#
```
var details = ctx.ExecuteStoreQuery<OrderDetail>
  ("Select * from OrderDetail");
```

VB
```
Dim details = ctx.ExecuteStoreQuery(Of OrderDetail)
  ("Select * from OrderDetail")
```

It's that easy. The query is executed and columns are automatically mapped to the entity. The mapping phase has a subtle caveat: it bypasses the EDM and uses another mechanism based on a property-column name match. This behavior is expressed in figure 4.4.

The extreme simplicity of this mapping solution has some limitations:

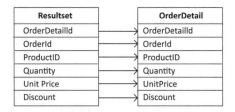

Figure 4.4   `ExecuteStoreQuery` performs a mapping based on the column name.

- If a property is named differently from the corresponding column, the mapping isn't performed and an exception is thrown. You can easily solve this problem by renaming the column in a query with the `AS` SQL clause.
- You can't map entities with complex properties because there's no way to match the name of a column with the name of a property inside a complex property.

Naturally, you can map the returning data to any type of class, and not only to those defined in the EDM. Suppose you created a class with the `Quantity`, `UnitPrice`, and `Discount` properties and called it `OrderDetailProjection`. You could write a query that extracts Quantity, UnitPrice, and Discount columns from the OrderDetail table and maps the result to `OrderDetailProjection`. In the end, it's a handmade projection, as this listing clearly shows.

Listing 4.24   Projecting the `OrderDetail`

C#
```
public class OrderDetailProjection
{
  public int Quantity { get; set; }
  public decimal UnitPrice { get; set; }
  public decimal Discount { get; set; }
}
```

```
var details = ctx.ExecuteStoreQuery<OrderDetailProjection>
  ("Select quantity, unitprice, discount from OrderDetail");
```

VB
```
Public Class OrderDetailProjection
  Public Property Quantity As Integer
  Public Property UnitPrice As Decimal
  Public Property Discount As Decimal
End Class

Dim details = ctx.ExecuteStoreQuery(Of OrderDetailProjection)(
  "Select quantity, unitprice, discount from OrderDetail")
```

Always keep in mind the projection option. It turns out to be useful sometimes.

> **NOTE** Through ExecuteStoreQuery<T>, you can launch a stored proce-
> dure too. We recommend not using this option, because Entity Frame-
> work natively supports stored procedures, and it offers a few more
> options regarding mapping than ExecuteStoreQuery<T> offers.

If the query takes some parameters (and what query doesn't?), you can use the over-load of the ExecuteStoreQuery<T> method, which accepts a list of parameters. This can be tricky, so let's take a closer look.

4.8.1 *Working with parameters*

When the Entity Framework team designed how parameters would be passed, there were plenty of options. The team narrowed the options, and the result is that now you have two ways of working with parameters:

- Using a numbered list, as in the String.Format method
- Using ADO.NET syntax

Let's investigate both options in detail.

USING NUMBERED LISTS

This is the easiest method. In the SQL query, you surround a number with curly brack-ets where the parameter should be. After that, you pass the parameters in the second argument of the method. The parameters can be either simple values or instances of the DbParameter class. Here are some recommendations to keep in mind:

- If you use a DbParameter instance, you have to use the concrete type dedicated to the database provider. For instance, you must use SqlParameter for SQL Server and OleDbParameter for OLE DB. If you use another instance, you'll get an InvalidCastException at runtime.
- If you have multiple parameters, you can't mix DbParameter instances and plain values. You have to choose one or the other; otherwise, you'll get an Invalid-OperationException at runtime.
- If you use simple values as parameters, they must be passed in the same order as they appear in the query.

This listing demonstrates all these methods.

Listing 4.25   Passing query parameters using a numbered list

C#

```
var names =
 ctx.ExecuteStoreQuery<string>
   ("SELECT name FROM company
➥   WHERE shippingcity = {0} and billingcity = {1}",
   "New York", "Seattle");
```
Pass parameters as simple values

```
var p0 = new SqlParameter("p0", DbType.String)
  { Value = "New York" };
var p1 = new SqlParameter("p1", DbType.String)
  { Value = "Seattle" };
var names = ctx.ExecuteStoreQuery<string>
  ("SELECT name FROM company
➥  WHERE shippingcity = {0}
➥  and billingcity = {1}", p0, p1);
```
Pass parameters using SqlParameter

VB

```
Dim names = ctx.ExecuteStoreQuery(Of String)(
  "SELECT name FROM company
➥ WHERE shippingcity = {0} and billingcity = {1}",
  "New York", "Seattle")
```
Pass parameters as simple values

```
Dim p0 = New SqlParameter("p0", DbType.String) _
  With {.Value = "New York"}
Dim p1 = New SqlParameter("p1", DbType.String) _
  With {.Value = "Seattle"}
Dim names = ctx.ExecuteStoreQuery(Of String)(
  "SELECT name FROM company
➥   WHERE shippingcity = {0}
➥   and billingcity = {1}", p0, p1)
```
Pass parameters using SqlParameter

As you can see, there's nothing particularly difficult here. Just pay attention to the pitfalls we mentioned.

> **NOTE**   Even if this syntax may lead you to think that you can be affected by a SQL injection attack, that's absolutely *not* the case. Parameters are always passed to the database as safe.

Now, let's move on and talk about using classic parameters.

USING CLASSIC PARAMETERS

When you write queries through classic ADO.NET, you're used to writing something like this to express parameters:

```
SELECT * FROM table WHERE id = @id
```

That syntax is valid for the SQL Server provider. If you're using the OLE DB provider, you use a question mark (?) character instead of the @paramname.

This approach is still perfectly valid using the ExecuteStoreQuery<T> method. Instead of the number surrounded by curly brackets, you put the parameter. All the rest remains exactly the same. The values of the parameters can still be passed as simple values or as parameters, and they have the same restrictions you saw in the previous section.

This listing shows all the possibilities.

Listing 4.26 Passing query parameters using a numbered list

C#
```
var names = ctx.ExecuteStoreQuery<string>
  ("SELECT name FROM company
➥   WHERE shippingcity = @p0 and billingcity = @p1",
  "New York", "Seattle");
```
> **Pass parameters as simple values**

```
var p0 = new SqlParameter("p0", DbType.String)
  { Value = "New York" };
var p1 = new SqlParameter("p1", DbType.String)
  { Value = "Seattle" };
var names = ctx.ExecuteStoreQuery<string>
  ("SELECT name FROM company
➥   WHERE shippingcity = @p0
➥   and billingcity = @p1", p0, p1);
```
> **Pass parameters using SqlParameter**

VB
```
Dim names = ctx.ExecuteStoreQuery(Of String)(
  "SELECT name FROM company
➥   WHERE shippingcity = @p0 and billingcity = @p1",
  "New York", "Seattle")
```
> **Pass parameters as simple values**

```
Dim p0 = New SqlParameter("p0", DbType.String) _
  With {.Value = "New York"}
Dim p1 = New SqlParameter("p1", DbType.String) _
  With {.Value = "Seattle"}
Dim names = ctx.ExecuteStoreQuery(Of String)(
  "SELECT name FROM company
➥   WHERE shippingcity = @p0
➥   and billingcity = @p1", p0, p1)
```
> **Pass parameters using SqlParameter**

If you compare this code with that in listing 4.25, you'll see that only the parameter declaration in SQL code changes. The rest remains identical, meaning that there's nothing more to learn.

So far, we've covered how to write powerful queries. Now let's see things from another perspective: how many related entities do you have to query? Should you retrieve related entities immediately, or only when needed by the code? This is clearly a *fetching* problem, and it's almost independent of whatever queries you write.

4.9   *Fetching*

We've already discussed the fetching mechanism in chapter 1, and you saw it in action in chapter 2. To make the terminology clear, *eager loading* refers to loading entities and their associated data in a single query, whereas *lazy loading* refers to the automatic loading of associated entities when they're used in the code.

> **NOTE**   Fetching isn't a LINQ to Entities–related task, but it fits in natu-
> rally when talking about querying.

Eager loading is often the most performant method for retrieving data. Although it retrieves lots of data from the database, it hits the database only once, avoiding the chatty communications that are a prerogative of lazy loading.

4.9.1   *Eager loading*

Eager loading is enabled via a special method of the `ObjectQuery` class: `Include`. This method accepts a string representing the navigation properties to be loaded. This string is referred to as the *navigation path* because it allows you to load an entire graph of related objects, and not only the properties associated with the one you're querying.

Let's start with the simplest example: an order with its details:

C#
```
from o in ctx.Orders.Include("OrderDetails")
select o;
```

VB
```
From o In ctx.Orders.Include("OrderDetails")
```

`OrderDetails` is a property of the `Order` class that's being queried here. As we said, the string parameter of `Include` is a path by which you can load an entire graph of properties. This turns out to be useful when you want to retrieve orders plus data about the details and even the products related to each of them. You simply build a path, separating the properties with a dot (`.`):

```
Include("OrderDetail.Product")
```

The `Include` method returns an `ObjectQuery<T>` instance, meaning that it can be chained with other calls to the `Include` method and LINQ to Entities methods.

The next snippet loads the orders and their details and chains another `Include` to load the customer too:

C#
```
from o in ctx.Orders.Include("OrderDetails.Product").Include("Customer")
select o;
```

VB
```
From o In ctx.Orders.Include("OrderDetails.Product").Include("Customer")
```

This query requires a noticeable amount of time to execute, and it returns to the application a huge amount of repeated data (because of the `JOIN` it generates in SQL code). There's no need to show the SQL here to make you understand how complex it is. Naturally, the more related entities you prefetch, and the more complex the query becomes, the more time it takes to execute and the more data is moved across the network.

> **NOTE**   You saw that the `Include` method can be chained with any method
> you have seen so far. We strongly recommend that you place `Include` at

the beginning of the query for two main reasons. The first is that placing the fetching strategy at the beginning makes queries more intuitive. The second one is more technical: `Include` belongs to the `ObjectQuery<T>` class, whereas LINQ extension methods return `IEnumerable<T>`. This means that after you've applied a LINQ method, you can no longer use `Include` unless you cast the `IEnumerable<T>` back to `ObjectQuery<T>`.

What data is loaded for a one-to-many association, and how is this data shaped? The first answer is that all the associated data is retrieved. If you eager-load the details of an order, you have no way of filtering them. LINQ to Entities allows you to apply conditions on eager-loaded data, but they're ignored. As for the *how*, data can't be either sorted or projected. If you need to apply any modification to the associated data, you have to resort to projecting the entire query, as we discussed in section 4.2.

> **NOTE** `Include` is translated to a SQL `OUTER JOIN` clause. Suppose you need orders and details. If an order doesn't have any details, you'll always get that order. This is correct behavior, because what you're looking for are orders.

When retrieving the data in a single round trip is too heavy, you can try obtaining them only when the code effectively uses them. This is what lazy loading does.

4.9.2 Lazy loading

To lazy-load an associated entity or list of entities, you don't have to learn anything new. You can obtain the related entities by accessing the navigation properties.

Suppose you've retrieved all the orders and need to cycle between the details. If you haven't prefetched them, you can access them by iterating over the `OrderDetails` property. The situation is the same when you're accessing navigation properties that refer to a single entity. For instance, if you want to retrieve the customer information, you can access the `Customer` property, and magically you have your data, as shown here.

Listing 4.27 Customer and details retrieved on demand

C#
```
foreach(var order in ctx.Orders)
{
  Console.WriteLine(order.Id + " " + order.Customer.Name);
  foreach(var detail in order.OrderDetails)
  {
    Console.WriteLine(detail.Id +  " " + detail.Quantity);
  }
}
```

VB
```
For Each order in ctx.Orders
  Console.WriteLine(order.Id & " " & order.Customer.Name)
  For Each detail in order.OrderDetails
```

```
      Console.WriteLine(detail.Id & " " & detail.Quantity)
    Next
  Next
Next
```

> **NOTE** Lazy loading is enabled by default. You can switch it off by setting the `ContextOptions.LazyLoadingEnabled` context property to `true`. More important, the entity must be attached to a context when the lazy loading is performed. If you access an entity's navigation property and the entity is outside the scope of the context that generated the entity, you'll get an `InvalidOperationException`.

How can a simple access of a property getter trigger a query? If you watch the code of the property, there's no trace of such a feature, so how does it happen? Do you remember the discussion of proxies in section 3.2.7? That's the answer to these questions.

When the context creates the proxy class, it detects all properties that navigate to another entity. For each of them, if they're marked as `virtual` for C# or `Overridable` for VB, the context overrides the getter, injecting the code necessary to perform a query to the database to retrieve data. If the property can't be overridden, the proxy can't inject the code, and lazy loading isn't active. Naturally, if you turn off proxy generation, the plain class is returned, and there's no proxy ... no lazy loading ... no party.

Figure 4.5 shows a simplification of the code for lazy loading inside a proxy.

Lazy loading is useful, but there are cases where you can't rely on it because you may have either disabled proxy generation or you may be outside of the context. Don't despair. Entity Framework can still help.

4.9.3 *Manual deferred loading*

Manual deferred loading is a way to dynamically retrieve a property without using lazy loading. This feature is enabled by the `LoadProperty` method of the object context, and it comes with two flavors: generic and nongeneric.

The generic version accepts the entity type whose property must be retrieved on the database as a generic argument, and then the object plus a lambda expression that states what property must be loaded:

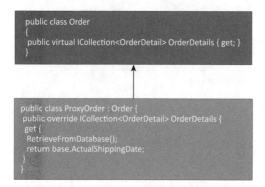

Figure 4.5 How the proxy overrides the code of a property that navigates to another entity

C#

```
void LoadProperty<T>(T entity, Expression<Func<T, object>> selector);
```

VB

```
Sub LoadProperty(Of T)(ByVal entity As T,
  ByVal selector As Expression(Of Func(Of T, Object)))
```

The nongeneric version accepts two arguments. The first one is the entity, and the second is the property to be loaded:

C#

```
void LoadProperty(object entity, string navigationProperty)
```

VB

```
Sub LoadProperty(ByVal entity As Object,
  ByVal navigationProperty As String)
```

The following listing manually loads the details for each order.

Listing 4.28 Manually retrieving the customer and details

C#

```
//Generic retrieval
ctx.LoadProperty<Order>(order, o => o.OrderDetails);

//Non generic retrieval
ctx.LoadProperty(order, "OrderDetails")
```

VB

```
'Generic retrieval
ctx.LoadProperty(Of Order)(order, o => o.OrderDetails)

'Non generic retrieval
ctx.LoadProperty(order, "OrderDetails")
```

In order for LoadProperty to work, the main entity must be attached to the context. If you're outside of a context, you can create a new one, attach the entity, and then load the property.

In a layered architecture, you can place such a method in the infrastructure so that data access remains encapsulated. Here's an example.

Listing 4.29 Generic method that manually retrieves a property of an entity

C#

```
public void LoadProperty<T>(T entity, Expression<Func<T, object>> selector)
  where T : class
{
  using (var ctx = new OrderITEntities())
  {
    ctx.CreateObjectSet<T>().Attach(entity);
    ctx.LoadProperty<T>(entity, selector);
  }
}
```

VB
```
Public Sub LoadProperty(Of T As Class)(ByVal entity As T,
  ByVal selector As Expression(Of Func(Of T, Object)))
  Using ctx = New OrderITEntities()
    ctx.CreateObjectSet(Of T)().Attach(entity)
    ctx.LoadProperty(Of T)(entity, selector)
  End Using
End Sub
```

That's all you need to know about fetching with Entity Framework.

4.9.4 *Choosing a loading approach*

Choosing the correct loading strategy makes a great difference in an application. Often, applications are developed without keeping this in mind, and you end up generating enormous queries to prefetch all data or plenty of little queries to retrieve associated data at runtime.

The second case is the most dangerous. We've seen applications where only the main entity was retrieved, and all associations were loaded at runtime. Everything worked because of the transparent lazy loading, but performance was at least poor, if not disastrous.

Generally speaking, eager loading is better. But you may find situations where you have to load associated entities only in certain circumstances. For instance, you may want to load the details only for orders of the last seven days. In this case, loading the details on demand may be a good choice. What's worse, SQL generated by eager loading doesn't always perform well. In some cases, the Entity Framework–generated SQL contains useless OUTER JOIN commands or retrieves more columns than required.

Determining the correct fetching strategy is a matter of testing and case-by-case analysis. There isn't a simple bulletproof technique.

4.10 *Summary*

In this chapter, you've learned all about the query capabilities of Entity Framework using LINQ to Entities. This LINQ dialect brings the expressiveness and power of the object-oriented world to the database querying mechanism in a very transparent way.

You have learned how to use LINQ to Entities to perform all of the important operations that you would usually perform in SQL. Projecting, filtering, sorting, grouping, and joining are all features that LINQ to Entities simplifies as no other framework has done in the past. What's more, you have seen how to combine these features to create complex queries that in SQL would require many, many lines of code and a heavy testing phase.

We also looked at fetching, which is an important feature. You have seen in practice how to prefetch and how to fetch on demand data from an associated entity. This is vital when tweaking performance.

You have now learned how to create a model, map it against a database, and query it. What you haven't seen yet is the EDM structure. You know it contains mapping information, but that's all. In the next chapter, we'll examine it in depth.

Domain model mapping

This chapter covers

- Introducing the Entity Data Model
- Creating Entity Framework domain model classes
- Describing classes
- Describing database
- Mapping classes to database

So far, you've learned how to create an application from scratch, defining a model, mapping it to the database, and performing queries on it. We also looked at creating and mapping classes using the Visual Studio designer, which hides a lot of complexity, making your life easier. But a strong knowledge of the Entity Data Model and the code in the model classes is fundamental to mastering Entity Framework. In this chapter, we'll dig deep into both subjects so that you'll be able to completely understand this aspect of Entity Framework. This chapter covers the mapping of tables or views to entities. Other features, like stored procedures and function mappings, will be discussed in later chapters.

We'll first look at the Entity Data Model, its concepts, and Microsoft's vision about its future. After that, we'll discuss how to create entities and map them. You'll learn how to write an entity from scratch and create the three mapping files that allow you to map it to the database. You'll see how Entity Framework 4.0 supports POCO (plain old CLR objects) entities and how this positively affects classes.

   Once classes and their mapping are clear to you, we'll create the association between them and describe everything in the Entity Data Model. You'll finally learn how to create an inheritance hierarchy and how to reflect it into the Entity Data Model.

   By the end of this chapter, you'll have the knowledge to manually modify the mapping files where needed (because the designer isn't all-powerful). When we talk about designer customization later, in chapter 13, this knowledge will help you a lot.

   Let's start by discussing what the Entity Data Model is and how it's made.

5.1   *The Entity Data Model*

The Entity Data Model (EDM) is the heart of the Entity Framework. Essentially, Entity Framework is a tool that decouples the object model from the database by creating an abstraction layer between them. You develop an application that works with Entity Framework, which in turn works with the database. This means the application works only with the object model classes, ignoring the database. It's the EDM that makes this decoupling possible.

   You already know that the EDM is split into three sections:

- *Conceptual schema* (CSDL)—Describes the object model. Classes and their relationships have their counterparts in this section.
- *Storage schema* (SSDL)—Describes the database structure. Tables, views, and even stored procedures and functions are put into this section.
- *Mapping schema* (MSL)—Maps the CSDL and SSDL. Each class is mapped to one or more tables, and each property has a corresponding column.

The object model is the reflection of the CSDL, and they must be in sync. (Well, that's not completely true. You can create properties in your object model class and avoid mapping them. They will be ignored by Entity Framework and won't cause any problem.)

   Now, you're probably wondering at least two things:

- Where is the EDM?
- Is there any relationship between the EDM and the EDMX file used by the Visual Studio designer?

These questions will both be answered in the next section.

5.1.1   *The Entity Data Model and Visual Studio designer*

When you double-click the EDMX file in the Solution Explorer, Visual Studio opens the designer, showing entities. But to discover the relationship between the EDM and EDMX files, let's follow another path. Right-click the EDMX file and select the Open With option, as shown in figure 5.1.

   The designer opens the dialog box shown in figure 5.2. Select the XML (Text) Editor option, and click OK.

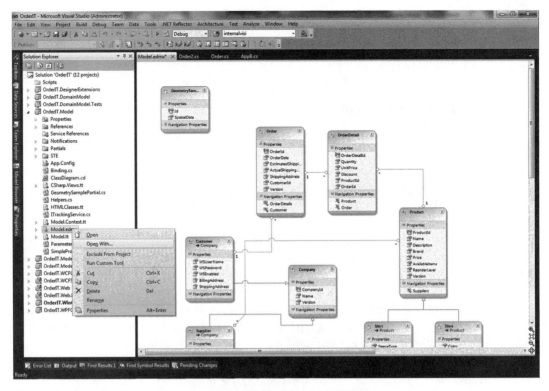

Figure 5.1   The context menu displayed when you right-click the EDMX file

Visual Studio will open a new window displaying an XML file that looks a lot like the EDM. (Note that if the designer is already open, you'll be prompted about that. Click Yes to close the designer and open the new window.) The EDMX file contains the three EDM files plus other information used by the designer, like the positions of the objects on the canvas, the zoom, the scroll position, and so on.

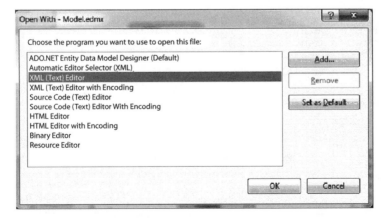

Figure 5.2   The Open With dialog box lets you open the EDMX file as an XML file instead of showing the designer.

NOTE The fact that EDM and designer data are mixed causes problems when working in teams. If one person works on the `Customer` and `Supplier` classes, he probably optimizes his view of the designer to see those entities. Someone else who works on the products will optimize her view for those classes. Each time the EDMX is checked in, it overrides the previous view. This problem will be solved in the future, using separate files: one for the EDM, shared by everyone; and one for the designer data, which can be kept out of source control.

You can see the collapsed EDMX file in figure 5.3.

The EDM is under the edmx:Edmx/edmx:Runtime path. Inside it, you can see the storage, conceptual, and mapping schemas. The designer-related information is stored in the edmx:Edmx/edmx:Designer path. For our discussion, the designer info isn't important, so we'll ignore it.

The EDMX file is an *artifact*—it's necessary to create the designer in Visual Studio. Entity Framework isn't interested at all in the EDMX file—it can't even parse it. Entity Framework only understands mapping files when they're split into three: one for the conceptual schema (*.csdl), one for the storage schema (*.ssdl), and one for the mapping schema (*.msl).

If you look at the `metadata` attribute of the connection string, you'll see a reference to the three mapping files:

```
metadata=res://*/OrderIT.csdl|res://*/OrderIT.ssdl|res://*/OrderIT.msl
metadata=c:\OrderIT.csdl|c:\OrderIT.ssdl|c:\OrderIT.msl
```

The EDMX file contains the EDM, but Entity Framework doesn't understand it. The connection string references three mapping files that are nowhere in the project: how does this work? The answer is that at compile time, the designer extracts the sections from the EDMX file and creates a separate file for each one.

```
Model.edmx  X  Start Page
  1    <?xml version="1.0" encoding="utf-8"?>
  2  ⊟ <edmx:Edmx Version="2.0"
  3      xmlns:edmx="http://schemas.microsoft.com/ado/2008/10/edmx">
  4      <!-- EF Runtime content -->
  5  ⊟   <edmx:Runtime>
  6        <!-- SSDL content -->
  7  ⊟     <edmx:StorageModels>
  8  ⊞       <Schema Namespace="OrderIT.DomainM" Alias="Self" Provider="S
222        </edmx:StorageModels>
223        <!-- CSDL content -->
224  ⊟     <edmx:ConceptualModels>
225  ⊞       <Schema Namespace="OrderIT.DomainM" Alias="Self" xmlns="http
345        </edmx:ConceptualModels>
346        <!-- C-S mapping content -->
347  ⊟     <edmx:Mappings>
348  ⊞       <Mapping Space="C-S" xmlns="http://schemas.">...</Mapping>
486        </edmx:Mappings>
487      </edmx:Runtime>
488      <!-- EF Designer content (DO NOT EDIT MANUALLY BELOW HERE) -->
489  ⊞   <Designer xmlns="http://schemas.">...</Designer>
554    </edmx:Edmx>
```

Figure 5.3   A collapsed view of the EDMX file. The `Runtime` section contains the EDM, and the `Designer` section contains the designer-related information.

These files are either embedded into the assembly or copied into the output directory. You can specify which by opening the designer properties and setting the Metadata Artifact Processing property to either Embed in Output Assembly or to Copy to Output Directory. The setting names are self-explanatory.

Now that you know the basics of the EDM and how it integrates with Visual Studio, you're ready to create and map models. The first thing you need to do when creating a model is design the entities. Designing a class is the same as writing, or creating, it.

5.2   Creating consumable entities

When the designer generates code to create entities, it performs the following steps:

1 Create the entity's code.
2 Create the conceptual schema.
3 Create the storage schema.
4 Create the mapping schema.

In the next sections, you'll manually perform these steps to reproduce the tables and entities involved in OrderIT's ordering process and see how mapping works under the covers.

> **NOTE** By default, the designer emits Entity Framework–aware non-POCO code—a choice that was made to maintain compatibility with the previous release. With Entity Framework 4.0, it's pointless using non-POCO code. We strongly recommend always using the POCO template that we introduced in chapter 2.

Let's start with the first step.

Why POCO is so important

POCO (plain old CLR object) classes lead to persistence ignorance (PI). PI allows the user to write code that only cares about the business problem without any infrastructure intrusion. The `Order` and `OrderDetail` classes know nothing about Entity Framework. The persistence engine could be a handwritten data layer, Entity Framework, NHibernate, or something else. What's more, a clean separation between the object model classes and the persistence engine allows you to put the classes in the model assembly (the object model or domain model, depending on your architecture), leaving to the infrastructure or the data layer (again, depending on the architecture) the burden of persistence. More separation leads to more maintainability; more maintainability leads to better reactions to application changes and bugs; better reactions lead to happier customers and lower costs; and all of this leads to a great success.

Nonetheless, *don't* be deceived by PI. It's not always needed. We have shipped many projects using Entity Framework 1.0 without worrying about PI. Those projects were well designed and efficient, and the customer is happy with them. PI is important and sometimes would have saved hundreds of lines of code, but it's not the only key to a winning project.

5.2.1 *Writing the entities*

The ordering process in OrderIT includes the `Order` and `OrderDetail` entities plus the `AddressInfo` complex type. Thanks to the POCO support, you can create such classes without worrying about persistence (as you'll notice in listing 5.1). For now, let's forget about associations. We'll discuss them later.

Listing 5.1   Creating the order scenario model

C#

```csharp
public class AddressInfo
{
  public virtual string Address { get; set; }
  Public virtual string ZipCode { get; set; }
  Public virtual string City { get; set; }
  Public virtual string Country { get; set; }
}

public class Order
{
  public virtual int OrderId { get; set; }
  public virtual DateTime OrderDate { get; set; }
  public virtual AddressInfo ShippingAddress { get; set; }
  public virtual DateTime EstimatedShippingDate { get; set; }
  public virtual DateTime ActualShippingDate { get; set; }
}

public class OrderDetail
{
  public virtual int OrderDetailId { get; set; }
  public virtual int Quantity { get; set; }
  public virtual decimal Price { get; set; }
  public virtual decimal Discount { get; set; }
}
```

VB

```vb
Public Class AddressInfo
  Public Overridable Property Address as String
  Public Overridable Property ZipCode as String
  Public Overridable Property City as String
  Public Overridable Property Country as String
End Class

Public Class Order
  Public Overridable Property OrderId as Int32
  Public Overridable Property OrderDate as DateTime
  Public Overridable Property ShippingAddress as AddressInfo
  Public Overridable Property EstimatedShippingDate as DateTime
  Public Overridable Property ActualShippingDate as DateTime
End Class

Public Class OrderDetail
  Public Overridable Property OrderDetailId as Int32
  Public Overridable Property Quantity as Int32
  Public Overridable Property Price as Decimal
  Public Overridable Property Discount as Decimal
End Class
```

That's all you need to create the entities. Isn't it great? It's 19 lines of code, and you're done. In Entity Framework 1.0, it would have taken about 70 lines. That's a huge step ahead.

Complex properties deserve more attention. When you instantiate Order, the address is null because it isn't created anywhere. This means that you should create the address every time you create an order, and that's repetitive and error-prone code.

You have two options for solving this problem: instantiate the address in the order constructor, or instantiate it lazily when it's accessed for the first time. Both options are shown in listing 5.2.

Listing 5.2 Two ways of instantiating complex properties

C#
```csharp
public Order()                                          <──── Constructor instantiation
{
  ShippingAddress = new AddressInfo();
}

private AddressInfo _ShippingAddress;                   <──── Lazy instantiation
public virtual AddressInfo ShippingAddress
{
  get
  {
    _ShippingAddress = _ShippingAddress ?? new AddressInfo();
    return _ShippingAddress;
  }
  set
  {
    _ShippingAddress = value;
  }
}
```

VB
```vb
Public Sub New()
  ShippingAddress = New AddressInfo()        <──── Constructor instantiation
End Sub

Private _ShippingAddress As AddressInfo
Public Overridable Property ShippingAddress() As AddressInfo
  Get
    _ShippingAddress =
      If(_ShippingAddress, New AddressInfo())              <──── Lazy instantiation
    Return _ShippingAddress
  End Get
  Set(ByVal value As AddressInfo)
    _ShippingAddress = value
  End Set
End Property
```

The constructor solution requires less code, so it's our favorite, but we have nothing against lazy instantiation. The result is the same, and the choice is up to you.

There is another step we skipped: the overriding of Equals and GetHashCode. When you create a model, implementing them for each class is important. There's lots of literature out there about how to best implement these methods, so we won't explain it here. Our suggestion is to write them as follows.

Listing 5.3   Implementing `Equals` and `GetHashCode` in the `Order` entity

C#
```csharp
public class Order
{
  ...
  public override bool Equals(object obj)
  {
    Order order = obj as Order;
    if (order == null) return false
    return order.OrderId == this.OrderId;
  }

  public override int GetHashCode()
  {
    return OrderId.GetHashCode();
  }
}
```

VB
```vb
Public Class Order
  ...
  Public Overloads Overrides Function Equals(ByVal obj As Object)
    As Boolean
    Dim order As Order = TryCast(obj, Order)
    If order Is Nothing Then
      Return False
    End If
    Return order.OrderId = Me.OrderId
  End Function

  Public Overloads Overrides Function GetHashCode() As Integer
    Return OrderId.GetHashCode()
  End Function
End Class
```

This code says that two orders are equal if their OrderId property has the same value.

In chapters 2 and 3, you were introduced to the runtime proxy subject. You learned that in order to be runtime extensible, a class must be open to inheritance and all properties must be virtual/Overridable. You can avoid these rules, but the obtained objects wouldn't provide features like object tracking and lazy loading. Because they're important in many scenarios, we always suggest making properties virtual.

> **NOTE**   It's important that you understand how to create classes. You may need to customize entity code generation to accommodate particular needs (as we'll do in chapter 13). This means that an understanding of classes is at least desirable.

The classes created in this section aren't consumable by Entity Framework yet. You must put the necessary information into the EDM. The starting point for doing this is the conceptual file.

5.2.2 *Describing entities in the conceptual schema*

The conceptual schema contains the description of the entities. Creating this schema isn't difficult at all, but because many XML tags are involved, you might find it confusing at first. Fortunately, these tags are reused in the storage schema, significantly simplifying the entire EDM.

In the EDMX file for OrderIT, the conceptual schema is at the path edmx:Edmx/edmx:Runtime/edmx:ConceptualModels. If you create the conceptual file manually, you can name it OrderIT.csdl and reference it in the database connection string. In the CSDL file, you must ignore the preceding XML path because it's part of the EDMX artifact. This applies also to the storage and the mapping files.

The basic structure of the CSDL is pretty simple. It has a main element named Schema, inside which there is an EntityContainer element plus an EntityType for each entity and a ComplexType for each complex type. Figure 5.4 shows the file structure.

Having a broad understanding of the structure is good, but knowing each node is essential to mastering mapping. Let's analyze them one by one, starting from the outermost: Schema.

SCHEMA

Schema is a pretty simple element. It contains the attributes Namespace and Alias to specify the namespace and an alias for it. Furthermore, it declares the base namespace via xmlns and an additional namespace with the store prefix:

```
<Schema xmlns="http://schemas.microsoft.com/ado/2008/09/edm"
xmlns:store="http://schemas.microsoft.com/ado/2007/12/edm/
➥    EntityStoreSchemaGenerator" Namespace="OrderITModel" Alias="Self">
    ...
</Schema>
```

Because Schema is a mere container, there is nothing special about its attributes. What we're more interested in is its inner content.

ENTITYCONTAINER

The EntityContainer element declares the entity sets and the relationship sets in the EDM; the entity sets declared here are used to generate the code of the context class. The element has only a Name attribute, which the designer sets to the name of the connection string you enter in the EDMX wizard. If you create the file manually, we suggest setting the attribute value to the name of the application, plus the suffix Entities.

If you look at the context-generated code, you'll see that all base constructors take a ContainerName argument. That argument is the container name as inserted in the EDM, so the context is linked with its description in the EDM.

```
<Schema Namespace="OrderIT.Model" Alias="Self" xmlns:store="htt
    <EntityContainer Name="OrderITEntities">...</EntityContainer>
    <ComplexType Name="AddressInfo">...</ComplexType>
    <EntityType Name="Order">...</EntityType>
    <EntityType Name="OrderDetail">...</EntityType>
</Schema>
```

Figure 5.4 The structure of the CSDL file. Schema is the main element, and EntityContainer, ComplexType, and EntityType are its children.

> **NOTE** You can have many `EntityContainer` tags, which means you can have many contexts. This may be useful when you want to logically separate different parts of your application. It's not supported by the designer, but you can do it if you want to edit files manually.

As you may expect, the `EntityContainer` is a mere wrapper. Inside it is one `EntitySet` element for each entity set. You learned in chapter 2 that there's an entity set for each class that doesn't inherit from another one in the model. For instance, `Order` has an entity set, and `Company` has an entity set, but `Supplier` and `Customer` don't because they inherit from `Company`.

`EntitySet` has two attributes:

- `Name` declares the entity set's unique name. (In chapter 2, you set the entity set name for each entity in the designer—that value was put into the `Name` attribute.)
- `EntityType` contains the fully qualified name (FQN) of the entity it exposes.

In the end, the entity container looks like the following listing.

Listing 5.4   Defining the entity sets in `EntityContainer`

```
<EntityContainer Name="OrderITEntities">
  <EntitySet Name="Orders" EntityType="OrderIT.DomainModel.Order" />
  <EntitySet Name="OrderDetails"
    EntityType="OrderITModel.OrderDetail" />
</EntityContainer>
```

Multiple entity sets per type (MEST)

You can define multiple entity sets for a single type. This feature is named multiple entity sets per type (MEST), and it may be extremely useful in some scenarios. Suppose you're developing a site that handles articles, blog posts, and forum posts. These items share the same structure: a posted date, a published date, text, a subject, and so on. They may be stored in different tables, but a single class represents them.

MEST allows you to reuse one class across different entity sets. Unfortunately, this approach has limitations when dealing with associations, and, what's worse, it isn't supported by the designer, so you have to create the class's code and mapping manually. In the end, MEST slows down productivity, so unless you have a strong reason to use it, don't.

Now that you understand the `EntityContainer`, we can move on to the model classes. The element that describes an entity is `EntityType`, whereas a complex type is represented by `ComplexType`.

COMPLEXTYPE AND ENTITYTYPE

`ComplexType` has only the `Name` attribute, which is set to the class FQN. Inside it is one `Property` node for each property of the complex type. `Property` has several attributes, which are described in table 5.1.

Table 5.1 Attributes of `Property` node in the conceptual schema

Attribute	Description	Required
`Name`	Specifies the name of the property.	Yes
`Type`	Specifies the CLR type of the property. If the property is a complex type, this should be set to the FQN of the complex type.	Yes
`Nullable`	Indicates whether the property can be `null`. The default value is `true`.	No
`FixedLength`	Indicates whether the property must have a fixed length.	No
`MaxLength`	Specifies the maximum length of the value.	No
`Scale`	Specifies how many numbers are allowed after a comma in a decimal type.	No
`Precision`	Specifies how many numbers are allowed in a decimal type.	No
`store:StoreGeneratedPattern`	Indicates how the column is set by the database during inserts and updates. It has three possible values: • `None`—The value from the application is used (default). • `Identity`—The value is calculated by the database during inserts, and the value from the application is used for updates. • `Computed`—The value is calculated by the database during inserts and updates.	No
`ConcurrencyMode`	Indicates whether the property participates in the concurrency check. To enable the check, set the value to `Fixed`.	No

When the complex type is ready, you can start creating entities that use it. `EntityType` is where you do this. It has a mandatory `Name` attribute, where the name of the class is specified. After that, there are two optional attributes:

- `Abstract`—Specifies whether the class is abstract
- `BaseType`—Specifies a base class

`Abstract` and `BaseType` become important when inheritance comes into play. (We'll get to inheritance in section 5.4.)

Inside `EntityType` is a `Property` element for each scalar and complex property in the class, and a `Key` element to specify which properties are in the entity's primary key. If the property is a complex property, you set its type to the full name of the complex type it represents through the `Type` attribute. The `Key` element has no attributes; it has only one `PropertyRef` node for each property that participates in the primary key. `PropertyRef` has only the `Name` attribute, which contains the name of the property.

Putting everything in action, the mapping fragment looks like this.

Listing 5.5   Describing complex types and entities

```
<ComplexType Name="AddressInfo">
  <Property Type="String" Name="Address" Nullable="false" MaxLength="50" />
  <Property Type="String" Name="City" Nullable="false" MaxLength="50" />
  <Property Type="String" Name="ZipCode" Nullable="false" MaxLength="15" />
  <Property Type="String" Name="Country" Nullable="false" MaxLength="30" />
</ComplexType>
<EntityType Name="Order">
  <Key>
    <PropertyRef Name="OrderId" />
  </Key>
  <Property Type="Int32" Name="OrderId" Nullable="false"
    store:StoreGeneratedPattern="Identity" />
  <Property Name="ShippingAddress" Type="OrderITModel.AddressInfo"
    Nullable="false" />
  <Property Type="DateTime" Name="EstimatedShippingDate" Nullable="false"
    Precision="29" />
  <Property Type="DateTime" Name="ActualShippingDate" Nullable="false"
    Precision="29" />
</EntityType>
<EntityType Name="OrderDetail">
  <Key>
    <PropertyRef Name=" OrderDetail Id" />
  </Key>
  <Property Type="Int32" Name="OrderDetailId" Nullable="false"
    store:StoreGeneratedPattern="Identity" />
  <Property Type="Int16" Name="Quantity" Nullable="false" />
  <Property Type="Decimal" Name="UnitPrice" Nullable="false" Precision="29"
    Scale="29" />
  <Property Type="Decimal" Name="Discount" Nullable="false" Precision="29"
    Scale="29" />
</EntityType>
```

That's all you need to know about the conceptual schema, but that's only the first part of the EDM. You still have to create the storage schema to describe the tables that will persist orders and their details. Later, you'll bridge the two models in the mapping file.

5.2.3   *Describing the database in the storage schema*

The storage-description file contains detailed information about the database structure. You can map several database objects here: tables, views, stored procedures, and functions. In this chapter, we'll focus on the first two objects only; the others will be discussed in chapter 10, which is dedicated to the use of stored procedures.

In the EDMX file for the OrderIT example, the storage schema is under the edmx:Edmx/edmx:Runtime/edmx:StorageModels path; but if you want to create the file manually, you can name it OrderIT.ssdl and reference it in the connection string.

We already mentioned that conceptual schema elements are reused in the storage schema. This is true, but some nodes have more attributes in the storage schema to accommodate specific database options. Let's start by looking at the Schema node.

SCHEMA

`Schema` is the root element of the storage schema. It has the same attributes as its counterpart on the conceptual side, plus two needed for database communication:

- `Provider`—Specifies the ADO.NET provider
- `ProviderManifestToken`—Specifies the version number of the database (for instance, SQL Server uses 2000, 2005, and 2008)

The following snippet contains an example of the `Schema` element:

```
<Schema Namespace="OrderITModel.Store" Alias="Self"
  Provider="System.Data.SqlClient" ProviderManifestToken="2008"
  xmlns:store="http://schemas.microsoft.com/ado/2007/12/edm/
     EntityStoreSchemaGenerator"
  xmlns="http://schemas.microsoft.com/ado/2009/02/edm/ssdl">
  ...
</Schema>
```

As in the conceptual file, `Schema` has both a container section and a detail section. You'll be happy to know that the container section is named the same way it is in the conceptual file.

ENTITYCONTAINER

`EntityContainer` declares all database objects described later in the file. Its only attribute is `Name`, which represents the name of the container. The designer sets its value to the namespace name plus the suffix `StoreContainer`. Although you can have multiple `EntityContainer` elements in the conceptual schema, that's nonsense in the storage schema, because the objects belong to a single database.

Inside `EntityContainer`, you create an `EntitySet` element for each table or view. `EntitySet` in the storage schema has more attributes than its counterpart on the conceptual side:

- `Name`—Specifies the *logical* name of the object. The designer uses the name of the table, but it's not mandatory.
- `EntityType`—Represents the FQN of the object and is set using the `{namespace}.{name}` pattern.
- `Schema`—Represents the owner of the table.
- `Table`—Represents the physical name of the table. `Table` isn't mandatory; when it's omitted, `Name` is used.
- `store:Type`—Identifies whether the object is a table (`Tables`) or a view (`Views`).

The result is the fragment shown here.

Listing 5.6   Defining database tables and views

```
<EntityContainer Name="OrderITModelStoreContainer">
  <EntitySet Name="Order" EntityType="OrderITModel.Store.Order"
    store:Type="Tables" Schema="dbo" />
  <EntitySet Name="OrderDetail"
```

```
        EntityType="OrderITModel.Store.OrderDetail"
        store:Type="Tables" Schema="dbo" />
</EntityContainer>
```

We've introduced a bunch of new attributes, and you've reused all the previous elements and declared the database objects. This is a successful case of code reuse. Now you need to describe the table structure.

ENTITYTYPE

Objects are described using the `EntityType` element, much as in the conceptual file. You must create one element for each `EntitySet` element that's put inside `Entity-Container`. In the conceptual file, classes that are part of an inheritance hierarchy have only one `EntitySet` but many `EntityType` elements. Databases don't support inheritance natively, so it isn't possible to have one entity set and more tables or views in the storage file.

Every `EntityType` node has a `Name` attribute whose value must match the `Name` attribute of the `EntitySet` in the entity container.

Inside the `EntityType` element, you have to include the elements that describe the database object. Again, you use `Property` to declare the columns and `Key` and `PropertyRef` to specify which ones compose the key.

`Property` has the same attributes as its counterpart in the CSDL, plus some additional ones to accommodate database needs:

- `Collation`—Specifies the collation of the column
- `DefaultValue`—Specifies the default value of the column
- `Unicode`—Specifies whether the value is Unicode

The result is the mapping fragment shown in the following listing.

Listing 5.7 Describing the `Order` and `OrderDetail` database tables

```
<EntityType Name="Order">
  <Key>
    <PropertyRef Name="OrderId" />
  </Key>
  <Property Name="OrderId" Type="int" StoreGeneratedPattern="Identity"
    Nullable="false" />
  <Property Name="ShippingAddress" Type="nvarchar" Nullable="false"
    MaxLength="50" />
  <Property Name="ShippingCity" Type="nvarchar" Nullable="false"
    MaxLength="50" />
  <Property Name="ShippingZipCode" Type="nvarchar" Nullable="false"
    MaxLength="15" />
  <Property Name="ShippingCountry" Type="nvarchar" Nullable="false"
    MaxLength="30" />
  <Property Name="EstimatedShippingDate" Type="datetime" Nullable="false"/>
  <Property Name="ActualShippingDate" Type="datetime" Nullable="false" />
  <Property Name="CustomerId" Type="int" Nullable="false" />
</EntityType>
<EntityType Name="OrderDetail">
```

```
  <Key>
    <PropertyRef Name="OrderDetailId" />
  </Key>
  <Property Name="OrderDetailId" Type="int"
    StoreGeneratedPattern="Identity" Nullable="false" />
  <Property Name="Quantity" Type="smallint" Nullable="false" />
  <Property Name="UnitPrice" Type="decimal" Nullable="false" Precision="29"
    Scale="29" />
  <Property Name="Discount" Type="decimal" Nullable="false" Precision="29"
    Scale="29" />
  <Property Name="OrderId" Type="int" Nullable="false" />
  <Property Name="ProductId" Type="int" Nullable="false" />
</EntityType>
```

The storage file is now ready. You're only missing the link between the conceptual and storage schemas. You already know that this bridge is created using the third file of the EDM: the mapping schema.

5.2.4 Creating the mapping file

The mapping file has the hard duty of bridging the gap between database and classes. When the model has one class for each table, the mapping is pretty simple; but as soon as things get more complicated, the mapping becomes complex.

In the EDMX file for the OrderIT example, edmx:Edmx/edmx:Runtime/ edmx:Mappings is the path of the mapping section. If you want to create the file on your own, you can create OrderIT.msl and reference it in the connection string.

The mapping file doesn't describe entities or tables—it maps them. As a result, this file's structure is completely different from the other two files. Unfortunately, this means you have to learn a bunch of new XML tags and attributes, as you can see in figure 5.5.

Differences emerge immediately at the root level. Although `Schema` is the root element for the conceptual and storage files, here you use `Mapping`.

```
<Mapping Space="C-S" xmlns="http://schemas.microsoft.com/ado/2008/09/mapping
  <EntityContainerMapping StorageEntityContainer="OrderITModelStoreContainer
    <EntitySetMapping Name="Companies">
      <EntityTypeMapping TypeName="IsTypeOf(OrderIT.Model.Company)">
        <MappingFragment StoreEntitySet="Company">
          <ScalarProperty Name="CompanyId" ColumnName="CompanyId" />
          <ScalarProperty Name="Name" ColumnName="Name" />
        </MappingFragment>
      </EntityTypeMapping>
      <EntityTypeMapping TypeName="IsTypeOf(OrderI">...</EntityTypeMapping>
      <EntityTypeMapping TypeName="IsTypeOf(OrderI">...</EntityTypeMapping>
    </EntitySetMapping>
    <EntitySetMapping Name="Orders">...</EntitySetMapping>
    <EntitySetMapping Name="OrderDetails">...</EntitySetMapping>
  </EntityContainerMapping>
```

Figure 5.5 The main structure of the mapping file

MAPPING AND ENTITYCONTAINERMAPPING

The declaration of the `Mapping` node is fixed, and you can't put any custom information in it. The only inner element it allows is `EntityContainerMapping`, where you specify the name of the containers whose entities must be mapped. (You have to specify the containers because you map entities and complex types used by the entity sets.) The `StorageEntityContainer` attribute identifies the storage schema container, and the `CdmEntityContainer` attribute is used for the conceptual schema container, as you can see in listing 5.8.

Listing 5.8 Defining the containers in the mapping

```
<Mapping Space="C-S"
  xmlns="http://schemas.microsoft.com/ado/2008/09/mapping/cs">
  <EntityContainerMapping CdmEntityContainer="OrderITEntities"
    StorageEntityContainer="OrderITModelStoreContainer">
    ...
  </EntityContainerMapping>
</Mapping>
```

After the entity containers are linked, the next step is to map tables and views against classes. This is accomplished by nesting an `EntitySetMapping` element inside the `EntityContainerMapping` element for each entity set.

ENTITYSETMAPPING, ENTITYTYPEMAPPING, AND MAPPINGFRAGMENT

Mapping an entity to a table is a four-step job. You start by defining the entity set and the entity inside it. Within the entity, you specify the table to which the entity is mapped, and finally you specify the column/property association between the two. Figure 5.5 shows the elements that must be used in the process.

`EntitySetMapping` is the node that lets you state what entity set you're going to map (remember that you can have multiple classes per entity set). The only attribute here is `Name`, and it's used to specify the entity set name.

Inside `EntitySetMapping`, you nest an `EntityTypeMapping` element for each entity that's part of the entity set. The type of the entity is set through the `TypeName` attribute and must follow the pattern `IsTypeOf(EntityName)`, where `EntityName` is the FQN of the entity.

Now we come to the mapped tables. Because a class can be mapped to one or more tables (`Order` maps to the Order table, but `Shirt` maps to both the Product and Shirt tables), inside the `EntityTypeMapping` element you specify a `MappingFragment` element for each table involved. It has only the `StoreEntitySet` attribute, and it must match the `Name` attribute of the entity set in the storage schema. The next listing shows this first part of the mapping.

Listing 5.9 Defining the entity set, the class, and the mapped table

```
<EntitySetMapping Name="Orders">
  <EntityTypeMapping TypeName="IsTypeOf(OrderITModel.Order)">
    <MappingFragment StoreEntitySet="Order">
      ...
```

```
      </MappingFragment>
    </EntityTypeMapping>
  </EntitySetMapping>
  <EntitySetMapping Name="OrderDetails">
    <EntityTypeMapping TypeName="IsTypeOf(OrderITModel.OrderDetail)">
      <MappingFragment StoreEntitySet="OrderDetail">
        ...
      </MappingFragment>
    </EntityTypeMapping>
  </EntitySetMapping>
```

Now you have the entity set, the class, and the table (or tables). That's all you need to start the property-to-column mapping process. In the next section, you'll see how this delicate part works.

SCALARPROPERTY AND COMPLEXPROPERTY

The `ScalarProperty` element maps a scalar property of the class to a column of the table or view. It has only two attributes:

- `Name`—Represents the property name
- `ColumnName`—Represents the mapped column

Easy as pie.

`ComplexProperty` is used to map a complex type. This node has two attributes too:

- `Name`—Specifies the name of the property in the class
- `TypeName`—Contains the FQN of the complex type

`ComplexProperty` on its own is useless. You have to map its properties to the columns, and this is done by nesting `ScalarProperty` elements.

> **NOTE** Because complex types can be nested, you can put a `Complex-Property` inside another `ComplexProperty`.

Putting it all together, the following listing shows the overall mapping schema for `Order` and `OrderDetail`.

Listing 5.10 Defining the mapping between properties and columns

```
<EntitySetMapping Name="Orders">
  <EntityTypeMapping TypeName="IsTypeOf(OrderITModel.Order)">
    <MappingFragment StoreEntitySet="Order">
      <ScalarProperty Name="Id" ColumnName="Id" />
      <ComplexProperty Name="ShippingAddress"
        TypeName="OrderITModel.AddressInfo">
        <ScalarProperty Name="Address" ColumnName="ShippingAddress" />
        <ScalarProperty Name="City" ColumnName="ShippingCity" />
        <ScalarProperty Name="ZipCode" ColumnName="ShippingZipCode" />
        <ScalarProperty Name="Country" ColumnName="ShippingCountry" />
      </ComplexProperty>
      <ScalarProperty Name="EstimatedShippingDate"
        ColumnName="EstimatedShippingDate" />
      <ScalarProperty Name="ActualShippingDate"
        ColumnName="ActualShippingDate" />
```

```
      </MappingFragment>
    </EntityTypeMapping>
  </EntitySetMapping>
  <EntitySetMapping Name="OrderDetails">
    <EntityTypeMapping TypeName="IsTypeOf(OrderITModel.OrderDetail)">
      <MappingFragment StoreEntitySet="OrderDetail">
        <ScalarProperty Name="Id" ColumnName="Id" />
        <ScalarProperty Name="Quantity" ColumnName="Quantity" />
        <ScalarProperty Name="UnitPrice" ColumnName="UnitPrice" />
        <ScalarProperty Name="Discount" ColumnName="Discount" />
      </MappingFragment>
    </EntityTypeMapping>
  </EntitySetMapping>
```

So far, we have covered entities and ignored the associations between them, but associations between entities are the real essence of a model. Mapping them isn't too complicated, but you still have to touch all three EDM schemas. Fortunately, you know something about the schemas, so it should be simpler.

5.3   *Defining relationships in the model*

Implementing associations is one of the most challenging tasks in any O/RM, but the Entity Framework makes it quite easy. Naturally, you'll have to write some code and modify the mapping, but you'll understand it at first sight.

In the OrderIT model, there are three types of associations: one-to-one, one-to-many, and many-to-many. Let's look at them in turn.

5.3.1   *One-to-one relationships*

A typical example of a one-to-one relationship is that between the order detail and its order. Creating this type of association isn't difficult, but it involves several steps:

1 Modify the `OrderDetail` class by adding the navigation property. If you opt for foreign-key associations (as we did), you'll have to add the foreign-key property too.

2 Modify the CSDL to add properties to the class description and introduce the relationship.

3 Modify the storage schema to introduce the foreign key between the tables (if it exists).

4 Modify the mapping schema to map the relationship (only for independent associations).

Now, let's look at each step.

MODIFYING THE CLASS

To create a reference to the order from the order detail, you need to create an `Order` property in the `OrderDetail` class. Because you're using foreign keys, you have to add a foreign key property, as shown in the next listing.

Listing 5.11 Creating properties that reference the order from the order detail

C#
```
public class OrderDetail
{
  ...
  public virtual Order Order { get; set; }
  public virtual int OrderId { get; set; }
}
```

VB
```
Public Class OrderDetail
  ...
  Public Overridable Property Order() As Order
  Public Overridable Property OrderId() As Integer
End Class
```

That's all you need to do to create the relationship in the code. All the plumbing that was necessary to create associations in the classes in v1.0 is gone. Lovely!

Now that the code is fine, let's get back to the EDM and look at the conceptual schema.

MODIFYING THE CONCEPTUAL SCHEMA

Because the conceptual schema describes the model, this is where you must add information about the new properties and the relationship. You need to add the new navigation and foreign-key properties to the OrderDetail entity description.

The navigation property is added to the EntityType node related to OrderDetail by using the NavigationProperty element. The Name attribute maps the element to the property in the object, Relationship requires the full name of the relationship, FromRole identifies its starting point, and ToRole identifies the ending point. In this way, you can move from OrderDetail to Order.

The foreign-key property is added as a simple scalar property. Both properties are shown here.

Listing 5.12 Adding navigation and foreign-key properties to the entity in the CSDL

```
<EntityType Name="OrderDetail">
  ...
  <NavigationProperty Name="Order"
    Relationship="OrderIT.Domain.OrderOrderDetail" FromRole="OrderDetail"
    ToRole="Order" />
  <ScalarProperty Name="OrderId" ColumnName="OrderId" />
</EntityType>
```

That's all you need to do for the entity description. Now, let's move on to the relationship description. In Entity Framework, associations are first-class citizens, like entities, so they must be treated equally in the EDM.

In the EntityContainer element, you need to declare an AssociationSet for each association. It has two attributes:

- Name—Represents the name of the relationship set (a sort of entity set for associations)
- Association—Specifies the type

Inside AssociationSet, you insert two End nodes (one for each entity involved), placing the name of the class in the Role attribute and the name of its entity set in EntitySet.

> **NOTE** When you use the designer, the Name attribute is set with the name you assign to the relationship in the Association wizard.

Outside EntityContainer, you need to describe the relationship using the Association element. Its Name attribute links the description to the AssociationSet in the container, whereas the nested End elements describe the types involved in the relationship and their cardinality. What's important in the End element is the Multiplicity attribute, which can have one of the following values:

- 1—One side of the cardinality
- 0..1—Zero or one side of the cardinality
- *—Multiple side of the cardinality

End allows you to specify the delete cascade behavior. This has nothing to do with the database; it states that when the parent entity is marked as deleted, children are marked too. Its definition in the mapping is shown in the following listing.

Listing 5.13 Declaring and defining associations

```
<EntityContainer ...>
  <AssociationSet Name="OrderOrderDetail"
    Association="OrderITModel.OrderOrderDetail">
    <End Role="Order" EntitySet="Orders">
      <OnDelete Action="Cascade" />
    </End>
    <End Role="OrderDetail" EntitySet="OrderDetails" />
  </AssociationSet>
</EntityContainer>

<Association Name="OrderOrderDetail">
  <End Role="Order" Type="OrderITModel.Order" Multiplicity="1" />
  <End Role="OrderDetail" Type="OrderITModel.OrderDetail"
    Multiplicity="*" />
</Association>
```

Order is the one side, and OrderDetail is the multiple side in this example. That means you're mapping a one-to-many relationship! A one-to-many relationship implicitly declares the one-to-one relationship too. The order can have multiple details, but a detail can have only one order. It would be useless repeating this relationship twice in the EDM, so you declare it only once.

An independent association is mapped in the MSL, but a foreign-key association is mapped in the CSDL. Because we've opted to use a foreign-key relationship in this example, you have to add mapping information to the association definition. This information is put in the ReferentialConstraint node inside the Association element, and it comes after the End nodes, as shown in the next listing.

Listing 5.14   Defining a foreign-key association

```
<Association Name="OrderOrderDetail">
  ...
  <ReferentialConstraint>
    <Principal Role="Order">
      <PropertyRef Name="OrderId" />
    </Principal>
    <Dependent Role="OrderDetail">
      <PropertyRef Name="OrderId" />
    </Dependent>
  </ReferentialConstraint>
</Association>
```

ReferentialConstraint is only the container element. The real mapping happens in the Principal and Dependent nodes, where you specify the primary key of the master class and the foreign-key property in the child class (through the PropertyRef element). It's much like defining a foreign key in a database.

The conceptual schema is now ready; the third step is modifying the storage. But wait a second; what if the database knows nothing about the relationship between the order and its details? The foreign-key constraint might not exist for performance or other reasons. It turns out that this means absolutely nothing for mapping. You can still enforce the relationship on the conceptual side without worrying about the database. Nevertheless, in the OrderIT example, you have a relationship in the database, so let's see how it's described.

MODIFYING THE STORAGE SCHEMA

Describing relationships in the storage schema is similar to describing them in the conceptual schema. You declare the relationships in the entity container, and then you describe them outside it.

To declare the foreign-key constraint, you use the AssociationSet with its children inside EntityContainer exactly the same way as before. To specify which columns compose the foreign key, you use the Association node outside EntityContainer, as in the following listing.

Listing 5.15   Defining a database foreign key in the storage schema

```
<EntityContainer ...>
  <AssociationSet Name="FK_OrderDetail_Order"
    Association=" OrderITModel.Store.FK_OrderDetail_Order">
    <End Role="Order" EntitySet="Order" />
    <End Role="OrderDetail" EntitySet="OrderDetail" />
  </AssociationSet>
</EntityContainer>

<Association Name="FK_OrderDetail_Order">
```

```
    <End Role="Order" Type="OrderITModel.Store.Order" Multiplicity="1">
      <OnDelete Action="Cascade" />
    </End>
    <End Role="OrderDetail" Type="OrderITModel.Store.OrderDetail"
      Multiplicity="*"/>
    <ReferentialConstraint>
      <Principal Role="Order">
        <PropertyRef Name="OrderId" />
      </Principal>
      <Dependent Role="OrderDetail">
        <PropertyRef Name="OrderId" />
      </Dependent>
    </ReferentialConstraint>
  </Association>
```

Hey, this declaration is identical to the one in the conceptual schema! Notice that this time the cascade constraint between the order and order details describes the one in the database.

> **NOTE**   When we talk about foreign keys here, we mean the database foreign keys. This has nothing to do with the conceptual model foreign keys.

You're almost done. You only need to put mapping information in the MSL.

MODIFYING THE MAPPING SCHEMA

The mapping schema knows nothing about foreign-key associations. It only needs to know how a foreign-key property is mapped to the foreign key in the database table.

In this example, you have to map the OrderId property of the OrderDetail class to the OrderId column in the OrderDetail table, as in the following snippet:

```
<EntitySetMapping Name="OrderDetails">
  <EntityTypeMapping TypeName="IsTypeOf(OrderITModel.OrderDetail)">
    <MappingFragment StoreEntitySet="OrderDetail">
      ...
      <ScalarProperty Name="OrderId" ColumnName="OrderId" />
    </MappingFragment>
  </EntityTypeMapping>
</EntitySetMapping>
```

The one-to-one relationship between the detail and its order is now set up. In the next section, you'll learn how to build the one-to-many relationship between the order and its details.

5.3.2   *One-to-many relationships*

Creating the one-to-many relationship is only slightly different from creating the one-to-one relationships. The process is exactly the same as before, but because you've already put association data in the EDM, you only need to modify the Order class and reflect the modifications inside the CSDL.

ADDING A PROPERTY TO THE PARENT CLASS

The `Order` class maintains a reference to its details with a collection property named `OrderDetails`. To be Entity Framework–compliant, the property must be of type `ICollection<OrderDetail>`, `ISet<OrderDetail>`, or any type that implements them such as `List<T>` or `HashSet<T>`.

A collection property needs to be initialized before it's accessed, or you'll get a `NullReferenceException`. How you create the property depends on the type you choose for the collection. If you use an interface, you'll have to instantiate it lazily. If you use a real type, you can instantiate it either in the constructor or lazily.

The reason for this behavior is that when a proxy for the instance is created, if the property is exposed using an interface, it creates a concrete type and assigns it to the property. When this is done, the property can't be reassigned; if you do, you'll get an `InvalidOperationException`. Furthermore, putting your instantiation code in the constructor would override the instantiation made by the proxy (if you have a proxy), causing the exception to occur. If you use a concrete type, the proxy ignores the property instantiation, so you're free to put instantiation code wherever you want.

We recommend always using the lazy approach, as shown in the next listing.

Listing 5.16 Creating a property that references a collection of objects

C#
```csharp
public class Order
{
  ...
  private ICollection<OrderDetail> _OrderDetails;
  public virtual ICollection<OrderDetail> OrderDetails
  {
    get
    {
      _OrderDetails = _OrderDetails ?? new HashSet<OrderDetail>();
      return _OrderDetails;
    }
    set
    {
      _OrderDetails = value;
    }
  }
}
```

VB
```vb
Public Class Order
  ...
  Private _OrderDetails As ICollection(Of OrderDetail)
  Public Overridable Property OrderDetails() As ICollection(Of OrderDetail)
    Get
      _OrderDetails = If(_OrderDetails, New HashSet(Of OrderDetail)())
      Return _OrderDetails
    End Get
    Set(ByVal value As ICollection(Of OrderDetail))
      _OrderDetails = value
```

```
    End Set
  End Property
End Class
```

There's nothing more to do. Notice that the foreign key to the order details doesn't exist here. Now, let's move on to the conceptual schema.

MODIFYING THE CONCEPTUAL SCHEMA

To add the new property to the Order description in the conceptual schema, you add a NavigationProperty as you did for OrderDetail, changing the Name attribute and inverting the roles because here you're moving from Order to OrderDetail. This is the property mapping:

```
<NavigationProperty Name="OrderDetails" FromRole="Order"
  ToRole="OrderDetail" Relationship="OrderITModel.OrderOrderDetail" />
```

And that's all. The relationship has already been defined in the CSDL and SSDL; and in the MSL, nothing changes because the navigation property doesn't need to be mapped.

The last relationship we need to analyze is the many-to-many. In the OrderIT example, such a relationship exists between the products and the suppliers. People are often afraid of many-to-many relationships because they can be intricate. But don't worry: many-to-many mapping isn't complicated at all.

5.3.3   *Many-to-many relationships*

The steps for creating a many-to-many relationship are always the same. First, you create collection properties in both classes to relate them to each other, and then you modify the EDM. The difference in this type of relationship is that there are no foreign-key properties. The relationship between classes is direct, so the link table in the database has no correspondence in the model. This means you have to use an independent association.

You've already seen the relevant code for classes, CSDL, and SSDL because we've dealt with collection properties before. Here's a quick recap of how to set up the many-to-many relationship between the product and supplier:

1   Product and Supplier need to be associated to each other using collection properties.
2   In the CSDL, you need to map classes and their association, without inserting information about the foreign-key association.
3   In the SSDL, you need to declare and define Product, Company, and Product-Supplier tables and their associations.
4   In the MSL, you need to map the relationship between Product and Supplier to the database.

At this point, because you haven't used a foreign-key association, you have to define how the classes are related. This is done in the mapping file.

MODIFYING THE MAPPING SCHEMA

In the mapping schema, you use the `AssociationSetMapping` element to map database columns to independent associations. The `AssociationSetMapping` element has three attributes:

- `Name`—Specifies the name of the association in the conceptual schema
- `TypeName`—Represents the full name of the association set in the conceptual schema
- `StoreEntitySet`—Contains the name of child table in the database

Inside `AssociationSetMapping`, you put two `EndProperty` elements whose `Name` attribute matches the `Role` attribute of the `End` element in the `Association` node of the conceptual schema. Finally, you include a `ScalarProperty` element that specifies the property of the class and the foreign key column in the linked table. This column is used in conjunction with the primary key of the linked table to create the join when generating the SQL.

The overall mapping fragment is shown in this listing.

Listing 5.17 Mapping an independent property

```
<AssociationSetMapping Name="ProductsSuppliers"
  TypeName="OrderItModel.ProductsSuppliers"
  StoreEntitySet="ProductSupplier">
  <EndProperty Name="Suppliers">
    <ScalarProperty Name="CompanyId" ColumnName="SupplierId" />
  </EndProperty>
  <EndProperty Name="Products">
    <ScalarProperty Name="ProductId" ColumnName="ProductId" />
  </EndProperty>
</AssociationSetMapping>
```

Finished. The many-to-many relationship just required a new tag in the mapping schema. Before we move on and talk about inheritance, let's look at a few points about relationships.

5.3.4 Some tips about relationships

The first thing to know about relationships is that you aren't obliged to use foreign-key associations. You can, for example, remove the `OrderId` from the `OrderDetail` class and map the association with `Order` using an independent association. But working with foreign associations is easier than working with independent associations, especially when you're persisting an object graph. When possible, we always recommended using foreign keys.

Another thing you should know is that you can't map an association using both foreign keys and independent associations. You have to choose in advance which strategy you want to use. The designer enforces this rule, disabling one option when the other is used.

If you don't want to work with independent associations in many-to-many scenarios, you can follow the LINQ to SQL approach: create a class that matches the link table, and associate the classes with that. This would allow using foreign keys, but it's poor design, and we discourage this technique.

You've now learned everything you need to know about relationships. It's time to investigate inheritance mapping. An expressive model often makes use of inheritance; in OrderIT, Customer and Supplier inherit from the Company class, whereas Shoe and Shirt are specializations of the Product class.

5.4   *Mapping inheritance*

OrderIT uses two different inheritance strategies: table per hierarchy (TPH) for the Customer and Supplier classes and table per type (TPT) for the product-related classes. The database doesn't support inheritance at all, but by using these inheritance strategies, you can simulate this behavior. Let's start with the TPH strategy.

5.4.1   *Table per hierarchy inheritance*

The TPH inheritance mapping model states that an entire hierarchy of objects is mapped into a single table. In OrderIT, the Customer and Supplier classes are persisted into the Company table. Company has a Type column that acts as a discriminator, identifying whether a particular row is about a customer or a supplier. In chapter 2, we discussed the benefits of this inheritance model; here we'll cover only the practical task of mapping, starting with the class code.

DESIGNING THE CLASSES

Inheritance doesn't require any additional effort during class development. You simply create the base class (Company, in this case) and then create the other classes (Customer and Supplier), letting them inherit from the base class. Notice that the discriminator column must not be mapped because it's handled by Entity Framework. The following listing shows the class-declaration code.

> **Listing 5.18   The Company, Customer, and Supplier classes**

C#
```
public abstract class Company
{
  ...
}
public class Customer : Company
{
  ...
}
public class Supplier : Company
{
  ...
}
```

VB

```
Public MustInherits Class Company
  ...
End Class
Public Class Customer
  Inherits Company
  ...
End Class
Public Class Supplier
  Inherits Company
  ...
End Class
```

As usual, describing the new classes in the EDM is the next step. We'll start with the conceptual schema.

MODIFYING THE CONCEPTUAL SCHEMA

Inside the EntityContainer element of the conceptual schema, you put only one entity set for the entire hierarchy. Describing the classes requires the Abstract and BaseType attributes. For Company, Abstract is set to true and BaseType is empty. For Customer and Supplier, Abstract is set to false and BaseType is set to the FQN of Company. Their mapping is shown in the following listing.

Listing 5.19 Defining inheritance in the conceptual schema

```
<EntityContainer ...>
  <EntitySet Name="Companies" EntityType="OrderIT.Domain.Company" />
</EntityContainer>

<EntityType Name="Company" Abstract="true">
  <Key>
    <PropertyRef Name="CompanyId" />
  </Key>
  <Property Type="Int32" Name="CompanyId" Nullable="false"
    store:StoreGeneratedPattern="Identity" />
  <Property Type="String" Name="Name" Nullable="false" MaxLength="50" />
</EntityType>

<EntityType Name="Customer" BaseType="OrderITModel.Company" >
  <Property Name="BillingAddress" Type="OrderITModel.AddressInfo"
    Nullable="false" />
  <Property Name="ShippingAddress" Type="OrderITModel.AddressInfo"
    Nullable="false" />
  <Property Type="String" Name="WSUsername" Nullable="true"
    MaxLength="20" />
  <Property Type="String" Name="WSPassword" Nullable="true" />
  <Property Type="String" Name="WSEnabled" Nullable="false" />
</EntityType>

<EntityType Name="Supplier" BaseType="OrderITModel.Company" >
  <Property Type="String" Name="IBAN" Nullable="false" FixedLength="true"
    MaxLength="26" />
  <Property Type="Int16" Name="PaymentDays" Nullable="false" />
</EntityType>
```

Notice that each `EntityType` node must define only the properties of the class it describes. The description of `Company` contains only the ID and the name. The description of `Customer` includes the addresses and web service properties, whereas the `Supplier` description adds payment information.

That's all you need to do in the conceptual schema, so we can move on to the storage. You've already seen the tables, so we'll go directly to the mapping schema.

MODIFYING THE MAPPING SCHEMA

As usual, the real power emerges in the mapping file. The `EntitySetMapping` element allows you to map multiple classes in one entity set.

We'll start by mapping `Company`. The `Name` attribute of `EntitySetMapping` must be set to `Companies`—that's the entity set defined in the conceptual schema. Inside `EntityTypeMapping`, `TypeName` must be set to `IsTypeOf(OrderITModel.Company)`. Finally, `StoreEntitySet` attribute inside the `MappingFragment` element must be set to `Company`—that's the storage entity set name (which, by default, matches the table name). Inside `MappingFragment`, you put all the properties defined in the conceptual schema.

Here's what it looks like:

```
<EntitySetMapping Name="Companies">
  <EntityTypeMapping TypeName="IsTypeOf(OrderITModel.Company)">
    <MappingFragment StoreEntitySet="Company">
      <ScalarProperty Name="CompanyId" ColumnName="CompanyId" />
      <ScalarProperty Name="Name" ColumnName="Name" />
    </MappingFragment>
  </EntityTypeMapping>
  ...
<EntitySetMapping Name="Companies">
```

In the `Customer` mapping, you don't create a new `EntitySetMapping`. Instead, you add an `EntityTypeMapping` node inside it. Into this new node, you put another `Mapping-Fragment` node. In the `EntityTypeMapping` node, you set the `TypeName` attribute to `IsTypeOf(OrderITModel.Customer)`. This way, you've changed only the mapped class, whereas the entity set and the database table have remained the same. Naturally, here you define only the properties described in the class, ignoring those inherited from `Company` *except* for the key properties. You can see that in the following snippet:

```
<EntityTypeMapping TypeName="IsTypeOf(OrderITModel.Customer)">
  <MappingFragment StoreEntitySet="Company">
    <Condition ColumnName="Type" Value="C" />
    <ScalarProperty Name="CompanyId" ColumnName="CompanyId" />
    <ScalarProperty Name="WSUsername" ColumnName="WSUsername" />
    <ScalarProperty Name="WSPassword" ColumnName="WSPassword" />
    ...
  </MappingFragment>
</EntityTypeMapping>
```

Mapping the `Supplier` entity is a matter of copying and pasting the `Customer` snippet, changing the `TypeName` attribute, and mapping the properties, as shown in the next snippet:

```
<EntityTypeMapping TypeName="IsTypeOf(OrderITModel.Supplier)">
  <MappingFragment StoreEntitySet="Company">
    <Condition ColumnName="Type" Value="S" />
    <ScalarProperty Name="CompanyId" ColumnName="CompanyId" />
    ...
  </MappingFragment>
</EntityTypeMapping>
```

The last tweak is the discriminator. You know that in the TPH mapping strategy you need a discriminator column to identify what type a row is mapped to. In OrderIT, the discriminator column specifies whether the row is about a customer or a supplier. This must be specified in the mapping schema; the conceptual side must have no knowledge of this plumbing because it's a storage requirement.

To specify the discriminator, you use the `Condition` element inside `Mapping-Fragment` to specify a value for the discriminator column. When the column has the specified value, the row belongs to the type that's being mapped. The value `C` specifies that the row is about a customer, whereas the value `S` identifies a supplier. You can see this tag at work in the previous snippets.

Well done! You've successfully mapped an inheritance hierarchy with the TPH strategy. It wasn't that hard. You've only had to learn one new node, `Condition`, and the rest were the same ones covered before.

Now that you're a master of TPH, we can move ahead and talk about the OrderIT product scenario, which uses the TPT inheritance mapping strategy. TPT has a completely different point of view compared to TPH, but the way you map it is similar.

5.4.2   *Table per type inheritance*

In the TPT approach, you map each entity in the hierarchy to a dedicated table. The table contains as many columns as the related type defines. In OrderIT, for example, you have Product, Shoe, and Shirt tables, and similarly named classes that hold their data.

In the TPH model, the discriminator column is responsible for distinguishing the customers from the suppliers. In the TPT model, there's no need for such a column because the primary keys specify the product type. For instance, if a product has ID 1 and it's in the Product and Shirt tables, it's a shirt; if it's in the Product and Shoe tables, it's a pair of shoes. With the use of ad hoc SQL joins, Entity Framework is able to determine the type of each product when querying and to correctly update data when persisting objects.

Mapping the TPT isn't complicated, because you already have all the necessary knowledge. The code is identical to that used for TPH; you define the classes and their inheritance chain as in the following listing.

> **Listing 5.20   The `Product`, `Shoe`, and `Shirt` classes**

C#
```
public abstract class Product
{
  ...
```

```
}
public class Shoe : Product
{
  ...
}
public class Shirt : Product
{
  ...
}
```

VB

```
Public MustInherits Class Product
  ...
End Class
Public Class Shirt
  Inherits Product
  ...
End Class
Public Class Shoe
  Inherits Company
  ...
End Class
```

What changes between the TPT and TPH strategies is the mapping and the storage schemas, not the way the classes are shaped.

In the conceptual schema, you define the entities exactly the same way as for the TPH strategy and create one `EntitySet` for the root of the hierarchy. The storage schema is different because you have more than one table for each entity, but you already know how to define tables, so we won't show that again.

In the mapping file, you use the `EntitySetMapping` element, nesting an `Entity-TypeMapping` node for each entity. Inside `EntityTypeMapping`, you include a `Mapping-Fragment` element to associate the table with the entity. Inside `MappingFragment`, you map only the properties declared in the entity plus the primary key. The mapping result is shown next.

Listing 5.21 Mapping TPT inheritance in the MSL

```
<EntitySetMapping Name="Products">
  <EntityTypeMapping TypeName="IsTypeOf(OrderITModel.Product)">
    <MappingFragment StoreEntitySet="Product">
      ...
    </MappingFragment>
  </EntityTypeMapping>
  <EntityTypeMapping TypeName="IsTypeOf(OrderITModel.Shirt)">
    <MappingFragment StoreEntitySet="Shirt">
      ...
    </MappingFragment>
  </EntityTypeMapping>
  <EntityTypeMapping TypeName="IsTypeOf(OrderITModel.Shoes)">
    <MappingFragment StoreEntitySet="Shoe">
      ...
    </MappingFragment>
  </EntityTypeMapping>
</EntitySetMapping>
```

For the umpteenth time, you've reused your knowledge without having to learn anything to create a brand-new feature. Despite its intricacies, EDM isn't so hard to master.

5.5 Extending the EDM with custom annotations

The EDM is made of three XML files. Like any other XML file, it can be extended by adding custom namespaces and linking nodes to them. Even if all the information about mapping is already there, adding custom information can be useful when you need additional data that isn't included in the default schema.

A simple example is validation. The `Supplier` class has an `IBAN` property (IBAN being an international format for identifying bank accounts). You could specify the format in the EDM and then use templates, as shown in chapter 2, to customize the class's code generation to add validation code in the IBAN property setter. Even better, you could generate a `DataAnnotation` attribute so that the class was compliant with ASP.NET MVC validation specifications. Whatever your choice, EDM customization is where it all begins.

Another example involves collection properties. Suppose that an order can't have more than 10 details. You can add this value to the property in the EDM and then create a CLR custom collection that, in the `Add` method, compares the number of details to the limit, raising an exception or performing some other action if there are too many lines.

There are several other cases where customization of the EDM is a winning choice. It's a powerful tool in your toolbox. Now that you know *why* you should customize the EDM, let's look at *how* to do it.

5.5.1 Customizing the EDM

Adding custom annotations is pretty straightforward. You just have to add a namespace, inside of which you put the tags.

Suppose you need to add IBAN validation information in the EDM. The easiest way to validate a string is with a regular expression. The following listing adds such an expression to the `IBAN` property.

Listing 5.22 Adding a custom tag to the EDM

```
<Schema xmlns:val="http://val" ...>                    ⟵──── Declares namespace
  <EntityType Name="Supplier">
    <Property Name="IBAN" ...>
      <val:regex>
        [a-zA-Z]{2}\d{2}[ ][a-zA-Z]\d{3}[ ]\d{4}[ ]\d{4}      Adds custom
⇥ [ ]\d{4}[ ]\d{3}|[a-zA-Z]{2}\d{2}[a-zA-Z]\d{22}            annotation
      </val:regex>
    </Property>
  </EntityType>
<Schema>
```

Naturally, you can add attributes following the same principle. There's no technical limitation—the choice is up to you.

Keep in mind that not all tags in the EDM accept inner custom tags. The following tags don't allow customizations:

- `Using`
- `Schema`
- `Key`
- `PropertyRef`

The reason for this limitation is that those tags don't have a correspondence in the Entity Framework metadata object model, so they can't be accessed. Similarly, MSL tags can't be customized, whereas SSDL and CSDL tags can.

> **NOTE**   That last sentence probably sounded like Jabba the Hutt speaking without subtitles, but don't worry; in chapter 12, which focuses on metadata, you'll learn about the metadata object model and tag customization.

For the moment, keep in mind that you can customize the EDM. The real power that comes from using this technique will be revealed later.

5.6   *Summary*

In this chapter, you've learned what you need to know to create and map entities to tables. We have not covered some very task-specific details, like the mapping of stored procedures, because they'll be discussed in depth in chapter 9.

Mapping is a complicated task at first, but when you understand the use of the five main elements of the mapping (`EntitySet`, `EntityType`, `AssociationSet`, `Association`, and `EntitySetMapping`), there's little more to learn. They, in combination, open the door to every mapping scenario.

Fortunately, creating the CLR classes is simpler than creating the EDM. Thanks to the POCO support, you can have classes that are completely ignorant of Entity Framework or any other persistence mechanism, allowing you to focus only on the business problem.

It was a long trip from defining classes to mapping them through to the database. If you have a complex model, you can end up spending a lot of time maintaining this infrastructure code. This is what drove the Entity Framework team to create a designer. By using the designer, you only need to worry about the business code, leaving to the designer the burden of creating the plumbing.

Now that you know how to map the domain model and how to use the power of querying with Entity Framework, it's time to learn how to modify objects and persist their modifications into the database. This will allow you to start developing real projects.

Understanding the entity lifecycle

This chapter covers

- Understanding entity states
- Understanding transitions between states
- Automatic and manual state changes

At this point in the book, you have two-thirds of the basics you need to implement Entity Framework–based data access code. You have learned how to create an object model, how to map it against the database using the EDM, how to perform queries to retrieve data, and how to transform data in objects. What you're still missing is an understanding of the entity lifecycle and how to persist modifications made to an entity into the database. This chapter is about the first part of that: the entity lifecycle.

In this chapter, you'll learn about the different states an entity can be in and what can be done in each one of them. This is a central subject because the changes you make to an entity affect its state, which in turn affects the way those modifications are later persisted.

Let's start our discussion by analyzing the lifecycle of an entity and its several states.

151

6.1   *The entity lifecycle*

During its lifetime, an entity has a state. Before looking at how to retrieve entity state, let's take a look at what entity state is. The state is an enum of type `System.Data.EntityState` that declares the following values:

- `Added`—The entity is marked as added.
- `Deleted`—The entity is marked as deleted.
- `Modified`—The entity has been modified.
- `Unchanged`—The entity hasn't been modified.
- `Detached`—The entity isn't tracked.

What do these states represent? What is the state related to? How can an entity pass from one state to another? Does the state affect the database? To answer these questions, we'll have to look at the concepts behind the object lifecycle.

6.1.1   *Understanding entity state*

As explained in chapter 3, the context holds a reference to all objects retrieved from the database. What's more important for our discussion, the context holds the state of an entity and maintains modifications made to the properties of the entity. This feature is known as *change tracking (or object tracking)*.

If you create an entity outside the context, its status is `Detached` because the context can't track it.

> **NOTE**   More precisely, an entity outside the context has no state. We referred to `Detached` status because in Entity Framework 1.0 that's the state an entity is in when it's not tracked by a context.

If you *attach* an entity to the context (more on this in section 6.2), it will move to the `Unchanged` state. If you retrieve an entity from the database and then get rid of the context, the entity state will be `Detached`. If you retrieve an entity, dispose of the context, and create a new context and *add* the entity to it, the entity will be in the `Added` state (again, this will be explained in section 6.2). As these examples make clear, the state is the relationship between the entity and the context that holds a reference to it.

At first, you might have thought that the entity state reflected the state of the entity compared to the corresponding row in the database, but it's not like that. The context is the application database; this is why entities relate their state to the context and not to the database.

> **NOTE**   The fact that the state of an entity relates to the context instead of the database often confuses people when they first approach Entity Framework. It's important to understand this point.

Let's look at an example. Suppose you have two methods in the OrderIT web service: the first retrieves data about a customer, and the second updates the data. The client uses the first method to retrieve the data and display it in a form. In this method, you create a context to retrieve the data and then destroy the context.

The user modifies some of the data, such as the shipping address, and then saves it, invoking the second method and passing in the updated customer data. In the web-service method, you create a new context and attach the entity to it. The new context can't know what data has been modified by the user (if any) unless it goes to the database and performs a comparison.

Going to the database would be too expensive, so it's not performed automatically. This means that when the entity is attached to the context, it enters the `Unchanged` state, because the context knows nothing about modifications. If the entity state reflected the actual state against the database, it would be `Modified`, but that's not the case. This example is simple, but it explains why the state indicates the relationship between the entity and the context, and not the entity and the database.

Naturally, the state of an entity affects the way it's persisted. Not surprisingly, when you persist entities, those in the `Added`, `Modified`, or `Deleted` state are saved using the `INSERT`, `UPDATE`, or `DELETE` command in the database.

6.1.2 How entity state affects the database

The state represents not only the state of the entity in the context, but also how the data will be persisted into the database. For each state, there is a corresponding SQL command.

An entity in `Added` state is persisted using an `INSERT` command to create a new row in the mapped tables. An entity that's `Modified` already has a correspondence with a table row, so it will be persisted using an `UPDATE` command. An entity in `Deleted` state has a correspondence with a table row, but it triggers a `DELETE` instead of an `UPDATE`.

The `Detached` and `Unchanged` states have no impact on the database: a detached entity isn't tracked by a context, so it can't be persisted, whereas an unchanged one has no modifications to persist.

During its lifetime, an entity can change its state. Let's look at how this happens and what API you can to use to make it happen manually.

6.1.3 State changes in the entity lifecycle

The state of an entity is sometimes set automatically by the context and can also be modified manually by the developer. Although all the combinations of switches from one state to another are possible, some of them are pointless. For instance, there's no point in moving an `Added` entity to the `Deleted` state, or vice versa. Figure 6.1 shows all the states and how an entity can pass from one to another.

The figure is quite clear. The only thing we need to add is that all the methods shown belong to the `ObjectContext` or to the `ObjectSet<T>` classes. Now, let's look more closely at the different states.

DETACHED STATE

When an entity is `Detached`, it isn't bound to the context, so its state isn't tracked. It can be disposed of, modified, used in combination with other classes, or used in any other way you might need. Because there is no context tracking it, it has no meaning to Entity Framework.

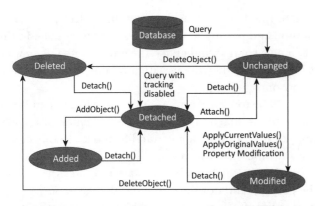

Figure 6.1   The different entity states and the context methods that make them change

As a consequence, Detached is the default state of a newly created entity (one created using the new constructor) because the context can't track the creation of any object in your code. This is true even if you instantiate the entity inside a using block of the context. Detached is even the state of entities retrieved from the database when tracking is disabled.

UNCHANGED STATE

When an entity is Unchanged, it's bound to the context but it hasn't been modified. By default, an entity retrieved from the database is in this state.

When an entity is attached to the context (with the Attach method), it similarly is in the Unchanged state. The context can't track changes to objects that it doesn't reference, so when they're attached it assumes they're Unchanged.

ADDED STATE

When an entity is in the Added state, you have few options. In fact, you can only detach it from the context using Detach.

Naturally, even if you modify some property, the state remains Added, because moving it to Modified, Unchanged, or Deleted would be nonsense—it's a new entity and has no correspondence with a row in the database. This is a fundamental prerequisite for being in one of those states (but this rule *isn't* enforced by the context).

MODIFIED STATE

When an entity is Modified, that means it was in Unchanged state and then some property was changed.

After an entity enters the Modified state, it can move to the Detached or Deleted state, but it can't roll back to the Unchanged state even if you manually restore the original values (unless you detach and reattach the entity to the context). It can't even be changed to Added (unless you detach and add the entity to the context, because a row with this ID already exists in the database, and you would get a runtime exception when persisting it.

> **NOTE**   The preceding rules can be overridden using an API we'll discuss in section 6.2.6.

DELETED STATE

An entity enters the `Deleted` state because it was `Unchanged` or `Modified` and then the `DeleteObject` method was used. This is the most restrictive state, because it's pointless changing from this state to any other value but `Detached`.

That covers what each state means and how an entity can have its status changed. Now, let's take the methods that are responsible for this process and put them into action.

6.2 *Managing entity state*

The change from the `Unchanged` to the `Modified` state is the only one that's automatically handled by the context. All other changes must be made explicitly using proper methods:

- `AddObject`—Adds an entity to the context in the `Added` state
- `Attach`—Attaches an entity to the context in the `Unchanged` state
- `ApplyCurrentValues` and `ApplyOriginalValues`—Change the state to `Modified`, comparing the tracked entity with another one
- `DeleteObject`—Marks an entity as `Deleted`
- `AcceptAllChanges`—Marks all entities as `Unchanged`
- `ChangeState` and `ChangeObjectState`—Change an entity from one state to another without any restrictions (except for `Detached`)
- `Detach`—Removes an entity from the context

These methods are exposed by the `ObjectContext` and `ObjectSet<T>` classes, with the exception of `AttachTo`, which is defined only by the context, and `ChangeState`, which is defined by the state manager (we'll look at this component shortly). The `Object-Set<T>` methods internally invoke the context methods, so there's no difference between them.

In the first release of Entity Framework, only the `ObjectContext` methods existed. The interface for these methods is muddy, so the team added the new ones to `ObjectSet<T>`, improving usability and simplifying code readability. Because of these advantages, we strongly recommend using the `ObjectSet<T>` methods and consider the context methods obsolete.

Let's look at each of these methods, starting with the one that adds an entity to the context.

6.2.1 *The AddObject method*

`AddObject` allows you to add an entity to the context in the `Added` state. When the entity is added to the context, it's added to those tracked by the context for modifications. When the persistence process is triggered, the context saves the object as a new row in the tables using INSERT commands. In the OrderIT example, persisting an order will cause an INSERT into the Order table, whereas persisting a shirt will cause an INSERT into the Product and the Shirt tables.

Let's look at the code. We'll first analyze the context method, and then we'll look at the entity-set method so that you understand why a new API was desirable.

The `AddObject` context method receives two arguments, the entity set name and the entity:

C#
```
public void AddObject(string entitySetName, object entity)
```

VB
```
Public Sub AddObject(ByVal entitySetName As String,
  ByVal entity As Object)
```

There are at least two weaknesses in this code. First, the entity set name is passed as a string. If you type it incorrectly, you'll get an exception only at runtime. Here's an example:

C#
```
ctx.AddObject("Companis", new Customer() { ... });
```

VB
```
ctx.AddObject("Companis", New Customer() With { ... })
```

Second, the entity argument is of type `Object`, meaning you can potentially pass any CLR object and receive an exception only at runtime if the object isn't correct. Here's an example that compiles, despite having the wrong object and wrong entity set name. It produces a runtime exception:

C#
```
ctx.AddObject("Companis", String.Empty);
```

VB
```
ctx.AddObject("Companis", String.Empty)
```

The following listing shows the correct code.

Listing 6.1   Adding an entity to the context via the `ObjectContext` method

C#
```
ctx.AddObject("Companies", new Customer() { ... });
```

VB
```
ctx.AddObject("Companies", New Customer() With { ... })
```

In the strong-typing era, such an API is unbearable. To overcome this bad design, the Entity Framework team introduced an equivalent API in the entity set interface. It accepts as input only the object that needs to be added:

C#
```
public void AddObject(TEntity entity)
```

VB
```
Public Sub AddObject(ByVal entity As TEntity)
```

`TEntity` is the type of the entity maintained by the entity set (remember that an entity set is an instance of a type implementing the IObjectSet<T> interface). Due to strong typing, you have no chance to pass an object of the incorrect type to the method. Furthermore, because the entity set knows its name, there's no need to specify it.

Listing 6.2 shows the code that uses the new method.

Listing 6.2 Adding an entity to the context with the `ObjectSet<T>` class method

C#
```
ctx.Companies.AddObject(new Product() { ... });

ctx.Companies.AddObject(new Customer() { ... });
```

VB
```
ctx.Companies.AddObject(New Product() With { ... })

ctx.Companies.AddObject(New Customer() With { ... })
```

In each case, the first line doesn't compile; Product isn't allowed. The second line compiles, and Customer inherits from Company.

Now, look at listings 6.1 and 6.2. Didn't you fall in love with the new syntax?

Adding an entity to the context using the method exposed by the entity set property of the context class is pretty straightforward. Later in the chapter, we'll deal with relationships, and you'll discover there are subtleties that can complicate your life.

Adding an entity to the context is useful when you need to persist the object as a new row in the database. But when the object already has a correspondence with a row in the database, it must be persisted using an UPDATE command. The flow changes, and you have to use the Attach method.

6.2.2 The Attach method

The Attach method attaches an object to the context in an Unchanged state. When the entity is *attached* to the context, it's tracked by the context for modifications made to *scalar* properties.

In a real-world application, there are plenty of situations where an entity needs to be attached. Web applications and web services are typical examples. Let's go back to the example from section 6.1, where a customer updates its data. In the method that retrieves the customer, you create a context, perform a query, return the object to the client, and then dispose of the context. In the update method, you create a brand-new context and then attach the customer to it. Finally, you persist the customer. (There's also something else to do, as you'll discover later in this chapter.)

Let's get back to the Attach method. The Attach context method receives two arguments: the entity-set name and the entity. This method suffers from the same limitations of AddObject and so has become obsolete. In its place, you can use the Attach entity-set method, which needs only the object to be attached, as you can see in the next listing.

Listing 6.3   Attaching an entity with the `Attach` method

C#
```
var c = new Customer { CompanyId = 1 };
...
ctx.Companies.Attach(c);
```

VB
```
Dim c as New Customer With { .CompanyId = 1 }
...
ctx.Companies.Attach(c)
```

You attach an object to the context because you want its data to be updated (or deleted, as you'll see later) in the database. The object must have a correspondence with a row in the database, and this correspondence is identified by the primary-key properties and columns.

> **NOTE**   As you have learned before, the context doesn't go to the database to check whether the object's primary key has a correspondence with a database row.

When you attach an object to the context, the primary-key columns must be set, or you'll get an `InvalidOperationException` at runtime. Furthermore, during the persistence phase, if the `UPDATE` command doesn't affect any row, the context throws an exception.

Because an attached entity goes to the `Unchanged` state, you must find a way to mark it as `Modified` to persist it in the database. The next methods we'll discuss can do this.

6.2.3   *The ApplyCurrentValues and ApplyOriginalValues methods*

In our customer web-service example, when you have attached the object, you need to persist it. The problem is that after it's attached, it's in `Unchanged` state, so you need to find a way to change it to `Modified` state. The simplest way is to query the database for the latest data, and compare it with the input entity.

You know that the object context keeps a reference to each entity read from the database or that is added through the `AddObject` or `Attach` method. What we haven't mentioned is that it keeps in memory both the *original* values and the *current* values of the scalar properties when the entity is bound to the context (you'll learn more about this in section 6.3).

The `ApplyOriginalValues` method takes an entity as input (the one coming from the database, in this case). The method then retrieves in the context's memory an object of the same type and with the same key as the input entity (we'll refer to this entity as the *context entity*). Finally, the method copies the values of the input entity's scalar properties into the original value of the context entity's scalar properties. At this point, the scalar properties' original values held in the context contain data from the database, whereas the scalar properties' current values held in the context contain the values of the entity from the web service. If original values are different from current values, the entity is set to Modified state; otherwise it remains Unchanged.

You can follow the opposite path too. Instead of attaching the entity and querying the database, you can query the database and then apply modifications from the web service's entity. This is what the ApplyCurrentValues method does. It takes an entity as input (the one from the web service, in this case). The method then retrieves in the context's memory an object of the same type and with the same key as the input entity (again, we'll call this the *context entity*). Finally, the method copies the values of the input entity's scalar properties into the current value of the context entity's scalar properties. At this point, the current values held in the context contain data from the web service entity, and the original values are the values from the database. If they are different, the entity is set to Modified state; otherwise it remains Unchanged.

When persistence is triggered, if the entity is in Modified state, it's persisted using UPDATE commands.

Like the previous methods we've discussed, the ApplyOriginalValues and Apply-CurrentValues methods belong to the ObjectContext and ObjectSet<T> classes, and we recommend using those exposed by the latter, as shown here.

Listing 6.4 Changing state with `ApplyOriginalValues` and `ApplyCurrentValues`

C#
```
Dim entityFromDb = GetEntityFromDb(entityFromService.CompanyId);
ctx.Companies.Attach(entityFromService);
ctx.Companies.ApplyOriginalValues(entityFromDb);

ctx.Companies.First(c => c.CompanyId == entityFromService.CompanyId);
ctx.Companies.ApplyCurrentValues(entityFromService);
```

VB
```
Dim entityFromDb = GetEntityFromDb(entityFromService.CompanyId)
ctx.Companies.Attach(entityFromService)
ctx.Companies.ApplyOriginalValues(entityFromDb)

ctx.Companies.First(Function(c) c.CompanyId = entityFromService.CompanyId)
ctx.Companies.ApplyCurrentValues(entityFromService)
```

You must be aware of a little trap here. Both methods *only* care about scalar and complex properties of the input entity. If a scalar property in an associated entity changes, or if a new line is added, removed, or changed in an associated collection, it won't be detected.

The other persistence operation in a database is DELETE. The DeleteObject method marks an entity for deletion.

6.2.4 *The DeleteObject method*

The DeleteObject method marks an entity as Deleted. The only caveat that you have to keep in mind is that the entity passed to this method must be attached to the context. The object must come from a query or have been attached to the context using the Attach method.

If the object isn't found in the context, an `InvalidOperationException` is thrown with this message: "The object cannot be deleted because it was not found in the ObjectStateManager."

The next listing shows how easy it is to use the `DeleteObject` method exposed by the `ObjectSet<T>` class.

Listing 6.5   Deleting an entity

C#
```
var c = ctx.Companies.OfType<Customer>()
  .Where(w => w.CompanyId == 1);
ctx.Companies.DeleteObject(c);
```
Connected scenario

```
var c = new Customer { ... };
ctx.Companies.Attach(c);
ctx.Companies.DeleteObject(c);
```
Disconnected scenario

VB
```
Dim c = ctx.Companies.OfType(Of Customer)().
  Where(Function(w) w.CompanyId = 1)
ctx.Companies.DeleteObject(c)
```
Connected scenario

```
Dim c as New Customer { ... }
ctx.Companies.Attach(c)
ctx.DeleteObject(c)
```
Disconnected scenario

When `DeleteObject` is invoked, the entity isn't deleted from the context; it's *marked* as deleted. When persistence is triggered, the entity is removed from the context, and `DELETE` commands are issued to delete it from the database.

The next method we'll explore is used to commit entity modification inside the context.

6.2.5   *The AcceptAllChanges method*

The `AcceptAllChanges` method takes all entities that are in `Added` and `Modified` states and marks them as `Unchanged`. It then detaches entities in `Deleted` state and eventually updates the `ObjectStateManager` entries (more on this in section 6.3).

`AcceptAllChanges` is exposed only by the `ObjectContext` and doesn't have a counterpart in the `ObjectSet<T>` class. That's why you need to use this code:

C#
```
ctx.AcceptAllChanges();
```

VB
```
ctx.AcceptAllChanges()
```

The methods you've seen so far are very strict. They change the entity state to a specific value. The next methods we'll look at are different because they give you the freedom to switch to any state.

6.2.6 The ChangeState and ChangeObjectState methods

The `ChangeState` and `ChangeObjectState` methods are the most flexible state-changing methods. They allow you to change the state of an entity to any other possible state (except `Detached`). When working with one entity, these methods are useful. But their importance grows when dealing with complex object graphs, as you'll discover later in this chapter.

`ChangeState` is exposed by the `ObjectStateEntry` class, whereas `ChangeObject-State` is exposed by the `ObjectStateManager` class (more on these classes in section 6.3). `ChangeState` only needs the new state, because the `ObjectStateEntry` instance already refers to an entity. `ChangeObjectState` accepts the entity and the new state as arguments. Both methods are shown in the following listing.

> **Listing 6.6 Changing object state using `ChangeObjectState` and `ChangeState`**

C#
```
var osm = ctx.ObjectStateManager;
osm.ChangeObjectState(entity, EntityState.Unchanged);
osm.GetObjectStateEntry(entity).ChangeState(EntityState.Unchanged);
```

VB
```
Dim osm = ctx.ObjectStateManager
osm.ChangeObjectState(entity, EntityState.Unchanged)
osm.GetObjectStateEntry(entity).ChangeState(EntityState.Unchanged)
```

These methods don't always physically change the entity state; sometimes they resort to using the previous methods. For instance, moving an entity to the `Unchanged` state means calling the `AcceptChanges` method of the `ObjectStateEntry` class (`AcceptChanges` is internally invoked by the `AcceptAllChanges` method we discussed in section 6.2.5). In contrast, changing the state from `Unchanged` to `Added` means changing the state.

Sometimes you don't need the entities to be persisted or to be tracked for modification by the context. In that case, you can remove the entities from the context by detaching them.

6.2.7 The Detach method

The `Detach` method removes the entity from the list of entities tracked by the context. Whatever the state of the entity, it becomes `Detached`, but entities referenced by the detached one aren't detached.

Invoking this method is pretty simple, as you see in listing 6.7, because it accepts only the entity that must be detached. (We show only the entity set method, which is the recommended one.)

> **Listing 6.7 Detaching an entity**

C#
```
ctx.Companies.Detach(c);
```
VB
```
ctx.Companies.Detach(c)
```

The precondition for successful detaching is that the entity must already be attached to the context. If that's not the case, you'll get an `InvalidOperationException` with the message, "The object cannot be detached because it is not attached to the ObjectStateManager."

You've now learned how to move an entity from one state to another, but there's still one missing piece. So far, we've said that the context is able to track modifications to the objects it references. This is true, but only to a certain extent. The truth is that the context delegates change-tracking management to another inner component: `ObjectStateManager`.

6.3   *Managing change tracking with ObjectStateManager*

The `ObjectStateManager` component (*state manager* from now on) is one of Entity Framework's hidden gems. It's responsible for everything related to object tracking in the context:

- When you add, attach to, or delete an entity from the context, you actually do that against the state manager.
- When we say that the context keeps an in-memory collection of all entities read from the database, it's the state manager that holds this data.
- When the context performs an identity-map check (discussed in chapter 3), it's really the state manager that performs the check.
- When we say that the context keeps track of relationships between entities, it's the state manager that keeps track of everything.

> **NOTE**   Because `ObjectContext` wraps the state manager, it's still valid to say that the *context* performs the tracking.

Tracking changes to entities is only one of the state manager's tasks. It also provides APIs for retrieving entity state and manipulating it.

The state manager isn't directly accessible. Because it's an inner component of the context, it's exposed as a property, named `ObjectStateManager`, of the `Object-Context` class. This is the code you use to access the state manager:

C#
```
var osm = ctx.ObjectStateManager;
```

VB
```
Dim osm = ctx.ObjectStateManager
```

> **NOTE**   For brevity, we'll use the variable `osm` to identify the state manager in the code.

The context is responsible for the lifecycle of the state manager. It handles its instantiation and disposal, and there's absolutely nothing you can do to change this behavior (nor is there any reason why you should).

Now that you know what the purpose of the state manager is, let's go deeper and look at how it accomplishes its tasks. Let's first investigate what data it manages.

6.3.1　*The ObjectStateEntry class*

When you query the state manager to retrieve an entity tracked by the context, it replies with an `ObjectStateEntry` object (*entry* from now on). This object contains more than the simple tracked entity. It holds data that fully represents the entity and its history inside the state manager. It also holds the relationships between the entity and other entities it references by navigation properties. More specifically, it exposes two types of members: properties and methods that reveal data about the entry (shown in table 6.1) and methods that manipulate entry data (discussed in section 6.3.3).

Table 6.1　Members exposed by the `ObjectStateEntry` class that give access to data in the entry

Member	Description
`Entity` property	Entity tracked by the state manager
`EntityKey` property	Key of the entity
`EntitySet` property	Entity set that the entity belongs to
`EntityState` property	State of the entity
`OriginalValues` property	Value of each entity property when it was attached
`CurrentValues` property	Current value of each entity property
`GetModifiedProperties` method	Properties modified since the entity was tracked
`IsRelationship` property	Flag that specifies whether the entry contains data about an entity or a relationship

This is a lot of information. The most important members for you are likely `Entity-State`, `OriginalValues`, and `CurrentValues`; the others are there mainly because Entity Framework itself is their first consumer.

> **NOTE**　`OriginalValues` and `CurrentValues` are of type `DbDataRecord`.

`ObjectStateEntry` is an abstract class that acts as a base class for two other classes: `EntityEntry` and `RelationshipEntry`. They're internal classes, so you'll never work with them directly. As their names suggest, `EntityEntry` contains data about an entity, and `RelationshipEntry` contains information about a relationship between entities. `EntityEntry` needs no explanation, but we'll get back to `RelationshipEntry` in section 6.3.5.

The `EntityKey` property is vital because it represents the key of the entity inside the state manager. The `EntityKey` concept is a little bit tricky, so it's worth looking into it.

UNDERSTANDING HOW THE STATE MANAGER IDENTIFIES AN OBJECT BY ITS KEY

The `EntityKey` property is what the state manager uses to ensure that only one entity of a given type with a given ID is tracked. The identity-map check is performed by inspecting the entity's `EntityKey` property and not the entity's key properties.

`EntityKey` contains two important properties: the entity set and the values of the properties that compose the entity's primary key.

When you add an object to the context, it's added to the state manager with a *temporary* entity key, because Entity Framework knows it must persist the object as a new row. This temporary key isn't evaluated by the identity-map check, so if you add the another object of the same type and with the same ID, it's added with another temporary key. When persistence is triggered, two `INSERT` commands are issued.

If the row ID is autogenerated on the database (as it is in OrderIT), persistence works fine. If you use natural keys (such as the SSN), the persistence process will throw a duplicate-key exception because the second `INSERT` command uses the same ID, causing a primary-key violation on the database.

When you attach an entity, the state manager automatically creates an `EntityKey` object and saves it in the entry created for the entity. This `EntityKey` object isn't temporary and is used by the identity-map check.

> **NOTE**   When you call `ChangeState` or `ChangeObjectState` to change the state from `Added` to `Unchanged` or `Deleted`, the `EntityKey` is regenerated. The new `EntityKey` isn't temporary and is filled with the key properties of the entity. If there's already an entity with that key, the state change triggers an exception.

Not only does `ObjectStateEntry` contain data, but it also incorporates behavior. It allows you to change the state of an entity and override its original and current values. In the rest of this section and chapter, we'll look at how to use the power of `Object-StateEntry` to solve problems.

The only way to obtain an `ObjectStateEntry` instance is to query the state manager. In the next section, you'll see how to do this and why this is a great feature.

6.3.2   *Retrieving entries*

You know perfectly well whether you're adding, attaching, or deleting entities, so why would you ever need to query the context for entity state? There are two situations where this is useful: first, Entity Framework itself needs to query object state; and second, you may want to report the entity state in some sort of generic logging or other scenario.

Suppose you want to log each persistence operation triggered by your application. One way to do this might be to create an extension method that performs an attach, add, or delete and then adds an entry to the logging storage. This implementation is naive because you might need to halt the persistence process for some reason, and you'd end up logging operations that hadn't happened. (Yes, you could roll back the logging, but that's not the point here.)

Another approach might be subscribing to the `SavingChanges` event, which is triggered before the persistence process begins (`SaveChanges`), retrieving entities in the `Added`, `Modified`, and `Deleted` states, and writing entries in the log. This solution, shown in the next listing, better serves your needs; it doesn't even require you to create and use extension methods.

Listing 6.8   Logging persisted objects

C#
```csharp
ctx.SavingChanges +=                                          ❶ Subscribes
  new EventHandler(ctx_SavingChanges);                           to event
ctx.SaveChanges();

void ctx_SavingChanges(object sender, EventArgs e)
{
  var osm = (sender as OrderITEntities).ObjectStateManager;
  var entries = osm.GetObjectStateEntries(                    ❷ Iterates over
    EntityState.Added | EntityState.Modified                    modified
    | EntityState.Deleted);                                     entities

  foreach(var entry in entries)
  {
    Logger.Write(entry.Entity.GetType().FullName +            ❸ Writes
      " - " + entry.State);                                      to log
  }
}
```

VB
```vbnet
AddHandler ctx.SavingChanges,                                 ❶ Subscribes
  AddressOf ctx_SavingChanges                                    to event
ctx.SaveChanges()

Private Sub ctx_SavingChanges(ByVal sender As Object, ByVal e As EventArgs)
  Dim osm = TryCast(sender, OrderITEntities).ObjectStateManager
  Dim entries = osm.GetObjectStateEntries(                    ❷ Iterates over
    EntityState.Added Or EntityState.Modified Or                modified
    EntityState.Deleted)                                        entities

  For Each entry In entries
    Logger.Write(entry.Entity.GetType().FullName &            ❸ Writes
      " - " & entry.State)                                       to log
  Next
End Sub
```

The first step is hooking up the SavingChanges event ❶. Next, in the handler, you retrieve all entries in a specific state by using the ObjectStateManager class's GetObjectStateEntries method ❷. It accepts an EntityState parameter representing the state to look for, and it returns a collection of all entries in that state. If you need entries in different states, you can combine them using the flag syntax. Eventually, you invoke the logger method to write the entry ❸.

Often, you'll only need to retrieve a single entry. GetObjectStateEntries is unusable in such scenario. What you need is another method that lets you pass an entity and get the corresponding state-manager entry. The state manager has a method that serves this purpose.

RETRIEVING A SINGLE ENTRY

To retrieve the entry related to a single entity, you can use the GetObjectStateEntry method, passing the entity as argument, as shown here:

Listing 6.9 Retrieving an entry from the `ObjectStateManager`

C#
```
var entry = osm.GetObjectStateEntry(entity);
```

VB
```
Dim entry = osm.GetObjectStateEntry(entity)
```

The input entity *must* have the key properties set, because when the state manager tries to retrieve the entry, it creates an EntityKey using them and performs a lookup. If no entry contains this EntityKey, the method throws an InvalidOperationException with the message, "The ObjectStateManager does not contain an ObjectStateEntry with a reference to an object of type 'type'."

To avoid the exception, you can use TryGetObjectStateEntry. It performs the same task as GetObjectStateEntry; but following the design guidelines of the .NET Framework, this method accepts the entity and an output parameter representing the entry found, and it returns a Boolean value indicating whether the entry was found. Should it return false, the output parameter is null. The following listing contains code using this method.

Listing 6.10 Safely retrieving an entry from `ObjectStateManager`

C#
```
ObjectStateEntry entry;
var found = osm.TryGetObjectStateEntry(c, out entry);
```

VB
```
Dim entry As ObjectStateEntry
Dim found = osm.TryGetObjectStateEntry(c, entry)
```

With the ObjectStateEntry class, you can modify the state of the entity, as you've seen before, by using the ChangeState method. But that's not your only option. In the next section, you'll discover other methods that allow you to change entity state.

6.3.3 *Modifying entity state from the entry*

When you have the entry, you can modify the state of the related entity because the context methods we looked at earlier in this chapter internally invoke the methods in the ObjectStateEntry class. These methods are listed in table 6.2.

> **NOTE** Technically, talking about *entity state* is incorrect. The actual state of an entity is the state of its entry in the state manager. However, the term *entity state* is intuitive and more commonly understood than *entry state*, so we'll continue using it.

Table 6.2 Methods exposed by the `ObjectStateEntry` class that modify entity state

Method	Description
Delete	Marks the entity as deleted. This method is also invoked by `DeleteObject` and `ChangeState` when moving to the `Deleted` state.
SetModified	Marks the entity and all of its properties as `Modified`. This method is internally invoked by `ChangeState` when moving to the `Modified` state.
SetModifiedProperty	Marks a property as `Modified`, and consequently marks the entity too.
AcceptChanges	Changes the entity's state to `Unchanged` and overrides the original values of the entry with the current ones.
ChangeState	Changes the entity's state to the input value.

These methods are pretty simple to use because most of them don't accept any parameters. The only exceptions are `SetModifiedProperty`, which accepts the name of the property to set as `Modified`, and `ChangeState`, which accepts the new state the entity should be changed to.

Previously we said that the only state change that's automatically performed by the state manager is from `Unchanged` to `Modified` when you modify a property, but we said that it's not always the case. In the next section, we'll dig deep into the object-tracking mechanism, discuss its internals, and see how to avoid its traps.

6.3.4 *Understanding object tracking*

Technically speaking, the state manager can't monitor modifications to properties inside an entity; it's the entity that notifies the state manager when a change is made. This notification mechanism isn't always in place—it depends on how you instantiate the entity. You can create the following kinds of entities:

- POCO entity *not wrapped* by a proxy (a plain entity)
- POCO entity *wrapped* by a proxy (a proxied entity)

A *wrappable* entity is a class written to enable extensibility via proxy. You have already discovered that a class is wrappable when it isn't closed to inheritance and its properties are virtual. In particular, a wrappable class enables change tracking if all *scalar* properties are virtual. A *wrapped* (or proxied) entity is an instance of such an entity that has been wrapped inside a virtual proxy.

The state manager doesn't care whether a class is wrappable or not. What's important to it is whether the entity has been instantiated as a proxy or as a pure POCO class. Let's look at some examples to clarify the distinctions in the preceding list.

CHANGE-TRACKING OF AN ENTITY NOT WRAPPED INSIDE A PROXY

An entity might be obtained from a web service, from the deserialization of the ASP.NET ViewState in a web page, from a query where the context has proxy creation disabled, or from instantiating it with a constructor. These objects aren't wrapped by a proxy, because only the context with proxy-creation enabled (the default setting) can create a wrapped entity. What's more, an entity may not be wrappable, so even if it comes from a context, it may not be proxied.

As you saw in chapter 5, entities' property setters have no knowledge of the state manager, so how can the state manager learn when a property is modified? You may be surprised to discover that it can't.

Let's look at an example. Suppose you need to modify a customer. You query the database to retrieve the customer, and you modify a property, such as the name, and then persist it. Because the state manager doesn't know that you have modified a property, the state of the entity remains Unchanged, as you can see here.

Listing 6.11 Modifying a customer using an entity not wrapped inside a proxy

C#
```
var customer = ctx.Customers.First();
var entry = osm.GetObjectStateEntry(customer);
customer.Name = "NewCustomer";              <──── State Unchanged
ctx.SaveChanges();
```

VB
```
Dim customer = ctx.Customers.First()
Dim entry = osm.GetObjectStateEntry(customer)
customer.Name = "NewCustomer"               <──── State Unchanged
ctx.SaveChanges()
```

When the SaveChanges method is invoked, the modifications are persisted into the database even if the state is Unchanged! How can this work? Why are modifications persisted if the state manager knows nothing about them?

The magic is buried inside the ObjectStateManager class's DetectChanges method, which is internally invoked by the SaveChanges method. This method iterates over all state-manager entries, and for each one compares the original values with those stored in the entity. When it detects that a property has been modified—the customer name, in this example—it marks the property as Modified, which in turn marks the entity as Modified and updates the current value of the entry. When DetectChanges has finished its job, the entities and their entries in the state manager are perfectly in sync, and SaveChanges can move on to persistence.

Because the state manager isn't automatically synchronized with the entities, whenever you need to work with its APIs, you must invoke the DetectChanges method to avoid retrieving stale data, as in the previous listing. You can do this as in the next snippet.

Listing 6.12 Invoking the DetectChanges method

C#
```
var entry = osm.GetObjectStateEntry(customer);
customer.Name = "NewCustomer";                      <──── State Unchanged
ctx.DetectChanges();            <──── State Modified
```

VB
```vb
Dim entry = osm.GetObjectStateEntry(customer)
customer.Name = "NewCustomer"                          <──── State Unchanged
ctx.DetectChanges()                        <──── State Modified
```

`DetectChanges` isn't problem-free. It iterates over all entities and evaluates all their properties. If lots of entities are tracked, the iteration may be expensive. Use it, but don't abuse it.

CHANGE TRACKING WRAPPED INSIDE A PROXY

When an entity is wrapped in a proxy, there is more magic under the covers. A proxied entity enables automatic change tracking, meaning that it immediately notifies the state manager when a property is modified. This happens because the proxy overrides property setters, injecting code that notifies the state manager about property changes. Figure 6.2 contains a simplified version of the code inside the proxy.

This feature is fantastic because, without any effort, you get automatic synchronization between the state manager entry and the entity. This behavior is clear in the next listing.

Listing 6.13 Modifying a customer inside a proxy

C#
```csharp
var entry = osm.GetObjectStateEntry(customer);       <──── State Unchanged
customer.Name = "NewCustomer";            <──── State Modified
```

VB
```vb
Dim entry = osm.GetObjectStateEntry(customer)        <──── State Unchanged
customer.Name = "NewCustomer"          <──── State Modified
```

In chapter 3, you learned that proxies enable lazy loading. In this chapter, you've learned that proxies also enable automatic change tracking. In Entity Framework 1.0, these features required tons of code, and now you get them *almost* for free. This is another huge step ahead in Entity Framework 4.0.

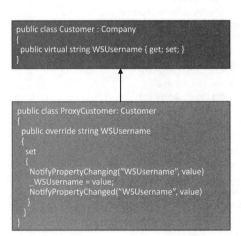

Figure 6.2   The code injected by the proxy notifies the state manager about changes in properties.

Not only can the context track single entities, but it also tracks entities' relationships. You might expect this to be done using the primary-key properties of associated objects or foreign keys; sometimes it's done that way, but sometimes it's done in other ways.

6.3.5   *Understanding relationship tracking*

When an entity is attached to the context, a new entry is added in the state manager. After that, the context scans the navigation properties to find associated entities. Those that aren't `null` are automatically attached. The same behavior holds true when adding entities.

When a related entity is attached, if the relationship is via an independent association, a new `RelationshipEntry` is added to the state manager, containing information about the related entities. For instance, if you attach an order that has a reference to a customer and many order details, the state manager will contain the order, its details, and its customer entries, along with their association entries. Figure 6.3 shows what the state manager looks like after such an attach process.

If the order is loaded using a query, things are slightly different. The state manager creates one entry for the order, one for the customer, and one for their relationship (order details are ignored because collection associations are ignored). This happens even if you don't retrieve the customer with the order. The customer entry contains only the primary key (taken from the CustomerId column in the Order table), whereas the relationship points to both entities, so the state manager has everything it needs.

A relationship can be in the `Added` or `Deleted` state but can't be in the `Modified` state. Usually, you won't need to modify relationship state, because it's handled by the

☐ ctx.ObjectStateManager.GetObjectStateEntries	{System.Data.Objects.ObjectStateEntry[11]}
☐ [System.Data.Objects.ObjectStateEntry[]]	{System.Data.Objects.ObjectStateEntry[11]}
⊞ [0]	{System.Data.Objects.RelationshipEntry}
⊞ [1]	{System.Data.Objects.RelationshipEntry}
⊞ [2]	{System.Data.Objects.RelationshipEntry}
⊞ [3]	{System.Data.Objects.RelationshipEntry}
⊞ [4]	{System.Data.Objects.RelationshipEntry}
⊞ [5]	{System.Data.Objects.EntityEntry}
⊞ [6]	{System.Data.Objects.EntityEntry}
⊞ [7]	{System.Data.Objects.EntityEntry}
⊞ [8]	{System.Data.Objects.EntityEntry}
⊞ [9]	{System.Data.Objects.EntityEntry}
⊞ [10]	{System.Data.Objects.EntityEntry}

Figure 6.3   The state manager entries after an order with independent associations is attached (shown in the QuickWatch window). There are six entities (one for the order, one for the customer, two for the order details, and two for their related products) and five entries for the relationships between the entities (one for the relationship between the order and the customer, two for the relationship between the order and its details, and two for the relationship between the order details and their product).

⊟ 🔧 ctx.ObjectStateManager.GetObjectStateEntrie	{System.Data.Objects.ObjectStateEntry[3]}
⊟ 🔹 [System.Data.Objects.ObjectStateEntry[]]	{System.Data.Objects.ObjectStateEntry[3]}
⊞ 🔹 [0]	{System.Data.Objects.EntityEntry}
⊞ 🔹 [1]	{System.Data.Objects.EntityEntry}
⊞ 🔹 [2]	{System.Data.Objects.EntityEntry}

Figure 6.4   The state manager after an order with foreign-key associations is attached. There are three entities (one for the order and two for the details). The relationship entries don't exist because foreign keys are used.

state manager. In the rare cases when you need to modify the relationship state, you can use the `ObjectStateManager` class's `ChangeRelationshipState` method or the `ObjectStateEntry` class's `ChangeState` method. Naturally, if you try to change the relationship state to `Modified`, you'll get a runtime exception.

If foreign-key associations are used, no relationship entries are created because you don't need the associated entity, just the foreign-key property. The result is that after attaching the same order as before, the state manager looks like what you see in figure 6.4.

When an entity is retrieved from the database, neither the entity entries nor the relationship entries are created in the state manager for the associated entities. Furthermore, changing a relationship is trivial because you only need to change the foreign-key property. As you can see, foreign-key associations make things simple and reduce the state manager's work.

Now that you know how the state manager tracks entities and relationships, let's investigate a couple of caveats.

CHANGES ARE TRACKED ONLY WHEN ENTITIES ARE TRACKED BY CONTEXT

When entities are outside the scope of the context, changes made to them aren't tracked. If you create an order, add a detail, or change its associated customer, and then attach the order to the context, the context will never know what happened. The order and the relationship entry will be in the `Unchanged` state when they're attached.

STATE MANAGER DOESN'T SUPPORT PARTIALLY LOADED GRAPHS

When you attach an entity, the context scans all navigation properties and attaches related objects as well. (The same happens if you add an object to the context.) All entities are put in `Unchanged` state if they're attached, and in `Added` state if they're added.

If the context already tracks an entity of the same type and with the same key as an entity in the graph, it raises an `InvalidOperationException` because it can't hold two objects of the same type with the same key.

When adding a graph, there's no risk of an exception because the entity key associated with the objects is temporary. A problem arises if the entity is later marked as `Unchanged` (which does happen, as you'll discover later in this chapter). In such a case, the `EntityKey` is regenerated and becomes permanent, and if there's already an entity with the same key, an `InvalidOperationException` is thrown with the message, "AcceptChanges cannot continue because the object's key values conflict with another object in the ObjectStateManager. Make sure that the key values are unique before calling AcceptChanges."

HOW RELATIONSHIPS CHANGE IN SINGLE-REFERENCE PROPERTIES

Suppose you have to change the customer associated with an order. You can find yourself in two situations:

- Customer *is already attached to the context.* If a foreign key association is in place, the property is synchronized and the Order object becomes Modified. If you use an independent association, only the RelationshipEntry is created between the entities.
- Customer *isn't attached to the context.* The Customer is added to the context (remember it doesn't support partial graphs) in the Added state. If the association is kept using a foreign-key association, the property is synchronized and the Order object becomes Modified. If you use an independent association, only the RelationshipEntry is created between the entities.

> **NOTE** If the instances are proxies, the state change is automatic. If the instances are plain objects, you'll see state changes only after a call to DetectChanges.

Suppose you have an order without a customer. If you use a foreign-key association, setting the foreign-key property to null makes the association between the order and the customer disappear. If you use an independent association, setting the Customer property to null leads to the same result (the RelationshipEntry becomes Deleted).

Keep in mind that only the association between the customer and the order is removed. None of the objects are deleted.

HOW RELATIONSHIPS CHANGE IN COLLECTION PROPERTIES

A call to the Remove method of a collection property causes the reference to the master to be removed from the detail. For instance, when you remove a detail from an order, its Order property is set to null, and its status is set as Modified. Because the foreign-key property (OrderId) isn't nullable, during persistence an Invalid-OperationException occurs with this message: "The operation failed: The relationship could not be changed because one or more of the foreign-key properties is non-nullable. When a change is made to a relationship, the related foreign-key property is set to a null value. If the foreign-key does not support null values, a new relationship must be defined, the foreign-key property must be assigned another non-null value, or the unrelated object must be deleted."

Although the message might look encrypted, its quite clear. The OrderId property of the detail can't be null because you can't have an *orphan* order detail. The detail must always be assigned to an order. If you supported orphan details, the OrderId column in the OrderDetail table would be nullable. Similarly, the OrderID property in the OrderDetail class would be nullable. In this case, persistence wouldn't throw any exception, so the order would be persisted and the order detail would become an orphan. (Of course, there's no point in having an orphan detail—we mention this only for completeness.)

If you use an independent association, you'll get a different message: "A relationship from the 'OrderOrderDetail' AssociationSet is in the 'Deleted' state. Given multiplicity constraints, a corresponding 'OrderDetail' must also in the 'Deleted' state." This means that the `RelationshipEntry` in the state manager is `Deleted`, but the entity is `Modified`, and that isn't allowed because orphan order details aren't allowed; the detail must be deleted too.

The solution to the problem is to invoke the context's `DeleteObject` method instead of the collection property's `Remove` method.

You're probably wondering why Entity Framework doesn't automatically delete the entity instead of simply removing the reference. The answer is that in other situations this isn't the correct behavior. Think about the many-to-many relationships between suppliers and products. In that case, you don't have to delete a product if you remove it from those sold by a supplier. You just have to delete the reference in the Product-Supplier table. Due to these different behaviors, the Entity Framework team decided conservatively to let you explicitly choose what to do.

> **NOTE** We hope that in the next release, the Entity Framework team will allow us to map what to do and add an element in the EDM that specifies whether the entity must be deleted or just the reference, when the entity is removed from a collection property. Having to explicitly call the `DeleteObject` method sounds less fluent than removing an element from the collection.

When you add an entity to a collection property (such as adding an order detail to an order), you can find yourself in two different situations depending on whether the entity is attached to the context or not:

- *The detail is attached to the context.* If foreign-key association is in place, the property *must* be synchronized with the ID of the order. If you use an independent association, only the `RelationshipEntry` is created between the entities.
- *The detail isn't attached to the context.* The `Customer` is added to the context in `Added` state (remember, the context doesn't support partial graphs). If the association is kept using a foreign-key association, the property must be synchronized with the ID of the order. If you use an independent association, a `RelationshipEntry` between the entities is also created.

There are a lot of rules, and knowing them in advance makes manipulating graphs easier and less scary.

Do you remember `MergeOption`? It's a way to specify how an entity that's tracked by the context is merged with an entity with the same key coming from a query. We looked at all the options in chapter 3, but we only analyzed them from a querying point of view. Now let's look at them from the state manager's point of view.

6.3.6 *Change tracking and MergeOption*

MergeOption is a property of the ObjectSet<T> class. It's an enum of type System. Data.Objects.MergeOption that contains the following values:

- AppendOnly
- NoTracking
- OverwriteChanges
- PreserveChanges

During an object's materialization, when AppendOnly is used (the default setting), the state manager checks whether there's already an entry with the same key. If so, the entity related to the entry is returned and data from the database is discarded. If not, the entity is materialized and attached to the context. In this case, the state manager creates the entry using the original and current values of the materialized entity. Eventually, the materialized entity is returned.

When NoTracking is used, the context doesn't perform the identity-map check, so data from the database is always materialized and returned, even if there's already a corresponding entity in the state manager. The entities returned when the NoTracking option is enabled are in Detached state, so they're not tracked by the context.

When OverwriteChanges is used, if the identity-map check doesn't find an entry in the state manager, the entity is materialized, attached to the context, and returned. If the entry is found, the related entity state is set to Unchanged, and both the current and original values are updated with values from the database.

When PreserveChanges is used, if the identity-map check doesn't find an entry in the state manager, the entity is materialized, attached to the context, and returned. If the identity-map check does find an entry in the state manager, there are a few things that can happen:

- If the state of the entity is Unchanged, the current and original values in the entry are overwritten with database values. The state of the entity remains Unchanged.
- If the state of the entity is Modified, the current values of the modified properties aren't overwritten with database values. The original values of the unmodified properties are overwritten with database values.
- If the current values of the unmodified properties are different from the values from the database, the properties are marked as Modified. This is a breaking change from version 1.0, because in that version properties aren't marked as Modified. If you need to restore the version 1.0 behavior, set the UseLegacy-PreserveChangesBehavior property to true as follows:

C#
```
ctx.ContextOptions.UseLegacyPreserveChangesBehavior = true;
```

VB
```
ctx.ContextOptions.UseLegacyPreserveChangesBehavior = true
```

Now you know all there is to know about `MergeOption`'s behavior. It's an important aspect of any application, and it's often misused or underestimated. In chapter 19, you'll discover that it dramatically affects performance.

6.4 *Summary*

Understanding the entity lifecycle will enable you to manage objects efficiently and avoid surprises. Because an entity's state affects how modifications are persisted into the database, its vital that you fully master this aspect of Entity Framework.

Correctly managing the various states and their transitions is very important and will prevent problems when objects are later persisted. This is particularly true when you're working with object graphs, where Entity Framework will automatically attach and add related objects.

You must also pay attention to tracking. When working with plain POCO entities, you have to remember that they aren't in sync with the state manager. If you plan to search entities in the state manager, always remember to synchronize it with the actual entities.

When you fully master these subjects, persistence will become much easier, as you'll discover in the next chapter.

Persisting objects into the database

7

This chapter covers

- Persisting modified objects into the database
- Persisting complex object graphs into the database
- Persisting with foreign-key and independent associations

Now that you know how to handle entity lifecycles, you're ready to take the next step: persisting modifications made to objects into the database.

In this chapter, we'll discuss how to insert, update, and delete entities in both connected and disconnected scenarios. We'll cover single-object updates, such as a customer, and complex *graph* updates, such as an order and its details. By the end of this chapter, you'll be able to manage updates through Entity Framework.

> **NOTE** In this chapter, we won't be discussing topics like transaction and concurrency management. They get a chapter of their own—chapter 8.

Let's start our discussion with how the persistence process works.

7.1   *Persisting entities with SaveChanges*

Entity persistence is the process that stores entities data inside the database. Triggering this procedure is simple as invoking the `SaveChanges` method of the `Object-Context` class (which is the class from which the `OrderITEntities` class in OrderIT inherits).

The following snippet shows an example of how to use `SaveChanges` to persist modifications made to a customer:

C#
```
var customer = from c in ctx.Companies
               where c.Id == 1
               select c;
customer.Name = "new name";
ctx.SaveChanges();
```

VB
```
Dim customer = From c In ctx.Companies Where c.Id = 1
customer.Name = "new name"
ctx.SaveChanges()
```

Using `SaveChanges` is easy. When it's invoked, it internally iterates over the entities in the `Modified`, `Deleted`, and `Added` states, generates the appropriate SQL statements, and executes them against the database. In the next section, we're going deeper into this subject.

`SaveChanges` performs all the plumbing required for persisting entities. Not only does it synchronize the state manager with the entities (as you learned in chapter 6), but it also detects dirty entities (entities in the `Added`, `Modified`, and `Deleted` states), starts the connection and the transaction with the database, generates the correct SQL and commits or rolls back everything depending on whether some exception occurred. Eventually, it removes deleted entities and sets added and modified ones to `Unchanged`. In the end, it's a complex process that uses the database, the state manager, and SQL to accomplish its task, as you see in figure 7.1.

Now let's look at each step, starting with the first.

7.1.1   *Detecting dirty entities*

Dirty entities are entities that are in the `Added`, `Modified`, or `Deleted` state. As you learned in chapter 6, entities and their related entries in the state manager aren't always in sync. The `SaveChanges` method needs to synchronize them.

This phase is the easiest one in the persistence process. The `SaveChanges` method invokes the `DetectChanges` method (introduced in chapter 6) so that entities and

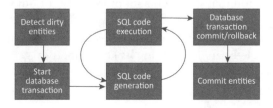

Figure 7.1   The steps performed by the `SaveChanges` method to persist entity state

entries in the state manager are synchronized. When `DetectChanges` has finished its work, the `SaveChanges` method queries the state manager to retrieve entries for entities in the `Added`, `Modified`, and `Deleted` states so that it can persist them.

Here is an excerpt of the code in the `SaveChanges` method that's executed during this phase:

C#
```
DetectChanges();
var entries = ObjectStateManager.GetObjectStateEntries(
  EntityState.Added | EntityState.Modified | EntityState.Deleted);
```

VB
```
DetectChanges();
Dim entries = ObjectStateManager.GetObjectStateEntries(
  EntityState.Added Or EntityState.Modified Or EntityState.Deleted);
```

The entries returned by the query to the state manager contains first the added entities, then the modified ones, and finally the deleted ones.

Our exploration of the state manager in the last chapter should make this step fairly easy to understand. Now we can move on to the second part.

7.1.2 *Starting database transactions*

At this point in the process, the `SaveChanges` method opens a connection to the database and starts a transaction. All commands that are executed in the following phase are executed in the context of this transaction.

> **NOTE** In chapter 8, you'll learn how to customize the transaction management.

This phase is simple. Let's move on and discuss the most complicated one.

7.1.3 *SQL code generation and execution*

SQL code generation is pretty complex compared with detecting the dirty entities or starting the transaction. Here the entries returned from the call to the `GetObject-StateEntries` method is iterated through, and for each entity in it, the appropriate SQL code is generated.

When it comes to persisting entities in `Added` state, generating the SQL code isn't difficult. A simple `INSERT` SQL statement is created.

The situation gets more complicated with entities in the `Modified` state. Because the state manager keeps track of both the original and current values of each loaded entity, Entity Framework generates `UPDATE` commands that modify only the changed properties. This is a great optimization that saves you a lot of work. Isn't Entity Framework lovely?

Probably the simplest SQL code to generate is the `DELETE` commands for entities in the `Deleted` state. The SQL code deletes an object using its key properties.

The SQL generation and execution is an iterative process because statements often need data from previous ones. For example, think about the order and its details. To insert each detail, Entity Framework needs the ID of the order saved previously, so the SQL for the order detail is generated only after the order has been persisted.

7.1.4 *Database transaction commit or rollback*

If every SQL command executed in the previous phase is executed correctly, the database transaction is committed. But if an error occurs during the execution of a SQL statement, the transaction is rolled back.

An error can occur for several reasons. For instance, the database can be temporarily down or there can be a network problem. Those are common hardware problems, and software problems are treated exactly the same way. A duplicate key or a not-nullable column receiving a `null` value causes the execution flow to terminate and the transaction to roll back.

Those sorts of errors are raised by the database, but there's another type of error that causes the persistence process to stop suddenly, even if the database doesn't raise an exception: a concurrency exception. This is a software exception, and it's raised by Entity Framework itself. We'll discuss concurrency in chapter 8.

7.1.5 *Committing entities*

By default, if the transaction terminates correctly, the context invokes the `AcceptAll-Changes` method, which internally invokes the `AcceptChanges` method of each dirty entry in the state manager. After its invocation, the entries are in sync with both the entities and the database, so you can think of this as a *commit* for entities. Entities in `Added` or `Modified` state become `Unchanged`, and entities in `Deleted` state are removed from the context (and the state manager).

You can manipulate this commit process by using an overload of `SaveChanges` that accepts an enum of type `SaveOptions` (namespace `System.Data.Objects`). The enum has three possible values:

- `None`—Neither the `DetectChanges` nor the `AcceptAllChanges` methods are invoked.
- `AcceptAllChangesAfterSave`—The `AcceptAllChanges` method is invoked.
- `DetectChangesBeforeSave`—The `DetectChanges` method is invoked before saving changes.

The enum is a flag, so you can combine the values.

> **NOTE** When no parameter is passed to `SaveChanges`, both the `Accept-AllChangesAfterSave` and `DetectChangesBeforeSave` values are automatically passed.

Earlier we mentioned that if an error occurs during persistence, the transaction rolls back. In that case, `AcceptAllChanges` isn't triggered, so if you invoke the `SaveChanges` method again, the context will try to persist the entities again, the same way it did when the exception occurred because nothing has been touched.

If no error occurs during persistence and the `AcceptAllChangesAfterSave` value isn't passed to `SaveChanges` method, the entities and the entries in the state manager remain untouched so a new call to `SaveChanges` would trigger persistence again.

7.1.6   Overriding SaveChanges

The `SaveChanges` method is virtual. You can override it in the context to inject any logic you need or even to completely override the persistence logic. Overriding `SaveChanges` is useful for building a logging system, as you saw in section 6.3.2. It could also be used to invoke a method on the entity, notifying it when it's updated, added, or deleted. That's not hard to do, especially if this method is exposed through an interface or a base class.

> **NOTE**   If you don't want to completely override the `SaveChanges` logic, remember to invoke the base implementation.

Now you have all the basics necessary to understand how Entity Framework persists entities. In the next section, we'll see some of these concepts in action and look at how they affect the database.

7.2   Persisting changed entities into the database

Persisting a single entity means saving it into the database. You have three ways to do this:

- Persisting it as a new row
- Using its properties to update an existing row
- Using its key properties to delete an existing row

We'll look at each of these options in this section.

In chapter 4, we introduced a user as the tester of OrderIT. In the next sections, this user will return to simulate a real-world scenario.

7.2.1   Persisting an entity as a new row

The first thing the user wants to do is create customers, suppliers, and products. You made the user happy about data retrieval, and you'll make the user happy about data insertion too.

The first thing you need to do is allow the user to create customers. This is extremely easy to do: you can use the `AddObject` method, pass the `Customer` instance, and then invoke `SaveChanges`. Here's what it looks like.

Listing 7.1   Persisting a new customer

C#
```
var cust = new Customer()
{
```

```
    Name = "Stefano Mostarda",
    BillingAddress = new AddressInfo()
    {
      Address = "5th street",
      City = "New York",
      Country = "USA",
      ZipCode = "0000000"
    },
    ShippingAddress = new AddressInfo()
    {
      Address = "5th street",
      City = "New York",
      Country = "USA",
      ZipCode = "0000000"
    },
    WSEnabled = true,
    WSUserName = "user1",
    WSPassword = "user1pwd"
};
ctx.Companies.AddObject(cust);
ctx.SaveChanges();
```

VB
```
Dim cust As new Customer() With
{
  .Name = "Stefano Mostarda",
  .BillingAddress = new AddressInfo() With
  {
    .Address = "5th street",
    .City = "New York",
    .Country = "USA",
    .ZipCode = "0000000"
  },
  .ShippingAddress = new AddressInfo() With
  {
    .Address = "5th street",
    .City = "New York",
    .Country = "USA",
    .ZipCode = "0000000"
  },
  .WSEnabled = true,
  .WSUserName = "user1",
  .WSPassword = "user1pwd"
}
ctx.Companies.AddObject(cust)
ctx.SaveChanges()
```

This listing shows how you can create a customer. Because the primary-key property is an identity, you don't need to set it; if you do, the value will be ignored.

> **NOTE** In the event that the key isn't an identity, you need to set it, or you'll get an `InvalidOperationException` at runtime.

Despite its simplicity, the code generates more than a simple insert. To better understand some of the background, let's look at the SQL that's generated.

Listing 7.2   The SQL generated by the insert

```
exec sp_executesql N'insert [dbo].[Company](
[Name],
[BillingAddress], [BillingCity], [BillingZipCode], [BillingCountry],
[ShippingAddress], [ShippingCity], [ShippingZipCode], [ShippingCountry],
[WSUserName], [WSPassword], [WSEnabled], [Type], [IBAN], [PaymentDays])
values
(@0,
@1, @2, @3, @4,
@5, @6, @7, @8,                                              ❶ Inserts
@9, @10, @11, @12, null, null)                                customer

select [CompanyId]
from [dbo].[Company]
where @@ROWCOUNT > 0 and [CompanyId] = scope_identity()',     ⊲─❷ Retrieves ID

N'@0 varchar(30), @1 varchar(20), @2 varchar(20), @3 varchar(10),
@4 varchar(20), @5 varchar(20), @6 varchar(20), @7 varchar(10),
@8 varchar(20), @9 varchar(20), @10 varchar(20), @11 bit,
@12 char(1)',
@0='Stefano Mostarda', @1='5th street', @2='New York', @3='0000000',
@4='USA', @5='5th street', @6='New York', @7='0000000', @8='USA',
@9='user1', @10='user1pwd', @11=1, @12='C'          ⊲─❸ Sets parameters
```

The first thing that's triggered is the insertion of the record ❶. Then, after the record is added, the database-generated ID is retrieved ❷. (The primary-key property is an `Identity`, which causes it to be assigned a database-generated ID.)

Notice that the discriminator column (Type) is automatically handled ❸. Because a customer was added, the value of the column is set to C. If a supplier was added, the value would have been S—these are the values of the discriminator specified in the mapping. This is a great feature that lets you code using the OOP paradigm and leave Entity Framework to handle the transformation to the relational jargon.

The same paradigm applies to products. If you want to add a new Shirt, you create an instance, add it to the context, and then persist it. The SQL generated will insert the record into both the Product and Shirt tables. Again, you code using OOP and let Entity Framework worry about the database.

Persisting new entities isn't tricky. Even if the persistence process involves complex stuff, it's nicely handled by the context and kept hidden from you. Next, we'll look at how to persist modifications to an entity.

7.2.2   Persisting modifications made to an existing entity

It's 4 p.m. Friday, and the phone rings. The user has saved a customer with an incorrect name, and now the record needs to be modified.

PERSISTENCE IN THE CONNECTED SCENARIO

The first path you can follow is to update data in a connected scenario—that's when an entity is retrieved from the database and modified in the same context. In this scenario, you can modify the properties and then call the SaveChanges method, as follows.

Listing 7.3 Persisting a modified entity in the connected scenario

C#
```
var cust = ctx.Companies.OfType<Customer>()
  .First(c => c.CompanyId == 1);
cust.Name = "Stefano Mostarda";
ctx.SaveChanges();
```

VB
```
Dim cust = ctx.Companies.OfType(Of Customer)().
  First(Function(c) c.CompanyId = 1)
cust.Name = "Stefano Mostarda"
ctx.SaveChanges()
```

This code is pretty simple and needs no explanation. What's more, because the state manager keeps track of the original and current values of entity properties, the SQL affects only columns mapped to modified properties. As a result, the UPDATE command is highly optimized, as you can see in the following snippet:

```
exec sp_executesql
N'update [dbo].[Company] set [Name] = @0 where ([CompanyId] = @1)',
N'@0 varchar(15), @1 int', @0='Stefano Mostarda', @1=13
```

There is an important point to understand here. When you modify a scalar property in a complex type, *all* properties of the complex type are persisted. For instance, if you modify the shipping address, the SQL will update the shipping city, country, and ZIP code even if they haven't been modified. This happens because the state-manager entry considers a complex property to be a unique block. The modification of a single property in the block causes the entire block to be considered modified.

This connected scenario is by far the easiest one to code. In the disconnected scenario, things are more complex.

PERSISTENCE IN THE DISCONNECTED SCENARIO

Suppose you have a method that accepts a Customer instance. You create a new context, attach the customer, and then persist it. The problem is that when you attach the entity to the context, it's Unchanged, and SaveChanges won't persist anything.

You have two ways to overcome this problem:

- Attach the input entity, and change its state to Modified by using the ChangeObjectState method.
- Query the database to retrieve the entity, and then use the ApplyCurrentValues method to overwrite properties of the database entity with the properties of the input entity.

The first solution is the simplest and the most used. It's shown in the following listing.

Listing 7.4 Updating an entity using `ChangeObjectState`

C#
```
void UpdateCustomer(Customer cust)
{
```

```
   using (var ctx = new OrderITEntities())
   {
     ctx.Companies.Attach(cust);
     ctx.ObjectStateManager.ChangeObjectState(cust, EntityState.Modified);
     ctx.SaveChanges();
   }
}
```

VB

```
Sub UpdateCustomer(ByVal cust as Customer)
  Using ctx = New OrderITEntities()
    ctx.Companies.Attach(cust)
    ctx.ObjectStateManager.ChangeObjectState(cust, EntityState.Modified)
    ctx.SaveChanges()
  End using
End Sub
```

SQL

```
exec sp_executesql
N'update [dbo].[Company]
    set [Name] = @0, [BillingAddress] = @1, [BillingCity] = @2,
        [BillingZipCode] = @3, [BillingCountry] = @4,
        [ShippingAddress] = @5, [ShippingCity] = @6,
        [ShippingZipCode] = @7, [ShippingCountry] = @8, [WSUserName] = @9,
        [WSPassword] = @10, [WSEnabled] = @11
  where ([CompanyId] = @12)',
N'@0 varchar(15), @1 varchar(10), @2 varchar(8),@3 varchar(5),
  @4 varchar(3), @5 varchar(10), @6 varchar(8), @7 varchar(5),
  @8 varchar(3), @9 varchar(3), @10 varchar(3), @11 bit,
  @12 int',
@0='newCustomerName', @1='7th Avenue', @2='New York', @3='98765',
@4='USA', @5='7th Avenue', @6='New York', @7='98765', @8='USA', @9='US1',
@10='US1',@11=1,@12=1
```

The drawback to this approach is that ChangeObjectState marks the entity and all its properties as Modified. As a result, the UPDATE command will modify *all* the mapped columns, even if they weren't really changed. If a property isn't set, its value will overwrite the one in the database, causing data loss.

Let's look at an example. Suppose you have a customer with ID 1. You create a Customer instance and set CompanyId to 1 and Name to NewName. You then attach the instance to the context, mark it as Modified, and call SaveChanges. The generated UPDATE command will update the Name column, and all the other columns will be assigned their default values (null for strings, 0 for integers, and so on), meaning that any previous data for that customer in the database is lost. Figure 7.2 illustrates this problem.

Figure 7.2 clearly shows the problem that arises when using ChangeObjectState to set a partially loaded entity in the Modified state. As you can see, if all the properties are correctly set, this is a powerful technique that offers good performance and simplicity, but it can be dangerous if you don't know the internals.

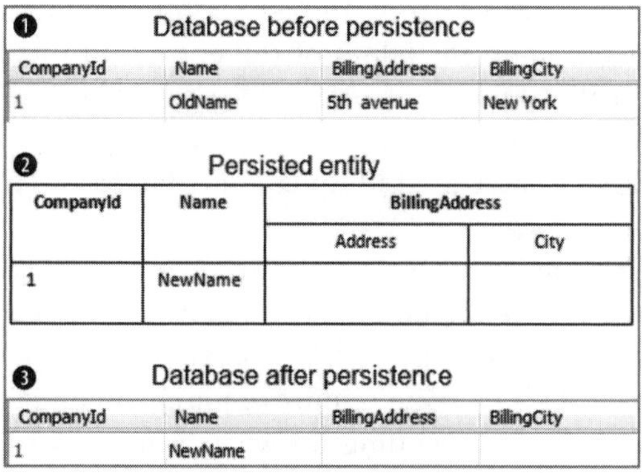

Figure 7.2 The billing address and city are empty in the persisted entity, so the database's original values are lost after persistence.

NOTE You could argue that updating all columns, even those that weren't modified, causes a slowdown in performance. In most databases, this cost is negligible. In fact, when the database has to perform an update, the biggest effort is in row retrieval. The column-update phase takes an insignificant percentage of the entire operation time.

The second solution for updating an object is pretty simple, even if it's slightly more complex than the one based on `ChangeObjectState`. For this second solution, you query the database to retrieve the entity you want to modify, and then you use the `ApplyCurrentValues` method to apply the values from the modified entity. Finally, you invoke `SaveChanges`. When the modifications are persisted, the most optimized SQL is generated because the state manager knows which properties have been modified. Here's the code for such a solution.

Listing 7.5 Updating an entity using `ApplyCurrentValues`

C#
```csharp
void UpdateCustomerWithApplyCurrentValues(Customer cust)
{
  using (var ctx = new OrderITEntities())
  {
    ctx.Companies.OfType<Customer>()
      .First(c => c.CompanyId == cust.CompanyId);
    ctx.Companies.ApplyCurrentValues(cust);
    ctx.SaveChanges();
  }
}
```

VB
```vb
Private Sub UpdateCustomerWithApplyCurrentValues(ByVal cust As Customer)
  Using ctx = New OrderITEntities()
    ctx.Companies.OfType(Of Customer)().
      First(Function(c) c.CompanyId = cust.CompanyId)
    ctx.Companies.ApplyCurrentValues(cust)
    ctx.SaveChanges()
  End Using
End Sub
```

Unfortunately, `ApplyCurrentValues` suffers from the same problem as `Change-ObjectState` because it overwrites the current values of the entry, and the attached entity properties, with those from the input entity. If a property in the input entity isn't set (if it's `null`, empty, or set to the type's default value), that property overwrites the current value of the entry, which is later used to update the database. The result, once again, is data loss.

`ApplyCurrentValues` suffers from another problem. It involves two round trips to the database: one to read data and one to update it. Performance can be hurt by this behavior. The problem gets even bigger when the data is separated in multiple tables, such as for the product data in OrderIT. Querying requires a join between tables, and updating can affect one or more tables, depending on what properties have been changed. If performance is critical, you'll probably have to choose the `ChangeObject-State` approach, because it goes to the database only for the update process.

In the end, both approaches work in some cases but may cause data loss if misused. If you know in advance that some properties aren't set and that you'll lose data using one of these approaches, you have two options:

- *Retrieve the customer from the database, and manually modify its properties one by one, based on the values in the input entity.* This approach works well because it works like the connected scenario.
- *Attach the input entity, and explicitly mark the properties to be updated.* This approach eliminates both the need to go to the database to retrieve the entity and the risks of data loss.

The last option is the best one. It requires some code, but it's effective because it offers the best performance while avoiding data loss.

CHOOSING WHAT PROPERTIES TO UPDATE IN THE DISCONNECTED SCENARIO

Let's look at updating the customer information. The user wants to update the customer name and addresses (web service–related properties are updated in another dedicated form).

To do this, you can create a method that attaches the entity and marks the specified properties as `Modified`. This marking process automatically puts the entity in the `Modified` state too. When you invoke the `SaveChanges` method, only the specified properties are persisted into the database.

The method that marks a property as `Modified` is `SetModifiedProperty`. It accepts only one parameter, which represents the name of the property to be updated, as you can see in the following snippet:

C#
```
var entry = osm.GetObjectStateEntry(customer);
entry.SetModifiedProperty("Name");
entry.SetModifiedProperty("ShippingAddress");
entry.SetModifiedProperty("BillingAddress");
```

VB
```
Dim entry = osm.GetObjectStateEntry(customer)
```

```
entry.SetModifiedProperty("Name")
entry.SetModifiedProperty("ShippingAddress")
entry.SetModifiedProperty("BillingAddress")
```

We've now covered all the possible ways of updating an entity. The user can update customer information and is happy. But only for a couple of hours, because now the user needs to delete a customer.

7.2.3 Persisting entity deletion

Deleting an entity is a simple task. You already know that marking an entity as `Deleted` is a simple matter of invoking the `DeleteObject` method and passing in the entity. After the entity is marked, the related row in the database is deleted when the `SaveChanges` method is invoked.

Before being marked as `Deleted`, the entity must be attached to the context. This will be the case if the entity has been queried (in the connected scenario) or if it has been attached (in the disconnected scenario). The following listing shows examples of both techniques.

Listing 7.6   Deleting an entity in both connected and disconnected scenarios

C#
```
var cust = ctx.Companies.OfType<Customer>().First();        Connected
ctx.DeleteObject(cust);                                      scenario
ctx.SaveChanges();

var cust = new Customer() { CompanyId = id };
ctx.Companies.Attach(cust);                                  Disconnected
ctx.DeleteObject(cust);                                      scenario
ctx.SaveChanges();
```

VB
```
Dim cust = ctx.Companies.OfType(Of Customer).First()         Connected
ctx.DeleteObject(cust)                                       scenario
ctx.SaveChanges()

Dim cust As new Customer() With { .CompanyId = id }
ctx.Companies.Attach(cust)                                   Disconnected
ctx.DeleteObject(cust)                                       scenario
ctx.SaveChanges()
```

Congratulations. You have successfully written code to modify customer data in any way the user may need. But that's just the beginning. The next step is to write a new part of OrderIT: order management. This is a brand-new environment because you'll be working with associations.

7.3   Persisting entities graphs

Order persistence requires you to work with up to four entities. Although you'll update only the order and its details, the customer that places the order and the products in the details are equally involved as read-only data. Because more entities are involved, we talk about an *entities graph* (or *objects graph*); sometimes its persistence can be challenging, because entities in the same graph may need different actions. For instance, some may be added while others are modified or ignored.

To see these problems in practice and how to solve them, let's get back to our user. To start with, the user needs a mask where they can choose the customer, fill in order data, and specify the products to be ordered.

7.3.1 Persisting a graph of added entities

When the user saves the order, the persistence process must be triggered. This is what you have to do:

1 Create an `Order` instance.
2 Associate the `Order` with a `Customer`.
3 Create an `OrderDetail` instance.
4 Associate the `OrderDetail` with a product.
5 Add the `OrderDetail` to the `Order`.
6 Repeat steps 3 to 5 for each detail.
7 Add the `Order` to the context.
8 Persist the modifications.

The code that performs these steps varies depending on whether you opt for foreign-key or independent associations, but the basic idea is the same. We'll look at both options in turn.

PERSISTING A GRAPH OF ADDED ENTITIES USING FOREIGN-KEY ASSOCIATIONS

Thanks to the foreign-key feature, associating a customer with the order is pretty easy; you just have to set the foreign-key property with the primary key of the related entity. Setting the `CustomerId` property of the order to 1 automatically associates the order with the customer that has that ID. The same thing happens when you set the ProductId column of the detail.

As we mentioned, Entity Framework doesn't support an object graph being partially loaded when an order is added—the details are added too. You can see this in the following listing.

> **Listing 7.7 Creating an order using foreign-key associations**

```
C#
var order = new Order
{
  CustomerId = 1,
  OrderDate = DateTime.Now.Date
};
order.ShippingAddress = new AddressInfo()
{
  Address = "2th street",
  City = "New York",
  Country = "USA",
  ZipCode = "0000001"
};
```

```
var detail1 = new OrderDetail()
{
  ProductId = 2,
  Quantity = 3,
  UnitPrice = 10
};
var detail2 = new OrderDetail()
{
  ProductId = 1,
  Quantity = 5,
  UnitPrice = 10
};
order.OrderDetails.Add(detail1);
order.OrderDetails.Add(detail2);
ctx.Orders.AddObject(order);
ctx.SaveChanges();
```

VB
```
Dim order As New Order With
{
  .CustomerId = 1, _
  .OrderDate = DateTime.Now.Date
}
order.ShippingAddress = New AddressInfo()
{
  .Address = "2th street",
  .City = "New York",
  .Country = "USA",
  .ZipCode = "0000001"
}
Dim detail1 As New OrderDetail()
{
  .ProductId = 2,
  .Quantity = 3,
  .UnitPrice = 10
}
Dim detail2 As New OrderDetail()
{
  .ProductId = 1,
  .Quantity = 5,
  .UnitPrice = 10
}
order.OrderDetails.Add(detail1)
order.OrderDetails.Add(detail2)
ctx.Orders.AddObject(order)
ctx.SaveChanges()
```

Persisting a new order isn't difficult thanks to foreign keys. They don't require you to load the associated customer and products. You only work with the Order and Order-Detail entities.

Foreign keys are simple to use, but they're not the only way to maintain relationships between entities. During model design, you may decide not to use foreign keys and to rely on independent associations instead. Or perhaps you're upgrading an application to Entity Framework 4.0 from Entity Framework 1.0, which has no concept of foreign keys.

PERSISTING A GRAPH OF ADDED ENTITIES USING INDEPENDENT ASSOCIATIONS

When you use an independent association, the CustomerId column of the Order table is mapped to the `CompanyId` property of the `Customer` class. There's no `CustomerId` property in the `Order` class. As a result, to associate a customer with an order, you have to create a customer instance and associate it with the order. The same process applies to the association between the details and their product.

Because you need only the ID of the customer and the ID of the product, instead of retrieving them from the database, you can create an instance (a *stub*) for each of them, set the ID, and then associate the instances with the order and the details. The following listing contains a first draft of the code for this technique.

Listing 7.8 Creating an order using independent associations

C#

```
var cust = new Customer() { CompanyId = 1 };
var product1 = new Product() { ProductId = 1 }
var product2 = new Product() { ProductId = 2 };

var order = new Order
{
  Customer = cust,
  OrderDate = DateTime.Now.Date
};
order.ShippingAddress = new AddressInfo()
{
  Address = "2th street",
  City = "New York",
  Country = "USA",
  ZipCode = "0000001"
};
var detail1 = new OrderDetail()
{
  Product = product1,
  Quantity = 3,
  UnitPrice = 10
};
var detail2 = new OrderDetail()
{
  Product = product2,
  Quantity = 5,
  UnitPrice = 10
};
order.OrderDetails.Add(detail1);
order.OrderDetails.Add(detail2);

ctx.Orders.AddObject(order);
ctx.SaveChanges();
```

VB

```
Dim cust As New Customer() With { .CompanyId = 1 }
Dim product1 As New Product() With { .ProductId = 1 }
Dim product2 As New Product() With { .ProductId = 2 }
```

```
Dim order As New Order With
{
  .Customer = cust,
  .OrderDate = DateTime.Now.Date
}
order.ShippingAddress As New AddressInfo() With
{
  .Address = "2th street",
  .City = "New York",
  .Country = "USA",
  .ZipCode = "0000001"
}
Dim detail1 As New OrderDetail() With {
  .Product = product1,
  .Quantity = 3,
  .UnitPrice = 10
}
Dim detail2 As New OrderDetail() With
{
  .Product = product2,
  .Quantity = 5,
  .UnitPrice = 10
}
order.OrderDetails.Add(detail1)
order.OrderDetails.Add(detail2)

ctx.Orders.AddObject(order)
ctx.SaveChanges()
```

Take a moment to look through the code again and ask yourself, "Will this code work?" The answer is, "No." It will raise an exception during the persistence phase. More precisely, you'll receive an `UpdateException` whose `InnerException` is a `SqlException` stating that you can't insert a `null` value into the Name column of the Company table.

This happens because the customer is marked as `Added`, due to the `AddObject` method, so the persistence process tries to insert the customer too. Because you've set only the ID, the insert fails because the name is `null`, and the database doesn't allow that.

To make everything work correctly, you have to use the `ChangeObjectState` method to mark the customer as `Unchanged` before calling `SaveChanges`. The same method must be invoked to set the products as `Unchanged`. This way, only the order and its details are persisted; the rest remains untouched. The following listing shows the code that must be added to listing 7.8 to make everything work.

Listing 7.9 Correctly creating an order with independent associations

C#
```
ctx.Orders.AddObject(order);
osm.ChangeObjectState(cust, EntityState.Unchanged);
osm.ChangeObjectState(product1, EntityState.Unchanged);
osm.ChangeObjectState(product2, EntityState.Unchanged);
ctx.SaveChanges();
```

VB
```
ctx.Orders.AddObject(order)
osm.ChangeObjectState(cust, EntityState.Unchanged)
osm.ChangeObjectState(product1, EntityState.Unchanged)
osm.ChangeObjectState(product2, EntityState.Unchanged)
ctx.SaveChanges()
```

As you can see, independent associations are harder to manage.

The user is happy for a while. But then the user discovers that when a new customer calls, the user can take the order but can't associate it with the customer, because the new customer hasn't been created yet. The user has to go back to the customers form, create the customer, and then reinsert the order. Instead, the user wants to be able to insert data about the new customer and the order in the same form.

PERSISTING A GRAPH OF ENTITIES IN DIFFERENT STATES

Achieving this goal is pretty easy. You can create a `Customer` instance with all the data, associate it with the order, and *not* set its state to `Unchanged`.

If you write the code directly in the form, you'll probably have a flag indicating whether the customer is new or not. If you use an external method, you could pass that flag, but a more *independent* solution would be better. The problem is how to decide whether the customer must be inserted into the database or not without having a flag.

The ID is the key. In the case of foreign-key associations, if the foreign-key property is 0, the customer is new; otherwise, the customer already exists. In the case of independent associations, if the ID of the `Customer` entity is 0, the customer is new; otherwise, the customer exists.

> **NOTE**   By following this simple rule, you can decide whether an instance is new or not and correctly persist any graph. If you have composed keys or you use GUIDs, another check might be needed, but the general idea remains the same. Using mapping information (*metadata*) you could even write an extension method that checks any graph in a generic way and set entity state automatically.

Persisting a graph of added entities isn't difficult. The real challenge comes when you have to save modifications made to the objects—to do this, you have to manually detect what's changed.

7.3.2   *Persisting modifications made to a graph*

You've just deployed the new version of OrderIT, and the user has called to congratulate you on the excellent job. Five minutes later, the user gets back to you saying that they've made a mistake in the shipping address of an order and need to change it. That's pretty easy to do. It doesn't even involve a graph, because you can update the order and ignore its details.

Soon the user is back again. A customer has changed their mind and needs more red shirts (`ProductId` 1), no shoes (`ProductId` 2), and a new green shirt (`ProductId` 3).

What's worse, the user discovered that the order has been erroneously associated with the wrong customer.

This is a big challenge. The data in the `Order` instance is untouched, but the association with the customer has changed. Some items in the details list must be changed or removed, and others must be added. Coordinating all the updates will require some effort.

PERSISTING MODIFICATIONS USING FOREIGN-KEY ASSOCIATIONS

If you're in a connected scenario, you read the data and show it on the form, and when the user saves the modifications, you apply them to the entities. In this case, everything is pretty simple, as the following listing shows, because you're always connected to the context, which tracks any modifications.

Listing 7.10   Updating an order in a connected scenario

C#
```csharp
order.ActualShippingDate = DateTime.Now.AddDays(2);

var product1 = new Product() { ProductId = 3 };
var detail1 = new OrderDetail()
{
  Product = product1,
  Quantity = 5,
  UnitPrice = 3
};
order.OrderDetails.Add(detail1);

order.OrderDetails[1].Quantity = 2;
ctx.OrderDetails.DeleteObject(order.OrderDetails[2]);
ctx.SaveChanges()
```

VB
```vb
order.ActualShippingDate = DateTime.Now.AddDays(2)

Dim product1 As New Product() With { .ProductId = 3 }
Dim detail1 As New OrderDetail() With
{
  .Product = product1,
  .Quantity = 5,
  .UnitPrice = 3
}
order.OrderDetails.Add(detail1)

order.OrderDetails(1).Quantity = 2
ctx.OrderDetails.DeleteObject(order.OrderDetails(2))
ctx.SaveChanges()
```

This code causes four operations to occur. The order shipping date is updated, a new detail is added, an existing quantity is modified, and another is deleted. Fairly easy to understand, isn't it?

In a disconnected scenario, everything is more difficult. Suppose you're putting persistence logic in an external method—it doesn't know anything about what has

Figure 7.3   An order and details with matching keys are updated. Details from the input order with a key of 0 have been added. Other details from the database order are deleted.

been modified, added, or removed. It receives the order and then needs a way to discover what's been changed. In a layered application, this is a common scenario.

The solution is simple. You query the database to retrieve the order and its details. After that, you use the `ApplyCurrentValues` method to update the order from the database with the value of the input order. Unfortunately, the `ApplyCurrentValues` method affects only the order, leaving the details untouched. To discover how the details have been modified, you have to use LINQ to Objects.

The added order details are in the input order but not in the order retrieved from the database. (Because their `OrderDetailId` property is 0, you could use that search condition to locate added order details too.) The removed order details are among those downloaded from the database, but they won't have been received by the method. The order details in both the database and the input order may have been modified, and by using `ApplyCurrentValues`, you can easily find out. Figure 7.3 illustrates this technique.

At the end of the matching process, the order you have read from the database is updated with the input data and is ready to be persisted. The following listing shows the overall code for this technique.

Listing 7.11   Updating an order in the disconnected scenario

C#
```
void UpdateOrder(Order order)
{
  using (var ctx = new OrderITEntities())
  {
    var dbOrder = ctx.Orders.Include("OrderDetails")
      .First(o => o.OrderId == orderId);
    var added = order.OrderDetails.Except(order2.OrderDetails);
    var deleted = order2.OrderDetails.Except(order.OrderDetails);
    var modified = order2.OrderDetails.Intersect(order.OrderDetails);
    ctx.Orders.ApplyCurrentValues(order);
    added.ForEach(d => dbOrder.OrderDetails.Add(d));
    deleted.ForEach(d => ctx.OrderDetails.DeleteObject(d));
    modified.ForEach(d => ctx.OrderDetails.ApplyCurrentValues(d));
    ctx.SaveChanges();
  }
}
```

VB
```
Sub UpdateOrder(ByVal order As Order)
```

```
Using ctx as New OrderITEntities()
  Dim dbOrder = ctx.Orders.Include("OrderDetails").
    First(Function(o) o.OrderId = orderId)
  Dim added = order.OrderDetails.Except(order2.OrderDetails)
  Dim deleted = order2.OrderDetails.Except(order.OrderDetails)
  Dim modified = order2.OrderDetails.Intersect(order.OrderDetails)
  ctx.Orders.ApplyCurrentValues(order)
  added.ForEach(Function(d) dbOrder.OrderDetails.Add(d))
  deleted.ForEach(Function(d) ctx.OrderDetails.DeleteObject(d))
  modified.ForEach(Function(d) ctx.OrderDetails.ApplyCurrentValues(d))
  ctx.SaveChanges()
End Using
End Sub
```

What's lovely about this approach is that, thanks to foreign keys, the association with the customer can be modified too, because the foreign-key property is tracked as a scalar property and so is affected by `ApplyCurrentValues`. Naturally, the same behavior applies to the relationship between a detail and the product.

> **NOTE** The LINQ queries work only because these entities implement `Equals` and `GetHashCode`. If that's not the case, you should pass an object that implements `IEqualityComparer`.

When independent associations are used, things are, once again, harder to figure out.

PERSISTING MODIFICATIONS USING INDEPENDENT ASSOCIATIONS

When independent associations are involved, the code that modifies the order and its details remains the same. What's different is the way you change the association with the customer.

Because you don't have the foreign-key property, `ApplyCurrentValues` doesn't change the association between the order and the customer. The only way to change the customer is to assign an instance representing the new customer to the `Customer` property of `Order`.

If the customer instance isn't attached to the context, it will be associated to the context in the `Added` state. That's clearly not what you need, because you don't want to insert the customer but just change the customer associated with the order. You have three possible ways to do that:

- Retrieve the customer from the database, so that it's already attached to the context, and assign it to the order.
- Associate the customer with the order, and then modify the entity state using the `ChangeObjectState` method.
- Attach the entity to the context, and then associate it with the order.

All of these options will work, so choosing one pattern or the other is a matter of personal taste and case-by-case circumstances. Naturally, you can change the association between an order detail and a product in the same way.

The following listing shows how to change the customer association using the third option. You've already seen the code for the other options. Note that the same code can be used to change the association between an order detail and a product.

> **Listing 7.12 Changing the customer of an order using independent associations**

C#
```
var order = GetOrder();
ctx.Companies.Attach(order.Customer);
dbOrder.Customer = order.Customer;
ctx.SaveChanges();
```

VB
```
Dim Order = GetOrder()
ctx.Companies.Attach(order.Customer)
dbOrder.Customer = order.Customer
ctx.SaveChanges()
```

Persisting modifications made to objects is difficult, because you need to check lots of things. When it comes to object deletion, the situation is simpler.

7.3.3 *Persisting deletions made to a graph*

Our user has just received sad news—a customer has cancelled an order. As a consequence, the order must be removed from the database. In this scenario, the association type between the order, the customer, the details, and the products makes the difference.

PERSISTING DELETIONS USING FOREIGN-KEY ASSOCIATIONS

Once again, foreign-key associations make everything simple. In a connected scenario, you retrieve the order, call `DeleteObject`, and then call `SaveChanges`.

In a disconnected scenario, you create an order instance populating the ID, attach it to the context, invoke `DeleteObject`, and invoke `SaveChanges`, and the game is done. There's no need for a graph here because details are useless. The following listing shows the simplicity of deleting a graph in the disconnected scenario.

> **Listing 7.13 Deleting an order with foreign-key associations, disconnected scenario**

C#
```
void DeleteOrder(int orderId)
{
  using (var ctx = new OrderITEntities())
  {
    Order order = new Order() { OrderId = orderId };
    ctx.Orders.Attach(order);
    ctx.Orders.DeleteObject(order);
    ctx.SaveChanges();
  }
}
```

VB
```
Sub DeleteOrder(ByVal Int32 As orderId)
```

```
   Using ctx as New OrderITEntities()
     Dim order As New Order() With { .OrderId = orderId }
     ctx.Orders.Attach(order)
     ctx.Orders.DeleteObject(order)
     ctx.SaveChanges()
   End Using
End Sub
```

There is a little performance caveat you need to be aware of. Even if the EDM is aware of the cascade constraint in the database, the context will issue a DELETE command for each child entity attached to the context.

Suppose you have an order with 30 details. You may expect that one delete for the entire order is issued, but it's not like that. In the conceptual schema, a cascade constraint between the order and order details is specified; so, if they're attached to the context, they're marked as deleted, and a delete for each of them is issued to the database.

Naturally, if you don't have the delete-cascade constraint, you *must* retrieve all details and mark them as deleted. Unfortunately, this solution is error prone, because in the time between retrieving the details and their physical deletion, a new detail could be added, and the context would know nothing about it. This would result in a foreign-key error when deleting data from the database, because this detail wouldn't be deleted and would remain an orphan when the order was deleted.

An alternative solution is to launch a custom database command that deletes all details and then lets the context issue a separate delete for the order. This spares the retrieval and deletion of all the details from the database, and this is good.

> **NOTE** You're probably thinking that if you're removing an order and someone else adds a detail in the meantime, there should be a concurrency check. In the next chapter, we'll talk about that, but let's ignore it for now.

In the end, if you use delete cascade, everything is simpler. The code doesn't care about details, and database performance improves. Without the cascade, you have more control over the deletion process, but that means more code and slower performance.

That's all there is to deleting entities using foreign-key associations. Independent associations are harder to manage because the relationships stored in the state manager claim their role.

PERSISTING DELETIONS USING INDEPENDENT ASSOCIATIONS

Conceptually speaking, deleting entities in a graph using independent associations is no different from deleting an entity in a graph using foreign-key properties. What changes is the code, because to delete an entity, the context requires all the one-to-one related entities to be attached. If you need to delete a customer, you don't need orders because they're on the many side. But if you need to delete an order, you need its customer, and this is *weird* because only the order ID should be needed.

The reason why deleting an order requires you to know the customer is that the state manager marks the relationship between the two entities as Deleted and translates this into SQL, adding the foreign-key column to the WHERE clause of the DELETE command for the order.

In the end, to delete an order, instead of issuing a statement like DELETE FROM Order WHERE OrderId = 1, the context emits DELETE FROM order WHERE OrderId = 1 AND CustomerId = 2. Unfortunately, this odd requirement is one of those things that you'll have to live with.

In the connected scenario, the difference between independent and foreign-key associations doesn't exist. When you retrieve the order, the state manager already knows about its customer and their relationship, so it has everything it needs.

In the disconnected scenario, you must attach the customer along with the order. This is trivial; all you need to do is create the order, associate the related customer, attach the order to the context, and then pass it to the DeleteObject method. Because the cascade constraint exists, details are automatically deleted too, as you can see in the following listing.

> **Listing 7.14 Deleting an order with independent associations**

C#
```csharp
void DeleteOrder(int orderId, int customerId)
{
  using (var ctx = new OrderITEntities())
  {
    var order = new Order() { OrderId = orderId };
    order.Customer = new Customer() { CompanyId = 1 };
    ctx.Orders.Attach(order);
    ctx.Orders.DeleteObject(order);
    ctx.SaveChanges();
  }
}
```

VB
```vb
Sub DeleteOrder(ByVal Int32 As orderId, ByVal Int32 As customerId)
  Using ctx as New OrderITEntities()
    Dim order As New Order() With { .OrderId = orderId }
    order.Customer = New Customer() With { .CompanyId = 1 }
    ctx.Orders.Attach(order)
    ctx.Orders.DeleteObject(order)
    ctx.SaveChanges()
  End Using
End Sub
```

If the delete cascade constraint doesn't exist, the same considerations made for foreign keys apply. The only thing to point out is that in order to delete the details, their related products must be loaded too (just as the customer is required by the order). To remove an order without delete-cascade constraints, you have to load the whole graph.

That's it. Now the user can manipulate orders any way they need. There's only one thing that the user needs to do now: associate products with a supplier.

7.3.4   *Persisting many-to-many relationships*

Many-to-many relationships introduce nothing new. You have learned everything you need in the previous sections. To add a product to a supplier, you create the supplier and the product instances, add the product to the supplier's list of products, and call SaveChanges.

The same result can be obtained the opposite way. You can create the supplier and product, add the supplier to the product's list of suppliers, and invoke SaveChanges.

When you have to remove a product from a supplier in the connected scenario, you remove the product from the supplier's list and call SaveChanges. In the disconnected scenario, you retrieve data from the database and compare it to the input data to identify the changes. As you can see, there's nothing new here.

Now we can look at a new question. What happens if you wrongly associate an order with a customer that doesn't exist? More generally, what happens when something goes wrong during persistence? And what if you need to execute a custom command? Those questions will be answered in the next section.

7.4   *A few tricks about persistence*

Many things may cause an error during persistence. A string that's too long, a foreign-key violation, a not-nullable column set to null, a duplicate key, and so on—these are typical reasons for exceptions. Let's look at how you can handle exceptions in code.

7.4.1   *Handling persistence exceptions*

Generally speaking, handling an exception is simple; you wrap the call to SaveChanges inside a try/catch block, and you're done. In terms of exceptions caused by Entity Framework, the situation is similar, but you have one specific exception to catch: UpdateException. UpdateException contains information about the entry whose entity persistence caused the error.

The entry is exposed by the StateEntries property, which is of type ReadOnly-Collection<ObjectStateEntry>. The StateEntries property is a list because it returns an EntityEntry for the entity that caused the exception, plus all its related RelationshipEntry instances. You receive only one entity, because as soon as the problem is encountered, the persistence process stops and the current entry is passed to the exception.

Important information is stored in the InnerException too. Here you'll find the raw SqlException raised by the managed provider.

If you mix up the information from the inner exception with that in the entries, you can build a log entry that is useful for understanding what went wrong. If you want to go further, you can build a form that gives the user enough information to understand what the problem was and how it can be solved (if possible). The following listing shows how to catch the exception and write it to a log.

Listing 7.15   Managing persistence exceptions

C#
```
try
{
  ...
  ctx.SaveChanges();
}
catch (UpdateException ex)
{
  Log.WriteError(ex.StateEntries, ex.InnerException);
}
```

VB
```
Try
  ...
  ctx.SaveChanges()
Catch ex As UpdateException
  Log.WriteError(ex.StateEntries, ex.InnerException)
End Try
```

Handling errors is simple; you can easily log information, rethrow the exception, display information to the user, or do whatever you need. We suggest wrapping SaveChanges in a method and invoking that when persisting entities. This way, you don't have to clutter your code with try/catch blocks every time you save data.

The next feature about persistence that you must know is how to send custom commands to the database to update data. This turns out to be particularly useful when manipulating orders and their details.

7.4.2   *Executing custom SQL commands*

Entity Framework can persist any modifications, but there are cases where a custom SQL command simplifies things compared to having Entity Framework persist everything. Let's see how a custom SQL command can help in the OrderIT application.

In OrderIT, there are always 0 items in stock. This value is never updated when the product is created or when an item is sold. That's because in chapter 5, you mapped the AvailableItems property to the AvailableItems column in the Product table and set the property as Computed. This means the property is never used to update the mapped column in the database; when an entity is persisted, the computed column value is immediately queried from the database and put into the property.

Essentially, this approach relieves the context from updating the available items by delegating the update to the database or a custom SQL command like a stored procedure. This approach was necessary to correctly calculate the value.

To correctly calculate the available items, you need to modify the code you have already written to add the following actions:

   1   When you create the product, you let the context create the row in the database and then issue a SQL command that updates the AvailableItems column.

2 When you create or update an order, if the detail is new, you issue a SQL command that subtracts the sold items from the number in stock; if the detail is removed, you issue a SQL command that adds the number of sold items to the number in stock; and if the detail is changed, you issue a SQL command that subtracts the old quantity and then adds the new quantity to the number in stock.

Why do it this way? Why not let Entity Framework persist the column? The reasons are two: *concurrency* and *simplicity.*

- *Concurrency*—Suppose two users create an order simultaneously. They both read the product data at the same time, and the first user then updates the data; the second user will subsequently be updating stale data. A concurrency check could be a solution, but this would be a waste of user time. The user shouldn't have to reinsert the order because the number of items in stock has changed since the data was last read.
- *Simplicity*—Updating a product requires the product to be attached, even if you use foreign-key associations. What's more, you have to update the `Available-Items` property and the overall entity state, resulting in more complex code. A manual `UPDATE` is more straightforward and less complex.

Performing the task this way is pretty simple. Before invoking `SaveChanges`, you take all the details in `Modified` state and add the quantity to `AvailableItems`. After `SaveChanges`, you take all the `Added` and `Modified` entities and subtract the quantity from `AvailableItems`. Finally, for each detail entity in `Deleted` state, you add the quantity to `AvailableItems`.

To execute a custom SQL command, you use the `ObjectContext` class's `Execute-StoreCommand` method. This method has the same features as the `ExecuteStore-Query<T>` method you saw in chapter 4. You can use a numbered list as well as classic ADO.NET parameters in SQL code, and the parameter values can be passed as `DbParameter` or simple values. This listing shows how you can use such a method.

Listing 7.16 Executing a custom SQL command to update data

C#
```
ctx.ExecuteStoreCommand("Update Product set
➥    AvailableItems = AvailableItems - 3 where productid = 1");
```

VB
```
ctx.ExecuteStoreCommand("Update Product set
➥    AvailableItems = AvailableItems - 3 where productid = 1")
```

You learned in chapter 4 that embedding SQL in the application code isn't always a good idea, because you tie the application to a specific database. This might not be problem in many situations, but a stored procedure can be more desirable. You'll learn how to replace the preceding code with a stored procedure in chapter 10.

7.5   *Summary*

You now know how to persist objects into the database. Although the order-detail scenario is simple, it introduced lots of caveats and intricacies. Delete-cascade constraints, connected and disconnected scenarios, foreign keys and independent associations, and frequently updated columns are situations that you'll often encounter during development. Now you're ready to master them. It doesn't matter whether it's an order-detail scenario or different types of data: the concepts remain the same.

You're almost ready to write a complete application, but we still have to cover two important concepts related to persistence: transaction management and concurrency checks. The first is particularly important when you need to launch custom commands that must be executed in the same transaction of the context. The second is essential to avoid updating stale data when multiple users work on the same entity at the same time. In the next chapter, we'll cover these two subjects.

Handling concurrency and transactions

This chapter covers

- Understanding the concurrency problem
- Configuring concurrency
- Managing concurrency exceptions
- Managing transactions

Suppose you want to book a flight online. You search for the flight you want and find an available seat, but when you click the reservation button, the system says the flight is fully booked. If you search for the flight again, it isn't shown.

What happened is that at the moment when you searched for the flight, a seat was available; but in the time between the search response and the booking attempt, someone else booked the last seat. There were *concurrent* searches for the last seat, and the first person to book it won. If the booking application hadn't checked for concurrency, the flight would have been overbooked.

When you book a flight, you register on the carrier's website, and your information is stored so it can be retrieved and updated anytime you want. This kind of data is rarely updated and is only modified by you or a carrier's employee. Contention in this context is so low that you can easily live without concurrency checks.

These examples demonstrate why and when concurrency management is essential for a serious application. This chapter will dig deep into this subject, because it's a simple Entity Framework feature to use, but it's easy to misunderstand.

The second subject covered in this chapter is transaction management. In the previous chapter, we looked at manually updating product-availability data before and after `SaveChanges`. These updates were not executed in the same transaction as the commands issued by the `SaveChanges` method, which would cause data inconsistency if exceptions occurred during persistence. The commands issued manually and the commands generated by `SaveChanges` *must* be executed in the same transaction.

Similarly data must often be updated on more than one database or sent to outside systems, like Microsoft Message Queuing (MSMQ), and everything must be transactional. Thanks to the classes in the `System.Transaction` namespace, it's easy to manage these scenarios. If you have never used these classes, you'll enjoy seeing them in action.

It's time to cover concurrency. The example of booking a flight gave a good picture of what concurrency is all about, so now we'll look at how the concurrency problem fits into OrderIT.

8.1   *Understanding the concurrency problem*

The user's business is growing every day, and the company now needs employees to register and manage incoming orders. This means that two or more people will be working on the application at the same time, accessing and sometimes modifying the same data. OrderIT needs to coordinate updates to avoid having two employees working on the same order at the same time and overriding each other's data.

8.1.1   *The concurrent updates scenario*

Consider this scenario: a big customer has different departments that place orders. Department 1 calls employee 1 to place an order. A few hours later, department 1 calls employee 1 again to update the order. At the same time, department 2 calls employee 2 to update the same order, adding some products. If you think about the code in the previous chapter, you can probably imagine where this is headed.

The two employees retrieve the order. Employee 1 modifies some details, adds a couple more, and saves the order. Employee 2 removes a detail and saves the order a minute later. What happens is that employee 1 saves data and employee 2 overrides it with other data. The two employees will never be aware of this problem, and an incorrect shipment will be delivered to the customer.

There's a worse scenario. If department 2 called to delete the order instead of modifying it, the customer would lose the entire order. Figure 8.1 illustrates potential problems arising from not managing concurrency during persistence.

Technically speaking, there could be contention on every editable entity in the application. It's always possible for two users to work contemporarily and unknowingly

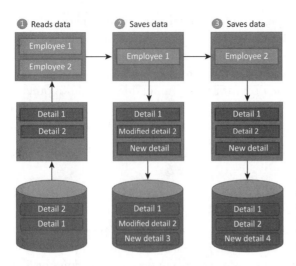

Figure 8.1 A typical concurrency scenario. Both users read the same data, employee 1 saves the records first, and employee 2 overrides them later. New detail 3 and the modifications to detail 2 are lost.

on the same data. But in the real world, very little data is subject to contention, and often it's not important enough to deserve a concurrency check.

For instance, order data is vital and must always be checked. Customer and supplier data is surely important, but not as important as orders. What's more, customers and suppliers are less frequently updated, reducing the risks a lot. As a result, it's probably not worth handling concurrency checks for them. The same considerations apply to products; after they're added to the database, they're rarely changed except for their prices (which is something you won't change often) and their quantity in stock (which is handled manually, as you saw in chapter 7).

Now that the problem is clear, let's look at the possible solutions. The first adopts a pessimistic approach, locking the database rows until they're updated. This approach has pros and cons, as you'll see in the next section.

8.1.2 A first solution: pessimistic concurrency control

When you need to update data and want to be sure that nobody else can do so at the same time, the safest way to go is exclusively physically locking the data on the database. When data is locked, other users can't access it either to read or update it. This way, nobody else can change the data until it's updated or unlocked. This approach is named *pessimistic*, and it's illustrated in figure 8.2.

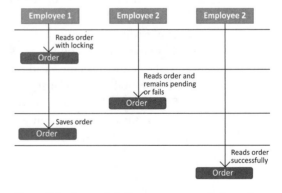

Figure 8.2 In pessimistic concurrency, employee 1 reads the data, and it can't be read by employee 2 until it's saved by employee 1.

What's good about pessimistic concurrency control is that it grants a single user exclusive access to the information, eliminating any possibility of contentions. What's bad is that exclusive locking produces many complications from a performance and usability point of view.

Locking the row exclusively makes it impossible for other users to read information. That means even if another user wants to see the order, they can't. If the user who holds the lock works on the order for a long time, they slow down other people's productivity. What's worse, if the application crashes (and don't say it shouldn't happen; it does), the lock remains there until it expires or a DBA manually removes it.

> **NOTE** A less aggressive policy might allow other users to read data but not to modify it.

Pessimistic concurrency is a good technique, but its cons often outweigh its pros. Unless you're obliged to use it, other approaches are preferable.

The basic idea behind pessimistic concurrency is that because there might be data contention, the data is locked by the first reader. Another technique that solves concurrency problems starts with an opposite approach: because data contention isn't frequent, it's pointless to lock data. The check for contention is performed only during the update phase.

8.1.3   *A better solution: optimistic concurrency control*

How often will multiple users work simultaneously on the same order or customer or whatever else? If this happens, is it a problem for the first person who updates the data to win, and for the others to have to reapply their modifications? Usually the answers to these questions are "almost never" and "no," respectively.

Locking in this sort of situation would be only a waste of resources, because there is low, or no, contention. A softer approach can be taken. You can allow all users to read and even change data, but when you update the database, you must check that nothing in the record has been changed since data retrieval. This is the *optimistic* approach.

The easiest way to do this is to add a version column that changes on every row modification. In the case of concurrent modifications, the first to save the data wins; the others can't update the data because the version has changed since they read it. Figure 8.3 illustrates this concept.

Checking the version column is as easy as including the value initially read from the database in the SQL WHERE clause, along with the ID of the order. This means the real key of the row is the primary-key columns plus the version column, as shown here:

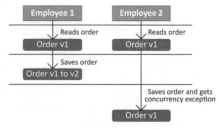

```
UPDATE [order]
SET ..., version = 2
WHERE OrderId = 1 AND version = 1
```

If the query updates the row, you know that the version hadn't changed since the order

Figure 8.3 With optimistic concurrency, employee 1 and employee 2 read order version 1. Employee 1 saves the order, which is updated to version 2. Employee 2 saves order version 1 and gets an exception.

was read. If the query doesn't update any rows, that's because the version number had changed, and there was a concurrency problem. In figure 8.3, the same UPDATE is issued by two employees: employee 1 wins, and employee 2 gets the exception because the version had changed.

When using optimistic concurrency, we recommend you use an autogenerated column for the row version (TimeStamp or RowVersion for SQL Server) so you don't have to manage its value manually.

> **NOTE** Sometimes you can't change the table structure to add a version column, such as when you have a legacy database. In this case, you can use some or all of the columns to perform a concurrency check. Those you choose for the concurrency check will end up in the WHERE clause.

By not using locks, optimistic concurrency improves system scalability and usability because the data is always available for reading. This improvement comes at the cost of managing versioning in the code, but that's not a heavy burden, as you'll discover later. The main drawback is that unless you write some sophisticated code, the users who get the concurrency exceptions will have to read the updated data and then reapply their modifications. It's a waste of time that is usually affordable, but sometimes it isn't.

8.1.4 *The halfway solution: pessimistic/optimistic concurrency control*

This last technique takes the pros of the previous approaches. It doesn't allow concurrent modifications to an order, nor does it physically lock the row on the database.

The way it works is pretty simple. First you add version and flag columns to the table. Then, when a user edits the data, the user's application issues a command to the database to set the flag column to true. If two users do this simultaneously, the first wins. After that, anyone can read the data, but nobody can modify it because the client checks the flag and denies any modifications until it's set back to false. This is the *pessimistic/optimistic* approach.

This technique minimizes contention over the data, but it suffers from the same limitations as pessimistic concurrency control. If the application crashes, the lock must be removed manually. If the user who's editing the order goes to get coffee or to a meeting without saving or canceling the modifications, other users are prevented from making modifications. You can create a demon that kills locks held for longer than a certain amount of time, but that increases the complexity needed do to manage concurrency.

This last technique isn't a perfect solution; it's another string in your bow. Broadly speaking, optimistic concurrency is the best choice in most scenarios. If it doesn't fit your needs, try the pessimistic/optimistic approach; and only if that isn't appropriate should you move on to pessimistic concurrency.

Now that you have a clear understanding of the concurrency problem, it's time to look at how you can take care of it from a database point of view. It's time to see how Entity Framework can help in managing concurrency.

8.2   Handling concurrency in Entity Framework

Entity Framework makes concurrency management easy. It handles most of the plumbing, leaving you only the burden of managing configuration and handling exceptions when they occur.

The first thing you need to know is that Entity Framework *doesn't* support pessimistic concurrency control. That's by design, and the development team doesn't intend to add this feature in the future. That gives you an idea of how little pessimistic concurrency is used in the real world.

By design, only optimistic concurrency is supported. The pessimistic/optimistic approach is an artifact that can be re-created in a few lines of code.

8.2.1   Enabling optimistic concurrency checking

It's time to enable optimistic concurrency in OrderIT. To do so, you need to follow these steps:

1   Add a version column to the Order, Company, and Product tables. Name the column Version, and set its type as `TimeStamp` (`RowVersion` if you SQL Server 2008 or higher).

2   Right-click the designer, and choose Update Model from Database. The designer opens a dialog box displaying the last form of the wizard, which lets you generate the model from the database (we discussed the wizard in chapter 2). Click the OK button.

3   The designer updates the `Order`, `Company`, and `Product` entities, adding a `Version` property and mapping it to the new Version column in the mapped tables. Because the `TimeStamp/Row-Version` type is managed by SQL Server, the columns in the SSDL and the property in the CSDL are automatically marked as `Computed`.

4   Right-click the `Version` property in the `Company` entity, and select Properties.

5   In the Properties window, change the Concurrency Mode to `Fixed`, as shown in figure 8.4.

6   Repeat steps 4 and 5 for the `Order` and `Product` entities.

In terms of EDM, step 5 sets the `Concurrency-Mode` attribute of the `Version` property to `Fixed`, as shown here:

```
<Entity Type="Company" Abstract="True">
    ...
```

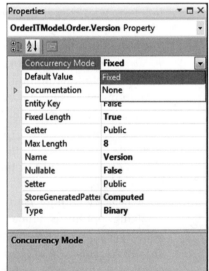

Figure 8.4   Enabling concurrency checking for a property in the designer

```
<Property Name="Binary" Type="timestamp" Nullable="false"
  a:StoreGeneratedPattern="Computed" ConcurrencyMode="Fixed" />
</Entity>
```

That's it. When you're done, the `Version` property will automatically be appended in the `WHERE` clause of the `UPDATE` and `DELETE` SQL commands.

It's important to note that the value used in the `WHERE` clause isn't the one from the entity but the one from the original value of the entry in the state manager. If you attach the entity to the context, and the `Version` property is 1, that value will be used in the query even if you set the property's value to 2 (which you should never do intentionally, but could be done by a bug). This makes sense because for concurrency you have to use the original value from the database and not a new one.

Now that the configuration is finished, it's time to move on to the code. Although Entity Framework manages all the plumbing, you still need to write code to introduce concurrency management into the persistence process. More specifically, you have to manage the version column and handle the concurrency exception.

8.2.2 *Optimistic concurrency in action*

In the previous chapter, we looked at how to persist entities in different scenarios using different techniques:

- Connected scenario
- Disconnected scenario with the `ChangeObjectState` method
- Disconnected scenario with the `ApplyCurrentValues` method
- Connected and disconnected scenarios with graphs

Let's analyze how concurrency affects these techniques.

HANDLING CONCURRENCY IN THE CONNECTED SCENARIO

The connected scenario is once again the easiest to code. It doesn't require any modification because the original value of the `Version` property is in sync with the database. If you read the entity from the database and `Version` is 1, that value will be used in the `WHERE` clause, so there is nothing you have to do.

HANDLING CONCURRENCY IN THE DISCONNECTED SCENARIO WITH CHANGEOBJECTSTATE

In the disconnected scenario, you have an entity and you have to attach it to the context and persist it. As in the connected scenario, the code doesn't change here. You must only make sure that the `Version` property has the same value as when the data was initially read.

For instance, suppose you have created a web form to display customer data. You read the `Customer` entity, display it, store its `Version` property in the ViewState, and then dispose of both the entity and the context. When the user saves the modifications, you create a new context and re-create the entity, populating properties with the form's data. When you attach the re-created entity to the new context, the value of the properties is used by the context to populate the original value of the entry in the state manager. The result is that the value of the `Version` property at the moment it's attached to the context is the value used in the `WHERE` clause.

If you set the value of the Version property to the value previously saved in ViewState *after* the entity is attached to the context, the original value of the Version property in the state manager entry is null because when the entity was attached, the Version property was null. The result is that the UPDATE command uses the NULL value in the WHERE clause, and the row isn't updated; this causes a concurrency exception to be raised by Entity Framework.

If you serialize the entire Customer entity in ViewState or in the ASP.NET session, you don't need to maintain the version. Because the object isn't disposed of when the form is displayed, when the user saves data you can retrieve the object from ViewState or the ASP.NET session and update the object's properties with the form values, leaving the version unmodified. When you attach the object to the context, the Version property is already set, so the original value in the entry is set too. When you persist the customer, the UPDATE command will place the correct value in the WHERE clause.

HANDLING CONCURRENCY IN THE DISCONNECTED SCENARIO WITH APPLYCURRENTVALUES

When you use the ApplyCurrentValues method in the disconnected scenario, you query for the current data in the database and then apply your changes. This means the original values of the entry are those read by the database. When you call Apply-CurrentValues, the current values in the entry are modified but the original values (which are those read from the database) aren't.

Here a big problem arises. When you invoke SaveChanges, the generated WHERE clause uses the original value of the Version property, which holds the current database value. The consequence is that the database's current value is used in the WHERE clause, causing the data to be modified even if it has since been changed by someone else.

Let's look at an example: employee 1 reads the customer with ID 1 and version 1 from the database. Later, employee 2 reads and updates the same customer (so that it's now ID 1, version 2 in the database). Then employee 1 updates the customer and saves it with ID 1, version 1.

When employee 1 triggers persistence, you read the customer from the database (ID 1, version 2) and use ApplyCurrentValues to update the customer data with the input customer object containing the modified data. After the call to ApplyCurrent-Values, the current values of the entry contain the modified data, but the original values are still those read from the database (ID 1, version 2). The result is that the UPDATE command generated during persistence will be the following:

```
UPDATE ...
WHERE CompanyId = 1 and Version = 2
```

As you see, even if the version of the customer has been changed since employee 1 read it, the updates are applied because the version isn't the original one read by employee 1 but the one last read from the database. The modifications made by employee 2 are *lost*.

Fortunately, there is a way to granularly change the original values of an entry. This allows you to modify the original value of the Version property, setting it to the one held by the entity (1 in the preceding example), ensuring that the WHERE clause is correct.

To accomplish this, you have to use the ObjectStateEntry's GetUpdatable-OriginalValues method, which returns an OriginalValueRecord instance. This class has a set of SetXXX methods that allow you to modify the values inside OriginalValue-Record. The following snippet shows how you can use the SetValue method, which is the most generic one:

C#
```
var entry = ctx.ObjectStateManager.GetObjectStateEntry(dbEntity);
var origValues = entry.GetUpdatableOriginalValues();
origValues.SetValue(origValues.GetOrdinal("Version"), entity.Version);
```

VB
```
Dim entry = ctx.ObjectStateManager.GetObjectStateEntry(dbEntity)
Dim origValues = entry.GetUpdatableOriginalValues()
origValues.SetValue(origValues.GetOrdinal("Version"), entity.Version)
```

SetValue is a nontyped method. We used it because Version is imported as a Byte[] and there isn't a SetByteArray (or similar) method. If you already know that you're updating a string or integer or another simple type, you can use SetString, SetInt32, SetDateTime, SetBoolean, and so on.

When you have updated the original value of Version, you can safely invoke SaveChanges. The complete code is shown in the following listing.

Listing 8.1   Performing concurrency checks with ApplyCurrentValues

C#
```
private void UpdateCustomerWithApplyCurrentValues(Customer cust)
{
  using (var ctx = new OrderITEntities())
  {
    var dbCust = ctx.Companies.OfType<Customer>()
      .First(c => c.CompanyId == cust.CompanyId);
    ctx.Companies.ApplyCurrentValues(cust);
    var entry = ctx.ObjectStateManager.GetObjectStateEntry(dbCust);
    var origValues = entry.GetUpdatableOriginalValues();
    origValues.SetValue(origValues.GetOrdinal("Version"), cust.Version);
    ctx.SaveChanges();
  }
}
```

VB
```
Private Sub UpdateCustomerWithApplyCurrentValues(ByVal cust As Customer)
  Using ctx = New OrderITEntities()
    Dim dbCust = ctx.Companies.OfType(Of Customer)().
      First(Function(c) c.CompanyId = cust.CompanyId)
    ctx.Companies.ApplyCurrentValues(cust)
    Dim entry = ctx.ObjectStateManager.GetObjectStateEntry(dbCust)
```

```
    Dim origValues = entry.GetUpdatableOriginalValues()
    origValues.SetValue(origValues.GetOrdinal("Version"), cust.Version)
    ctx.SaveChanges()
  End Using
End Sub
```

You have now seen that performing a concurrency check on an entity is mostly a matter of configuration. A little tweak in the code is required only in this particular scenario. But when graphs come into play, more changes must be made.

HANDLING CONCURRENCY WITH GRAPHS IN THE CONNECTED AND DISCONNECTED SCENARIOS

You know that order persistence involves a graph consisting of the order and its details. Technically speaking, we could put a `Version` property in both entities, but we've chosen to put it only on the order for this example. We made this choice because the details can't exist without an order; even if you modify only one detail, the order version should be updated.

If yours is the only application working on the database, everything is fine. If other applications also work on the database, all have to respect the rule of updating the order when a detail is touched. If this didn't happen, the concurrency checks would be inconsistent, and you should add a version property in the order details too. (We won't take this route in this chapter.)

To update the order version even if only a detail is changed, you have to make sure the `Order` instance is in `Modified` state; otherwise, no update will be performed and no concurrency check will happen.

If you work in a connected scenario and don't change any properties, or if you use `ApplyCurrentValues` and nothing was modified, the state of the entity remains `Unchanged`. Using `ChangeObjectState` to set the order to `Modified` ensures that everything is updated properly.

OPTIMISTIC CONCURRENCY AND INHERITANCE

When dealing with inheritance, there is an important rule to know: you can't use a property of an inherited type for concurrency. For instance, you couldn't use a property in the `Customer` or `Supplier` entity for concurrency checks; only properties in the `Company` entity can be used. If, to enable concurrency, you use properties from an inherited type, you'll get a validation error from the designer or a runtime exception when instantiating the context. In OrderIT, this would also apply to the `Product` hierarchy.

Products are persisted using the TPT strategy (as discussed in chapter 2). When dealing with TPT, you may need to update only a property of an inherited entity (for example, `Shirt` or `Shoe` in OrderIT). When `SaveChanges` generates the SQL, it updates only the table containing the column mapped to the modified property. The table containing the versioning column isn't touched, because there aren't any modified properties that must be persisted to it. This way, the concurrency check isn't performed.

To perform the concurrency check, Entity Framework performs a nice trick. Suppose a user modifies a shirt and changes only the size. Size is a column in the Shirt table, so its modification doesn't affect the Product table, which contains the version column. When SaveChanges is called, Entity Framework issues a fake UPDATE command against the Product table to perform a concurrency check, as you can see in this listing.

Listing 8.2 Performing concurrency checks with TPT hierarchies

C#
```
var dbProduct = ctx.Products.OfType<Shirt>()
  .First(p => p.ProductId == 2);
dbProduct.Gender = "f";
ctx.SaveChanges();
```

VB
```
Dim dbProduct = ctx.Products.OfType(Of Shirt)().
  First(Function(p) p.ProductId = product.ProductId)
dbproduct.Gender = "f"
ctx.SaveChanges()
```

SQL
```
exec sp_executesql N'declare @p int
update [dbo].[Product]
set @p = 0
where (([ProductId] = @0) and ([Version] = @1))
select [Version]
from [dbo].[Product]
where @@ROWCOUNT > 0 and [ProductId] = @0',N'@0 int,@1
    binary(8)',@0=2,@1=0x000000000000084F

exec sp_executesql N'update [dbo].[Shirt]
set [Gender] = @0
where ([ProductId] = @1)
',N'@0 char(1),@1 int',@0='f',@1=2
```

① Issues fake update on Product table

② Retrieves current version of product

③ Updates Shirt table

The first query executes the fake UPDATE on the Product table to see if the command would update a row **①**. If the update affects 0 records, a concurrency exception is thrown. The SELECT **②** is executed only because Version property is marked as Computed, so its value is immediately retrieved from the database after any command. Finally, if no concurrency exception has been raised, the UPDATE on the Shirt table is executed **③**.

You've now seen how to make Entity Framework generate the correct SQL to check for concurrency. What we haven't done yet is handle the exception generated when you update stale data.

8.2.3 *Catching concurrency exceptions*

When an update doesn't affect any rows, the context raises an OptimisticConcurrency-Exception exception, which inherits from UpdateException and doesn't add any methods or properties. Its only purpose is letting you handle exceptions related to persistence and concurrency. Handling this exception is simple, as shown in this listing.

Listing 8.3   Intercepting concurrency exception

C#
```
try
{
  ...
  ctx.SaveChanges();
}
catch (OptimisticConcurrencyException ex)
{
  Log.WriteError(ex.StateEntries, ex.InnerException);
}
catch (UpdateException ex)
{
  //Some logic
}
```

VB
```
Try
  ...
  ctx.SaveChanges()
Catch ex As OptimisticConcurrencyException
  Log.WriteError(ex.StateEntries, ex.InnerException)
Catch ex As UpdateException
  //Some logic
End Try
```

The catching logic is pretty simple. Just keep in mind that if you handle both concurrency and update exceptions, you have to catch the concurrency exception first. Because OptimisticConcurrencyException inherits from UpdateException, if you put the catch block with UpdateException first, the code in that block is executed and the other catch blocks are ignored even if the exception is of type OptimisticConcurrency-Exception.

Catching the exceptions is straightforward, but what should you do when you catch them? Logging the exception is pointless, because it isn't caused by a bug in the code. Letting the system solve the problem is too risky. The right approach is to create instruments to let the user decide what to do.

8.2.4   *Managing concurrency exceptions*

Suppose that employee 1 and employee 2 are unknowingly modifying data about a customer at the same time. Employee 1 changes the web-service password and saves the data. Employee 2 changes the name, saves the data, and gets the exception. It would be great if employee 2 could see what's been changed since the data was read and try to fix the problem, instead of reloading the form and modifying the data from scratch. In this example, employee 2 could reload the form and enter the new name again; in bigger forms with lots of information, this might be an unbearable waste of time.

Your best ally is the `ObjectContext` class's `Refresh` method, which restores entry and entity values, depending on your choice, with data from the database. It accepts the entity to be refreshed and an enum specifying what data must be refreshed. The enum is of type `System.Data.Objects.RefreshMode` and has two possible values: `ClientWins` and `StoreWins`.

If you pass `ClientWins`, the method updates the original values of the entry in the state manager (the object context cache) with those from the data source. The current values and the entity remain untouched. Furthermore, all properties are marked as `Modified` even if they're unchanged.

If you pass `StoreWins`, the original and current values of the entry and the entity are refreshed with data from the data source. Furthermore, the state is rolled back to `Unchanged` because the entity now reflects the database's state. This means all the modifications made by the user are lost.

Getting back to the example, you can use the `Refresh` method and then use the current and original values of the entry to show the user how things have changed on the database since the data was last read. Users can review the changes and choose between the database version and their own entries.

REFRESHING VALUES FROM THE DATABASE

Refreshing values from the database is fairly easy: you invoke `Refresh` and pass in the `ClientWins` value, as shown in the following listing. This way, the original values in the state manager entry reflect the server data, and the current values in the state manager entry reflect the data edited by the user.

> **Listing 8.4 Refreshing entities with values from the server**

C#

```csharp
try
{
  ctx.SaveChanges();
}
catch (OptimisticConcurrencyException ex)
{
  var errorEntry = ex.StateEntries.First();
  ctx.Refresh(RefreshMode.ClientWins, errorEntry.Entity);
  ...
}
```

VB

```vb
Try
  ctx.SaveChanges()
Catch ex As OptimisticConcurrencyException
  Dim errorEntry = ex.StateEntries.First()
  ctx.Refresh(RefreshMode.ClientWins, errorEntry.Entity)
  ...
End Try
```

If you invoke `SaveChanges` after `Refresh`, the database is correctly updated with employee 2's new name value, because all properties are marked as `Modified`. What's bad about this is that employee 1's password change is updated with employee 2's value, which is the old one before employee 1's modification. That's why employee 2 must see the changes and confirm them.

Figure 8.5   The tree view showing original and current values of the conflicting `Customer` entry. Employee 2 is changing the name from "Giulio Mostarda" to "Stefano Mostarda". In the meantime, employee 1 has changed the password from "PWD1" to "password1".

BUILDING THE COMPARISON FORM

There are many ways to show original and current values to the user. You can take a form-by-form approach or opt for a generic solution. We'll take the generic approach here because it's quicker.

At first, you might consider creating a form that displays a grid with the name and original and current values of each property. The problem with this implementation is that complex types can't be represented in a row. We choose a tree view. It has check boxes that allow the user to specify which properties to save and which to ignore. Figure 8.5 shows such a form.

The form may seem complex at first, but it's easy to understand when you get used to it.

> **NOTE**   Including check boxes for properties of complex properties and for original and current value nodes is pointless. They're included because we're lazy and didn't want to override the tree-view rendering.

Here's the main code used to create the form in figure 8.5.

Listing 8.5   Showing entry values in a tree view display

C#
```
private void EntriesComparer_Load(object sender, EventArgs e)
{
  var modifiedProperties = _entry.GetModifiedProperties();
  for (int i=0;
    i<_entry.OriginalValues.FieldCount; i++)
  {
    var isModified = modifiedProperties.Any(n => n ==
      _entry.OriginalValues.GetName(i));

    TreeNode node = new TreeNode(CreateNodeText(
      _entry.OriginalValues.GetName(i), isModified));
```

```
        node.Tag = _entry.OriginalValues.GetName(i);
        tree.Nodes.Add(node);

        if (_entry.OriginalValues[i] is DbDataRecord)
          DrawComplexType(node,
            _entry.OriginalValues[i] as DbDataRecord,
            _entry.CurrentValues[i] as DbDataRecord);
        else
          DrawProperty(node, _entry.OriginalValues[i],
            _entry.CurrentValues[i]);
      }
    }
```

VB
```
Private Sub EntriesComparer_Load(ByVal sender As Object,
  ByVal e As EventArgs)
  Dim modifiedProperties = _entry.GetModifiedProperties()
  For i As Integer = 0 To
    _entry.OriginalValues.FieldCount - 1
    Dim isModified = modifiedProperties.Any(
      Function(n) n = _entry.OriginalValues.GetName(i))

    Dim node As New TreeNode(CreateNodeText(
      _entry.OriginalValues.GetName(i), isModified))
    node.Tag = _entry.OriginalValues.GetName(i)
    tree.Nodes.Add(node)

    If TypeOf _entry.OriginalValues(i) Is DbDataRecord Then
      DrawComplexType(node,
        TryCast(_entry.OriginalValues(i), DbDataRecord),
        TryCast(_entry.CurrentValues(i), DbDataRecord))
    Else
      DrawProperty(node, _entry.OriginalValues(i),
        _entry.CurrentValues(i))
    End If
  Next
End Sub
```

DrawProperty generates a node whose text indicates the name of the property and whether it's marked as Modified. It then renders two child nodes for the current and original values of the property. DrawComplexType creates a node and then invokes DrawProperty to generate a child node for each of its properties.

In the end, building the visualizer is straightforward. What's challenging is writing the code to let users persist its modifications. In this case, employee 2 selects the Name property to mark it as *to-persist* and then clicks the Merge button. At this point, you have to roll back the state to Unchanged and then manually mark the properties selected by the user (Name in this case) as Modified.

To switch the state to Unchanged, you use the entry's ChangeState method. But the problem with this method is that not only does it change the state, it also overrides the original values with the current ones (remember, it calls the AcceptChanges method of the ObjectStateEntry class). This poses a problem, because the current value of Version still contains the old value, which will overrides the original (most updated) value. If you invoke SaveChanges now, you'll still get an exception.

Let's consider this step by step. Employee 1 and employee 2 read the customer with Version 1. Employee 1 updates Version to 2. Then, employee 2 saves the data using Version 1 and gets an exception. When Refresh is invoked, the original value of Version becomes 2, but the current Version remains 1. When ChangeState is then invoked, the original value of Version becomes 1 because it's overwritten with the original value. This way the UPDATE will always fail. Table 8.1 shows this workflow. The last row shows that the original value is set to the incorrect value.

Table 8.1   The update workflow and the problem with the version value

Employee	Action	Database version	Current version	Original Version
Employee 1	Reads customer	1	1	1
Employee 2	Reads customer	1	1	1
Employee 1	Saves customer	2		
Employee 2	Saves customer and gets exception	2	1	1
Employee 2	Refresh method	2	1	2
Employee 2	ChangeState to Unchanged	2	1	1
Employee 2	Saves customer and gets exception	2	1	1

The trick to resolving this is the same one you saw in listing 8.1. You save the original value of Version into a variable, modify the state to Unchanged, and then restore the original value using the variable by using the GetUpdatableOriginalValues method and the OriginalValueRecord class's methods that you saw in section 8.2.2. This listing shows the code.

Listing 8.6   Persisting only selected columns

C#

```
private void Merge_Click(object sender, EventArgs e)
{
  ApplyChanges = true;
  object version = _entry.OriginalValues["Version"];
  _entry.ChangeState(EntityState.Unchanged);
  _entry.GetUpdatableOriginalValues()
    .SetValue(
      _entry.OriginalValues.GetOrdinal("Version"),
      version);

  foreach (TreeNode node in tree.Nodes)
  {
    if (node.Checked)
      _entry.SetModifiedProperty(node.Tag.ToString());
  }
  Close();
}
```

VB
```
Private Sub Merge_Click(ByVal sender As Object, ByVal e As EventArgs)
  ApplyChanges = True
  Dim version As Object =
    _entry.OriginalValues("Version")
  _entry.ChangeState(EntityState.Unchanged)
  _entry.GetUpdatableOriginalValues().
    SetValue(
      _entry.OriginalValues.GetOrdinal("Version"),
      version)

  For Each node As TreeNode In tree.Nodes
    If node.Checked Then
      _entry.SetModifiedProperty(node.Tag.ToString())
    End If
  Next
  Close()
End Sub
```

This code saves the version, rolls back the entity to Unchanged, sets the version, and then sets the checked properties as Modified. The visualizer form is a generic form that is opened by another form to resolve conflicts. ApplyChanges is a property of the visualizer form that informs the calling form that the SaveChanges method must be invoked after the user has finished checking the changed values. The complete code for the method that saves the data from the edit form now looks like the following.

> **Listing 8.7 Complete code for managing concurrency exceptions**

C#
```
try
{
  ctx.SaveChanges();
}
catch (OptimisticConcurrencyException ex)
{
  var errorEntry = ex.StateEntries.First();
  ctx.Refresh(RefreshMode.ClientWins, errorEntry.Entity);
  var form = new EntriesComparer(errorEntry);
  form.ShowDialog();
  if (form.ApplyChanges)
    ctx.SaveChanges();
}
```

VB
```
Try
  ctx.SaveChanges()
Catch ex As OptimisticConcurrencyException
  Dim errorEntry = ex.StateEntries.First()
  ctx.Refresh(RefreshMode.ClientWins, errorEntry.Entity)
  Dim form = New EntriesComparer(errorEntry)
  form.ShowDialog()
  If form.ApplyChanges Then
    ctx.SaveChanges()
  End If
End Try
```

Under some circumstances, you can handle concurrency problems automatically, without user involvement. For instance, you may have a rule stating that if the Name is modified, the user must check what happened. Another rule may state that if a user modifies the shipping address while another modifies the billing address, the system must reconcile everything automatically. Fortunately, by working with Refresh, this shouldn't be too difficult to achieve.

> **NOTE**   In this example, we assumed that concurrency is handled by a property named Version. Using metadata from the EDM (which we'll discuss more in chapter 12), you can write a generic method that looks for properties that have the ConcurrencyMode attribute set to Fixed, and use those properties instead of embedding a property name in code.

Congratulations. You have achieved the master level in concurrency management. As a reward, you can go on to the next stage, which is transaction management. It mostly involves persistence processes, but you'll discover that it might even have an impact on queries.

8.3   *Managing transactions*

When you invoke SaveChanges, the context automatically starts a transaction and commits or rolls it back depending on whether the persistence succeeded. This is all transparent to you, and you'll never need to deal with it.

But sometimes persistence is complex. Think about the product-availability calculation in the previous chapter. When you update an order, you iterate over each detail, adding the old quantity using a custom command, and then invoke SaveChanges. Then you add, for each detail, the new quantity using another custom command.

The problem with such a solution is that the custom commands aren't executed in any transaction. If a problem occurs during SaveChanges, the first set of custom commands is executed and committed, the order isn't committed, and the second set of custom commands isn't even executed. The result is that the product availability values are compromised.

That's a simple example. A more complex scenario is when you have to integrate your application with an external system. For instance, when you save the order, you may have to send a message over MSMQ or update another database. Everything must be executed in the scope of a transaction.

Even if these actions have different natures and use different technologies, they can be grouped together in the same transaction by using the TransactionScope class. It's defined in the System.Transactions namespace inside the System.Transactions assembly.

The TransactionScope class is pretty simple to use. You instantiate it in a using statement, and before disposing of it, you either invoke its Complete method to mark the transaction as committed or do nothing to roll it back. In the using block, you put all the code that must execute in the scope of the transaction. The following snippet shows how simple the code is:

C#

```
using (var transaction = new TransactionScope())
{
  ...
  scope.Complete();
}
```

VB

```
Using transaction = New TransactionScope()
  ...
  scope.Complete()
End Using
```

It's that easy. But how is it possible? How can a class handle transactions that span multiple databases and different technologies? The answer lies in the Microsoft Distributed Transaction Coordinator (MSDTC or simply DTC). It's a component embedded in Windows that coordinates transactions across different platforms.

Connecting to the DTC is an expensive task, so `TransactionScope` tries not to do it unless it's necessary. When you connect to the database, the DTC starts a classic transaction: `SqlTransaction`, `OleDbTransaction`, or another as appropriate. If you connect to a second database or another platform like MSMQ, `TransactionScope` automatically *promotes* the transaction to the DTC. As the following listing shows, this behavior is totally transparent; you don't have to change your code to adapt to the different transaction technology.

> **Listing 8.8 An example of transaction promotions**

C#

```
using (var ctx = new OrderITEntities())
{
  var cust = new Customer() { ... };
  ctx.Companies.AddObject(cust);
  using (var transaction = new TransactionScope())
  {
    ctx.SaveChanges(SaveOptions.DetectChangesBeforeSave);
    using (var altCtx = new OrderITEntities("name=OrderIT2"))
    {
      var newCust = new Customer() { ... };
      altCtx.Companies.AddObject(newCust);
      altCtx.SaveChanges(
        SaveOptions.DetectChangesBeforeSave);     │ Transaction
    }                                             │ is promoted
    transaction.Complete();
    ctx.AcceptAllChanges();
    altCtx.AcceptAllChanges();
  }
}
```

VB

```
Using ctx = New OrderITEntities()
  Dim cust = New Customer() With { ... }
  ctx.Companies.AddObject(cust)
```

```
Using transaction = New TransactionScope()
  ctx.SaveChanges(SaveOptions.DetectChangesBeforeSave)
  Using altCtx = New OrderITEntities("name=OrderIT2")
    Dim newCust = New Customer() With { ... }
    altCtx.Companies.AddObject(newCust)
    altCtx.SaveChanges(
      SaveOptions.DetectChangesBeforeSave)
  End Using
  transaction.Complete()
  ctx.AcceptAllChanges()
  altCtx.AcceptAllChanges()
End Using
End Using
```

**Transaction
is promoted**

Consider the calculation of product availability during order persistence. To execute all the commands in a single transaction, you can wrap them in a `TransactionScope` using block. What's absolutely great is that because only one database is involved, the transaction isn't promoted to the DTC, sparing resources and gaining performance.

> **NOTE** SQL Server 2008 has improved its capabilities in avoiding transaction promotion. With SQL Server 2008, transaction promotion happens less frequently than it does with SQL Server 2005.

If you want to know whether some code will cause a transaction to be promoted, you have to use SQL Profiler, because it always specifies when this happens. You can see an example in figure 8.6.

SQL Profiler is useful during development and debugging. If you want to control how many transactions are promoted and monitor related statistics, you'll have to resort to performance counters, which have a category dedicated to DTC.

In listing 8.7, the value `SaveOptions.DetectChangesBeforeSave` is passed to the `SaveChanges` method. Passing such a value without combining it with the `SaveOptions.AcceptAllChangesAfterSave` value guarantees that the entities' modifications in the context aren't committed after the `SaveChanges` has finished executing.

8.3.1 The transactional ObjectContext

You know that `SaveChanges` accepts an enum of type `SaveOptions`, indicating whether it has to invoke `DetectChanges` and `AcceptAllChanges`. If no value is passed to `SaveChanges`, or if the value `SaveOptions.AcceptAllChangesAfterSave` is specified,

TM: Begin Tran completed	BEGIN TRANSACTION
RPC:Completed	exec sp_executesql N'insert [dbo].[...
Audit Logout	
RPC:Completed	exec sp_reset_connection
Audit Login	-- network protocol: LPC set quote...
TM: Promote Tran completed	
Audit Logout	
RPC:Completed	exec sp_reset_connection
Audit Login	-- network protocol: LPC set quote...
RPC:Completed	exec sp_executesql N'insert [dbo].[...
TM: Commit Tran completed	COMMIT TRANSACTION

**Figure 8.6 The first
INSERT is executed under
a database transaction.
Later, the transaction is
promoted, and then the
second INSERT is issued.**

then when SaveChanges has finished its job, the objects in Modified and Added states return to Unchanged, and the ones in Deleted state are removed from the context. (This is the SaveChanges method's commit phase for entities that you learned about in chapter 7.)

If you pass the value SaveOptions.DetectChanges to the SaveChanges method and don't pass SaveOptions.AcceptAllChangesAfterSave, the entities' commit phase isn't triggered. This is exactly what you need when extending the transaction span, because if something fails in commands executed after the SaveChanges method, the transaction is rolled back and the entities in the context maintain their state.

After you've committed the transaction, you can manually call the AcceptAll-Changes method to bring the objects into a clean state. This is necessary because the entities' commit phase in the object context isn't transactional. You have to manually take care of keeping everything synchronized.

Transactions are widely used to provide an all-or-nothing method of saving data on databases, but they're useful when reading data too.

8.3.2 *Transactions and queries*

You can't roll back a read; it's pure nonsense. But you can use a transaction to control an important aspect of data retrieval: the *isolation level.* You can use it to decide what types of records can be read and whether they can be modified. For instance, you may decide to search for rows that are in the database, including those that aren't committed yet. Or you may decide to include uncommitted rows and enable their modifications too.

These options are configurable via the IsolationLevel property of the TransactionScope class. It's an enum of type IsolationLevel and can have the following values:

- Unspecified
- Chaos
- ReadUncommitted
- ReadCommitted
- RepeatableRead
- Serializable
- Snapshot

If you're used to database transactions, you'll know what these levels correspond to. We won't cover them here, but if you want to delve more into this subject, the MSDN documentation is a good starting point: http://mng.bz/hGel. The following snippet shows how to set the isolation level of a transaction:

C#

```
var transaction = new TransactionScope(TransactionScopeOption.Required,
  new TransactionOptions()
```

```
  {
    IsolationLevel = IsolationLevel.ReadUncommitted
  }
);
```

VB
```
Dim transaction As New TransactionScope(TransactionScopeOption.Required,
  New TransactionOptions() With
  {
    .IsolationLevel = IsolationLevel.ReadUncommitted
  }
)
```

Some years ago, transactions would have been a complex subject. Nowadays, thanks to the DTC component and the TransactionScope class, controlling them is incredibly simple.

8.4   *Summary*

You've now finished the second part of this book, which means you have enough knowledge to develop an application using Entity Framework as a persistence engine. Concurrency and transaction management complete the circle, because they integrate with persistence, which was covered in the previous chapter.

Now you can handle concurrent writes to the same data and make custom SQL commands work in the same transaction as the SaveChanges method, even if those SQL commands are external to Entity Framework. That makes you an Entity Framework pro.

It's time to become a master by learning a few other features. For instance, Entity SQL isn't as easy to use as LINQ to Entities is, but sometimes it makes life easier. Another feature that you must learn about is the use of stored procedures. In environments where the DBA is the governor of the database, learning how to use stored procedures and functions is fundamental. These and other topics will be the subject of the next part of the book.

Part 3

Mastering Entity Framework

In part 1, you learned about Entity Framework's fundamentals, and in part 2 you put Entity Framework to work. In part 3, you'll learn about some advanced features that are necessary to get the best out of Entity Framework.

Mapping data between database and entities, reading data from the database, and updating data is vital to creating an application, but there's still a lot to learn. What about stored procedures? How can you customize the generated code? How can you use the mapping metadata to write generic code? We'll answer these questions in this part of the book.

Chapter 9 covers Entity SQL. Although LINQ to Entities is the most attractive language for querying the model, Entity SQL is still useful. There are tasks that require lots of lines of LINQ to Entities code that you can do with a single clause in Entity SQL.

Chapter 10 is about stored procedures. You'll learn how to integrate them in Entity Framework and how to use them to read and update data.

Chapter 11 is about the `DefiningQuery` element and about reusing code through the use of database and user-defined functions in LINQ to Entities. You'll see how you can dramatically simplify query code.

Chapter 12 introduces one of the hidden gems of Entity Framework: code and database generation. Code-generation templates enable you to fully customize code generation. You'll also learn about database-generation customization and about extending the designer.

Chapter 13 describes how to read mapping information and how to take advantage of that information to write generic code. Such code can make applications much easier to write and maintain.

An alternative way
of querying: Entity SQL

This chapter covers

- Executing queries using Entity SQL
- Executing queries using query-builder methods
- Using the Entity Client data provider

In this chapter, we'll cover one of the hidden gems of Entity Framework: Entity SQL. LINQ to Entities has made this language almost obsolete, and developers don't feel comfortable with it—its string-based nature is less expressive than the object-oriented LINQ. But thinking that Entity SQL is useless is a huge mistake, because some types of queries are easier to write using such a language.

In the first part of the chapter, we'll discuss the querying capabilities of Entity SQL, focusing on different types of common operations, exactly as we did in chapter 4 when discussing LINQ to Entities. After that, we'll explain how to easily use query-builder methods to use Entity SQL in combination with the `ObjectContext`. Later, we'll talk about some advantages Entity SQL has over LINQ to Entities and look at the Entity Client data provider, which is the lowest level of Entity Framework and is used to interact almost directly with the database.

We'll begin by looking at the basics of querying.

A brief history of Entity SQL

When Entity Framework was first presented at Tech-Ed EMEA in 2006, it was called ADO.NET vNext. (Visual Studio 2008, codenamed Orcas, was no more than a prototype, and the LINQ project was taking its first steps.) To perform queries, the speaker used a strangely familiar syntax. It was a string-based language that used a SQL-like syntax.

At that time, creating a new language to query the model was the only choice, because LINQ wasn't ready yet. The Entity Framework team decided not to start from scratch but to use a syntax that was developer-friendly: the SQL syntax. That's why the language was named Entity SQL.

Initially, the language was very similar to SQL; you almost couldn't spot the difference. But SQL is meant to query tabular database structures, and it lacks concepts like inheritance, polymorphism, and other OOP features. Because Entity Framework must accommodate these characteristics, Entity SQL had to be adapted. This led to the introduction of new keywords, and the language began to evolve. Now it's grown to the point where it shares just a few keywords with SQL.

When LINQ to Entities came around, Entity SQL, which had little appeal, became a secondary query language, because its counterpart was far more intuitive and productive. LINQ expressiveness immediately made LINQ to Entities the principal query language. Articles began talking about LINQ to Entities as if it were the entire Entity Framework technology, and people weren't even aware that Entity SQL was in the game.

Nonetheless, Entity SQL is still included in Entity Framework; and due to some LINQ to Entities limitations, it remains the most powerful (although hidden) language for querying. Entity SQL will remain an integral part of Entity Framework. Even if the presence of LINQ to Entities puts it in second place, it will be maintained and evolved like any other part of the framework.

9.1   Query basics

Entity SQL's SQL-like structure makes it more familiar for developers. Let's look at this similarity by analyzing a simple Entity SQL query. The following query retrieves all orders.

Listing 9.1   A simple Entity SQL query

```
SELECT
VALUE c
FROM OrderITEntities.Orders
AS c
```

The SELECT keyword is mandatory, and each query must begin with it. After SELECT, you must specify what data you want to retrieve. In this case, you're retrieving a known CLR type, so you use the keyword VALUE. Next, you use the FROM keyword, followed by the full name of the entity set that you're querying. Finally, you specify the alias of the entity set with the AS keyword.

> **NOTE** Unlike in SQL, the alias is mandatory and is commonly referred to as the *defining variable*. This is important, because in Entity SQL queries, you always refer to a property starting from the defining variable.

You've now written your first Entity SQL query. There are several ways to execute it:

- Through `ObjectContext`
- Through `ObjectContext` with query-builder methods
- Through Entity Client

For now, you'll use `ObjectContext` features to execute Entity SQL queries. In section 9.8, we'll talk about query-builder methods, and in section 9.9 we'll show you how to use Entity SQL in combination with Entity Client.

To execute an Entity SQL query through the `ObjectContext` class, you have to invoke its `CreateQuery<T>` method, passing the Entity SQL query as the parameter, and the return type as the generic parameter. Here's an example of consuming such a method:

C#

```
using (var ctx = new OrderITEntities())
{
  ObjectQuery<Order> result = ctx.CreateQuery<Order>(
    "SELECT VALUE c FROM OrderITEntities.Orders AS c");

  foreach(var item in result)
  {
    //code that handles orders
  }
}
```

VB

```
Using ctx = New OrderITEntities()
  Dim result = ctx.CreateQuery(Of Order)(
    "SELECT VALUE c FROM OrderITEntities.Orders AS c")

  For Each item As var In result
    'code that handles orders
  Next
End Using
```

The `result` variable contains a list of `Order` objects that you can use for whatever you need. Keep in mind that, as for LINQ to Entities, the query isn't executed until the data are actually used by the code. This means the query is executed when the code reaches the `foreach` loop and not before.

Now that you understand the basics of Entity SQL, we can move on and start covering queries. As we mentioned, we'll follow the same path as chapter 4, so we'll begin with filtering and then move to projecting, grouping, sorting, and joining.

> **NOTE** We won't show the context instantiation in the examples again. The `ctx` variable will represent it.

The first query we looked at returns all orders without applying any filters. In the next section, we'll look at how to restrict the data returned.

9.2 *Filtering data*

Filtering the data you want returned is the most common operation of a query. Entity SQL performs this basic operation exactly as SQL does, with the WHERE clause. The following listing shows how to retrieve orders that must be shipped to New York.

> **Listing 9.2   Retrieving all orders shipped to New York**

C#
```
var result = ctx.CreateQuery<Order>("SELECT VALUE c
    FROM OrderITEntities.Orders as c
    WHERE c.ShippingAddress.City =
    @city");
result.Parameters.Add(new ObjectParameter("city", name));
return result.ToList();
```

VB
```
Dim result = ctx.CreateQuery(Of Order)("SELECT VALUE c
    FROM OrderITEntities.Orders as c
    WHERE c.ShippingAddress.City  =
    @city ")
result.Parameters.Add(New ObjectParameter("city", name))
Return result.ToList()
```

In the WHERE clause, two features come up clearly. The first is the syntax when dealing with complex properties . When you refer to the scalar value of a complex property, you have to reach it as if you were navigating to it in VB or C# code.

The second feature is the parameter syntax, which is the same syntax used when executing queries through the classic ADO.NET provider for SQL Server. After declaring the parameter in the query, you have to create an ObjectParameter and add it to the collection that contains parameters for the query.

> **NOTE**   From now on, we won't show the code required to run the query; we'll focus on the Entity SQL syntax.

The query in listing 9.2 is fairly simple and deals with only one entity. In the real world, such queries are very rare; usually, multiple related entities are involved in a query. Understanding how to work with associations is fundamental to writing Entity SQL queries, and we'll look at that next.

9.2.1 *Working with associations*

You know that in a model, associations are one-to-one, one-to-many, or many-to-many. Let's start with one-to-one associations, like the one between an order and its customer.

FILTERING WITH A SINGLE ASSOCIATION

Filtering based on a single association is easy: you navigate to the property as if you were using it in code. Because the property represents a single instance, it's seen as an extension of the main object, so its use is trivial.

The following snippet shows an example of filtering on an association and retrieving all orders that are placed by customers in New York:

```
SELECT VALUE o FROM OrderITEntities.Orders AS o
WHERE o.Customer.BillingAddress.City  = 'New York'
```

Like LINQ to Entities and unlike SQL, you don't have to worry about joins between tables. The Entity Framework generator creates the SQL, making use of the mapping information.

FILTERING WITH COLLECTION ASSOCIATIONS

Filtering based on a collection property is a bit more complicated than filtering based on a single reference property. This is because the filter must be applied on a value *calculated* on the collection data. It may be a count, a sum, or the mere existence of data in the associated collection.

For example, the next snippet retrieves orders that have at least one detail related to a product whose brand property is `MyBrand`:

```
SELECT VALUE o FROM OrderITEntities.Orders as o
WHERE EXISTS
   (SELECT d FROM o.OrderDetails AS d WHERE d.Product.Brand = 'MyBrand')
```

`EXISTS` is an Entity SQL function that's equivalent to the `Any` method of LINQ to Entities and to the SQL `EXISTS` clause. In this case, it's used to filter the orders based on the presence of at least one detail that contains a product with brand `MyBrand`.

> **NOTE** The LINQ to Entities syntax is different than that used by Entity SQL, but if you compare the SQL generated by the two languages, you'll find it's exactly the same. The only difference is in the parameter name; in LINQ to Entities, you can't specify parameter names, whereas in Entity SQL you're forced to do so.

Checking for the existence of a child element in a collection isn't the only filter you may want to apply. Often, an aggregated value is the discriminator for a filter. For example, if you wanted to retrieve all orders with no discount, you could take those where the sum of the discount in the details was 0, as in the following snippet:

```
SELECT VALUE o FROM OrderITEntities.Orders as o
WHERE SUM(SELECT VALUE d.discount FROM o.OrderDetails as d) = 0
```

As you can see, the `SUM` function takes as input another query that returns the discount of each detail. In SQL, it would be impossible to write a query with this structure because `SUM` can be used only in the `SELECT`, `HAVING`, and `GROUP BY` clauses. Here you can use it in the `WHERE` clause, which makes the query more natural from a logical point of view. Thumbs up for Entity SQL!

Another example of filtering based on aggregated data is searching for orders that contain more than one product. In OrderIT, due to the discount policy, a single product can appear twice in an order, so you can have two details but one product. That means you can't simply count the details to find orders with more than one product sold. By using the `COUNT` and `DISTINCT` functions, you can easily determine how many different products are in an order, as follows:

```
SELECT VALUE o FROM OrderITEntities.Orders AS o
WHERE COUNT(
        SELECT VALUE DISTINCT(d.product.productid) FROM o.OrderDetails AS d
      ) > 1
```

The `DISTINCT` clause removes duplicates, and then `COUNT` adds up how many products are in the order. Like `SUM`, the `COUNT` clause is used inside the `WHERE` clause. As you can see, this way of querying is more intuitive than plain old SQL.

Filtering based on a collection isn't difficult when you understand the mechanism of working on aggregated values. But filtering based on data is only part of the game. You can also perform filtering on a count basis. The simplest example is when you want to retrieve only the first *n* rows, or you need to page data in a grid on a web page.

9.2.2   Paging results

How many times have you been asked to create a report containing the top 10 of something? It's a common request. The top 10 (or 100) request can be considered a filtering matter because you're narrowing down the number of objects returned.

To take only the first *n* occurrences, you use the `LIMIT` clause. It must be put at the end of the statement, followed by the number of objects you want returned, as in the following snippet:

```
SELECT VALUE o FROM OrderITEntities.Orders AS o ORDER BY o.OrderId LIMIT 5
```

Notice the use of the `Order By` clause. It's mandatory when using `LIMIT`. If you don't specify the sort field explicitly, you'll get a runtime exception.

Another typical requirement is paging data in web applications. This goal is easily achievable by combining the use of `LIMIT` with `SKIP`. The latter's task is to skip *n* rows before retrieving the number of rows specified by `LIMIT`.

Suppose you want to retrieve the second page of a grid that shows five records per page. In this case, you have to skip the first five rows and limit the retrieved ones to five. That's what the following example does:

```
SELECT VALUE o FROM OrderITEntities.Orders AS o
ORDER BY o.orderid SKIP 5 LIMIT 5
```

It's not mandatory to put `SKIP` before `LIMIT`, but inverting them would result in the query returning the first five occurrences, because the parser considers clauses in the order it receives them.

All the preceding queries return full entities. More precisely, the preceding queries return a list of `Order` objects. Often you don't need the full instance, but only some of its properties. What you need is a projection.

9.3   Projecting results

The process of projecting data in Entity SQL is natural. As in SQL, you specify the projected data in the Entity SQL `SELECT` clause. What's different between a query that returns an entity and one that returns a projection is that the `VALUE` keyword must be omitted for the projection.

Projecting with Entity SQL is also different from projecting in LINQ to Entities because the output result is different. Due to its typed syntax, LINQ to Entities can return an anonymous type with the selected properties. Entity SQL is string-based, and the compiler can't create a class from strings.

9.3.1 Handling projection results

The output of a projected query is an `ObjectQuery<DbDataRecord>` instance. As you know, `DbDataRecord` is the class that represents a row in a `DbDataReader`. This means you have to forget strong typing and use a generic object, as in the following listing.

Listing 9.3 Using projected data

C#
```
var result = ctx.CreateQuery<DbDataRecord>("SELECT c.CompanyId, c.Name
    FROM OrderITEntities.Companies AS c");

foreach (var item in result)
  Console.WriteLine((int)item["CompanyId"] + "-" + (string)item["Name"]);
```

VB
```
dim result = ctx.CreateQuery(Of DbDataRecord)("SELECT c.CompanyId,
    c.Name FROM OrderITEntities.Companies AS c")

For Each item In result
  Console.WriteLine(item("CompanyId") + "-" + item("Name"))
Next
```

Returning data as a list of DbDataRecord objects isn't the most desirable approach. First, the invoking code needs to be aware of the column names. Second, you lose the strong typing and compile-time checking.

Returning a class (DTO) in this case is the best way to go, but it's a more time-consuming approach because it involves more steps. First you have to create an ad hoc class to hold the data. Then you have to execute the query. Finally, you need to use a LINQ to Objects query to move data from the DbDataRecord to the class. You can see the code in the following listing.

Listing 9.4 Returning projected data as typed objects

C#
```
public class KeyValue<T, K>
{                                                    DTO class
  public T Id { get; set; }
  public K Value { get; set; }
}

public List<KeyValue<int, string>> GetCompaniesProjection()
{
  var q = ctx.CreateQuery<DbDataRecord>(             Data-access
    "SELECT c.CompanyId, c.Name                      method
      FROM OrderITEntities.Companies AS c").ToList();
  return q.Select(i => new KeyValue<int, string>(
    (int)i["CompanyId"], i["Name"].ToString())).ToList();
}
```

```
foreach (var item in GetCompaniesProjection())
  Console.WriteLine(item.Id, item.Value);
```
Data-access consumer

VB
```
Public Class KeyValue(Of T, K)
  Public Property Id() As T
  Public Property Value() As K
End Class
```
DTO class

```
Public Function GetCompaniesProjection() As
  List(Of KeyValue(Of Integer, String))

  Dim q = ctx.CreateQuery(Of DbDataRecord)(
    "SELECT c.CompanyId, c.Name
      FROM OrderITEntities.Companies AS c").ToList()
  Return q.Select(Function(i)
    New KeyValue(Of Integer, String)
      (i["CompanyId"], i["Name"]))).ToList()
End Function
```
Data-access method

```
For Each item In GetCompaniesProjection()
  Console.WriteLine(item.Id, item.Value)
Next
```
Data-access consumer

As you can see, the invoking code is now much more readable. The dirty stuff of converting the projection from a DbDataRecord to an object is handled by the data-access method. The invoker doesn't need to worry about typing and column names because it works directly with objects.

> **NOTE** Instead of creating the DTO class, you could create a Company instance, setting only the CompanyId and Name properties. Although using the Company class works perfectly, this approach results in an object that's only partially filled with values. A DTO is much better.

Another thing you can do with projections is concatenate properties. You can join all the billing-address properties of an order into a scalar property, as in the following snippet. This makes data binding easier:

```
SELECT (o.ShippingAddress.Address + '-' + o.ShippingAddress.City + '-' +
  o.ShippingAddress.Country + '-' + o.ShippingAddress.ZipCode)
  AS ShippingAddress
FROM OrderITEntities.Orders AS o
```

You can also group properties into a complex property. In this case, the column in the DbDataRecord doesn't hold a scalar value, but another DbDataRecord, which in turn contains the scalar values. This nifty method of organization allows you to nest complex properties infinitely.

Grouping is achieved through the ROW function. The following query shows an example that returns only the city and street address of an order grouped into a single property:

```
SELECT o.OrderId, o.OrderDate,
ROW(o.ShippingAddress.City, o.ShippingAddress.Address)
```

```
AS ShippingAddress
FROM OrderITEntities.Orders AS o
```

The way you access the scalar columns doesn't change, but when you access the column that contains the grouping property, the situation is different because it contains a DbDataRecord instance containing the scalar columns. Figure 9.1 displays how the grouping property is organized.

OrderId	OrderDate	ShippingAddress	
		City	**Address**
10	27/11/2008 00:00:00	New York	7th Avenue
		City	**Address**
11	27/11/2008 00:00:00	Washington	7th Avenue

Figure 9.1   The ShippingAddress column in the DbDataRecord is a DbDataRecord representing the complex property.

As a result of this organization, you have to cast the inner DbDataRecord's column to DbDataRecord in order to access the scalar column's value. The next snippet shows the simplicity of the code:

C#
```
var sa = ((DbDataRecord)item["ShippingAddress"])["Address"];
```

VB
```
Dim sa = DirectCast(item("ShippingAddress"), DbDataRecord)("Address")
```

There's nothing more you need to know about projections based on single entities, so let's move on to projecting with associations.

9.3.2   Projecting with associations

It's no surprise that associations can participate in projections. As with filtering, you have to distinguish between projections that involve one-to-many associations and projections with a one-to-one association. That's the only similarity between projecting and filtering.

PROJECTING WITH SINGLE ASSOCIATIONS

Handling projections for single associations is simple. Because a single association can be seen as a sort of extension of the class, retrieving it is easy.

You have two options when projecting a single association: return a projection of the main entity plus the entire associated one, or return a projection of the main entity plus a projection of the associated one.

In the first case, you need to put the name of the associated property in the SELECT clause, as follows:

```
SELECT o.OrderId, o.OrderDate, o.Customer FROM OrderITEntities.Orders AS o
```

In the output result, the column containing the associated property directly exposes the object (Customer). To retrieve its data, you cast the column to Customer and then access its properties.

If you project the association too, you need to put the properties in the SELECT clause using the usual navigation syntax, like this:

```
SELECT o.OrderId, o.OrderDate, o.Customer.CompanyId, o.Customer.Name
FROM OrderITEntities.Orders AS o
```

The result is flat because all properties are scalar values. There's no need to do any additional processing.

PROJECTING WITH COLLECTION ASSOCIATIONS

There are three main ways you can project with collection associations, depending on what you need:

- Return partial data from the main entity, plus all the data from the collection.
- Return partial data from both the main entity and the associated collection.
- Return calculated values from the list of associated data.

Let's start with the first case.

A typical situation is when you retrieve parts of the selected orders and their full details. To do this in Entity SQL, you have to put the property in the SELECT clause. The column containing the collection holds a List<T> instance, where T is the type of object in the collection. The value of the column must be cast to List<T> and then iterated. This is what the next listing does.

Listing 9.5　Projecting an order plus full details

C#
```
var result = ctx.CreateQuery<DbDataRecord>("SELECT o.OrderId,
    o.OrderDate, o.OrderDetails
    FROM OrderITEntities.Orders AS o");          ◁— Retrieves
foreach (var item in result)                            association
{
  Console.WriteLine(item["OrderId"]);
  var details =
    (List<OrderDetail>)item["OrderDetails"];     ◁— Iterates over
  foreach (var detail in details )                      association
    Console.WriteLine("  " + detail.OrderDetailId);
}
```

VB
```
Dim result = ctx.CreateQuery(Of DbDataRecord)("SELECT o.OrderId,
    o.OrderDate, o.OrderDetails
    FROM OrderITEntities.Orders AS o")           ◁— Retrieves
For Each item In result                                 association
  Console.WriteLine(item("OrderId"))
  Dim details = DirectCast(item["Details"],      |  Iterates over
    List(Of OrderDetail)                         |  association
  For Each detail in details)
    Console.WriteLine("  " & detail.OrderDetailId);
  Next
Next
```

The second case, returning partial data from both the main entity and the associated collection, often happens when you retrieve parts of the selected orders, plus the quantities, IDs, and products from their details. In Entity SQL, to project collection data, you insert a subquery in the SELECT specifying the columns of the association you want to retrieve. The subquery is shown in bold in the following example.

```
SELECT o.OrderId, o.OrderDate,
  (SELECT d.OrderDetailId, d.Product.ProductId, d.Quantity
   FROM o.OrderDetails As d) as Details
FROM OrderITEntities.Orders AS o
```

The output result is a three-column `DbDataRecord` whose third column is a collection. The difference between this collection and the one generated by the previous query is that because it contains a projected detail, it holds a list of `DbDataRecord` instances.

Even if the objects are different, the concept still remains the same: to access the association data, you have to cast the column to `List<DbDataRecord>` and iterate over the items in the list. Figure 9.2 illustrates the column data in this case.

The last case, returning calculated values from a list of associated data, is common and useful when you need to retrieve orders and their total amounts. In this case, you don't get a collection; you get a scalar value that is easier to manage. From the query perspective, the amount is calculated using a subquery, in the `SELECT` clause that returns only a property, as in the next snippet:

OrderId	OrderDate	Details	
		DetailId	**Quantity**
10	27/11/2008 0:00:00	20	5
		21	2
		DetailId	**Quantity**
11	27/11/2008 0:00:00	22	5
		23	5

Figure 9.2 The result of projecting both orders and details

```
SELECT o.OrderId, o.OrderDate,
  SUM(SELECT VALUE (d.UnitPrice - d.Discount) * d.Quantity
      FROM o.OrderDetails As d) AS Total
FROM OrderITEntities.Orders AS o
```

The result is a list of `DbDataRecord` objects containing the OrderId, OrderDate, and Total columns. Because the Total column is a simple scalar value, it's retrieved as a classic scalar column.

Now you understand two important pieces of Entity SQL: filtering and projecting. The next step is learning how to group data using this language.

9.4 Grouping data

Grouping data is a basic function of any advanced query language. SQL, LINQ, LINQ to Entities, and Entity SQL have this feature in their toolbox. Once again, grouping data in Entity SQL is similar to doing so in SQL. You use a `GROUP BY` clause to specify the grouping fields. That's all.

As a first example, let's extract the orders and group them by shipping city:

```
SELECT o.ShippingAddress.City,
  (SELECT VALUE o2
   FROM OrderITEntities.Orders AS o2
   WHERE o.ShippingAddress.City = o2.ShippingAddress.City) AS Orders
FROM OrderITEntities.Orders AS o
GROUP BY o.ShippingAddress.City
```

The output of this query is an `ObjectQuery<DbDataRecord>`, where each record contains a column for the shipping city and another for the orders, as shown in figure 9.3.

City	details							
Miami	**OrderId**	**OrderDate**	**EstimatedShippingDate**	**ActualShippingDate**	**ShippingAddress**			
					Street	**City**	**ZipCode**	**Country**
	15	27/11/2008 0:00:00	NULL	NULL	7th Avenue	Miami	24323	USA
					Street	**City**	**ZipCode**	**Country**
	16	27/11/2008 0:00:00	NULL	NULL	7th Avenue	Miami	34631	USA
New York	**OrderId**	**OrderDate**	**EstimatedShippingDate**	**ActualShippingDate**	**ShippingAddress**			
					Street	**City**	**ZipCode**	**Country**
	3	27/11/2008 0:00:00	20/10/2008 0:00:00	NULL	7th Avenue	New York	98765	USA
					Street	**City**	**ZipCode**	**Country**
	10	27/11/2008 0:00:00	NULL	05/02/2009 14:47:38	7th Avenue	New York	98765	USA

Figure 9.3   The result of a grouping query. The first column contains the grouping field—City, in this case. The second column contains the orders shipped to the city.

To process the records extracted by the query, you need to iterate over them. Remember that the second column contains a List<Order> object and not a List<DbData-Record> object because the query didn't perform any projection.

You can also group data on more than one property. For instance, you might have to group orders by shipping city and zip code. To do this, you'd include both columns in the GROUP BY clause, separating them with a comma (,) as in the following query:

```
SELECT o.ShippingAddress.City, o.ShippingAddress.ZipCode,
  (SELECT VALUE o2
   FROM OrderITEntities.Orders AS o2
   WHERE o.ShippingAddress.City = o2.ShippingAddress.City) AS Orders
FROM OrderITEntities.Orders AS o
GROUP BY o.ShippingAddress.City, o.ShippingAddress.ZipCode
```

The DbDataRecord output contains the columns in the SELECT clause.

Data retrieved by the query can be projected; you aren't forced to return an entire entity. To do so, remove the VALUE keyword from the SELECT clause, and select the properties you need, as shown in the next snippet. The difference between this and the previous example is that the column that contains the projected data isn't a List<Order> instance but a List<DbDataRecord> instance:

```
SELECT o.ShippingAddress.City,
  (SELECT o2.OrderId, o2.OrderDate
   FROM OrderITEntities.Orders AS o2
   WHERE o.ShippingAddress.City = o2.ShippingAddress.City) AS details
FROM OrderITEntities.Orders AS o
GROUP BY o.ShippingAddress.City
```

Sometimes you may need to filter data after it's grouped. More often, you may need to filter on an aggregated value. For instance, you may want to retrieve data only for those cities that have more than two orders.

As with SQL, the solution is the HAVING clause. It must be put after the GROUP BY clause and can specify any valid Entity SQL expression (COUNT is used in the following example):

```
SELECT o.ShippingAddress.City,
  (SELECT VALUE o2 FROM OrderITEntities.Orders AS o2
   WHERE o.ShippingAddress.City = o2.ShippingAddress.City) AS details
```

```
FROM OrderITEntities.Orders AS o
GROUP BY o.ShippingAddress.City
HAVING COUNT(o.ShippingAddress.City) > 2
```

As you can see, grouping data is a fairly easy task. By mixing GROUP BY and HAVING, you can perform powerful queries. Next, it's time to look at sorting.

9.5 Sorting data

Sorting in Entity SQL is *identical* to sorting in SQL. The ORDER BY clause is used, followed by a list of comma-separated columns that the sorting is based on. You can even set the sorting direction with the DESC and ASC keywords:

Here's an example of sorting on one column:

```
SELECT VALUE o
FROM OrderITEntities.Orders AS o
ORDER BY o.ShippingAddress.City
```

And here's a similar example of sorting on multiple columns:

```
SELECT VALUE o
FROM OrderITEntities.Orders AS o
ORDER BY o.ShippingAddress.City, o.ShippingAddress.ZipCode
```

Sorting is a simple matter of using the ORDER BY clause. But when associations are involved, you can do interesting things.

9.5.1 Sorting data based on associations

The first thing you may want to do when associations are involved is to sort data on the basis of an aggregated value calculated on a collection association. For instance, the next example sorts the orders based on their total amounts:

```
SELECT VALUE o
FROM OrderITEntities.Orders AS o
ORDER BY
  Sum(SELECT VALUE (d.UnitPrice - d.Discount) * d.Quantity
      FROM o.OrderDetails AS d)
```

What's great in this query is that you can use a subquery in the ORDER BY clause. This is something SQL doesn't allow—it's another Entity SQL feature that makes life easier.

Another interesting Entity SQL feature is the ability to retrieve an entity, or a projection of it, and have only its associated collection data sorted. The following example retrieves the orders and sorts their details by the items sold:

```
SELECT o.OrderId, o.OrderDate,
  (Select VALUE d
  FROM o.OrderDetails AS d
  ORDER BY d.Quantity) AS Details
FROM OrderITEntities.Orders AS o
```

When it comes to associations that point to a single reference, sorting is trivial. The reference points to a single instance, so you can navigate to properties as usual. In the following snippet, the orders are sorted by their customer city:

```
SELECT VALUE o
FROM OrderITEntities.Orders AS o
ORDER BY o.Customer.ShippingAddress.City
```

That's all you need to know about sorting. In the next section, we'll talk about another feature: joins between objects.

9.6   *Joining data*

You already discovered in chapter 4 that manually joining data is unnecessary because Entity Framework automatically takes care of relationships when generating SQL. But there are some situations where you may need to manually join objects, so you must be aware of this mechanism.

Once again, Entity SQL syntax for joins is identical to SQL syntax; you use the JOIN clause. In the following example, orders and companies are joined by the shipping city and the customer ID:

```
SELECT o.OrderId, o.OrderDate
FROM OrderITEntities.Orders AS o
JOIN OrderITEntities.Companies AS c ON o.Customer.CompanyId = c.CompanyId
  AND o.ShippingAddress.City = c.ShippingCity
```

The last feature needed to query data is the inheritance-querying mechanism. This is a bit different from what you've seen so far, because it's something that doesn't exist in SQL.

9.7   *Querying for inheritance*

When talking about inheritance, two types of queries can be performed:

- Queries that return objects, exposing them through the base class
- Queries that return only objects of a specified type

The first type of query is pretty simple and doesn't involve any Entity SQL inheritance knowledge. Because the entity set you query exposes objects through the base class, you perform a query using properties on that class. At runtime, Entity Framework generates the concrete classes by analyzing the mapping information.

The second type of query requires some explanation, because Entity SQL inheritance features come into play via the OFTYPE function. This function is placed immediately after the FROM clause and accepts the full entity-set name and the full type name to be retrieved, as shown in the next snippet:

```
SELECT VALUE c
FROM OFTYPE(OrderITEntities.Companies, OrderIT.Model.Customer) AS c
```

Naturally, you can add filters. Because this query retrieves customers, you can add a WHERE clause on the customer properties. The next snippet looks for customers who are enabled to use the web service:

```
SELECT VALUE c
FROM OFTYPE(OrderITEntities.Companies, OrderIT.Model.Customer) AS c
WHERE c.WSEnabled = true
```

Not only can you filter data, but you can also project, sort, and group it any way you want.

This is all you really need to know to consider yourself an Entity SQL master, but Entity SQL is wide subject. It has a lot of functions and operators. MSDN has great documentation for the Entity SQL Language; you can find the MSDN language reference at http://mng.bz/f3ew.

So far, you've used the `CreateQuery<T>` method for querying, passing in the entire Entity SQL string. To simplify the creation of Entity SQL queries, you can use a set of methods, named *query-builder methods*, to shorten the code.

9.8 *Using query-builder methods*

Query-builder methods are a convenient way to organize Entity SQL queries and can often simplify dynamic query creation. These methods do exactly what their name suggests: they let you build an Entity SQL query using methods instead of having to write the entire Entity SQL on your own. Query-builder methods don't cover all aspects of querying, but, in our experience, 90% of a project's queries can be developed using them.

Query-builder methods aren't extension methods like the LINQ to Entities methods. They're included in the `ObjectQuery<T>` class and implement the fluent technique, which allows them to be chained, because they return an `ObjectQuery<T>` instance. The query-builder methods are listed in table 9.1.

Table 9.1   The query-builder methods

Method	Functionality
Distinct	Specifies that returned data must be unique
Except	Limits query results by excluding results based on the results of another object query
Include	Eager-loads related associations
Intersect	Limits query results by including only the results that exist in another object query
OfType<T>	Retrieves only instances of objects of the specified type
OrderBy	Defines the sorting properties
Select	Defines the properties to retrieve
SelectValue<T>	Defines the properties to retrieve, and returns them in the object specified
Skip	Sorts the data by a key, and skips the first n occurrences
Top	Returns only the first n occurrences
Union	Merges the results of two queries, removing duplicates
UnionAll	Merges the results of two queries
Where	Defines filters

Let's see a simple query in action. This one retrieves all orders shipped to New York:

C#
```
var result = ctx.Orders.Where("it.ShippingAddress.City = 'New York'");
```

VB
```
Dim result = ctx.Orders.Where("it.ShippingAddress.City = 'New York'")
```

This query is simple; it uses the `Where` method to filter returned data. Despite its simplicity, there is one thing to point out: the `it` defining variable. `it` is the name of the defining variable, but the name can be changed programmatically using the `Object-Query<T>` instance's `Name` property.

Note that you must be aware of some caveats when changing the defining variable. It's bound to the chaining mechanism, which we'll cover next.

9.8.1   *Chaining methods*

Chaining multiple query-builder methods together is a simple and powerful mechanism for shaping a query at runtime. Suppose you have a method with many filter parameters. When you create the query, you have to apply the filters only for the input parameters that have a value. In this case, you can call the `Where` method multiple times, as shown here.

Listing 9.6   Chaining query-builder methods

C#
```
ObjectQuery<Order> result = ctx.Orders;
if (city != String.Empty)
  result = result.Where("it.ShippingAddress.City = '" + city + "'");
if (zipCode != String.Empty)
  result = result.Where("it.ShippingAddress.ZipCode = '" + zipCode + "'");
```

VB
```
Dim result As ObjectQuery<Order> = ctx.Orders
If city <> String.Empty
  result = result.Where("it.ShippingAddress.City = '" + city + "'")
End If
If zipCode <> String.Empty
  result = result.Where("it.ShippingAddress.ZipCode = '" + zipCode + "'")
End If
```

The Entity SQL code generated by a chaining method isn't necessarily what you may expect. If you were to create the Entity SQL string on your own, you would probably create a `WHERE` clause with multiple `AND`s. Entity SQL behaves differently, generating a nested query for each call to the `Where` method. Although this may seem to be a cumbersome approach, it guarantees the needed flexibility in code generation.

The following query is the Entity SQL generated by the code in listing 9.6, obtained by inspecting the `CommandText` property of the `ObjectQuery<T>` class:

```
SELECT VALUE it
FROM
  (
```

```
    SELECT VALUE it
    FROM ([Orders]) AS it
    WHERE it.ShippingAddress.City = 'New York'
  ) AS it
WHERE it.ShippingAddress.ZipCode = '98765'
```

As you see, the second WHERE causes a query-nesting process.

Earlier, we said you can change the defining variable name programmatically, but you should be aware of a caveat when doing so. When you have just one method call, you can change the defining variable name and then use it in the method:

VB

```
ctx.Orders.Name = "o"
ctx.Orders.Where("o.ShippingAddress.ZipCode = '98765'")
```

C#

```
ctx.Orders.Name = "o";
ctx.Orders.Where("o.ShippingAddress.ZipCode = '98765'");
```

But if you're chaining multiple methods, you have to change the name before each method. This is mandatory, because queries are nested, and it is automatically used as the defining variable name for each one:

VB

```
Dim result As ObjectQuery<Order> = ctx.Orders
result.Name = "o"
result = result.Where("o.ShippingAddress.ZipCode = '98765'")
result.Name = "o2"
result = result.Where("o2.ShippingAddress.ZipCode = '98765'")
```

C#

```
ObjectQuery<Order> result = ctx.Orders;
result.Name = "o";
result = result.Where("o.ShippingAddress.ZipCode = '98765'");
result.Name = "o2";
result = result.Where("o2.ShippingAddress.ZipCode = '98765'");
```

You should now understand why, despite its power, Entity SQL isn't famous among Entity Framework adopters. Its string-based nature makes it less appealing than LINQ to Entities. Nevertheless, query-builder methods make things easier and are fantastic when the query must be created at runtime. Entity SQL is friendlier than LINQ to Entities in such cases.

9.8.2 *Query-builder methods vs. LINQ to Entities methods*

A typical situation when a query must be built dynamically is when the sorting field is decided at runtime based on user input. This often happens if the user can sort a grid by clicking a column header. Due to LINQ to Entities' strong typing nature, this task can be handled only by using a set of if or switch statements.

Because Entity SQL is string-based, query-builder methods, and Entity SQL in general, make runtime construction easy. The following listing shows the code required for runtime query construction using both LINQ to Entities and query-builder methods.

Listing 9.7   Chaining query-builder methods vs. chaining LINQ to Entities methods

C#
```
IEnumerable result;
if (sortField == "city")
  result = ctx.Orders.OrderBy(
    o => o.ShippingAddress.City);
else if (sortField == "ZipCode")
  result = ctx.Orders.OrderBy(
    o => o.ShippingAddress.ZipCode);
else
  result = ctx.Orders.OrderBy(
    o => o.ShippingAddress.Country);

var result = ctx.Orders.OrderBy(
  "it.ShippingAddress." + sortField);
```

❶ Dynamic sorting with LINQ to Entities

❷ Dynamic sorting with Entity SQL

VB
```
Dim result as IEnumerable
if sortField == "city"
  result = ctx.Orders.OrderBy(Function(o)
    o.ShippingAddress.City)
elseif (sortField == "ZipCode")
  result = ctx.Orders.OrderBy(Function(o)
    o.ShippingAddress.ZipCode)
else
  result = ctx.Orders.OrderBy(Function(o)
    o.ShippingAddress.Country)

Dim result = ctx.Orders.OrderBy(
  "it.ShippingAddress" & sortField)
```

❶ Dynamic sorting with LINQ to Entities

❷ Dynamic sorting with Entity SQL

Wow. Just one statement ❷, as compared to seven ❶. Isn't that great? You should now understand why we said that Entity SQL in combination with query-builder methods is more useful than LINQ to Entities in such cases.

Listing 9.6 uses string concatenation to create a query; this is bad. We just wanted to demonstrate that Entity SQL offers great flexibility in creating a query. But in that sort of situation, there's no doubt that the best way to go is to use parameters. We introduced them in section 9.2, and we'll discuss them in more detail in the next section.

9.8.3   *Using parameters to prevent injection*

Lots of queries are parameterized through arguments. For instance, a query that looks for customers by their billing city accepts the customer's city as an argument. In this type of query, we strongly recommend you to use *parameters* to avoid SQL injection attacks. You should never concatenate user input to create Entity SQL code. If you have already developed solutions using ADO.NET, you should be accustomed to parameters. If not, you'll find them easy to use.

> **NOTE**   You can learn more about SQL injection and about how parameters help you in avoiding this type of attack from the MSDN article "SQL Injection" at http://mng.bz/76s4.

To simplify the use of parameters, each query-builder method that requires parameters (the majority) accepts a list of `ObjectParameter` objects as a second argument. The parameters are accepted as `param`/`ParamArray`, so you can declare and instantiate them in a single statement, as shown in the following snippet:

C#

```
ctx.Orders.Where("it.ShippingAddress.City = @city",
  new ObjectParameter("city", city));
```

VB

```
ctx.Orders.Where("it.ShippingAddress.City = @city",
  New ObjectParameter("city", city))
```

The SQL code generated by a LINQ to Entities query uses parameters, so there's nothing you have to do to use them; with Entity SQL, you must explicitly use parameters in your query.

We've never seen it happen, but if you encounter a situation where you can't use parameters, you'll have to check the user input for malicious data. Even if the user input is smarter than your validation process, it still has to perform a complicated action: inject code that's perfectly valid for Entity SQL and in turn SQL. Although Entity SQL and SQL are similar, there are subtle differences. For instance, Entity SQL doesn't support the semicolon (`;`) character, which is often used in SQL injection to interrupt a SQL statement and create a new malicious one.

This doesn't mean Entity SQL is more secure than plain old ADO.NET, but it surely makes life harder for attackers. Nevertheless, the greater difficulty of injection doesn't mean you can lower your defenses; always take care of this aspect of security.

Naturally, all of these considerations apply to Entity SQL in general, and not only to query-builder methods.

PARAMETER TRANSLATION

When an Entity SQL query with parameters is translated into SQL, the generated SQL uses the parameter feature of each database engine. For instance, OrderIT uses SQL Server, which has the `sp_executesql` stored procedure. This stored procedure accepts a string that represents both the SQL string and a set of parameters that are used to execute the query.

Generic solutions like O/RM have a generic structure that makes them ready for any situation. When it comes to parameters, this means many O/RM tools use the maximum size of the parameter type. For instance, a string parameter is translated in SQL as a `varchar(8000)`.

This is one place where Entity Framework is optimized. It uses the real size of the value of the parameter, instead of assuming the maximum size for the type. Although it may seem negligible, this is a huge optimization.

So far, we've used the context as the gateway to the data. But Entity Framework has another layer that lets you communicate with the database: the Entity Client data provider.

9.9   *Working with the Entity Client data provider*

You learned in chapter 1 that the Object Services layer isn't directly connected to the database. It's situated on the *Entity Client data provider* (Entity Client from now on), which is an ADO.NET data provider built for Entity Framework. Entity Client is responsible for many Entity Framework internal behaviors (like transforming data read from the database into a format that's later transformed into objects by the Object Services layer), and it uses the ADO.NET data provider specified in the connection string to physically interact with the database.

Because the Entity Client is an ADO.NET data provider, like `OracleClient`, `Sql-Client`, and `OleDb`, it contains a set of classes that implement the standard ADO.NET base classes:

- `EntityConnection`—Inherits from `DbConnection` and represents the connection to a database. It adds some functionality to the base class.
- `EntityTransaction`—Inherits from `DbTransaction` and represents a transaction to the database. It's a wrapper needed to implement a full ADO.NET provider.
- `EntityCommand`—Inherits from `DbCommand` and represents the class necessary to execute any command to the database.
- `EntityParameter`—Inherits from `DbParameter` and represents a parameter of a query.
- `EntityDataReader`—Inherits from `DbDataReader` and contains the result of a query executed by the `EntityCommand` class.

If you're familiar with ADO.NET development, these classes will be nothing new.

Keep in mind that the Entity Client doesn't physically connect to the database; it relies on the underlying ADO.NET provider. Entity Client is a wrapper that works with the EDM to generate SQL from queries and to shape the results of queries. The only language you can use to query the database via Entity Client is Entity SQL (LINQ to Entities works only with Object Services).

The following listing shows how you can retrieve orders by writing an Entity SQL query, not a SQL one.

Listing 9.8   Retrieving orders with Entity Client

C#

```
using (var conn = new EntityConnection(
  Parameters.ConnectionString))
{
  using (EntityCommand comm = new EntityCommand("SELECT VALUE o
     FROM OrderITEntities.Orders AS o", conn))
  {
    conn.Open();
    EntityDataReader reader =
      comm.ExecuteReader(
        CommandBehavior.SequentialAccess);
    while (reader.Read())
    {      ...
```

```
      }
    }
  }
```

VB
```
Using conn As New EntityConnection(
  Parameters.ConnectionString)
  Using comm As New EntityCommand("SELECT VALUE o
➡️    FROM OrderITEntities.Orders AS o", conn)
    conn.Open()
    Dim reader As EntityDataReader =
      comm.ExecuteReader(
        CommandBehavior.SequentialAccess)
    While reader.Read()
      ...
    End While
  End Using
End Using
```

This example is quite simple: it creates a connection, creates a command, executes a query, and consumes data. If you have written at least one query in your life, you should be able to follow what it does. Let's focus on the objects that are used in it, starting with the connection.

9.9.1 Connecting with EntityConnection

`EntityConnection` is the class that establishes a connection with the underlying ADO.NET provider. Two main points are worth looking at here.

The first point to highlight is the connection string that's passed to the `Entity-Connection` class. In chapter 3, you learned the different ways you can pass the connection string to the `ObjectContext`. The same paths can be followed when using the `EntityConnection` class. You can pass the full connection string, or a formatted string that contains the keyword `Name` followed by an equal sign (=) and then the name of the connection string in the configuration file:

```
Name=OrderITEntities
```

The second thing to note is that `EntityConnection` exposes the `StoreConnection` property that represents the physical connection to the database. The property is of `DbConnection` type, but the real underlying type is the one you specified in the connection string.

Having access to the real database connection turns out to be particularly useful in scenarios that aren't natively supported by Entity Framework. For instance, Entity Framework doesn't support stored procedures that return multiple resultsets. To bypass this limitation, you can retrieve the physical connection to the database, launch the stored procedure, and then handle the result manually.

> **NOTE** You can also use this method to execute native queries on the database. But although this is technically possible, we strongly discourage it. As you'll discover in the next chapter, you have other ways to launch native commands against the database.

EntityConnection is a gateway to the metadata of the EDM too. Through its Get-MetadataWorkspace method, you can access all of the information of the EDM and get information about the objects, their relationships, and their mapping to the database. We'll talk more about this subject in chapter 12.

9.9.2   *Executing queries with EntityCommand*

The EntityCommand class doesn't introduce any new concepts that you haven't seen in any other ADO.NET-specific provider. The only additional feature it introduces is the ability to enable or disable the caching of the query. The property involved is Enable-PlanCaching, which is a Boolean whose default value is true. We'll talk more about the plan-caching feature in chapter 19, which is dedicated to performance.

The ExecuteReader method has a peculiarity: you have to pass the Command-Behavior.SequentialAccess parameter. This indicates that when reading columns from the reader, you have to access them *sequentially*, not randomly. If you access the columns randomly, you'll get an InvalidOperationException. The reason for this requirement is to avoid excessive memory usage. The following snippet shows examples of correct and incorrect code:

C#
```
var f1 = Reader[1];        Incorrect (random)
var f2 = Reader[0];        access

var f1 = Reader[0];               Valid (sequential)
var f2 = Reader[1];               access
```

VB
```
Dim f1 = Reader(1)         Incorrect (random)
Dim f2 = Reader(0)         access

Dim f1 = Reader(0)                Valid (sequential)
Dim f2 = Reader(1)                access
```

The situation doesn't change if you access columns by name. You always have to access them in sequential order.

The EntityCommand class has a unique feature: the way it sizes parameters. In the previous section, you saw that Entity Framework automatically adjusts the size and type of a query parameter based on the value it contains. Although that's a good thing, in some scenarios you may want full control over parameter sizes or types. In this situation, the EntityParameter class comes into play.

EntityParameter isn't any different from other providers. Its instantiation process, properties, and methods are exactly the same. The fact that you can control parameter type and size is all that makes it different from the LINQ to Entities and ObjectParameter implementations of parameters.

9.9.3   *Processing query results with EntityDataReader*

Hardly surprisingly, the EntityDataReader class is the container for data returned by the EntityCommand's ExecuteReader method. As you'll discover, this DbDataReader implementation is likely the most different from any of the other providers you have seen.

OrderId	OrderDate	EstimatedShippingDate	ActualShippingDate	ShippingAddress			
				Street	**City**	**ZipCode**	**Country**
3	27/11/2008	20/10/2008 0:00:00	NULL	NewAddress1	NewCity1	NewZipC	NewCountry1

Figure 9.4   The structure of an `EntityDataReader` record returned by listing 9.8

In terms of query results, what's their format in the data reader? Are the results shaped like the database query, or are they formatted like classes? The answer is two-fold. The data is shaped like classes, but it's held in a generic structure like the `DbDataRecord` instead of a typed object.

This has two effects. First, when the data is retrieved from the database, the Entity Client uses the projection, if present, or queries the EDM to understand how the data should be returned to the code. Figure 9.4 illustrates how the data is organized in logical, not in database, format.

Second, although you work with a data reader, you aren't connected to the database. The underlying ADO.NET provider data reader that contained the data pulled off by the query has already been processed by the Entity Client. This may seem unusual if you're accustomed to ADO.NET development.

Now you know how the data is shaped, but how do you access it? When the column holds a scalar value, you get the value by name or index; but when the column contains a complex property, you have to cast it to `DbDataRecord` and then access its scalar columns. In the case shown in figure 9.4, casting the ShippingAddress columns to `DbDataRecord` gives you access to the inner columns.

> **NOTE**   Columns inside the inner `DbDataRecord` must be accessed sequentially too.

Wouldn't it be good if you could transform a `DbDataReader` into objects? This would make your code easier to understand. Well, thanks to the `ObjectContext` class's `Translate` method, this is possible.

TRANSFORMING A DBDATAREADER INTO OBJECTS

Working with a `DbDataReader` isn't type safe and is extremely error prone. Working with objects is far more appealing. Thanks to the `ObjectContext` class's `Translate` method, you can transform a `DbDataReader` into a list of objects in a single line of code. This method uses the same materialization process used by the `ObjectContext`'s `ExecuteStoreQuery` method: it sets properties by comparing their names with the columns in the reader.

The `Translate` method accepts a generic parameter representing the object that's materialized and the `DbDataReader` instance, as shown in the following listing.

Listing 9.9   Materializing order details

C#
```
using (var conn = new EntityConnection(Parameters.ConnectionString))
{
  using (var comm = new EntityCommand("SELECT value o
➥    FROM OrderITEntities.OrderDetails AS o", conn))
```

```
    {
        conn.Open();
        var reader = comm.ExecuteReader(CommandBehavior.SequentialAccess);
        using (var ctx = new OrderITEntities())
        {
            var result = ctx.Translate<OrderDetail>(reader);

            foreach(var item in result)
            {
                ...
            }
        }
    }
}
```

Invokes
Translate
❶ method

VB

```
Using conn = New EntityConnection(Parameters.ConnectionString)
    Using comm = New EntityCommand("SELECT value o FROM
➥       OrderITEntities.OrderDetails AS o", conn)

        conn.Open()
        Dim reader = comm.ExecuteReader(CommandBehavior.SequentialAccess)
        Using ctx = New OrderITEntities()
            Dim result = ctx.Translate(Of OrderDetail)(reader)

            For Each item In result
                ...
            Next
        End Using
    End Using
End Using
```

Invokes
Translate
❶ method

What's good about Translate is that it accepts a DbDataReader ❶. Because DbData-Reader is the base class for all ADO.NET data readers, you can use this method to materialize data readers from queries made through any ADO.NET provider (SQL Server, OLE DB, and so on). Furthermore, Translate isn't bound to the EDM, so it can materialize any CLR object. The only rule is that *all* properties must have a counterpart in the data reader.

What's bad about Translate is that because it uses the same materialization mechanism used by ExecuteStoreQuery, it suffers from the same limitations.

So far, you've used the Entity Client to query the database. In almost all cases, this is how you'll use this layer. But occasionally, you may need to execute a Create, Update, Delete (CUD) operation that you can't or don't want to perform using the context. In that situation, the Entity Client is the only way to go.

9.9.4   *Going beyond querying with Entity Client*

Often there are scenarios where it's wiser to adopt a manual solution, even if you could use Entity Framework. A typical example is when you need to perform a bulk operation. Suppose that in OrderIT you wanted to increase the price of all products by 5 percent.

If you handle this requirement the Entity Framework way, you'll have to retrieve the all products, modify their prices, and send the updates back to the database. If you have 100 products, you'll have to launch 101 commands: 1 for retrieval and 100 for the updates. Awful.

You can avoid this waste of resources by using a stored procedure that performs an update. You'll learn exactly how to perform such a task in the next chapter, which discusses stored procedures; the point here is that you can invoke such a stored procedure using the Entity Client.

The method that allows you to invoke stored procedures is `EntityCommand`'s `ExecuteNonQuery`. To use this method, you set the `CommandType` property of the command to `CommandType.StoredProcedure` and set the command text to the name of the stored procedure. Naturally, everything must be mapped in the EDM, but you'll see more about that in the next chapter.

Entity SQL vs. LINQ to Entities

At first glance, there's no comparison between Entity SQL and LINQ to Entities. Why use the string-based approach of Entity SQL when you can have the autocompletion, IntelliSense, and compile-time checking features of LINQ to Entities? It's a common question. Throughout the chapter, you've seen many situations where the Entity SQL syntax is ugly and awkward compared with the LINQ to Entities syntax.

But there are cases where Entity SQL is the only or the most reasonable way to achieve something. The most noticeable of Entity SQL's benefits is the dynamicity introduced by the query-builder methods. They simplify query composition for scenarios where the fields to be used are retrieved at runtime.

Entity SQL is also sometimes cleaner than LINQ to Entities. When a query becomes complex, the LINQ to Entities syntax grows ungracefully, keeping readability low. If you're accustomed to the SQL language, the SQL-like syntax of Entity SQL can help in keeping the query more comprehensible for developers.

In the end, we suggestion you use LINQ to Entities to write most of your queries. When things become too complex, query-builder methods should be your second choice. When the situation is extreme, you can resort to using Entity SQL.

9.10 Summary

In this chapter, you have seen the full querying potential of Entity SQL. You're now aware of all the querying mechanisms of Entity Framework. The only part you haven't learned about yet is the use of database functions in Entity SQL—that's a subject we'll cover in chapter 11.

After reading this chapter, you should understand how to use Entity SQL for projecting, grouping, filtering, and sorting data, and to perform other typical query-related tasks. You have even learned how to simplify the generation of Entity SQL queries by using query-builder methods. We also covered the subject of combining LINQ to Entities queries and query-builder methods to further ease query composition at runtime. You also learned about possible security breaches, and how to mitigate the problem by using parameters.

In the last part of the chapter, you learned how to use the Entity Client data provider to execute queries on a layer closer to the database and to process the results as generic objects and not as typed ones.

Now it's time to investigate how Entity Framework deals with stored procedures. There's a lot to learn about this subject, because you can both query and update data, and many scenarios aren't particularly obvious.

Working with
stored procedures

This chapter covers

- Mapping stored procedures in the EDM
- Retrieving data using stored procedures
- Embedding SQL commands in the EDM
- Updating data using stored procedures

Now that you've mastered Entity SQL, we can move forward and take a closer look at another advanced feature of Entity Framework: the use of stored procedures.

Because LINQ to Entities makes it so easy to write queries, leaving the burden of creating SQL code to the framework, you may think that stored procedures are no longer needed. From a developer's point of view, writing queries against the domain model with LINQ to Entities is more natural than writing a stored procedure that returns raw data. But there is another side to this coin: the DBA.

Often, DBAs want full control over the commands that are executed against the database. Furthermore, they want only authorized users to have read and write permissions on the tables, views, and so on. A well-defined set of stored procedures gives the DBA this control over the database and guarantees that the SQL is highly optimized.

Another situation where stored procedures are useful is when you want to put some logic in them. In OrderIT, when an order is placed, you have to update the quantity of in-stock products by subtracting the items sold. A stored procedure is the ideal place to put such logic.

The first half of this chapter discusses stored procedures that read data. You may encounter several different situations when using such stored procedures, and each one deserves attention. We'll cover this topic in great detail. After that, we'll look at how to use stored procedures to persist data instead of using dynamically generated SQL.

Before digging into querying with stored procedures, let's start with the basics: how to make stored procedures available to Entity Framework.

10.1   *Mapping stored procedures*

Entity Framework doesn't allow a stored procedure to be queried until it's mapped in the EDM. As usual, this is a three-step affair: import the stored procedure into the storage schema, create its counterpart in the conceptual schema, and finally map everything in the MSL.

The designer is powerful enough to let you perform all these operations graphically without touching the EDMX file manually. But you'll learn as you read this chapter that you need a deep knowledge of the EDM to use its stored procedure–related features. Such knowledge is necessary because the designer doesn't cover all EDM capabilities; to use specific features, you'll have to manually modify the EDMX file.

In this section, we'll map the following stored procedure, which returns all the details of an order, given its ID:

```
CREATE PROCEDURE GetOrderDetails
  @OrderId as int
As
SELECT OrderDetailId, Quantity, UnitPrice, Discount, ProductId, OrderId
  FROM OrderDetail
 WHERE OrderId = @OrderId
```

Let's see how to make it available to the code. You'll use the designer to accomplish this task. When that's done, you'll see how the steps made using the designer modify the EDMX file.

10.1.1   *Importing a stored procedure using the designer*

The designer doesn't allow you to write stored procedures and bring them into the database. That means it doesn't matter whether you opt for the model-first or database-first approach; you always have to create your stored procedures in the database and later import them into the EDM.

Here you'll import the stored procedure mentioned at the end of the previous section into the EDM, but these general steps can be used to import any stored procedure. Follow these steps:

1 Right-click the designer, and select the Update Model from Database option.

2 In the wizard, expand the Stored Procedures node, and check the `GetOrderDetails` stored procedure, as shown in figure 10.1.

3 Click Finish to import the stored procedure.

4 In the Model Browser, open the `OrderITModel.Store` node, open its Stored Procedures child folder, and right-click GetOrderDetails, as shown in figure 10.2. In the context menu, select Add Function Import.

5 In the Returns a Collection Of section of the wizard, click the Entities radio button and select the `OrderDetail` entity from the drop-down list, as shown in figure 10.3.

Figure 10.1 The `GetOrderDetails` stored procedure in the wizard

Figure 10.2
The `GetOrderDetails` stored procedure in the Model Browser window

Now the EDM contains all the information needed to invoke the stored procedure. In the Model Browser window (shown in figure 10.4) you can see that the stored procedure has been imported into the conceptual side of the EDM.

That was easy—with a bunch of clicks, everything is ready.

But what happened under the covers? What does the EDM look like now that the stored procedure has been imported and mapped? We'll look at that next.

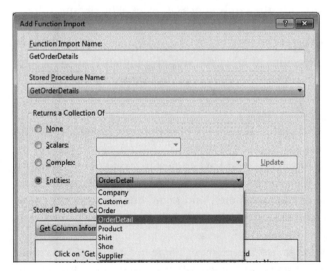

Figure 10.3 The wizard makes the stored procedure available on the conceptual side and maps its result to the `OrderDetail` class.

Figure 10.4 Once imported, the `GetOrderDetails` stored procedure is visible in the Model.

10.1.2 *Importing stored procedures manually*

The wizard steps in the previous section can be performed manually by modifying the EDM. As you'll discover, it's not a difficult task. There are three main steps:

1 Declare the stored procedure in the storage schema.
2 Declare the function in the conceptual schema (so that it becomes available to the code).
3 Create the mapping between the stored procedure in the storage schema and the function in the conceptual schema.

We'll look at these steps in turn.

DEFINING A STORED PROCEDURE IN THE STORAGE SCHEMA

The first EDM schema involved is the storage schema. Here you define the shape of the stored procedure via the `Function` node inside the `Schema` element, as in the next snippet:

```
<Function Name="GetOrderDetails" IsComposable="False"
  ParameterTypeSemantics="AllowImplicitConversion" Schema="dbo">
  <Parameter Name="OrderId" Type="int" Mode="In" />
</Function>
```

The `Name` attribute contains the logical name of the function inside the EDM, and `StoreFunctionName` specifies the name of the stored procedure in the database. If `StoreFunctionName` isn't specified, `Name` must be set to the name of the stored procedure. The ability to specify a name that is different from the stored procedure name turns out to be useful when procedures have meaningless names and you want to use more friendly ones.

The `ParameterTypeSemantics` attribute is an enumeration that specifies how the .NET parameter types are converted to the equivalent SQL types. The default value is `AllowImplicitConversion`, which instructs the runtime to take care of the conversion so you don't have to worry about it.

The `IsComposable` attribute specifies whether the stored command can be used to create other commands or not. Its default value is `true`, but for stored procedures it must be set to `false` because stored procedures can't be queried on the server. (You can't write `SELECT * FROM StoredProcName`.)

Finally, the `Schema` attribute identifies the owner of the stored procedure (it has nothing to do with EDM schemas).

If the stored procedure has parameters, you have to nest a `Parameter` element for each one. In this element, the `Name` attribute contains the name of the parameter, `Type` specifies the *database* type of the parameter, and `Mode` identifies the direction. `Mode` is an enumeration that contains one of three values: `In` (input-only), `Out` (output-only), and `InOut` (input-output).

The preceding attributes of the `Parameter` element are mandatory, but `Parameter` has other optional attributes. The first is `MaxLength`, which is used when the parameter is a string and you need to specify the maximum length for its value. If you have decimal parameters, you can also use `Precision` and `Scale` to specify how much data the number can contain.

At this point, you've imported the stored procedure in the EDM. This is the same thing you achieve when completing step 3 of the wizard we discussed in section 10.1.1. Now you need to declare the function in the conceptual schema so that it becomes available to the code.

DEFINING A FUNCTION IN THE CONCEPTUAL SCHEMA

In the conceptual schema, a stored procedure is referred to as *function*. When you create a function in the conceptual schema, you're actually importing a stored procedure from the storage schema. This is why, in the conceptual layer, the element responsible for declaring the function is called `FunctionImport` and is nested in the `Entity-Container` node.

In the next snippet, you can see that not only does `FunctionImport` declare the function, it also describes the function's parameters and results:

```
<FunctionImport Name="GetOrderDetails" EntitySet="OrderDetails"
  ReturnType="Collection(OrderITModel.OrderDetail)">
  <Parameter Name="orderid" Mode="In" Type="Int32" />
</FunctionImport>
```

The `Name` attribute represents the name of the function in the conceptual layer and is the only mandatory attribute. This name is decoupled from the stored-procedure name in the storage schema because it's the mapping schema that binds the function to the stored procedure. `EntitySet` specifies the entity set returned by the stored procedure, and `ReturnType` declares the type returned. The `Collection` keyword is mandatory because even if the function returns only a single record, it's included in a list.

> **NOTE** When the function returns an entity, specifying the entity set and the type may seem to be a duplication. But when you deal with objects that are part of an inheritance hierarchy, you may have different types for the same entity set, so you have to specify both to clearly identify the result of the function. What's more, in situations where you don't retrieve an entity but a custom type, you can omit `EntitySet` and declare only the `ReturnType` attribute.

Not all stored procedures are used for querying—many are used to update data in tables and don't return any results. In this case, you don't include the `EntitySet` and `ReturnType` attributes.

The `Parameter` element is used to specify function parameters (which match the stored-procedure parameters). Its attributes are exactly the same as those for the `Parameter` element in the storage file, with the only difference being that here `Type` is expressed as a .NET type: `Int32`, `String`, `DateTime`, and so on.

The last step is creating the mapping between the stored procedure in the storage schema and the function in the conceptual schema. Not surprisingly, this is done in the mapping file.

BINDING A STORED PROCEDURE TO A FUNCTION IN THE MAPPING SCHEMA

Mapping a stored procedure to a function is trivial. The following mapping fragment shows that you just need to add a `FunctionMapping` element inside `EntityContainer-Mapping`:

```
<FunctionImportMapping FunctionImportName="GetOrderDetails"
  FunctionName="OrderITModel.Store.GetOrderDetails" />
```

`FunctionImportName` is the name of the function in the conceptual schema, and `FunctionName` is the name of the stored procedure in the storage schema.

   The EDM is now ready. It contains everything needed to invoke the stored procedure on the database and have the results returned as objects. It's time to talk about the code.

10.2 *Returning data with stored procedures*

Retrieving data with stored procedures is a common task in any data-centric application. What's different when using an O/RM tool is that the results must be poured into objects that are then returned to the application. What's more, the results of the stored procedures are just resultsets with columns, and these columns may be anything. The columns may match the properties of an entity, they may come from multiple joined tables, they may contain a single scalar value, or they can be anything else.

   We'll discuss the following scenarios in the upcoming sections:

- Stored procedures whose columns match the properties of an entity
- Stored procedures whose columns don't match the properties an entity
- Stored procedures that return scalar values
- Stored procedures that return objects in an inheritance hierarchy

   NOTE Stored procedures can return output parameters too. You must keep this in mind in any of the preceding scenarios.

Each of these cases has a different solution and has its particular needs. The first three cases are the easiest to deal with. Thanks to the designer's capabilities, you can handle them visually without getting your hands dirty in the EDM. The fourth case is a little more complicated, but it's not too difficult.

   Let's start with the first and analyze how a stored procedure's results become an entity.

10.2.1 *Stored procedures whose results match an entity*

Executing a stored procedure is pretty easy. Once it's imported into the conceptual side of the EDM, you can use the `ExecuteFunction<T>` method, whose signature is shown in the following snippet:

C#
```
public ObjectResult<TElement> ExecuteFunction<TElement>(string functionName,
    MergeOption mergeOption, params ObjectParameter[] parameters)
```

VB
```
Public Function ExecuteFunction(Of TElement) _
  (ByVal functionName As String, ByVal mergeOption As MergeOption, _
  ByVal ParamArray parameters As ObjectParameter()) _
  As ObjectResult(Of TElement)
parameters)
```

The generic parameter is the class returned by the query. The arguments represent the function name as imported in the CSDL, the MergeOption for the returned entities, and the parameters passed to the stored procedure.

The following snippet shows how to use the ExecuteFunction<T> method to invoke the stored procedure:

C#
```
ObjectParameter orderidParameter = new ObjectParameter("orderid", 1);
var result = ctx.ExecuteFunction<OrderDetail>("GetOrderDetails",
  orderidParameter);
```

VB
```
Dim orderidParameter As New ObjectParameter("orderid", 1)
Dim result = ctx.ExecuteFunction(Of OrderDetail)("GetOrderDetails",
    orderidParameter)
```

The POCO template that generates code automatically generates a convenient wrapper method for each function. The stored-procedure parameters are exposed as method arguments, so the invocation code is simplified. Due to this simplicity, we strongly recommend using these autogenerated methods, as shown in listing 10.1, instead of directly invoking ExecuteFunction<T>.

> **Listing 10.1 The autogenerated method to invoke a stored procedure**

C#
```
public virtual ObjectResult<OrderDetail> GetOrderDetails(
  Nullable<int> orderid)
{
  ObjectParameter orderidParameter;
  if (orderid.HasValue)
    orderidParameter = new ObjectParameter("orderid", orderid);
  else
    orderidParameter = new ObjectParameter("orderid", typeof(int));

  return base.ExecuteFunction<OrderDetail>("GetOrderDetails",
    orderidParameter);
}
```

VB
```
Public Overridable Function GetOrderDetails _
  (ByVal orderid As Nullable(Of Integer)) As ObjectResult(Of OrderDetail)
  Dim orderidParameter As ObjectParameter
  If orderid.HasValue Then
    orderidParameter = New ObjectParameter("orderid", orderid)
  Else
    orderidParameter = New ObjectParameter("orderid", GetType(Integer))
  End If
```

```
Return MyBase.ExecuteFunction(Of OrderDetail)
   ("GetOrderDetails", orderidParameter)
End Function
```

Notice that parameters are passed as *nullable*. The database allows you to pass a `null` value to any stored procedure parameter, so this possibility is left open in the code.

The last piece of background you need to know is how the result of the stored procedure becomes an entity. In the world of mapping, you would expect the stored procedure result to be explicitly mapped against a class. Well, it's not like that.

HOW A STORED PROCEDURE'S RESULTS ARE MAPPED TO A CLASS

An object is materialized from each row of the result based on the column and scalar property names. It's *almost* the same materialization mechanism used by the `Object-Context` class's `ExecuteStoreQuery<T>` method.

> **NOTE** We said *almost* because later you'll see that you can slightly tweak the materialization process using the EDM.

Let's look at the `GetOrderDetails` stored procedure. The `OrderDetail` entity that the `GetOrderDetails` stored procedure result is mapped to has the following scalar properties: `OrderDetailId`, `Quantity`, `UnitPrice`, `Discount`, `ProductId`, and `OrderId`. To map the stored procedure result to the entity, the stored procedure *must* return a resultset containing the columns OrderDetailId, Quantity, UnitPrice, Discount, ProductId, and OrderId. The order in which they're returned isn't important, but the names of the class properties and the resultset column names must match exactly or you'll get an `InvalidOperationException` with the message, "The data reader is incompatible with the specified 'TypeName'. A member of the type, 'PropertyName', does not have a corresponding column in the data reader with the same name."

Figure 10.5 illustrates how the mapping works.

Navigation properties are ignored by the materialization process. They are handled by class code. If they aren't initialized within the constructor, they're null; otherwise they're set to whatever value the constructor gives them. This is true even if the foreign-key properties are set.

If the query returns more columns than there are entity properties, the extra columns are ignored. If the query doesn't return enough columns to match the entity

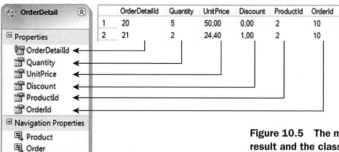

Figure 10.5   The mapping between the function result and the class is based on the match between column and property names.

properties, the materialization process fails, and you get the runtime exception mentioned earlier.

The example shown here is the easiest case: the stored procedure results line up perfectly with an entity. In the next section, we'll discuss how to handle resultsets that don't match up with an entity.

10.2.2 *Stored procedures whose results don't match an entity*

When a stored procedure's results don't match up with an entity, you can resort to *complex types*. You can create a new complex type in the designer (as you learned how to do in chapter 2) and map the stored procedure's results to it. The materialization mechanism is the same as is used for entities; there are no differences.

There are three possible situations where the stored procedure's results don't align with an entity:

- The resultset is an aggregation or contains columns that don't match with any entity.
- The resultset columns contain data that match up with an entity but that have different names.
- The entity has complex properties.

Let's start with the first case, where the result of the stored procedure isn't an entity but is something else: a set of columns plus other aggregated columns, a set of columns that partially fill an entity, or perhaps a set of columns coming from a query that joins multiple tables and that don't fit any entity.

STORED PROCEDURES WHOSE RESULTS HAVE COLUMNS
THAT DON'T LINE UP WITH AN ENTITY

In OrderIT, the `GetTopOrders` stored procedure returns the top ten orders sorted by their total amount. Its code is as follows:

```
CREATE PROCEDURE GetTopOrders
AS
   SELECT TOP 10 c.Name, o.OrderId, o.OrderDate,
     SUM(od.UnitPrice * (Quantity - Discount)) as Total
   FROM [order] o
   JOIN company c ON o.CustomerId = c.CompanyId
   JOIN orderdetail od ON od.OrderId = o.OrderId
   GROUP BY c.Name, o.OrderId, o.OrderDate
   ORDER BY Total DESC
```

This stored procedure returns a resultset that doesn't match the `Order` class or any other entity in OrderIT. You can see the result in figure 10.6.

In figure 10.7, you can see a class that matches the result of the stored procedure.

There's no entity like this in OrderIT, so how do you map the result of the stored procedure, and to which class? The solution is simple: you map the results to an ad hoc class; more precisely, you map the results to a complex type (the `TopOrder` class in this case).

Name	OrderId	OrderDate	Total
Bill Clay	24	5/27/2010	270.2000
Bill Clay	11	11/27/2008	255.0000
Bill Clay	17	11/27/2008	252.0000
Michael Douglas	32	8/10/2009	201.0000
Bill Clay	13	11/27/2008	152.0000
Bill Clay	29	8/9/2009	135.0000
Michael Douglas	12	11/27/2008	100.0000
Michael Douglas	31	8/9/2009	100.0000
Bill Clay	30	8/9/2009	90.0000

Figure 10.7   The class that matches the results of the `GetTopOrders` stored procedure

Figure 10.6   The result of the `GetTopOrders` stored procedure

> **NOTE**   Because the results of the stored procedure are specified in the EDM, the class must be in the EDM. You can't use a class that isn't in the EDM.

Once again, the designer comes to the rescue by simplifying the plumbing. After you've imported the stored procedure from the database, you can import it into the conceptual side by using the form you saw earlier in figure 10.3.

What's different in this case is that instead of mapping the result to an entity, you map it to a complex type. If there are no complex types that match the stored procedure's results, you can let the form inspect the stored procedure and create the complex type for you. Your productivity will increase to an incredible extent thanks to this feature.

Follow these steps to import the stored procedure into the conceptual schema of the EDM:

1 Right-click the designer, and choose Update Model from Database.

2 In the wizard (shown earlier in figure 10.1), expand the Stored Procedures node, and check the `GetTopOrders` item.

3 Click Finish to import the stored procedure.

4 In the Model Browser, open the `OrderITModel.Store` node, open its Stored Procedures child, and then right-click the `GetTopOrders` item. In the context menu, select the Add Function Import option.

5 In the Returns a Collection Of section of the Add Function Import dialog box, click the Complex radio button.

6 In the Stored Procedure Column Information section of the dialog box, click the Get Column Information button. The stored procedure's results structure will be displayed in a grid, as shown in figure 10.8.

7 Click the Create New Complex Type button to create a complex type from the results' structure.

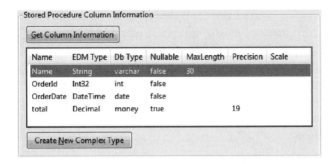

Figure 10.8 The structure of the stored procedure's results

8 A new item is added in the Complex drop-down list, and you can change its name. By default, the name follows the pattern *FunctionName_Result,* but you can change the name to whatever you want. (We opted for `TopOrder`.)

9 Click OK to finish the import.

10 Right-click the POCO templates that generate the context and entities' code. Click the Run Custom Tool item in the context menu that pops up. At the end of the process, you'll have the `GetTopOrders` method (which invokes the stored procedure) in the context class, and the `TopOrder` class that the result of the stored procedure is mapped to.

It's that easy. Now you have the EDM, the code to invoke the stored procedure in the context, and the code for the class that holds the results. All that with just a few clicks.

Invoking the stored procedure is simple. You can call the `ExecuteFunction<T>` method directly (not recommended):

C#

```
var orders = ctx.ExecuteFunction<TopOrder>("GetTopOrders");
```

VB

```
Dim orders = ctx.ExecuteFunction(Of TopOrder)("GetTopOrders")
```

Or you can use the autogenerated `GetTopOrders` context method (recommended):

C#

```
var orders = ctx.GetTopOrders();
```

VB

```
Dim orders = ctx.GetTopOrders()
```

Naturally, stored procedures are mutable, meaning that you can add, remove, and rename columns in the results. In such cases, you need to realign the complex type with these changes. Once again, the designer lets you do this visually by following these steps:

1 In the Model Browser window, expand the `OrderITModel` > `Entity Container`: `OrderITEntities` > `FunctionImport` nodes, and double-click the `GetTopOrders` item.

2   Click the Update button next to the Complex drop-down list. Doing so triggers the stored procedure inspection and automatically updates the complex type structure.

3   In the Explorer Solution window, right-click the template that generates code for entities, and select Run Custom Tool to regenerate the class's code. The class that the stored procedure maps to is updated to reflect the changes in the stored-procedure results). There's no need to update the context because its code doesn't change.

Again, the designer spares you a lot of work. It's fantastic being able to use stored procedures and simply configure everything from the designer.

Another scenario where the stored procedure's results don't fit an entity is when the results don't contain all of an entity's data. For instance, a stored procedure may return the ID and the name of all customers, and ignore all other properties. In this case, one possible way to go would be to modify the stored procedure to return all columns. This approach has two problems: you may not be able to modify the stored procedure, and returning unused data is a waste of resources. Once again, complex types are the best solution.

So far, we've assumed that the stored procedure's column names match the properties of the entity. But sometimes entity properties are named differently from database columns, or the stored procedure may rename the result columns for some reason.

STORED PROCEDURES WHOSE RESULT COLUMNS' NAMES ARE DIFFERENT FROM ENTITY PROPERTIES

A typical case where column names in a stored procedure's results differ from entity property names is when you have a legacy database with meaningless table and column names. For example, some legacy databases still have table and column names that are limited to eight characters. Due to this limitation, columns names are almost or totally meaningless (such as USISAPPM standing for USer IS APPlication Manager). In such a situation, it's best to rename all the classes and properties in the model so they're clearer for developers.

When a stored procedure is run, and the column names in the results don't match property names in the entity, the materialization fails. To solve this problem, you can use the FunctionImportMapping section in the mapping schema to manually specify how a column maps to a property. Once again, the designer spares you from the manual work by adding a new window to visually perform this task.

In the following steps, you'll modify the GetOrderDetails stored procedure to return a result with column names that don't line up with the OrderDetail entity, and you'll see how to make the mapping work:

1   Modify the GetOrderDetails stored procedure by changing the name of the Quantity column as shown in the following code:

```
SELECT orderDetailId, Quantity as q, UnitPrice, Discount, orderid
  FROM orderdetail
 WHERE orderid = @orderid
```

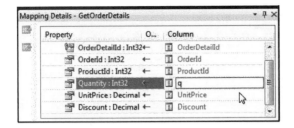

Figure 10.9   Mapping a column to a property with a different name

2   In the Model Browser window, expand the `OrderITModel` > `Entity Container:` `OrderITEntities` > `FunctionImport` nodes, right-click the `GetOrderDetails` item, and select the Function Import Mapping item.

3   In the mapping window, the properties are displayed on the left and the columns on the right. Change the name of the Quantity column to q (as shown in figure 10.9), and you're done.

It's that easy. This approach is better than using a complex type just because a property name doesn't match, isn't it?

Before moving on to the next subject, take a look at this snippet to see what the EDM's MSL schema looks like after this modification:

```
<FunctionImportMapping FunctionImportName="GetOrderDetails"
  FunctionName="OrderITModel.Store.GetOrderDetails" >
  <ResultMapping>
    <EntityTypeMapping TypeName="OrderITModel.OrderDetail">
      <ScalarProperty Name="Quantity" ColumnName="q" />
    </EntityTypeMapping>
  </ResultMapping>
</FunctionImportMapping>
```

This code is saying that the return type is `OrderDetail` and that the property `Quantity` maps to the column q. Only the differently named columns must be included; by default, the other ones are matched by name. What's good is that only the mapping schema changes; the conceptual and storage schemas are untouched.

We've now talked about entities with scalar and navigation properties. The situation gets more challenging when complex properties come into play.

STORED PROCEDURES THAT RETURN RESULTSETS OF AN ENTITY WITH COMPLEX TYPES
Mapping a function to an entity or a complex type with a complex property is tricky. The flat nature of a stored procedure's results and the complex nature of objects make the materialization impossible, as you see in figure 10.10.

The only way to go is to use a *defining query*, but as you'll discover in chapter 11, this requires the database to be adapted and that's not always possible.

Stored procedures, and queries in general, return not only entities, but also scalar values. Using a class to contain a single value is pointless; other approaches are preferable.

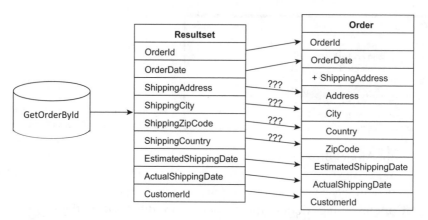

Figure 10.10   Mapping function result to a class with a complex property is impossible due to the names mismatch.

10.2.3   *Stored procedures that return scalar values*

In OrderIT, the GetTotalOrdersAmount stored procedure returns the amount of all orders placed. This stored procedure returns a single decimal value; neither complex types nor entities are involved:

```
CREATE PROCEDURE GetTotalOrdersAmount
AS
   SELECT sum(Quantity * (UnitPrice - Discount))
   FROM orderdetail
```

Let's see how to import this stored procedure in the EDM and how to use it.

With the designer you import the stored procedure from the database and then import it in the conceptual side. In the wizard form (shown in figure 10.11), select the Scalar option, and select the Decimal type from the drop-down list.

Finally, you need to update the context code using the POCO template, and you're done.

The autogenerated method in the context returns an ObjectResult<Int32> object. Because it implements the IEnumerable<T> interface, and you already know that only one item is returned, you can call the LINQ First method to retrieve the value. Remember that everything is generated as nullable; the result is no exception, as the following code demonstrates:

C#

```
decimal? amount = ctx.GetTotalOrdersAmount().First();
```

VB

```
Nullable(Of Decimal) amount = ctx.GetTotalOrdersAmount().First()
```

If, instead of using the designer, you want to manually modify the EDM, you'll have to declare the stored procedure in the SSDL and map it to the MSL as you've seen before. In the CSDL, the situation is slightly different.

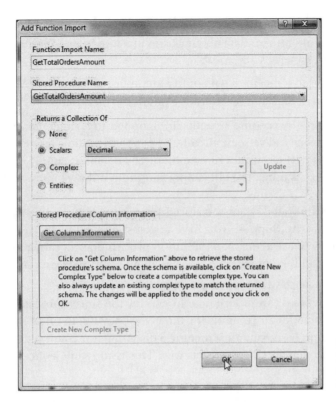

Figure 10.11 The wizard imports into the conceptual schema a stored procedure that returns a single decimal value.

First of all, because you aren't retrieving an entity, you don't have an entity set, and consequently an entity, to associate the result to. This means the `EntitySet` attribute in the `FunctionImport` element isn't needed.

Second, even if the function returns a single value, Entity Framework can't know in advance whether the stored procedure returns more than one result, so it's always mapped as a collection. This is clearly indicated by the use of the `Collection` keyword in the next mapping fragment:

```
<FunctionImport Name="GetTotalOrdersAmount"
  ReturnType="Collection(Decimal)" />
```

Naturally, it's possible that a stored procedure returns a collection of scalar values. For instance, you may need to retrieve a list of order IDs. In that case, you can simply loop over the results of the function, and you're finished.

So far, we haven't talked about polymorphic stored procedures. You know that you can query a hierarchy using LINQ to Entities and Entity SQL to obtain only a specified type or an entire hierarchy, regardless of the mapping strategy you choose. Stored procedures allow you to do this too, but the implementation is a bit more complex.

10.2.4 *Stored procedures that return an inheritance hierarchy*

When the stored procedure returns data about classes involved in an inheritance hierarchy, two very different scenarios are possible:

- The resultset maps to a specified type of the hierarchy.
- The resultset returns data about different types in the hierarchy.

In the first case, the stored procedure's results are mapped to a single entity. That's not any different from what you've seen already. The materialization process doesn't care whether the class is part of an inheritance hierarchy or not. It simply creates an instance and populates it. As usual, the only important thing is that column and property names match.

Things get more complicated when the stored procedure returns data about different types in the hierarchy. Suppose you have a stored procedure that returns all customers and suppliers. Because the materialization process doesn't care about mapping information, how can it know whether a row is about a customer or a supplier?

RETURNING A HIERARCHY MAPPED WITH THE TPH STRATEGY

To map a result to all types of an inheritance hierarchy, the stored procedure must return a resultset that includes all columns for the involved types. Because the resultset is mapped on a column basis, you must include a discriminator column that identifies which class must be generated from each row. This is the same concept you've seen for the TPH mapping strategy.

> **NOTE**   For this section, we'll assume that there aren't any complex properties but just scalar ones; otherwise, the following code won't work. This section just explains how to use stored procedures to query an inheritance graph persisted with TPH. In chapter 11, you'll see how to make complex properties, inheritance, and stored procedures work together.

Let's start by analyzing the customer/supplier scenario. In the model, the `Get-Companies` stored procedure returns all the companies without worrying whether they're customers or suppliers. In this situation, the return type can't be `Customer` or `Supplier` but must be `Company`.

`Company` is abstract,, and mapping the stored procedure as described in the preceding paragraph generates an exception at runtime. What's worse, because the use of stored procedures bypasses any inheritance configuration, if `Company` isn't abstract, all the objects returned by the invocation of the stored procedure are of `Company` type, even if the result contains rows about customers and suppliers.

To solve the previous problems, you still use `Company` as the return type, but you also have to manipulate the mapping file of the EDM, specifying a discriminator column and what concrete type corresponds to each value of that column.

The node responsible for this configuration is `FunctionImportMapping`. Inside it, you nest a `ResultMapping` node containing as many `EntityTypeMapping` elements as there are possible return types. Each `EntityTypeMapping` element specifies the full name of the mapped type, and inside that you add a `Condition` node for each column of the function that acts as a discriminator. The result of this configuration is shown here.

Listing 10.2 Mapping resultset rows to types with a discriminator

```
<FunctionImportMapping FunctionImportName="GetCompanies"
  FunctionName="OrderITModel.Store.GetCompanies">
  <ResultMapping>
    <EntityTypeMapping TypeName="OrderITModel.Supplier">
      <Condition ColumnName="Type" Value="S"/>
    </EntityTypeMapping>
    <EntityTypeMapping TypeName="OrderITModel.Customer">
      <Condition ColumnName="Type" Value="C"/>
    </EntityTypeMapping>
  </ResultMapping>
</FunctionImportMapping>
```

The conceptual file and storage file don't specify any additional information other than what you've seen previously.

Finally, here's the code for the stored procedure. As you can see, it's trivial:

```
CREATE PROCEDURE GetTotalOrdersAmount
AS
SELECT * FROM company
```

Now you can invoke the stored procedure. Thanks to the inheritance mapping settings and the correct names of the columns, everything works fine.

> **NOTE** We haven't used the designer here because it doesn't support this feature. You have to change the EDM manually.

Using stored procedures to retrieve entities mapped using the TPH strategy is pretty easy. Mapping classes using a discriminator is something you're familiar with. But what about the TPT approach? You don't have a discriminator in this situation, so how do you map inheritance?

RETURNING A HIERARCHY MAPPED WITH THE TPT STRATEGY

The product scenario uses the TPT approach. Even if the data organization is different from the TPH strategy, the way inheritance is mapped with stored procedures doesn't change at all. You still have to use a discriminator. You can't rely on the relationship between tables, because here you're dealing only with the resultset. This is why the only thing that changes in the TPT approach is the stored procedure code—it must perform the join between the tables and create a discriminator column on the fly.

In OrderIT, the `GetProducts` stored procedure returns all the products in the database. As you'll see, this stored procedure is more complicated than you may think, because there are columns with the same names in different tables, and they must be handled carefully, as the following stored procedure demonstrates:

```
ALTER PROCEDURE GetProducts
AS
  SELECT p.*, isnull(sho.Color, shi.color) Color,
    isnull(sho.Size, shi.Size) Size,
    isnull(sho.Gender, shi.gender) Gender,
    sho.Sport, shi.SleeveType, shi.Material,
    case isnull(sho.gender, '0')
      when '0' then 'SHIRT' else 'SHOE' end as type
  FROM Product p
  LEFT JOIN Shoes sho ON (p.ProductId = sho.ProductId)
  LEFT JOIN Shirt shi ON (p.ProductId = shi.ProductId)
```

This SQL takes the Product table and joins it to the tables that contain product-specific data. Naturally, it's a left join, so you're sure that all products are returned. Additional columns for shoes are left `null` when the row belongs to a shirt and vice versa. In addition to joining data, this query creates a column that's used in the mapping file to identify the row type: `Type`.

As you can see, there are many `ISNULL` statements in this T-SQL command. In T-SQL, `ISNULL` returns the value of the first parameter unless it's `null`. If it's `null`, the second value is returned. You do this because the Shirt and Shoe tables share the same column names. If you extract them twice, the materializer will always use the first column, ignoring the second one.

This means that if you extract shoe size and then shirt size as different columns, only the first one will be used to populate the property of both objects. If the object to be created is `Shoe`, everything works fine; but when the object is `Shirt`, it receives a `null` value, leading to exceptions or bugs due to erroneous data. Figure 10.12 illustrates this problem.

Using the `ISNULL` function allows you to have a single column that contains data for both records. This way, the value of the column will be used to populate both classes. In figure 10.13 you can see that the problem is solved.

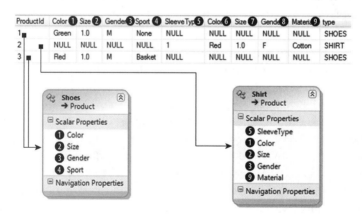

Figure 10.12 Mapping between the function result and the objects. Values in the first Color column are used to set both Shirt and Shoe entity properties. The second Color column is ignored.

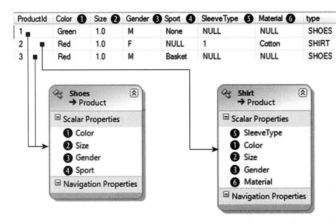

Figure 10.13 Mapping between the function result and the objects. The Color, Size, and Gender columns are used to fill properties of both classes.

The type column acts as a discriminator, letting you map the results as if they were coming from a TPH strategy. Here's the mapping code.

Listing 10.3 Mapping resultset rows to types via a discriminator with TPT hierarchies

```xml
<FunctionImportMapping FunctionImportName="GetProducts"
  FunctionName="OrderITModel.Store.GetProducts">
  <ResultMapping>
    <EntityTypeMapping TypeName="OrderITModel.Store.Shirt">
      <Condition ColumnName="Type" Value="SHIRT"/>
    </EntityTypeMapping>
    <EntityTypeMapping TypeName="OrderITModel.Store.Shoe">
      <Condition ColumnName="Type" Value="SHOES"/>
    </EntityTypeMapping>
  </ResultMapping>
</FunctionImportMapping>
```

Stored procedures return resultsets, but in some cases you may want them to return additional information. The best way to do this is to use output or input-output parameters.

10.2.5 Stored procedures with output parameters

A typical example where you need an output parameter is when creating a stored procedure that returns paged data. To build an efficient paging system, you must retrieve only the data that needs to be bound to a control (such as a grid) and the number of records to create a pager. In OrderIT, the `GetPagedOrderDetails` stored procedure retrieves the order details based on paging information and sets an output parameter with the total number of details. Its code is as follows.

Listing 10.4 Stored procedure that returns a resultset plus an output parameter

```sql
CREATE PROCEDURE GetPagedDetails
  @pageIndex int,
  @rowsPerPage int,
  @count int output
AS
```

```
BEGIN
  WITH PageRows
  AS (
    SELECT TOP(@pageIndex * @rowsPerPage)
    RowNumber = ROW_NUMBER() OVER (ORDER BY orderdetailid), *
    FROM orderdetail
  )
  SELECT *
  FROM PageRows
  WHERE RowNumber > ((@pageIndex - 1) * @rowsPerPage);

  select @count = COUNT(*) from orderdetail
END
```

Entity Framework natively supports output parameters for stored procedures. When you import a stored procedure by the designer, Entity Framework automatically inspects the stored procedure looking for output parameters and marking them in the EDM.

If you modify the EDM manually, you need to set the Mode attribute of the Parameter element to Out for output parameters or InOut for both input and output, as in the next fragment:

```
<Parameter Name="count" Type="int" Mode="Out" />
```

The context code autogenerated by the POCO template is more complicated than it may seem. So far, you've used the automatically generated methods, passing in a value for each input parameter of the function. Output parameters are a bit different. They must still be passed to the method, but as ObjectParameter objects instead of simple values. This is due to the way Entity Framework retrieves the output parameter's value after execution.

The fetching of stored procedure results is lazy. First the resultset is processed, and only after that are the output parameters retrieved. This means you can't get the output parameter values until you've fetched all the resultset records. To avoid this, the template code generates the method parameter related to the stored procedure output parameter as an object of ObjectParameter type. If you pass an out value for C# or ref for VB, you will always have an empty value because the results have not been iterated yet. The following listing contains the correct code.

Listing 10.5   Output parameters returned as ObjectParameter objects

C#
```
public ObjectResult<OrderDetail> GetPagedOrderDetails(
  int pageIndex, int rowsPerPage,                         ┐ Output parameter
  ObjectParameter parameter)                              ◁┘ as ObjectParameter
{
  return ExecuteFunction<OrderDetail>("GetPagedOrderDetails",
    new ObjectParameter("pageIndex", pageIndex),
    new ObjectParameter("rowsPerPage", rowsPerPage), parameter);
}

var par = new ObjectParameter("count", 0);
var result = ctx.GetPagedOrderDetails(pageIndex, rowsPerPage,     ┐ Result
  par).ToList();                                                 ◁┘ iteration
count = Convert.ToInt32(par.Value);            ◁— Parameter setting
```

VB

```
Public Function GetPagedOrderDetails( _
  ByVal pageIndex As Integer, ByVal rowsPerPage As Integer, _
  ByVal parameter As ObjectParameter) _                         Output parameter
  As ObjectResult(Of OrderDetail)                                as ObjectParameter

  Return ExecuteFunction(Of OrderDetail)("GetPagedOrderDetails", _
    New ObjectParameter("pageIndex", pageIndex), _
    New ObjectParameter("rowsPerPage", rowsPerPage), parameter)
End Function

Dim par = New ObjectParameter("count", 0)
Dim result = ctx.GetPagedOrderDetails(pageIndex, rowsPerPage, _     Result
  par).ToList()                                                     iteration
count = Convert.ToInt32(par.Value)        ◁— Parameter setting
```

What's bad about this approach is that the invoking code needs to know the names of the output parameters. This makes it impossible to encapsulate the logic of the function call.

An alternative is shown in the following listing. Here you iterate over the results directly into the context function, so that inside it you have both the results and the values of the parameters.

Listing 10.6   Output parameters returned as simple values

C#

```
public List<OrderDetail>  GetPagedOrderDetails      ◁—❶ Result is list
  (int pageIndex, int rowsPerPage, int count)           ◁⌐  Output parameter
{                                                       ❷ as simple value
  Dim outParam = new ObjectParameter("count", 0);
  var result = ExecuteFunction<OrderDetail>("GetPagedOrderDetails",
    new ObjectParameter("pageIndex", pageIndex),
    new ObjectParameter("rowsPerPage", rowsPerPage),     ❸ Result
      outParam).ToList();                                   iteration
  count = Convert.ToInt32(outParam.Value);        ◁⌐
  return result;                                   ❹ Parameter setting
}

var count = 0;
var result = ctx.GetPagedOrderDetails(pageIndex, rowsPerPage, out count);
```

VB

```
Public Function GetPagedOrderDetails( _
  ByVal pageIndex As Integer, ByVal rowsPerPage As Integer, _
  ByVal count As Integer)                             ◁⌐  Output parameter
  As List(Of OrderDetail)     ◁—❶ Result is list      ❷ as simple value

  Dim outParam = New ObjectParameter("count", 0)
  Dim result = ExecuteFunction(Of OrderDetail)("GetPagedOrderDetails", _
    New ObjectParameter("pageIndex", pageIndex), _
    New ObjectParameter("rowsPerPage", rowsPerPage),    ❸ Result
      outParam).ToList()                                   iteration
  count = Convert.ToInt32(outParam.Value)        ◁⌐
  Return result                                   ❹ Parameter setting
End Function
```

```
Dim count as Integer
Dim result = ctx.GetPagedOrderDetails(pageIndex, rowsPerPage, count)
```

The function result is no longer an `ObjectResult<T>` instance but a `List<T>` **❶**, because the data is fetched inside it. The method no longer accepts an `Object-Parameter` parameter but a simple value **❷**. Inside the method, you execute the function and immediately iterate its result using the `ToList` method **❸**. Finally, you set the simple output parameter value **❹**.

Remember that returning results as a `List<T>` is different from returning them as an `ObjectResult<T>`. Choose each option on a one-by-one basis.

Sometimes, instead of using output parameters, data is returned in a second resultset. Let's see what you can do in this case.

OUTPUT PARAMETERS IN A SECOND RESULTSET

If you opt for a solution where the additional data is returned as a second resultset instead of in output parameters, you must keep in mind that `ExecuteFunction<T>` doesn't support multiple resultsets. It doesn't fail if more than one resultset is returned from the stored procedure; it takes the first and ignores the others. The workaround is to use the Entity Client and its internal physical connection to manually invoke the stored procedure and iterate over its results. This goes beyond Entity Framework, so you're better off directly using ADO.NET.

Now you know everything about reading data using stored procedures. But sometimes you don't have a stored procedure, and you'd like to. If you can't create one because you don't have permissions (or for any other reason) you can create one inside the EDM.

10.3 *Embedding functions in the storage model*

Although the storage file describes the database, you can add information to it that isn't related to the real database structure. More precisely, you can create functions that don't exist in the database but that are still seen as functions by the engine. Figure 10.14 shows the flow of a storage model function's execution.

Naturally, you have to define the SQL code for such functions, and you have to do it using the database-specific SQL code (for instance, T-SQL for SQL Server or PL-SQL for Oracle).

This feature turns out to be useful when you want to optimize a query and you don't have an appropriate stored procedure. Another situation where it's useful is

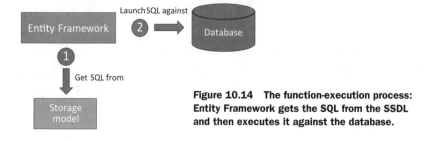

Figure 10.14 The function-execution process: Entity Framework gets the SQL from the SSDL and then executes it against the database.

when you must use a particular database feature that neither LINQ to Entities nor Entity SQL allows you to use. The power of this feature really shines when you have to update data using stored procedures; we'll cover this subject in section 10.4.

Defining a function in the storage model is similar to defining a stored procedure. The only difference is that the `Function` element has a nested `CommandText` element, inside which you put the SQL code. Should the function need any parameters, you use the `Parameter` element. (The `CommandText` element *must* be put before `Parameter` elements.) The following snippet shows the definition of a function:

```
<Function Name="GetOrderDetailsByIdUsingEmbeddedFunction"
  IsComposable="false" Schema="dbo">
  <CommandText>
    select * from [orderdetail] where orderid = @orderid
  </CommandText>
  <Parameter Mode="In" Name="orderid" Type="int"/>
</Function>
```

> **NOTE** If the SQL code contains the < or > sign, you *must* use its escaped versions: > or <. This is necessary to avoid any conflict with the XML format of the mapping files.

The conceptual and mapping schemas aren't even aware that the function is embedded in the storage schema. As a result, the declaration of the function in the CSDL, and the mapping between the function and the stored procedure in the MSL, don't change. The code generated by the POCO template and the way you use the code isn't affected either. You can invoke the function exactly as you do for stored procedures.

> **NOTE** This feature isn't supported by the Visual Studio Designer. What's worse, every time you update the model from the database, it re-creates the storage schema from scratch, and the function is lost. Despite these limitations, this feature is a great example of mapping flexibility in Entity Framework and a great example of the advantages of EDM decoupling.

The SQL embedded in the function can contain more than one command. It can contain any SQL command you need. Potentially, you could avoid writing stored procedures in the database and put all of them into the storage schema. But naturally, we wouldn't recommend this practice to our worst enemies, let alone to you.

So far, you've learned how to query data using stored procedures and storage-model functions, but that's only half of the story. Stored procedures can perform any operation on the database, including making modifications. In the next section, we'll investigate how to make Entity Framework interact with this type of stored procedure.

10.4 *Updating data with stored procedures*

Updating data using stored procedures is a common way of hiding SQL and database complexity from the code. Sometimes such complexity can be difficult to manage in code, and a stored procedure may be a good place to put the logic.

For instance, using a stored procedure is useful when an operation on one entity requires updating another entity. In OrderIT, adding an order requires updating the stock of the ordered products. You've seen how to update the number of items in stock via code, but using a stored procedure would probably have been simpler.

Sometimes, handling the update via Object Services isn't convenient because of concurrency or other reasons. In OrderIT, this was the case with updating the number of items in stock when new items are added to the available ones. You learned in chapter 8 that if you update the number of items in stock, you risk concurrency check problems even if you don't need the check to be performed. In such a case, a stored procedure is a good way to avoid concurrency checks.

These are the possible scenarios when updating entities using stored procedures:

- A stored procedure persists a standalone entity.
- A stored procedure persists an entity in an inheritance hierarchy.
- A stored procedure upgrades and downgrades an entity in an inheritance hierarchy.
- A stored procedure performs an arbitrary operation not connected to any entities.

The first two cases are straightforward and are almost identical in terms of how you handle them. The third case is a bit more complex and deserves particular handling. The last one covers launching commands other than those executed by Entity Framework for persistence.

Let's start by analyzing the simplest scenario, where a standalone entity is updated using stored procedures.

10.4.1 *Using stored procedures to persist an entity*

Persisting an entity using stored procedures is an all-or-nothing affair. You can't use a stored procedure that inserts data into the database and leave Entity Framework to generate the SQL for UPDATE and DELETE operations. That isn't supported, and if you try it you'll get a runtime exception.

To demonstrate using a stored procedure to persist an entity, you'll persist an Order. This is probably the most complex entity in the model, and it uses all the function-mapping features. It has foreign keys and complex properties, and it's the parent of a relationship, which means its database-generated ID is necessary for inserting the details.

The following steps will show you specifically how to map the stored procedure to insert an order, but the same process applies to updates and deletions:

1 Create the stored procedure as in the following listing.

> **Listing 10.7   A stored procedure that inserts an order**

```
CREATE PROCEDURE InsertOrder
  @OrderDate datetime,
  @CustomerId int,
```

```
  @ShippingAddress varchar(50),
  @ShippingCity varchar(50),
  @ShippingZipCode varchar(15),
  @ShippingCountry varchar(50),
  @EstimatedShippingDate datetime,
  @ActualShippingDate datetime
as
INSERT INTO [Order] (OrderDate, CustomerId , ShippingAddress, ShippingCity,
  ShippingZipCode, ShippingCountry, EstimatedShippingDate,
  ActualShippingDate)
VALUES (@OrderDate, @CustomerId, @ShippingAddress, @ShippingCity,
  @ShippingZipCode, @ShippingCountry, @EstimatedShippingDate,
  @ActualShippingDate)                                    ⟵  Inserts order

SELECT SCOPE_IDENTITY() AS OrderId                        ⟵  Returns ID
```

2 Import the stored procedure the same way as before. (You don't need to create the function in the conceptual schema.)

3 Right-click the `Order` entity, and select the Stored Procedure Mapping item.

4 In the Mapping Details window, associate each operation to the related stored procedure, as shown in figure 10.15.

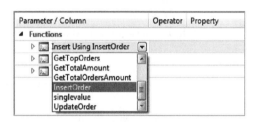

Figure 10.15 Mapping a stored procedure to persist a new order. The same process applies for modifications and deletions.

5 Map the stored procedure's parameters to the `Order` class's properties. The designer automatically maps columns and properties whose names match. Complex properties must be mapped manually.

6 In the Result Column Bindings section (shown in figure 10.16), write `OrderId` in Parameter/Column column, and associate it to the `OrderId` property. This way, the column containing the autogenerated ID returned by the stored procedure (see the last line of listing 10.7) is used to set the `OrderId` property of the order after the stored procedure has been executed. Naturally, this is only needed for database-generated values; if you generate primary keys on your own, it's not necessary.

The preceding steps can also be used to map stored procedures that perform updates and deletions. The only difference is that step 6 isn't required because `UPDATE` and `DELETE` commands don't generate the ID of the row.

That's it. You don't need to invoke these stored procedures manually. Because Entity Framework knows how they're mapped to the properties, it invokes the stored procedures when it needs to persist the entity, instead of generating SQL code.

To demonstrate this, suppose that you added an order and two details to the context. When you call the `SaveChanges` method, the SQL Profiler would look like figure 10.17.

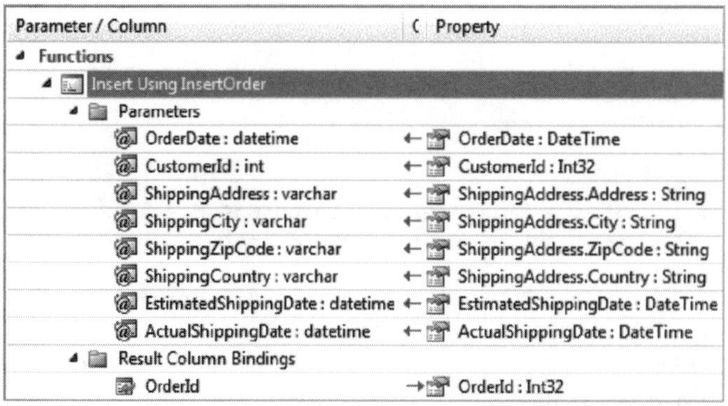

**Figure 10.16
Mapping the stored
procedure's parameters to
the entity's properties**

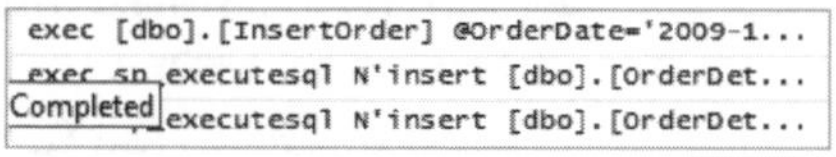

What's great about this technique is that if you decide to switch from using Entity Framework–generated SQL code to stored procedures, it's completely transparent to you. What's dangerous is that although the Entity Framework code updates only the modified properties of the entity, the stored

**Figure 10.17   The order is inserted using a
stored procedure; details are stored using
Entity Framework–generated code.**

procedures you write generally update all the properties. Always remember that, because if you persist a partially loaded entity (an entity where not all properties are set), you may end up losing your data.

Before passing on to the next subject, let's take a quick look at how the EDM is affected when you map stored procedures to persist an entity, as in the previous series of steps.

STORED PROCEDURES THAT PERSIST AN ENTITY AND THE EDM

From the SSDL point of view, the stored procedures are declared as usual; there's nothing new about that. The same thing happens for the CSDL. Because the stored procedures are invoked automatically by Entity Framework, there's no need to import them to the conceptual schema: you'll never use them.

What really changes is the mapping schema, as you see here.

Listing 10.8   Mapping an entity to persistence stored procedures in the MSL

```
<EntityTypeMapping TypeName="OrderITModel.Order">
  <ModificationFunctionMapping>
    <InsertFunction FunctionName="OrderITModel.Store.InsertOrder">
      <ScalarProperty Name="ActualShippingDate"
        ParameterName="ActualShippingDate" />
      <ScalarProperty Name="EstimatedShippingDate"
        ParameterName="EstimatedShippingDate" />
      <ScalarProperty Name="CustomerId" ParameterName="CustomerId" />
      <ScalarProperty Name="OrderDate" ParameterName="OrderDate" />
      <ComplexProperty Name="ShippingAddress"
        TypeName="OrderITModel.AddressInfo">
        <ScalarProperty Name="Country" ParameterName="ShippingCountry" />
```

```
                <ScalarProperty Name="ZipCode" ParameterName="ShippingZipCode" />
                <ScalarProperty Name="City" ParameterName="ShippingCity" />
                <ScalarProperty Name="Address" ParameterName="ShippingAddress" />
            </ComplexProperty>
            <ResultBinding Name="OrderId" ColumnName="OrderId" />
        </InsertFunction>
        <UpdateFunction ...> ... </UpdateFunction>
        <DeleteFunction ...> ... </DeleteFunction>
    </ModificationFunctionMapping>
</EntityTypeMapping>
```

In the `EntityTypeMapping` element related to the `Order` type, you include a
`ModificationFunctionMapping` element. It instructs Entity Framework that the persistence of the entity is delegated to the stored procedure defined in this element. Inside
`EntityTypeMapping`, you define three nodes that correspond to the insert, update, and
delete stored procedures: `InsertFunction`, `UpdateFunction`, `DeleteFunction` (the
order isn't important).

We'll focus on the mapping information for the insert function here, but this
information is valid for the other elements too. The `InsertFunction` element contains the `FunctionName` attribute, which defines the full name of the stored procedure
as declared in the storage schema. Inside it, you declare a set of `ScalarProperty`
nodes to map scalar-entity properties to stored-procedure parameters; complex properties are mapped using the `ComplexProperty` node. Furthermore, using the `Result-
Binding` element, you define the mapping for data returned by the function. It's
particularly important for insert functions that can return the ID of the row just added
to the database.

After you've mapped all the parameters for the insert function, you have to map
the update and delete ones too, and then you're ready to go.

What about concurrencies? You know that the automatically generated SQL
reflects the concurrency settings. Because with stored procedures you have to manage
everything manually, you have to handle concurrency too.

10.4.2 *Using stored procedures to update an entity with concurrency*

Entity Framework natively supports optimistic concurrency. With stored procedures,
this support is totally up to you, but the infrastructure and the designer help a lot.
Because the state manager keeps track of the original values, you can pass them to the
stored procedure along with the current ones. When you have both, you can perform
the concurrency check in the stored procedure.

What's absolutely great is that the retrieval of the original values is hidden from the
code. You specify it directly in the mapping using the designer. In the Mapping Details
window (shown in figure 10.18), next to the Property column is a Use Original Value
column containing check boxes. If Use Original Value is checked, the original value
of the property is used; otherwise, the current value is used.

Parameter / Column	(Property	Use Original Value
▲ 🗔 Update Using UpdateOrder		
▲ 🗀 Parameters		
📵 OrderDate : datetime	← 📝 OrderDate : DateTime	☐
📵 CustomerId : int	← 📝 CustomerId : Int32	☐
📵 ShippingAddress : varchar	← 📝 ShippingAddress.Address : String	☐
📵 ShippingCity : varchar	← 📝 ShippingAddress.City : String	☐
📵 ShippingZipCode : varchar	← 📝 ShippingAddress.ZipCode : String	☐
📵 ShippingCountry : varchar	← 📝 ShippingAddress.Country : String	☐
📵 EstimatedShippingDate : datetime	← 📝 EstimatedShippingDate : DateTime	☐
📵 ActualShippingDate : datetime	← 📝 ActualShippingDate : DateTime	☐
📵 OrderId : int	← 🔑 OrderId : Int32	☐
📵 Version : timestamp	← 📝 Version : Binary	☑

Figure 10.18   The original value of the Version field is passed to the stored procedure. The other parameters take the property's current value.

Manually mapping the version in the EDM is simple. Just add the `Version` attribute of the `ScalarProperty` element, and set it to `Original` to pass the original value, as in the following fragment:

```
<ScalarProperty Name="Version" ParameterName="Version"
  Version="Original" />
```

Or set `ScalarProperty` to `Current` to use the current value.

> **NOTE**   Remember that even if you don't need concurrency, the `Version` attribute is mandatory for the parameters declared in an `UpdateFunction`.

A standalone entity is easy to map. The situation gets more complicated when the entity is part of an inheritance hierarchy. In the next section, we'll investigate such a scenario.

10.4.3   *Persisting an entity that's in an inheritance hierarchy*

When inheritance comes into play, there are some additional considerations. Once again, all or nothing is the main rule: if you want to use stored procedures to persist an entity that's part of an inheritance hierarchy, *all* of the concrete (non-abstract) entities that belong to the same hierarchy *must* be persisted using stored procedures.

In the customer/supplier scenario, you have to create three stored procedures for the customer and three stored procedures for the supplier. It works like a charm without you needing to learn anything new.

But the difference between the customer and supplier stored procedures is just a few fields. It would be nice to create a stored procedure that manages one operation for both entities. For instance, you could create a stored procedure that handles the insert for both customers and suppliers, and do the same for updates and deletions. This would spare some lines of code and keep the set of stored procedures smaller.

USING ONE STORED PROCEDURE TO PERSIST A HIERARCHY

The idea behind this technique is to create a single stored procedure to perform a type of update for both classes. (Potentially, you could write a single stored procedure that performs all CUD operations for all classes, but it would be a mess.)

After the stored procedure is created, you can create two functions in the SSDL and personalize the command to invoke the real stored procedure with different parameters. This can be done using the `CommandText` element, as you saw in section 10.3. This technique is shown in listing 10.9. (For the sake of clarity, we have hidden the parameter declarations.)

Listing 10.9 Declaring functions and letting them invoke stored procedures

```
<Function Name="CreateCustomer" IsComposable="false"
  ParameterTypeSemantics="AllowImplicitConversion" Schema="dbo">
  <CommandText>
    exec CreateCompany @Name,
       @BillingAddress, @BillingCity,
       @BillingZipCode, @BillingCountry,
       @ShippingAddress, @ShippingCity,          Invokes SP
       @ShippingZipCode, @ShippingCountry,       for customer
       @WSUserName, @WSPassword,
       @WSEnabled, null, null, 'C')
  </CommandText>
  <Parameter Name="Name" Type="varchar" Mode="In" />
  <Parameter Name="BillingAddress" Type="varchar" Mode="In" />
  <Parameter Name="BillingCity" Type="varchar" Mode="In" />
  <Parameter Name="BillingZipCode" Type="varchar" Mode="In" />
  <Parameter Name="BillingCountry" Type="varchar" Mode="In" />
  <Parameter Name="ShippingAddress" Type="varchar" Mode="In" />
  <Parameter Name="ShippingCity" Type="varchar" Mode="In" />
  <Parameter Name="ShippingZipCode" Type="varchar" Mode="In" />
  <Parameter Name="ShippingCountry" Type="varchar" Mode="In" />
  <Parameter Name="WSUserName" Type="varchar" Mode="In" />
  <Parameter Name="WSPassword" Type="varchar" Mode="In" />
  <Parameter Name="WSEnabled" Type="bit" Mode="In" />
</Function>
<Function Name="CreateSupplier" IsComposable="false"
  ParameterTypeSemantics="AllowImplicitConversion" Schema="dbo">
  <CommandText>
    exec CreateCompany @Name, null, null,
       null, null, null, null, null,            Invokes SP
       null, null, null, null, @IBAN, @PaymentDays, 'S'   for supplier
  </CommandText>
  <Parameter Name="Name" Type="varchar" Mode="In" />
  <Parameter Name="IBAN" Type="char" Mode="In" />
  <Parameter Name="PaymentDays" Type="smallint" Mode="In" />
</Function>
```

The last step is mapping the stored procedures to the `InsertFunction` node of the customer and the supplier classes. That's done the same way as before, so we won't show it again here. Naturally, the same technique applies to update and deletion stored procedures.

> **NOTE**   We didn't use the designer because this feature isn't supported. Everything must be done manually. And remember that the storage schema is rewritten each time you update the model from the database, so you'll lose any changes when that happens.

We have now analyzed the customer/supplier (TPH) scenario, but everything we have done is perfectly valid for the product (TPT) scenario. In both mapping strategies, you can encounter a case where you need to upgrade or downgrade an entity. Let's see what that means.

10.4.4   Upgrading and downgrading an entity that's in an inheritance hierarchy

In OrderIT, you can't persist a company or a product. You have to use the specialized classes (Customer, Supplier, Shoe, and Shirt) because the base classes have no meaning in the business (in fact, they're abstract). In other situations, the base classes may have meaning as well as the inheriting classes. Think about a contact list where a simple contact can become a customer. You can model this situation using the TPH strategy: Contact is the base class, and Customer inherits from it.

When you create a new contact, it's persisted in the table with a discriminator value of CO. At a certain point, the contact decides to buy something and becomes a customer. Lots of additional data is required, and the discriminator column must be changed to CU. We'll call this process *upgrade*. If for some reason you need to delete the customer but keep the person or company as a contact, you perform a *downgrade*.

Entity Framework doesn't support this functionality. This means you have to perform all the updates manually using stored procedures or custom SQL commands. If you aren't comfortable with this approach, you can use the classic ADO.NET approach to modify data in the table. If you use the TPH strategy, you just have to modify the discriminator column to change the type. If you use the TPT strategy, you have to delete the record from the specialized table, leaving the data only in the main table.

It's important to highlight that the domain-driven design rules state that the type of an entity *must* always be the same during its lifetime. What we have described here is a situation where we're changing the type of an entity. This is a situation we have encountered several times and have solved using stored procedures without any problems, but you could also achieve the same goal in other ways. Because there are many variables involved, every case must be evaluated on its own.

Sometimes you need to perform an update on the database that's not connected to the persistence of an entity. For instance, you may want to log each time a user signs in. In this case, you don't have a Log entity; what you need to do is add a record in a table. Using a stored procedure to do this is pretty simple. Let's see how to do that.

10.4.5   Executing stored procedures not connected to an entity

In chapter 7 you saw that a custom command can be executed using the Execute-StoreCommand method, but this has the disadvantage of breaking the database-independence model, because it accepts a SQL string. A stored procedure is definitely a better way to go; it encapsulates the logic, makes the application database-agnostic, and keeps the DBA happy. You kill three birds with one stone.

Having said that, to invoke a stored procedure that doesn't return data, you have to use the `ExecuteFunction` method. It's different from `ExecuteStoreCommand` because it doesn't accept a generic parameter and returns only an `Int32` containing the number of affected rows. The only arguments it accepts are the stored procedure name plus an array of `ObjectParameter` objects representing the parameters.

Naturally, to be invoked via the context class, the stored procedure must be imported to the conceptual schema. Even if you import the stored procedure in the conceptual schema, the POCO template you've been using so far to generate code doesn't generate a context method to invoke these types of stored procedures. Fortunately, with a little bit of work on the POCO template, you can change that. You'll learn how to do that in chapter 13.

10.5 Summary

Stored procedures are a key feature of any database, and they're used in almost every project we have developed. It's very important that you understand how to best use them in any situation.

This chapter has given you some great insight into what you can do with Entity Framework and stored procedures. In this version of Entity Framework, native support for stored procedures has been greatly improved, but there's still a lot to do to make them work seamlessly.

The designer offers great productivity improvements and the template-generated context class offers better integration, but the ability to map stored procedure to entities with complex types and support for eager loading are still missing. We'll probably see these features in the next release, but for the moment we have to live without them.

We're now finished with stored procedures, but there's another similar feature that's key in Entity Framework: database and model functions, which are discussed in the next chapter, together with defining queries.

11

Working with functions and views

11

This chapter covers

- Using defining queries
- Creating custom database functions
- Creating model defined functions

In the previous chapter, you saw that you can embed native SQL commands into the storage model of the EDM to simulate stored procedures. The same idea can be applied to create custom views that aren't on the database. Creating such views can allow you to write simpler queries, easing the development process.

Another thing that eases querying is the use of database and model functions. These are pieces of code that can be reused across different queries, avoiding repetitive code. In Entity Framework 1.0, these functions could be used only via Entity SQL, but now they're available in LINQ to Entities too. What's even better, now you can create your own set of functions in the EDM, allowing further customization and even more reuse.

This chapter is all about these feature. First we'll discuss embedding views in the EDM, and specifically the defining query feature, which is one of the most powerful, and hidden, features of Entity Framework. Then, we'll talk about custom database functions and user-defined functions. By the end of this chapter, you'll graduate from the university of the EDM.

Let's first look at how you can embed views into the storage model.

11.1 Views in the storage model: defining queries

Conceptually, stored procedures and views are quite different. A stored procedure is a block of statements that optionally returns data; a view is an object that contains data obtained by a predefined query. But the main difference is that stored procedures can't be *combined* on the server, whereas views can. If the stored procedures at your disposal already cover all your needs, you may not need views, but in our experience, views are often worth a place in your toolbox.

There are two ways to handle views in Entity Framework:

- *Map them as if they were tables*—In this case, Entity Framework makes no difference between views and tables. If you modify properties of the entities returned by the query to a view, the context will keep track of them and will generate the statements required to update them on the database (which will fail). Although technically possible, we don't recommend this approach.

- *Map them using a defining query*—In this case, Entity Framework knows that the entity is read-only, and unless you specifically instruct it on how to update data, it disables this option. This is the most common scenario because, in most cases, data coming from a view is read-only.

The storage schema is where you decide which approach to use. If you opt for the first choice, chapter 5 contains all the information you need, because Entity Framework treats views as tables. If you opt for the second option, the next section contains all you need to know.

11.1.1 Creating a defining query

Views are a storage affair. It's not surprising that when you have learned how to define them in the SSDL, there's nothing more you have to learn. In fact, when you map an entity to a view, the conceptual and the mapping schemas simply define the entity and map it to the view as if it were a normal table.

Before delving into the storage schema, let's look at a query that generates a view. The following query retrieves the total amount of the orders, grouped by customer:

```
CREATE VIEW SalesByCustomer
AS
  SELECT c.Name, SUM(d.Quantity * (d.UnitPrice - d.Discount)) AS Total
  FROM dbo.[Order] AS o
  INNER JOIN dbo.Company AS c ON c.CompanyId = o.CustomerId
  INNER JOIN dbo.OrderDetail AS d ON o.OrderId = d.OrderId
  GROUP BY c.Name
```

Defining a view in the SSDL is simple. In the `EntitySet` element inside `Entity-Container`, you put a `DefiningQuery` node, and inside it you write the `SELECT`, in database-native SQL code, from the database view. The next snippet shows how this is done:

```
<EntitySet Name="SalesByCustomer"
  EntityType="OrderITModel.Store.SalesByCustomer">
  <DefiningQuery>
    SELECT Name, Total FROM SalesByCustomer
  </DefiningQuery>
</EntitySet>
```

When it comes to the entity description, you must choose a key. In this example, you could use the name of the customer, because there is one row per customer, and two customers can't have the same name. In situations where there isn't a unique natural key, consider including in the view an autogenerated column that acts as a key.

After you've created a class, mapped it against the view, and generated the related entity set in the context, you can query it as if it were a table. The following listing demonstrates this.

Listing 11.1   Code for querying a view, and the generated SQL

C#
```
from s in ctx.SalesByCustomer
orderby s.Total descending
select s
```

VB
```
From s In ctx.SalesByCustomer
Order By s.Total Descending
```

SQL
```
SELECT
[Extent1].[Name] AS [Name],
[Extent1].[Total] AS [Total]
FROM (
  SELECT Name, Total
  FROM SalesByCustomer
) AS [Extent1]
ORDER BY [Extent1].[Total] DESC
```

As you can see, when the SQL generator creates the code, the SQL in the `Defining-Query` node is embedded in a nested query, and operations defined in the LINQ to Entities or Entity SQL query act on the nested one.

You have seen that the query in the `DefiningQuery` element isn't the query that defines the view, but is a command that returns all of its data. This means that in a `DefiningQuery` element, you can write SQL code to cover any needs you may have. This is the real power of the defining query: if there's something you can't map using EDM, a defining query is the solution.

An example of this power is when you have to map a stored procedure to an entity with complex properties.

11.1.2 *Mapping stored procedures to classes with complex properties*

You know that a stored procedure can't be mapped to an entity that defines a complex property. This is because the mapping is based on column and property names, and complex properties break this model. A defining query creates a sort of EDM view, so an entity with complex properties can be mapped against it. If the SQL in the defining query returns data from a stored procedure (such as EXEC GetOrders 1), you can easily map it to an entity with complex properties, overcoming the current limitations. If it seems too good to be true, that's because it isn't completely true.

You must keep a couple of caveats in mind when following this path:

- *A defining query creates a read-only entity.* A defining query specifies a query by which you retrieve data. If you need to update data retrieved using a defining query, Entity Framework can't generate INSERT, UPDATE, and DELETE (CUD) commands based on such a query. To solve this problem, you have to map CUD operations to ad hoc stored procedures.
- *Stored procedures can't be queried.* You can't query stored procedures on the server; you can't write a SQL statement like SELECT * FROM GetOrders.

In spite of the second limitation, you can still achieve the goal of mapping a database function (not a stored procedure) to an entity with complex properties by bending the database model. The technique we'll look at uses a SQL Server feature known as *table-valued functions.*

Like stored procedures, table-valued functions expose the result of a query, but they *can* be queried on the server. The following snippet shows the code that invokes the table-valued function in the DefininqQuery:

```
<EntitySet Name="Orders"
  EntityType="OrderITModel.Store.Order">
  <DefiningQuery>
    SELECT * FROM GetOrders()
  </DefiningQuery>
</EntitySet>
```

GetOrders is the table-valued function. Now you can easily map this view to the Order class, even if it contains the Address complex property.

What happens when relationships come into play? Order has a relationship with its details and with the customer. Because Order is mapped to a query and not directly to a table, the SQL code may get complicated. Fortunately, the runtime query composition of Entity Framework is what the Entity Framework team has concentrated more of its efforts on. An entity mapped to a storage object that uses a defining query can participate in relationships like any other table without any additional effort. The query-nesting process during SQL generation for a defining query is valid even when relationships are taken into account. The result is that the following queries work exactly as expected:

C#
```
var order = ctx.Orders.Include("Details");
var customer = order.Customer;
```

VB
```
Dim order = ctx.Orders.Include("Details")
Dim customer = order.Customer
```

Mapping an entity to a defining query that invokes a table-valued function that returns all the records of a table may seem useless, but this way you can have database functions that map against entities with complex property too. It's a good example of the power of the EDM.

Now you know everything about functions and views that return data. The next things we'll look at help in the reuse of queries: user-defined functions and scalar-valued functions. They allow you to define logic in (sort of) functions that can be reused in querying, so that writing queries becomes simpler.

11.2   *User-defined functions and scalar-valued functions*

You often need to calculate the total amount of an order detail. The formula is pretty simple: `(unit price - discount) * quantity`. If you need to calculate this amount in lots of queries, you end up placing the same formula in many different places, and then if you need to change things, you have to check lots of queries. In a large project, this is unacceptable.

To overcome this problem, you can create a function that performs the calculation for you. You can't use a CLR function because LINQ to Entities isn't able to translate it into SQL, and Entity SQL has no knowledge of CLR functions; so how can you solve the problem? The answer is to use a scalar-valued function.

11.2.1   *Scalar-valued functions*

A scalar-valued function is a special type of database function that accepts any parameter you have and returns a scalar value. The following SQL code represents the `(unit price - discount) * quantity` function:

```
CREATE FUNCTION GetTotalAmount
(@unitprice as money, @quantity as int, @discount as money)
RETURNS money
AS
BEGIN
  return (@unitprice - @discount) * @quantity
END
```

When you have the function, you need to import it into the storage schema using the designer, as you did for stored procedures. Then you can invoke the database function using the following Entity SQL query:

```
SELECT o.OrderId,
  SUM(SELECT VALUE OrderITModel.Store.GetTotalAmount(d.UnitPrice,
      d.Quantity, d.Discount)
```

```
      FROM o.OrderDetails As d)
  FROM OrderITEntities.Orders AS o
```

In Entity Framework 1.0, only Entity SQL lets you use the database functions. There's no way to use it in a LINQ to Entities query even if you import the function to the conceptual schema. This is because LINQ to Entities knows nothing about the EDM; it works on .NET classes and methods.

Fortunately, this limitation was lifted in Entity Framework version 4.0. To use a scalar-valued function in LINQ to Entities, you need to create a stub method, as shown in the following listing, which acts as a bridge between LINQ to Entities and the EDM.

Listing 11.2 Stub method that maps a function in the storage to a CLR method

C#
```csharp
[EdmFunction("OrderITModel.Store", "GetTotalAmount")]
public static Nullable<decimal> GetTotalAmount(Nullable<decimal> unitprice,
  Nullable<int> quantity, Nullable<decimal> discount)
{
  throw new NotImplementedException("Cannot invoke this method");
}
```

VB
```vb
<EdmFunction("OrderITModel.Store", "GetTotalAmount")> _
Public Shared Function GetTotalAmount( _
  ByVal unitprice As Nullable(Of Decimal), _
  ByVal quantity As Nullable(Of Integer), _
  ByVal discount As Nullable(Of Decimal)) As Nullable(Of Decimal)
    Throw New NotImplementedException("Cannot invoke this method")
End Function
```

This function has many prerequisites:

- It *must* be static.
- It *must* return the same type as the database function.
- It *must* be marked with the EdmFunction attribute. (The attribute needs two mandatory parameters: the storage schema namespace and the name of the function.)
- Its body should throw an exception. (This isn't mandatory, but because the function is only a stub for LINQ to Entities, its code is never really invoked.)

  NOTE Unfortunately, the POCO template doesn't generate the stub method, so you have to write everything on your own. In chapter 13, we'll show you how to modify the template to generate this code too.

After you've created the stub method, LINQ to Entities knows that this stub method is mapped to the database function in the storage schema, so you can consume it in your queries as shown in the following listing. We prefer putting the method in the context class, but you can place it wherever you like.

Listing 11.3   Using the stub function in LINQ to Entities

C#
```
from o in ctx.Orders
select new
{
  o.OrderId,
  Amount = o.OrderDetails.Sum(d => OrderITEntities.GetTotalAmount(
                               d.UnitPrice,
                               d.Quantity,
                               d.Discount))

}
```

VB
```
From o In ctx.Orders
Select New With
{
  .o.OrderId,
  .Amount = o.OrderDetails.Sum(Function(d) OrderITEntities.GetTotalAmount(
                                 d.UnitPrice,
                                 d.Quantity,
                                 d.Discount))
}
```

Placing querying logic in a database function facilitates code reuse and maintainability. This is probably one of the greatest features in Entity Framework 4.0 because in large-scale projects, reusability and maintainability are essential in the long term.

But what if you can't add the function to the database? What if you need a function that returns more than a scalar value? The database can't help in such scenarios, so you have to resort to user-defined functions.

11.2.2 *User-defined functions*

When the database can't help, the EDM comes to the rescue. In this case, it lets you define a *conceptual* function that can be used in both Entity SQL and LINQ to Entities (always via a stub).

The function is defined in the CSDL, which knows nothing about SQL. So the question is, how do you conceptually define a function? The answer is, using Entity SQL. You can create a function whose body is an Entity SQL expression that returns a result. This function is a *user-defined function.*

The output result can be anything. It can be a scalar value, an object, or a DbData-Record. This is the big difference between user-defined functions and scalar-valued functions—the latter can only return scalar values. This doesn't mean you should only adopt user-defined functions; they're just more powerful. The choice is entirely up to you.

User-defined functions have one big problem: they aren't supported by the designer. You have to manually change the EDM to use them. If you don't like touching the raw XML, this is a real pain.

The first step is to create the function in the conceptual schema, as shown here.

Listing 11.4 User-defined function that returns and accepts scalar values

```
<Schema ...>
  <Function Name="GetUDFTotalAmount" ReturnType="Decimal">
    <Parameter Name="UnitPrice" Type="Decimal" />
    <Parameter Name="Quantity" Type="Int32" />
    <Parameter Name="Discount" Type="Decimal" />
    <DefiningExpression>
      (UnitPrice - Discount) * Quantity
    </DefiningExpression>
  </Function>
</Schema>
```

The declaration is straightforward. In the Function node, you declare the function name and return type. Then, you include a Parameter node for each input parameter. Finally, you create a DefiningExpression node, inside which the function code is written using Entity SQL. That's it for the EDM.

Next, you have to create the CLR stub method for the function to make it available to LINQ to Entities. That's done the same way as for a scalar-valued function except that the first parameter of the EdmFunction attribute must contain the namespace of the conceptual schema, not the namespace of the storage one. Of course, the name must be changed too. The final code is shown in the following snippet:

C#

```
[EdmFunction("OrderITModel", "GetUDFTotalAmount")]
```

VB

```
<EdmFunction("OrderITModel", "GetUDFTotalAmount")> _
```

Now you can invoke the function in both LINQ to Entities and Entity SQL queries. In LINQ to Entities queries, you won't see the difference between a scalar-valued function and a user-defined one. The code is exactly the same, because you simply invoke a method. In Entity SQL, you have to change the way you invoke the function compared with how you invoke the database scalar-valued function because the user-defined function is defined on the conceptual side. The difference is highlighted in the next snippet:

```
SELECT o.OrderId,
  SUM(SELECT VALUE OrderITModel.GetUDFTotalAmount(d.UnitPrice,
       d.Quantity, d.Discount)
       FROM o.OrderDetails As d)
  FROM OrderITEntities.Orders AS o
```

So far, scalar-valued functions and user-defined functions have reached the same goal. From now on, you'll see how user-defined functions are more powerful. We'll start with an interesting feature: the ability to pass objects as parameters.

PASSING AN OBJECT AS A PARAMETER OF A FUNCTION

Suppose that, in the future, you're asked for another type of discount. To achieve this goal, you add a new column and property to the OrderDetail table and class. Naturally, this affects the way the total amount is calculated, because the new discount comes into play.

You need to change the `GetUDFTotalAmount` function to accept a fourth parameter, and that means changing all callers to pass that parameter. If the function is used in several places, this work can be tedious and error prone. The alternative is to change your approach and to pass the entire `OrderDetail` object. This way, if you need to add another parameter, you won't have to change the code but just the function in the EDM. That's shown in this snippet:

```
<Function Name="GetUDFTotalAmount" ReturnType="Decimal">
  <Parameter Name="detail" Type="OrderITModel.OrderDetail" />
    <DefiningExpression>
      (detail.UnitPrice - detail.Discount) * detail.Quantity
    </DefiningExpression>
</Function>
```

Notice that now there is only one `Parameter` node, and its type is a class mapped in the EDM (`OrderDetail`). The code is Entity SQL, so you can refer to the parameter properties as in a classic Entity SQL query.

The stub signature is different because now it accepts an `OrderDetail` instance as a parameter, and not the unit price, quantity, and discount parameters. Naturally, both LINQ to Entities and Entity SQL queries must be adapted to this different parameter list.

Passing an object as a parameter is only half of the game. You can even let the function return objects.

RETURNING A NONTYPED OBJECT FROM A FUNCTION

Suppose that you often perform projections. Repeating this in every query is error prone and troublesome when something changes. It would be great if you could encapsulate the projection in a function and then reuse it.

The following listing takes out the customer's name and the main information about the shipping and billing addresses.

> **Listing 11.5   User-defined function that accepts an object and returns a `DbDataRecord`**

```
<Function Name="GetUDFAddresses">
  <ReturnType>
    <RowType>
      <Property Name="Name" Type="String" />
      <Property Name="BillingAddress" Type="String"/>
      <Property Name="BillingCity" Type="String"/>
      <Property Name="ShippingAddress" Type="String"/>
      <Property Name="ShippingCity" Type="String"/>
    </RowType>
  </ReturnType>
  <Parameter Name="customer" Type="OrderITModel.Customer" />
  <DefiningExpression>
    ROW(detail.Name, detail.BillingAddress.Address,
        detail.BillingAddress.City, detail.ShippingAddress.Address,
        detail.ShippingAddress.City)
  </DefiningExpression>
</Function>
```

The return type of this function is a `DbDataRecord` that contains the columns specified in the `ReturnType`/`RowType` node. It's important that the Entity SQL expression return the columns in the same order as they're declared, and that they're wrapped inside the `ROW` function.

The stub method returns a `DbDataRecord`. There's nothing more you need to do. Now you can use the function in listing 11.5 in both LINQ to Entities and Entity SQL queries, as in the following code:

C#
```
from c in ctx.Companies.OfType<Customer>()
select OrderITEntities.GetUDFAddresses(c)
```

VB
```
From c In ctx.Companies.OfType(Of Customer)()
Select OrderITEntities.GetUDFAddresses(c)
```

Entity SQL
```
SELECT OrderITModel.GetUDFAddresses(c)
FROM OFTYPE(OrderITEntities.Companies, OrderIT.Model.Customer) As c
```

Working with the `DbDataRecord` isn't bad, but having a class returned is much better. This is another great opportunity you can take advantage of.

RETURNING A TYPED OBJECT FROM A FUNCTION

The tweaks needed to switch from a `DbDataRecord` instance to a typed object are very minor. First, you have to create the class that holds the data. Because it must be in the CSDL, you can easily create that using the designer. Then you have to create the function shown in the following fragment:

```
<Function Name="GetUDFTypedAddresses">
  <ReturnType Type="OrderITModel.CustomerProjection"/>
  <Parameter Name="customer" Type="OrderITModel.Customer" />
  <DefiningExpression>
    OrderITModel.CustomerProjection(customer.Name,
      customer.BillingAddress.Address, customer.BillingAddress.City,
      customer.ShippingAddress.Address, customer.ShippingAddress.City)
  </DefiningExpression>
</Function>
```

The first thing to notice here is that the return type is neither a scalar value nor a generic class, but a specific type (the complex one generated in the designer). The second point is that the return columns aren't wrapped in a Row function, but in the return type class. This is an Entity SQL feature that allows the return of a typed object instead of a generic `DbDataRecord`. The stub method for such a function returns the object instead of a `DbDataRecord`.

> **NOTE** It's mandatory to place the method parameters in the same order in which the properties of the class are declared.

The LINQ to Entities and Entity SQL queries don't change. The only thing that changes is the way the application manages the result, because now it's a class and that's much better.

All of the preceding functions have one thing in common—they return a single instance. Because functions are all about reuse and encapsulation, it would be a pity if you couldn't return collections too. Fortunately, that's possible.

11.2.3 *User-defined functions and collection results*

Suppose that in many queries, you need to return only the order details that have no discount. Repeating these conditions in all the queries would be a problem; a ready-to-use function would definitely be better.

User-defined functions can return an enumerable of scalar values, an enumerable of DbDataRecord instances, or an enumerable of objects. There's no limit to what you can do.

RETURNING A LIST OF SCALAR VALUES

Let's start with the basics and return the IDs of the details that have no discount. Creating this function is pretty easy, as you can see in this snippet:

```
<Function Name="GetUDFDetailsWithNoDiscount_Scaar"
  ReturnType="Collection(Int32)">
  <Parameter Name="o" Type="OrderITModel.Order" />
  <DefiningExpression>
    SELECT VALUE d.OrderDetailId FROM o.OrderDetails AS d
    WHERE d.discount == 0
  </DefiningExpression>
</Function>
```

The ReturnType attribute contains the Collection keyword, which says that this function returns a *list* of Int32 instances and not a single value. In the Entity SQL code in the DefiningExpression element, you place a full query, not just a simple expression. With these simple tweaks, a function can return a collection of items.

The stub method must return an IEnumerable<Nullable<Int32>> object. That's the only tweak needed to make the stub method work. Once again, you can use the method in your queries.

RETURNING A LIST OF GENERIC OBJECTS

You may need more information than just the ID of the details. For instance, you may need the quantity and the unit price. The following listing shows how you can do that using the DbDataRecord class.

Listing 11.6 User-defined function that returns a list of `DbDataRecord` objects

```
<Function Name="GetUDFDetailsWithNoDiscount_Record">
  <ReturnType>
    <CollectionType>
      <RowType>
        <Property Name="OrderDetailId" Type="Int32"/>
        <Property Name="UnitPrice" Type="Decimal"/>
        <Property Name="Quantity" Type="Int32"/>
      </RowType>
    </CollectionType>
```

```
  </ReturnType>
  <Parameter Name="o" Type="OrderITModel.Order" />
  <DefiningExpression>
    SELECT d.OrderDetailId, d.UnitPrice, d.Quantity
    FROM o.OrderDetails AS d
    WHERE d.discount == 0
  </DefiningExpression>
</Function>
```

The `ReturnType` attribute disappears, and you create the `ReturnType` node to specify the shape of the result. Because it's a list, you use a `CollectionType` element and then use `RowType` to specify the output properties.

The stub returns an `IEnumerable<DbDatarecord>`. You're ready again to use the function in your queries.

RETURNING A LIST OF TYPED OBJECTS

Returning a list of typed objects is fairly simple. You just have to specify the type of the object returned and prepare the Entity SQL query using the following code:

```
<Function Name="GetUDFDetailsWithNoDiscount_Object"
  ReturnType="Collection(OrderITModel.OrderDetail)">
  <Parameter Name="o" Type="OrderITModel.Order" />
  <DefiningExpression>
    SELECT VALUE d FROM o.OrderDetails AS d WHERE d.discount == 0
  </DefiningExpression>
</Function>
```

This code is very similar to that used for returning a scalar value, and it needs no further explanation.

The stub method for such function is simple. In fact, it returns an `IEnumerable` `<OrderDetail>` object.

In the end, scalar-valued functions enable a great level of reuse in your code. That's worth taking into account when you're developing a project.

11.3 Summary

Mastering functions and defining queries is important in any real-world project. Functions, in particular, really make a difference when you're writing queries. They avoid repetitive code and promote code reuse to an incredible extent. No technology before this has ever enabled such code reuse in queries. You can't help falling in love with them.

What's great about functions is that in addition to enabling the use of database functions in LINQ to Entities, they also enable you to write your own custom functions in Entity SQL and make them available to LINQ to Entities. Thumbs up!

Now you have a complete understanding of the EDM, and you've been introduced to its potential and its intricacies. What you need to know next is how you can access EDM metadata in code. That's the subject of the next chapter.

12

Exploring
EDM metadata

This chapter covers

- Reading the EDM
- Retrieving entity structures
- Retrieving function structures
- Writing generic code

Roughly speaking, the EDM consists of three XML files carrying information about classes, database, and their mappings. It's no surprise that Entity Framework is the first consumer of these XML files, using them to generate the SQL code for CRUD operations, to understand whether a column is an identity on the database, and much more.

Reading XML files with LINQ to XML is easier than ever, but it will never be like having a set of well-designed APIs that access the same data. Entity Framework's regular need to access EDM metadata led to the need for simplicity, which in turn led to a set of APIs. At the beginning, the APIs were for internal use only, but they were later made public so that everyone could access them.

Metadata retrieval introduces the possibility of writing generic code. By *generic*, we mean code that works with entities without even knowing what type the entities are. For instance, you could write a clever extension method that takes an entity and decides whether to perform an `AddObject` or an `Attach` based on the key value, as we described in chapter 6.

Thanks to metadata, you can discover the key property at runtime, retrieve the value via reflection, and then perform the correct operation. By using custom annotations, you can even specify in the EDM which value causes an `AddObject` and which causes an `Attach`. Although this is a simple example, it makes clear why metadata is important.

This chapter discusses all these subjects starting from the basics. First we'll show how metadata can be reached and what pitfalls you may encounter when accessing it. After that, we'll take a tour of the API system. Finally, you'll finally put everything into action by building a metadata viewer and completing an example that chooses between the `AddObject` and `Attach` methods.

12.1 Metadata basics

You know where the EDM is, but how are the APIs to access its data exposed? How are the different files in the EDM identified? And when is the metadata loaded?

The APIs are accessible via three different classes: `ObjectContext`, `Entity-Connection`, and `MetadataWorkspace`. This may sound confusing, but there's a good reason for this variety, which we'll get to shortly.

To identify the different files during data retrieval, you have to specify the *dataspace* when you query for a certain object, or a list of objects. The same APIs retrieve metadata for both the conceptual and storage models, so you must state each time which file should be inspected. (MSL isn't available via the APIs; you can only access it via LINQ to XML.)

As for when the metadata is loaded, the CSDL is immediately available, but the SSDL can be inspected only after a request that requires that metadata is triggered (a query, for example).

Those short answers will barely get you started. Let's look at each of these topics in more detail.

12.1.1 Accessing metadata

The class that exposes APIs to access metadata is `MetadataWorkspace`. It can be instantiated directly using one of its constructors or accessed through the `Object-Context` or `EntityConnection` class. Manually instantiating the `MetadataWorkspace` class can be tough because it requires lots of code; you're better off using one of the other methods.

> **NOTE** We've directly instantiated the `MetadataWorkspace` class only when generating code via a template (in chapter 13, you'll see why this is extremely useful). In all other cases, we've accessed the `Metadata-Workspace` class through the context, and only in very rare cases through the connection.

Let's look at how you can access metadata through the `ObjectContext`.

ACCESSING METADATA USING THE CONTEXT

When you work with objects, the context is your gateway to the database. To correctly handle objects, the context works with the conceptual schema of the EDM. It must know whether a property is an identity, which properties are used for concurrency, and so on.

Fortunately, the context constructor already knows about metadata because the connection string, which contains the metadata's location, is passed in the constructor. That's why you only need to access the `MetadataWorkspace` property, as shown in the next snippet:

C#
```
var ctx = new OrderITEntities();
var mw = ctx.MetadataWorkspace;
```

VB
```
Dim ctx As New OrderITEntities()
Dim mw = ctx.MetadataWorkspace
```

That's really all you need to do when you have a context around. But this isn't always the case—you may be working with a connection.

ACCESSING METADATA USING THE CONNECTION

The `EntityConnection` class exposes metadata through the `GetMetadataWorkspace` method, which returns a `MetadataWorkspace` object. After the connection is created, you can invoke the method:

C#
```
var ctx = new EntityConnection(connString);
var mw = conn.GetMetadataWorkspace();
```

VB
```
Dim conn As New EntityConnection(connString)
Dim mw = conn.GetMetadataWorkspace()
```

> **NOTE** From now on, we'll use the variable `mw` to identify a `MetadataWork-space` in the code.

In chapters 3 and 7, you learned that the context relies on the underlying `Entity-Connection` to access the database. It turns out that the context relies on the connection to access metadata too. When the context is instantiated, it creates the connection and then internally clones the metadata, making it available to the context consumer.

We've developed many projects using Entity Framework and have never needed to access metadata without having a context or a connection in place. Obviously, that doesn't mean it can't happen to you. In that case, working directly with the `Metadata-Workspace` class may be the only way.

ACCESSING METADATA USING THE METADATAWORKSPACE CLASS

When you work with the context or the connection, you always have a connection string. When working with `MetadataWorkspace` class, metadata in the class can be initialized in the constructor or via specific methods.

When you use the constructor, you have to pass in the paths of the three EDM files plus the assemblies containing the CLR classes. If the three EDM files are embedded in an assembly, that assembly must be passed to the constructor.

Note that if the three EDM files aren't embedded in an assembly, you have to reference them using their full paths; but if they're embedded, you can use the same syntax used in the connection string, as the following listing demonstrates.

Listing 12.1 Accessing the metadata using the `MetadataWorkspace` class

C#
```
Assembly asm = Assembly.LoadFile("C:\\OrderIT\\OrderITModel.dll");   Embedded
var mw1 = new MetadataWorkspace                                      files
   (new string[] { "res://*/ Model.csdl", "res://*/ Model.ssdl" },
   new Assembly[] { asm });
var mw2 = new MetadataWorkspace
   (new string[] { "C:\\OrderIT\\Model.csdl", "C:\\OrderIT\\Model.ssdl" },
   new Assembly[] { asm });                                          Plain files
```

VB
```
Dim asm = Assembly.LoadFile("C:\OrderIT\OrderITModel.dll")
Dim mw1 = New MetadataWorkspace                                      Embedded
   (New String() { "res://*/Model.csdl", "res://*/ Model.ssdl" },    files
   New Assembly() { asm })
Dim mw2 = New MetadataWorkspace
   (New String() { " C:\OrderIT\Model.csdl", " C:\OrderIT\Model.ssdl" },
   New Assembly() { asm })                                           Plain files
```

If you opt for creating the `MetadataWorkspace` class without passing EDM information in the constructor, the job gets harder. `MetadataWorkspace` internally registers a set of collections for each file type. What you have to do is initialize these collections one by one and register them using the `RegisterItemCollection` method.

Each collection is of a different type, depending on the EDM file it handles. For instance, if you want to register metadata about the storage layer, you need to create a `StoreItemCollection` instance and pass in the SSDL file; the `EdmItemCollection` instance is used for the CSDL.

Even without seeing the code, you can see that this approach isn't desirable, because you have to write lots of code to instantiate and load the collections. We've never used this approach in the past and are unlikely to ever do so in the future. But if you encounter a case where this is the only way to make things work, you now know how to handle it.

We mentioned earlier that the assembly containing the CLR classes must be passed to the `MetadataWorkspace` class constructor. Have you wondered why? Aren't EDM metadata only about CSDL, SSDL, and MSL? That's what we'll look at next.

12.1.2 *How metadata is internally organized*

What's great about the metadata APIs is that they're reused across the different schemas of the EDM. It doesn't matter if you're scanning through the storage or the conceptual model, the APIs you use remain the same. So the question is, how do you specify what schema to look for?

The answer is that the dataspace lets you specify what schema to look in. The dataspace is an enum of type `DataSpace` (`System.Data.Metadata.Edm` namespace) that contains the following values:

- `CSpace`—Identifies the conceptual schema.
- `SSpace`—Identifies the storage schema.
- `CSSpace`—Identifies the mapping schema. Unfortunately, support for the mapping schema is minimal; you can't retrieve anything useful about it using the APIs. The best way to retrieve this metadata is to use LINQ to XML.
- `OSpace`—Identifies the CLR classes. This may seem weird, but CLR classes are included in the metadata. That's why you have to include them when instantiating the `MetadataWorkspace`. Naturally, only object-model classes are included, and you'll discover that this is feature is handy.
- `OCSpace`—Identifies the mapping between the CLR classes and the CSDL. In .NET Framework 1.0, the mapping between CLR classes and properties with the conceptual schema is based on custom attributes. In .NET Framework 4.0, it's based on the names of the classes and properties. This mapping information can be queried, but it's there more for Entity Framework's internal use than for helping you.

The `DataSpace` is passed to all `MetadataWorkspace` methods, as you can see in the following snippets:

C#
```
mw.GetItems<EntityType>(DataSpace.CSpace);
mw.GetItems<EdmFunction>(DataSpace.SSpace);
```

VB
```
mw.GetItems(Of EntityType)(DataSpace.CSpace)
mw.GetItems(Of EdmFunction)(DataSpace.SSpace)
```

The first method returns all entities in the conceptual space, and the second returns all stored procedures in the storage schema.

> **NOTE** Keep the `EntityType` and `EdmFunction` classes in mind. They are pretty useful, as you'll discover later in this chapter.

You now know how to access the metadata and how to specify what schema you're extracting data from. The next step is understanding *when* you can retrieve the data.

12.1.3 Understanding when metadata becomes available

Metadata information is lazily loaded by Entity Framework; because Entity Framework doesn't need it, you can't access it. For example, when you instantiate a context, the conceptual schema is immediately loaded because the context works with it. If you try to query the storage schema, you'll get a runtime `InvalidOperationException` with the message. "The space 'SSpace' has no associated collection." No query has been performed, so Entity Framework hasn't needed to access the MSL and SSDL.

Naturally, wherever there's an inconvenient limitation like this, a workaround is nearby. Most of the `MetadataWorkspace` methods come with an exception-safe version. For instance, you have `GetItem<T>` as well as `TryGetItem<T>`. You can use the `Try*` methods, and if data the data isn't ready yet, you can artificially cause it to be loaded.

The easiest way to force loading is to perform a query, but you won't want to waste a round trip to the database. Fortunately, the `ToTraceString` method, used in the following listing, does the trick. It causes Entity Framework to load the MSL and SSDL schemas to prepare a query, but it doesn't actually execute it.

> **Listing 12.2 Forcing the loading of the storage and mapping schemas**

C#
```
ItemCollection coll = null;
var loaded = mw.TryGetItemCollection(DataSpace.SSpace, out coll);
if (!loaded)
   ctx.Orders.ToTraceString();          ◁── Forces
                                            schema loading
```

VB
```
Dim coll As ItemCollection
Dim loaded = mw.TryGetItemCollection(DataSpace.SSpace, coll)
If Not loaded Then
   ctx.Orders.ToTraceString()           ◁── Forces
End If                                      schema loading
```

You now have enough background to advance to the next stage: querying. You've had a sneak peek with the `GetItems<T>`, `GetItem<T>`, `TryGetItem<T>`, and `GetItemCollection` methods, and now it's time to look at them more closely.

12.2 Retrieving metadata

`MetadataWorkspace` has many methods for retrieving metadata, but you'll generally only be using a few of them. All the metadata can be reached using a single generic API, but some types of metadata have dedicated retrieval methods (such as `GetEntityContainer` and `GetFunctions`). We discourage the use of such dedicated methods because using a single generic one makes the code easier to read.

These are the generic methods for accessing metadata:

- `GetItems`—Retrieves all items in the specified space
- `GetItems<T>`—Retrieves all items of type `T` in the specified space
- `GetItemCollection` and `TryGetItemCollection`—Retrieve all items in the specified space returning a specialized collection
- `GetItem<T>` and `TryGetItem<T>`—Retrieve a single item in the specified space

The first three of these methods do almost the same thing, with tiny differences. In the example that you'll create in this chapter, we'll only use GetItem<T>, TryGetItem<T>, and GetItems<T>. As you'll see, the other methods aren't all that necessary.

You're probably wondering what type T can be. If you want to retrieve all entities in the conceptual space, what should you pass as T? It's important to understand this before going deeper into the various retrieval methods.

12.2.1 *Understanding the metadata object model*

The metadata object model consists of classes that are in the System.Data.Metadata. Edm namespace, but not all classes in this namespace are related to the EDM. For instance, MetadataWorkspace acts as the gateway, but it doesn't work with metadata.

What we're interested in are the classes strictly related to metadata. Each node in the CSDL and SSDL has a corresponding class (with some exceptions). What's good is that in almost all cases, classes have the same name as their corresponding nodes. What's even better is that because the SSDL and CSDL share the same structure, even the classes are the same. Table 12.1 shows the correspondences between EDM nodes and metadata classes.

All the other EDM elements you learned about in chapter 5 are exposed as properties of the classes in table 12.1. For instance, the EntityContainer class has a BaseEntitySets property, which lists the AssociationSet and EntitySet elements, and a FunctionImports property, which exposes the FunctionImport elements, all in the EDM's EntityContainer element.

The EntityType class has a similar structure. It exposes the Properties property, containing all the Property elements inside the EntityType node in the EDM; and KeyMembers, which lists the PropertyRef elements inside the Key element that is nested in the EntityType node of the EDM.

The ComplexType class is pretty simple because it contains only the properties, whereas EdmFunction exposes the Parameters and ReturnParameter properties.

The AssociationType class is the most complex because it exposes the Role property, plus ReferentialConstraint, which has Principal and Dependent properties that in turn have PropertyRef elements.

Now that you know about the classes, it's time to look closely at the methods for accessing metadata that we introduced before.

EDM node	Metadata class name
EntityContainer	EntityContainer
EntityType	EntityType
ComplexType	ComplexType
Function	EdmFunction
Association	AssociationType

Table 12.1 The correspondence between metadata classes and EDM nodes

12.2.2 *Extracting metadata from the EDM*

Querying the EDM is just a matter of invoking methods on the `MetadataWorkspace` class. Let's analyze these methods one by one; later, you'll put everything in action. We'll start with the `GetItems` method.

EXTRACTING METADATA WITH GETITEMS

When you need all the items in a schema, `GetItems` is the best method to use. Not only does it return objects you've defined, but also primitive types and function types that are embedded in the EDM. It's easy to invoke, as the next snippet shows:

C#
```
var items = ctx.MetadataWorkspace.GetItems(DataSpace.CSpace);
```

VB
```
Dim items = ctx.MetadataWorkspace.GetItems(DataSpace.CSpace)
```

The variable `items` contains 272 elements! It contains all EDM primitive types, like `Edm.String`, `Edm.Boolean`, and `Edm.Int32`; primitive functions like `Edm.Count`, `Edm.Sum`, and `Edm.Average`; and the objects you've defined.

The preceding query operates on the conceptual schema, but the same considerations hold true for the storage schema. The only difference is that primitive types are in another namespace dedicated to the database. `SqlServer.varchar`, `SqlServer.Bit`, `SqlServer.int`, `SqlServer.COUNT`, `SqlServer.SUM`, and `SqlServer.AVERAGE` are just an example of what you'll get. Figure 12.1 shows an excerpt from the Visual Studio Quick Watch window containing types from the CSDL and SSDL.

The objects returned by `GetItems` are of type `ReadOnlyCollection<GlobalItem>`, which implements `IEnumerable<T>`. That means you can query the data using LINQ. For instance, if you want to retrieve all primitive types, you can perform the following query:

C#
```
ctx.MetadataWorkspace.GetItems(DataSpace.CSpace)
  .Where(i => i.BuiltInTypeKind == BuiltInTypeKind.PrimitiveType);
```

VB
```
ctx.MetadataWorkspace.GetItems(DataSpace.CSpace).
  Where(Function(i) i.BuiltInTypeKind = BuiltInTypeKind.PrimitiveType)
```

Like `GetItems`, `GetItemCollection` returns all the items that belong to a specific schema, but with a subtle difference: the type returned is different.

Name	Value	Name	Value
⊞ ● [10]	{Edm.Int32}	⊞ ● [29]	{SqlServer.ntext}
⊞ ● [11]	{Edm.Int64}	⊞ ● [30]	{SqlServer.text}
⊞ ● [12]	{Edm.String}	⊞ ● [31]	{SqlServer.uniqueidentifier}
⊞ ● [13]	{Edm.Time}	⊞ ● [32]	{SqlServer.xml}
⊞ ● [14]	{Edm.DateTimeOffset}	⊞ ● [33]	{SqlServer.AVG}
⊞ ● [15]	{Edm.Max}	⊞ ● [34]	{SqlServer.AVG}
⊞ ● [16]	{Edm.Max}	⊞ ● [35]	{SqlServer.AVG}
⊞ ● [17]	{Edm.Max}	⊞ ● [36]	{SqlServer.AVG}
⊞ ● [18]	{Edm.Max}	⊞ ● [37]	{SqlServer.CHECKSUM_AGG}

Figure 12.1   On the left side is a snapshot of items returned by `GetItems` in the `CSpace`. On the right side are items returned by `GetItems` in the `SSpace`.

EXTRACTING METADATA WITH GETITEMCOLLECTION AND TRYGETITEMCOLLECTION

The `GetItemCollection` method retrieves all items in the specified schema, and it returns them in an `ItemCollection` instance. `ItemCollection` inherits from `Read-OnlyCollection<GlobalItem>`, meaning that you can use LINQ to query its data, and it adds some convenient methods. Its use is shown in the following snippet:

C#
```
var items = ctx.MetadataWorkspace.GetItemCollection(DataSpace.CSpace);
```

VB
```
Dim items = ctx.MetadataWorkspace.GetItemCollection(DataSpace.CSpace)
```

The `items` variable contains the same data extracted by `GetItems`. The difference is that now you can call additional methods like `GetItems<T>`, `GetFunctions`, and others that are also exposed by the `MetadataWorkspace` class. These methods act on the data extracted by `GetItemCollection`, whereas the methods invoked on `Metadata-Workspace` need the schema to scan through.

These additional methods exposed by the `ItemCollection` class don't particularly simplify development. What really helps development is the `TryGetItemCollection` method, which you can use to check whether metadata in that space is loaded, as you saw in listing 12.2.

Both `GetItems` and `GetItemCollection` return all data from the queried dataspace. If you want to filter it, you have to use LINQ or, in the case of `GetItem-Collection`, some specific methods. Either way, the core behavior doesn't change; you retrieve all the data and then pick up what you need.

But wouldn't it be better to only have the items you wanted, without having to filter them after retrieving them?

EXTRACTING METADATA WITH GETITEMS<T>

The `GetItems<T>` method enables you to retrieve items of a certain type immediately. No additional methods and no LINQ queries are needed: just a method call. Isn't that better?

`GetItems<T>` returns a `ReadOnlyCollection<T>`, where `T` is the type searched for. If you searched all entities in the conceptual schema, the result would be a `ReadOnly-Collection<EntityType>`. The following example shows how to use this method:

C#
```
var items = ctx.MetadataWorkspace.GetItems<EntityType>(DataSpace.CSpace);
```

VB
```
Dim items = ctx.MetadataWorkspace.GetItems(Of EntityType)(DataSpace.CSpace)
```

Because `ReadOnlyCollection<T>` implements `IEnumerable<T>`, you can perform LINQ queries on the result returned by `GetItems<T>`. This is full control.

Unfortunately, `GetItems<T>` doesn't have an exception-safe version, meaning that the metadata for the searched space must be loaded, or this method will raise an exception.

All the methods we've seen so far return a list of items, but often you'll just need one item. For instance, you may need to inspect the `Supplier` item to validate the `IBAN` property with a regular expression (remember the example in chapter 5?).

EXTRACTING METADATA WITH GETITEM<T> AND TRYGETITEM<T>

The `GetItem<T>` method retrieves a single entity. It accepts the dataspace and a string representing the *full* name of the entity.

It's important that you understand what we mean by the *full name*. When you search through the `CSpace` or the `SSpace`, the namespace is the one specified in the `Schema` element. When you search through `OSpace`, the namespace is the CLR class namespace that *doesn't* necessarily match with its counterpart in the CSDL. In the following listing, you can see the difference in how data from different spaces is retrieved.

Listing 12.3 Using `GetItem<T>` to retrieve metadata

C#

```
var csItem = ctx.MetadataWorkspace.GetItem<EntityType>
  ("OrderITModel.Supplier", DataSpace.CSpace);
var osItem = ctx.MetadataWorkspace.GetItem<EntityType>
  ("OrderIT.Model.Supplier", DataSpace.OSpace);
```

VB

```
Dim csItem = ctx.MetadataWorkspace.GetItem(Of EntityType)(
  "OrderITModel.Supplier", DataSpace.CSpace)
Dim osItem = ctx.MetadataWorkspace.GetItem(Of EntityType)(
  "OrderIT.Model.Supplier", DataSpace.OSpace)
```

The object returned by `GetItem<T>` is of the type specified in the generic parameter. In this listing, `csItem` and `osItem` are of `EntityType` type.

If an element isn't found, or if the metadata for the dataspace isn't loaded, `GetItem<T>` throws an exception. If you're sure that the metadata is loaded and that the item exists in the space, `GetItem<T>` is for you; otherwise, the exception-safe version `TryGetItem<T>`, used in the following listing, is a better choice.

Listing 12.4 Using `TryGetItem<T>` to retrieve metadata

C#

```
EntityType osItem = null, csItem = null;
var csloaded = ctx.MetadataWorkspace.TryGetItem<EntityType>
  ("OrderITModel.Supplier", DataSpace.CSpace, out csItem);
var osloaded = ctx.MetadataWorkspace.TryGetItem<EntityType>
  ("OrderIT.Model.Supplier", DataSpace.CSpace, out osItem);
```

VB

```
Dim osItem As EntityType = Nothing
Dim csItem As EntityType = Nothing
Dim csloaded = ctx.MetadataWorkspace.TryGetItem(Of EntityType)(
  ("OrderITModel.Supplier", DataSpace.CSpace, csItem)
Dim osloaded = ctx.MetadataWorkspace.TryGetItem(Of EntityType)(
  "OrderIT.Model.Supplier", DataSpace.CSpace, osItem)
```

Congratulations! You're close to becoming a metadata Jedi. You have the knowledge; now it's time to see how to use it. Let's look at how you can build powerful stuff using what you've learned.

12.3 *Building a metadata explorer*

The best way to use all you've seen in this chapter is to create a metadata explorer. The metadata explorer is a simple form with a tree view showing all elements defined in the conceptual and storage schemas. The elements are grouped in nodes, and the most important properties of each type of element are shown.

For instance, for each entity, all properties are shown with the primary-key properties displayed in bold and the foreign-key properties shown in bold and red. Function return values and parameters are listed along with their types.

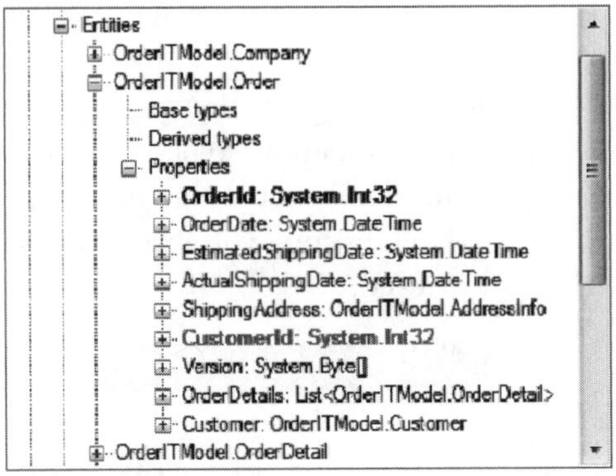

After the metadata is loaded, the

Figure 12.2   The tree view where metadata is shown. The conceptual side is divided into entities, complex types, functions, and containers. The same is done for the storage side.

metadata explorer form is very similar to the designer's Model Browser window. Figure 12.2 shows the metadata browser you're going to build.

Take a quick look at the tree in figure 12.2. Doesn't it remind you the structure of the conceptual and storage schemas? You have entities, complex types, functions, and containers. It's much easier to read than raw XML, isn't it?

Representing both the conceptual and the storage schemas takes about 120 lines of code in the editor (but only about 80 if you don't count blank lines and lines with only curly brackets). In the tree view, each schema is represented with two root nodes, labeled `Conceptual Side` and `Storage Side`, with four inner nodes: `Entities`, `ComplexTypes` (only for the conceptual schema), `Functions`, and `Containers`. Let's see how you can populate the tree view, starting with the `Entities` node.

12.3.1 *Populating entities and complex types*

The entities node has a child for each entity in the schema. Listing all the entities is just a matter of using `GetItems<T>`, passing `EntityType` as the generic parameter, and creating a node for each item.

Each entity node has three children:

- *Base types*—Contains all classes that the entity inherits from
- *Derived types*—Contains all classes that inherit from the entity
- *Properties*—Contains all entity properties

The following code creates the entities node.

Listing 12.5   Creating the entities node

C#
```csharp
var entities = ctx.MetadataWorkspace.GetItems<EntityType>
  (DataSpace.CSpace);
foreach (var item in entities)
{
  var currentTreeNode = tree.Nodes[0].Nodes[0]            Node for entity
    .Nodes.Add(item.FullName);
  WriteTypeBaseTypes(currentTreeNode, item);
  WriteTypeDerivedTypes(currentTreeNode,                 Nodes for
    item, entities);                                     entity details
  WriteProperties(currentTreeNode,
    item, ctx, DataSpace.CSpace);
}
```

VB
```vbnet
Dim entities = ctx.MetadataWorkspace.GetItems(Of EntityType)(
  DataSpace.CSpace)
For Each item In entities
  Dim currentTreeNode = tree.Nodes(0).Nodes(0).          Node for entity
    Nodes.Add(item.FullName)
  WriteTypeBaseTypes(currentTreeNode, item)
  WriteTypeDerivedTypes(currentTreeNode, item, entities)  Nodes for
  WriteProperties(currentTreeNode,                        entity details
    item, ctx, DataSpace.CSpace)
Next
```

So far, everything is pretty easy. The core code lies in the three internal methods
`WriteTypeBaseTypes`, `WriteTypeDerivedTypes`, and `WriteProperties`, whose names
explain perfectly what they do.

RETRIEVING ENTITY BASE TYPES

The `WriteTypeBaseTypes` method retrieves the base types. It uses the `BaseType` property of `EntityType`, which points to another `EntityType` object representing the base
class. For instance, the entity type representing `Order` has the `BaseType` property set to
null, and the one representing `Customer` has the property set to `Company`. Here's the
code.

Listing 12.6   Creating the base types nodes

C#
```csharp
private void WriteTypeBaseTypes(TreeNode currentTreeNode, EntityType item)
{
  var node = currentTreeNode.Nodes.Add("Base types");
  if (item.BaseType != null)
    node.Nodes.Add(item.BaseType.FullName);
}
```

VB
```vbnet
Private Sub WriteTypeBaseTypes(ByVal currentTreeNode As TreeNode,
  ByVal item As EntityType)
  Dim node = currentTreeNode.Nodes.Add("Base types")
```

```
   If item.BaseType IsNot Nothing Then
      node.Nodes.Add(item.BaseType.FullName)
   End If
End Sub
```

As you can see, looking for the base type is trivial. Finding types that inherit from an entity is a little more complicated.

RETRIEVING ENTITY-DERIVED ENTITIES

Retrieving which entities inherit from the current one requires a simple LINQ query that searches for entities whose base type matches the current entity. The Write-TypeDerivedTypes method that retrieves this data is shown in this listing.

Listing 12.7   Creating the derived type nodes

C#
```csharp
private void WriteTypeDerivedTypes(TreeNode currentTreeNode,
   EntityType item, ReadOnlyCollection<EntityType> entities)
{
   var node = currentTreeNode.Nodes.Add("Derived types");
   var derivedTypes = entities                              // ❶ Retrieves
      .Where(e => e.BaseType != null &&                     //   derived
         e.BaseType.FullName == item.FullName);             //   entities
   foreach (var entity in derivedTypes)
   {
      node.Nodes.Add(entity.FullName);
   }
}
```

VB
```vb
Private Sub WriteTypeDerivedTypes(ByVal currentTreeNode As TreeNode,
   ByVal item As EntityType,
   ByVal entities As ReadOnlyCollection(Of EntityType))
   Dim node = currentTreeNode.Nodes.Add("Derived types")
   Dim derivedTypes = entities.Where(Function(e)            ' ❶ Retrieves
      e.BaseType IsNot Nothing AndAlso                      '   derived
      e.BaseType.FullName = item.FullName)                  '   entities
      For Each entity In derivedTypes
         node.Nodes.Add(entity.FullName)
      Next
End Sub
```

The LINQ query is fairly simple ❶. You just match the FullName property of the current entity with the FullName property of all entities' base types. That's all.

So far, everything has been simple. The next, and last, method retrieves properties and their information. That's a bit harder, compared with what you've done so far.

RETRIEVING PROPERTIES

The method that writes properties for the current entity in the tree view is Write-Properties. This method accepts the entity to be inspected as a StructuralType instance. Because EntityType inherits from StructuralType, passing the parameter as an EntityType instance is perfectly valid.

StructuralType has a property named Member that lists all the entity's properties. Highlighting the primary key ones is a simple matter of checking whether the current property name is included in the KeyMembers property, which is a list of primary-key properties.

Determining whether a property is a foreign-key property is a bit more complex. It requires a LINQ query that looks for foreign-key associations where the end role is the current entity and the dependent properties contain the current property. These and other features are shown in the following listing.

Listing 12.8 Creating the properties nodes

C#
```csharp
private void WriteProperties(TreeNode currentTreeNode, StructuralType item,
  OrderITEntities ctx, DataSpace space)
{
  var node = currentTreeNode.Nodes.Add(
    (space == DataSpace.CSpace) ? "Properties" : "Columns");        // ❶ Enumerates
  foreach(var prop in item.Members)                                 //     properties
  {
    var propNode = node.Nodes.Add(
      GetElementNameWithType(prop.Name,                             // ❷ Gets
        prop.TypeUsage, space));                                    //     property name

    var entityItem = item as EntityType;
    if (entityItem != null)
    {
      if (entityItem.KeyMembers
        .Any(p => p.Name == prop.Name))
      {                                                             // ❸ Checks if
        propNode.NodeFont =                                        //     property is
          new Font(this.Font, FontStyle.Bold);                     //     primary key
      }

      if (ctx.MetadataWorkspace                                    // ❹ Checks if
        .GetItems<AssociationType>(space)                         //     property is
          .Where(a => a.IsForeignKey).Any(a =>                     //     foreign key
            a.ReferentialConstraints[0]
              .ToProperties[0].Name == prop.Name &&
            a.ReferentialConstraints[0]
              .ToRole.Name == item.Name))
      {
        propNode.NodeFont = new Font(this.Font, FontStyle.Bold);
        propNode.ForeColor = Color.Red;
      }
    }

    var metaNode = propNode.Nodes.Add("Metadata Properties");
    foreach (var facet in prop.TypeUsage.Facets)                  // ❺ Retrieves
    {                                                             //     property
      propNode.Nodes.Add(facet.Name + ": " + facet.Value);       //     facets
    }

    foreach (var meta in prop.MetadataProperties)                // ❻ Retrieves
    {                                                            //     property
      metaNode.Nodes.Add(meta.Name + ": " + meta.Value);        //     metadata
```

```
        }
      }
    }
```

VB

```vb
Private Sub WriteProperties(ByVal currentTreeNode As TreeNode,
  ByVal item As StructuralType, ByVal ctx As OrderITEntities,
  ByVal space As DataSpace)
  Dim node = currentTreeNode.Nodes.Add(
    If((space = DataSpace.CSpace), "Properties", "Columns"))
  For Each prop In item.Members
    Dim propNode = node.Nodes.Add(
      GetElementNameWithType(prop.Name,
        prop.TypeUsage, space))

    Dim entityItem = TryCast(item, EntityType)
    If entityItem IsNot Nothing Then
      If entityItem.KeyMembers.Any(Function(p)
        p.Name = prop.Name) Then
        propNode.NodeFont =
          New Font(Me.Font, FontStyle.Bold)
      End If

      If ctx.MetadataWorkspace.
        GetItems(Of AssociationType)(space).
        Where(Function(a) a.IsForeignKey).
        Any(Function(a)
          a.ReferentialConstraints(0)
            .ToProperties(0).Name = prop.Name AndAlso
          a.ReferentialConstraints(0)
            .ToRole.Name = item.Name) Then
        propNode.NodeFont = New Font(Me.Font, FontStyle.Bold)
        propNode.ForeColor = Color.Red
      End If
    End If

    For Each facet In prop.TypeUsage.Facets
      propNode.Nodes.Add(facet.Name & ": " & facet.Value)
    Next

    Dim metaNode =
      propNode.Nodes.Add("Metadata Properties")
    For Each meta In prop.MetadataProperties
      metaNode.Nodes.Add((meta.Name & ": ") & meta.Value)
    Next
  Next
End Sub
```

① Enumerates properties

② Gets property name

③ Checks if property is primary key

④ Checks if property is foreign key

⑤ Retrieves property facets

⑥ Retrieves property metadata

Wow, that's a huge amount of code. But don't worry. It's the only long function in this chapter.

As we mentioned before, the input entity is of type StructuralType and not EntityType. This happens because this function can be used to write complex types too, and both ComplexType and EntityType inherit from StructuralType.

In the code, all properties are iterated via the Members property **①**. For each property, the following actions are taken:

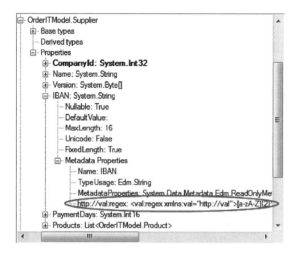

Figure 12.3 The regular expression of the IBAN is reachable through the property metadata.

- A node is created, setting the text with the result of the `GetElementNameWith-Type` method, which returns the property name and its type ❷. The code for this method isn't shown here because it's of no interest for this discussion. You can look at it in the book's source code.
- If the input item is an entity, a check is performed to see whether the property is part of the primary key ❸ and if it's a foreign key ❹.
- A node for each *facet* is added. The facets are the attributes of the property node (`nullable`, `maxLength`, and so on) ❺.
- A node for each metadata property is shown ❻.

It's important to note that metadata properties are exposed by every EDM-related class and that they contain the custom nodes you may add to an element. Do you remember the custom node that expresses the validation of the `IBAN` property of `Supplier`? You can see it in figure 12.3.

Now that the entities are described, it's time to talk about complex types.

RETRIEVING COMPLEX TYPES

Complex types are similar to entities, but they're simpler to manage because they can't be inherited, which means there are no `Base Type` and no `Derived type` nodes, and they have no primary or foreign keys. Only the `Properties` node is shared between entities and complex types.

The method that writes properties is already aware of complex types, so you can reuse it as the following listing demonstrates (note that in this listing and the rest of the chapter, the `tree` variable refers to the tree view in the form).

Listing 12.9 Creating the complex types nodes

C#
```
foreach (var item in ctx.MetadataWorkspace.GetItems<ComplexType>
  (DataSpace.CSpace))
```

```
{
  var currentTreeNode = tree.Nodes[0].Nodes[2].Nodes.Add(item.FullName);
  WriteProperties(currentTreeNode, item, ctx, DataSpace.CSpace);
}
```

VB

```
For Each item In ctx.MetadataWorkspace.GetItems(Of ComplexType)(
  DataSpace.CSpace)
  Dim currentTreeNode = tree.Nodes(0).Nodes(2).Nodes.Add(item.FullName)
  WriteProperties(currentTreeNode, item, ctx, DataSpace.CSpace)
Next
```

That's it! You retrieve complex types and then call `WriteProperties` for each of them. Cool, isn't it?

The second step is populating the functions. What's nice here is that you only have parameters and results to show, so there's not a lot to learn.

12.3.2 *Populating functions*

The functions node contains a child for each function, which in turn has a child node for each parameter. The text shown in the root node for each function is formatted with the name followed by the return type.

The technique is always the same: you retrieve all the functions using `Get-Items<EdmFunction>`, and for each of them you call a method that populates the parameters and return types. Here's the code that does that.

Listing 12.10 Creating the functions nodes

C#

```
var functions = ctx.MetadataWorkspace.GetItems<EdmFunction>      ❶ Extracts only
  (DataSpace.CSpace)                                                functions
    .Where(i => i.NamespaceName != "Edm");                    ◁─    defined by you
foreach (var item in functions)
{
  var currentTreeNode = tree.Nodes[0].Nodes[1].Nodes.Add(
    GetElementNameWithType(item.FullName, item.ReturnParameter.TypeUsage,
    DataSpace.CSpace));
  WriteFunctionParameters(currentTreeNode, item.Parameters,
    DataSpace.CSpace);
}
```

                                                      Extracts only ❶
                                                        functions
VB   **defined by you**

```
Dim functions = ctx.MetadataWorkspace.GetItems(Of EdmFunction)(
  DataSpace.CSpace)
    .Where(Function(i) i.NamespaceName <> "Edm")              ◁─
For Each item In functions
  Dim currentTreeNode =    tree.Nodes(0).Nodes(1).Nodes.Add(
    GetElementNameWithType(item.FullName, item.ReturnParameter.TypeUsage,
    DataSpace.CSpace))
  WriteFunctionParameters(currentTreeNode, item.Parameters,
  DataSpace.CSpace)
Next
```

Notice the filter applied to the items returned by `GetItems<EdmFunction>` ❶. It's applied because primitive functions are returned too, and the namespace is the only way to differentiate them from those defined by you (which are the ones you're interested in).

The `WriteFunctionParameters` method is trivial, as you can see in the following listing. It iterates over function parameters, leveraging the `GetElementNameWithType` method to get their names and types, and adding the directions: `In`, `Out`, or `InOut`.

> **Listing 12.11 Creating parameter nodes for each function**

C#
```
private void WriteFunctionParameters(TreeNode parentNode,
  ReadOnlyMetadataCollection<FunctionParameter> parameters,
  DataSpace space)
{
  foreach (var param in parameters)
    parentNode.Nodes.Add(
      GetElementNameWithType(param.Name,              Name, type, and
        param.TypeUsage, space) + ": " + param.Mode); direction creation
}
```

VB
```
Private Sub WriteFunctionParameters(ByVal parentNode As TreeNode,
  ByVal parameters As ReadOnlyMetadataCollection(Of FunctionParameter),
  ByVal space As DataSpace)
  For Each param In parameters
    parentNode.Nodes.Add(
      (GetElementNameWithType(param.Name,             Name, type, and
        param.TypeUsage, space) & ": ") + param.Mode) direction creation
  Next
End Sub
```

The code is self-explanatory. We can move on and talk about the last part of the conceptual schema: the containers.

12.3.3 Populating containers

The containers node contains a child node for each container found. Each container has three children: entity sets, association sets, and function imports. Association sets and entity sets are very similar and, in terms of metadata, share the base class. Function imports are identical to functions, so this listing reuses the code from the previous section.

> **Listing 12.12 Creating the containers nodes**

C#
```
var containers = ctx.MetadataWorkspace.GetItems<EntityContainer>
  (DataSpace.CSpace);                                     Function
foreach (var item in containers)                      imports nodes
{
  var currentTreeNode = tree.Nodes[0].Nodes[3].Nodes.Add(item.Name);
  WriteFunctionImports(currentTreeNode, item);
```

```
    WriteEntitySets<EntitySet>(currentTreeNode, item);                    Entity sets
    WriteEntitySets<AssociationSet>                    Association       nodes
      (currentTreeNode, item);                          sets nodes
}
```

VB

```
Dim containers = ctx.MetadataWorkspace.GetItems(Of EntityContainer)
  (DataSpace.CSpace)                                                Function
For Each item In containers                                     imports nodes
  Dim currentTreeNode = tree.Nodes(0).Nodes(3).Nodes.Add(item.Name)
  WriteFunctionImports(currentTreeNode, item)
  WriteEntitySets(Of EntitySet)(currentTreeNode, item)              Entity sets
  WriteEntitySets(Of AssociationSet)(            Association       nodes
    currentTreeNode, item)                       sets nodes
Next
```

Here you retrieve all the containers, using `GetItems<EntityContainer>`, and then invoke the methods that build the inner nodes. Those methods are the interesting part, as you can see in the next in listing.

Listing 12.13   Creating the entity sets and function imports nodes

C#

```
private void WriteEntitySets<T>(TreeNode currentTreeNode,
  EntityContainer item) where T: EntitySetBase
{
  var entitySetsNode = currentTreeNode.Nodes.Add(
    typeof(T) == typeof(EntitySet) ? "Entity sets" : "Association sets");
  foreach (var bes in item.BaseEntitySets.OfType<T>())
  {
    var node = entitySetsNode.Nodes.Add(bes.Name + ": " + bes.ElementType);
  }
}

private void WriteFunctionImports(TreeNode currentTreeNode,
  EntityContainer item)
{
  var funcsNode = currentTreeNode.Nodes.Add("FunctionImports");
  foreach (var func in item.FunctionImports)
  {
    var funcNode = funcsNode.Nodes.Add(func.Name);
    WriteFunctionParameters(funcNode, func.Parameters, DataSpace.CSpace);
  }
}
```

VB

```
Private Sub WriteEntitySets(Of T As EntitySetBase)(
  ByVal currentTreeNode As TreeNode, ByVal item As EntityContainer)
  Dim entitySetsNode = currentTreeNode.Nodes.Add(
    IIf(GetType(T) = GetType(EntitySet), "Entity sets","Association sets"))
    For Each bes In item.BaseEntitySets.OfType(Of T)()
      Dim node = entitySetsNode.Nodes.Add((bes.Name & ": ") &
        bes.ElementType)
    Next
End Sub
```

```
Private Sub WriteFunctionImports(ByVal currentTreeNode As TreeNode,
  ByVal item As EntityContainer)
  Dim funcsNode = currentTreeNode.Nodes.Add("FunctionImports")
  For Each func In item.FunctionImports
    Dim funcNode = funcsNode.Nodes.Add(func.Name)
    WriteFunctionParameters(funcNode, func.Parameters, DataSpace.CSpace)
  Next
End Sub
```

The WriteEntitySets method is the most interesting. The classes representing entity sets and association sets are EntitySet and AssociationSet, both of which inherit from the EntitySetBase class. The EntityContainer class has a BaseEntitySets property that exposes both sets via their base class. To show them in different nodes, you pass the type as a generic parameter and then use the OfType<T> LINQ method to extract only the sets for that type. Then for each set, a node with the name and base type is created.

The WriteFunctionImports method is less complex. It creates a node for each function and then describes it using the WriteFunctionParameters method you've seen before.

The conceptual node is now populated. It contains all the conceptual schema items, so it's time to move on to the storage-schema representation. Fortunately, because CSDL and SSDL share the same schema, all the functions can be reused.

12.3.4 Populating storage nodes

Populating the storage-side nodes is slightly easier than populating the conceptual-side modes. In a database, you don't have complex types; there's only one container because you can't describe more databases, and there's no function-import concept. These differences lead to simpler code, as you can see in the following listing.

> **Listing 12.14 Creating the containers nodes**

C#
```
foreach (var item in
  ctx.MetadataWorkspace.GetItems<EntityType>(DataSpace.SSpace))
{
  var currentTreeNode = tree.Nodes[1].Nodes[0].Nodes.Add(item.ToString());
  WriteProperties(currentTreeNode, item, ctx, DataSpace.SSpace);
}
foreach (var item in
  ctx.MetadataWorkspace.GetItems<EdmFunction>(DataSpace.SSpace)
    .Where(i => i.NamespaceName != "SqlServer"))
{
  var currentTreeNode = tree.Nodes[1].Nodes[1].Nodes.Add(item.ToString());
  WriteFunctionParameters(currentTreeNode, item.Parameters,
    DataSpace.SSpace);
}
var container = ctx.MetadataWorkspace.GetItems<EntityContainer>
  (DataSpace.SSpace).First();
var currentNode = tree.Nodes[1].Nodes[2].Nodes.Add(container.ToString());
```

```
WriteEntitySets<EntitySet>(currentNode, container);
WriteEntitySets<AssociationSet>(currentNode, container);
```

VB

```
For Each item In ctx.MetadataWorkspace.GetItems(Of EntityType)
  (DataSpace.SSpace)
  Dim currentTreeNode = tree.Nodes(1).Nodes(0).Nodes.Add(item.ToString())
  WriteProperties(currentTreeNode, item, ctx, DataSpace.SSpace)
Next
For Each item In ctx.MetadataWorkspace.GetItems(Of EdmFunction)
  (DataSpace.SSpace).Where(Function(i) i.NamespaceName <> "SqlServer")
  Dim currentTreeNode = tree.Nodes(1).Nodes(1).Nodes.Add(item.ToString())
  WriteFunctionParameters(currentTreeNode, item.Parameters,
    DataSpace.SSpace)
Next
Dim container = ctx.MetadataWorkspace.GetItems(Of EntityContainer)
  (DataSpace.SSpace).First()
Dim currentNode = tree.Nodes(1).Nodes(2).Nodes.Add(container.ToString())
WriteEntitySets(Of EntitySet)(currentNode, container)
WriteEntitySets(Of AssociationSet)(currentNode, container)
```

As you can see, the differences are small:

- The `SSpace` value, instead of `CSpace`, is used to extract items from the storage side.
- The namespace for removing primitive functions is `SqlServer`, not `Edm`.

The rest of the code makes extensive reuse of the existing methods, making everything easier than you may have thought.

We've covered a lot, but now you've mastered metadata. This academic exercise was a good way to learn a new feature, but you may find a bite of the real world more interesting. In the next section, we'll show you how metadata can positively affect your real code.

Why there's no mapping representation

You surely have noticed that there's no MSL metadata in the tree. That's because there are no methods to access the mapping schema. Although there's the `CSSpace` value in the `DataSpace` enum, it's of absolutely no use. The classes representing the mapping metadata aren't exposed by Entity Framework, so you can't access them.

If you think there's some esoteric reason for this lack, you're wrong. There has just been no developer interest in having such APIs. The Entity Framework team decided to keep the APIs internal, suggesting that you use LINQ to XML to search for the necessary information. It's not nice, but it's not difficult to do once you get used to the mapping structure.

12.4   *Writing generic code with metadata*

In chapter 6, we introduced a smart method that adds or attaches an entity to the context depending on the value of the primary key. That method works with a fixed entity, meaning that if you have 100 entities, you have to duplicate it 100 times. That's unbearable. Fortunately, thanks to metadata, you can write a single method that can handle any class.

Another interesting method is the one that allows you to retrieve any type of entity using just its keys. Every project has a `GetById` method for almost every entity. This requires some coding for the types of the properties and the returning types. Using metadata, you can write a generic method and save some lines of code.

We'll look at these examples in the next sections so you can understand how to use metadata in such real-world scenarios.

12.4.1 Adding or attaching an object based on custom annotations

Let's assume you're adding a new customer. Its `CompanyId` property is 0 because the real value is calculated on the database. If you need to update a customer, the `CompanyId` property is already set to a value that matches the value in the database (a value that is higher than 0).

In chapter 6, you created a method that decided whether to attach or add an entity to the context based on the value of the primary key properties. If the value is 0, the entity is added; otherwise, it's attached. Wouldn't it be good if such a method could decide whether to add or to attach an entity based on a value configured in the EDM?

The steps are pretty simple:

1 Add a custom annotation to the key properties in the EDM, indicating what value causes the `AddObject` method to be invoked.

2 Create an extension method (say, `SmartAttach`) that accepts the entity. It then checks the key properties' values, and if they match the ones expressed in the custom annotation, it invokes the `AddObject` method; otherwise it invokes the `Attach` method.

The first point needs no explanation. We covered it in depth in chapter 5. You just need to add the `efex` (or any name you like) namespace, and then use the `Insert-When` element inside the `CompanyId` attribute:

```
<Schema xmlns:efex="http://efex" ...>
  ...
  <EntityType Name="Company" Abstract="true">
    <Property Name="CompanyId" ...>
      <efex:InsertWhen>0</efex:InsertWhen>
    </Property>
    ...
  </EntityType>
  ...
</Schema>
```

The fun part is the second point. Look at the following listing.

Listing 12.15   Adding or attaching an entity depending on the value in the EDM

C#

```
public static void SmartAttach<T>(this ObjectSet<T> es, T input)
  where T : class
{
  var objectType = ObjectContext.GetObjectType(input.GetType());
  var osItem = es.Context.MetadataWorkspace.GetItem<EntityType>
    (objectType.FullName, DataSpace.OSpace);
  var csItem = (EntityType)es.Context
    .MetadataWorkspace.GetEdmSpaceType(osItem);
  var value = ((XElement)(csItem.KeyMembers.First()
    .MetadataProperties.First(p =>
      p.Name == "http://efex:InsertWhen").Value)).Value;
  var idType = input.GetType().GetProperty(csItem.KeyMembers.First().Name)
    .PropertyType;
  var id = input.GetType().GetProperty(csItem.KeyMembers.First().Name)
    .GetValue(input, null);
  if (id.Equals(Convert.ChangeType(value, idType)))
    set.AddObject(input);
  else
    set.Attach(input);
}
```

❶ Retrieves conceptual entity

❷ Retrieves insert value annotation

❸ Adds or attaches object based on entity and metadata value

VB

```
<System.Runtime.CompilerServices.Extension>
Public Shared Sub SmartAttach(Of T As Class)(
  ByVal es As ObjectSet(Of T), ByVal input As T)
  Dim objectType = ObjectContext.GetObjectType(input.GetType ())
  Dim osItem = es.Context.MetadataWorkspace.GetItem(Of EntityType)(
    objectType.FullName, DataSpace.OSpace)
  Dim csItem = DirectCast(es.Context.
    MetadataWorkspace.GetEdmSpaceType(osItem),
    EntityType)
  Dim value = DirectCast((csItem.KeyMembers.First()
    .MetadataProperties.First(Function(p) _
      p.Name = "http://efex:InsertWhen").Value),
    XElement).Value
  Dim idType = input.[GetType]().GetProperty _
    (csItem.KeyMembers.First().Name).PropertyType
  Dim id = input.GetType().GetProperty(csItem.KeyMembers.First().Name).
    GetValue(input, Nothing)
  If id.Equals(Convert.ChangeType(value, idType)) Then
    es.AddObject(input)
  Else
    es.Attach(input)
  End If
End Sub
```

❶ Retrieves conceptual entity

❷ Retrieves insert value annotation

❸ Adds or attaches object based on entity and metadata value

The method signature is simple; it extends the `ObjectSet<T>` class and accepts the entity to be added or attached.

The first two statements retrieve the POCO type of the entity (remember that it could be a proxied instance) and look for the entity in the object space of the metadata. The object retrieved is then passed to the `GetEdmSpaceType` method to obtain its conceptual space counterpart ❶.

Next, the key property is retrieved, and its custom annotation value is extracted, obtaining the value that determines whether the entity should be marked for addition ❷. The first thing to notice here is that the custom annotation is retrieved using its full name, `http://efex:InsertWhen`, and not using the namespace alias. The second thing is that the custom annotation is exposed as an XML fragment. It's first cast to `XElement`, and then the value is extracted.

Finally, the value from the metadata is converted to a key property type and compared with the key property value ❸. If they match, the entity is marked as added; otherwise, it's attached.

> **NOTE** In this example, we've made the assumption that the entity has only one key property. Naturally, this isn't always the case, because you may have many key properties. Accommodating this case doesn't change the code a lot; instead of dealing with a single property, you must deal with an array of properties. Have fun.

The next example we'll look at involves a generic `GetById<T>` method. If you've used NHibernate, you'll know that this method is already provided by the session. Let's realize it using Entity Framework.

12.4.2 Building a generic GetById method

`ObjectContext` has a `GetObjectByKey` method that searches for an object using its key. This method has two drawbacks: it returns an `object` instance that requires casting to the actual entity type, and it requires an `EntityKey` instance as input. These drawbacks make the `GetObjectByKey` method awkward. Let's see how to create a smarter method.

The `GetById<T>` method you'll create in this section overcomes the limitations of the `GetObjectByKey` method. First, the `GetById<T>` method makes use of generics, eliminating the need for casting the result to the entity type you need. Second, the `GetById<T>` method accepts only the key properties' values, so that the method interface is extremely simple.

`GetById<T>` internally uses `GetObjectByKey`, and `GetObjectByKey` needs an `EntityKey` instance as parameter. `GetById<T>` automatically retrieves, through metadata, the values necessary to create the `EntityKey` instance that is then passed to `GetObjectByKey`.

The code of the `GetById<T>` method is shown in the following listing.

Listing 12.16 The `GetById<T>` implementation

C#
```
public static T GetById<T>(this ObjectContext ctx, object id)
{
  var container = ctx.MetadataWorkspace.GetEntityContainer
    (ctx.DefaultContainerName, DataSpace.CSpace);
  var osItem = ctx.MetadataWorkspace.GetItem<EntityType>
    (typeof(T).FullName, DataSpace.OSpace);
```

```
var csItem = (EdmType)ctx.MetadataWorkspace.GetEdmSpaceType(osItem);

while (csItem.BaseType != null)
  csItem = csItem.BaseType;

var esName = container.BaseEntitySets
   .First(s => s.ElementType.FullName == csItem.FullName).Name;
var fullEsName = container.Name + "." + esName;
var keyName = ((EntityType)csItem).KeyMembers.First().Name;
return (T)ctx.GetObjectByKey(new EntityKey(fullEsName, keyName, id));
}
```

❶ Retrieves first base type

VB

```
<System.Runtime.CompilerServices.Extension>
Public Shared Function GetById(Of T)(
  ctx As ObjectContext, id As Object) As T

  Dim container = ctx.MetadataWorkspace.
    GetEntityContainer(ctx.DefaultContainerName, DataSpace.CSpace)
  Dim osItem = ctx.MetadataWorkspace.GetItem(Of EntityType)(
    GetType(T).FullName, DataSpace.OSpace)
  Dim csItem = DirectCast(
    ctx.MetadataWorkspace.GetEdmSpaceType(osItem), EdmType)

  While csItem.BaseType IsNot Nothing
    csItem = csItem.BaseType
  End While

  Dim entitySetName = container.BaseEntitySets.First(
    Function(s) s.ElementType.FullName = csItem.FullName).Name
  Dim esName = container.Name + "." & entitySetName
  Dim keyName = DirectCast(csItem, EntityType).KeyMembers.First().Name
  Return DirectCast(
    ctx.GetObjectByKey(New EntityKey(esName, keyName, id)), T)
End Function
```

❶ Retrieves first base type

At this point in the chapter, you should have no difficulty understanding this method. The first part retrieves the container and the entity in the metadata. They're necessary to get the entity set name that is then used to create the EntityKey instance.

Because the entity set points to the base entity of an inheritance hierarchy, the base class for the input entity is retrieved through the BaseType property ❶. The loop is required because the inheritance can be more than one level deep. When BaseType is null, the base class has been reached.

The full entity set name is required by GetObjectByKey, so the entity set name is appended to the container name. After that, the key property name is retrieved from the entity. Now every parameter necessary for GetObjectByKey to work has been retrieved. You just invoke it, cast the result to the generic type, and then return it to the caller.

Hopefully these examples have given you an idea of what you can do with metadata. You may still be somewhat uncertain of its usefulness, but if you give metadata a chance, you won't regret it.

12.5 *Summary*

In this chapter, you've learned about a powerful, often underestimated, feature of the Entity Framework: metadata retrieval.

You've learned how to read the conceptual and storage schemas, and you've learned what the object space is useful for and why the mapping layer doesn't have a set of public APIs. All this knowledge makes you a Padawan of metadata.

What takes you to the Jedi Master level is the ability to find places where metadata helps you cut down on the code. We presented two examples at the end of the chapter, but there are many others, and your duty is to find them.

Understanding metadata is also vital to code and database generation, which we'll discuss in the next chapter. Code generation uses metadata to create CLR classes from the model, and database generation creates mapping schema, storage schema, (and the SQL DDL from this last schema) starting from the conceptual model.

Customizing code and the designer

13

This chapter covers

- Understanding the Visual Studio T4 mechanism
- Customizing code generation
- Customizing database DDL generation
- Customizing the designer

You know that by default the Visual Studio designer generates Entity Framework 1.0–style classes. You also know that these classes are generated through a *template*. What's great is that you can modify this template, or create new templates, to generate classes to fit your needs. You've already seen an example in chapter 2, when we introduced the POCO template provided by Microsoft. Another point where templates help in generating code is during database DDL generation from the storage model (when you use the model-first approach). You'll learn about that later in this chapter.

When you modify templates to change the way CLR code or database DDL is generated, you have to deal with different Entity Framework features and other products in the .NET framework.

Metadata is an important feature that you must use to be able to modify templates. When you create or modify classes in the designer, only the EDMX file is modified; the template generates the code on demand. It reads the conceptual schema metadata and generates the code based on that data. The same way, when the database DDL is generated, the storage and mapping schema are generated. After that, the storage schema data is used to create the DDL. Everything is metadata-driven.

To modify templates, a minimal knowledge of Windows Workflow Foundation (WF) is necessary too, because during database script generation (when using the model-first approach), the MSL, SSDL, and DDL are generated by a custom workflow action.

Finally, having good knowledge of the designer helps simplify code generation, because it can be customized to make things easier for you. For instance, it can be extended to write custom annotations in the EDMX file without you having to do it manually.

This chapter will cover all of these subjects—templates, metadata, Workflow Foundation, and designer extensions—putting them into action to help you customize your development environment.

13.1 How Visual Studio generates classes

When Visual Studio 2008 shipped, it introduced a text-generation engine named Text Template Transformation Toolkit (better known as *T4*). It's a template-file-based engine that can generate any data you need.

We said *data*, but T4's generation potential is unlimited. You can create text strings and save them to a file, or you can create images, Word documents, and so on. Despite its enormous potential, the goal here is using it for creating classes, which are just text files.

Creating a template file is pretty simple. If you've already used code-generation tools (such as CodeSmith), you won't find it difficult. If you have a Classic ASP background, you'll see many similarities between a template and an ASP page.

A template is a plain-text file with a .tt extension. It has a dedicated icon in the Solution Explorer window, as figure 13.1 illustrates.

A template contains code that generates data. This code is executed automatically when you open the template and save it. A simpler way to trigger generation is right-clicking the template and selecting the Run Custom Tool item from the context menu.

A template file is divided into two main sections:

- *Directives (pragmas)*—Declares assemblies, namespaces, includes, and other *global* information
- *Code*—Contains the code that actually generates the code (classes, in our case)

Each of these parts is identified by tags that are a key aspect of the template. We'll first discuss the tags and then look at the two sections of the file.

Figure 13.1 A template file shown in the Solution Explorer

Template-editing extension

When you open a template, the editor doesn't offer any help. Autocompletion isn't enabled, and there's no syntax highlighting. Fortunately, Tangible Engineering has created an extension for Visual Studio that offers features to make editing and comprehension easier. You can install it directly from Extension Manager inside Visual Studio:

1 Click the Tools menu, and select Extension Manager to open the Extension Manager pop-up window.
2 In that window, click the Online Gallery item at left.
3 Type T4 Editor in the search box at upper right (see the figure).

The free version of this extension offers a limited set of features; if you want the full version, you can buy it from the Tangible website (http://mng.bz/WAxC).

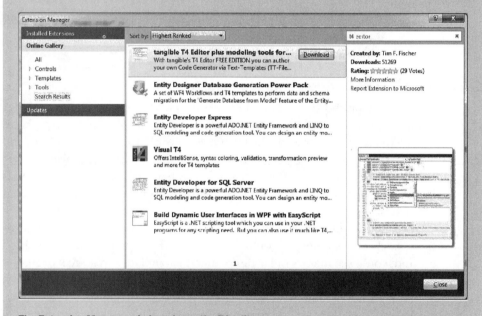

The Extension Manager window shows the T4 editors.

13.1.1   *Understanding template tags*

We already said that a template is a text file that is interpreted by an engine to generate code. To interpret the template file, the engine relies on specific *markup* in the template itself.

We also said that a template file is very similar to a Classic ASP page; the template is a mix of directives, code, and dynamic text, with the code and directives being identified by special tags. One difference is that in Classic ASP pages, the server code is surrounded by <% %> tags; but in the template file, both the code and the directives are surrounded by <# #> tags. Everything inside the tags is interpreted by the engine as code that must be executed (also known as a *block*); the text that's not included inside the tags is what is written to the output file.

In some cases, you may need to append a special character to the opening tag to perform special tasks. The first special character is @, which specifies that the block is a directive:

```
<#@ template language="C#" debug="false" hostspecific="true" #>
```

Another important character is =. The block inside this tag returns a value, and it's written in the generated code:

```
public class <#= ClassName #> { }
```

This block is also known as an *evaluation block*.

The last special character is +. It specifies that the code inside the block is class-like. If you have to create properties or methods, you have to use this character.

```
<#+
void WriteClassName() {
  ...
}
#>
```

This block is also known as a *class block*.

Understanding tags is only the first step toward understanding templates. We'll look at the pragma section next.

13.1.2 *Understanding directives*

The first directive of a template is `template`. It identifies the file as a template, and it *must* be the first element. It also specifies the language and enables or disables debugging:

```
<#@ template language="C#" debug="false" hostspecific="true"#>
```

Although the `template` directive is mandatory, all the other directives are optional. The first one is `assembly`. It imports an assembly, making its classes available to the code. The assembly is specified in the `name` attribute:

```
<#@ assembly name="System.Core" #>
```

Once the assembly is declared, you can use the `import` directive to import a namespace so you can use classes inside the namespace in the code without fully referencing them. This directive has the same purpose as the `Imports` and `using` statements in VB and C#:

```
<#@ import namespace="System" #>
```

Another useful directive is `output`. With it, you can specify the extension of the file generated by the template, through the `extension` attribute, and the encoding of the file, through `encoding`:

```
<#@ output extension=".cs" #>
```

The last directive is `include`. It allows you to import a code file whose classes can be used by the template:

```
<#@ include file="EF.Utility.CS.ttinclude"#>
```

> **NOTE** The file to be included must be placed in the %ProgramFiles%\ Microsoft Visual Studio 10.0\Common7\IDE\Extensions\Microsoft\Entity Framework Tools\Templates\Includes folder, or in the same folder as the template.

You're two-thirds of the way through learning about templates. The last third, and the most complex, is the code section.

13.1.3 Writing code

Suppose you need to write a template that generates an HTML page that displays all the files in a specific directory. This isn't an Entity Framework–related example, but don't worry; you'll learn about more real-world scenarios later.

To accomplish this task, you need to add a new file of Text Template type to the project and write code to retrieve the files in the directory that you need to display; then, you have to create tags that will write files to the output stream. The following listing shows an example of a template that generates HTML.

Listing 13.1 Template that creates an HTML file that lists a directory's files

C#
```
<#@ template language="C#" debug="false" hostspecific="true"#>
<#@ output extension=".html"#>

<#var files = System.IO.Directory.GetFiles("D:\\");#>      ❶ Retrieves files
<html>
<head><title>Files</title></head>                         ❷ Writes
<body>                                                        static HTML
<#foreach (var file in files){#>
  <#=file#><br />                                          ❸ Writes
<#}#>                                                         dynamic HTML
</body>
</html>
```

VB
```
<#@ template language="VB" debug="false" hostspecific="true"#>
<#@ output extension=".html"#>

<#                                                        ❶ Retrieves files
Dim files = System.IO.Directory.GetFiles("D:\")
Dim file
#>
<html>
<head><title>Files</title></head>                        ❷ Writes
<body>                                                       static HTML
<#For Each file In files#>
  <#=file#><br />                                         ❸ Writes
<#Next#>                                                     dynamic HTML
</body>
</html>
```

In the first line of this listing, a code block is opened and the files are retrieved **❶**. The block is then closed to write the beginning part of the HTML **❷**. This part, not included in code tags, is written in the output stream as is. Next, a new code block starts the iteration over the files. For each item, an evaluation block adds the filename to the result stream. Finally, another code block closes the iteration: } for C# and Next for Visual Basic **❸**.

The HTML file generated by the preceding template looks like this:

```
<html>
<head><title>Files</title></head>
<body>
  D:\file1.txt<br />
  D:\file2.txt<br />
</body>
</html>
```

This example writes the names of the files in a folder. In many cases, you may need a more complex result whose calculation is better encapsulated in a method (for readability reason). Doing that is easy. First, you add a class block inside which you put a method that accepts the filename and returns the calculated result. Then, you change the evaluation block to invoke the method. The new method and the code that invokes the method are shown here.

Listing 13.2 Creating methods in the template

C#

```
...
<#=GetFileName(file)#><br />
...
<#+
string GetFileName(string file){
  return file;
}
#>
```

VB

```
...
<#=GetFileName(file)#><br />
...
<#+
Private Function GetFileName(ByVal file As String) As String
  Return file
End Function
#>
```

The GetFileName function is trivial because it just returns the filename. We created it only to explain how to create and consume methods in the template.

The result is automatically saved in a file that's named after the template file and whose extension matches the template language. If the template name is test.tt, then the filename is test.cs or test.vb. But wouldn't it be better to force the extension to be .html? The output pragma does the trick:

```
<#@ output extension=".html"#>
```

It's that simple. The next step is to modify Entity Framework templates to adapt them to your needs. You'll learn how to do that next.

13.2   *Customizing class generation*

In chapter 2, we introduced a template released by the Entity Framework team that generates POCO classes. Actually, there are two templates: one that generates object model classes and one that generates the context class. In OrderIT, you placed them in a single assembly; to keep things simple, we decided to use a single assembly with data-access code and object model classes.

In the next chapter, you'll see that in a well-layered architecture, you put object-model classes in one assembly and the context class in another. The Entity Framework team kept this in mind when they decided to deliver two different templates.

In sections 13.2.2 and 13.2.3, we'll show you how to customize those templates; but first, you need to understand how they're structured so that modifying them will be easier.

13.2.1   *Understanding the available POCO template*

Creating a template that reads the EDMX file and generates classes isn't difficult. You know that the EDMX file combines the three EDM files in one, so you need metadata APIs to read conceptual and storage-schema metadata.

As you learned in chapter 12, accessing metadata using the `ObjectContext` class or the `EntityConnection` is easy. Because the template must generate the context class, you can't use the `ObjectContext` class, and using the `EntityConnection` class is too complicated. The only way to access EDMX file metadata is by using the `Metadata-Workspace` class directly.

You learned in chapter 12 that directly creating an instance of `MetadataWorkspace` class is complicated. Fortunately, the Entity Framework team has created a helper file containing a set of classes that expose metadata. What's even better, the metadata is exposed as an `ItemCollection`, so you can reuse the APIs as you learned in chapter 12.

The helper file is named EF.Utility.CS.ttinclude for C# and EF.Utility.VB.ttinclude for VB, and it's in the Visual Studio includes folder. The main class in the helper file is `MetadataLoader`, and it exposes metadata through the `CreateEdmItemCollection` method, which returns an `EdmItemCollection` instance. You know that this class holds conceptual data only. If you want to retrieve the storage data, you have to do it on your own. But don't worry; we'll show you how to do that in section 13.2.2.

There are other important classes. The first is `MetadataTools`, which exposes methods that work on EDM types. For instance, its `ClrType` method accepts the EDM type and returns the CLR equivalent. `IsKey` accepts a property and returns a Boolean indicating whether it's part of its entity's primary key.

The `CodeGenerationTools` class performs the dirty work on strings. Its `Escape` function has many overloads that accept metadata objects like `EdmFunction`, `Edm-Property`, `EntityType`, and so on, and returns their escaped names so they don't conflict with language keywords. The `SpaceAfter` and `SpaceBefore` methods ensure that the string they accept as input has a space after or before, respectively, so the string isn't bound to the next or the preceding text.

The last interesting class is `Accessibility`. It contains static methods that read the visibility of a type or property defined in the EDM and return a string in the chosen language. For instance, if a property is defined as `public` in the EDM, the `For-Property` method returns the string `"public"` for C# and `"Public"` for VB.

Both templates instantiate these classes at the very beginning of the code section so you can use them without any effort. That's another point for Entity Framework's productivity, isn't it?

It's finally time to put all this knowledge to work. The first thing we'll show you is how to modify the context template to generate user-defined and scalar-valued functions, as we hinted in the previous chapter.

13.2.2 Generating user-defined and scalar-valued functions

User-defined functions are part of the CSDL; scalar-valued functions are defined in the SSDL because they're defined in the database. We said previously that `MetadataLoader` only returns data about the conceptual schema, so to retrieve scalar-valued functions defined in the storage schema, you have to write the code on your own.

Retrieving the storage schema isn't that hard. What you need to do is retrieve the raw XML representing the SSDL and pass it to the `MetadataItemCollectionFactory.` `CreateStoreItemCollection` method. It returns a `StoreItemCollection` instance that can be queried, as you saw in the previous chapter.

You can embed the code to retrieve the storage schema in a class-block method inside the template. You could even add the code to the `MetadataLoader` class, but we don't recommend that because the file containing the `MetadataLoader` class isn't under source control, and you should maintain it manually on each workstation. What's worse, if the Entity Framework team releases a new version of the file containing the `MetadataLoader` class, your modifications will be overwritten.

This listing shows the code you need in the template to retrieve the storage schema.

> **Listing 13.3   Retrieving the storage schema**

C#

```
<#+
StoreItemCollection CreateStoreItemCollection(string sourcePath)
{
  var _textTransformation = DynamicTextTransformation.Create(this);
  sourcePath =
    _textTransformation.Host.ResolvePath(sourcePath);      Gets EDMX file
                                                            absolute path

  XNamespace edmx =
    MetadataConstants.EDMX_NAMESPACE_V2;
  var model =
    XDocument.Load(sourcePath)
    .Element(edmx + "Edmx")                                 Gets
    .Element(edmx + "Runtime")                              storage
    .Element(edmx + "StorageModels")                        node
```

```
        .Elements().First();
  using (XmlReader reader = model.CreateReader())
  {
    IList<EdmSchemaError> errors = null;
    return MetadataItemCollectionFactory.
      CreateStoreItemCollection(
        new List<XmlReader> { reader }, out errors);
  }
}
#>
```
Loads storage schema

VB

```
<#+
Private Function CreateStoreItemCollection _
  (ByVal sourcePath As String) As StoreItemCollection
  Dim _textTransformation = DynamicTextTransformation.Create(Me)
    sourcePath =
      _textTransformation.Host.ResolvePath(sourcePath)

  Dim edmx As XNamespace = MetadataConstants.EDMX_NAMESPACE_V2
  Dim model = XDocument.Load(sourcePath).
    Element(edmx + "Edmx").
    Element(edmx + "Runtime").
    Element(edmx + "StorageModels").
    Elements().First()
  Using reader As XmlReader = model.CreateReader()
    Dim errors As IList(Of EdmSchemaError) = Nothing
    Return
      MetadataItemCollectionFactory.
        CreateStoreItemCollection(
          New List(Of XmlReader)(), errors)
  End Using
End Function
#>
```
Gets EDMX file absolute path

Gets storage node

Loads storage schema

In addition to the schema, you need the namespace. It's required in order to build the stub methods. Retrieving the namespace requires a new method whose code is quite similar to listing 13.3. The difference is that when you have the Schema element, you return its namespace attribute instead of the whole element:

C#

```
string GetStoreNamespace(string sourcePath)
{
  ...
  return model.Attribute("Namespace").Value;
}
```

VB

```
Private Function GetStoreNamespace(ByVal sourcePath As String) As String
  ...
  Return model.Attribute("Namespace").Value
End Function
```

Now that the plumbing is ready, you can write the code that creates the stubs for the functions. First, you retrieve all the functions from both the conceptual and storage schemas using a LINQ query. Then, you iterate over the elements, and for each one you retrieve the return type and the parameters. When you have them, you can write the stub methods' code. That's all shown in the following listing.

Listing 13.4 Creating the code for stub methods

C#

```
<#
var modelNamespace = loader.                          ❶ Retrieves model
  GetModelNamespace(inputFile);                           namespaces
var storeNamespace = GetStoreNamespace(inputFile);
var functions = CreateStoreItemCollection(inputFile)  ⟵  Retrieves scalar-valued
  .GetItems<EdmFunction>()                            ❷  and user-defined functions
  .Where(f => (bool)f.MetadataProperties
                 .First(p => p.Name == "IsComposableAttribute").Value
                         && f.NamespaceName == storeNamespace)
  .Select(f => new { Namespace = storeNamespace, Function = f })
  .Union(ItemCollection.GetItems<EdmFunction>()
          .Where(i => i.NamespaceName == modelNamespace)
          .Select(f => new { Namespace = modelNamespace, Function = f }));

foreach(var item in functions){
  string returnTypeElement = String.Empty;
  try
  {
    returnTypeElement = code.Escape(ef.GetElementType(
      item.Function.ReturnParameter.TypeUsage));
  }                                                        ❸ Generates
  catch                                                       function return
  {                                                           type string
    returnTypeElement = "DbDataRecord";
  }
  if (item.Function.ReturnParameter
        .TypeUsage.EdmType is CollectionType)
    returnTypeElement =
      "IEnumerable<" + returnTypeElement + ">";

  var parameters = FunctionImportParameter.Create          ❹ Generates
    (item.Function.Parameters, code, ef);                     parameter
  string paramList = String.Join(", ", parameters.Select(     string
    p => p.FunctionParameterType + " " +
    p.FunctionParameterName).ToArray());
#>
  [EdmFunction("<#=item.Namespace#>",                       ❺ Writes
    "<#=item.Function.Name#>")]                                functions
  public static <#=returnTypeElement#>
    <#=item.Function.Name#> (<#=paramList#>)
  {
    throw new NotImplementedException
      ("Cannot call this method");
  }<#
}#>
```

VB

```vb
<#
Dim modelNamespace =
  loader.GetModelNamespace(inputFile)
Dim storeNamespace = GetStoreNamespace(inputFile)
Dim functions = CreateStoreItemCollection(inputFile)
  .GetItems(Of EdmFunction)()
  .Where(Function(f) CBool(f.MetadataProperties
        .First(Function(p) p.Name = "IsComposableAttribute").Value)
      AndAlso f.NamespaceName = storeNamespace)
  .Select(Function(f)
        New With { .Namespace = storeNamespace, .Function = f })
  .Union(ItemCollection.GetItems(Of EdmFunction)()
        .Where(Function(i) i.NamespaceName = modelNamespace)
        .Select(Function(f)
            New With { .Namespace = modelNamespace, .Function = f }))

For Each item In functions
  Dim returnTypeElement As String = String.Empty
  Try
    returnTypeElement = code.Escape(ef.GetElementType(
      item.Function.ReturnParameter.TypeUsage))
  Catch
        returnTypeElement = "DbDataRecord"
  End Try
  If TypeOf item.Function.ReturnParameter.TypeUsage.EdmType Is
    CollectionType Then
    returnTypeElement =
      "IEnumerable(Of" & returnTypeElement & ")"
  End If

  Dim parameters = FunctionImportParameter.Create(item.Function.Parameters,
    code, ef)
  Dim paramList As String = String.Join(", ", parameters.Select(
    Function(p) (p.FunctionParameterType & " ") +
                p.FunctionParameterName).ToArray())
#>
  <EdmFunction("<#=item.Namespace#>",
    "<#=item.Function.Name#>")> _
  Public Shared Function <#=item.Function.Name#>
    (<#=paramList#>) As <#=returnTypeElement#>
    throw new NotImplementedException(
      "Cannot call this method");
  End Function<#
Next#>
```

① Retrieves model namespaces

② Retrieves scalar-valued and user-defined functions

③ Generates function return type string

④ Generates parameter string

⑤ Writes functions

Lots of interesting things happens in this listing. First, the namespace from both models is retrieved so it can be later used to create the stubs ①. The `loader` variable is an instance of the `MetadataLoader` class, and it's used to retrieve the conceptual schema namespace. `GetStoreNamespace` is the method that returns the storage schema namespace. `inputFile` is the EDMX file.

After that, a LINQ query joins the storage and conceptual functions ②. Notice how only the objects in the specified namespace are extracted, and in the case of the storage schema how only scalar-valued functions (functions whose `IsComposable-Attribute` attribute value is `true`) are retrieved.

Next, a loop over the functions is started, and for each one the string representing the return type is retrieved. The key point here is that you get the type as a string by invoking the MetadataTools class's GetElementType method, and you don't have to deal with the complexity of converting information from EDM to CLR format ❸. If the method throws an exception, the function returns a DbDataRecord. If the return value is a list, it's wrapped by the IEnumerable<T> class.

The next step is creating the string for the parameters ❹. First, the Function-ImportParameter class's Create method creates an array of parameters where each one exposes the type and the name as a string. Then, a LINQ query joins this information, separating the individual parameters with commas.

Finally, you have the function namespace, name, parameters, and return type. You now can close the block method and create the function using markup text and evaluation blocks ❺.

This is the result of the template in listing 13.4:

C#

```
[EdmFunction("OrderITModel", "GetUDFTypedAddresses")]
public static CustomerProjection GetUDFTypedAddresses
  (Customer customer)
{
  throw new NotImplementedException("Cannot call this method");
}
```

VB

```
<EdmFunction("OrderITModel", "GetUDFTypedAddresses")> _
Public Shared Function GetUDFTypedAddresses(ByVal customer As Customer) _
  As CustomerProjection
  Throw New NotImplementedException("Cannot call this method")
End Function
```

Modifying the template that generates object model classes isn't any different from modifying the context template. Naturally the type of data to be treated changes, but the technique is the same: you use a mix of code blocks and generated text.

13.2.3 Generating data-annotation attributes

In chapters 5 and 12, we showed you how to add custom information to EDM and how to retrieve it in the code. Here we'll complete the circle and show you how to generate data annotation attributes from those custom EDM annotations.

The example we looked at in those chapters added validation information to the Supplier class's IBAN property. What you'll do now is generate an attribute for that property, as shown in the following snippet:

C#

```
[RegularExpression(@"[a-zA-Z]{2}\d{2}[ ][a-zA-Z]\d{3}[ ]\d{4}
➥[ ]\d{4}[ ]\d{4}[ ]\d{4}[ ]\d{3}|[a-zA-Z]{2}\d{2}[a-zA-Z]\d{22}")]
```

VB

```
<RegularExpression("[a-zA-Z]{2}\d{2}[ ][a-zA-Z]\d{3}[ ]\d{4}[ ]
➥\d{4}[ ]\d{4}[ ]\d{4}[ ]\d{3}|[a-zA-Z]{2}\d{2}[a-zA-Z]\d{22}")> _
```

As you can imagine, the template that generates object-model classes retrieves the entities' metadata from the EDM's conceptual schema and iterates over them, generating classes, properties, and so on. We're interested in the property-creation process because you have to add the preceding code to the IBAN property. You need to plug in the code before the *scalar* properties are written. You can easily find the point where scalar properties are generated by looking for the LINQ query that retrieves them from the entity's properties.

Listing 13.5 adopts another technique. Instead of mixing text and code blocks, it uses a method that takes the property and returns a string containing the attribute. Just before the property is written, the method is invoked in an evaluation block.

Listing 13.5 Creating a data annotation containing a regular expression for a property

C#

```
<#+
string WriteAttribute(EdmMember edmProperty)
{
  var meta = edmProperty.MetadataProperties.FirstOrDefault(      ❶ Searches for
    mp => mp.Name.IndexOf("http://val") > -1);                     custom node
  if (meta != null)
  {
    XElement xe = meta.Value as XElement;
    return "[RegularExpression(@\"" + xe.Value + "\")]";         ❷ Writes
  }                                                                  attribute
  return String.Empty;
}#>
```

VB

```
<#+
Private Function WriteAttribute(ByVal edmProperty As EdmMember) As String
  Dim meta = edmProperty.MetadataProperties.FirstOrDefault(      ❶ Searches for
    Function(mp) mp.Name.IndexOf("http://val") > -1)               custom node
  If meta IsNot Nothing Then
    Dim xe As XElement = DirectCast(meta.Value, XElement)
    Return "<RegularExpression(""" & xe.Value & """)> _ "        ❷ Writes
  End If                                                            attribute
  Return String.Empty
End Function
#>
```

This code should look familiar to you. The first noticeable thing is that the method scans the input property's metadata, looking for an item with the validation namespace (the one specified in the Schema element) ❶.

If the metadata exists, it's cast to XElement, and its value is used to create the data annotation attribute ❷. You can then invoke the WriteAttribute method before a property is created, in the following way:

```
<#=WriteAttributes(edmProperty)#>
```

The use of the template increases productivity. If it didn't generate the scalar-valued and user-defined functions, you would have to write and maintain them, which means writing and maintaining a lot of code. Thanks to the template, these functions are generated and maintained by a single Visual Studio command.

Class generation greatly benefits from templates. The creation of POCO classes is just one of the possible scenarios. The ability to create attributes, to customize setters, and so on speeds things up to a great extent. We consider templates to be a great new feature in Entity Framework 4.0.

Classes don't consist only of data from the database. They can also contain methods and properties that aren't persisted in the database. The EDM knows nothing about them, so you have to find a way to create them.

13.2.4 *Extending classes through partial classes*

Suppose you need to create a `FullShippingAddress` string property in the `Customer` class. This property will be read-only and flattens the `ShippingAddress` complex property into a string.

Templates can't generate such a property for you, and if you add such a property to the class generated by the template, the property will be lost at the next code regeneration. To add this code to the class manually without losing it when the class is regenerated, you have to create it in a *partial* class.

Partial classes are a feature introduced in .NET Framework 2.0 that allow you to split a class into multiple files in the *same* assembly. At compile time, the compiler joins the files and generates only one class. The basic requirement for a class to be partial is that all files that define it contain the `partial` keyword in the definition, as shown in the following code:

C#
```
public partial class Customer
{
  . . .
}
```

VB
```
Public Partial Class Customer
  . . .
End Class
```

The template already generates partial classes, so you don't have to touch it. What you have to do is add a new class to the project, name it `Customer`, sign it with the `partial` keyword for C# or `Partial` keyword for Visual Basic, and then add the property as the following listing shows.

> **Listing 13.6 Creating a partial class**

C#
```
public partial class Customer
{
  public string FullShippingAddress
  {
    get
```

```
    {
      return String.Concat(ShippingAddress.Address, ",",
        ShippingAddress.ZipCode, ", ",
        ShippingAddress.City);
    }
  }
}
```

VB
```
Public Partial Class Customer
  Public ReadOnly Property FullShippingAddress() As String
    Get
      Return String.Concat(ShippingAddress.Address, ",",
        ShippingAddress.ZipCode, ", ",
        ShippingAddress.City)
    End Get
  End Property
End Class
```

With this technique, you can extend your classes and add any code you need.

Nevertheless, there are things you can't do with partial classes. For instance, you can't add an attribute to a property or method defined in another file, nor can you change the implementation of a method or property defined in another file. You can only add code, and nothing more.

> **NOTE**   Properties added in partial classes can't be used in LINQ to Entities or Entity SQL queries because they aren't mapped in the EDM.

We mentioned before that just as you can generate code from the EDM, you can create a script to generate the database from the storage schema. This is what model-first design is all about. You design the conceptual schema, and then the mapping schema, the storage schema, and the database script are generated on that basis. The good part is that the database generation is completely customizable.

13.3 *How Visual Studio generates database DDL*

As we said in chapter 2, the model-first support in the designer is still naive. Its current limitations make it impractical to use. Fortunately, the designer has been built on a great extension mechanism that you can use to modify the designer's default behavior. This extension mechanism isn't simple. It requires the use of Workflow Foundation, templates, metadata, and EDM knowledge. Due to this complexity, we'll go slowly and explain it all in detail.

The Entity Framework team that built the designer's extensibility mechanism has also published a toolkit that simplifies the process of building designer extensions to generate databases. The extensions are still a bit difficult to create, but it's a lot simpler when you use the toolkit. The toolkit, Entity Designer Database Generation Power Pack, can be downloaded here: http://mng.bz/ssf0; or you can download it via Visual Studio's Extension Manager window.

Before delving into the details, let's take a quick look at the steps involved when you adopt the model-first approach and generate a database script. In the model-first

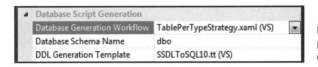

Figure 13.2 The designer properties that manage database script generation

scenario, you design entities without worrying about how they're mapped, because you don't have a database yet. When you've finished designing the model, you right-click the designer and select the Generate Model from Database option.

The command opens a pop-up window in which you can add the database connection string (required the first time you generate the database). After some internal processing, a new window opens, displaying the database script.

How does this happen? It's all based on a Windows Workflow Foundation workflow launched by the designer. We'll look at that next.

13.3.1 Choosing the workflow

To choose which workflow the designer should use to generate mapping schema, storage schema, and database script, you have to open the designer, right-click it, and select properties. Figure 13.2 shows the interesting part of the Properties toolbox.

The Database Generation Workflow property indicates what workflow is used to generate the database. The only workflow available out of the box is TablePerType-Strategy.xaml. The designer knows about it because it looks for files with an .xaml extension in the %ProgramFiles%\Microsoft Visual Studio 10.0\Common7\IDE\ Extensions\Microsoft\Entity Framework Tools\DBGen directory.

As you can see in figure 13.2, the workflow property has a drop-down list, meaning you can choose a different workflow. To do that, you need to create another .xaml workflow file inside the DBGen directory. The Properties Window will automatically list it in the drop-down menu when it's expanded.

Whatever workflow you choose, it has to do three things:

1 Generate the storage schema from the conceptual schema.
2 Generate the mapping schema.
3 Generate the database script from the storage schema.

The default workflow separates these steps into two actions. The first action takes care of steps 1 and 2, and the second action performs step 3. The entire workflow can be seen in the following listing.

Listing 13.7 Workflow that generates a script to persist inheritance with TPT

```
<Activity x:Class="GenerateDatabaseScriptWorkflow"
  xmlns="http://schemas.microsoft.com/netfx/2009/xaml/activities"
  xmlns:x="http://schemas.microsoft.com/winfx/2006/xaml"
  xmlns:s="clr-namespace:System;assembly=mscorlib"
  xmlns:sde="clr-namespace:System.Data.Metadata.Edm;
➥assembly=System.Data.Entity"
  xmlns:edm="clr-
➥namespace:Microsoft.Data.Entity.Design.DatabaseGeneration.Activities;
```

```
➥assembly=Microsoft.Data.Entity.Design.DatabaseGeneration"
  xmlns:edm1="clr-
➥namespace:Microsoft.Data.Entity.Design.DatabaseGeneration.Activities;
➥assembly=Microsoft.Data.Entity.Design">
  <x:Members>
    <x:Property Name="Csdl" Type="InArgument(sde:EdmItemCollection)" />
    <x:Property Name="ExistingSsdl" Type="InArgument(s:String)" />
    <x:Property Name="ExistingMsl" Type="InArgument(s:String)" />
    <x:Property Name="Ssdl" Type="OutArgument(s:String)" />
    <x:Property Name="Msl" Type="OutArgument(s:String)" />
    <x:Property Name="Ddl" Type="OutArgument(s:String)" />
  </x:Members>
  <Sequence>
    <edm:CsdlToSsdlAndMslActivity CsdlInput="[Csdl]"
      SsdlOutput="[Ssdl]" MslOutput="[Msl]"
OutputGeneratorType="Microsoft.Data.Entity.Design.DatabaseGeneration.
➥OutputGenerators.CsdlToSsdl,
➥Microsoft.Data.Entity.Design.DatabaseGeneration"
MslOutputGeneratorType="Microsoft.Data.Entity.Design.DatabaseGeneration
➥.OutputGenerators.CsdlToMsl,
➥Microsoft.Data.Entity.Design.DatabaseGeneration" />
    <edm1:SsdlToDdlActivity ExistingSsdlInput="[ExistingSsdl]"
      SsdlInput="[Ssdl]" DdlOutput="[Ddl]" />
  </Sequence>
</Activity>
```

Even if you aren't a workflow expert, you should be able to understand what this workflow does. The `CsdlToSsdlAndMslActivity` activity reads the CSDL and generates SSDL and MSL, whereas `SsdlToDdlActivity` creates the database script starting from the SSDL. It's that simple.

13.3.2   *Generating SSDL, MSL, and DDL*

The `CsdlToSsdlAndMslActivity` activity doesn't require you to do anything. It already has everything it needs to accomplish its task. That's not true of the `SsdlToDdlActivity` activity, which needs an input from you.

In figure 13.2, you see two important properties: Database Schema Name and DDL Generation Template. The first is the database schema, and by default it's set to dbo. You're free to modify it as you like, but keep in mind that all tables will be generated under that schema. The second property is more important because it specifies the template that will be invoked by the second workflow action (`SsdlToDdlActivity`).

The default template is SSDLToSQL10.tt, and it's situated in the same folder as the workflow file. Like the workflow property, the template property has a drop-down list. The designer looks for *.tt files in the DBGen folder to populate the drop-down list with templates.

Let's quickly recap:

- You can customize the way MSL and SSDL are generated (for instance, to apply a TPH strategy instead of TPT, which is the default).
- You can customize the way the database script is generated (for instance, to create an Oracle database or to generate a script that contains only the modifications made to the model since the last time the database script was generated).

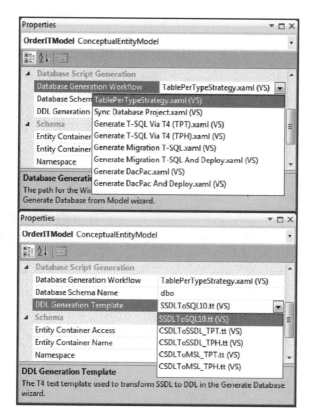

Figure 13.3   The workflows and templates installed by the Database Generation Power Pack

That's complete control.

It's now time to talk about the Entity Designer Database Generation Power Pack toolkit.

13.4   Customizing DDL generation

The Database Generation Power Pack installer copies a set of .xaml and .tt files into the Visual Studio template folder. When you open the drop-down lists for the Database Generation Workflow and DDL Generation Template properties, you'll see many more options, as shown in figure 13.3.

> **NOTE**   The templates installed by this CTP are written in C# only, so we won't show VB versions.

This gives you lots of new toys to play with. As you may imagine based on its name, the Generate T-SQL Via T4 (TPH).xaml file is the workflow that generates tables to persist inheritance hierarchies using the TPH strategy. We're going to talk about this workflow and show you how the Database Generation Power Pack works.

Here's the Sequence section from the XAML file:

```
<Sequence>
  <dbtk:CsdlToSsdlTemplateActivity SsdlOutput="[Ssdl]"
    TemplatePath="$(VSEFTools)\DBGen\CSDLToSSDL_TPH.tt"/>
```

```
  <dbtk:CsdlToMslTemplateActivity MslOutput="[Msl]"
    TemplatePath="$(VSEFTools)\DBGen\CSDLToMSL_TPH.tt"/>
  <ded:SsdlToDdlActivity ExistingSsdlInput="[ExistingSsdl]"
    SsdlInput="[Ssdl]" DdlOutput="[Ddl]" />
</Sequence>
```

The three activities started here create the SSDL, the MSL, and the DDL. What's really smart about these workflow actions is that instead of consisting of lots of code, they generate SSDL, MSL, and DDL by running the CSDLToSSDL_TPH.tt, CSDLToMSL_TPH.tt, and SSDLToSQL10.tt templates, respectively. Let's take a quick look at each of them so you understand how they work.

13.4.1 Understanding the conceptual-to-storage template

The first node to be created in the storage model is `Schema`. It needs the data-store namespace, the database type, and the database version. Database information is retrieved via the connection string, and the namespace name is based on the conceptual schema name. This information is available in the template because it's passed in by the workflow action.

This is the template code that generates the `Schema` element:

```
<Schema Namespace="<#=ssdlModelNamespace#>" Alias="Self"
  Provider="<#=providerInvariantName#>"
  ProviderManifestToken="<#=providerManifestToken#>"
  xmlns="<#=ssdlNamespace#>" xmlns:store="<#=essgNamespace#>">
```

And this is the generated output:

```
<Schema Namespace="OrderITModel.Store" Alias="Self"
  Provider="System.Data.SqlClient"
  ProviderManifestToken="2008"
  xmlns:store="http://schemas.microsoft.com/ado/2007/12/edm/
➥ EntityStoreSchemaGenerator"
  xmlns="http://schemas.microsoft.com/ado/2009/02/edm/ssdl">
```

> **NOTE** The variables `ssdlModelNamespace`, `providerInvariantName`, and so on are populated in the template before this piece of code. If you want to see how the variables are populated, look at the template.

After the `Schema` element, the container and the entity set are created. The code generates a table for each base class and a table for each many-to-many relationship (the famous link table). To easily obtain information about base classes and many-to-many relationships from the EDM, the template uses a set of extension methods that the Entity Framework team has created. For instance, the `GetAllEntityTypes` method wraps a call to the `GetItems<EntityType>` method of the `EdmItemCollection` class. The following listing shows this code.

Listing 13.8   Container and entity-set creation

```
<EntityContainer
  Name="<#=this.WriteEntityContainerName(csdlModelNamespace)#>">
<#
```

```
foreach (EntityType entityType in edm.GetAllEntityTypes()
  .Where(e => !e.IsDerivedType()))
{#>

  <EntitySet Name="<#=WriteEntityTypeName(entityType, edm)#>"
    EntityType="<#=ssdlModelNamespace#>.
    <#=WriteEntityTypeName(entityType, edm)#>" store:Type="Tables"
    Schema="<#=databaseSchemaName#>" />
<#}
foreach (AssociationSet associationSet in edm.GetAllAssociationSets()
  .Where(set => set.GetAssociation().IsManyToMany())) { #>

  <EntitySet Name="<#=associationSet.Name#>"
    EntityType="<#=ssdlModelNamespace#>.
    <#=associationSet.ElementType.Name#>" store:Type="Tables"
    Schema="<#=databaseSchemaName#>" />
<#}
```

The association sets are also created at this point, but showing that code here would bore you and take up too much space. You can find the code in the template if you're interested.

The next thing the template does is describe the tables. This involves a lot of code to correctly generate the storage schema:

- Complex properties don't exist in the database, so their inner properties must be correctly named to avoid conflicts (think about `BillingAddress` and `ShippingAddress` in OrderIT's `Customer` entity). The pattern used to avoid collisions is `ComplexPropertyName_SubPropertyName`.
- In tables containing an inheritance hierarchy, a discriminator column must be added.
- Foreign-key columns must be added even if they aren't specified in the entity, because they're required in the database to maintain relationships.

The following listing shows an excerpt of what the template code looks like. The table, key, and discriminator definitions are shown here—the property definition requires a lot more code.

Listing 13.9 Table, primary key, and discriminator definitions

```
<EntityType Name=
  "<#=WriteEntityTypeName(csdlEntityType, edm)#>">         ◁─── Table definition
  <Key>
  <#foreach (EdmMember key in csdlEntityType.GetRootOrSelf()
      .GetKeyProperties())
  {#>
    <PropertyRef Name="<#=key.Name#>" />                   ◁─── Primary key columns
  <#}#>
  </Key>
...
<#if (csdlEntityType.GetEntitySet(edm).ContainsInheritanceHierarchy(edm)){
#>
  <Property Name="__Disc__" Type="nvarchar" MaxLength="Max"
    Nullable="false" />                                    ◁─── Discriminator column
<#}#>
```

We didn't cover associations here because they would involve a lot of code. If you want to learn more, look at the template.

That's pretty much all there is to know about the storage-schema generation. Let's move on to the mapping schema, which is relatively simpler.

13.4.2   *Understanding the conceptual-to-mapping template*

The concept that drives the generation of the mapping schema is the same as for the storage schema. Entities are retrieved using metadata, and each standalone entity has a one-to-one mapping with the corresponding table. Entities that are part of an inheritance hierarchy have all their properties grouped into a single table.

Following these principles, writing a template is straightforward, as the following listing demonstrates.

Listing 13.10   Mapping entities to tables

```
<#foreach (EntitySet set in edm.GetAllEntitySets()) {#>
  <EntitySetMapping Name="<#=set.Name#>">
  <#
  IEnumerable<EntityType> containingTypes = set.GetContainingTypes(edm);
  bool containsInheritanceHierarchy = containingTypes.Count() > 1;
  foreach (EntityType type in containingTypes)
  {#>
    <EntityTypeMapping TypeName="<#=type.FullName#>">
      <MappingFragment
        StoreEntitySet="<#=WriteEntityTypeName(set.ElementType, edm)#>">
    <#foreach (EdmProperty property in                      ❶ Retrieves key
       set.ElementType.GetKeyProperties())                    properties
      {
  #>
        <ScalarProperty Name="<#=property.Name#>"
          ColumnName="<#=property.Name#>" />
  <#}
      foreach (EdmProperty property in
        (type.GetPropertiesInAllBaseTypes().                ❷ Retrieves all
          Except(set.ElementType.GetKeyProperties()           other properties
            .Distinct())
      {
        if (property.IsComplexProperty())
        {
          ConstructComplexProperty(property, property.Name,
            csdlModelNamespace);
        }
        else
        {#>
          <ScalarProperty Name="<#=property.Name#>"
            ColumnName="<#=property.Name#>" />
        <#}
      }
      if (containsInheritanceHierarchy)                     ❸ Maps discriminator
      {#>                                                     for hierarchies
        <Condition ColumnName="__Disc__"
```

```
        Value="<#=type.Name#>" />
      <#}#>
      </MappingFragment>
    </EntityTypeMapping>
  <#}#>
  </EntitySetMapping>
<#}#>
```

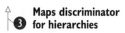

Maps discriminator
③ for hierarchies

The method names are so self-explanatory that the code is easy to follow. It first retrieves all the entity sets, and for each one retrieves the table mapping, first for the key properties **❶**, and then for all other properties of the entity that are part of the entity set **❷**. At the end, the discriminator column is mapped if the entity is part of an inheritance hierarchy **❸**.

You've now seen how the workflow activities generate the EDM (more precisely, how the templates generate text that is saved and encapsulated in the EDMX). The step for us to look at is how the database script is generated from the storage schema.

13.4.3 *Understanding the storage-to-database script template*

The database-script-generation process is very similar to the process we looked at in the previous section. The template reads metadata from the storage schema and generates DDL script like what you see in the following listing.

Listing 13.11   Generating database tables

```
<#
foreach (EntitySet entitySet in Store.GetAllEntitySets())
{
  string schemaName = Id(entitySet.GetSchemaName());
  string tableName = Id(entitySet.GetTableName());
#>
CREATE TABLE [<#=schemaName#>].[<#=tableName#>] (
<#
  for (int p = 0; p < entitySet.ElementType.Properties.Count; p++)
  {
    EdmProperty prop = entitySet.ElementType.Properties[p];
#>
    [<#=Id(prop.Name)#>] <#=prop.ToStoreType()#>
    <#=WriteIdentity(prop, targetVersion)#>
    <#=WriteNullable(prop.Nullable)#>
    <#=(p < entitySet.ElementType.Properties.Count - 1) ? "," : ""#>
  <#}#>
);
<#}#>
```

This code retrieves all the storage entity sets (the database tables) and then builds the CREATE TABLE statements by iterating over all the properties.

Congratulations. You've just learned how the Database Generation Power Pack creates the code that builds a database script based on the entities created in the designer.

What you have seen so far is an *external* extension to the designer; the designer always remains the same. Prepare yourself, because in the next section we'll show you how to add new behavior to the designer.

13.5   *Creating designer extensions*

The Entity Framework team has added a lot of extensibility points into the designer. You can plug in custom behaviors via these four interfaces:

- `IEntityDesignerExtendedProperty`—Allows you to add custom properties to any item on the designer surface: entities, properties, associations, and so on.
- `IModelTransformExtension`—Lets you customize the EDMX file in two phases: after it's loaded (but before it's shown by the designer) and before it's saved.
- `IModelConversationExtension`—Lets you transform a mapping file in a custom format to the EDMX format, which is then passed to the designer for visualization. There's also a reverse method that takes the EDMX and allows you to save it in your format.
- `IModelGenerationExtension`—Exposes methods that let you customize behavior when the EDMX file is generated by the initial wizard and when it's updated by the Update Model wizard.

Unless you need very particular customizations, the last three interfaces are of little interest; the first one may save you from having to make some manual EDMX modifications.

Let's take a step back and look at the `SmartAttach<T>` extension method created in chapter 12. That method takes an entity as input and decides whether to add or attach it to the context based on the value of the primary key specified in a custom EDM annotation: if the primary-key property value is 0, the method adds the entity to the context; otherwise, the method attaches the entity to the context.

You know that you have to manually modify the EDMX file to add the custom annotation that specifies the value that determines whether the input entity must be added or attached to the context. Wouldn't it be absolutely fantastic if you could set this value by using the designer, without manually touching EDMX? It would look something like what's shown in figure 13.4.

We bet you're whispering, "wow." In the rest of this section, we'll show you how to build this designer extension.

13.5.1   *How the property-extension mechanism works*

Customizing a designer is generally thought to be tough work, and often that's true. Lots of base classes and interfaces to implement, plus a lack of documentation, make thing really difficult sometimes. Fortunately, the Entity Framework designer is an exception. Its extensibility model is built on the Managed Extensibility Framework (MEF), which already takes care of all the plumbing.

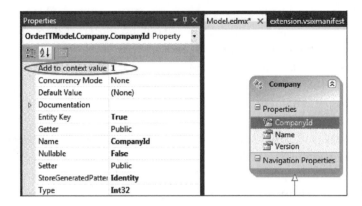

Figure 13.4 The custom annotation value is shown in the Property Editor when the entity property is selected.

The result is that you only have to create two classes to extend the designer. The first (which we'll call the *property class*) reads and writes values from and to the EDMX, and the second (often known as the *factory*) acts as the bridge between the designer and the first class.

When you select an item in the designer and then go to the Properties window, the designer goes to the factory and asks for an object containing the property to be added to the Properties window. The factory instantiates the property class and returns it to the designer.

The designer sends the object to the Properties window, which retrieves the exposed property and shows it in the designer. From that moment on, when you modify the property, the getter and setter work directly with the EDMX. Figure 13.5 illustrates this workflow.

The first step in extending the designer is creating the extension project.

13.5.2 Setting up the project containing the extension

A designer-customization project requires two classes: the manifest file that installs the generated extension, and a couple of references. To create these, follow these steps:

1 Create a new Class Library project inside the OrderIT solution, and name it `OrderIT.DesignerExtensions`.

2 Delete the Class1.* file.

3 Add a reference to the `System.ComponentModel.Composition` assembly that's situated in the .NET Framework 4.0 folder (%ProgramFiles%\Reference Assemblies\Microsoft\Framework\.NETFramework\v4.0).

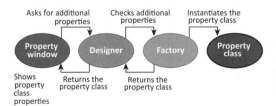

Figure 13.5 The Property window asks the designer for additional properties to display. The designer delegates the factory, which instantiates the property class that is then displayed by the Properties window.

4 Add a reference to the `Microsoft.Data.Entity.Design.Extensibility` assembly located in the Visual Studio assemblies folder (%ProgramFiles% \Microsoft Visual Studio 10.0\Common7\IDE\PublicAssemblies).

5 Add a new class, and name it `InsertWhenValue`. It's the property class that manipulates the EDMX file.

6 Add a new class, and name it `InsertWhenFactory`. It's the bridge class, or factory.

7 Add a new XML file, and name it `extension.vsixmanifest`. It's needed to install the extension in Visual Studio.

8 Right-click the XML file, and select Properties. In the Properties window, set the Build Action property to `VsixContent`.

The project is now set up. What you need to do next is put some code inside the classes. We'll start with the property class that handles the EDMX file; it's the most important.

13.5.3 Creating the property class

The property class has two purposes: exposing the properties that must be added to the Properties window, and reflecting their values in the EDMX. In this example, when you set the value in the Properties window, the property setter has to create, or update, the custom annotation in the EDMX. Similarly, when the property is read, the getter must retrieve the custom annotation and return its value, which is then shown in the Properties window.

Here's the code for the property class.

Listing 13.12   Creating the designer property class

C#
```
class InsertWhenValue
{
  internal static XName ELEMENTNAME = XName.Get("InsertWhen",
    "http://EFEX");

  private XElement _property;
  private PropertyExtensionContext _context;

  public InsertWhenValue(XElement parent,              ❶ Accepts designer context
    PropertyExtensionContext context)                     and EDM element
  {
    _context = context;
    _property = parent;
  }

  [DisplayName("Add to context value")]
  [Description("Gets or sets the value that adds an entity the context")]
  [Category("Extensions")]
  [DefaultValue(false)]
  public string Value
```

```
  {
    get
    {
      XElement child = _property.Element(ELEMENTNAME);
      return (child == null)
        ? String.Empty : child.Value;
    }
    set
    {
      if (String.IsNullOrEmpty(value)) return;
      using (EntityDesignerChangeScope scope =
        _context.CreateChangeScope("Set InsertWhen"))
      {
        var element = _property.Element(ELEMENTNAME);
        if (element == null)
          _property.Add(
            new XElement(ELEMENTNAME, value));
        else
          element.SetValue(value);
        scope.Complete();
      }
    }
  }
}
```

❷ Returns EDM element value

❸ Creates scope for designer undo command

❹ Sets EDM element value

VB

```
Class InsertWhenValue
  Friend Shared ELEMENTNAME As XName = XName.Get("InsertWhen", _
    "http://EFEX")

  Private _parent As XElement
  Private _context As PropertyExtensionContext

  Public Sub New(ByVal property As XElement, _
    ByVal context As PropertyExtensionContext)
    _context = context
    _parent = property
  End Sub

  <DisplayName("Add to context value")> _
  <Description("Gets or sets the value that adds an entity the context")> _
  <Category("Extensions")> _
  <DefaultValue(False)> _
  Public Property Value() As String
    Get
      Dim child As XElement =
        _property.Element(ELEMENTNAME)
      Return If((child Is Nothing),
        String.Empty, child.Value)
    End Get
    Set(ByVal value As String)
      If String.IsNullOrEmpty(value) Then
        Return
      End If
      Using scope As EntityDesignerChangeScope =
        _context.CreateChangeScope("Set InsertWhen")
```

❶ Accepts designer context and EDM element

❷ Returns EDM element value

❸ Creates scope for designer undo command

```
        Dim element = _property.Element(ELEMENTNAME)                    ❹ Sets EDM
        If element Is Nothing Then                                        element
          _property.Add(                                                  value
            New XElement(ELEMENTNAME, value))
        Else
          element.SetValue(value)
        End If
        scope.Complete()
      End Using
    End Set
  End Property
End Class
```

Notice how the class is POCO. You don't have to implement any interfaces or inherit from any class!

Another important thing to notice is the constructor. It accepts an XElement object, representing the XML element inside the EDMX, and a PropertyExtension-Context object, which carries context information about the designer environment ❶. As you may imagine, the XElement object is the Property node of the EDMX. Modifying and reading it means modifying and reading the EDMX.

When the Properties window needs to show a label for the Value property, it takes the string contained in the DisplayName attribute of that property (it's the Add to Context Value property in this case, as you can see in figure 13.4). When the Properties window needs the property value, the getter is triggered, and the custom annotation element is searched for. If found, its value is returned; otherwise, an empty string is returned ❷.

The setter is slightly more complex then the getter. The first thing to notice is its use of the context received by the constructor. The setter invokes the context's CreateChangeScope method, which creates a scope that's needed for Visual Studio to create the undo list, so that any modification can be undone ❸.

> **NOTE** Creating the scope is mandatory. Any attempt to modify the XElement outside of a scope throws an exception.

Once inside the scope, the custom annotation is searched for. If it's not found, it's added to the property; otherwise, it's updated ❹.

The simplicity of this feature may be a surprise to you. You'll be glad to know that creating the factory class is even easier.

13.5.4 *Creating the factory class*

The factory class is a very simple class that, in many cases, contains only one line of code! It must implement the IEntityDesignerExtendedProperty interface, and it must be decorated with two attributes, as you can see in this listing.

Listing 13.13 Creating the bridge class

C#

```csharp
[Export(typeof(IEntityDesignerExtendedProperty))]
[EntityDesignerExtendedProperty(
  EntityDesignerSelection.ConceptualModelProperty)]
class InsertWhenFactory :
  IEntityDesignerExtendedProperty
{
  public object CreateProperty(XElement element,
    PropertyExtensionContext context)
  {
    var edmXName = XName.Get("Key",
      "http://schemas.microsoft.com/ado/2008/09/edm");
    var keys = element.Parent.Element(edmXName)
      .Elements().Select(e =>
        e.Attribute("Name").Value);
    if (keys.Contains(element.Attribute("Name").Value))
      return new InsertWhenValue(element, context);
    return null;
  }
}
```

1 Integrates class with designer

2 Specifies which EDM element is extended

3 Declares required interface/

4 Retrieves key properties

5 Returns property class if current property is a key

VB

```vb
<Export(GetType(IEntityDesignerExtendedProperty))> _
<EntityDesignerExtendedProperty( _
  EntityDesignerSelection.ConceptualModelProperty)> _
Class InsertWhenFactory
  Implements IEntityDesignerExtendedProperty
  Public Function CreateProperty(ByVal element As XElement, _
    ByVal context As PropertyExtensionContext) As Object
    Dim edmXName = XName.[Get]("Key", _
      "http://schemas.microsoft.com/ado/2008/09/edm")
    Dim keys = element.Parent.Element(edmXName)
      .Elements().Select(Function(e)
        e.Attribute("Name").Value)
    If keys.Contains(
      element.Attribute("Name").Value) Then
      Return New InsertWhenValue(element, context)
    End If
    Return Nothing
  End Function
End Class
```

1 Integrates class with designer

2 Specifies which EDM element is extended

3 Declares required interface

4 Retrieves key properties

5 Returns property class if current property is a key

There's a lot to say about this little listing. First, notice the `Export` attribute **1**. It's defined in the `System.ComponentModel.Composition` namespace and accepts the implemented interface type.

The `EntityDesignerExtendedProperty` attribute tells the designer which EDM element the factory class applies to. When the designer invokes the factory class, the designer also specifies what object is currently selected (an entity, a property, the designer itself, and so on) **2**. If the selected object doesn't match the attribute definition, the factory class is ignored.

The object to which the factory class applies to is expressed by an enum of type `EntityDesignerSelection`. It has lots of values, but these are the most important:

- `DesignerSurface`—The factory class is invoked if the selected object is the designer surface.
- `ConceptualModelEntityType`—The factory class is invoked if the selected object is an entity.
- `ConceptualModelProperty`—The factory class is invoked if the selected object is an entity's property.
- `ConceptualModelNavigationProperty`—The factory class is invoked if the selected object is an entity's navigation property.
- `ConceptualModelAssociation`—The factory class is invoked if the selected object is an association between two entities.
- `ConceptualModelComplexType`—The factory class is invoked if the selected object is a complex type.
- `ConceptualModelComplexProperty`—The factory class is invoked if the selected object is an entity's complex property.
- `ConceptualModelFunctionImport`—The factory class is invoked if the selected object is a function in the conceptual schema.
- `ConceptualModelFunctionImportParameter`—The factory class is invoked if the selected object is a parameter of a function in the conceptual schema.

In this example, you're working on entity properties only.

The factory class has to implement the `IEntityDesignerExtendedProperty` interface—that's required by the extensibility mechanism ❸. This interface has only the `CreateProperty` method, which is invoked by the designer to obtain the property class. It accepts both the element that represents the property in the EDMX and a context. These parameters are then passed to the property class constructor when the property class is instantiated.

By default, the factory class applies to all properties of an entity. That means the designer enables you to put the custom annotation on all of an entity's properties, and this isn't what you need; only key properties should have these annotations. That's why the code navigates from the property to the parent element (the `EntityType` element), taking the `Key` node and retrieving its children, which contain the key properties' names ❹.

If the current property is in the key properties list, the property class is instantiated and returned. Otherwise, `null` is returned so that the Properties window doesn't show any additional properties ❺.

There are about 30–40 lines of real code in this example. That's all there is to the code—isn't it great? What still remains is the manifest file.

13.5.5 *Creating the manifest extension file*

The manifest file is required by Visual Studio to install any extension. It contains basic information, like the author, description, and version, and important information such as the Visual Studio supported version, the range of .NET Framework versions supported, and the assembly containing the extension. Here's an example of a manifest file.

Listing 13.14 The manifest file

```xml
<?xml version="1.0" encoding="utf-8"?>
<Vsix Version="1.0.0"
  xmlns="http://schemas.microsoft.com/developer/vsx-schema/2010" >
  <Identifier Id="OrderIT.DesignerExtensions">
    <Name>OrderIT.DesignerExtensions</Name>
    <Author>Stefano Mostarda</Author>
    <Version>1.0</Version>
    <Description>Add InsertWhen to key properties</Description>
    <Locale>1033</Locale>
    <InstalledByMsi>false</InstalledByMsi>
    <SupportedProducts>
      <VisualStudio Version="10.0">
        <Edition>VST_All</Edition>
        <Edition>Express_All</Edition>
      </VisualStudio>
    </SupportedProducts>
    <SupportedFrameworkRuntimeEdition MinVersion="3.5" MaxVersion="4.0">
    </SupportedFrameworkRuntimeEdition>
  </Identifier>
  <References />
  <Content>
    <MefComponent>OrderIT.DesignerExtensions.dll</MefComponent>
  </Content>
</Vsix>
```

The XML contains the name of the package, along with the author, the version, a long description, the list of supported Visual Studio and .NET Framework versions, and much more. If you're accustomed to XML (and we know you are, or the EDM would have scared you to death), this listing will be a piece of cake.

> **NOTE** The Entity Framework team has published an ADO.NET Entity Data Model Designer Extension Starter Kit that adds a project template to Visual Studio for creating designer extensions. It's available here: http://code.msdn.microsoft.com/DesignerExtStartKit.

You've now finished from the code point of view, but there are still a few subjects that are worth a look: installing, debugging, and uninstalling.

13.5.6 *Installing, debugging, and uninstalling the extension*

After you've built the assembly, Visual Studio creates the extension as a VSIX file in the bin\debug|release folder. The extension is a zip file containing the manifest and the compiled assembly.

To install the extension, you simply need to run it; the next time you open Visual Studio, the extension will be there. When you open the Entity Framework designer and select a key property of an entity in the designer, you'll see the additional property in the Property window.

To uninstall the extension, open the Extension Manager window, select the `OrderIT.DesignerExtensions` item, and click the Uninstall button in the box. That's it.

When it comes to debugging, the procedures are a bit more involved. Because the host of the extension is Visual Studio, you have to debug Visual Studio, which means you need to start a second instance of Visual Studio to debug the first one. By properly configuring the project properties, you can make things go smoothly.

To configure the project properties, follow these steps:

1 Open the project properties by right-clicking the project in the Solution Explorer window and choosing the Properties item.
2 In the project properties form, choose the Debug tab, and select the Start External Program radio button.
3 In the text box next to the radio button, insert the path to the Visual Studio executable file: `%ProgramFiles%\Microsoft Visual Studio 10.0\Common7\ IDE\\devenv.exe`. The forms looks like figure 13.6.

The effect of this configuration is that when you run the extension project, a second instance of Visual Studio will be started, and the debugger will automatically be attached. When the extension code is hit, the first instance enables debugging.

The tricky part comes in when you make modifications and need to debug them. Each time you have to rebuild the extension, you need to uninstall it, close all your Visual Studio instances, reinstall the extension, restart Visual Studio, and rerun the extension project. This is annoying, but it's the only way to go.

The example you've built in this section is very simple, but it should give you an understanding of how extending the designer could simplify your life. With a mix of template customization, database-generation customization, and designer extensions, you can create powerful frameworks that simplify your use of the designer and generate a lot of code for you. This can make the difference between an easily maintainable project and a real nightmare.

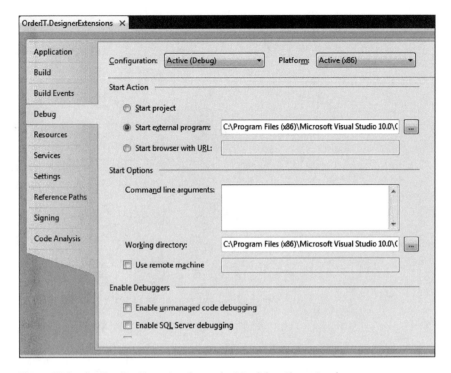

Figure 13.6   Configuring the extension project to debug the extension

13.6   *Summary*

In this chapter, you learned about features that greatly increase productivity. Code generation isn't only about POCO classes. You can also write tests, mocks, repositories, and anything else that can be automatically generated. That's a big step forward. Customizing database generation isn't a step toward productivity but a step toward a different way of designing models. By using a powerful template, you could perform a match between an existing database and the SSDL and create a script for the differences. It could make model-first design much more usable than it is now.

Finally, customizing the designer makes its usage simpler. By creating ad hoc extensions, you can avoid getting your hands in the EDMX, making everything simpler and less error prone.

Now it's time to talk about how to design a real-world application that uses Entity Framework to access data.

Part 4

Applied
Entity Framework

You've learned how Entity Framework can simplify application development and make code more readable and usable. In part 4, you'll discover how Entity Framework behaves in the real world. Web and Windows applications have different needs and different architectures, and by making Entity Framework entities aware of these needs, you can easily integrate them into any application. The context lifecycles of these applications differ too; web applications and web services are disconnected by nature, whereas Windows applications are connected, so different approaches are required.

In the real world, an application's architecture must be aware of Entity Framework for both data access and testing. The domain-driven design philosophy is growing in popularity, and you'll learn how Entity Framework can be integrated with it.

Performance is also critical in any data-access application. Even if applications do what they've been created for, if they do it too slowly, it's like having a nonfunctional application.

In chapter 14, we'll tour the different types of architectures. We'll start with a classic three-layer application and move on to a domain-model-driven one. Finally, we'll look at how Entity Framework fits into a domain-model-driven application.

Chapters 15, 16, and 17 talk about Entity Framework inside the different application types. ASP.NET applications, web services, Windows Forms applications, and WPF applications are covered in these chapters.

Chapter 18 covers the subject of testing. Here you'll learn how to make applications testable even when Entity Framework and LINQ to Entities are in place.

Chapter 19 discusses performance. By the end of this chapter, you'll be a master of Entity Framework.

14

Designing the application around Entity Framework

This chapter covers

- Basic concepts of layered architectures
- Principles of domain-driven design
- Repository pattern implementation with Entity Framework

This chapter moves slightly away from what you may expect from a book about ADO.NET Entity Framework. We've faced the matter of persistence from a technical point of view, trying to understand how to use this O/RM tool to store a graph of objects in a relational database. In this chapter, we're going to discuss the same topic but from an architectural point of view.

First, we'll look at how to integrate Entity Framework in a typical three-layer architecture, which represents a good and widely used strategy for designing modern applications. But layering itself may not be helpful in handling the complex business logic typical of enterprise applications; in these cases, your design must move toward a more suitable domain-driven design modeling style. Finally, we'll look at how you can shape your object model to handle this kind of architecture and how Entity Framework fits in.

14.1 The application design process

As software architects, we tend to work on two kinds of applications: those that will never see a second release, because they're built for a specific need of the moment; and meaningful products that are destined to last through time, perhaps evolving as the years go by. In the latter case, despite the complexity of the problems to be handled, we don't need something that just works. We must try to achieve a result that meets the following requirements:

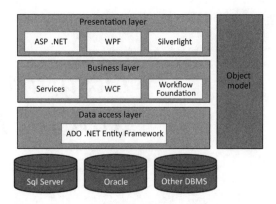

Figure 14.1   A diagram of the three-layer architecture

- *Robust*—This guarantees that the code does its job in every situation.
- *Maintainable*—This makes future bug fixes as easy as possible.
- *Expandable*—This means you can implement new functionality or improvements with little effort, and without greatly affecting the overall architecture.

Meeting these requirements isn't easy. A common technique to improve your chances is to split the application into simpler parts, called *layers*, with each one having its own specific functional responsibilities.

Three-layer applications, whose conceptual schema is shown in figure 14.1, are the most common example of such a layered architecture.

Starting from the bottom, a three-layer application consists of these layers:

- *Data access layer*—Interacts with the database and shields the rest of the application from its specific logic. Concepts like connections, commands, and tables only make sense within this layer and should never be exposed to the upper layers. This is also where Entity Framework fits in; in most cases, it can be considered the entire data access layer on its own.
- *Business layer*—Holds all the business logic and provides services that implement the real-world processes that the application is built to take care of. Although it doesn't care where its inputs come from, it knows whether a fund transfer can take place between two bank accounts and how to handle it correctly, invoking the data access layer when it needs to query the database or store something there.
- *Presentation layer*—Contains all the logic for interacting with the user, correctly rendering windows or web pages, and interpreting user commands, translating them to business method invokes.

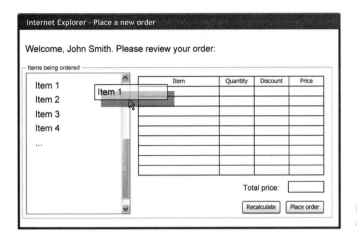

Figure 14.2   An interface for an order-placing web page

Each layer can interact only with the one immediately lower, sending and receiving messages in the form of classes that belong to the application's object model, which is a sort of common language shared among them all.

Although it's designed to bring simplicity to our software, this layered architecture requires more effort on the part of the developer compared to applications that have a monolithic structure. Layered applications have more class libraries, references, classes, and so on—in other words, more code! But the layered architecture offers the tremendous advantage of splitting this complexity across simpler elements that are easier to implement, test, and maintain, with obvious benefits on the overall result.

14.2   A typical three-layer architecture

To better understand how concerns should be separated into the three layers, let's consider a practical example. Let's go back to the OrderIT application to reconsider some of its requirements and rethink its architecture. We'll implement the feature that allows customers to place orders. Imagine you're building an ASP.NET web application with a Place a New Order page like the one shown in figure 14.2.

This page features some nice rich client interaction, like allowing drag and drop from the list box on the left to the grid on the right to compose an order, and it has a couple of buttons to calculate the total amount and to eventually place the order.

14.2.1   Filling the product list

The first task the web page has to accomplish, once loaded, is filling the list on the left with all the products currently available, as in the following listing.

Listing 14.1   Filling the `productsList` list box

C#
```
protected void Page_Load(object sender, EventArgs e)
{
  if (!IsPostBack)
```

```
  {
    var availableProducts = ProductsService.GetAvailableProducts();
    this.productsList.DataSource = availableProducts;
    this.productsList.DataBind();
  }
}
```

VB

```
Protected Sub Page_Load(ByVal sender As Object, ByVal e As EventArgs)
  If Not IsPostBack Then
    Dim availableProducts = ProductsService.GetAvailableProducts()
    Me.productsList.DataSource = availableProducts
    Me.productsList.DataBind()
  End If
End Sub
```

In this listing, a lot of presentation logic, like triggering the Load event or the ListBox data binding, is provided under the hood by the ASP.NET Framework. But you should notice that page code has absolutely no knowledge of where the list of available products comes from, nor does it know when a product is *available* according to the business logic.

A static ProductsService class holds the code that retrieves the available products; its code can be seen in the next listing.

Listing 14.2   Retrieving available products

C#

```
public static class ProductsService
{
  public static List<Product> GetAvailableProducts()
  {
    using (OrderITEntities ctx = new OrderITEntities())
    {
      return ctx.Products
                .Where(p => p.QuantityInStock > 0)
                .ToList();
    }
  }
}
```

VB

```
Public Module ProductsService
  Public Function GetAvailableProducts() As List(Of Product)
    Using ctx As New OrderITEntities()
      Return ctx.Products.Where(Function(p) p.QuantityInStock > 0) _
                .ToList()
    End Using
  End Function
End Module
```

The ProductsService class is part of the business layer, and it has a single responsibility: it models the business rule that makes a product available. That rule could be something like, "we still have stock for that item," or "this item can be sold in the

current period of the year." Its logic is implemented within the `GetAvailableProd-`
`ucts` method, which knows how to query the data access layer to retrieve a list based
on the rule. In any case, `ProductsService` can't see what its caller is going to do with
that list of products, nor does it know how the context is actually retrieving them.

As we said in the previous section, Entity Framework can be considered the application's data access layer, because it shields the business layer from concepts like connecting to a relational database and executing a query. To establish communication
among the layers, you need them to share a common vocabulary in terms of an object
model (for the `Product` class in the previous example) and to use it to exchange information with each other.

This example showed a case where a requirement can be fulfilled with the cooper-
ation of all the three application layers. Despite this being the most common situation, there are also cases in which functionalities don't traverse a layer boundary: the
form's drag-and-drop logic, for example, belongs entirely to the presentation layer
and is totally unknown to the layers below.

14.2.2 Calculating order totals and saving them to the database

The user can recalculate the order total by clicking the Recalculate button. When the
button is clicked, the application has to evaluate whether discount lines have to be
created, according to the business requirements:

> *If the customer buys more than five items of the same product, there is a discount of 10
> percent for each subsequent item. Should the discount be applicable, the order must
> contain two details: the first contains data about the first five items with no discount,
> and the other contains data about the additional items and the related discount.*

When the user clicks the Recalculate button, the web page executes code similar to
the following.

Listing 14.3   Calculating the order total

C#
```
private void btnCalculateTotal_Click(object sender, EventArgs e)
{
    Order order = getCurrentOrder();
    OrdersService.PreProcess(order);
    this.bindOrderData(order);
}
```

VB
```
Private Sub btnCalculateTotal_Click(ByVal sender As Object,
  ByVal e As EventArgs)
    Dim order As Order = getCurrentOrder()
    OrdersService.PreProcess(order)
    Me.bindOrderData(order)
End Sub
```

Even though you're triggering this logic from the presentation layer, the rule belongs
to the business layer. Thus it would be incorrect to pollute the click event handler

with code that explores the order details and decides whether it should benefit from a discount; it makes much more sense to encapsulate that logic within a specific class, called `OrdersService`, which has the responsibility and the knowledge to rearrange order details according to the discount logic.

We won't dive into the actual implementation of the `PreProcess` method, but you should appreciate how a layered architecture offers an undeniable advantage in terms of code simplicity, logic, and reusability (which often leads to easier maintainability). The code that implements the discount logic is always the same, regardless of the client. If you were to change from using a web page to a WPF application, you could easily reuse it. At the same time, any bug fixes or changes to the business rules have no impact on the user interface code and remain confined in the `OrderService` class.

When it comes time to save an order, things tend to become tricky, because you have to pursue several steps:

1. Verify whether user inputs are correct.
2. Verify whether there's enough stock of the item being ordered.
3. Update the item stock.
4. Save the order and its details to the database.
5. Notify the user that the order was correctly placed, perhaps sending an email.

While dealing with such a workflow, the presentation, business, and data access layers interact according to logic that can become rather complex. In such cases, a UML sequence diagram like the one in figure 14.3 can help to represent all the interactions.

This diagram illustrates how messages flow across the various application layers, and shows the actors involved with the exchange and their lifecycle.

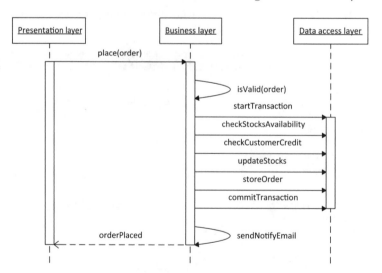

Figure 14.3   A sequence UML diagram of the order-placing process

14.2.3 *Dealing with higher levels of complexity*

Earlier in this chapter, we mentioned the concept of an application's object model, which represents a common library that all the application layers can use to communicate with each other and to store information. The `Order` class is part of OrderIT's object model, so it holds all the order data, such as the details, the customer that placed the order, and the order time.

There aren't any rules carved in stone about how an object model has to be made. For example, nothing prevents you from building it upon the well-established `Data-Set/DataTable` infrastructure we've been using since .NET Framework 1.0. But when dealing with a layered architecture, it's common to see object models made of various classes, whose shapes come directly from the tables of the underlying data source. Each instance maps to a specific row of the database and stores the row's primary key value to keep track of this relationship. Often, those classes are somehow interconnected, sometimes by holding a reference to another object, or sometimes only by storing its key.

Unfortunately, as complexity arises, this kind of architecture begins to show its limits. There's nothing wrong with layering itself, but the model we just presented has two main issues that need to be addressed:

- All the logic resides outside the object model and tends to concentrate within a series of business methods, giving the application a potentially dangerous procedural flavor.
- There's no guidance on how the object model itself should be built, which is the main reason for it to mime the database schema, regardless of whether you implement it using plain classes or `DataTables`. Although the data is ultimately stored in a relational database, you still have a full object-oriented programming language at your disposal, and this model leaves a lot of its peculiarities unused; there may be a way to use them to achieve a better design.

In conclusion, we need a different starting point: something that isn't strictly related to how data is shaped in our database, but that helps us model the real-world domain the application is supposed to manage. The result of this process is called the *domain model*, and it's the central concept behind domain-driven design.

14.3 *Principles of domain-driven design*

The first thing we should point out when talking about domain-driven design (DDD) is that it isn't a brand-new kind of architecture, different from layering. It's a bunch of rules and formalizations to effectively design the application's business layer or, better said, the domain model.

As we've discussed, every class in a layered architecture has a specific functionality, and that means easier coding and improved maintainability. But everything is designed by keeping in mind the precise role that the object will have in the application ecosystem.

In contrast, with DDD you start from a different and innovative point of view: the aim of the designer is to let the domain model be the object-oriented alter ego of the real-world concepts the application is supposed to handle, keeping track of their attributes and relationships and implementing the same behaviors. It interacts with three other application layers, defining an architectural partitioning much like what you're used to, as shown in figure 14.4.

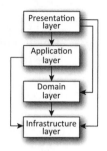

Once again, starting from the bottom, the first layer is the infrastructure layer, which carries a slightly broader responsibility than its data access layer counterpart. The infrastructure layer encompasses all the technical functionality that the upper layers may need, such as sending email, interacting with a database, or opening TCP/IP channels.

**Figure 14.4
Application layering
according to DDD**

Entity Framework as part of the infrastructure layer

When layering according to DDD, the infrastructure layer doesn't just manage data access, although this feature represents a big part of it. You'll see shortly that you can use Entity Framework's designer in Visual Studio to build an Entity Data Model, which can be thought as a raw domain layer. Thanks to that, when it comes time to fetch or store data to the database, Entity Framework completely shields you from what's needed under the hood to communicate with it: you won't have to open connections or use commands to execute stored procedures anymore, because you won't code over tables but over a fully object-oriented model.

That's why, when dealing with a three-layer architecture, we pointed out that Entity Framework fits inside the data access layer or, in some cases, can be considered the entire data access layer on its own; this is still valid in DDD, when talking about the infrastructure layer. Should other services (emails, third-party web services, and so on) be needed, they're implemented in other assemblies. These assemblies, along with the Entity Framework ones, together form the application's infrastructure layer.

We already talked about the domain layer. The application layer coordinates the interactions between the various layers and objects of the application. Usually this layer is kept thin; it shouldn't hold any business concepts, because those belong to the domain layer.

On the side, the presentation layer is much the same as before, taking care of anything that concerns displaying data and reacting to user input.

DDD introduces a few new concepts related to how a domain model should be created. Let's explore them in the context of OrderIT.

14.3.1 Entities

Let's start building the OrderIT domain model following the application requirements, as you did in chapter 2, looking particularly at the first feature you need to fulfill:

- OrderIT must store data about customers.
- Each customer has a name, billing address, and shipping address.

The customer is the first business concept that finds a place in the application, and you also have a small subset of data you need to track for it: name, billing address, and shipping address. Let's imagine that you did such a great job that the application will be a commercial success in the near future, having hundreds of registered customers. Probably among them you'll find many with the same names, such as John Smith (or Mario Rossi, if you lived in Italy); moreover, some of them could move over the years, so the users would need to update their addresses.

OrderIT will need to keep on correctly placing orders and dispatching items, no matter how many matching names are in the database and how many times they change locations. If OrderIT wasn't able to do so, users would probably end up sending goods to the wrong people and wouldn't receive payments for their bills.

In other words, some business concepts (like a customer) own a well-defined, sometimes implicit, identity that isn't related to their attributes and that remains the same for their entire lifecycle within the application. Objects with such features are called *entities*.

`Order`, too, is an entity for this application: an order has its own lifecycle, and while it lasts, it should always be unambiguously identifiable; that's why after it's created, every order is given a unique and immutable number that represents its identity field. Every entity should have one, and that's the first aspect deserving attention when a brand-new entity appears in your domain.

> **Different scenarios require different identities**
>
> The entity concept is strictly related to the application's purpose, and not to the real-world object that's being modeled. If you were working on an inventory-management application that used the concept of incoming and outgoing orders to increase and decrease the stock of a given item, you probably wouldn't care about an order's lifecycle and identity: you'd just want to know whether it contains a certain item or not. In other words, two orders for the same amount of the same item would be identical for that business process. In this example, `Order` wouldn't be an entity for your domain model. We'll get back to this distinction shortly.

In OrderIT, `Order` and `Customer` have a relationship with each other that's called an *association*. Figure 14.5 shows an early version of the domain model you're building.

Another concept that the domain-model philosophy has is the *value object*.

Figure 14.5
An `Order` and `Customer` UML diagram

14.3.2 *Value objects*

Let's go back for a moment to the requirement of storing customer data:

- *OrderIT must store data about customers.* Each customer has a name, billing address, and shipping address. The address isn't plain text, but consists of four separate pieces of data: street, city, ZIP code, and country.

We can easily identify another business concept in that statement: the address. But the nature of this object is considerably different from `Order` or `Customer`. Does OrderIT really need an addresses catalog? Does an address have its own lifecycle? Are two addresses different even though they're pointing to the exactly the same location? The answer is no. You only need a customer's address to correctly deliver bills and goods, so two addresses with the same attributes can be considered absolutely the same address. That means there are objects whose equality is solely determined by their attributes. These objects are called *value objects.*

Typically value objects are small classes that group one or more attributes used in many points of the domain model, maybe encapsulating some sort of behavior. They're not independent, which means a value object can't exist on its own: in OrderIT, for example, an address has no business meaning unless it's related to an order, to store its delivery address.

Relationships that involve value types are called *compositions.* Figure 14.6 shows how `Address` fits into the domain model to represent one customer's billing and shipping addresses.

Considering their nature, value objects can be freely exchanged. Given two customers, the following statement can be used to copy the first customer's billing address data to the other:

C#
```
customer2.BillingAddress = customer1.BillingAddress;
```

VB
```
customer2.BillingAddress = customer1.BillingAddress
```

You may argue that a statement like this isn't completely free of side effects: we're talking about .NET classes, and modifying customer1's billing address would result in a harmful bug, because customer2 would inherit the change as well.

A possible solution for that (and absolutely a best practice) is always designing value objects as immutable, which means giving them read-only properties and fields. This rule has also has a more philosophical reason behind it: because a value object's identity is completely defined by its attributes, modifying one of them should result in a brand-new object. That's why it's more correct to create a new instance when its values need to be changed.

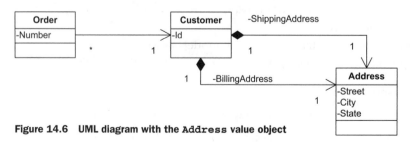

Figure 14.6   UML diagram with the `Address` value object

14.3.3 *Handling associations correctly: domain roots and aggregates*

Each order must keep track of the products and quantities it involves. Hence, it's pretty clear that you need to add a collection of `OrderDetail` objects.

Is OrderDetail an entity or a value object?

Based on what we said in the previous pages, you may wonder whether `OrderDetail` should be considered an entity or a value object. Two order details that relate to the same item and have the same quantity could be considered exactly the same thing, so at first sight, you may consider `OrderDetail` a value object.

When it comes to dealing with domain-model persistence, though, you must be aware of how the domain design impacts the infrastructure layer. Saving a detail table of value objects isn't easy, because they don't have their own identity field that maps the instance to a specific and well-identified database row. That's why it's sometimes worth sacrificing the model's pureness to achieve an easier implementation when writing the code.

This chapter's concepts work whether `OrderDetail` is modeled as an entity or as a value object.

`Order` and `OrderDetail` provide a typical example of a master-detail relationship. To make the relationship navigable in both directions, you need an `Order` property in the `OrderDetail` class that references the order to which it belongs, and you need a collection of details (`OrderDetails` property) in the `Order` object.

Does it make sense to blindly apply this pattern to every association in the domain model? Earlier in this chapter, for example, you saw that `Customer` and `Order` have a similar association, but you designed it as navigable only from the `Order`. Should you add an `Orders` property to the `Customer` entity?

There's a subtle difference between these two examples: an order detail is useless if taken away from its root; the `Order` entity along with all its details encompasses the business concept of a real-world order. Using a term specific to DDD, they form an *aggregate* of entities, whose root is the order itself. When you're dealing with aggregates, you're never supposed to directly reference an entity that isn't the aggregate's root: following this rule results in a more polished domain, in which external objects only refer to the order as a whole and never deal with its internal composition.

That said, implementing a master-detail relationship between the two makes a lot of sense, because you're always going to access order details from the main `Order` entity. Figure 14.7 shows how to represent an aggregate in a UML diagram.

Notice that the `Customer` entity, along with its addresses, also forms an aggregate. Note also that you're allowed to reference other entities from within an aggregate, as it happens between `OrderDetail` and `Product`.

The relationship between a customer and its orders now appears clearly different from the relationship between an order and its details, because they aren't part of the same aggregate! In fact, there's nothing wrong with directly referencing an order

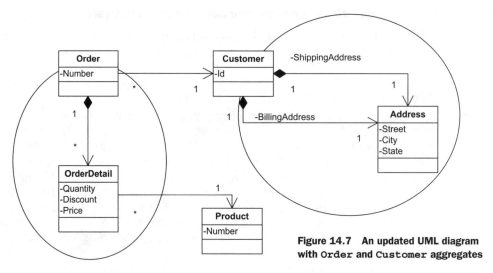

Figure 14.7   **An updated UML diagram with `Order` and `Customer` aggregates**

without coming from the customer that placed it. An order makes a lot of sense (and has a huge business meaning) even if you don't consider which customer it belongs to. In DDD terms, a customer and its orders aren't an aggregate.

Why should you a avoid master-detail relationship between customers and orders? Because associations are easy to navigate, but they don't come for free: they have a significant cost in terms of complexity and performance. Moreover, getting all the orders for a given customer doesn't have a great business meaning; more often, you'll need to recover orders placed within a certain period of time, or orders that are still waiting to be delivered. *Repositories* are better candidates for accomplishing these tasks, because they provide full object-oriented querying features. We'll cover repositories later in this chapter; now we need to work a bit more on the order entity.

14.3.4 *Refining the model*

Now that the `Order` and `Customer` parts of your domain model are well defined, it's time to think about how the discount calculation fits in:

> *The policy for discounts states that if the customer buys more than five of the same product, there is a discount of 10 percent for each subsequent item. Should the discount be applicable, the order must contain two details: the first contains data about the first five items with no discount, and the other contains data about the additional items and the related discount.*

You implemented this feature earlier as a method in the `OrderService` class. Now you're starting from a different perspective, because you're trying to model an object-oriented representation of the order business concept. In this context, it's natural to include a `ComputeDiscount` method in the `Order` class. This method should explore the details collection and eventually add discount rows where needed.

Listing 14.4 shows a sample implementation of this method. Notice that it often refers to `this` when the `Order` entity is involved, because it's an instance method.

Listing 14.4   Computing an order's discount

C#
```csharp
public void ComputeDiscount()
{
  compactOrderDetails();
  var detailsToDiscount =
    this.Details.FindAll(d => d.Quantity > 5);

  foreach(var orderDetail in detailsToDiscount)
  {
    int exceedingQuantity = orderDetail.Quantity - 5;
    orderDetail.Quantity = 5;
    OrderDetail discountDetail = new OrderDetail
    {
      Order = this,
      Item = orderDetail.Item,
      Quantity = exceedingQuantity,
      Discount = 0.1
    }
    this.Details.Add(discountDetail);
  }
}
```

VB
```vb
Public Sub ComputeDiscount()
    compactOrderDetails()
    Dim detailsToDiscount = Me.Details.FindAll( _
      Function(d)  d.Quantity > 5)

    For Each orderDetail In detailsToDiscount
        Dim exceedingQuantity As Integer = orderDetail.Quantity - 5
        orderDetail.Quantity = 5
        Dim discountDetail As New OrderDetail() With _
        { _
          .Order = me, _
          .Item = orderDetail.Item, _
          .Quantity = exceedingQuantity, _
          .Discount = 0.1 _
        }

        Me.Details.Add(discountDetail)
    Next
End Sub
```

The domain model isn't anemic anymore!

A domain model is called *anemic* when it only contains data, and no code. Many people think that a domain should be modeled that way, because usually processes change, but data doesn't, and modifying a domain class after the application has shipped could require great effort, given its centrality in the overall architecture. But remember that your ultimate goal is to take a real-world order and describe it as a class. As a general rule, there's nothing bad about adding logic to a domain class if you're sure it belongs to the class. In any case, you'll shortly see that there are better options in this case, and the model can be further improved.

Now let's imagine that, after some months of OrderIT running in production, this promotion discount expires, perhaps to be replaced with another one with different logic. This would force you to roll up your sleeves and modify the domain code; but besides that, isn't there something conceptually wrong with a changing promotion requiring maintenance on the order class? Should an order discount really belong to the order itself?

When you added the discount logic to the order, you hid a concept that you must make explicit to improve the overall design: the logic that determines whether an order is suitable for a discount or not. This logic is a new element of the OrderIT domain model, which we'll call `Discount-Policy`. Figure 14.8 shows the updated UML diagram.

The `CalculateDiscount` method can now be refactored, as shown in the following listing.

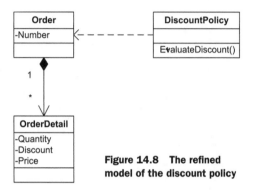

Figure 14.8   The refined model of the discount policy

Listing 14.5   Computing an order's discount with `DiscountPolicy`

C#
```csharp
public void ComputeDiscount()
{
  compactOrderDetails();
  this.DiscountPolicy.EvaluateDiscount(this);
}
```

VB
```vb
Public Sub ComputeDiscount()
  compactOrderDetails()
  Me.DiscountPolicy.EvaluateDiscount(Me)
End Sub
```

Notice how the `DiscountPolicy` class encapsulates the whole discount calculation logic.

This design isn't applicable to every situation. Sometimes the business process is too complex and involves too many objects, and you don't want to include all that logic in a single entity; sometimes there isn't a specific entity to which the processes belong. In such cases, you can introduce specific objects in your domain, called *domain services,* to handle those tasks. In OrderIT, you can use a domain service to

---

Why making DiscountPolicy explicit results in a better design

The step you just made brings great benefits to our design. The domain model is formally more correct, because you introduced a new business concept that avoids polluting the `Order` entity with responsibilities that don't belong to it. Moreover, it gives you the chance to use the object-oriented paradigm, using the Strategy pattern to easily support new discount policies to come.

implement the order-placing logic, which involves saving the new order, updating the stock, notifying the customer by email, and so on.

But beware of abusing domain services, or you'll soon be dealing again with procedural code. A process must be implemented as a service only when it meets all of these criteria:

- The service represents flows that don't directly belong to an entity or a value object, but that interact with various domain model elements.
- The service interface is solely composed of domain model objects.
- The service logic is stateless, which means an invocation result doesn't depend on previous results.

So far, we've focused on how the domain model must be shaped, without caring whether its building blocks are already in memory or need to be fetched from a database or created as new. In the next section, you'll discover which tools you can use to retrieve references to entities and value objects so you can use and manipulate them in the code.

14.4 Retrieving references to a domain's entities

If domain objects spend their whole lifecycle in memory, they should always be reachable from your code; otherwise, the garbage collector will wipe them out. Thanks to the persistence layer, objects are also stored in other ways, such as in databases, so they can be kept alive even if the application quits, the server restarts, or the code doesn't keep references to them. Sooner or later, you'll want to recover that reference. You could do it by navigating object references within an object graph, but you'd still need an aggregate root to start from. This is where repositories fit in.

14.4.1 Repositories at a glance

In DDD, you model the application's business concepts in the form of classes, and the most intuitive way for the object-oriented programmer to group a set of instances of the same class is using collections. In fact, if you put aside for a moment the need to store entities in a relational database, it would probably be most convenient to hold all the customer references in a globally reachable AllCustomers collection somewhere in the application design. For OrderIT, a customer would exist only if it was in that collection, and removing a customer from the collection would mean deleting it.

Unfortunately, in the real world, durable data needs to be stored in a durable platform, but it would still be great to abstract the storage as if it were made of collections. That would offer the best of both worlds. A *repository* is an object that acts like a collection of aggregate roots, giving the client the illusion that every entity it contains is already in memory. Entities can be added or removed from a repository to carry out inserts and deletes, and a repository can be queried to get references to the entities it holds.

Let's try to find a way to implement a generic repository that uses Entity Framework to interact with the relational database.

14.4.2 *Implementing a repository*

Implementing a repository is an almost trivial task, because Entity Framework already uses a repository-like pattern internally: each entity belongs to a well-defined entity set, and you only need to wrap them.

> ### Why you should build your own repositories
>
> If Entity Framework already provides entity sets, why would you need to build your own repositories? To answer this question, we must go back for a moment to the application layering we introduced in section 14.3. If you look at figure 14.4, you can see that repository implementations belong to the infrastructure layer, because they can interact with the underlying database to fetch customer data and rebuild a customer entity. This requires a reference from the infrastructure layer to the domain layer.
>
> This works perfectly when the interactions between the domain and infrastructure layers are orchestrated by the application layer: for example, when a web page must query the database to get a customer list. But it's not uncommon for domain entities to require the repository's services too. For example, a `DiscountPolicy` may need to check a customer's order history to determine whether a discount should be applied.
>
> For this reason, you must separate repository implementations from their interfaces (thus building your own repository library). The repository implementations belong to the infrastructure layer, and the interfaces are part of the domain layer. A domain class would only reference the interface, but an Inversion of Control (IoC) container would then inject the actual implementation.
>
> Another important reason to build your own repositories is for testing purposes. We'll explore this topic later in the book.

Because repositories must act as if they were in-memory collections, it's logical to inherit the generic interface from `ICollection<T>`, which provides Add, Remove, and other typical collection methods and properties. You can then add some specific functionalities. You'll start by defining the repository interface as shown in this listing.

Listing 14.6   A generic `IRepository<T>` interface

C#

```
public interface IRepository<T> : ICollection<T> where T : class
{
  IEnumerable<T> Query(Func<T, bool> predicate);
  T GetSingle(Func<T, bool> predicate);
  void Update(T entity);
}
```

VB

```
Public Interface IRepository(Of T As Class)
  Inherits ICollection(Of T)
  Function Query(ByVal predicate As Func(Of T, Boolean)) As _
           IEnumerable(Of T)
  Function GetSingle(ByVal predicate As Func(Of T, Boolean)) As T
```

```
   Sub Update(ByVal entity As T)
End Interface
```

The IRepository<T> interface adds three methods. Query and GetSingle can be used to query the repository's content and retrieve an enumerable or a single entity, respectively. Both methods accept a predicate as an argument (that's a delegate that accept an instance of a T and returns true or false) and can be easily invoked using a lambda expression, as you're used to doing with LINQ's Where extension method. Last but not least, you can use Update to attach an existing entity to the repository.

The concrete Repository<T> class has some prerequisites to work properly: first, it must be instantiated within a persistence context, which means it must operate on a valid and alive Entity Framework context. This is why, in order to initialize a repository, you need a context whose reference will be held for further use.

This isn't enough, though, because you can't query or add entities directly to the context. You also need a reference to the entity's entity set. The following listing shows the Repository<T> constructor.

Listing 14.7   Repository constructor

C#
```csharp
public class Repository<T> : IRepository<T> where T : class
{
  private ObjectContext context;
  private ObjectSet<T> entitySet;

  public Repository(ObjectContext context)
  {
    if (context == null)
      throw new ArgumentNullException("context");

    this.context = context;
    this.entitySet = context.CreateObjectSet<T>();
  }
}
```

VB
```vb
Public Class Repository(Of T As Class)
  Implements IRepository(Of T)
  Private context As ObjectContext
  Private entitySet As ObjectSet(Of T)

  Public Sub New(ByVal context As ObjectContext)
    If context Is Nothing Then
      Throw New ArgumentNullException("context")
    End If

  Me.context = context
    Me.entitySet = context.CreateObjectSet(Of T)()
  End Sub
End Class
```

Now you can get back to the interface and look at the Query method. As you can see in listing 14.8, when you have a reference to the object set, its implementation is straightforward. All you need to do is query the object set, forwarding the predicate to LINQ's `Where` extension method. `GetSingle` uses the same code, but it returns a single instance of the `T` entity.

Listing 14.8   Query and GetSingle implementations

C#
```
public IEnumerable<T> Query(Func<T, bool> predicate)
{
  return this.entitySet.Where(predicate);
}

public T GetSingle(Func<T, bool> predicate)
{
  return this.Query(predicate).Single();
}
```

VB
```
Public Function Query(ByVal predicate As Func(Of T, Boolean)) As _
                IEnumerable(Of T)
    Return Me.entitySet.Where(predicate)
End Function

Public Function GetSingle(ByVal predicate As Func(Of T, Boolean)) As T
    Return Me.Query(predicate).[Single]()
End Function
```

`IRepository<T>` provides two methods to connect an entity to the underlying `ObjectSet<T>`: `Add` comes from the base `ICollection<T>` interface you're inheriting from, whereas the `Update` method was explicitly defined in listing 14.6. You have to implement them for the context to be able to track every change you make to the entity and generate proper persistence queries. A third method, `Remove`, also belongs to the base `ICollection<T>` interface, and it can be used to flag the given entity for deletion. The following listing shows what we just described.

Listing 14.9   Add, Remove, and Update implementations

C#
```
public void Add(T entity)
{
  if (!this.Contains(entity))
    this.entitySet.AddObject(entity);
}

public void Update(T entity)
{
  if (!this.Contains(entity))
    this.entitySet.Attach(entity);
}

public bool Remove(T entity)
{
  if (!this.Contains(entity))
    return false;
```

```
    this.entitySet.DeleteObject(entity);

    return true;
}
```

VB

```
Public Sub Add(ByVal entity As T)
  If Not Me.Contains(entity) Then
    Me.entitySet.AddObject(entity)
  End If
End Sub

Public Sub Update(ByVal entity As T)
  If Not Me.Contains(entity) Then
    Me.entitySet.Attach(entity)
  End If
End Sub

Public Function Remove(ByVal entity As T) As Boolean
  If Not Me.Contains(entity) Then
    Return False
  End If

  Me.entitySet.DeleteObject(entity)

  Return True
End Function
```

All these methods internally use Contains (which you can see in listing 14.10) to determine whether the entity already belongs to the object context. Contains, in turns, asks the state manager for the entity's state and evaluates it.

Listing 14.10 `ICollection<T>.Contains` implementation

C#

```
public bool Contains(T item)
{
  ObjectStateEntry state;

  if (!this.context.ObjectStateManager
          .TryGetObjectStateEntry(item, out state))
    return false;

  return (state.State != EntityState.Detached);
}
```

VB

```
Public Function Contains(ByVal item As T) As Boolean
    Dim state As ObjectStateEntry

    If Not Me.context.ObjectStateManager.TryGetObjectStateEntry _
            (item, state) Then
        Return False
    End If

    Return (state.State <> EntityState.Detached)
End Function
```

In order to successfully implement `ICollection<T>`, the compiler requires you to also write members like `Clear` or `GetEnumerator` that aren't useful in this scenario. We won't cover their implementation here.

Let's move on to the client's point of view, and imagine how you would typically use a repository in your code. For example, if a discount should be applied to a customer's first order, the discount rule could be defined as follows.

Listing 14.11   Typical repository usage

C#
```csharp
public bool ApplyDiscount(Customer customer)
{
  IRepository<Order> orderRepository =
    container.Get<IRepository<Order>>();

  return orderRepository.Query(o => o.Customer == customer).Count() == 0;
}
```

VB
```vb
Public Function ApplyDiscount(ByVal customer As Customer) As Boolean

  Dim orderRepository As IRepository(Of Order) = _
    container.[Get](Of IRepository(Of Order))()

  Return orderRepository.Query(Function(o) o.Customer = customer) _
    .Count() = 0
End Function
```

Notice how the `FirstOrderDiscountRule` doesn't directly reference the concrete repository class but uses it via its interface. You can achieve this by using an Inversion of Control container to keep the interface separated from the actual implementation; this is the meaning of the `container` variable the code refers to.

Inversion of Control is a well-known and widely used pattern for loosely coupling various application dependencies; if you're interested in this topic, an internet search will turn up hundreds of related articles and libraries.

14.4.3 *Getting a reference to a brand new entity*

When you're dealing with complex domains, building new entities can be challenging and require interactions between various aggregates in your domain model. Consider the `Order` entity and its relationship with `DiscountPolicy`, as discussed in section 14.3.4: what has the responsibility to associate an order to the proper discount policy? It can't be the order itself, which hasn't any knowledge of the various policies the application supports; at the same time, you don't want the developer, who will use the domain model, to have the deep knowledge required to select the correct discount policy—that would reveal too many details of the `Order` class's internal structure. In such cases, *factories* are what you need: they're domain objects that are responsible for creating instances of aggregates.

Factories can also be useful when you need to invoke infrastructure services (like a logging service) and you don't want to expose this logic to the end user.

> ### Factories that use Entity Framework's foreign keys
>
> Although in your entity data model you have navigation properties to traverse relations, Entity Framework 4.0 introduces the concept of foreign-key properties, which are plain scalar properties containing the associated entity's ID. You can set them to modify this association if you want to. When you fetch an entity from the database, the foreign-key properties and their corresponding navigation properties are bound together, and changing the former results in an automatic update of the latter. To achieve the same behavior with new entities, you can use the `ObjectContext.CreateObject<T>` method.
>
> In DDD, you shouldn't use foreign keys, because they're a technical and infrastructural concept that you shouldn't pollute your domain model with. For the same reason, you shouldn't explicitly invoke `ObjectContext.CreateObject<T>` within the domain model. But it's also true that foreign-key features can be very useful in your infrastructure layer.
>
> To keep the best of both worlds, you can use a factory to encapsulate this logic and use it when the time comes to create new entities.

14.5 Summary

In this chapter, we explored the basics of an application's structure. We introduced a layered architecture, showing how the overall application design can benefit from better code organization and separation of concerns.

Then we moved on to domain-driven design (DDD), which aims to encapsulate the pure business logic in an object-oriented model, referred to as the application's domain. We introduced some key building blocks, like entities, value objects, repositories, and factories, giving examples of how you could use them to rethink the OrderIT application you've been working on in this book. If you want to explore all these concepts more deeply, we recommend reading *Domain-Driven Design*, by Eric Evans (Addison-Wesley, 2003), which is considered the "bible" of DDD. Although these DDD concepts are abstract and don't necessarily require a persistence framework such as Entity Framework, we showed how you can integrate Entity Framework with DDD.

Application architecture is a great place to start to achieve robustness and maintainability, but it covers only half of the journey. In the next chapters, you'll apply these concepts to some typical real-world applications, and then we'll focus on another technique that dramatically improves software quality: automatic code testing.

Entity Framework and ASP.NET

15

This chapter covers

- Binding data with the `EntityDataSource` control
- Using Dynamic Data controls and Entity Framework
- Understanding the `ObjectContext` lifecycle
- Common scenarios related to integrating ASP.NET and Entity Framework

ASP.NET is the technology used in the .NET Framework to build web applications. In this chapter, we'll analyze the ASP.NET and Entity Framework integration, so a basic knowledge of data-binding techniques in ASP.NET is required. You can find more information on this topic on MSDN, in the "ASP.NET Data-Bound Web Server Controls Overview" article at http://mng.bz/c3k4.

You can use Entity Framework's features in two different ways: you can use ASP.NET RAD support to directly tie them together; or you can manually manage the `ObjectContext` lifecycle by writing more code. The first approach has the main advantage of not requiring code, whereas the latter gives you maximum control over what is performed under the hood. Which is the best approach for your application is up to you: typically, the former is indicated in small (or quick-and-dirty) applications, because you can be very productive, whereas the latter is for enterprise applications. We'll start with the simpler approach and then look at how to directly manage the ObjectContext lifecycle in a typical ASP.NET application.

Before we can move on, it's useful to note that Entity Framework's ObjectContext can be instantiated only once per page. If you want to build some kind of layer over Entity Framework (as you did in chapter 14), you'll have to handle this task manually. If you prefer to let ASP.NET do the magic for you, just sit down and relax: there is a special control, called EntityDataSource that will perform most of the tasks for you. Let's start by looking at what EntityDataSource can do.

15.1 EntityDataSource, a new approach to data binding

Starting with version 2.0, ASP.NET offered a new approach to data binding, using a new set of web controls named *data source controls*. Data source controls are, in fact, used to enable a development approach ·based on Rapid Application Development (RAD) in Visual Studio, providing a drag-and-drop-based development environment.

15.1.1 A practical guide to data source controls

You can build an entire application based on data source controls with the wizards and RAD tools integrated in Visual Studio. The result is markup code that includes the configuration for extracting data and for binding to the associated data control, such as the GridView or Repeater.

Several data source controls are available for different scenarios. These are the most used:

- SqlDataSource—Makes a direct connection to a database structure
- ObjectDataSource—Enables the business logic to access business objects in common three-tier applications
- LinqDataSource—Adds support to LINQ to SQL's DataContext
- EntityDataSource—Implements support for Entity Framework's data model and ObjectContext

Every data source has a different set of pros and cons, depending on the approach you want to use in your application architecture.

THE SQLDATASOURCE CONTROL

SqlDataSource is used when you want to couple your database to your web interface. This situation isn't ideal in common applications, but it may be useful in quick-and-dirty scenarios, when all you want is a GUI to manipulate your data. When you use SqlDataSource, the connection string and SQL query are saved directly in the markup, so this isn't the best choice in terms of flexibility.

THE OBJECTDATASOURCE CONTROL

ObjectDataSource provides an alternative method of access in three-tier applications, where you have a separation between the data layer and business logic, and you manipulate data using object representations. This approach is suitable when you want a better architecture and the ability to build the graphical interface using a RAD approach. ObjectDataSource can use an EDM, but you'll have no benefits: you're using objects in a simple form.

THE LINQDATASOURCE AND ENTITYDATASOURCE CONTROLS

LinqDataSource and EntityDataSource offer the same functionality against different data sources: LINQ to SQL's DataContext and Entity Framework's ObjectContext, respectively. They both use the same approach; they don't use a tier to separate the data access from the interface, but use the O/RM capabilities directly. You can add your own validation and loading logic to both DataContext and ObjectContext by using partial classes.

Using the LinqDataSource and EntityDataSource controls prevents you from separating your data access strategy from your business rules. It may not be a good idea to directly expose the data access in the page. Putting the data access in the business logic tier is a better choice in terms of modularity and maintenance, resulting in a better application architecture. But if keeping the data access separate from the business rules isn't a problem for you and your application, the EntityDataSource control is a very practical and productive way to go.

Using a data source control has the advantage of avoiding code in your pages, because the DataBind method is performed automatically, during the PreRender event, by the data control itself. If you have a Repeater control on your page, you simply have to set the DataSourceID property to the ID of your data source control. The magic behind the scenes is done by ASP.NET: the resulting page will print data out of your data source.

15.1.2 *The EntityDataSource control in depth*

From a technical perspective, the EntityDataSource control is very similar to Linq-DataSource, because they're both based on the System.Web.Extensions.IDynamic-DataSource interface. This interface is primarily used to ensure compatibility in applications based on Dynamic Data controls (which will be discussed in section 15.2).

EntityDataSource in ASP.NET 3.5

In order to use EntityDataSource with ASP.NET 3.5, you need to reference the System.Web.Entity assembly, located in the Global Assembly Cache (GAC) and installed by .NET Framework 3.5 Service Pack 1. Entity Framework was added with Service Pack 1 and isn't directly available with ASP.NET 3.5.

ASP.NET 4.0 directly supports this control.

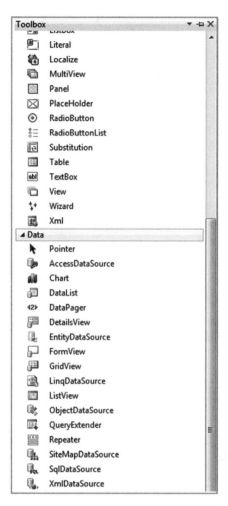

To explore `EntityDataSource`'s capabilities, let's build a simple application to show its features. You'll build a simple web page that will show the products available from OrderIT. You'll use this database in all the examples presented in this chapter.

To begin this little project, you need to locate the `EntityDataSource` control. You can find the `EntityDataSource` control in your toolbox, as shown in figure 15.1.

You can start by adding a data control, like a `Repeater` or `ListView`. Select the New Data Source option from the Choose Data Source smart task, as shown in figure 15.2. This smart task will appear when the editor is in design view.

The Data Source Configuration Wizard will guide you through a series of options. The most important step is the selection of your EDM and the entity that you want to display.

Figure 15.1   You can insert an `EntityDataSource` control via the Visual Studio toolbar. It can be found under the Data category.

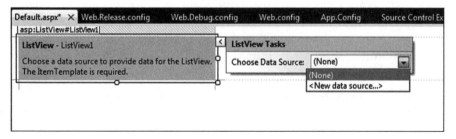

Figure 15.2   It's possible to directly define a new `EntityDataSource` using the associated Visual Studio smart task. Choose the New Data Source option to open a specific wizard.

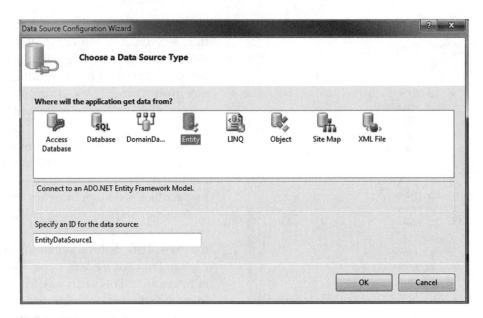

Figure 15.3   By selecting Entity in the Data Source Configuration Wizard, you can later define all the details associated with the to-be-created EntityDataSource.

The first wizard step is shown in figure 15.3.

In this example, you're using the OrderIT database hosted in the local SQL Server instance: choose Products as the EntitySetName in order to display all the products in the database. This step is shown in figure 15.4.

If you want to automatically let EntityDataSource handle inserts, updates, and deletes, all you have to do is select the corresponding check boxes in the wizard screen shown in figure 15.4. Given the common nature of ObjectContext, Entity-DataSource knows how to manipulate entities: the control uses the ObjectContext to persist your actions in the corresponding database, using the previously defined model. When you click the Finish button, the wizard exits, and the corresponding markup is generated in the page.

If you look at the resulting ASP.NET page markup, you'll see what the EntityData-Source control needs to make things work. The markup is shown in this listing, with the key properties in bold.

Listing 15.1   EntityDataSource markup code that displays a list of products

```
<asp:ListView ID="ListView1" runat="server" DataKeyNames="ProductId"
  DataSourceID="EntityDataSource1">
  ...
</asp:ListView>
<asp:EntityDataSource ID="EntityDataSource1" runat="server"
    ConnectionString="name=OrderITEntities"
    DefaultContainerName=" OrderITEntities"
    EntitySetName="Products">
</asp:EntityDataSource>
```

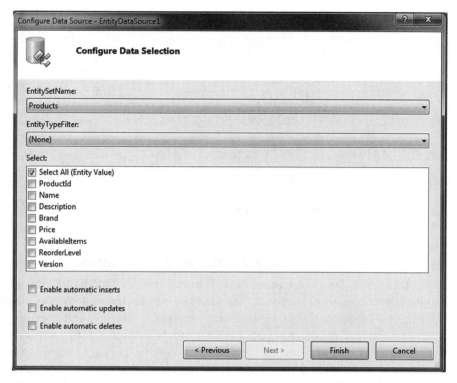

Figure 15.4   Choose the entity from the `EntitySetName` drop-down list. If you don't need to create a partial view of your entity, Select All is the preferred option in the Select box.

As you can see, `ListView`'s `DataSourceID` property is used to configure the corresponding data source control, so it can get the data from the source and display the value.

Speaking of `EntityDataSource`, the `ConnectionString` property is used to refer to the EDM previously defined, whereas `DefaultContainerName` is used to identify the `ObjectContext`. Finally, `EntitySetName` contains the entity set from which to get objects (and data).

In listing 15.1, you're taking all the data from a table named Products, located in the OrderIT database, mapped on an `EntitySet` named `Products`, using the `Object-Context` named `OrderITEntities`.

All you need to do to display the value is run the page shown in figure 15.5.

You don't need to write any code to get this result: all the magic is done by the `EntityDataSource` and the associated data control, which in this example is a `ListView`.

Your mileage with this approach may vary. As already mentioned, if you want more control over what happens under the hood, don't worry. We'll soon look at a more powerful approach to integrating ASP.NET and Entity Framework. First, though, we need to look at Dynamic Data controls, because their features are interesting if you simply need to manipulate data using a nice looking interface.

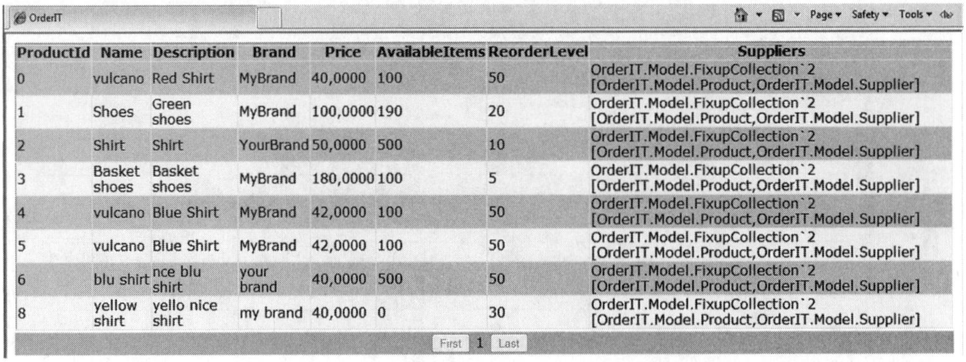

ProductId	Name	Description	Brand	Price	AvailableItems	ReorderLevel	Suppliers
0	vulcano	Red Shirt	MyBrand	40,0000	100	50	OrderIT.Model.FixupCollection`2 [OrderIT.Model.Product,OrderIT.Model.Supplier]
1	Shoes	Green shoes	MyBrand	100,0000	190	20	OrderIT.Model.FixupCollection`2 [OrderIT.Model.Product,OrderIT.Model.Supplier]
2	Shirt	Shirt	YourBrand	50,0000	500	10	OrderIT.Model.FixupCollection`2 [OrderIT.Model.Product,OrderIT.Model.Supplier]
3	Basket shoes	Basket shoes	MyBrand	180,0000	100	5	OrderIT.Model.FixupCollection`2 [OrderIT.Model.Product,OrderIT.Model.Supplier]
4	vulcano	Blue Shirt	MyBrand	42,0000	100	50	OrderIT.Model.FixupCollection`2 [OrderIT.Model.Product,OrderIT.Model.Supplier]
5	vulcano	Blue Shirt	MyBrand	42,0000	100	50	OrderIT.Model.FixupCollection`2 [OrderIT.Model.Product,OrderIT.Model.Supplier]
6	blu shirt	nce blu shirt	your brand	40,0000	500	50	OrderIT.Model.FixupCollection`2 [OrderIT.Model.Product,OrderIT.Model.Supplier]
8	yellow shirt	yello nice shirt	my brand	40,0000	0	30	OrderIT.Model.FixupCollection`2 [OrderIT.Model.Product,OrderIT.Model.Supplier]

First 1 Last

Figure 15.5 The rows are materialized into entities and displayed in the web page using the EntityDataSource control's capabilities. This is performed without writing code.

15.2 Using Dynamic Data controls with Entity Framework

ASP.NET Dynamic Data is a feature initially introduced in ASP.NET 3.5 Service Pack 1 and further enhanced in version 4. The idea behind this technology is to simplify the typical actions related to working with data: displaying, filtering, and altering data.

Dynamic Data controls ship with ASP.NET, and they support both Entity Framework and LINQ to SQL, using the LinqDataSource and EntityDataSource controls discussed previously. Dynamic Data is based on a simple assumption: because the ObjectContext has a fixed set of features that won't change, even for different mappings, its calls can be generically created. Using generics and reflection, the typical operations performed by the ObjectContext can be standardized. The same principles are valid for LINQ to SQL.

Dynamic Data controls work with a special kind of project—the Dynamic Data Entities Web Application, which can be found with the other ASP.NET projects. You can see it highlighted in figure 15.6.

Dynamic Data controls are composed of a set of templates and pages, located in the DynamicData directory. In this directory, you can find the templates used to represent different types, such as strings, integers, Booleans, and so on.

15.2.1 Registering the model

To start with Dynamic Data, you define the model you're going to work against, and the rest of the work will be performed by using the information already present in it. The model contains the list of entities, and each entity describes itself, so each set of entities can be represented and edited automatically.

The model and routes are registered in listing 15.2. The necessary code is partially generated by the wizard, but you need to add your context in order to use it with Dynamic Data.

Figure 15.6 Dynamic Data Entities Web Application is the template project you need to select to start using Dynamic Data controls with Entity Framework. The other templates won't work for this purpose.

Listing 15.2 The model and routes registration

C#

```
public class Global : System.Web.HttpApplication
{
  private static MetaModel s_defaultModel = new MetaModel();
  public static MetaModel DefaultModel
  {
    get
    {
      return s_defaultModel;
    }
  }

  void Application_Start(object sender, EventArgs e)
  {
    // model registration
    DefaultModel.RegisterContext(typeof(OrderITEntities),
                    new ContextConfiguration() {
                        ScaffoldAllTables = true });
    // routes
    RouteTable.Routes.Add(new DynamicDataRoute("{table}/{action}.aspx")
```

Uses
ObjectContext
as model

Enables
1 scaffolding

```
        {
          Constraints = new RouteValueDictionary(new {
                                   action = "List|Details|Edit|Insert" }),
          Model = DefaultModel
        });
      }
    }
```

VB

```
Public Class Global_asax
  Inherits System.Web.HttpApplication
  Private Shared s_defaultModel As New MetaModel()
  Public Shared ReadOnly Property DefaultModel() As MetaModel
    Get
      Return s_defaultModel
    End Get
  End Property

  Public Sub Application_Start(ByVal sender as Object, ByVal e as EventArgs)
    ' model registration
    Dim config As New ContextConfiguration()                    ❶ Enables
    config.ScaffoldAllTables = True                                scaffolding
    DefaultModel.RegisterContext(GetType(OrderITEntities),
                              config)                           Uses ObjectContext
                                                                as model
    ' routes
    RouteTable.Routes.Add(New DynamicDataRoute("{table}/{action}.aspx")
  ➥With {
            .Constraints = New RouteValueDictionary(New With {
                                   .Action = "List|Details|Edit|Insert"}),
            .Model = DefaultModel})
  End Sub
End Class
```

This code explicitly sets the scaffold feature ❶, so every entity is automatically displayed in the start page. If you prefer to control this list, you must turn it off. If you use the routing features from ASP.NET 4.0, the resulting URL will be similar to /Customers/List.aspx, where Customers is the entity set to be managed, and List is the action. As you can see in listing 15.2, the Details, Edit, and Insert actions can be used to manage the respective statuses.

15.2.2 *Working with data annotations*

In figure 15.7, you can see the default results you'll get when you display the Customer list from the model.

By default, the display template is inferred from the column's type, but it can be specified too. Generally, you specify templates by creating a new class, specifically for this scenario, that extends the entity using the MetadataTypeAttribute attribute. Dynamic Data controls work with *data annotations*, a feature introduced in .NET Framework 3.5 SP1 and further enhanced in version 4. In this example, we're using POCO entities, so the annotations are directly generated using the T4 engine (which was introduced in chapter 13). If you're using the default entity-generation engine,

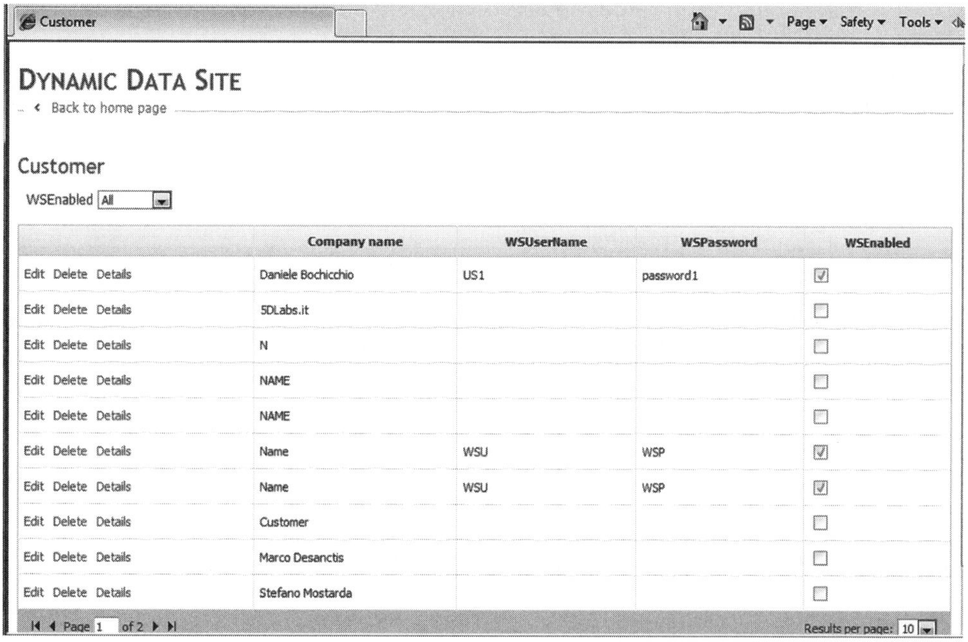

Figure 15.7 Dynamic Data controls are capable of displaying any mapped entity. As shown here, the display can be customized.

you can use a partial class and the aforementioned `MetadataTypeAttribute`. More information on this topic is available from MSDN in the "MetadataTypeAttribute Class" article: http://mng.bz/q9hA.

In this example, we added some custom logic to the default generation engine by altering the CDSL inside the EDMX file to generate the exact code used to represent the additional properties required by data annotations. Data annotations work with attributes, as you can see in the following listing, which contains an entity generated with these annotations.

Listing 15.3   POCO entities generated by a template with data annotations

C#
```
public abstract partial class Company : INotifyPropertyChanged,
    IEditableObject
{
  ...
  [DisplayName("Company name")]
  [Required(ErrorMessage = "Company name is required")]
  [DataType("MultilineText")]
  [RegularExpression("[\\w]{2,}",
ErrorMessage = "At least 2 chars.")]
  public virtual string Name
  {
    get { return _name; }
```

Attributes for data annotations

```
    set { _name = value; NotifyPropertyChanged("Name"); }
  }
}
```

VB
```
Public MustInherit Partial Class Company
  Implements INotifyPropertyChanged
  Implements IEditableObject

  ...
  <DisplayName("Company name")>
  <Required(ErrorMessage := "Company name is required ")>
  <DataType("MultilineText")>
  <RegularExpression("[\w]{2,}",
          ErrorMessage := "At least 2 chars.")>
  Public Overridable Property Name() As String
    Get
      Return _name
    End Get
    Set(ByVal value As String)
      _name = value
      NotifyPropertyChanged("Name")
    End Set
  End Property
End Class
```

> **Attributes for data annotations**

The annotations influence the way the property is displayed and how its value is validated:

- `DisplayNameAttribute`—Sets a more friendly name to be displayed
- `RequiredAttribute`—Lets you define the property as required, associating an error message to be displayed
- `DataTypeAttribute`—Specifies a new template
- `RegularExpressionAttribute`—Specifies a regular expression for validation

You can see how Dynamic Data controls handles these attributes in figure 15.8.

Data annotations are a very important way of using Entity Framework in ASP.NET. Their use isn't limited to working with Dynamic Data controls but can be expanded to ASP.NET MVC model validation. You can find more information on the available attributes in the "System.ComponentModel.DataAnnotations Namespace" article on MSDN: http://mng.bz/2cWi.

We're now finished with Dynamic Data controls. It's time to learn how to directly manage the `ObjectContext`'s lifecycle in a typical ASP.NET application, how to handle it properly, and what the main aspects to consider are.

15.3 *The ObjectContext lifecycle in ASP.NET*

`EntityDataSource` and Dynamic Data controls are interesting if you want to be very productive, or if you just need a simple interface to display and manipulate your data. In real-world applications, though, where enterprise techniques are needed, this approach won't work.

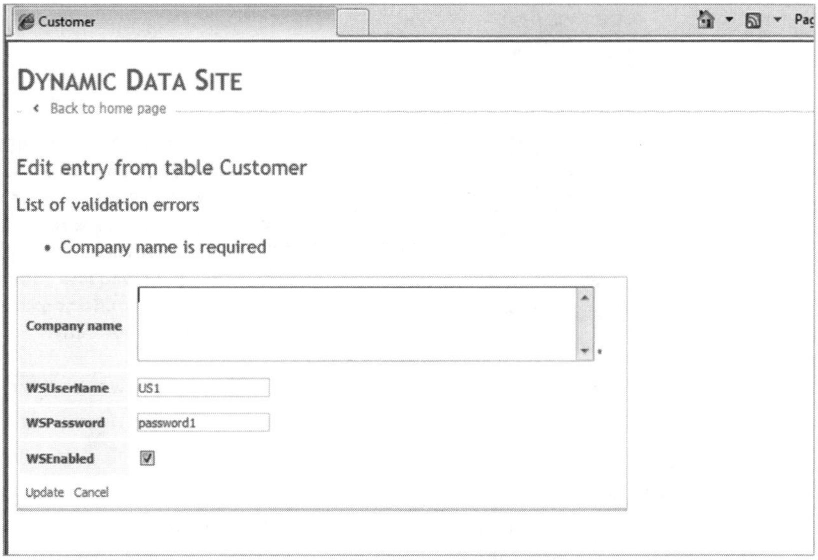

Figure 15.8   The data-annotation attributes modify the way the properties are displayed and how their values are handled. By using them, you can influence what Dynamic Data does.

As you learned in chapter 14, it's possible to isolate Entity Framework's dependency from the application, using a different approach from the one already introduced in this chapter. By using *repositories,* you can avoid coupling and maintain better control over what is performed under the hood. The examples provided in chapter 14 introduced you to the basics of this subject. The purpose of using a repository is to simplify testability, and, at the same time, to provide flexibility. By using a clean approach, primarily based on interfaces, the use of repositories also avoids coupling, generally thanks to an Inversion of Control (IoC) container that wraps the complexity.

> **NOTE**   The example provided in this section is based on *Unity,* an IoC container that's part of the Enterprise Library, created by the Microsoft Pattern & Practice team. The configuration is performed in the web.config file.

By using an IoC container, you can reuse part of the code already presented in chapter 14, which didn't incorporate ASP.NET. We can reuse it here because we designed the application with great flexibility in mind.

15.3.1 *The Context-per-Request pattern*

To make sure your strategy-based repositories can be implemented, you need to build a set of classes that will encapsulate the logic, as illustrated in figure 15.9.

There are different ways to handle the ObjectContext's lifecycle, but the best in web applications, in terms of flexibility and functionality, is to handle it *per-request* (as

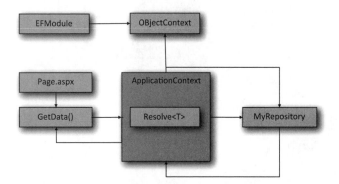

Figure 15.9 By using the IoC container, both the `ObjectContext` and repositories are resolved at runtime. This helps to avoid coupling and lets you manage the `ObjectContext`'s lifecycle correctly.

in the Context-per-Request pattern). Every request will have its own `ObjectContext` instance, shared by different repositories, with there generally being one instance of the `ObjectContext` per entity set.

This simplifies the problem in many ways, because different parts of the page can access the same context, and multiple actions can be completed at the same time. Thanks to the `IQueryable` interface, the real query to the database will be performed only when the entity set is effectively enumerated, so no tangible overhead is associated with this approach.

15.3.2 *Wrapping the context*

In order to support this scenario, you first need to create a basic implementation that gets the `ObjectContext`. We previously prepared an interface called `IObjectContext` that can support more scenarios, like unit testing, or Windows applications. The implementation is shown in the following listing.

Listing 15.4 Context wrapper creating an instance of the `ObjectContext`

C#

```csharp
public class WebContextWrapper : IObjectContext
{
  public WebContextWrapper()
  {
  if (HttpContext.Current.Items[ConfigurationKeys.ConnectionString] ==
                                                                  null)
    throw new
        InvalidProgramException("You must register the HttpModule first.");

    this.Context = ((OrderITEntities)
        HttpContext.Current
      .Items[ConfigurationKeys.ConnectionString]);             Populates item
    this.objectStateManager = new                              from module
                ObjectStateManagerWrapper(Context.ObjectStateManager);
  }

  public IObjectSet<T> CreateObjectSet<T>() where T : class
  {
    return this.Context.CreateObjectSet<T>();          ⊲──── Creates object
```

```
  }

  public IObjectStateManager ObjectStateManager
  {
    get { return this.objectStateManager; }
  }

  public OrderITEntities Context { get; set; }
  private IObjectStateManager objectStateManager;
}
```

VB
```
Public Class WebContextWrapper
  Implements IObjectContext
  Public Sub New()
    If HttpContext.Current.Items(ConfigurationKeys.ConnectionString) Is
                                                        Nothing Then
      Throw New
InvalidProgramException("You must register the HttpModule first.")
    End If

    Me.Context = DirectCast(
        HttpContext.Current
        .Items(ConfigurationKeys.ConnectionString),
        OrderITEntities)
    Me.m_objectStateManager = New
            ObjectStateManagerWrapper(Context.ObjectStateManager)
  End Sub

  Public Function CreateObjectSet(Of T As Class)() As IObjectSet(Of T)
    Return Me.Context.CreateObjectSet(Of T)()
  End Function

  Public ReadOnly Property ObjectStateManager() As IObjectStateManager
    Get
      Return Me.m_objectStateManager
    End Get
  End Property

  Private _Context As OrderITEntities
  Public Property Context() As OrderITEntities
    Get
      Return _Context
    End Get
    Set(ByVal value As OrderITEntities)
      _Context = value
    End Set
  End Property
  Private m_objectStateManager As IObjectStateManager
End Class
```

Annotations in the code above:
- "Populates item from module" (points to `Me.Context = DirectCast(...)` / `.Items(ConfigurationKeys.ConnectionString)`)
- "Creates object" (points to `Return Me.Context.CreateObjectSet(Of T)()`)

The repositories were created in chapter 14, so we won't address that topic here. The next step is to create the module to handle the per-request instance. This can easily be accomplished by writing an `HttpModule`.

15.3.3 *A module to handle the lifecycle*

You've handled the context, so now you need to build the module to manage the `ObjectContext` instance using the Context-per-Request pattern. The code is very simple, as you can see here.

> **Listing 15.5** `HttpModule` that instantiates the `ObjectContext` per request

C#
```csharp
public class WebContextModule : IHttpModule
{
  public void Dispose() {}

  public void Init(HttpApplication context)
  {
    context.BeginRequest += new EventHandler(context_BeginRequest);
    context.EndRequest += new EventHandler(context_EndRequest);
  }

  void context_BeginRequest(object sender, EventArgs e)
  {
    HttpContext.Current.Items[ConfigurationKeys.ConnectionString] =
      new OrderITEntities(Configuration.ConnectionString);        ◁┐  Creates
  }                                                                ❶ instance

  void context_EndRequest(object sender, EventArgs e)
  {
    var ctx = ((ObjectContext)
        HttpContext.Current.Items[ConfigurationKeys.ConnectionString]);
    if (ctx != null)
      ctx.Dispose();                                  ◁┐  Disposes of
  }                                                    ❷ instance
}
```

VB
```vb
Public Class WebContextModule
  Implements IHttpModule
  Public Sub Dispose()Implements IHttpModule.Dispose
  End Sub

  Public Sub Init(ByVal context As HttpApplication)
                  Implements IHttpModule.Init
    AddHandler context.BeginRequest, AddressOf context_BeginRequest
    AddHandler context.EndRequest, AddressOf context_EndRequest
  End Sub

  Private Sub context_BeginRequest(ByVal sender As Object,
                        ByVal e As EventArgs)
    HttpContext.Current.Items(ConfigurationKeys.ConnectionString) =
      New OrderITEntities(Configuration.ConnectionString)      ◁┐  Creates
  End Sub                                                       ❶ instance

  Private Sub context_EndRequest(ByVal sender As Object,
                        ByVal e As EventArgs)
    Dim ctx = DirectCast(
        HttpContext.Current.Items(ConfigurationKeys.ConnectionString),
        ObjectContext)
```

```
  If ctx IsNot Nothing Then
    ctx.Dispose()
  End If
End Sub
```
◁┐ **Disposes of**
❷ **instance**

```
End Class
```

The code speaks for itself: at the beginning of every request, the context is created ❶, and then it's destroyed at the end ❷. Note that you must dispose of the Object-Context, or memory leaks may occur. Remember also to register the module, which is an ASP.NET HttpModule, under the appropriate section in the web.config file; otherwise, you'll receive an error informing you that the module isn't configured.

15.3.4 *Using the repository in a page*

In order to use the repository to display customers in the page, you need to use this code in a Web Form page:

C#
```
Products.DataSource =
  ApplicationContext.Current.Companies.OfType<Customer>();
Products.DataBind();
```

VB
```
Products.DataSource =
  ApplicationContext.Current.Companies.OfType(Of Customer);
Products.DataBind()
```

As you can see, the access to repositories is wrapped in a singleton class, named ApplicationContext, which holds the reference to the repositories. The rest of the code you have already seen.

This approach, with POCO entities, gives you the freedom to change the implementation at any given time, because there's no deep coupling between ASP.NET and Entity Framework. The approach based on repositories and the Context-per-Request patterns gives you good control over the ObjectContext lifecycle, too. The resulting web page is shown in figure 15.10, where an ASP.NET MVC view is used.

If you need more advanced features in your repositories, you can easily add more complexity to them using this design. Each piece is interchangeable, thanks to the IoC container.

Now we need to look at some common ASP.NET and Entity Framework scenarios and see what needs to be addressed when they're used together.

15.4 *Common scenarios involving ASP.NET and Entity Framework*

You have to know a few things when working with Entity Framework in an ASP.NET application:

- *Serializing objects in ViewState*—By default, POCO entities aren't serializable when they're *proxied*. If you need to save an entity in ASP.NET's ViewState, for example, this may be an issue. If a proxy isn't in place, the entities must be decorated

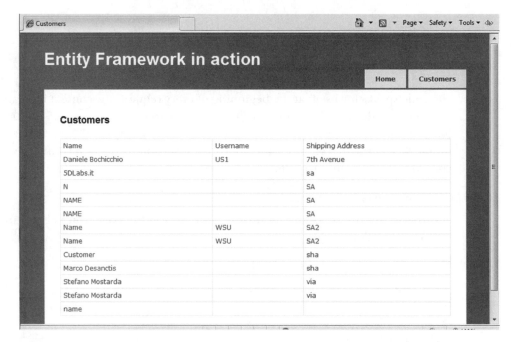

Figure 15.10   The customers in the database are displayed using the new design.

with `SerializableAttribute`. You can manually disable the proxy created or use a DTO (if that's suitable for your needs). This is discussed in chapter 16, in the context of analyzing Entity Framework in *n*-tier applications.

Non-POCO entities (the ones generated by default) are serializable by default because they're generated with `SerializableAttribute`.

- *Using transactions and concurrency*—ASP.NET applications are disconnected by nature. Between different requests there isn't a real state bag, so entities are created and destroyed frequently. If you need to handle transactions or concurrency, you have to keep this in mind. You can find more on this topic in chapter 8.

- *Attaching entities*—Attaching previously detached entities is a common scenario in web applications, because this atomic action is composed of two different steps: first, you get and display the data from the entity; then, you alter its properties, getting the value from the previous form. This problem is very similar to the previous point, and is specifically addressed in chapters 6 and 7.

Now you know how to create web sites using ASP.NET WebForm technology.

15.5 *Summary*

In this chapter, we discussed the two main options offered by ASP.NET for handling Entity Framework's `ObjectContext`. You can easily integrate them either automatically or manually.

Both `EntityDataSource` and Dynamic Data controls can make you very productive. In particular, Dynamic Data controls can work with the custom T4 template to generate rich data-editing interfaces, using data annotations to further enhance the generated interface. This approach has some limits in terms of controlling the `ObjectContext` creation, and it can't be used to wrap the `ObjectContext` behind a domain model.

If you prefer to isolate Entity Framework, you can manually manage the `ObjectContext`. Doing so gives you great flexibility; but `ObjectContext`'s lifecycle needs to be carefully managed in web applications, where multiple instance of the same object may occur per request—this situation must be resolved. You can address this scenario by writing a specific set of classes that automatically instantiate the `ObjectContext` at the beginning of every request and destroy it when the request is completed. In this scenario, using an IoC container gives you the flexibility to control what happens when common tasks related to your entities are performed.

ASP.NET is the most common way to use Entity Framework; but as a part of the .NET Framework, Entity Framework isn't limited to web pages: you can use Entity Framework in virtually any kind of application. The following chapters will look at using Entity Framework in *n*-tier and Windows-based applications.

16

Entity Framework and n-tier development

This chapter covers

- Solving *n*-tier development problems
- Developing Windows Communication Foundation services
- Developing with self-tracking entities

You can solve many problems with a service-oriented application. Sometimes these types of applications are used by client applications (*clients* from now on) within a larger system. Other times, clients are developed by third-party organizations, and your duty is to build services. This means that you have no GUI to develop—just *services*.

Whatever the client is, the application must be separated into different physical tiers that are completely disconnected from each other and that communicate through a specific interface: the *contract*. In the context of Entity Framework, working in a disconnected way is the obvious pattern for these types of applications because the context can't be propagated from the server to the client tier, which means modifications made on the client side can't be tracked, and a new context for each request is required on the server side.

In chapter 6, you learned that a degree of discipline is required to work in a disconnected scenario. Although the code on the client side is simple (the client code isn't even aware that Entity Framework is used by the server), persisting modifications on the service side requires a certain amount of code.

In this chapter, you'll learn what problems services have to face and what techniques you can use to solve them. You'll also learn that under some circumstances, Entity Framework can simplify *n*-tier applications so that you can stay more focused on the business code and not spend as much time on persistence problems.

16.1 n-*Tier problems and solutions*

Distributed applications introduce challenges that don't exist for applications that are always connected (such as Windows applications), including client change-tracking and entity serialization. We'll look at these *n*-tier problems and solutions in the next few sections, so we can spend the rest of the chapter looking at how to implement *n*-tier applications.

16.1.1 *Tracking changes made on the client*

The biggest challenge you face when developing *n*-tier applications is that the context exists only on the server side, so changes made to entities on the client aren't tracked (this is a typical example of a disconnected scenario). Suppose you have a web service with one method that reads the customer and another that updates it (an example we've looked at previously). Figure 16.1 shows how such a web service handles the context.

In the method that retrieves the customer, you create a context, retrieve the customer, return it to the caller, and then destroy the context. In the method that saves the customer, you create a context, but it has no knowledge of what has been modified on the client side. The result is that you have two ways to update the customer:

- Retrieve the customer from the database, compare it with the input version, update the database with the differences, and destroy the context.
- Attach the input customer to the context, mark it as `Modified`, persist all its data, and destroy the context.

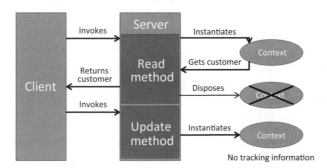

Figure 16.1 The path of an update in a *n*-tier application. The context that's used to read a customer is different from the one used to update it. Furthermore, client change-tracking isn't available.

Both solutions are simple because `Customer` is a single entity; but what happens with orders? Creating and deleting an order is pretty easy, but how do things change if you have to update one? You have to handle its relationships with the customer and with the details, which must in turn keep their relationships with the products. You have to know which details have been updated, added, or deleted.

A possible solution is to compare details from the database with the ones in the input order. Another option is adopting a convention where details with ID 0 are added, those with ID greater than 0 are updated, and those with ID greater than 0 and with all properties set to their default values are deleted. Whatever your choice is, you have to arrange a sort of *logic* contract between the client and the server, and the client must know how to let the service understand what happened. This logic contract requires lots of code on both the client and the server.

Another alternative is to use *self-tracking entities* (STEs). These are POCO entities that contain data plus logic that internally stores the modifications made to the properties. Thanks to this feature, the client can send the entities back to the server, which can read the internal state and save the modifications to the database. STEs aren't bulletproof. They're perfect in some scenarios, but in others they're unusable. Later in this chapter, we'll discuss when and why you can use them.

In addition to the change-tracking problem, another problem that arises when working in *n*-tier scenarios is the contract between the client and server. Usually you won't want to send full entities to the client because they could contain sensitive information.

16.1.2 *Choosing data to be exchanged between server and client*

In OrderIT, each customer has a username/password combination that grants access to the web service they can use to modify personal data and to create and modify orders. You should *never* let the password flow through the web service. You can let the customer reset the password, send it to the customer via mail, or let the system administrator change it, but you shouldn't let the password flow to the customer through the service (especially if the channel isn't secured by HTTPS).

What's more, it's the system administrator who decides whether a customer can access the web service and what username is assigned, so the customer can't change web service–related information through the web service.

Now, suppose that you're realizing the web service methods that let customers read and modify their personal data. The first thing you have to decide is how to exchange data with the client. Because the `Customer` entity has the `WSPassword`, `WSUsername`, and `WSEnabled` properties (which we'll refer to collectively as the `WS*` properties), and you don't want to send them to the web service client, you have two choices:

- *Send the `Customer` entity to the client, emptying the `WS*` properties.* This approach works. You just need to pay attention to not filling the `WS*` properties when sending data to the client and to not using the `WS*` properties' values to update the database when data comes back from the client. The obvious drawback is that because you're ignoring the WS* properties, there's not much point in sending them back and forth. The next option is better than this one.

- *Create a* CustomerDTO *class, a data transfer object (DTO) class, containing only the data needed for communication, and expose it to the client.* This approach works really well. You just need to create an ad hoc class (a DTO), pour data into it when reading the Customer entity, and pour data from it to the Customer entity when updating the database (not updating the WS* properties). This way, you have a much cleaner design, with the only drawback being that you need to maintain one more class.

   But remember that T4 templates can help you generate such classes. Just create a custom property (as you did in the Add/Attach example in chapter 13) that states whether the entity property must be included in the DTO, and then create a template that generates the DTO for you. If this doesn't make you fall in love with T4, nothing will.

The class you expose to the client is known as the *contract*. Choosing what type of contract to expose to the client isn't strictly related to Entity Framework; it's more related to application design. Nonetheless, choosing whether to send the full entity or a DTO to the client has an impact on how you work with Entity Framework.

Let's now look at another common problem. Generally speaking, to let data flow over the wire, the data must be *serialized*. You know that when an entity is returned by a query, the real type is a proxy (unless you disable proxy generation). This creates a problem, because Windows Communication Foundation (WCF), which is the framework we'll use to create the web service, isn't able to serialize a proxy instance.

16.1.3 *The serialization problem*

By default, when you query for a customer, you get an instance of an object that inherits from Customer (such as CustomerProxy). WCF can serialize only types it knows about (referred to as *known types*), and CustomerProxy, although it inherits from Customer, isn't a known type. The consequence is that serializing it throws an exception, as illustrated in figure 16.2.

The problem isn't only on the server side, but on the client side also. The client can be an application that uses Entity Framework for its own purposes. Suppose the client reads customer data from its own database and then calls the service to synchronize local database data with server data. In this case, the client could have a proxy instance that would need to be serialized by WCF: different layers, but the same problem.

Often you don't need a proxy. If you only need to read an entity from the database and send this

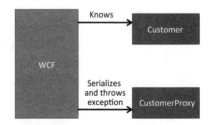

Figure 16.2   WCF knows Customer but not CustomerProxy, so it throws an exception when serializing CustomerProxy.

entity over the wire, you don't need either change-tracking or lazy-loading behavior. In such cases, you can disable proxy generation.

> **NOTE** If you have a proxy instance, remember to disable lazy loading before serializing, or you'll end up sending unwanted data to the client. This happens because the WCF serializer extracts *all* properties, including navigation properties, and this causes them to be lazily loaded.

In some cases, though, you may need to have a proxy instance and to serialize it. The Entity Framework team considered this possibility and used a new WCF 4.0 feature to serialize proxies: the *contract resolver*. WCF's DataContractResolver class allows you to dynamically map one type to another type.

The Entity Framework team created the ProxyDataContractResolver class, which inherits from DataContractResolver, to map the proxy type to the POCO type that the proxy wraps (for example, from CustomerProxy to Customer). To resolve the mapping, ProxyDataContractResolver invokes the ObjectContext class's static GetObjectType method, which returns the base type of the proxy, which is the POCO entity (for example, Customer is the base type of CustomerProxy).

Because WCF knows the POCO entity, WCF treats the proxy as if it were the POCO entity, so WCF serializes the entity without any problem. It's that easy.

ProxyDataContractResolver is great, but it does nothing on its own. You must plug it into the WCF pipeline. We'll look at how to do this in the next section, where you'll start to develop a service.

You now have a clear idea of what intricacies you face when developing a service application. In the next sections, you'll develop services that use plain entities, DTOs, and STEs so that the full spectrum of options will be covered. By the end of the chapter, you'll have a solution for each situation.

16.2 *Developing a service using entities as contracts*

In many projects, entities are fully exposed through a web service (so DTOs aren't used). If the client can access all of an entity's properties, using the entity to exchange data between client and server isn't an issue. If the client shouldn't access some entity's properties, using the entity to exchange data between client and server isn't the best solution. For instance, as we mentioned in the previous section, exposing the Customer entity in OrderIT poses a problem because you don't want to send WS* properties back and forth. However, as long as you don't set them when you send the entity to the client, and you don't update them when the entity comes back, you can let the properties flow across the tiers.

Let's look at how you can create a service that uses the Customer entity to let the customer read and update its personal data. The first thing to do is to create a service interface like the one in this listing.

Listing 16.1   The interface exposed by the service

C#

```csharp
[ServiceContract]
public interface IOrderITService
{
  [OperationContract]
  Customer Read();

  [OperationContract]
  void Update(Customer customer);
}
```

VB

```vb
<ServiceContract()> _
Public Interface IOrderITService
  <OperationContract()> _
  Function Read() As Customer

  <OperationContract()> _
  Sub Update(ByVal customer As Customer)
End Interface
```

The Read method returns the current customer. There's no CustomerId parameter because the web service is secured, and the security check returns the id of the logged-in customer. This way, you're sure that a call to Read returns data about the current customer.

The Update method takes the customer back and updates it.

> **NOTE**   Update accepts a Customer entity, but it could have accepted single properties (shipping address, city, name, and so on). There are pros and cons in both techniques, so choosing one approach or the other is a matter of personal taste.

The implementation of Read queries for the customer by the ID, blanks out the WS* properties, and returns the entity to the caller. The code is shown in the following listing.

Listing 16.2   The implementation of the Read method

C#

```csharp
public Customer Read()
{
  using (var ctx = new OrderITEntities())
  {
    var result = ctx.Companies
      .OfType<Customer>()
      .FirstOrDefault(
        c => c.CompanyId == _customerId);
    result.WSPassword = String.Empty;
    result.WSUsername = String.Empty;
    result.WSEnabled = false;
```

```
      return result;
   }
}
```

VB

```
Public Function Read() As Customer
  Using ctx = New OrderITEntities()
    Dim result = ctx.Companies.
      OfType(Of Customer)().
      FirstOrDefault(
        Function(c) c.CompanyId = _customerId)
    result.WSPassword = String.Empty
    result.WSUsername = String.Empty
    result.WSEnabled = False
    Return result
  End Using
End Function
```

The query to retrieve the customer is simple, and you've seen it several times before. Blanking out the WS* properties is pretty simple too. The entire method is definitely trivial.

At runtime, the code performs correctly; but when WCF serializes the entity, a serialization exception is thrown because result is a proxied instance of the Customer entity. In the next section, you'll see how to overcome this problem, but for the moment we'll let it stand and examine how to handle the Update method.

Update takes the modified customer and persists it. The problem here is that it should only update the address-related properties and the name, and ignore the others.

If you mark the entity as Modified using the ChangeObjectState method, all the properties will be modified even if they're blank or null. If you retrieve the customer from the database and then use ApplyCurrentValues to update it with the values from the input entity, you'll have the same problem. The password is blank in the input entity, and it has a value in the one coming from the database. Because Apply-CurrentValues overrides database entity values with ones from the input entity, the blank value would be persisted.

The ideal solution should allow you to set the entity as Modified but for only some of the properties to be updated. This result can be achieved using the Object-StateEntry class's SetModifiedProperty method, which marks a property (and the entry) as Modified. You see it in action in this listing.

Listing 16.3 The implementation of the Update method

C#

```
public void Update(Customer customer)
{
  using (var ctx = new OrderITEntities())
  {
    ctx.Companies.Attach(customer);
    var entry = ctx.ObjectStateManager.
```

```
        GetObjectStateEntry(customer);
      entry.SetModifiedProperty("ShippingAddress");
      entry.SetModifiedProperty("BillingAddress");
      entry.SetModifiedProperty("Name");
      ctx.SaveChanges();
  }
}
```

VB
```
Public Sub Update(ByVal customer As Customer)
  Using ctx = New OrderITEntities()
    ctx.Companies.Attach(customer)
    Dim entry = ctx.ObjectStateManager.
      GetObjectStateEntry(customer)
    entry.SetModifiedProperty("ShippingAddress")
    entry.SetModifiedProperty("BillingAddress")
    entry.SetModifiedProperty("Name")
    ctx.SaveChanges()
  End Using
End Sub
```

First the entity is attached to the context. After that, the related entry is retrieved and the properties that were updatable by the user are marked as `Modified`. Finally, the entity is persisted. This way, only marked properties are persisted.

Updating a single entity is fairly simple. But as we said before, when it comes to orders and details, the situation becomes more complex.

16.2.1 Persisting a complex graph

Updating just the order or a detail is pretty simple, because you can reuse the same technique used for the customer. What's difficult is understanding what details have been added or removed.

In section 7.3.3, you learned how to detect what's been changed. The drawback in that code is that it requires a comparison between details in the database and the details you've been passed by the client. To avoid this, you can establish a logic contract with the client: deleted details are always sent to the server with only the ID set (and with all other properties at their default values), added details are assigned an ID of 0, and other details are considered to be modified. This way, you can retrieve deleted, added, and modified details in a snap using simple LINQ queries.

The disadvantage of this technique is that you move some business logic to the client, and that's not good from a design point of view. That's why we disregard this pattern and opt for the comparison with the database, despite its additional querying.

Naturally, customers can't change an order's estimated or actual shipping dates, nor can they change an order detail's discount. To prevent customers from updating this data, you can use the same technique discussed in the preceding section.

So far, you've sent full entities over the wire, taking care to blank out properties that shouldn't be seen by the client. But wouldn't it be better if the properties that shouldn't be shown to the client weren't exposed by the service at all, so you could avoid writing the code that blanks these properties out? Let's look at how to do that.

16.2.2 *Optimizing data exchanges between client and server*

If you want to fully customize the way you send data back and forth, using DTOs is the best way. You can use plain entities and have them behave *sort of* like DTOs, but this solution has some disadvantages that we'll analyze in this section.

By default, WCF exposes all entities' public properties to the client. You can change this behavior and selectively decide what properties to expose by applying WCF-specific attributes on classes and properties. For example, you can apply attributes on the `CompanyId`, `Name`, `ShippingAddress`, and `BillingAddress` properties so that only they are available to the client. The following listing shows how to apply such attributes to classes.

Listing 16.4   Marking entities for WCF custom serialization

C#

```csharp
[DataContract(IsSerializable=true)]          ❶ Marks class
public partial abstract class Company
{
  [DataMember]
  public virtual int CompanyId { ... }
  [DataMember]                                ❷ Marks
  public virtual string Name { ... }            properties
  [DataMember]
  public virtual byte[] Version { ... }
}

[DataContract(IsSerializable=true)]          ❶ Marks class
public partial class Customer : Company
{
  ...
  [DataMember]
  public virtual AddressInfo BillingAddress { ... }    ❷ Marks
  [DataMember]                                           properties
  public virtual AddressInfo ShippingAddress { ... }
}
```

VB

```vbnet
<DataContract(IsSerializable := True)> _          ❶ Marks class
Public MustInherit Partial Class Company
  <DataMember()> _
  Public Overridable Property CompanyId() As Int32
  <DataMember()> _                                 ❷ Marks
  Public Overridable Property Name() As String       properties
  <DataMember()> _
  Public Overridable Property Version() As Byte()
End Class

<DataContract(IsSerializable := True)> _          ❶ Marks class
Public Partial Class Customer
  Inherits Company
  ...
  <DataMember()> _
  Public Overridable Property BillingAddress() As AddressInfo    ❷ Marks
  <DataMember()> _                                                 properties
```

```
Public Overridable Property ShippingAddress() As AddressInfo
End Class
```

The attributes to use are `DataContract` ❶ and `DataMember` ❷. `DataContract` must be applied on the class to specify that only properties decorated with `DataMember` should be exposed by the service. The result of listing 16.4 is that in the WSDL exposed by the service, `Company` contains the `CompanyId`, `Name`, and `Version` (required for concurrency checks) properties, and `Customer` contains only the `Shipping-Address` and `BillingAddress` properties. When the client generates its classes from the WSDL, it will create them with only those properties and will never know that on the server, the classes contain more properties.

> **NOTE** Manually modifying entities isn't the best practice because the modifications are lost at each code generation. It's better to create a custom annotation in the EDM and then modify the template that generates the code (as we discussed in chapter 13).

Exposing only the correct properties is optimal not only from a design point of view but for performance too. When you send full entities with blanked-out properties, the empty properties are still sent to the client. Not sending the `WS*` properties over the wire means that less data is sent and more requests can be served.

In the code for reading the customer, the only difference is that you don't need to blank out the `WS*` properties because they're not sent to the client. In the update phase, nothing changes because only the addresses and name properties must be updated.

> **NOTE** Even if the `Customer` entity that goes over the wire is different from the actual one (it has fewer properties), WCF is able to map it to the original one by using the `DataContract` and `DataMember` attributes.

We've already talked about the serialization problem, but we haven't talked much about its solution. Let's look at that now.

16.2.3 *Dealing with serialization in WCF*

The easiest way to make an entity that's returned by a query serializable by WCF is to set the `ContextOptions.ProxyCreationEnabled` property of the context to `false` (by default, it's `true`) before performing the query. This way, you obtain the plain entity instead of a proxied one, eliminating any serialization problem.

Disabling proxy generation isn't always possible because you may need lazy loading or change tracking. In such cases, you need to serialize a proxied instance.

In section 16.1.3, you've learned that `ProxyDataContractResolver` is the key to proxy serialization. The contract resolution is a WCF feature that enables you to map the actual type (the proxy) to a WCF known type (the entity exposed) using the workflow illustrated in figure 16.3.

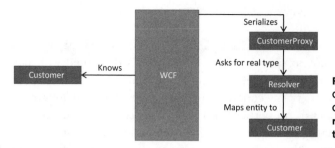

Figure 16.3   WCF knows `Customer`, **and when it receives** `CustomerProxy`, **it uses the resolver to map** `CustomerProxy` **to** `Customer`.

`ProxyDataContractResolver` performs such mappings but it isn't able to interfere with the WCF pipeline. That's something you have to do manually. Fortunately, this process is pretty simple; you just have to create an attribute and decorate the service interface methods with it. You can see the code for the attribute in the following listing.

Listing 16.5   Class that plugs the contract resolver into WCF

C#

```
public class ProxyResolverAttribute : Attribute, IOperationBehavior
{
  public void AddBindingParameters(OperationDescription description,
    BindingParameterCollection parameters) { }

  public void ApplyClientBehavior(OperationDescription description,
    ClientOperation proxy)
  {
    SetResolver(description);
  }

  public void ApplyDispatchBehavior(OperationDescription description,
    DispatchOperation dispatch)
  {
    SetResolver(description);
  }

  public void Validate(OperationDescription operationDescription) { }

  private void SetResolver(OperationDescription description)
  {
    var dataContractSerializerOperationBehavior =
        description.Behaviors.Find
          <DataContractSerializerOperationBehavior>();

    dataContractSerializerOperationBehavior.
      DataContractResolver =
        new ProxyDataContractResolver();
  }
}
```

❶ Sets client-side resolver

❷ Sets service-side resolver

❸ Retrieves serializer behavior

❹ Sets resolver on serializer behavior

VB

```
Public Class ProxyResolverAttribute
  Inherits Attribute
  Implements IOperationBehavior

  Public Sub AddBindingParameters(
```

```
    ByVal description As OperationDescription,
    ByVal parameters As BindingParameterCollection)
  End Sub

  Public Sub ApplyClientBehavior(ByVal description As OperationDescription,
    ByVal proxy As ClientOperation)
    SetResolver(description)                          ◁─┐  Sets client-side
  End Sub                                              ❶  resolver

  Public Sub ApplyDispatchBehavior(
    ByVal description As OperationDescription,
    ByVal dispatch As DispatchOperation)
    SetResolver(description)                          ◁─┐  Sets service-side
  End Sub                                              ❷  resolver

  Public Sub Validate(ByVal operationDescription As OperationDescription)
  End Sub

  Private Sub SetResolver(ByVal description As OperationDescription)
    Dim dataContractSerializerOperationBehavior =        ❸  Retrieves
      description.Behaviors.Find(                             serializer
        Of DataContractSerializerOperationBehavior)()         behavior

    dataContractSerializerOperationBehavior.            ❹  Sets resolver
      DataContractResolver =                                 on serializer
        New ProxyDataContractResolver()                       behavior
  End Sub
End Class
```

The ProxyResolverAttribute class intercepts both the client ❶ and service ❷ serialization processes, setting the actual resolver to a ProxyDataContractResolver instance. The SetResolver method is the most important, because it's here that you retrieve the serialization behavior ❸ and set its resolver to ProxyDataContract-Resolver ❹.

After the attribute class is created, you decorate the Read interface method with the attribute, as shown in the next snippet:

C#

```
[OperationContract]
[ProxyResolverAttribute]
Customer Read();
```

VB

```
<OperationContract()> _
<ProxyResolverAttribute()> _
Function Read() As Customer
```

From now on, each time WCF tries to serialize entities in the Read method, it will use the Entity Framework resolver. By applying the attribute to all service methods, you can work with both plain and proxied entities everywhere, without worrying about their serialization. This is a huge step forward for productivity and simplicity.

Working with proxies introduces the problem of lazy loading during serialization. This problem deserves a brief discussion.

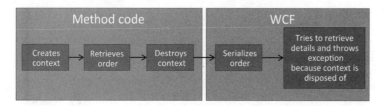

Figure 16.4   The flow when the context is disposed of and a proxied entity is later serialized. Accessing the navigation properties (`OrderDetail`) causes the navigation properties to be lazy loaded and a serialization exception to be thrown because the context is disposed of.

BEWARE LAZY LOADING WHEN SERIALIZING

The `Customer` entity doesn't have any navigation properties. `Order` is the opposite, because it references the customer and the details.

Suppose you want to write a method that returns just the order without details and customer. When WCF serializes the order, it uses all public properties, or those marked with the `DataMember` attribute. If the `Order` instance is a proxy, the access to its navigation properties causes them to be lazy-loaded and then serialized to be sent to the client. Depending on how you write the code, two things can happen.

One option is to instantiate the context in a `using` statement. When the WCF serializer accesses the properties, the context is gone. This causes the access to navigation properties by the serializer to throw an exception, because the lazy-loading code needs the context. Figure 16.4 shows this flow.

The second option is to not use the `using` statement. When the WCF serializer accesses the properties, the context is still there because it's referenced by the proxied entity, and the properties are lazy-loaded. For instance, when the `OrderDetails` property is accessed, details are dynamically loaded and added to the message sent to the client. Because the details are proxy instances, the access to the `Product` property causes it to be, once again, lazy loaded and added to the message. Finally, because `Product` has a reference to the suppliers, they're loaded too.

The result in this case is that a method that should return an order returns an enormous quantity of useless and unwanted data. Depending on how many associations are in the model, the entire database could be sent to the client (or you'll receive a WCF exception due to message size). What's even worse than sending a huge and useless message to the client is for the database to be flooded by lots of queries generated by the lazy-loading feature. Figure 16.5 shows this nightmare!

There are two ways to solve these problems:

- Disable proxy creation (and use `Include` if you need to eager load some properties).
- Disable lazy loading before sending data to the client.

Both options work, so which you choose must be evaluated on a case-by-case basis.

You've learned in this section that there are some tricks to developing a service using Entity Framework–generated entities. Let's see how to overcome these potential problems using the DTO approach.

16.3 Developing a service using DTOs

A DTO is a standalone class used only for communication purposes. By creating a DTO, you can easily control what data is sent to the client. In fact, customizing entities to add serialization attributes can be a real pain due to the complexity of modifying the EDM and template (unless you generate the model once, modify it manually, and never regenerate it … but that's an extremely improbable scenario).

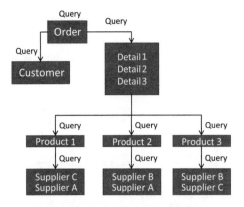

Figure 16.5 When lazy loading is active, serialization can generate lots of unwanted queries to the database, which may lead to an entire graph being loaded.

Creating a DTO for the `Customer` class is just a matter of creating a class containing the properties you need to expose to the client. You can create and maintain such a class manually, but nothing prevents you from using custom annotations in the EDM and a template to generate the class. The DTO class is simple, as you see in this listing.

Listing 16.6   The DTO class for the customer

C#
```
public class CustomerDTO
{
   public int CompanyId { get; set; }
   public string Name { get; set; }
   public AddressInfo ShippingAddress { get; set; }
   public AddressInfo BillingAddress { get; set; }
   public Byte[] Version { get; set; }
}
```

VB
```
Public Class CustomerDTO
   Public Property CompanyId() As Integer
   Public Property Name() As String
   Public Property ShippingAddress() As AddressInfo
   Public Property BillingAddress() As AddressInfo
   Public Property Version() As Byte()
End Class
```

Let's leave the `Read` and `Update` methods working with the full entities and create two new methods: `ReadDTO` and `UpdateDTO`. These methods won't work with `Customer` but with `CustomerDTO`. Adding methods to the service interface is trivial, so we'll move directly to their implementation. Here's the `ReadDTO` method.

> ### Listing 16.7   The `ReadDTO` method using DTO

C#

```csharp
public CustomerDTO ReadDTO()
{
  using (var ctx = new OrderITEntities())
  {
    return ctx.Companies
      .OfType<Customer>()
      .Select(c => new CustomerDTO
      {
        BillingAddress = c.BillingAddress,
        CompanyId = c.CompanyId,
        Name = c.Name,
        ShippingAddress = c.ShippingAddress,
        Version = c.Version
      })
      .FirstOrDefault(c => c.CompanyId == _customerId);
  }
}
```

❶ Creates returned DTO

VB

```vb
Public Function ReadDTO() As CustomerDTO
  Using ctx = New OrderITEntities()
    Return ctx.Companies.
      OfType(Of Customer)().
      Select(Function(c) New CustomerDTO With
      {
        .BillingAddress = c.BillingAddress,
        .CompanyId = c.CompanyId,
        .Name = c.Name,
        .ShippingAddress = c.ShippingAddress,
        .Version = c.Version
      }).
      FirstOrDefault(Function(c) c.CompanyId = _customerId)
  End Using
End Function
```

❶ Creates returned DTO

The `ReadDTO` implementation is trivial because you can create a `CustomerDTO` instance directly in the LINQ to Entities query ❶ and return it.

The `UpdateDTO` implementation consists of more code, but it's still pretty simple.

> ### Listing 16.8   The `UpdateDTO` method using DTO

C#

```csharp
public void UpdateDTO(CustomerDTO customer)
{
  using (var ctx = new OrderITEntities())
  {
    var newCustomer = new Customer
    {
      CompanyId = customer.CompanyId,
      Version = customer. Version
    };
```

❶ Creates stub

```
      ctx.Companies.Attach(newCustomer);
      newCustomer.ShippingAddress =
        customer.ShippingAddress;
      newCustomer.BillingAddress =
        customer.BillingAddress;
      newCustomer.Name = customer.Name;
      ctx.SaveChanges();
  }
}
```

❸ Sets stub properties

② Attaches stub

VB
```
Public Sub UpdateDTO(ByVal customer As CustomerDTO)
  Using ctx = New OrderITEntities()
    Dim newCustomer As New Customer() With {
      .CompanyId = custmer.CompanyId,
      .Version = customer.Version }
    ctx.Companies.Attach(newCustomer)
    newCustomer.ShippingAddress =
      customer.ShippingAddress
    newCustomer.BillingAddress =
      customer.BillingAddress
    newCustomer.Name = customer.Name
    ctx.SaveChanges()
  End Using
End Sub
```

❶ Creates stub

② Attaches stub

❸ Sets stub properties

You don't have a `Customer` entity, so you need to create one using DTO properties. Because you don't have all of the `Customer` entity's properties, the best solution is creating a `Customer` *stub* (an entity where only key properties are set), setting its `CompanyId` and `Version` properties ❶, attaching it to the context ②, and then setting other properties using DTO properties ❸. This way, the context will persist only properties modified after the entity was attached to the context and won't care if other properties (such as username and password) are empty or `null`; it won't persist them.

> **NOTE** Unlike `CompanyId`, the `Version` property isn't necessary for the attaching process. The reason it's set before attaching in listing 16.8 is that we care about *concurrency*. To perform the concurrency check, Entity Framework uses the value in the `OriginalValues` property of the entry. If you didn't set the `Version` property before attaching the entity, the entry's original value would be `null` because the original values are set with the value of the properties when the entity is attached to the context. In that case, the persistence would fail, raising an `Optimistic-ConcurrencyException`.

Even with DTOs, updating a single entity isn't complex. Let's look at what it takes to use DTOs to maintain the order graph.

16.3.1 Persisting a complex graph

Assume that you've created the DTOs for both order and details. After the client updates the data and sends it back, you can use the code from the previous section to modify the order.

To determine which details have been added, deleted, and modified, you can go to the database (arguably a best practice) and perform a comparison, or use the logic contract (arguably a worst practice).

If you choose the first option, there's a caveat you have to know about. Because the OrderDetailDTO and the OrderDetail classes are different, you can't use the Intersect and Except LINQ methods, as we discussed in chapter 7, because they work on classes of the same type. The workaround is to compare only the IDs of the objects, instead of comparing the objects, as you did in chapter 7. This is shown in the following listing (where order is the DTO instance and dbOrder is the order from the database).

Listing 16.9   Detecting added, deleted, and modified details in an order

C#

```
var added = order.OrderDetails.Where(d =>
  !dbOrder.OrderDetails.Any(od => od.OrderDetailId == o.OrderDetailId));
var deleted = dbOrder.OrderDetails.Where(d =>
  !order.OrderDetails.Any(od => od.OrderDetailId == o.OrderDetailId));
var modified = order.OrderDetails.Where(d =>
  dbOrder.OrderDetails.Any(od => od.OrderDetailId == o.OrderDetailId));
```

VB

```
Dim added = order.OrderDetails.Where(Function(d) _
  Not dbOrder.OrderDetails.Any(Function(od) _
    od.OrderDetailId = o.OrderDetailId))
Dim deleted = dbOrder.OrderDetails.Where(Function(d) _
  Not order.OrderDetails.Any(Function(od) _
    od.OrderDetailId = o.OrderDetailId))
Dim modified = order.OrderDetails.Where(Function(d) _
  dbOrder.OrderDetails.Any(Function(od) _
    od.OrderDetailId = o.OrderDetailId))
```

When you know what's changed, the hardest part is done and you can persist entities easily. Added details are added to the details collection of the dbOrder variable, deleted ones are removed through a call to the DeleteObject method of the details entity set, and updated ones are modified by setting their properties to the DTO settings. Easy, isn't it?

If you compare development using DTOs with development using Entity Framework–generated entities, you'll find that DTOs don't increase complexity, they guarantee optimal performance, and they decouple your entities from the service interface. These are all great reasons to adopt DTOs.

So far, the client has received an object (the client doesn't know whether it's an entity or a DTO), modified it, and sent it back to the service. Let's now investigate another scenario where the client and server exchange both information about the entity and information about what entity's properties have been modified on the client, so the service can update the database easily. Objects that contain both data and information about what's changed on the client are called STEs.

16.4 Developing a service using STEs

So far, we've followed a pattern where the client invokes a method on the service to obtain entities. The client modifies these entities and sends them back to the service. These entities contain data and nothing else.

If they contained information about what's changed on the client (change-tracking information), it would be much easier for the service to update the database. It would even be better if these entities themselves contained the *behavior* to detect and store changes made on the client. Self-tracking entities (STEs) contain all these features: entity data and internal change-tracking behavior.

By having an inner change-tracking manager, the entity can set its actual state as `Modified` when a property is modified, so the server doesn't need to discover what's been changed. The same way, when a linked entity is removed or added (think about details in an order), the entity keeps track of the change. When the entity is sent back to the service, the context reads the tracking information in the entity's change-tracker component and immediately knows what to do without your having to write code to detect changes on your own.

Figure 16.6 shows the entire workflow of an entity sent from the server to the client, which modifies it and then sends it back to the server.

As you may expect, STEs are generated through template. The template that generates STEs, in addition to creating the entities and their properties adds the inner change-tracking code to the entities. The template that generates the context code creates an `ObjectContext` extension method that accepts an STE, reads change-tracking information from it, and then sets the state manager so that it reflects the entity changes.

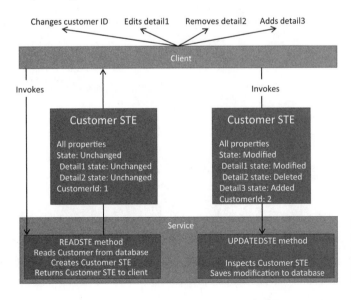

Figure 16.6 The client reads the STE, modifies it, and then sends it back. During the process, the STE keeps track of the changes.

Naturally, tracking information must be part of the entity, and this entity structure is described in the WSDL. But the WSDL doesn't describe behavior. How does the client know how to populate the change-tracking information? The answer is the *logic contract*.

An STE exposes a structure containing entity data and change-tracking data. It's up to the client to correctly populate the latter. As we've said, exposing such business logic to the client isn't optimal, but STEs introduce so many benefits that in *some cases* we can make exceptions.

We say "some cases" because STEs aren't always the best option. We'll discuss this more at the end of this section. First, let's create a service using STEs.

16.4.1 Enabling STEs

The first step in adding STEs to a project is creating them. Entity Framework ships with a template for generate this type of entity:

1 In OrderIT.Model, add a STE folder named STE.
2 Inside the folder, add a new template of type ADO.NET Self-Tracking Entities Generator and name it STE, as shown in figure 16.7. Two templates are added to the solution: one for the context (STE.Context.tt) and one for the entities (STE.tt).
3 Open the context template, and set the inputFile variable to the path of the EDMX file (../model.edmx).
4 Create a new assembly, name it OrderIT.Model.STE, cut the entities template file, and paste it inside this new assembly.

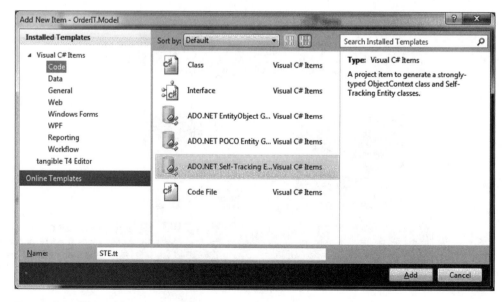

Figure 16.7   Adding STEs to the project

5 Open the entities template, and set the `inputFile` variable to the relative path of the EDMX (../OrderIT.Model/model.edmx).

6 In the `OrderIT.Model` assembly, add a reference to the `OrderIT.Model.STE` assembly.

Now you have an assembly with all the entities and the context in `OrderIT.Model`. This is the best configuration, as you'll discover later.

Next, let's investigate how the STE template generates the entities and the context.

16.4.2 Inside an STE

An STE is a POCO entity that has properties plus some infrastructure code that manages serialization and adds change-tracking capabilities to the entity itself. The infrastructure code that manages serialization is made of the `DataContract`, `DataCollection`, and `DataMember` attributes, which decorate the entity and its properties to be serialized. The change-tracking infrastructure code in the entity consists of the `IObjectChangeTracker` interface and its implementation in the entity. This interface is vital for change tracking.

UNDERSTANDING THE ENTITY CHANGE TRACKER

The `IObjectChangeTracker` interface declares the `ChangeTracker` property, which is of type `ObjectChangeTracker`. As you may guess from the name, the `ObjectChangeTracker` class is responsible for entity's change-tracking behavior. You can consider the `ObjectChangeTracker` to be equivalent to the `ObjectStateManager` class, but limited to one entity.

The `ObjectChangeTracker` (*change tracker* from now on) is particularly complex. It has the following properties:

- `ChangeTrackingEnabled`—Specifies whether the change tracking is enabled or not, with a Boolean value
- `ObjectState`—Specifies the state of the entity
- `ObjectsRemovedFromCollectionProperties`—Contains objects removed from a collection navigation property (for instance, details removed from an order)
- `OriginalValues`—Contains the original values for properties that were changed
- `ExtendedProperties`—Contains extended properties needed for Entity Framework internals (for instance, if you use independent associations, it contains the keys of the referenced entities)

Each of these properties is related to a key feature of the change tracker. `ChangeTrackingEnabled` is `true` by default, and it's mostly there because the change tracker needs to set it appropriately during the entity's serialization and deserialization phase. You'll probably never need to turn it off, but doing so will pose no problem other than the fact that modifications won't be tracked.

`ObjectState` is important because when the entity is sent back to the server, it's attached to the context, which analyzes the entity and sets its state to the value specified by the `ObjectState` property. By default, an STE is in `Added` state, not `Unchanged`.

`ObjectsRemovedFromCollectionProperties` is one of the most important properties. When you use DTOs or entities to exchange data between the server and the client, and an object from a collection navigation property is removed (for instance, a detail is removed from an order) that object is removed from the collection and it isn't sent to the service. The consequence is that on the service you have to perform a comparison between the database's and the entity's data to determine which details have been removed.

When you use STEs, if an object is removed from a collection navigation property, it's moved into the `ObjectsRemovedFromCollectionProperties` property. When the entity is sent back to the server, you don't need to perform a comparison with the database to discover which objects have been removed from the collection navigation property because these objects are in the `ObjectsRemovedFromCollectionProperties` property of the STE's change tracker. The context on the server sets all objects in the `ObjectsRemovedFromCollectionProperties` property to `Deleted` state.

`OriginalValues` maintains the original values of properties that are required for concurrency management. In the case of the `Customer` entity, it contains the original value of the `Version` property. This way, concurrency management is handled without you having to do anything.

`ExtendedProperties` is a repository for properties needed by Entity Framework, and you never have to deal with it.

HOW THE CHANGE TRACKER DETECTS ENTITY MODIFICATION

In addition to `IObjectChangeTracker`, an STE implements `INotifyPropertyChanged`. The change tracker subscribes to the `PropertyChanged` event that's raised by the setter of entity properties. In the handler of the event, the change tracker sets the entity state to `Modified` (if it's not already in `Added` or `Deleted` state) and registers the original value of the property if it's used for concurrency or is part of the key.

Collection properties are of type `TrackableCollection<T>`, which inherits from `ObservableCollection<T>`. This collection exposes the `CollectionChanged` event, which is raised when an item is added or removed. The change tracker subscribes to this event so it knows when an object is removed from the collection and can store the object in the `ObjectsRemovedFromCollectionProperties` internal property.

MANAGING ENTITY STATE

STEs also offer some interesting methods. The most important methods are the `MarkAs*` methods (where the asterisk stands for a state), which allow you to manually modify the internal state of an entity.

- `MarkAsAdded`—Marks an entity as `Added`
- `MarkAsUnchanged`—Marks an entity as `Unchanged`
- `MarkAsModified`—Marks an entity as `Modified`
- `MarkAsDeleted`—Marks an entity as `Deleted`

The `StartTracking` and `StopTracking` methods allow you to enable and disable change tracking, respectively. They do this by setting the `ChangeTrackingEnabled` property of the change tracker.

Finally, the `AcceptChanges` method accepts all modifications and sets the state of the entity to `Unchanged`. You can think of it as a sort of commit for modifications.

That covers how an STE tracks its modifications, keeps its internal state, and lets you manually modify it. The next thing you need to know is how the context is generated and how it reads the STEs internal state.

16.4.3 Inside the context

The context generated by the STE template isn't any different from the one generated by the POCO template, except for one thing: in the constructor, the proxy creation is disabled so that plain entities are returned. The STE template also generates another class that contains an extension method to the `ObjectContext` class.

The extension method is `ApplyChanges<T>`, and it's responsible for accepting an STE, attaching it to the context, analyzing its properties, and reflecting the changes stored in the entity change tracker to the context state manager. After the `Apply-Changes<T>` invocation, the state of the entry in the context-state manager will be the same as that of the entity in its change tracker.

What's more, if the entity attached has navigation properties that contain other entities, those entities are attached to the context too, and their state is poured into the state manager. This way, in a single method call, you've prepared a whole graph for persistence. Sounds cool, doesn't it?

Now let's write some code.

16.4.4 Using STEs

When the client generates classes from the WSDL, it knows it has to populate data in the change-tracking properties, but it doesn't know how to do that. You could write this code manually, but that's a pain.

Fortunately, because the STE template generates classes with both data and behavior, you can reference the assembly with STE from both server and client. This is why you created a separated assembly for the STE earlier. This way, when Visual Studio generates the classes from the WSDL, it doesn't create entities but just WCF classes for communicating with the service, because the entities are already referenced.

> **NOTE** As you can imagine, there are several problems arising from this configuration. We'll talk about the problems and solutions shortly.

On the service, let's add two new methods that use the `Customer` STE: `ReadSTE` and `UpdateSTE`. Implementing the interface to add these methods is extremely simple. You don't even need to apply the serialization behavior required to serialize a proxy, because the STE context disables proxied-class generation. Let's skip the interface code and move on to the method implementation.

The ReadSTE method is pretty simple. You instantiate the context and return data for the logged-in customer.

Listing 16.10   The ReadSTE method implementation

C#
```
public Customer ReadSTE()
{
  using (var ctx = new OrderITEntities())
  {
    return ctx.Companies
      .OfType<Customer>()
      .FirstOrDefault(c => c.CompanyId == _customerId);
  }
}
```

VB
```
Public Function ReadSTE() As Customer
  Using ctx = New OrderITEntities()
  Return ctx.Companies.
    OfType(Of Customer)().
    FirstOrDefault(Function(c) c.CompanyId = _customerId)
  End Using
End Function
```

This code is straightforward, but ... wait: the Customer entity contains web service–related data that you don't want sent over the wire. Because the Customer STE is shared between the client and the service, you can modify the entity, removing the DataMember attribute from the properties (as discussed in section 16.2.2) or blanking them before returning the entity (see section 16.2). So far, there's nothing new.

What's different is the UpdateSTE method. In this method, you can create the context, call the ApplyChanges<T> method to copy the entity's change tracker information to the context state manager, and call the SaveChanges method.

Listing 16.11   The UpdateSTE method implementation

C#
```
public void UpdateSTE(Customer customer)
{
  using (var ctx = new OrderITEntities())
  {
    ctx.Companies.ApplyChanges(customer);
    ctx.SaveChanges();
  }
}
```

VB
```
Public Sub UpdateSTE(ByVal customer As Customer)
  Using ctx = New OrderITEntities()
    ctx.Companies.ApplyChanges(customer)
    ctx.SaveChanges()
  End Using
End Sub
```

The internal state of the `Customer` STE is `Modified`. The `ApplyChanges<T>` method attaches the entity to the context, reads the state, and invokes the `ChangeState` method to synchronize the state in the state manager. You learned in chapter 6 that when you use the `ChangeState` or `ChangeObjectState` method, all properties are marked as `Modified`, so the `UPDATE` statement will update all the properties.

This is what you have to avoid, because you don't want the customer to be able to change the web service information. The solution is awkward because after `Apply-Changes<T>`, you should mark the entity as `Unchanged` and then mark the single properties as `Modified`, as in listing 16.3. In this case, STE fails to be useful.

Let's now look at a case where STEs show their full power: persisting complex graphs.

UPDATING A COMPLEX GRAPH WITH STES

So far, you've used a single entity. You may think that updating an order may be different, but it's not, because the `ApplyChanges<T>` method scans navigation properties too. Thanks to the properties of the `ObjectTracker` class, having a single entity or an object graph makes no difference.

An `UpdateOrderSTE` method would look like this:

C#
```
ctx.Orders.ApplyChanges(order);
ctx.SaveChanges();
```

VB
```
ctx.Orders.ApplyChanges(order)
ctx.SaveChanges()
```

If the order contains details, they're attached to the context too. Added, removed, and modified details are stored in the `Order` entity change-tracker. When `Apply-Changes<T>` is invoked, the state of each detail is poured into the context state manager so you don't have to do anything. The logic contract between the client and the server is handled by STE change tracker and the `ApplyChanges<T>` method.

Having the logic contract handled automatically, and having a single API to manage everything, is a strong point for STEs. Unfortunately, they're useful only in scenarios where the client can change all the entity's properties. In scenarios where only some properties can be updated, STEs are more likely to complicate your life than ease it.

ADDING OR DELETING AN ENTITY USING STES

STEs show their enormous power when updating an entity or a complex graph. In other scenarios they're valid, but not that powerful.

When you need to add an entity, you don't have either concurrency problems or need to compare with data in the database. There's not even any need to resort to `ApplyChanges<T>`, although it works perfectly well, because you can directly invoke `AddObject`.

Deleting an entity is even simpler, because only the ID and the concurrency token (if used) are required. You can pass these properties to the service method, create a stub inside it with just these properties, attach the stub to the context, and invoke `DeleteObject`.

MANY-TO-MANY RELATIONSHIPS AND STES

Suppose you have to develop a method that updates a product and its associated suppliers. This method will accept the `Product` STE, which contains the `Suppliers` property listing the suppliers.

Suppose that on the client side, you have to associate a new supplier to a product. If you create a `Supplier` instance, add it to the `Suppliers` property of the `Product` instance, and send the product back to the service, you'd expect the association to be created. But it doesn't work like that. Previously we mentioned that an STE is, by default, in `Added` state. On the service, after the call to `ApplyChanges<T>`, the `Supplier` entry is marked as `Added`, so when `SaveChanges` is invoked, Entity Framework tries to create a new row for the supplier in the Company table of the database. This causes an exception to be raised, because the properties required to persist the supplier aren't set. This problem can be solved both on the client and on the service.

On the client side, you can invoke the `Supplier` entity's `MarkAsUnchanged` method. This way, the entity state becomes `Unchanged`, and when `ApplyChanges<T>` is invoked, the entry in the context will become `Unchanged` as well.

The problem with this approach is that it requires some code on the client, meaning that if a client doesn't follow this path, exceptions are raised on the server. It's much better to solve the problem in the service to cut down on the possibility of errors.

On the service, there are two ways of solving the problem. The first one, shown in the next snippet, is to invoke the `MarkAsUnchanged` method on all entities in the `Suppliers` property before calling `ApplyChanges<T>`:

C#
```
product.Suppliers.ForEach(s => s.MarkAsUnchanged);
ctx.ApplyChanges(product);
```

VB
```
product.Suppliers.ForEach(s => s.MarkAsUnchanged)
ctx.ApplyChanges(product)
```

The second approach is to call `ApplyChanges<T>`, retrieve all `Added` entities of type `Supplier` in the state manager, and invoke `ChangeObjectState` to set their states to `Unchanged`. The following code demonstrates this technique:

C#
```
ctx.ApplyChanges(product);
ctx.ObjectStateManager
   .GetObjectStateEntries(EntityState.Added)
   .Where(e => e.Entity is Supplier)
   .ForEach(s => s.ChangeState(EntityState.Unchanged));
```

VB
```
ctx.ApplyChanges(product)
ctx.ObjectStateManager.
```

```
GetObjectStateEntries(EntityState.Added).
Where(Function(e) TypeOf e.Entity Is Supplier).
ForEach(Function(s) s.ChangeState(EntityState.Unchanged))
```

That's all you need to do. We have demonstrated this process on many-to-many relationships because it fits in perfectly with OrderIT, but the same technique can be applied to other types of relationships.

INTERNAL STATE AND CONTEXT STATE

There's a caveat that's worth mentioning. If you have an STE attached to the context, modifying it (by changing a property or invoking a MarkAs* method) will cause the STE change tracker to change the entity state, but it won't have any effect on the context state manager until the DetectChanges method is invoked. This happens because the context generated by the STE template disables proxy creation, so the instances created queries are plain entities, which, as you learned in chapter 6, aren't connected to the context.

Now that you know how to use STEs, it's time to talk a bit about their pros and cons.

16.4.5 *STE pros and cons*

The code that tracks changes within STEs isn't simple. That's why the Entity Framework team added the STE template, which reads data from the EDMX file and generates the STE.

If you're the client developer, you can freely use the STE assembly. If the clients can be developed by any consumer, you can distribute the STE assembly to those who develop on .NET 4.0 and beyond. If the clients can be heterogeneous (such as Java or PHP), client developers are responsible for creating their entities and for creating the change-tracking behavior to ensure that the contract with the service is honored (guaranteeing that the state is correct, that entities removed from collection properties are stored in the change tracker, and so on). As we've said before, creating change-tracking behavior in entities isn't easy, so non-.NET clients are pretty hard to create; that's a big obstacle.

Another con of STEs is that they expose the full entity to the clients. As we've mentioned in this chapter, that's bad because often you don't want to send all of an entity's properties to the client.

We already hinted that when an STE is in Modified state, the ApplyChanges<T> method uses the ObjectStateManager class's ChangeObjectState method to set the entity state to Modified in the context state manager. You know that when the ChangeObjectState method is used to set an entity's state to Modified, all the entity's properties are marked as Modified, so all of them will be persisted on the database. In cases where only some properties must be updated, this is an inconvenience because allowing only some properties to be updated requires manually reworking the entry in the state manager.

It's clear that STEs are the answer only in cases where full entities can be sent over the wire without any problems. In such cases, STEs greatly simplify development, and you should *always* use them. In all other cases, we strongly recommend using DTOs.

16.5 *Summary*

Developing a service is challenging. The disconnected nature of services makes it impossible to track changes made to entities on the client side. This requires you to write code on the service side to detect what's been changed on the client. To further complicate the scenario, not all entities' properties should be sent to the clients.

Using the entities generated by the POCO template is a viable solution, but it results in full entities going back and forth. That's good in some cases but not optimal in others. If some properties shouldn't be sent over the wire, using WCF attributes may optimize things, but you have a better solution.

In such cases, the best way to go is to use a DTO so you achieve full control over the data that's sent over the wire, and you ensure complete decoupling between the service and the entities used for persistence.

Eventually, in scenarios where you have full control over the clients, you can use STEs so that changes made on the client side are stored inside the entities and made available to the service when they're sent back.

Now you're ready for the next subject: integrating Entity Framework in Windows Forms and WPF applications.

Entity Framework and Windows applications

This chapter covers

- Customizing entities for binding
- Data binding with Windows Forms
- Data binding with WPF

In a web application, the browser receives HTML and then renders it. When the rendering is finished, the browser relies on JavaScript to add behavior to the page. There are many JavaScript libraries (jQuery, Ext JS, Scriptaculous, and so on) that can help with this, but whatever your choice is, you work on *client*-side objects.

Applications that use web services to manage data take the same approach. In the application, you use classes that are generated by the WSDL inspector. These classes contain the same data as the service classes (which can be Entity Framework entities), but they're just local copies. This means that you always work with objects that aren't generated by Entity Framework.

But loads of Windows applications don't have a tiered architecture and directly access the database through Entity Framework. In such situations, you can model your classes to let them interact with the binding capabilities of both Windows Forms and Windows Presentation Foundation (WPF) applications.

These applications have rich binding systems that rely on specific aspects of classes. For instance, if you create a form for manipulating orders, you'll surely have a grid displaying some orders and a set of components that show the selected order properties. The synchronization between the components, the data grid, and the orders can be completely handled by the binding system.

In this chapter, you'll learn how to adapt classes to make them binding-aware and what pattern to follow to get the best out of Windows applications. We'll look at both Windows Forms and WPF technologies. Although Windows Forms is less powerful, it's still widespread, and tons of applications are based on it, so it's worth looking at. WPF is the future. Nowadays, creating a new Windows application using Windows Forms is a nuisance; WPF is far more powerful and rich.

Before we look at the technologies, though, let's look at the example we'll use in this chapter.

17.1 An example application

We're going teo create a form that allows the user to create, modify, and delete orders and their details. Figure 17.1 shows the final result.

We'll make extensive use of both Windows Forms and WPF binding capabilities. You'll see that with some binding-related interfaces, a binding engine, and Entity Framework, you can create such a form in a snap and with few lines of code.

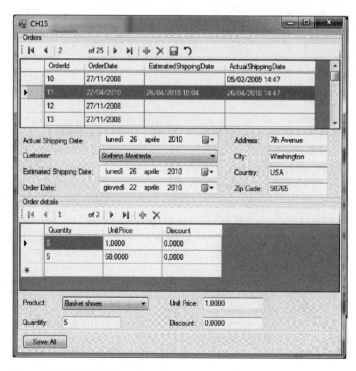

Figure 17.1 The Windows form shows orders and their data in the Orders box and the details related to the current order in the Order Details box.

Before you create the form, though, let's look at what interfaces the model classes must implement to interact with the binding.

17.2 Designing model classes for binding

To fully support the binding capabilities in both Windows Forms and WPF applications, classes must implement a few specific interfaces:

- `INotifyPropertyChanged`—Notifies a client that the value of a property has been modified
- `IEditableObject`—Allows an entity to roll back modifications made to a property
- `IDataErrorInfo`—Lets entity errors flow to the binding system

Mastering these interfaces isn't difficult. Don't believe it? Let's look at the first interface right now.

17.2.1 Implementing INotifyPropertyChanged

When you modify a property, you must notify the binding system so that every related component (data grids, text boxes, and another components) can update their values. For instance, in figure 17.1, when the user modifies the estimated shipping date in the text box, the grid above the text boxes should display the value modified. Similarly, if the user edits a value in the grid showing the orders, the text boxes must be updated as well.

> **NOTE** From now on, we'll discuss the `Order` class, but the same rules apply to all other classes.

By implementing `INotifyPropertyChanged`, you can raise an event that sends a change notification to subscribers, which can then react to the modification. In the example, the subscriber is the binding system, and its reaction is to update the components bound to the modified property. The implementation of `INotifyProperty-Changed` is shown in the following listing.

Listing 17.1 Implementing the `INotifyPropertyChanged` interface

C#
```csharp
public partial class Order : INotifyPropertyChanged
{
  public event PropertyChangedEventHandler PropertyChanged;

  protected void NotifyPropertyChanged(String info)
  {
    if (PropertyChanged != null)
      PropertyChanged(this, new PropertyChangedEventArgs(info));
  }
}
```

VB
```vb
Public Partial Class Order
  Implements INotifyPropertyChanged
  Public Event PropertyChanged As PropertyChangedEventHandler
```

```
   Protected Sub NotifyPropertyChanged(ByVal info As String)
     RaiseEvent PropertyChanged(Me, New PropertyChangedEventArgs(info))
   End Sub
End Class
```

Implementing INotifyPropertyChanged is just a matter of declaring the Property-Changed event. The NotifyPropertyChanged method is a convenient way to inform the subscribers of the event (the input parameter represents the name of the modified property).

On its own, this interface is useless. You have to call NotifyPropertyChanged, passing the modified property name to make the binding aware of the modification. This call must be made in the setters of the entity's properties, which means that you no longer use automatic properties in entities. This listing clearly shows that.

Listing 17.2   Raising the data-changed event

C#
```
public virtual Nullable<DateTime> EstimatedShippingDate
{
  get { return _estimatedShippingDate; }
  set
  {
    _estimatedShippingDate = value;
    NotifyPropertyChanged("EstimatedShippingDate");    ◁—— Change notification
  }
}
private Nullable<DateTime> _estimatedShippingDate;
```

VB
```
Public Overridable Property EstimatedShippingDate() _
  As Nullable(Of DateTime)
  Get
    Return _estimatedShippingDate
  End Get
  Set(ByVal value As Nullable(Of DateTime))
    _estimatedShippingDate = value                      ◁—— Change notification
    NotifyPropertyChanged("EstimatedShippingDate")
  End Set
End Property
Private _estimatedShippingDate As Nullable(Of DateTime)
```

What's great about this technique is that you don't have to do anything on the form to update values; you simply configure the connections between the Order properties and the form components at design time, and at runtime the binding system takes care of everything.

INotifyPropertyChanged is trivial to implement. Let's move on to the next interface.

17.2.2 *Implementing IEditableObject*

Like everyone else, you've probably modified a value in a text box and then wanted to roll back your modifications. This feature is useful, and you can enable it in your application by implementing the IEditableObject interface, which allows *transactional* modifications of an entity.

Implementing IEditableObject is pretty simple, as you can see in this listing.

Listing 17.3 Implementing the `IEditableObject` interface

C#
```csharp
public partial class Order : IEditableObject
{
  void IEditableObject.BeginEdit()                      ◁━① Starts transaction
  {
    BeginEditProtected();
  }

  void IEditableObject.EndEdit()                        ◁━② Commits changes
  {
    EndEditProtected();
  }

  void IEditableObject.CancelEdit()                     ◁━③ Rolls back changes
  {
    CancelEditProtected();
  }

  private bool isEditing = false;

  protected virtual void BeginEditProtected()
  {
    if (!isEditing)                                     ④ Stores
    {                                                      initial
      OrderIdEdit = OrderId;                               values
      OrderDateEdit = OrderDate;
      EstimatedShippingDateEdit = EstimatedShippingDate;
      ActualShippingDateEdit = ActualShippingDate;
      CustomerIdEdit = CustomerId;
      VersionEdit = Version;
      isEditing = true;
    }
  }

  protected virtual void EndEditProtected()
  {
    isEditing = false;                                  ◁━⑤ Stops editing
  }

  protected virtual void CancelEditProtected()
  {
    OrderId = OrderIdEdit;                               ⑥ Restores
    OrderDate = OrderDateEdit;                              initial
    EstimatedShippingDate = EstimatedShippingDateEdit;     values
    ActualShippingDate = ActualShippingDateEdit;
    CustomerId = CustomerIdEdit;
    Version = VersionEdit;
    isEditing = false;
  }
}
```

VB

```
Public Partial Class Order
  Implements IEditableObject
  Private Sub BeginEdit() _                          ❶ Starts
    Implements IEditableObject.BeginEdit               transaction
    BeginEditProtected()
  End Sub

  Private Sub EndEdit() _                             ❷ Commits
    Implements IEditableObject.EndEdit                 changes
    EndEditProtected()
  End Sub

  Private Sub CancelEdit() _                          ❸ Rolls back
    Implements IEditableObject.CancelEdit              changes
    CancelEditProtected()
  End Sub

  Private isEditing As Boolean = False

  Protected Overridable Sub BeginEditProtected()
    If Not isEditing Then                             ❹ Stores
      OrderIdEdit = OrderId                             initial
      OrderDateEdit = OrderDate                         values
      EstimatedShippingDateEdit = EstimatedShippingDate
      ActualShippingDateEdit = ActualShippingDate
      CustomerIdEdit = CustomerId
      VersionEdit = Version
      isEditing = True
    End If
  End Sub

  Protected Overridable Sub EndEditProtected()
    isEditing = False                          ◁—❺ Stops editing
  End Sub

  Protected Overridable Sub CancelEditProtected()
    OrderId = OrderIdEdit                              ❻ Restores
    OrderDate = OrderDateEdit                            initial
    EstimatedShippingDate = EstimatedShippingDateEdit    values
    ActualShippingDate = ActualShippingDateEdit
    CustomerId = CustomerIdEdit
    Version = VersionEdit
    isEditing = False
  End Sub
End Class
```

Even though the code is long, it's pretty simple. There are three interface methods:

- BeginEdit—Invoked when an entity is selected in the grid ❶
- EndEdit—Invoked when the selected entity modifications are committed ❷
- CancelEdit—Invoked when the selected entity modifications are rolled back ❸

Each method internally invokes another method, but that's not a requirement. The BeginEditProtected method checks whether the selected entity is already in transaction mode. If not, it saves the properties of the entity in the backup properties ❹.

NOTE The *Edit properties are simple duplicates of the original properties. They don't contain any logic and are used only for transaction purposes. In fact, they're implemented using automatic property syntax.

The EndEditProtected method puts the entity in committed mode ❺.

The CancelEditProtected method resets the properties using the backup ones, returning the entity to its initial state when the BeginEdit method was invoked. After that, the entity is put in the committed state ❻.

NOTE You're probably wondering why we created different methods and made them overridable, instead of putting the code in the interface methods. The reason is that if, in the future, you have to create a class that inherits from Order, you can override these methods and add transaction support for additional properties.

Easy, isn't it? Now let's move on to the last interface, which is responsible for notifying the binding system of errors in the entity's properties.

17.2.3 Implementing IDataErrorInfo

When the user sets the actual shipping date of an order, it can't be earlier than the estimated one. This rule can be enforced in the setter of the ActualShippingDate property. The real question is how to notify the user when an invalid date is entered. The IDataErrorInfo interface is the solution.

The IDataErrorInfo interface is another piece of binding magic. The binding system invokes the interface's methods to determine whether there are any errors in the entity, and then it dispatches any errors received to the error providers. Here's the implementation of this interface.

Listing 17.4 Implementing the `IDataErrorInfo` interface

C#

```
Dictionary<string, string> errors = new Dictionary<string, string>();

string IDataErrorInfo.Error
{
  get { return errors.Any() ? "There are errors" : String.Empty; }
}

string IDataErrorInfo.this[string columnName]
{
  get
  {
    if (errors.ContainsKey(columnName))
      return errors[columnName];
    else
      return String.Empty;
  }
}
```

VB

```
Private errors As New Dictionary(Of String, String)()

Private ReadOnly Property [Error]() As String
  Implements IDataErrorInfo.Error
  Get
    Return If(errors.Any(), "There are errors", String.Empty)
  End Get
End Property

Default ReadOnly Property Item(ByVal columnName As String) As String
  Implements IDataErrorInfo.this
  Get
    If errors.ContainsKey(columnName) Then
      Return errors(columnName)
    Else
      Return [String].Empty
    End If
  End Get
End Property
```

The interface comprises the `Error` property and the default property. The `Error` property returns a string representing an error message related to the entire entity. The default property accepts a property name, and if there's an error for that property then the default property returns the error message; otherwise, it returns an empty string.

Listing 17.4 shows the interface implementation where the errors are extracted from a dictionary (the `errors` variable) whose key is the property name and whose value is the error message. But where is the dictionary filled with errors? The answer is obvious: the properties setter. The following listing shows that.

Listing 17.5   Adding errors to the dictionary

C#

```
public virtual Nullable<System.DateTime> ActualShippingDate
{
  get { return _actualShippingDate; }
  set
  {
    _actualShippingDate = value;
    NotifyPropertyChanged("ActualShippingDate");
    errors.Remove("ActualShippingDate");                    ❶ Avoids duplicate
    if (value.HasValue &&                                      key exception
      EstimatedShippingDate.HasValue &&
      value.Value < EstimatedShippingDate.Value)
    {                                                       ❷ Adds error if
      errors.Add("ActualShippingDate",                        rule is broken
        "Actual shipping date cannot
        be lower that estimated shipping date");
    }
  }
}
```

VB
```
Public Overridable Property ActualShippingDate()
  As Nullable(Of System.DateTime)
  Get
    Return _actualShippingDate
  End Get
  Set(ByVal value As Nullable(Of System.DateTime))
    _actualShippingDate = value
    NotifyPropertyChanged("ActualShippingDate")
    errors.Remove("ActualShippingDate")
    If value.HasValue AndAlso
      EstimatedShippingDate.HasValue AndAlso
      value.Value < EstimatedShippingDate.Value Then
        errors.Add("ActualShippingDate",
          "Actual shipping date cannot
          be lower that estimated shipping date")
    End If
  End If
  End Set
End Property
```

1 Avoids duplicate key exception

2 Adds error if rule is broken

As you can see in this listing, the code in the property's setter checks that the actual shipping date isn't earlier than the estimated shipping date. Before performing the check, any error related to the property is removed from the errors dictionary **1**. Then, if the check fails, a new entry for the property is added to the errors dictionary **2**. The binding system invokes the default property once for each property that's bound, and it uses the returned information to display the errors.

The interfaces you've seen so far have opened up a brand-new problem: because the code is generated via templates, each time you run the template your customizations are lost. Nevertheless, there's nothing preventing you from modifying the template to generate the code you need, based on custom annotations in the EDM.

17.2.4 *Using a template to generate the binding code*

In chapter 13, you learned about code generation. Binding code is another good candidate for template-driven code generation.

> **NOTE** We won't show any code in this section because it would be unnecessarily lengthy. You'll find the templates in the book's source code.

Adding code to the `INotifyPropertyChanged` interface isn't difficult. Its implementation is static, so the steps are always the same:

1 Modify the class declaration, adding the interface.
2 Add the code for the event.
3 Add the code for the method that notifies subscribers.
4 Modify the properties setter to invoke the preceding method.

The only point you have to remember is that the code in steps 1–3 must be generated only for base classes. For example, the `Product` class must have those methods and events; but `Shirt` and `Shoes` inherit them, so you don't have to declare them again.

When it comes to adding code for the IEditableObject interface, the situation is slightly different. The steps are similar, but you have to pay more attention to inheritance details:

1 Modify the class declaration, adding the interface.
2 Add the code for the interface methods.
3 Add the code for backup properties.
4 Add the code for the internal methods.

Steps 1 and 2 must be done only for base classes and not in inherited classes, as we discussed before. Step 3 must always be performed, and step 4 is the trickiest. In base classes, you have to declare the internal methods as virtual for C# or Overridable for VB, whereas in inherited classes they must be declared as override for C# or Overrides for VB. What's more, in inherited classes these methods must invoke the base class implementation to ensure that all properties are backed up.

Adding code for IDataErrorInfo is more complicated than for the other interfaces. Here the code is dynamic, because the rules must be modified by you and can't be generated unless you create a set of designer extensions, which add new elements to the EDM and then customize the template to read those elements and generate validation code (you saw something similar in chapter 13).

If you opt for writing the code on your own, you must modify the template to place a hook in the property setter to inject the validation code, and here partial methods come to the rescue:

1 Modify the class declaration, adding the interface.
2 Add the code for the method.
3 Add the code for the default property.
4 Add the partial method declaration.
5 Create a partial class where you implement partial methods, adding validation.

In the partial method implementation, you write the validation code and add errors to the dictionary. There's no need to do anything else, because the rest of the code is template-generated.

Now that you know how to adapt classes for binding, it's time to start using them in a Windows Forms application, so that you can see the benefits of implementing such interfaces.

17.3 *Binding in Windows Forms applications*

The form you'll create enables users to create, modify, and delete orders and details. You have to perform several tasks:

- Create the grid for orders.
- Create the text box for editing orders.
- Create the grid for the selected order's details.
- Create the components for editing details.

- Link order and detail data to create a master-detail relationship.
- Enable transactional editing, property-changed notifications, and error notifications

Don't worry, this is going be fun.

17.3.1 Showing orders

The first step is creating the grid for displaying orders and binding it to the orders coming from database. To do this, you have to add a data source to the application, use it to create the order-related controls, and bind them. Follow these steps:

1. From the Visual Studio menus, select Data > Show Data Sources. Visual Studio opens the Data Source window.
2. In the window, click the Add New Data Source button to start the Data Source Configuration Wizard.
3. In the first wizard page, select Object, and click Next.
4. In the second wizard page, shown in figure 17.2, expand the OrderIT.Model assembly node and the OrderIT.Model namespace, select the OrderIT.Model. Order class, and click Finish.
5. The Data Source window now shows the Order class. Drag it onto the form to insert a grid, a toolbar to navigate through grid rows (we'll refer to it as the *orders toolbar*) and a BindingSource component, which points to the Order class.

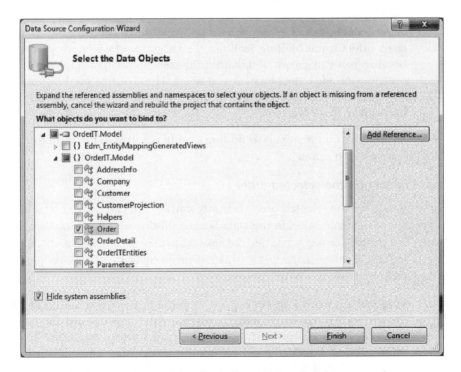

Figure 17.2 **The second page of the wizard allows you to select data-source classes.**

6 Declare a form-level variable of `OrderITEntities` type (the context).

7 Add the following code in the `Load` form's `Load` event:

C#
```
ctx = new OrderITEntities();
orderBindingSource.DataSource = new BindingList<Order>
  (ctx.Orders.Include("OrderDetails").ToList());
```

VB
```
ctx = new OrderITEntities()
orderBindingSource.DataSource = New BindingList(Of Order)(
   ctx.Orders.Include("OrderDetails").ToList())
```

8 Run the example. The form shows the grid with all the orders.

There are a couple of important points to highlight in this code. First, you have a form-level context. Instead of creating a new instance each time you perform a query, you create an instance when loading the form and destroy that instance when closing the form. The result is that all modifications made to objects are tracked by the same context that retrieved them, making things a lot easier.

> **NOTE**   This is the recommended pattern, and it's known as the Context-per-Form pattern.

The second thing to notice is the `BindingList<T>` class. It offers special binding behaviors, and we strongly suggest you use it.

> **NOTE**   Instead of using the `BindingList<T>` class, you could use the `ObjectSet<T>` class's `Execute` method, which, like the `BindingList<T>` class, offers some binding facilities. `BindingList<T>` is more powerful, because you can create a class that inherits from `BindingList<T>` and overrides or adds any behavior you need. The `Execute` method returns an `ObjectResult<T>` instance, and there's no way for you to modify the behavior of that class.

Now you can move on the next task: adding a set of controls to the form to display the data for the selected order.

17.3.2 *Showing data for the selected order*

Showing data for the selected order is pretty simple. You can do that by selecting the properties of the `Order` class in the Data Source window and dragging them onto the form. The properties are `ActualShippingDate`, `EstimatedShippingDate`, `OrderDate`, `CustomerId`, and `ShippingAddress` (this last property is a complex property, so you create a text box for each inner property).

> **NOTE**   When a property is dropped onto the form, Visual Studio detects the property's type and automatically uses the best control for it. For instance, `DateTime` properties are rendered using a `DateTimePicker`, whereas check boxes are used for Boolean properties. The other properties are rendered as text boxes.

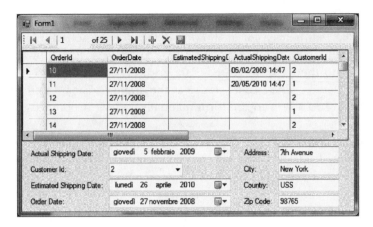

Figure 17.3   The form
shows the orders and
the current order data.

At this point, the form looks like figure 17.3.

Have you noticed that ugly number in the Customer Id combo box? That's the ID of the customer who placed the order. In terms of usability, this form is unacceptable. Let's see how to enable a lookup combo box that shows the customer name and works with the ID behind the scenes.

ADDING A LOOKUP COMBO BOX FOR DISPLAYING AND CHANGING A CUSTOMER

The combo box is the best control to display and change the customer who placed an order, but you have to make it customer-aware.

The first thing to do is to add a data source that points to the `Customer` class, as you did before for `Order`. After that, select the combo box smart tag (shown in figure 17.4), and set the Data Source property to the `OrderIT.Model.Customer` object (this automatically imports a `BindingSource` into the form), set Display Member to `Name`, set Value Member to `CompanyId`, and set Selected Value to the `CustomerId` property of the `orderBindingSource` object. This last setting is important, because it binds the `CustomerId` property of the order to the `CompanyId` property of the customer, enabling the lookup.

At this point, you have a form with controls to display and edit order data. The next step is to show the details of the selected order.

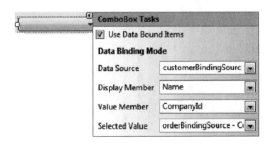

Figure 17.4   Configuring the
combo box. The `CompanyId` and
`CustomerID` properties are bound
to enable the lookup.

17.3.3 *Showing details of the selected order*

The binding mechanism helps a lot in showing details for the selected order. What you have to do is add a new data source that points to `OrderIT.Model.OrderDetail`, and then drag it onto the form to create a data grid. (The toolbar used to navigate through the order details, which we'll refer to as the *details toolbar,* isn't created automatically, so you have to add it to the form manually and let it point to the details binding source.)

The data grid points to the details data source, but you have to bind it to the details of the selected order. To do this, you add the following two lines of code in the `Load` event:

C#

```
orderDetailBindingSource.DataSource = orderBindingSource;
orderDetailBindingSource.DataMember = "OrderDetails";
```

VB

```
orderDetailBindingSource.DataSource = orderBindingSource
orderDetailBindingSource.DataMember = "OrderDetails"
```

Now run the form, and you'll see that when you change the selected order in the grid, its details are shown in the second grid. (For clarity, we removed some columns from the order and details grids, but you don't need to.) Figure 17.5 illustrates the details of the selected order.

Naturally, controls to show and edit the current details are needed in this form. Let's see how to add them.

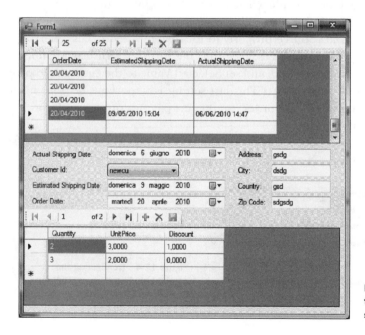

Figure 17.5 Details related to the selected order are shown in the second grid.

17.3.4 *Showing selected detail information*

The binding between the details grid and the controls that show the selected detail's data can be done at design time. But in this case, you're binding the details grid to the selected order using code, so you have to do the same for controls that show selected detail information. There's no rule that states which pattern is better; this is a choice you have to make on a case-by-case basis. Fortunately, the binding engine is easy to use both at design time and runtime.

The first step in binding components that show data of the selected detail to the details data source is adding text boxes for the `Quantity`, `UnitPrice`, and `Discount` properties and a combo box for `Product`. This combo box must be configured the same way as the combo box that displays the customer that placed the order, with the obvious difference that it must point to a data source related to the `OrderIT.Model.Product` class and that it must not be bound to the details binding source.

Next, you need to express bindings between the controls and the details binding source in the code. Once again, you can place this code in the `Load` event, as the following listing demonstrates.

Listing 17.6 Binding controls in code

C#

```
productBindingSource.DataSource = ctx.Products.ToList();
discountTextBox.DataBindings.Add("Text",
    orderDetailBindingSource, "Discount");
productIdComboBox.DataBindings.Add("SelectedValue",
    orderDetailBindingSource, "ProductId");
quantityTextBox.DataBindings.Add("Text",
    orderDetailBindingSource, "Quantity");
unitPriceTextBox.DataBindings.Add("Text",
    orderDetailBindingSource, "UnitPrice");
```

VB

```
productBindingSource.DataSource = ctx.Products.ToList();
discountTextBox.DataBindings.Add("Text",
    orderDetailBindingSource, "Discount")
productIdComboBox.DataBindings.Add("SelectedValue",
    orderDetailBindingSource, "ProductId")
quantityTextBox.DataBindings.Add("Text",
    orderDetailBindingSource, "Quantity")
unitPriceTextBox.DataBindings.Add("Text",
    orderDetailBindingSource, "UnitPrice")
```

The `Add` method accepts the bound property, the original data source, and the property of the data source.

You now have the complete form with all grids and controls, but the form simply displays information. Let's modify it so you can use it to add and modify data.

17.3.5 *Adding code to persist modifications*

The user must be able to use this form to modify orders, creating new ones or edit or delete existing ones. In this section, you're see how much little code is required to enable these features.

MODIFYING AN ORDER

The first operation a user would want to do is modify an order or one of its details. Suppose the user modifies the estimated and actual shipping dates for an order and then wants to save it. You need a Save button at the bottom of the form.

> **NOTE** You might consider using the Save button (the one with the disk icon) in the orders toolbar instead of adding one to the form. But that button isn't database-aware and does nothing on the database; it only commits changes in the data source. You could add code to the toolbar button so it issues commands to the database, but we're fans of the classic Save button at the bottom-right corner of the form.

In the method that handles the click of the Save button on the form, you call the SaveChanges method of the context instance you declared at form level. Because the context tracks the objects it has read from database and it's alive for the lifetime of the form, you're in a connected scenario. The context has tracked all modifications made to objects, so there's nothing more you need to do.

The same approach applies to details. If the user modifies a detail, the call to SaveChanges will cause that change to be persisted into the database.

Naturally a user can delete an order too, and that requires a bit of extra work.

DELETING AN ORDER

When the user clicks the Delete button in the order toolbar, the order is removed from the data source and disappears from the list but it's not removed from the database until the user confirms deletion by clicking the Save button. The problem is that if the user clicks the Save button, no command hits the database because even if the order has been removed from the data source, nothing told the context to delete it from the database. To trigger the deletion on the database, you have to handle the click event of the Delete button on the orders toolbar and call the DeleteObject method, passing in the current order obtained via the Current property of the order-related binding source, as shown in this snippet:

C#

```
ctx.Orders.DeleteObject((Order)orderBindingSource.Current);
```

VB

```
ctx.Orders.DeleteObject(DirectCast(orderBindingSource.Current, Order))
```

As you know, this doesn't actually delete the order. The physical deletion from the database is triggered only when the user clicks the Save button, which invokes the context SaveChanges method.

DELETING A DETAIL

When the user clicks the Remove button on the details toolbar, the detail is removed from the order. If the user clicks the Save button, an exception is raised because, as you learned in chapter 7, Entity Framework doesn't delete the detail but tries to remove the reference to the order, and this isn't possible in this scenario because you can't have a detail without an order.

Because only the reference to the order is removed, the Order property of the detail is set to null and its state is Modified. This means that before calling SaveChanges, you have to search all modified entities of type OrderDetail whose Order property is null, and mark them as Deleted. That code is shown in this listing.

Listing 17.7   Detecting deleted details

C#

```
ctx.ObjectStateManager
  .GetObjectStateEntries(EntityState.Modified)
  .Select(c => c.Entity)
  .OfType<OrderDetail>()
  .Where(c => c.Order == null)
  .ToList()
  .ForEach(c => ctx.DeleteObject(c));
```

VB

```
ctx.ObjectStateManager.
  GetObjectStateEntries(EntityState.Modified).
  Select(Function(c) c.Entity).
  OfType(Of OrderDetail)().
  Where(Function(c) c.Order Is Nothing).
  ToList().
  ForEach(Function(c) ctx.DeleteObject(c))
```

The LINQ query combines Entity Framework methods and several LINQ methods. It first retrieves all entities in the Modified state, then filters them out to retrieve only those of type OrderDetail whose OrderDetail property is null, and finally marks them as Deleted.

Deletions are pretty simple. Let's move on and see what you need to do to create a new order.

CREATING AN ORDER

To create a new order, the user just clicks the Add button in the order toolbar, enters the order information, clicks the Add button in the details toolbar, enters information for the detail, and continues adding more details as necessary. This way, the user can create many orders. When the user has finished creating orders, they click the Save button to send the new orders to the database.

As with deletions, the call to the SaveChanges method causes nothing to be persisted because although the orders and details were added to the data source, nothing told the context to add the objects that were created when the Add button was clicked. What you need to do is add the new orders (which have their OrderId properties set to 0) to the context before invoking `SaveChanges` when the Save button is clicked. That code is shown in this listing.

> **Listing 17.8   Marking new orders as added before saving changes**

C#

```csharp
var datasource = ((BindingList<Order>)orderBindingSource.DataSource);
foreach (var order in datasource.Where(o => o.OrderId == 0))
{
  ctx.Orders.AddObject(order);
}
SaveChanges();
```

VB

```vb
Dim datasource =
  DirectCast(orderBindingSource.DataSource, BindingList(Of Order))
For Each order In datasource.Where(Function(o) o.OrderId = 0)
    ctx.Orders.AddObject(order)
Next
SaveChanges()
```

That's it. Easy, wasn't it? With a few lines of code, you have enabled users to manipulate orders in every way they need. That's productivity.

But you haven't yet seen how to take advantage of the interfaces you've implemented in the entities. That's the subject of the next section.

17.3.6   *Taking advantage of binding interfaces*

The advantage offered by `INotifyPropertyChanged` is that when you modify a property, the binding engine modifies all controls bound to that property. You can easily verify this by modifying the value in the actual shipping date text box, removing the focus from the text box, and noticing that the grid cell that shows the actual shipping date for the current order reflects the new value. This synchronization is very important, because, internally, the binding engine makes extensive use of the `INotify-PropertyChanged` interface.

Regarding `IEditableObject`, you have to know that when the user selects a row in the grid, the binding engine checks whether the entity implements the `IEditable-Object` interface; if so, the binding engine automatically invokes the binding source's `BeginEdit` method, which in turns invokes the current object's `BeginEdit` method. When you move to another row, the binding engine invokes the `EndEdit` method, committing the modifications. To let the user roll back modifications to an object, you have to create an Undo button in the order toolbar and in its handler for the click event invoke the `CancelEdit` method of the related binding source. Because the properties are restored, their setters are invoked and the `INotifyPropertyChanged` interface comes in handy because it triggers updates for all controls, aligning them to the entity properties.

Finally, `IDataErrorInfo` is completely useless unless you combine it with an `ErrorProvider` component. By dragging this component onto the form and binding it to the orders binding source (through the `DataSource` property), the user is automatically notified of errors related to each property, displayed as a red circle next to the control representing the property or a red circle in the cell of the grid.

Although they're fairly simple to create, Windows Forms applications are doomed. With the advent of WPF and good designers, more and more developers are moving toward this platform. This is why in the next section we'll show you how to achieve the same results using a WPF application.

17.4 Binding in WPF applications

The WPF binding engine is far more powerful than the Windows Forms one. After reading this section, you'll probably want to migrate all your applications from Windows Forms to WPF to take advantage of its binding capabilities.

For instance, in Windows Forms, showing inner properties of a complex property in the grid requires you to write code. In WPF, this can be done declaratively. Furthermore, the binding between orders and details is declarative too. You don't have to write any code. These are the features we're using in this section, but there's much more you can do with WPF that you can't do with Windows Forms.

> **NOTE** We won't show the full XAML code in the examples in this section. We'll look at the binding-related attributes and ignore the style ones.

Let's re-create the Windows Forms application using WPF. As before, the first step is creating a grid that displays all orders in the database.

17.4.1 Showing orders

WPF 4.0 has a useful `DataGrid` control that you can use to show orders easily. This listing shows the XAML needed to use it.

Listing 17.9 A `DataGrid` that shows orders

```
<DataGrid
  AutoGenerateColumns="False"
  ItemsSource="{Binding}"
  Name="orderDataGrid"
  CanUserDeleteRows="True"
  CanUserAddRows="True">
  <DataGrid.Columns>
    <DataGridTextColumn Binding="{Binding Path=OrderDate}"/>
    <DataGridTextColumn Binding="{Binding Path=EstimatedShippingDate}"/>
    <DataGridTextColumn Binding="{Binding Path=ActualShippingDate}"/>
  </DataGrid.Columns>
</DataGrid>
```

The `Binding` attribute on the `DataGrid` element is the most important, because it binds the data grid to the data context of the container (the form, in this case). In code you set the context to the orders retrieved from the database.

Binding is also used in the DataGridTextColumn node to bind the column to a property of the source object. It's worth noticing that you can refer to inner properties by navigating to them, as you would do in code. For instance, the following binding expression retrieves the city of the shipping address:

```
{Binding Path=ShippingAddress.City}
```

The code to bind orders to the form context is pretty simple. Because the form exposes a DataContext property, you just need to set it with the result of the query, with a little caveat. Instead of using a BindingList<T> to wrap the data, you use the ObservableCollection<T> class, which is specifically designed to work with WPF binding, as shown in the following snippet:

C#
```
var orders = new ObservableCollection<Order>
  (ctx.Orders.Include("OrderDetails").ToList());
DataContext = orders;
```

VB
```
Dim orders As New ObservableCollection(Of Order)(
  ctx.Orders.Include("OrderDetails").ToList())
DataContext = orders
```

So far, it's been straightforward. Now, let's see how to create controls that show information about the order selected in the grid.

17.4.2 *Showing data for the selected order*

We said that the WPF binding engine is very powerful—now you're going to see why. To add data-bound controls to the form, you just add the XAML in the following listing to the form.

Listing 17.10   Controls that show order information

```
<Grid Name="orderInfo"
  DataContext="{Binding ElementName=orderDataGrid,            ❶ Sets context for
    Path=SelectedItem}">                                          child controls
  ...
  <ComboBox Name="Customers"
    DisplayMemberPath="Name"
    SelectedValuePath="CompanyId"                               ❷ Binds lookup
    SelectedValue="{Binding Path=CustomerId}"                      properties
    ItemsSource="{Binding}" />
  <DatePicker Name="orderDateDatePicker"                        ❸ Binds a simple
    SelectedDate="{Binding Path=OrderDate}" />                     property
  <TextBox Name="addressTextBox"                                ❹ Binds a
    Text="{Binding Path=ShippingAddress.Address}" />               complex property
</Grid>
```

This little snippet contains lots of magic. First, the grid's DataContext property sets the data context of the controls inside the grid to the order selected in the orders data grid ❶.

The lookup combo box control displays customer names (via `DisplayMemberPath`) and uses the `CompanyId` property to perform the lookup with the `CustomerId` property of the order ❷. Next, a `DatePicker` control allows the user to edit the date of the order, and it binds the date to the `OrderDate` property ❸. Finally, a text box shows the address property of the shipping address ❹. Notice how easy it is to navigate the complex properties.

The combo box control must be filled with customer names from the database, so you must add the following query to the form's `Loaded` event:

C#

```
Customers.ItemsSource = ctx.Companies.OfType<Customer>().ToList();
```

VB

```
Customers.ItemsSource = ctx.Companies.OfType(Of Customer)().ToList()
```

Listing 17.10 shows the XAML code that creates components that display only some properties. The full XAML code is included in the source code for the book.

Now it's time to display the order details.

17.4.3 Showing selected order details

Showing the details of the selected order is easy. First, you have to create a `DataGrid` and set its `DataContext` property using a `Binding` expression that points to the `SelectedItem` property of the orders data grid (the current order). Then, you have to set the `ItemsSource` property to the `OrderDetails` property of the order. The following snippet shows the XAML code:

```
<DataGrid Name="detailsDataGrid"
  AutoGenerateColumns="False"
  DataContext="{Binding ElementName=orderDataGrid, Path=SelectedItem}"
  ItemsSource="{Binding Path=OrderDetails}">
  <DataGrid.Columns>...<DataGrid.Columns>
</DataGrid>
```

There's nothing more to do. When the user selects an order, the data grid is populated with the details. XAML makes things much easier, doesn't it?

The last thing to do to complete the form is adding controls to the form so the user can view and edit the detail information.

17.4.4 Showing selected detail information

You can add controls that let the user view and edit information related to the selected order detail the same way you did for orders. The only difference here is that you have to point to the details data grid, as the following listing shows.

> **Listing 17.11 Controls that show detail information**

```
<Grid
  DataContext="{Binding
    ElementName=detailsDataGrid, Path=SelectedItem}">
  ...
```

```
<TextBox Name="quantityTextBox"
  Text="{Binding Path=Quantity}" />
<ComboBox Name="Products"
  DisplayMemberPath="Name"
  SelectedValuePath="ProductId"
  SelectedValue="{Binding Path=ProductId}" />
</Grid>
```

Once again, the `Grid` control's `DataContext` property is set to the current detail, and child controls are bound to properties of the detail.

The lookup combo box needs to be populated with the products. Again, you can use the form's `Loaded` event, adding the following code:

C#

```
Products.ItemsSource = ctx.Products.ToList();
```

VB

```
Products.ItemsSource = ctx.Products.ToList()
```

When you run the application, you'll see the form shown in figure 17.6.

Building a display form was simple, thanks to XAML and the WPF binding engine. Now let's see how you can write code to allow modifications.

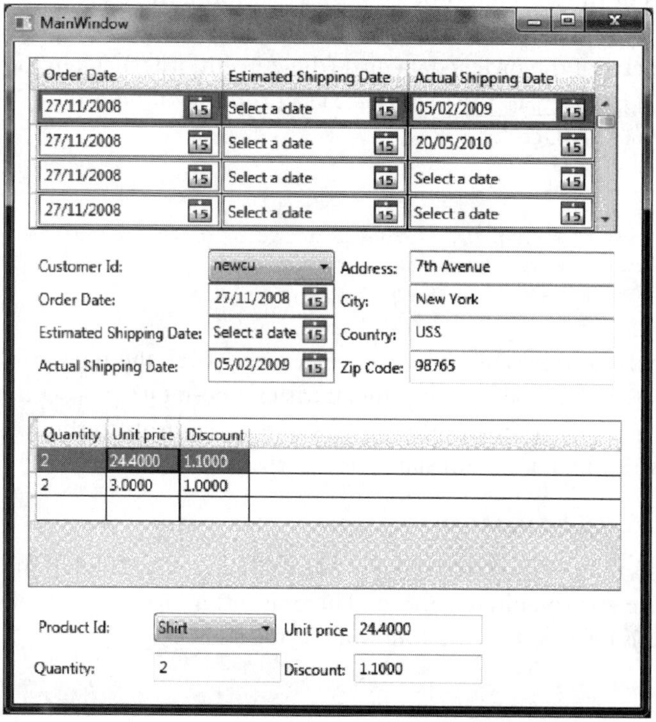

Figure 17.6   The WPF form showing orders and details

17.4.5 Adding code to persist modifications

Persisting modifications is just a matter of adding a Save button and invoking the
SaveChanges method when the user clicks it. But even in this case, you have to write
some code to notify the context about what objects to add and delete.

DELETING AND ADDING AN ORDER

The ObservableCollection<T> class you used to populate the form's DataContext
has a CollectionChanged event that's invoked when items in the collection are added
or removed. You can subscribe to this event and in its handler call AddObject when an
order is added and DeleteObject when one is deleted. Here's the code.

Listing 17.12 Intercepting an order's removal and addition for context notification

C#
```
orders.CollectionChanged +=
  new NotifyCollectionChangedEventHandler(order_CollectionChanged);
void order_CollectionChanged(object sender,
  NotifyCollectionChangedEventArgs e)
{
  if (e.Action == NotifyCollectionChangedAction.Remove)
    foreach (Order item in e.OldItems)
      ctx.Orders.DeleteObject(item);
  else if (e.Action == NotifyCollectionChangedAction.Add)
    ctx.Orders.AddObject((Order)e.NewItems[0]);
}
```

VB
```
AddHandler orders.CollectionChanged, AddressOf order_CollectionChanged

Private Sub order_CollectionChanged(
  ByVal sender As Object, ByVal e As NotifyCollectionChangedEventArgs)
    If e.Action = NotifyCollectionChangedAction.Remove Then
        For Each item As Order In e.OldItems
            ctx.Orders.DeleteObject(item)
        Next
    ElseIf e.Action = NotifyCollectionChangedAction.Add Then
        ctx.Orders.AddObject(DirectCast(e.NewItems(0), Order))
    End If
End Sub
```

The situation changes when you want to notify the context about removing an order
detail. In this case, you can't rely on the CollectionChanged event because it doesn't
get fired when an order is modified (the ObservableCollection<T> class monitors
orders, not their details).

DELETING A DETAIL

When a detail is removed from an order, the reference is deleted, its Order property is
set to null, and its state is Modified. This means that before calling SaveChanges, you
have to use the same code as in listing 17.7 to mark orphan details as Deleted.

This can be accomplished without many problems. As you have seen, Entity Framework–related code isn't very invasive, so you can concentrate mostly on your business code. Once again, that means *productivity*.

17.5 Summary

If you're an experienced Windows Forms or WPF developer, you have surely been happy to discover that Entity Framework gracefully integrates with the binding engines of both technologies. You can even create classes that inherit from `Binding-List<T>` and `ObservableCollection<T>` and handle context communication internally, so you don't have to write anything in your form.

Thanks to POCO support, you can easily implement interfaces and customize code so that binding is even easier. Most of this code can be generated via templates, so things have been simplified a lot. All this simplicity means you can write very little Entity Framework–related code in your form and concentrate your effort on the business code.

Now that you've seen how to use Entity Framework in web applications, web services, and Windows applications, it's time to move on to another important subject: testing.

Testing Entity Framework

This chapter covers

- Unit-testing basics
- Dependency isolation and mock objects
- Persistence testing with Entity Framework

Testing is a critical part of the software development lifecycle—development can't be considered complete until you've verified that the code you wrote works as expected. Unfortunately, testing code is rarely a trivial task for two main reasons:

- Test complexity strongly depends on the complexity of the application itself. It tends to grow in a nonlinear manner as you add functionality, objects, tiers, or dependencies with external systems.
- Fixing bugs or adding new features can potentially lead to regressions, harming your software stability and reliability. In these cases, you can't be sure you didn't damage existing functionality until you've reexecuted all the tests on them.

But what does "testing" a feature or a portion of code involve? It can mean launching your application and using UI to verify whether an order is correctly placed and that the stock of a given product is correctly adjusted, or it can mean building small console applications that invoke a method, so you can debug it and step through its

447

code to check it behaves as expected. Or it can mean something smarter and auto-mated, such as a durable and stable test suite that you can run on a daily basis (or after every build) to check that everything is working properly.

This chapter focuses on this last technique, showing the tools you can use and how you should design the code of an application using Entity Framework so it's effectively testable.

18.1 Unit tests at a glance

Automatic unit testing is a well-established concept in computer programming. It was initially introduced in Smalltalk, and then spread to a number of different technolo-gies, including .NET. Today, unit testing is considered a fundamental step in quality software development.

A unit test is no more than a series of methods that execute some code from the application being tested, providing well-known inputs and checking the outputs. In OrderIT, for example, you'll often need to handle an order total, perhaps because you want to show it to the end user or because you need to send it to a credit card payment service. You already implemented a simple read-only property within the `Order` class that performs the calculation on the fly and returns the order total.

Listing 18.1   Calculating an order total

C#

```csharp
public decimal Total
{
  get
  {
    decimal result = 0;
    this.OrderDetails.ForEach(d => result += d.UnitPrice * d.Quantity);

    return result;
  }
}
```

VB

```vb
Public ReadOnly Property Total() As Decimal
  Get
    Dim result As Decimal = 0
    Me.OrderDetails.ForEach(
      Function(d)
        result = result + d.UnitPrice * d.Quantity
      End Function)

    Return result
  End Get
End Property
```

Because this is such a critical part of the application, you want to be sure it always behaves as expected, so it needs to be tested. You could run the application, create an order, and see if the `Total` property shown in the page was correct, but you'd have to deal with all sorts of details (like authenticating in OrderIT, or selecting items that are in stock) that you don't want to be concerned with. An easier path is creating a simple console application that references the `OrderIT.DomainModel` assembly. You can write code like the following listing.

> **Listing 18.2   Console application that tests order's `Total` calculated property**

C#
```
public static void Main(string[] args)
{
  var order = new Order();

  order.OrderDetails.Add(
    new OrderDetail { Quantity = 2, UnitPrice = 10});      ⟵  Provides
  order.OrderDetails.Add(                                       dummy data
    new OrderDetail { Quantity = 3, UnitPrice = 15});

  Debug.Assert(order.Total == 65);                         ⟵  Checks for
}                                                              correct result
```

VB
```
Public Shared Sub Main(ByVal args As String())
    Dim order = New Order()

    Dim od = New OrderDetail()                            ⟵  Provides
    od.Quantity = 2                                           dummy data
    od.UnitPrice = 10
    order.OrderDetails.Add(od)

    od = New OrderDetail()
    od.Quantity = 3
    od.UnitPrice = 15
    order.OrderDetails.Add(od)                            ⟵  Checks for
                                                             correct result
    Debug.Assert(order.Total = 65)
End Sub
```

Although this is only a few lines of code, it has a great result—a *durable* test method that you can run from time to time to make sure you haven't broken any working logic (for example, after introducing support for discounts within `Order.Total`).

   We call this a *unit* test because it tests a simple and atomic part of the application. `Order.Total` doesn't rely on external resources to perform its task, like methods of external classes, databases, or web services. Later in this chapter, we'll talk about faking dependencies and perform integration testing, which do test how different pieces of code work with each other. For now, you only need to notice that, if the test fails, you can assert with certainty that one or the other of the following is true:

- There's a bug in the method being tested, and the test method was able to track it and identify it.
- The test method has a bug.

Bugs are something you want to absolutely avoid, and one of the best ways to do that is to keep the logic of the test method as simple as possible.

How to make sure a test method doesn't have any bugs

Although we're just starting to look at testing, it's already clear that having bug-free unit tests is essential; and the first rule to achieving this is keeping the test methods as simple as possible. That means avoiding `if` branches and cycles and using inheritance and other object-oriented peculiarities such as polymorphism or overrides as moderately as possible.

An interesting extreme programming technique, called *test-driven development* (TDD) consists of writing tests prior to the programming unit; when you have the test, the next step is writing the application code to let the test project compile, but without implementing any kind of logic. The purpose is making the test fail, so you can check out its effectiveness; if the test doesn't fail when the logic has not yet been implemented, that probably means there's something wrong with it. Only after a test failure do you code the new method.

Another recent trend is using *fault injection*, such as by using the CLR's Profiler API to artificially let the code under test return the wrong results. A sample library that allows you to do this is an open source project called TestApi, which can be downloaded from CodePlex at http://testapi.codeplex.com/.

A typical enterprise application needs hundreds of unit tests to verify its features properly, and using a console application for this would be inappropriate. Moreover, there are advanced development scenarios in which unit tests are completely integrated into the source control system (in some organizations, you need to provide the test code along with the application code in order to check a new feature into the source control) or into the build process (after every build, the tests are executed, and only if they all pass will the new version be released to customers).

A test tool is essential for writing, managing, and executing tests because it provides a runtime environment for executing the test code and producing reports like the one shown in figure 18.1, which allows you to immediately identify and locate errors in the code.

	Result	Test Name	Project	Error Message
	Passed	EqualGetPropInfoWorksWithBirthDayExternallyInitialized	Crad.MappingVerifier.Tests	
	Passed	GetPropInfoThrowsExWithNullArgument	Crad.MappingVerifier.Tests	
☑	Failed	MustThrowExpressionNotSupported3	Crad.MappingVerifier.Tests	Assert.Fail failed.
	Passed	CanStoreEqualExpressions	Crad.MappingVerifier.Tests	
	Passed	CanBuildPersister	Crad.MappingVerifier.Tests	
	Passed	EqualGetPropInfoWorksWithNameProperty	Crad.MappingVerifier.Tests	
☑	Failed	VerifyReturnsFalseWithIncorrectInput	Crad.MappingVerifier.Tests	Assert.Fail failed.
	Passed	ObjectContextCannotBeNull	Crad.MappingVerifier.Tests	
	Passed	PersisterCanSaveAndRetrieve	Crad.MappingVerifier.Tests	
	Passed	CanGetTheEntitySet	Crad.MappingVerifier.Tests	
	Passed	VerifyReturnsTrueWithCorrectInput	Crad.MappingVerifier.Tests	
	Passed	UnknownTypeThrowsException	Crad.MappingVerifier.Tests	
	Passed	ServiceRepositoryIsInitalizedIfProvided	Crad.MappingVerifier.Tests	

Test run failed Results: 76/78 passed; Item(s) checked: 2

Figure 18.1 A typical test report

There are a number of unit-testing tools out there, with NUnit and MSTest being the most widely used today. NUnit is an open-source port of the well-established Java JUnit test framework, and MSTest is provided by Microsoft and is completely integrated into the Visual Studio IDE. It's included in every edition of Microsoft Visual Studio 2010, and it's the one you'll use for the rest of this chapter.

In the next section, you'll see how to use MSTest to effectively test OrderIT.

18.2   Writing a test suite in Visual Studio 2010

The first step in testing the OrderIT project is creating a new test project in Visual Studio 2010. You can do that by selecting the Test Project template from the New Project dialog box shown in figure 18.2. Name the new project `OrderIT.DomainModel.Tests`, because it will contain all the tests for the classes belonging to `OrderIT.DomainModel`.

This is the first naming convention we'll introduce in this chapter, and others will follow. Good naming of test projects and classes is critical in real-world scenarios because, as we stated before, it's common to have hundreds of tests scattered among different assemblies, and naming them correctly helps identify which part of your application is failing.

Now it's time to dive into the code and writing your first test class.

18.2.1   Testing a simple method

As a first example, let's test the `Total` property we introduced at the beginning of the chapter. Because it belongs to the `Order` class, you'll add a new class to the test project that will be conventionally named `OrderTests`.

In order to make the class recognizable to the test framework, you need to decorate it with the `TestClass` attribute. Here's the code.

Figure 18.2   Creating a new test project in Visual Studio 2010

Listing 18.3   OrderTests class

C#

```csharp
[TestClass]
public class OrderTests
{
  [TestMethod]
  public void Total_CalculateWithoutDiscount_ReturnsTheCorrectSum()
  {
    var order = new Order();                                    ❶ Sets up test
                                                                   environment
    order.OrderDetails.Add(
      new OrderDetail { Quantity = 2, UnitPrice = 10 });
    order.OrderDetails.Add(
      new OrderDetail { Quantity = 3, UnitPrice = 15 });

    var result = order.Total;                                   Executes code
                                                               ❷ being tested
    Assert.AreEqual(65, result);      ❸ Checks result
  }
}
```

VB

```vb
<TestClass()> _
Public Class OrderTests

  <TestMethod()> _
  Public Sub Total_CalculateWithoutDiscount_ReturnsTheCorrectSum()
    Dim order = New Order()

    Dim od = New OrderDetail()
    od.Quantity = 2                                            ❶ Sets up test
    od.UnitPrice = 10                                             environment
    order.OrderDetails.Add(od)

    od = New OrderDetail()
    od.Quantity = 3
    od.UnitPrice = 15
    order.OrderDetails.Add(od)
                                                               ❷ Executes code
    Dim result = order.Total                                      being tested

    Assert.AreEqual(65, result)      ❸ Checks result
  End Sub
End Class
```

The method's name is, once again, built according to a naming convention that allows it to be absolutely self-explanatory. The name is composed of three parts:

- The program unit being tested
- The action being taken and any other useful information (in this example, that's the fact that you aren't considering discounts in the test)
- The expected result

The method's body follows a pattern called Arrange, Act, Assert (AAA) , which consists in setting up the environment ❶, executing the code ❷, and then verifying the result obtained ❸. It's similar to what you wrote in the console application in listing 18.2,

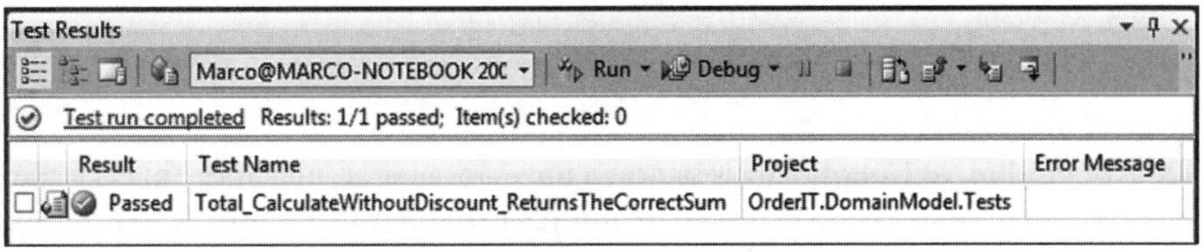

Figure 18.3 `Order.Total` test-results report

but this uses `Assert.AreEqual` instead of `Debug.Assert`. With `Assert.AreEqual`, you can express the conditions of the failure or success of the test.

The testing framework is completely integrated into the Visual Studio IDE. Because the method in listing 18.3 has the `TestMethod` attribute, after building the project, you can execute it by right-clicking its name and selecting the Run Tests option from the context menu. Visual Studio will run the code and, we hope, will return a test-passed report similar to the one in figure 18.3.

Based on the test report, you may decide to run another test, debug a failing one, check out a detailed test report, or even get a historic view of the results of every test.

But those aren't the sole advantages of using this test tool. In the following section, we'll look at some other useful features you can take advantage of while building a test suite.

18.2.2 Advanced features of Microsoft's Unit Testing Framework

In chapter 14, you designed a class called `DiscountPolicy` that analyzes an order to determine if the customer deserves a discount. Its method `EvaluateDiscount` accepts an instance of an `Order` and, as a coding best practice, should throw an `Argument-NullException` if invoked with a `null` argument.

Because testing the raising of expected exceptions is as important as testing the correctness of a method's results, every test framework provides built-in support for doing this. In Microsoft's Unit Testing Framework, for example, you can decorate the test code with the attribute `ExpectedException`, as shown in this listing.

Listing 18.4 Testing the raising of an exception

C#
```
[TestMethod,
 ExpectedException(typeof(ArgumentNullException))]     ❶ Exception
public void EvaluateDiscount_InvokedWithNull_ThrowsArgumentNullEx()     expectation
{
  var discountPolicy = new DiscountPolicy();
  discountPolicy.EvaluateDiscount(null);
}
```

VB
```
<TestMethod(),                                           ❶ Exception
 ExpectedException(GetType(ArgumentNullException))> _      expectation
Public Sub EvaluateDiscount_InvokedWithNull_ThrowsArgumentNullEx()
```

```
Dim discountPolicy = New DiscountPolicy()
discountPolicy.EvaluateDiscount(Nothing)
```

End Sub

Notice that, although this test don't have an `Assert` method, this is still code that can fail or succeed because the assertion part of the AAA pattern is written in a declarative manner. It has an attribute ❶ that is then consumed and checked by the runtime itself.

In many other cases, while testing the `DiscountPolicy` class, you must provide a valid `Order` instance, perhaps also adding some details and assigning a customer to it. We're probably talking about several lines of code for the arrange stage. Even if you build a helper method like this

```
Order order = buildTestOrder();
```

you'd still have to put it in every test method of your `DiscountPolicyTests` class.

To avoid this code redundancy, you can write an initialization method like this.

> **Listing 18.5   Test initialization method**

C#
```
private Order order;

[TestInitialize]
public void Init()
{
  this.order = new Order();

  this.order.Customer = new Customer
  {
    Name = "Marco De Sanctis"
  };

  // more initialization code here...
}
```

VB
```
Private order As Order

<TestInitialize()> _
Public Sub Init()
  Me.order = New Order()

  Me.order.Customer = New Customer()
  Me.order.Customer.Name = "Marco De Sanctis"

  ' more initialization code here...

End Sub
```

Because the method is marked with the `TestInitialize` attribute, the runtime will automatically execute it before every test method, so every test will be provided with its own new and isolated instance of the `Order` class. Should you need to execute code at the end of a test method, the `TestCleanup` attribute serves this purpose. Similar attributes exist to execute custom code before the first test method and after the last one of an entire test class (`ClassInitialize` and `ClassCleanup`) or of a whole assembly (`AssemblyInitialize` and `AssemblyCleanup`).

At this point, you're able to use Microsoft's Unit Testing Framework to write your test code and keep it simple and easy to maintain. But so far we've only dealt with atomic code units, which don't rely on external dependencies to perform their tasks. In the next section, we'll remove this limitation and still keep the test execution independent of these resources.

18.3 Isolating dependencies

We usually design applications with classes that cooperate with each other or that access external resources. For example, when accepting a new order in OrderIT, you need to check the database to see if the items are in stock, and when the order is placed, you want to notify the customer by sending an email. Moreover, providing a delivery-tracking system means querying the carrier's web service.

Suppose you wanted to implement this last requirement and query the web service. You might write a method within the `Order` class similar to the one shown here.

Listing 18.6 Accessing a remote web service to check delivery status

C#
```csharp
public DeliveryStatus CheckDeliveryStatus()
{
  CarrierWebService service = new CarrierWebService();

  string res = service.GetTracking(this.TrackingTicket);

  if (res == "delivered")
    return DeliveryStatus.Delivered;

  return DeliveryStatus.Dispatching;
}
```

VB
```vb
Public Class Order
  ' more code here

  Public Function CheckDeliveryStatus() As DeliveryStatus
    Dim service As New CarrierWebService()

    Dim res As String = service.GetTracking(Me.TrackingTicket)

    If res = "delivered" Then
      Return DeliveryStatus.Delivered
    End If

    Return DeliveryStatus.Dispatching
  End Function

End Class
```

Effectively testing such a method is nearly impossible. First, you need to know which ticket number to send to the web service. Usually, service suppliers provide developer environments with services operating on dummy data, and this could ease your job. But even in this case, you'd probably end up with a poor test that would be slow to run and, worse than that, could fail for a number of reasons:

- There's a bug in the CheckDeliveryStatus method.
- The network is down when you run the test.
- The remote service is offline.
- The remote service has a bug and throws an exception.

The CheckDeliveryStatus method *depends* on external systems, so there's a dependency problem. Unfortunately, there is nothing you can do with the implementation of CheckDeliveryStatus shown in listing 18.6. Let's modify it slightly to make it more testable.

18.3.1 *Refactoring for testability*

What's wrong with the current CheckDeliveryStatus implementation is that there's no way to avoid the call to the remote service. You could replicate it locally and modify a configuration file to invoke its URL, but you'd still have to rely on an external component that runs in a web server, and that wouldn't solve any of the issues introduced in the previous section.

It would be much better to simulate the service with a plain .NET class that has the same interface; this class could work in-process and provide hard-coded results to known inputs. To do this, you must modify CheckDeliveryStatus, as in the following listing, to inject the fake service instance at runtime,

---

Listing 18.7   A testable version of CheckDeliveryStatus

C#
```
internal DeliveryStatus CheckDeliveryStatus(ITrackingService service)
{
  string res = service.GetTracking(this.TrackingTicket);

  if (res == "delivered")
    return DeliveryStatus.Delivered;

  return DeliveryStatus.Dispatching;
}

public DeliveryStatus CheckDeliveryStatus()
{
  return this.CheckDeliveryStatus(new CarrierWebService());
}
```

VB
```
Friend Function CheckDeliveryStatus(ByVal service As ITrackingService) As
     DeliveryStatus
  Dim res As String = service.GetTracking(Me.TrackingTicket)

  If res = "delivered" Then
    Return DeliveryStatus.Delivered
  End If
```

```
    Return DeliveryStatus.Dispatching
End Function

Public Function CheckDeliveryStatus() As DeliveryStatus
    Return Me.CheckDeliveryStatus(New CarrierWebService())
End Function
```

This code still provides an overload without parameters, which allows you to keep the same interface you had before towards a *normal* caller. The internal (or Friend in VB) overload can be left visible only to the assembly that holds all the unit tests by decorating the assembly with the InternalsVisibleTo attribute, as in the next snippet:

C#
```
[assembly:InternalsVisibleTo("OrderIT.DomainModel.Tests")]
```

VB
```
<Assembly: InternalsVisibleTo("OrderIT.DomainModel.Tests")>
```

In order to compile the code without errors, you still have to let the service implement ITrackingService. This can be done directly on the service's proxy class if the auto-generated code is a partial class, or you can build a simple wrapper. With this small refactoring, you're finally able to build a *stub* for your tracking service.

> **STUB** A class or a method that mimics the behavior of an external dependency, accepting the same inputs and providing likely outputs. You can use a stub to replace that dependency for testing purposes, and you can also use stubs to temporarily substitute for code that has yet to be written.

For example, the fake service in the following listing is a stub for ITrackingService, simulating the service's behavior and providing hard-coded results.

Listing 18.8 The ITrackingService interface and its fake implementation

C#
```
public interface ITrackingService
{
    string GetTracking(string trackingTicket);
}

public class FakeTrackingService : ITrackingService
{
    public string GetTracking(string trackingTicket)
    {
        return "delivered";
    }
}
```

VB
```
Public Interface ITrackingService

    Function GetTracking(ByVal trackingTicket As String) As String

End Interface

Public Class FakeTrackingService
    Implements ITrackingService
```

```
Public Function GetTracking(ByVal trackingTicket As String) As String
   Return "delivered"
End Function

End Class
```

The advantage of the refactoring is that `CheckDeliveryStatus` will consider the fake service to be a valid tracking service. Now, writing the unit test is straightforward, as you can see.

Listing 18.9   Unit test for `CheckDeliveryStatus`

C#
```csharp
[TestMethod]
public void CheckDeliveryStatus_WhenOrderIsDelivered_ReturnsDelivered()
{
  var order = new Order();

  DeliveryStatus result = order.CheckDeliveryStatus(
    new FakeTrackingService());

  Assert.AreEqual(DeliveryStatus.Delivered, result);
}
```

VB
```vb
<TestMethod()> _
Public Sub CheckDeliveryStatus_WhenOrderIsDelivered_ReturnsDelivered()
  Dim order = New Order()

  Dim result As DeliveryStatus = order.CheckDeliveryStatus(New
    FakeTrackingService())

  Assert.AreEqual(DeliveryStatus.Delivered, result)
End Sub
```

Building stubs and refactoring the application code so it's loosely coupled with external resources is the way to successfully build unit test that execute quickly and that are reproducible and independent of the environment's conditions.

In doing this, though, you ended up with an additional class (`FakeTracking-Service`) that can potentially contain bugs. More than that, it represents more code to be maintained. Fortunately, this is something you can avoid. There are many frameworks out there that allow you to dynamically build stubs at runtime, and we'll look at them next.

18.3.2   *Using a mocking framework to fake dependencies*

A *mocking framework* is a library you can use to dynamically replace your dependencies and set up their behavior without needing to pollute your test assemblies with fakes like `FakeTrackingService`. As for unit-testing tools, various *mockers* are available on the market, some of them free and open source, and others sold as commercial products. Among the first group, the de facto standard is Rhino Mocks, built by Oren Eini and freely downloadable at www.ayende.com/projects/rhino-mocks.aspx.

To better understand how such a tool can help in writing tests, let's rewrite the previous example and use Rhino Mocks to build the stub. All the concepts we have introduced to loosely couple `CheckDeliveryStatus` with the web service remain valid, because you still need to inject a test stub in the code. Here's the new version of the test method.

Listing 18.10   Testing with a Rhino Mocks stub

C#
```
ITrackingService trackingService;
MockRepository mocks;

[TestInitialize]
public void SetUp()
{
  mocks = new MockRepository();
  trackingService = mocks.Stub<ITrackingService>();
}

[TestMethod]
public void CheckDeliveryStatus_WhenOrderIsDelivered_ReturnsDelivered()
{
  SetupResult.On(trackingService)
    .Call(trackingService.GetTracking(null))
    .Return("delivered")
    .IgnoreArguments();
  mocks.ReplayAll();

  var order = new Order();

  DeliveryStatus result =
    order.CheckDeliveryStatus(trackingService);

  Assert.AreEqual(DeliveryStatus.Delivered, result);
}
```

❶ Creates **TrackingService** stub

❷ Sets up stub's behavior

❸ Switches to Replay mode

❹ Executes test

VB
```
Private trackingService As ITrackingService
Private mocks As MockRepository

<TestInitialize()> _
Public Sub SetUp()
  mocks = New MockRepository()
  trackingService = mocks.Stub(Of ITrackingService)()
End Sub

<TestMethod()> _
Public Sub CheckDeliveryStatus_WhenOrderIsDelivered_ReturnsDelivered()
  SetupResult.[On](trackingService)._
    [Call](trackingService.GetTracking(Nothing))._
    [Return]("delivered").IgnoreArguments()
  mocks.ReplayAll()

  Dim order = New Order()

  Dim result As DeliveryStatus = _
    order.CheckDeliveryStatus(trackingService)

  Assert.AreEqual(DeliveryStatus.Delivered, result)
End Sub
```

❶ Creates **TrackingService** stub

❷ Sets up stub's behavior

❸ Switches to Replay mode

❹ Executes test

This listing uses a `TestInitialize` method ❶ to create a stub of the service, which is then stored in a local field. The arrange phase ❷ of the subsequent test configures that stub to simulate the service; notice the fancy fluent interface instructing it that a call to the `GetTracking` method should return `delivered` no matter what arguments it's invoked with. Then, after placing the stub in replay mode ❸, the code unit is executed ❹, exactly as if it were working with a handmade fake class.

The main advantage of using a mocking framework is that instead of building and maintaining a fake class, you have a dynamic stub whose responses can be easily configured. But there's still something you can improve on in the test code. You now know that the method can correctly parse results returned by the service, but you don't have any code to verify that it's invoked with the correct input. The best way to do that is to use a *mock* instead of a stub.

> **MOCK**   A class dynamically generated by a mocking framework, which you can configure to provide results to well-known inputs, similar to a stub. In addition, a mock has the ability to set up expectations on the members being called, and to verify them at the end of the test.

With Rhino Mocks, building a mock is similar to building a stub; the only difference is that with a mock you can set up and verify your expectations, as in the following listing.

Listing 18.11   Testing with a mock

C#

```
ITrackingService trackingService;
MockRepository mocks;

[TestInitialize]
public void SetUp()
{
  mocks = new MockRepository();
  trackingService =
    mocks.DynamicMock<ITrackingService>();        Creates mock
}

[TestMethod]
public void CheckDeliveryStatus_WhenOrderIsDelivered_ReturnsDelivered()
{
  var order = new Order();
  order.TrackingTicket = "test";

  Expect.Call(trackingService.GetTracking(order.TrackingTicket))
    .Return("delivered");
  mocks.ReplayAll();                           ◁  Sets up
                                               ❶ expectation
  DeliveryStatus result = order.CheckDeliveryStatus(trackingService);

  mocks.VerifyAll();                           ◁  Verifies that
  Assert.AreEqual(DeliveryStatus.Delivered, result);   expectation
}                                              ❷ has been met
```

VB

```
Private trackingService As ITrackingService
Private mocks As MockRepository
```

```vb
<TestInitialize()> _
Public Sub SetUp()
  mocks = New MockRepository()
  trackingService =                                    Creates mock
    mocks.DynamicMock(Of ITrackingService)()
End Sub

<TestMethod()> _
Public Sub CheckDeliveryStatus_WhenOrderIsDelivered_ReturnsDelivered()
  Dim order = New Order()
  order.TrackingTicket = "test"

  Expect.Call(trackingService.GetTracking(order.TrackingTicket))._
    Return("delivered")                                   Sets up
  mocks.ReplayAll()                                    ❶ expectation

  Dim result As DeliveryStatus = _                     ❷ Verifies that
    order.CheckDeliveryStatus(trackingService)            expectation
                                                          has been met
  mocks.VerifyAll()
  Assert.AreEqual(DeliveryStatus.Delivered, result)
End Sub
```

If the code under test doesn't invoke the service's `GetTracking` method, providing test as an input, according the expectation ❶, `mocks.VerifyAll` would throw an exception causing the test to fail ❷, which would result in a report like the one in figure 18.4.

Figure 18.4   A mock is able to track unexpected invocations.

As you can see, mocks and stubs give you the chance to dynamically fake external dependencies to isolate the code being tested. Stubs are useful if you want to replace a dependency and provide hard-coded results, whereas mocks are also able to check whether the external method was invoked as expected or not. Both are essential tools when you have complex code, and you're going to use them in the next section, where you'll use them with Entity Framework to test the data layer.

18.4   *Unit-testing the data access layer*

Before you start writing tests for the data layer, you need to identify which parts of it deserve to be tested. When you build an object model using the Entity Framework designer, you have a lot of automatically generated code, including the `Object-Context` and all the entities.

The test that may first come to mind is whether the O/RM tool is able to correctly get those entities from and persist them to the database. Because such tests require interactions with external resources, they're considered integration tests. They're as important as unit tests, and we'll cover them later this chapter.

When we talk about *unit-testing the data access layer*, we don't mean verifying whether a customer is correctly stored in its table; we mean checking whether our infrastructure interacts with Entity Framework in the way we expect.

18.4.1 *A test infrastructure for a repository*

In chapter 14, you designed the domain layer so it wasn't directly exposed to the Entity Framework classes and API. You created a set of repositories, which use Entity Framework to access the data source, but provide to the upper layer an abstract collection-like interface. Repositories were designed to contain a lot of logic, such as logic to check the uniqueness of a customer's email address while creating it, so they deserve their own test suite.

As a first step, you'll test that when the repository's Add method is invoked, the entity is added to the underlying object set by calling AddObject. You can see the Add method in the excerpt in listing 18.12. Notice that, for the sake of simplicity, you're not checking whether the entity already belongs to the object set, as you should do in a real-world scenario.

Listing 18.12 Repository's Add method

C#

```
public Repository(ObjectContext context)
{
  if (context == null)
    throw new ArgumentNullException("context");

  this.context = context;
  this.objectSet = context.CreateObjectSet<T>();        ❶ Dependency on
}                                                            ObjectSet<T>

private IObjectSet<T> entitySet;

public virtual void Add(T entity)
{                                                         ❷ Method that needs
  this.objectSet.AddObject(entity);                          to be mocked
}
```

VB

```
Public Sub New(ByVal context As ObjectContext)
  If context Is Nothing Then
    Throw New ArgumentNullException("context")
  End If

  Me.context = context
  Me.objectSet = context.CreateObjectSet(Of T)()         ❶ Dependency on
End Sub                                                      ObjectSet<T>

Private entitySet As IObjectSet(Of T)

Public Overridable Sub Add(ByVal entity As T)            ❷ Method that needs
  Me.objectSet.AddObject(entity)                             to be mocked
End Sub
```

This code has dependencies on two external classes that need to be mocked:

- `ObjectContext`—It needs to be faked because it's used to create an `Object-Set<T>` ❶, but you don't need to check anything on it, so it can be a stub.
- `IObjectSet<T>`—You need to check whether this object invokes its `AddObject` method ❷, so it needs to be a mock.

Unfortunately, Rhino Mocks can't effectively mock concrete entities unless they have only virtual methods. This is because the repository and its context are tightly coupled. But you can easily work around this by creating an `IObjectContext` interface and a wrapper around the real `ObjectContext`. The new class diagram is shown in figure 18.5.

Supporting the new `IObjectContext` interface obviously requires a little refactoring on the `Repository` constructor, but the result is that everything is loosely coupled and so is testable. Listing 18.13 shows the new version of code.

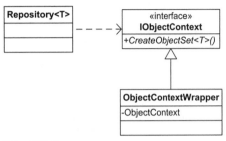

Figure 18.5
`Repository` and `ObjectContextWrapper`

Listing 18.13 Refactoring the `RepositoryConstructor`

C#

```csharp
public interface IObjectContext                          ◁┐ Object context's
{                                                           interface
  IObjectSet<T> CreateObjectSet<T>();
}
public class ObjectContextWrapper : IObjectContext       ◁┐ Object context's
{                                                           wrapper
  public ObjectContextWrapper(ObjectContext context)
  {
    this.Context = context;
  }

  public IObjectSet<T> CreateObjectSet<T>()
  {
    return this.Context.CreateObjectSet<T>();            ◁┐ Call redirection
  }                                                        to object context

  public ObjectContext Context { get; set; }
}
public class Repository<T> : IRepository<T>
{
  private IObjectContext context;                        ◁┐ Constructor with
                                                            IObjectContext
  public Repository(IObjectContext context)              ◁  argument
  {
    if (context == null)
      throw new ArgumentNullException("context");

    this.context = context;
    this.entitySet = context.CreateObjectSet<T>();
```

```vb
    }
  }
```

VB

```vb
Public Interface IObjectContext                                         Object context's
  Function CreateObjectSet(Of T)() As IObjectSet(Of T)            ◁┘    interface
End Interface

Public Class ObjectContextWrapper
  Implements IObjectContext
                                                                        Object context's
  Public Sub New(ByVal context As ObjectContext)                 ◁┘    wrapper
    Me.Context = context
  End Sub

  Public Function CreateObjectSet(Of T)() As IObjectSet(Of T)
    Return Me.Context.CreateObjectSet(Of T)()                    ◁┐    Call redirection
  End Function                                                         to object context

  Public Property Context() As ObjectContext

End Class

Public Class Repository(Of T)
  Implements IRepository(Of T)
                                                                        Constructor with
  Private context As IObjectContext                                     IObjectContext
                                                                 ◁┘    argument
  Public Sub New(ByVal context As IObjectContext)
    If context Is Nothing Then
      Throw New ArgumentNullException("context")
    End If

    Me.context = context
    Me.entitySet = context.CreateObjectSet(Of T)()
  End Sub
End Class
```

Now it's time to return to the main goal, which is testing the repository's Add method. The test code is pretty simple to write, because you're allowed to mock all the repository dependencies. The following code is completely isolated from all Entity Framework classes.

Why use a wrapper?

You might disagree with building a wrapper instead of implementing the interface directly on the designer-generated ObjectContext using partial classes. In this example, the same result could be achieved in both ways; but in a real-world scenario, repositories depend also on ObjectStateManager, which is another tightly coupled non-testable class within the Entity Framework assembly. Using a wrapper is the only way to successfully abstract the ObjectStateManager. The full code is omitted here for the sake of simplicity, but it's included in the book's source code.

You should avoid inserting any kind of logic into those wrappers and keep them as simple as possible; ideally, they should only forward the calls. Otherwise, you'd need to test them too, and this isn't possible because of the tight coupling with untestable classes such as ObjectContext and ObjectStateManager.

Listing 18.14   Test code for the `Add` method

C#

```
[TestInitialize]
public void SetUp()
{
  mocks = new MockRepository();                                    ➊ Sets up stub for
  objectContext = mocks.Stub<IObjectContext>();                       ObjectContext
  objectSet = mocks.DynamicMock<IObjectSet<Customer>>();           ➋ Sets up mock
                                                                      for ObjectSet
  SetupResult.On(objectContext)
    .Call(objectContext.CreateObjectSet<Customer>())
    .Return(objectSet);                                            Sets up result
}                                                                  for call on
                                                                   ➌ CreateObjectSet
MockRepository mocks;
IObjectContext objectContext;
IObjectSet<Customer> objectSet;

[TestMethod]
public void Repository_Add_CallsAddObject()
{                                                                  ➍ Sets up
  Customer customer = new Customer();                                 expectation
  Expect.Call(() => objectSet.AddObject(customer));                   to test
  mocks.ReplayAll();

  CustomerRepository repository =
    new CustomerRepository(objectContext);                         ➎ Verifies
  repository.Add(customer);                                           AddObject has
                                                                      been called
  mocks.VerifyAll();
}
```

VB

```
<TestInitialize()> _
Public Sub SetUp()
  mocks = New MockRepository()                                     ➊ Sets up stub for
  objectContext = mocks.Stub(Of IObjectContext)()                    ObjectContext
  objectSet = mocks. _                                             ➋ Sets up mock
    DynamicMock(Of IObjectSet(Of Customer))()                        for ObjectSet

  SetupResult.[On](objectContext)._
    [Call](objectContext.CreateObjectSet(Of Customer)())._
    [Return](objectSet)                                            Sets up result
End Sub                                                            for call on
                                                                   ➌ CreateObjectSet
Private mocks As MockRepository
Private objectContext As IObjectContext
Private objectSet As IObjectSet(Of Customer)

<TestMethod()> _
Public Sub Repository_Add_CallsAddObject()                        ➍ Sets up
  Dim customer As New Customer()                                     expectation
  Expect.Call(Function() objectSet.AddObject(customer))              to test
  mocks.ReplayAll()

  Dim repository As New CustomerRepository(objectContext)         ➎ Verifies
  repository.Add(customer)                                           AddObject has
                                                                      been called
  mocks.VerifyAll()
End Sub
```

The test initialization builds a stub ❶ and a mock ❷ for the `ObjectContext` and the `ObjectSet<T>`, respectively. They're then injected into the repository via its constructor, after setting up the `ObjectContext` to return the mock on ❸. Next comes the test, which is straightforward and verifies that the `AddObject` method ❹ is called before `repository.Add` ❺ is invoked. You can easily verify that modifying `repository.Add` to artificially introduce a bug results in the test failing.

This test infrastructure was worth the effort of building it. In the next section, you'll see that it's flexible enough to cover a wide range of needs.

18.4.2 *Testing LINQ to Entities queries*

Mocks work perfectly when you know exactly how the object under test interacts with the mocked instance, but you get into trouble when dealing with the extension methods LINQ is built on. Let's take the `Repository.Query` method in this listing as an example.

Listing 18.15   Query method of `Repository<T>`

C#
```
public virtual IEnumerable<T> Query(Func<T, bool> predicate)
{
  return this.objectSet.Where(predicate);
}
```

VB
```
Public Overridable Function Query(ByVal predicate As Func(Of T, Boolean)) _
  As IEnumerable(Of T)
  Return Me.objectSet.Where(predicate)
End Function
```

If `Where` was an `ObjectSet<T>` instance method, `Query` would be trivial to test, because you would only have to build a mock object and check that this call happens. Unfortunately, despite the syntax, `Where` is an extension method that belongs to a class named `System.Linq.Queryable`, whose implementation is anything but simple! (You can check it out using a tool like Reflector.) Mocking such a call, testing that arguments are passed correctly, and setting up method results would be tricky. Although less precise, using a fake data source to test LINQ queries is preferable.

Let's dig more into this additional technique. When customers register in OrderIT, they must provide a valid and unique email address. The following code belongs to the `CustomerRepository`'s `Add` method, and it checks that the email address is unique in the database by executing a simple query.

Listing 18.16   The `CustomerRepository.Add` method

C#
```
public class CustomerRepository : Repository<Customer>
{
  public override void Add(Customer entity)
  {
    if (this.GetSingleOrDefault(c => c.Email == entity.Email) != null)
```

```
        throw new ArgumentException("Email already used");   ◁┐ Checks email
                                                               │ address
    base.Add(entity);
  }
}
public class Repository<T> : IRepository<T>
{
  public virtual T GetSingleOrDefault(Func<T, bool> predicate)
  {
    return this.Query(predicate).SingleOrDefault();        ◁┐ Executes LINQ to
  }                                                          │ Entities query
                                                            ❶ on ObjectSet
  // ... more code here
}
```

VB

```
Public Class CustomerRepository
  Inherits Repository(Of Customer)
  Public Overloads Overrides Sub Add(ByVal entity As Customer)
    If Me.GetSingleOrDefault(Function(c) c.Email = entity.Email)_
      IsNot Nothing Then
        Throw New ArgumentException("Email already used")   ◁┐ Checks email
    End If                                                    │ address

    MyBase.Add(entity)
  End Sub
End Class

Public Class Repository(Of T)
  Implements IRepository(Of T)

  Public Overridable Function GetSingleOrDefault(_
    ByVal predicate As Func(Of T, Boolean)) As T

    Return Me.Query(predicate).SingleOrDefault()           ◁┐ Executes LINQ to
                                                             │ Entities query
  End Function                                              ❶ on ObjectSet

  ' ... more code here
End Class
```

The code at ❶ uses the Query method, which relies on the ObjectSet<T>. The idea is to fake the object set, in terms of having a class that implements IObjectSet<T> but does its job with in-memory and hard-coded data. You can easily query such an object as you'd do with the database, but without worrying about data or transactions, and you can reset it for every test by building another instance.

Building a fake object set is trivial, although it's a bit tedious because of the many methods IObjectSet<T> requires to be implemented. The following listing contains an excerpt from the FakeObjectSet class.

Listing 18.17 FakeObjectSet implementation (an excerpt)

C#

```
internal class FakeObjectSet<T> : IObjectSet<T>
{                                                         │ Stores data in
  private List<T> innerList = new List<T>();              ◁┘ internal list
```

```
  public List<T> InnerList
  {
    get { return this.innerList; }
  }

  public void AddObject(T entity)
  {
    this.innerList.Add(entity);          ◁──── Adds object to list
  }

  public void Attach(T entity)
  {
    if (!this.innerList.Contains(entity))
      this.innerList.Add(entity);
  }

  // ... more code here
}
```

VB

```
Friend Class FakeObjectSet(Of T)
  Implements IObjectSet(Of T)                    Stores data in
  Private m_innerList As New List(Of T)()    ◁── internal list
  Public ReadOnly Property InnerList() As List(Of T)
    Get
      Return Me.m_innerList
    End Get
  End Property

  Public Sub AddObject(ByVal entity As T)
    Me.m_innerList.Add(entity)          ◁──── Adds object to list
  End Sub

  Public Sub Attach(ByVal entity As T)
    If Not Me.m_innerList.Contains(entity) Then
      Me.m_innerList.Add(entity)
    End If
  End Sub

  ' ... more code here
End Class
```

As we mentioned before, you can inject the fake object set into a repository using an
ObjectContext stub. Then, using it in a test is only a matter of providing some fake
data to work on. For example, testing the email address while adding a new customer
looks like this.

Listing 18.18 Testing `CustomerRepository.Add` method with `FakeObjectSet`

C#

```
[TestMethod,
  ExpectedException(typeof(ArgumentException))]          ❶ Expects
public void Add_WithNotUniqueEmail_ThrowsException()        ArgumentException
{
  var customerSet = new FakeObjectSet<Customer>();

  SetupResult.On(objectContext)
```

```
        .Call(objectContext.CreateObjectSet<Customer>())
        .Return(customerSet);
```
◁ **Sets up ObjectContext to return FakeObjectSet**

```
    mocks.ReplayAll();

    Customer c = new Customer();
    c.Id = 3;
    c.Email = "sample@email.com";
    customerSet.AddObject(c);
```
❷ **Adds test data to FakeObjectSet**

```
    CustomerRepository repo = new CustomerRepository(this.objectContext);
    repo.Add(new Customer { Email = c.Email });
```
❸ **Should always fail**

```
    Assert.Fail();
}
```

VB
```
<TestMethod(), ___
 ExpectedException(GetType(ArgumentException))> _
Public Sub Add_WithNotUniqueEmail_ThrowsException()
    Dim customerSet = New FakeObjectSet(Of Customer)()
```
❶ **Expects ArgumentException**

```
    SetupResult.On(objectContext)._
        Call(objectContext.CreateObjectSet(Of Customer)())._
        Return(customerSet)
    mocks.ReplayAll()
```
Sets up ObjectContext to return FakeObjectSet

```
    Dim c As New Customer()
    c.Id = 3
    c.Email = "sample@email.com"
    customerSet.AddObject(c)
```
❷ **Adds test data to FakeObjectSet**

```
    Dim repo As New CustomerRepository(Me.objectContext)
    Dim c1 as New Customer()
    c1.Email = c.Email
    repo.Add(c1)

    Assert.Fail()
End Sub
```
❸ **Should always fail**

This test expects an exception to be thrown ❶ by the repository, and it uses a Fake-ObjectSet containing a sample customer ❷. At ❸ it tries to add another customer with the same email address. Internally, the repository queries the ObjectSet<T> and, in this case, throws an ArgumentException.

Testing a repository built on Entity Framework isn't a trivial task, because although the 4.0 release brings some improvements to testability, there are still classes that aren't directly mockable. In the last two sections, we presented two different strategies for working around this limitation and writing effective unit tests: one was more rigorous and exclusively based on mocks and stubs, and the other used fake object sets to work with in-memory data. The first solution should be always the preferred option, unless mocking becomes too complex. When that happens, fake object sets offer a good alternative.

In the next section, we'll drop the isolation requirements. We'll test whether entities are correctly stored and retrieved in the database. You're going to use integration tests to test the whole system as an ensemble, to make sure all the components integrate perfectly.

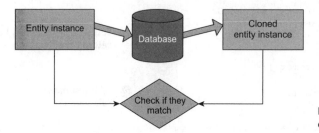

Figure 18.6　Conceptual flow of a persistence test

18.5　*Testing the persistence and retrieval of an entity*

Making sure all your repositories work as expected is only half the job of testing a data access layer. That doesn't prove whether Entity Framework is correctly parsing the mapping and successfully generating queries for the CRUD operations against the database. Even if it works now, that doesn't shield you from trouble in the future, because schemas evolve with time. Having a test suite that constantly verifies that Entity Framework's data is constantly up to date with the storage schema is valuable and is worth a little effort to build.

The basic idea is simple, and it's illustrated in figure 18.6. You build a new entity, save it to the database, fetch it back, and test whether its property values match what you originally stored.

A persistence test that applies this workflow to a Customer entity would look like this.

> **Listing 18.19　Persistence test for the Customer entity**

C#

```csharp
[TestMethod]
public void Customer_IsStoredAndRetrievedCorrectly()
{
  Customer original = new Customer
  {
    Name = "Marco De Sanctis",
    Email = "test@email.com"
  };

  using (Context context = new Context())
  {
    context.AddToCustomers(original);
    context.SaveChanges();
  }

  using (Context context = new Context())
  {
    Customer customer = context.Customers
      .Where(c => c.Id == original.Id).Single();

    Assert.AreEqual(original.Name, customer.Name);
    Assert.AreEqual(original.Email, customer.Email);
    //...
  }
}
```

VB

```vb
<TestMethod()> _
Public Sub Customer_IsStoredAndRetrievedCorrectly()
  Dim original As New Customer()

  Using context As New Context()
    context.AddToCustomers(original)
    context.SaveChanges()
  End Using

  Using context As New Context()
    Dim customer As Customer = context.Customers._
     Where(Function(c) c.Id = original.Id)._
     [Single]()

    Assert.AreEqual(original.Name, customer.Name)
    Assert.AreEqual(original.Email, customer.Email)
    '...

  End Using
End Sub
```

This test could work, at least the first time; there will likely be a unique constraint on the Email column on the Company table, so the second time you run it, you're going to get a `SqlException` due to a constraint violation. Every execution perturbs the test environment, so the test isn't repeatable.

You could get around this problem by using a `TestCleanUp` method and deleting the new `Customer`, but a far better solution is using transactions to ensure database consistency among different tests. This is pretty easy to do by using the `Test-Initialize` and `TestCleanUp` attributes, as in the following listing.

Listing 18.20   Using transactions in persistence tests

C#

```csharp
private TransactionScope transaction;

[TestInitialize]
public void SetUp()
{
  transaction = new TransactionScope();       ❶ Creates transaction
}                                                 before test starts

[TestCleanup]
public void CleanUp()
{                                             ❷ Doesn't commit
  transaction.Dispose();                         transaction
}
```

VB

```vb
Private transaction As TransactionScope

<TestInitialize()> _
Public Sub SetUp()                            ❶ Creates transaction
  transaction = New TransactionScope()           before test starts
End Sub
```

```
<TestCleanup()> _
Public Sub CleanUp()
  transaction.Dispose()
End Sub
```

② **Doesn't commit transaction**

This code starts a transaction **❶**, under which you can execute the test code. Then you release it without committing it **❷**, ensuring that nothing remains in the database. But from test to test, this will involve a lot of repetitive code, because the flow in figure 18.6 will repeat a number of times.

To address this issue, we've built a simple tool called EF Mapping Verifier; the original idea behind it belongs to Fluent NHibernate, one of the many open source projects born around this famous .NET O/RM. The tool uses lambda expressions to write persistence tests in a simple, concise, and intuitive way. EF Mapping Verifier supports a more versatile set of expressions, and it's included in the book's source code.

After you've referenced EF Mapping Verifier's assembly in your test project, the previous example of customer persistence looks like this.

Listing 18.21 Persistence test of the `Customer` entity using EF Mapping Verifier

C#

```csharp
[TestMethod]
public void Customer_IsStoredAndRetrievedCorrectly()
{
  using (Context context = new Context())
  {
    VerifyMapping.For<Customer>(context)
      .Test(c => c.Name, "Marco De Sanctis")
      .Test(c => c.Email, "test@email.com")
      .Execute();
  }
}
```

VB

```vb
<TestMethod()> _
Public Sub Customer_IsStoredAndRetrievedCorrectly()
  Using context As New Context()
    VerifyMapping.For(Of Customer)(context)._
      Test(Function(c) c.Name, "Marco De Sanctis")._
      Test(Function(c) c.Email, "test@email.com")._
      Execute()
  End Using
End Sub
```

In this example, the EF Mapping Verifier creates a new instance of `Customer` and sets its properties to the values provided by the test method. Then it uses the given context instance to store and subsequently retrieve the `Customer` instance, automatically checking whether all the properties match. This testing tool supports a wide range of use cases: it can test lookup relationships, master-detail relationships, and complex types.

18.6 *Summary*

This chapter covered a wide range of topics related to automatic testing of software. A test suite is worth the effort of building it, because it gives you a chance to react to changes, avoiding that sense of uncertainty when you need to modify the code. With a test tool, you can effectively and constantly monitor how those changes affect the application.

We first looked at the challenges of writing unit tests, starting from the first trivial examples and then moving deeper to more complex cases. We looked at some techniques you can use to refactor the code to make it more testable, making it more feasible to build mocks and stubs to fake the dependencies on external resources.

Then, we focused on Entity Framework and the testing of the data access layer in general. We applied the concepts discussed before to writing unit tests for the repositories we introduced in chapter 14.

Finally, we looked at integration testing. We examined how you can check whether Entity Framework is able to store and retrieve your entities, and we introduced an open source tool that can help you write simple, readable, and concise integration code.

Keeping an eye
on performance

When people first approach Entity Framework, one of their first questions is, "What about performance?" This is a great question that involves many aspects of Entity Framework.

Entity Framework is a layer in your application, and it's not news that additional layers slow down performance. But that's not always bad. Entity Framework simplifies development so much that the decreased performance can be a reasonable tradeoff. Naturally, you must still take care of performance. Fortunately, Entity Framework has several internal behaviors that you can use to gain much more performance benefit than you might imagine.

Optimizing SQL is only part of the game. For instance, LINQ to Entities queries can benefit from *query compilation*, whereas Entity SQL queries can be optimized by enabling *plan caching*. Change tracking plays a role too. When you only read entities, disabling change tracking ensures better performance.

All these optimizations are the key to a well-performing data access layer, and in this chapter you'll learn how to use them. Furthermore, you'll learn how much Entity Framework slows down performance, compared with the classic ADO.NET approach, and you'll see how performance optimizations can make them extremely close in certain scenarios. By the end of the chapter, you'll be able not only to write robust applications, but also to make them perform smoothly.

Let's start by building a testing application that will demonstrate the performance of the Entity Framework and ADO.NET queries we'll look at.

19.1 Testing configuration and environment

The database we'll use for our tests is OrderIT, and it's installed on the same machine where the test application will be run. The machine has the following configuration:

- 8 GB of RAM
- T9600 dual core processor, 2.80 GHz
- Solid state disk, 250 MBps (read) and 220 MBps (write)
- Windows 7, 64-bit operating system
- SQL Server 2008

This is a good configuration for a desktop machine, but a server would be much more powerful. As a result, the performance numbers in this chapter are intended only for comparing ADO.NET and Entity Framework, or different techniques in Entity Framework itself. They aren't intended as absolute performance numbers.

To ensure an exact comparison, we'll follow these guidelines:

- *All queries must be performed 50 times.* To ensure that the context doesn't use state-manager caching to return objects, the context is created and destroyed for each query. This means a connection is opened and closed each time. In ADO.NET code, you do exactly the same thing, which ensures that ADO.NET and Entity Framework perform exactly the same tasks.
- *In* ADO.NET, *all fields must be iterated.* Entity Framework reads all data from a query to shape it into its internal format. When using ADO.NET, you have to read all columns to simulate the same behavior.
- *500 customers and suppliers are added in the scope of a transaction.* A good test can't ignore updates to the database. You insert 500 records in a single `SaveChanges` call, which opens a transaction, issues the commands to the database, and then commits it. The same steps are reproduced in ADO.NET.
- *An Entity Framework warm-up query must be executed before issuing the commands.* This is necessary to ensure that metadata and other stuff necessary to Entity Framework is already in place when running the test. Otherwise, the test might be influenced by initialization processes.

The tests are performed in a Windows Forms application that offers a nice way of seeing the results.

19.1.1 *The performance test visualizer*

The test application is easy to understand. It contains a single form with a set of buttons on the left to start the tests, and a ListView on the right to show the results. The ListView shows the test type, the total execution time, the average command-execution time, the first command-execution time, and the execution time for all the other commands (each time is shown in milliseconds). This form is shown in figure 19.1.

It's particularly important to separate the first execution time from subsequent times because, as you'll discover, in Entity Framework the first command is the slowest and the others are much faster. You'll learn in this chapter how to mitigate this issue and how much it improves performance.

To test performance, you need to measure, and to measure you need a timer.

19.1.2 *Building the timer*

To build the timer, you create a class that wraps the System.Diagnostics.Stopwatch class: Watch. Its purpose isn't only measuring execution time, but also writing the result to the output ListView so that showing the result has minimal impact on the

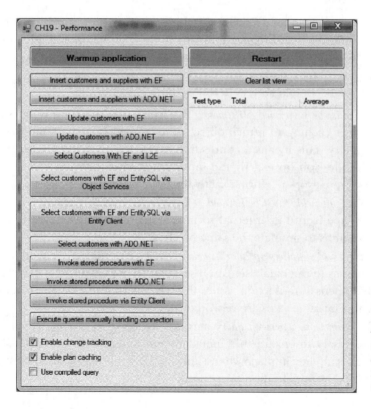

Figure 19.1 The testing application. On the left are the buttons to start the tests and check boxes to enable various optimizations. The right ListView shows the results of each test.

test code. (We could have used the Template Method pattern, but we opted for the "get in and out quick" approach). Here's the Watch class.

Listing 19.1   The custom timer

C#
```
public class Watch
{
  Stopwatch _sw;
  ListView _result;
  string _testType;
  List<long> _laps;

  public Watch(ListView result)                  ❶ Stores output
  {    _result = result;                             ListView
  }

  public void Start(string testType)
  {
    _laps = new List<long>();                    ❷ Sets up
    _sw = new Stopwatch();                           timer
    _testType = testType;
    _sw.Start();
  }

  public void SaveLap()
  {                                              ❸ Stores
    _laps.Add(_sw.ElapsedMilliseconds);             iteration length
  }

  public void Stop()
  {
    _sw.Stop();                        ❹ Stops timer
    if (_laps.Count > 0)
    {
      string[] localTimes = new string[_laps.Count-1];
      for (int i = 1; i < _laps.Count-1; i++)
      {
        localTimes[i-1] =
          (_laps[i] - _laps[i - 1]).ToString();
      }
      _result.Items.Add(new ListViewItem(new[] {   ❺ Writes result
        _testType,                                     in ListView for
        _sw.ElapsedMilliseconds.ToString(),            iterations
        ((double)_sw.ElapsedMilliseconds /
         (double)_laps.Count).ToString(),
        _laps[0].ToString(),
        String.Join(", ", localTimes) }));
    }
    else
      _result.Items.Add(new ListViewItem(new[] {   ❻ Writes result
        _testType,                                     in ListView for
        _sw.ElapsedMilliseconds.ToString(),            single query
        _sw.ElapsedMilliseconds.ToString(),
          "0", String.Empty }));
  }
}
```

VB

```vb
Public Class Watch
  Private _sw As Stopwatch
  Private _result As ListView
  Private _testType As String
  Private _laps As List(Of Long)

  Public Sub New(ByVal result As ListView)
    _result = result
  End Sub

  Public Sub Start(ByVal testType As String)
    _laps = New List(Of Long)()
    _sw = New Stopwatch()
    _testType = testType
    _sw.Start()
  End Sub

  Public Sub SaveLap()
    _laps.Add(_sw.ElapsedMilliseconds)
  End Sub

  Public Sub [Stop]()
    _sw.Stop()
    If _laps.Count > 0 Then
      Dim localTimes As String() =
        New String(_laps.Count - 2)
      For i As Integer = 1 To _laps.Count - 2
        localTimes(i - 1) =
          (_laps(i) - _laps(i - 1)).ToString()
      Next
      _result.Items.Add(New ListViewItem(New () {
        _testType,
        _sw.ElapsedMilliseconds.ToString(),
        (CDbl(_sw.ElapsedMilliseconds) /
          CDbl(_laps.Count)).ToString(),
          _laps(0).ToString(),
          String.Join(", ", localTimes)}))
    Else
      _result.Items.Add(New ListViewItem(New () {
        _testType,
        _sw.ElapsedMilliseconds.ToString(),
        _sw.ElapsedMilliseconds.ToString(),
        "0", String.Empty}))
    End If
  End Sub
End Class
```

1 Stores output ListView

2 Sets up timer

3 Stores iteration length

4 Stops timer

5 Writes result in ListView for iterations

6 Writes result in ListView for single query

Watch's constructor **1** takes as input the list view the result are written into when a test is finished.

The Start method resets the list view internal state, saves the test type that's passed as an argument, and then starts the timer **2**.

SaveLap saves in a list the number of milliseconds that have passed since Start was invoked **3**. Calling SaveLap at each iteration allows you to know how long each operation takes to execute.

The Stop method stops the timer ❹. If any laps are stored, it first calculates the exact execution time for each iteration and then reports it in the list view ❺. If no laps are stored, there's no calculation, and the data is reported as a single execution ❻.

Now you know what you're going to do, how you're going to do it, and how you'll measure it. It's time to see some real tests. Because you can't query empty tables, you'll start by using both Entity Framework and classic ADO.NET to pour data into a table. You'll then measure the performance of both approaches and compare them.

19.2 *Database-writing comparison*

Writing data to the database means adding, modifying, and deleting rows. From a database perspective, these operations affect performance in very different ways; but we're interested only in caller performance so we'll only use the INSERT command to make comparisons.

> **NOTE** Because the test code is verbose and of no great interest, we'll only show the C# code in this chapter. The VB code is included in the book's source code.

The test of the INSERT commands creates 500 Customer and 500 Supplier objects, adds them to the context, and calls the SaveChanges method, as shown in the following listing.

> **Listing 19.2 Inserting customers and suppliers using Entity Framework**

```
using (OrderITEntities ctx = new OrderITEntities())
{
  for (int i = 0; i < 500; i++)
  {
    Customer c = CreateCustomer();
    ctx.Companies.AddObject(c);

    Supplier s = CreateSupplier();
    ctx.Companies.AddObject(s);
  }
  _watch.Start("Insert 500 customers and
➥     500 suppliers with EF");
  ctx.SaveChanges();
  _watch.Stop();
}
```

This listing creates a customer and adds it to the context, creates a supplier and adds it to the context, and then measures persistence performance. The object-creation phase isn't timed. You only care about the SaveChanges duration, because that code performs the same work you'd perform when using ADO.NET: it opens a connection, starts a transaction, and issues 500 commands to insert customers and 500 to insert suppliers. The comparable ADO.NET code is shown in the following listing.

Listing 19.3   Inserting customers and suppliers using ADO.NET

```
_watch.Start("Insert 500 customers and
    500 suppliers with ADO.NET");              ◁——— Starts timer
using (var conn = new SqlConnection(connString))    ◁——— Creates connection
{  conn.Open();
  using (SqlTransaction tr = conn.BeginTransaction())    ◁——— Starts transaction
  {
    try
    {
      for (int i = 0; i < 500; i++)
      {
        using (SqlCommand comm = new SqlCommand("", conn, tr))
        {
          comm.CommandText = GetCustomerSQL();
          comm.Parameters = GetCustomerParams();
          comm.ExecuteNonQuery();              ◁——— Saves customer
        }
      }
      for (int i = 0; i < 500; i++)
      {
        using (SqlCommand comm = new SqlCommand("", conn, tr))
        {
          comm.CommandText = GetSupplierSQL();
          comm.Parameters = GetSupplierParams();
          comm.ExecuteNonQuery();              ◁——— Saves supplier
        }
      }
      tr.Commit();
    }
    catch (Exception er)
    {
      tr.Rollback();
    }
  }
}
_watch.Stop();
```

The `GetCustomerSQL` and `GetSupplierSQL` methods return the SQL to insert a customer and a supplier, respectively. And as you may guess, `GetCustomerParams` and `GetSupplierParams` return the parameters for the SQL.

We executed both tests three times, but we wanted more. We also wanted to find out what would happen with lower and higher numbers of records to write to the table. Table 19.1 shows the results with 100, 5,000, and 10,000 records.

These results offer lots of information. First, the percentage difference between Entity Framework and ADO.NET when performing bulk inserts of a small number of objects the difference is negligible; but as number of objects grows, the difference increases to an unacceptable level. What's interesting is that the more objects there are, the more slowly the difference grows.

It's rare that an application created for human beings inserts a huge number of objects in a single transaction, so don't worry too much about the preceding statistics. For small numbers of inserts, you can hardly spot the difference.

Table 19.1 Comparing the performance of Entity Framework and ADO.NET with different numbers of records

Technology	Items	1st attempt	2nd attempt	3rd	Difference
ADO.NET	100	493 ms	491 ms	486 ms	—
Entity Framework	100	530 ms	513 ms	521 ms	+6.39%
ADO.NET	1,000	4,626 ms	4,892 ms	4712 ms	—
Entity Framework	1,000	5,386 ms	5,385 ms	5,660 ms	+15.46%
ADO.NET	5,000	24,906 ms	25,325 ms	24,968 ms	—
Entity Framework	5,000	30,536 ms	29,914 ms	29,535 ms	+19.66%
ADO.NET	10,000	48,308 ms	47,496 ms	48,324 ms	—
Entity Framework	10,000	58,297 ms	57,659 ms	58,325 ms	+20.92%

In contrast, if you have to perform a bulk insert, Entity Framework and other O/RM tools are your enemy. O/RM tools simplify development, but using them for bulk transactions is a capital sin. You're better off relying on ADO.NET or database-specific tools.

When it comes to updates and deletes, the situation doesn't change. Updating 1,000 rows is slower than inserting them, but that's due to database internals. Both Entity Framework and ADO.NET suffer equally from this performance slowdown. Entity Framework is obviously slower than ADO.NET, but in both cases you can do nothing to improve performance for database updates.

Let's now move on to talk about queries.

19.3 *Query comparisons in the default environment*

To test queries, you'll first test them in the environment you created. Then, you'll start introducing the tweaks necessary to speed up things a little.

As we mentioned in section 19.1, the query you'll use returns customers whose names start with *C*, and it's performed 50 times. To embrace the spectrum of querying technologies, we've created tests for ADO.NET, LINQ to Entities, Entity SQL via the `ObjectContext`, and Entity SQL via Entity Client.

Unlike the insert test, you won't warm up the application for this test. Each test is isolated from the others; after each test, the application is restarted to make sure the test is performed in a clean environment. We wanted you to see the performance with the default configuration, and how much performance improves when you optimize some aspects.

In chapter 3, you learned that you can perform queries through the Object Services layer and through the Entity Client. In the following listing, you see the test code that uses Object Services. Later in this section, we'll show you the test code that uses Entity Client. Here's the test.

Listing 19.4 Retrieving customers using Object Services

```
private void SelectCustomersViaObjectServices(string testType,
  bool enableTracking, bool useCompiledQuery, bool enablePlanCaching,
  bool useEntitySQL)
{
  _watch.Start(testType);
  for (int i = 0; i < 50; i++)
  {
    using (OrderITEntities ctx = new OrderITEntities())
    {
      List<Customer> items;
      if (!enableTracking)                              ❶ Sets change-tracking
        ctx.Companies.MergeOption =
          MergeOption.NoTracking;

      if (!useEntitySQL)
      {
        if (useCompiledQuery)                           ❷ Uses compiled LINQ
        {                                                 to Entities query
          var it = compQuery.Invoke(ctx, "C");
          foreach (var item in it)
            object o = item;
        }
        else
        {
          string name = "C";                            ❸ Uses classic LINQ
          items = ctx.Companies.OfType<Customer>()        to Entities query
            .Where(c => c.Name.StartsWith(name))
            .ToList();
        }
      }
      else                                              Uses ❹
      {                                                 EntitySQL
        var oq = ctx.CreateQuery<Customer>("SELECT VALUE c  query
⇒   FROM OFTYPE(OrderITEntities.Companies, OrderIT.Model.Customer)
⇒     AS c WHERE c.name LIKE @name");

        if (!enableTracking)                            ❶ Sets
          oq.MergeOption = MergeOption.NoTracking;         change-tracking

        if (!enablePlanCaching)                         ❺ Sets plan
          oq.EnablePlanCaching = false;                   caching

        oq.Parameters.Add(new ObjectParameter("name", "C%"));
        items = oq.ToList();
      }
    }
    _watch.SaveLap();
  }
  _watch.Stop();
}
```

This code tests the queries via Object Services using LINQ to Entities compiled queries
❷ (more about that in the next section), LINQ to Entities ❸, and Entity SQL ❹. It
also considers plan caching ❺ and change-tracking ❶ depending on the parameters.

The following listing performs queries via the Entity Client.

Listing 19.5 Retrieving customers using Entity Client

```
string testType = "Select Customers using EntitySQL via Entity Client. ";
_watch.Start(testType);
for (int i = 0; i < 50; i++)
{
  using (var conn = new EntityConnection(connString)      ❶ Opens connection
  {
    conn.Open();
    using (var comm = new EntityCommand(                   ❷ Creates
      "SELECT VALUE c                                         command
        FROM OFTYPE(OrderITEntities.Companies,
        OrderITModel.Customer)
        AS c WHERE c.name LIKE @name", conn))
    {
      comm.EnablePlanCaching =                              ❸ Sets plan
        enablePlanCaching.Checked;                            caching
      comm.Parameters.AddWithValue("name", "C%");
      using (EntityDataReader reader =
        comm.ExecuteReader(                                 ❹ Executes
          CommandBehavior.SequentialAccess))                  query
      {
        while (reader.Read())
        {
          var x = reader.GetValue(0);                       ❺ Iterates over
          var x1 = reader.GetValue(1);                        query result
          var x2 = reader.GetValue(2);
          var x3 = reader.GetValue(3);
          var x4 = reader.GetValue(4);
        }
      }
    }
  }
  _watch.SaveLap();
}
_watch.Stop();
```

This code tests queries via Entity Client. It first opens a connection ❶, and then it creates a command ❷, enables plan-caching depending on a check box in the form ❸, executes the query ❹, and iterates over the records returned by it ❺.

The code for ADO.NET is identical to listing 19.5, except that the Entity* objects are replaced by Sql* objects, and the connection string is in plain old ADO.NET format. You can find it in the book's source code.

Table 19.2 shows the performance comparison between the various techniques. Ouch! We knew Entity Framework was likely to lose, but we didn't expect LINQ to Entities to take *six* times longer than ADO.NET (LINQ to Entities is the most-adopted query technique).

Things get better when Entity SQL comes into play, because it's much easier to parse than LINQ to Entities. But when used via the ObjectContext class's Create-Query<T> method, it takes almost *five* times longer than ADO.NET!

Table 19.2   Comparing performance of Entity Framework and ADO.NET in querying customers whose names start with *C*

Technology	Total	Average	Difference
ADO.NET	171 ms	3.42 ms	—
LINQ to Entities	1,078 ms	21.56 ms	+530%
Entity SQL via Object Services	843 ms	16.86 ms	+392%
Entity SQL via Entity Client	420 ms	8.4 ms	+145%

If you skip object generation and opt for the Entity Client, Entity Framework takes more than twice the time ADO.NET takes. This is because, as you learned in chapter 3, Entity Client creates a `DbDataReader` whose columns match the conceptual format instead of the database format. This is one of the heaviest tasks Entity Client performs in the query pipeline (remember that this task is performed even when using LINQ to Entities and Entity SQL via `ObjectContext`).

A couple of years ago, the ADO.NET team published an interesting blog post about Entity Framework performance: "Exploring the Performance of the ADO.NET Entity Framework, Part 1" (http://mng.bz/27XQ). What is great about this post is that it separates tasks performed in the query pipeline, showing how long each of them takes to execute. You're going to use that information to make Entity Framework much faster.

19.4   Optimizing performance

The numbers shown in table 19.2 could make you think that Entity Framework isn't worth the effort. You'll be glad to know that there are four areas where you can do a lot to improve performance, and in this section we'll look at them in detail:

- View generation
- LINQ to Entities query compilation
- Entity SQL plan caching
- Change tracking

If you optimize these points, you'll be surprised by how much Entity Framework gains on ADO.NET. Let's start with the first point, which is very important.

19.4.1   Pregenerating views

Views are Entity SQL statements that retrieve data from entity sets and association sets declared in the SSDL and CSDL. These commands are used internally by the Entity Client to generate the final SQL.

According to the blog post we mentioned earlier, generating views is the most expensive task in the query pipeline, taking 56% of overall time. Fortunately, views are generated once per `AppDomain`, so when they're created, the other queries can reuse them, even if you use other contexts or the Entity Client.

As a result of view generation, the first query is tremendously slow. If you had warmed up the application by issuing a dummy query, the results in table 19.2 would have been much different because the views would have already been generated.

Table 19.3 shows the results after the warmup.

Table 19.3 Comparing performance of Entity Framework and ADO.NET querying customers whose names start with C" after a warmup

Technology	Total	Average	Difference
ADO.NET	171 ms	3.42 ms	—
LINQ to Entities	975 ms	19.5 ms	+470%
Entity SQL via Object Services	788 ms	15.76 ms	+360%
Entity SQL via Entity Client	416 ms	8.32 ms	+143%

Queries executed via Object Services (rows 2 and 3 of table 19.3) are now faster, and Entity Framework gains on ADO.NET. In contrast, queries issued using Entity Client perform pretty much the same as before (compare table 19.3 with table 19.2).

But although issuing a dummy query works, it's a waste. What's worse, when you deal with large models, Entity Framework takes its time to generate views. You don't want users to wait a long time before starting to use an application. To improve on this, you can generate the views at design time using the *EdmGen* tool, as shown in the following listing, and then compile them into the project.

Listing 19.6 Using EdmGen to generate views

```
"%windir%\Microsoft.NET\Framework\v4.XXXX\EdmGen.exe"
/nologo
/language:C#
/mode:ViewGeneration
"/inssdl:c:\OrderIT\model.ssdl"
"/incsdl:c:\OrderIT\model.csdl"
"/inmsl:c:\OrderIT\model.msl"
"/outviews:c:\OrderIT\School.Views.cs"
```

EdmGen needs the CSDL, SSDL, and MSL files, and it returns a C# or VB file, depending on the /language switch, containing the views. Now you just need to add the file to the project and compile everything.

The problem with this approach is that you need the three EDM files, but you only have the EDMX. You can let the designer generate the three files, but then you need to remember to reference them differently in the connection string and deploy them along with the rest of the application. This process is awkward.

There's another path you can follow:

1 Set the designer to generate the three files on build.
2 Build the application.

  3 Launch EdmGen in a post-build event.

  4 Reset the designer to embed the files in the application.

  5 Build it again.

This is even worse than the previous option.

What you really want is a simpler way to generate the views at design time, without touching the designer. Fortunately, the solution is astonishingly simple: use a template.

PREGENERATING VIEWS VIA TEMPLATE

Although view generation happens internally, the APIs are public, which means you can generate views from code. You can write a template that reads the EDMX, extracts the three files, and invokes the API to generate the views. Listing 19.7 contains the main code of such a template.

Listing 19.7 The main part of the template that generates views

C#

```
using (StreamWriter writer = new StreamWriter(new MemoryStream()))
{
  XmlReader csdlReader = null;
  XmlReader mslReader = null;
  XmlReader ssdlReader = null;

  GetConceptualMappingAndStorageReaders(edmxFilePath,
    out csdlReader, out mslReader, out ssdlReader);
  var edmItems = new EdmItemCollection(
    new XmlReader[] { csdlReader });            ❶ Creates EDM
  var storeItems = new StoreItemCollection(       files from EDMX
    new XmlReader[]{ssdlReader});
  var mappingItems = new StorageMappingItemCollection(
    edmItems, storeItems,
    new XmlReader[] { mslReader });

  EntityViewGenerator viewGenerator =
    new EntityViewGenerator();               ❷ Generates
  viewGenerator.LanguageOption =               view code
    LanguageOption.GenerateCSharpCode;
  IList<EdmSchemaError> errors =
    viewGenerator.GenerateViews(mappingItems, writer);

  foreach (EdmSchemaError e in errors)      ❸ Enumerates
    this.Error(e.Message);                    errors

  MemoryStream memStream =                   ❹ Writes
    writer.BaseStream as MemoryStream;          view code
  this.WriteLine(                               in file
    Encoding.UTF8.GetString(memStream.ToArray()));
}
```

VB

```
Using writer As New StreamWriter(New MemoryStream())
  Dim csdlReader As XmlReader = Nothing
  Dim mslReader As XmlReader = Nothing
  Dim ssdlReader As XmlReader = Nothing
```

```
GetConceptualMappingAndStorageReaders(
    edmxFilePath, csdlReader, mslReader, ssdlReader)

Dim edmItems As New EdmItemCollection(                    ❶ Creates EDM
    New XmlReader() {csdlReader})                            files from EDMX
Dim storeItems As New StoreItemCollection(
    New XmlReader() {ssdlReader})
Dim mappingItems As
    New StorageMappingItemCollection(edmItems,
        storeItems, New XmlReader() {mslReader})

Dim viewGenerator As New EntityViewGenerator()           ❷ Generates
viewGenerator.LanguageOption =                              view code
    LanguageOption.GenerateVBCode
Dim errors As IList(Of EdmSchemaError) =
    viewGenerator.GenerateViews(mappingItems, writer)

For Each e As EdmSchemaError In errors                   ❸ Enumerates
    Me.Error(e.Message)                                     errors
Next

Dim memStream =                                          ❹ Writes
    TryCast(writer.BaseStream, MemoryStream)                view code
Me.WriteLine(                                               in file
    Encoding.UTF8.GetString(memStream.ToArray()))
End Using
```

In the first part of this code, a stream for each EDM file is extracted from the EDMX, and the item collections are instantiated using those streams ❶. When that's done, the `EntityViewGenerator` class (situated in the `System.Data.Entity.Design` namespace inside the `System.Data.Entity.Design` assembly) is instantiated, and its `GenerateView` method is invoked, passing the item collections joined into one, and the writer that the code will be written into ❷. Finally, any errors are sent to the output ❸, and the stream containing the file is serialized as a string and is written to the output file ❹.

This template has already been created and has been made available for download by the Entity Framework team through a blog entry entitled, "How to use a T4 template for View Generation" (http://mng.bz/8ZNK).

We strongly recommend pregenerating views via a template. You'll gain all the runtime benefits of the already-compiled views without any design-time drawbacks.

Naturally, pregeneration speeds up things only at startup. Let's now look at a mechanism every LINQ to Entities query can benefit from: *query compilation*.

19.4.2 Compiling LINQ to Entities queries

LINQ to Entities queries are parsed at runtime by the Object Services layer. The more complex a query is, the more time the parsing process takes. The Entity Framework team knows that, and they've added the option to compile queries. By compiling queries, you tell Object Services to parse the query and cache the generated command tree. The next time the query is executed, the Object Services layer doesn't have to parse the query again; it uses the cached command instead.

Table 19.4   Comparing performance of Entity Framework and ADO.NET with and without LINQ to Entities query compilation

Technology	1st query	Other query average
ADO.NET	4 ms	2.59 ms
LINQ to Entities (no compilation)	378 ms	12.38 ms
LINQ to Entities (with compilation)	378 ms	10.01 ms

Obviously, the first time you execute a particular query, you get no benefits. The benefits become evident from the second execution on, as you see in table 19.4.

As you can see, compiling queries helps hugely in improving performance, but it requires a different style of coding. You must choose during development which queries must be compiled and which must not; introducing this feature later means changing a lot of code.

WRITING A COMPILED QUERY

At first sight, creating a compiled query may look odd because it involves the CompiledQuery class in association with a predicate. Don't worry—after a bit of practice, it will look familiar.

To create a compiled query, you have to write a predicate. It must accept the context and any parameters you need for the query, and it must return an IQueryable <Customer> instance. To instantiate the predicate, you have to invoke the CompiledQuery class's Compile method, passing in the LINQ to Entities query. The last thing you need to do is make the predicate static.

In this example, the predicate accepts the context plus a string containing the first letter of the customers' names you're looking for in the query. (Remember, in the previous examples you looked for customers whose names start with *C*.) Here's an example of a compiled query.

Listing 19.8   The compiled query code

C#

```
static Func<OrderITEntities, string, IQueryable<Customer>> compQuery =
  CompiledQuery.Compile<OrderITEntities, string, IQueryable<Customer>>(
    (ctx, name) => ctx.Companies
                    .OfType<Customer>()
                    .Where(c => c.Name.StartsWith(name)
  )
);
```

VB

```
Shared compQuery As Func(Of OrderITEntities, String,
  IQueryable(Of Customer)) =
  CompiledQuery.Compile(Of OrderITEntities, String,
    IQueryable(Of Customer))
      (Function(ctx, name) ctx.Companies
                        .OfType(Of Customer)()
```

```
                    .Where(Function(c) c.Name.StartsWith(name)
    )
)
```

The first generic parameter of the predicate *must* be the context, and the last represents the return type. Between those two, you can specify any parameters you need.

To use the query you just need to invoke the predicate, passing in the context and the string "C":

C#

```
var result = compQuery.Invoke(ctx, "C").ToList();
```

VB

```
Dim result = compQuery.Invoke(ctx, "C").ToList()
```

That's all you need to do to compile a LINQ to Entities query. As you can see, it's pretty simple. The Object Services layer takes care of compiling the query and reusing the compiled version after the first execution. When the Object Services layer looks for an existing compiled query, it uses the parameters too. This means that if you search for customers whose names start with *C* and then for customers whose names start with *A*, Object Services caches two command trees.

Despite their simplicity, compiled queries have some nasty internals that are worth mentioning.

COMPILED QUERY INTERNALS

The first thing to know about compiled queries is that nothing happens until they're executed. CompiledQuery.Invoke does nothing unless a ToList, ToArray, foreach, or Execute forces the query to execute.

Another aspect of compiled queries is that if you combine them with other LINQ to Entities operators, you lose all benefits: the entire query is recompiled. For instance, if you use the query in listing 19.8 and then attach the First operator, as shown here, the entire command is reparsed and nothing is reused:

C#

```
var result = compQuery.Invoke(ctx, "C").First();
```

VB

```
Dim result = compQuery.Invoke(ctx, "C").First()
```

To mitigate this problem, you can call the AsEnumerable method, as in the following snippet. It fetches data from the database and then uses LINQ to Object operators or creates a brand-new compiled query:

C#

```
var result = compQuery.Invoke(ctx, "C").AsEnumerable().First();
```

VB

```
Dim result = compQuery.Invoke(ctx, "C").AsEnumerable().First()
```

Things get trickier when MergeOption comes into play, because MergeOption is set at query level. This means that when the query is compiled, the merge option is saved along with the compiled version. After it's created, you can't change the merge option of a compiled query. The next piece of code shows what problems you might face:

C#
```
ctx1.Companies.MergeOption = MergeOption.NoTracking;
var c = compiledQuery(ctx1, "C").AsEnumerable().First();

ctx2.Companies.MergeOption = MergeOption.AppendOnly;
var c = compiledQuery(ctx2, "C").AsEnumerable().First();
```

VB
```
ctx1.Companies.MergeOption = MergeOption.NoTracking
var c = compiledQuery(ctx1, "C").AsEnumerable().First()

ctx2.Companies.MergeOption = MergeOption.AppendOnly
var c = compiledQuery(ctx2, "C").AsEnumerable().First()
```

In the first case, `MergeOption` is set to `NoTracking`, so the object is in the `Detached` state. In the second case, even if the merge option has changed, the state of the object remains `Detached` because the query was compiled with the `NoTracking` option. If you need to perform the same query with different merge options, it's best to create two separate predicates.

This is a nasty behavior, and it's likely to change in future versions. For the moment, you need to be aware of it so you can avoid the pitfalls.

19.4.3 Enabling plan caching for Entity SQL

When you execute an Entity SQL query, the Entity Client parses it and then saves it in a cache along with its counterpart in native SQL. The second time the query is executed, before it parses the query again, the Entity Client checks whether a copy already exists in the cache.

The check is based on the Entity SQL string and query parameters, and it's case sensitive. "SELECT VALUE ..." is different from "Select Value ...". If you create two queries like those, you'll end up with two different entries for the same query, and that's a waste of resources.

We strongly recommend choosing a convention so you can avoid that problem. For example, use uppercase for keywords and write object names using Pascal case, as in the following query:

```
SELECT VALUE c FROM OrderITEntities.Companies AS c
```

Plan caching is enabled by default, so you have it for free. Should you need to disable it, you can do so via the `EnablePlanCaching` property of the `ObjectSet<T>` and `EntityCommand` classes. Table 19.5 shows the benefits of having plan caching enabled.

Table 19.5 Entity SQL performance with plan caching enabled and disabled

Technology	Plan caching enabled	Plan caching disabled
Entity SQL via Object Services	9.66 ms	11.66 ms
Entity SQL via Entity Client	3.82 ms	4.84 ms

There's one last optimization to keep in mind, and it regards change tracking. Often you read objects but don't need to update them. Let's see how this scenario can be optimized.

19.4.4 Disabling tracking when it's not needed

When you display customers in a grid, you probably don't allow them to be modified. In such a scenario, change tracking is unnecessary, so you can disable it by setting the `MergeOption` of a query property to `MergeOption.NoTracking`.

This optimization lets object generation in the context skip many steps, and it has a dramatic impact on performance, as you can see in table 19.6.

Table 19.6   Performance with change tracking enabled and disabled (average)

Technology	Enabled	Disabled	Difference
ADO.NET	2.59	2.59 ms	—
LINQ to Entities (with compilation)	10.21 ms	3.44 ms	+32%
Entity SQL via Object Services	9.62 ms	3.33 ms	+28%

As you can see, disabling change tracking makes object generation much quicker. We strongly recommend removing change tracking from your application wherever it's unnecessary.

You have optimized a lot. For LINQ to Entities queries, you went from +530% to +32% greater time, as compared with ADO.NET. This is why we always suggest checking not only your SQL code but your Entity Framework code too. We have encountered many cases where the problem wasn't the SQL produced by Entity Framework, but the total, or sometimes partial, lack of code optimization.

Another area where you can make some optimizations is in stored-procedure execution. These types of queries are interesting, because they involve a different materialization process.

19.4.5 Optimizing stored procedures

You know that invoking a stored procedure triggers a different materialization mechanism. To cover the various cases, we created a stored procedure that returns all order details and invoked it from Object Services, Entity Client, and ADO.NET so we could compare the results, which are shown in table 19.7.

Table 19.7   Stored-procedure execution performance

Technology	Total	Average	Difference
ADO.NET	11 ms	0.22 ms	—
Object Services	23 ms	0.46 ms	+109%
Entity Client	19 ms	0.38 ms	+72%

As you may have expected, ADO.NET is faster than any other technique. What's interesting here is that Entity Framework isn't that much slower. If you compare these results with those in table 19.3, you'll see that the materialization mechanism used by stored procedures is much faster than that used for queries. We've used a table that contains less data here, but that's not the point. What we wanted to stress is the performance of the different materialization mechanisms.

You know that the methods added to the context for calling the stored procedures hide the internal call to the context's `ExecuteFunction<T>` method. This method has two overloads: the first accepts the function name and the parameters, and the second accepts both of those plus the `MergeOption`. The methods added to the context for calling stored procedures internally use only the first overload, so by default you have the `AppendOnly` behavior.

If you don't need change tracking for entities returned by the stored procedure, you can directly invoke the `ExecuteFunction<T>` method using the second overload and passing the `MergeOption.NoTracking` value, as shown in the next example:

C#
```
var parameters = CreateParameters();
var details = ctx.ExecuteFunction<OrderDetail>("GetDetails",
  MergeOption.NoTracking, parameters);
```

VB
```
Dim parameters = CreateParameters()
Dim details = ctx.ExecuteFunction(Of OrderDetail)("GetDetails",
  MergeOption.NoTracking, parameters)
```

Even better, you can modify the template that generates the context to create two overloads for each stored procedure, so you don't have to manually invoke the `ExecuteFunction<T>` method. (This book's source code contains such a template.)

There's nothing more to add about performance. Now you know what the bottlenecks are, what you can do to avoid common pitfalls, and, most important, what you can do to make database access via Entity Framework much quicker. It's not as fast as ADO.NET, but it surely makes your life easier.

19.5   Summary

Performance is a key point of almost any data-driven application. If you're developing a simple catalog for your DVD collection, performance probably won't even cross your mind; but in enterprise applications with lots of clients and lots of queries, you can't ignore it.

Entity Framework was built with one eye always on performance. Almost every aspect of it has been optimized or made a target for an opt-in optimization. Plan caching and LINQ to Entities query compilation are great examples of opt-in optimizations. Unfortunately, generated SQL isn't always as good as you might like, but you can resort to stored procedures and live happily.

Always remember these golden rules: check the SQL with a profiler, use compiled LINQ to Entities queries, and disable change tracking as much as possible. That's your take-away.

Congratulations! You've reached the end of the book. It's been a long journey, but now you have a solid understanding of Entity Framework. You can develop an application using Entity Framework and solve most of the problems you're likely to encounter.

appendix A:
Understanding LINQ

You're likely already familiar with the various C# and Visual Basic language innovations and their importance in bringing LINQ to life. But if you haven't come across LINQ yet, this appendix will introduce you to the project and enumerate its advantages, its requirements in terms of language modifications, and its vision. This is important, because the main query language in Entity Framework is LINQ to Entities, which in the end is a LINQ *dialect*. Having a solid knowledge of LINQ's foundations will help you understanding LINQ to Entities queries.

In the first part of this appendix, we'll cover the reasons why the Microsoft architects decided to embed query extensions into the language, and the broad vision of the LINQ platform. After that, we'll introduce the features that have made LINQ a success. These features are the language innovations that have been introduced in C# 3.0 and VB 9. There are lots of innovations to cover, so this will be a long discussion.

By the end of the appendix, you'll be able to fully understand and write any LINQ query.

A.1   Why was LINQ created?

Each data technology has its own language for performing queries. Data from databases can be pulled out using SQL commands; XML data can be retrieved using the XPath syntax; even Active Directory and ADO.NET `DataTable` information can be accessed using their own syntaxes.

Whatever the data source is, retrieving data requires that you have specific knowledge of its query language and related .NET framework classes, as shown in figure A.1. Although this is an obvious consequence of adopting different technologies, a common way of retrieving data is still desirable.

LINQ bridges this gap between data technologies and code development by providing a set of common extensions that can be used to query any data source.

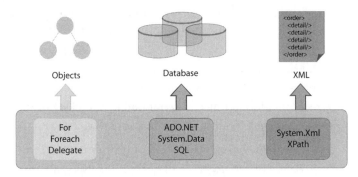

Figure A.1 Searching data from different sources without LINQ requires a wide knowledge of retrieval methods.

These extensions aren't related to a specific data technology but can be used across all of them, creating a unique language for all data sources.

Another point that makes LINQ a great innovation is its way of shaping query results. When you retrieve data from a database, they're returned in `DataTable` or `DbDataReader` objects. The same happens for XML data, which is represented as `Xml-Node` objects.

The search for a common coding style can't ignore such diversity. Not only does LINQ enable a brand-new opportunity for standardizing the query language, but it also returns the results of a query in a single well-known format: in *objects*. This is another significant step toward flattening the data access differences, as figure A.2 illustrates.

The real power of LINQ lies in its extensibility. Versions 1.0 and 1.1 of the .NET Framework class library had many features that were provided as black boxes, where you couldn't plug in or modify any behavior. Fortunately, lots of things have changed since version 2.0, and one of the guidelines has become *extensibility*. For instance, the *provider model* was introduced so that you can change the underlying behavior of a feature without touching its interface. And many classes that were sealed have been opened for inheritance, offering developers much more flexibility and freedom.

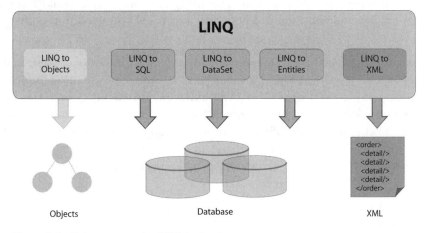

Figure A.2 Data access using LINQ technology

The current version of the .NET Framework class library has continued this trend, and LINQ has a provider-based architecture that allows you to write providers to query any data source. .NET Framework 3.5 introduced four *flavors* of LINQ:

- *LINQ to Objects*—Queries in-memory lists of objects
- *LINQ to XML*—Queries XML files or in-memory structures
- *LINQ to SQL*—Queries the domain model generated by the LINQ to SQL O/RM
- *LINQ to DataSet*—Queries data in all the `DataTables` of a `DataSet`

The evidence of LINQ's extensibility lies in the myriad of providers that have been created to query any data source. Further proof is the LINQ to Entities provider, which enables you to query models based on Entity Framework.

LINQ has also introduced a conceptual change. When you write a LINQ query, you express what you want to retrieve, but you don't specify how to do that. That's a big shift for .NET languages, because for the first time, they introduce some of the functional programming concepts. When you perform a SQL query, for example, you have no idea of how the database will execute it; you just state what you want, and leave the search to the internal system. The same thing happens with LINQ.

To make this concept clearer, look at the following snippet:

C#
```
var result = from o in orders
             where o.OrderDate.Date == DateTime.Now.Date
             select o;
```

VB
```
Dim result = From o in orders _
             Where o.OrderDate.Date = DateTime.Now.Date
```

This query filters orders, returning only those placed today. You don't specify anything about the retrieval method, and you don't know how LINQ will perform it.

> **NOTE** LINQ uses a simple in-memory loop over the orders, but that's completely hidden from you. The LINQ implementation could change one day, and you wouldn't notice it, nor would you need to modify the code.

The LINQ technology has its foundations in language innovations. Most of the new features that have shown up in C# 3.0 and VB 9 are there because LINQ requires them. In this appendix, we'll provide a brief introduction to LINQ and the language improvements, but you can find plenty of books and online material that discuss this in great detail. For further information, we strongly recommend the book *LINQ in Action* by Fabrice Marguerie, Steve Eichert, and Jim Wooley (Manning, 2007).

The advent of LINQ brought about improvements in the following areas:

- Type inference
- Extension methods
- Lambda expressions
- Object initializers

- Anonymous types
- Query syntax

We'll look at these topics in the following sections.

A.2 Type inference

Type inference is the new ability of the compiler to understand the type of an object without you having to explicitly declare it. To let you declare a variable without specifying the type, C# offers the var keyword. VB doesn't need a new keyword, because it already has one that can be used for the same purpose: Dim. The compiler automatically infers the type of the variable from the expression used to initialize it.

In C# it's mandatory to initialize a variable; otherwise, the compiler wouldn't be able to understand the type automatically and would throw a compile-time exception. In VB, a variable that isn't initialized becomes of type Object. The following listing shows this behavior.

Listing A.1 How type inference understands an object's type

C#
```
string s = "Hello";          ❶ Declares
int i = 10;                     variable's type

var s = "Hello";      ❷ Infers variable's
var i = 10;             type from initializer   ❸ Throws compile
                                                   time error
var x = null;
```

VB
```
Dim s as string = "Hello"     ❶ Declares
Dim i as int = 10;              variable's type

Dim s = "Hello";      ❷ Infers variable's
Dim i = 10;             type from initializer   ❹ Sets variable's
                                                   type to Object
Dim x = null;
```

The code generated by the compiler is exactly the same for the first two blocks of each of these snippets ❶ ❷, because it infers the types from the values assigned to the variables when they're declared. The x variable declaration in C# ❸ throws an exception because it's initialized to null, so the type can't be inferred. The x variable declaration in VB ❹ is valid because the type of the x variable is Object.

In C#, using the var keyword comes in handy when you have to declare a complex type with many generic declarations, as in the following code:

```
Dictionary<string, Dictionary<int, Order>> variable = new
  Dictionary<string, Dictionary<int, Order>>();
```

Repeating the type for such a long piece of code is at least annoying. Using var allows you to write the type only once, in the assignment part of the statement:

```
var variable = new Dictionary<string, Dictionary<int, Order>>();
```

In addition to making your code smaller, var can also make it less readable. C# developers are used to seeing the type of a variable at the beginning of the declaration.

Cluttering the code with var forces developers to read the full statement to determine the variable's type, and some developers argue that this is a waste of time. Apart from a few cases that you'll see later in this appendix, using var or declaring the variable type is a matter of personal taste.

> **NOTE**   Be aware that the var keyword in C# has nothing to do with the var keyword in JavaScript. The var keyword in C# allows neither late binding nor VB variant-like features.

We've only scratched the surface of type inference. As you'll see in the next sections (in particular, when we talk about lambda expressions), this feature allows you to cut even more code than you've seen so far.

A.3   *Extension methods*

An *extension method* is a method that's defined in a class but is invoked using another class to which it's attached by the compiler. This definition might seem a bit awkward, but the use of extension methods will be clear enough when we look at some examples.

Suppose you have a list of orders, and you want to serialize those created on a specified date in JSON format. Without using extension methods, the only way to go is to write a method that accepts the orders as input and iterates over them, serializing those that correspond to the requirement, and returning the JSON string when the iteration is done. The code would look like this.

Listing A.2   Creating and using a helper method without extension methods

C#
```
namespace EFInaction.Common
{
  public static class Utilities
  {
    public static string SerializeOrders(List<Order> orders, DateTime date)
    {
      JavaScriptSerializer serializer = new JavaScriptSerializer();
      StringBuilder builder = new StringBuilder();
      foreach(var order in orders)
      {
        if (order.OrderDate.Date == date.Date)
          builder.Append(serializer.Serialize(order));
      }
      return builder.ToString();
    }
  }
}

namespace EFInaction.UI
{
  ...
  List<Order> orders = ctx.Order.ToList();
  string serializedOrders = Utilities.SerializeOrders(orders, DateTime.Now);
  ...
}
```

```vb
VB
Namespace EFInAction.Common
  Class Utilities
    Public Shared Function SerializeOrders( _
      ByVal orders As List(Of Order), _
      ByVal now As DateTime) As String
      Dim serializer As New JavaScriptSerializer()
      Dim builder As New StringBuilder()
      For Each order In orders
        If order.OrderDate.Date = now.Date Then
          builder.Append(serializer.Serialize(order))
        End If
      Next
      Return builder.ToString()
    End Function
  End Class
End Namespace

Namespace EFInAction.UI
  ...
  Dim orders = ctx.Order.ToList()
  Dim serializedOrders = EFInAction.Common.Utilities.SerializeOrders( _
    orders, DateTime.Now)
  ...
End Namespace
```

The code in listing A.2 is fine, except that the caller code has to resort to calling another class to perform steps that are closely related to the orders. Wouldn't you feel more comfortable if you could invoke the SerializeOrders method using the orders instance instead the Utilities class?

By using extension methods, you can invoke SerializeOrders on the orders instance even if the method is defined in another class, as is demonstrated in the following listing. This is a modified version of listing A.2.

Listing A.3 Creating and using a helper method with extension methods

```csharp
C#
public static string SerializeOrders(            ❶ Extension
  this List<Order> orders, DateTime date)          method
{ ... }                                            declaration

using EFInAction.Common;                         ❷ Extension
                                                   method import

string serializedOrders =                        ❸ Extension method
  orders.SerializeOrders(DateTime.Now);            invocation
```

```vb
VB
<System.Runtime.CompilerServices.Extension()> _   ❶ Extension
Public Function SerializeOrders(                   method
  ByVal orders As List(Of Order), _                declaration
  ByVal now As DateTime) As String
  ...
End Function

using EFInAction.Common;                          ❷ Extension
                                                   method import

string serializedOrders =                         ❸ Extension method
  orders.SerializeOrders(DateTime.Now)             invocation
```

In the method declaration ❶, you have to indicate what type the method must be attached to. In VB, this is accomplished by specifying in the first parameter the class that's extended, and adding the Extension attribute to the method. In C#, you only need to add the this keyword before the extended type without using any attribute. If the method accepts other parameters, they must be added after the first parameter; if the type isn't first, you'll get a compile-time error. There is one caveat in both languages: in VB, an extension method can be defined only in a module; and in C#, it must be defined in a static class, and the method must be static too.

In the caller code, the first thing you have to do is to add a using statement for C# (Imports for VB) ❷ to import the namespace that contains the class that declares the extension method. Without that, the compiler can't detect the class and can't apply the extension method. As shown in figure A.3, Visual Studio offers autocompletion for extension methods; but if you don't use the using or Imports keyword, they don't even appear in the autocompletion list.

The second change you have to apply to the caller code is to invoke the extension method from the orders object ❸. The parameters for the method must be modified too. The parameter for the extended class must be omitted, and only those that come after it should be included.

To enable extension methods in LINQ, you must add the System.LINQ namespace to the class. This namespace contains the Enumerable class, which in turn contains all the LINQ extension methods.

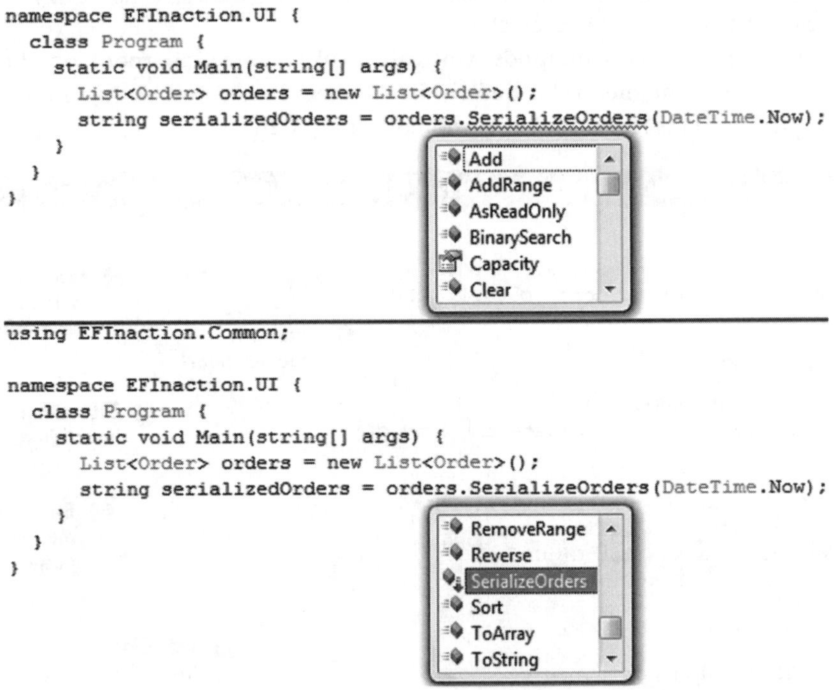

```
namespace EFInaction.UI {
  class Program {
    static void Main(string[] args) {
      List<Order> orders = new List<Order>();
      string serializedOrders = orders.SerializeOrders(DateTime.Now);
    }
  }
}
```

Add
AddRange
AsReadOnly
BinarySearch
Capacity
Clear

```
using EFInaction.Common;

namespace EFInaction.UI {
  class Program {
    static void Main(string[] args) {
      List<Order> orders = new List<Order>();
      string serializedOrders = orders.SerializeOrders(DateTime.Now);
    }
  }
}
```

RemoveRange
Reverse
SerializeOrders
Sort
ToArray
ToString

Figure A.3   Visual Studio autocompletion without and with the using statement

In section A.1, we said that LINQ was been conceived as a set of extensions to the VB and C# languages for querying any data source. At the highest level, you can think about LINQ as a set of extension methods that you can use to perform queries. Table A.1 lists all the LINQ methods grouped by type.

Table A.1 LINQ methods grouped by type

Type	Methods
Projection	`Select, SelectMany`
Filtering	`Where`
Sorting	`OrderBy, OrderByDescending, Reverse`
Grouping	`GroupBy`
Set	`Distinct, Union, Intersect, Except`
Generation	`Range, Repeat, Empty`
Conditional	`Any, All, Contains`
Element	`Last, LastOrDefault, ElementAt, ElementAtOrDefault, First, FirstOrDefault, Single, SingleOrDefault, SequenceEqual, DefaultIfEmpty`
Paging	`Take, TakeWhile, Skip, SkipWhile`
Aggregation	`Count, LongCount, Sum, Min, Max, Average, Aggregate`

What's great about LINQ methods is that they enable the fluent technique so they can be combined in a single statement.

A.3.1 *Method chaining*

The power of extension methods becomes clear when you combine them to perform a more complex query. Suppose you have to sort the orders before serializing them. You could perform this operation in the `SerializeOrders` method, but if you also need to sort orders in other parts of your application, this isn't the most convenient approach.

This is the optimal solution:

1 Create an extension method that sorts the orders and returns the ordered list.
2 Invoke the `SerializeOrders` method to serialize the objects.

With this approach, you achieve the goal of code reuse. Because the sorting method returns a list of orders, you can invoke the `SerializeOrders` method on it in the same line of code (which is why this technique is named method chaining). Here's an example:

C#

```
var x = orders.Sort().SerializeOrders(DateTime.Now);
```

VB

```
Dim x = orders.Sort().SerializeOrders(DateTime.Now)
```

LINQ offers a wide range of extension methods. Most of the methods extend the `IEnumerable<T>` interface, which is directly or indirectly implemented by all generic lists in the .NET Framework, enabling query capabilities on any set of objects. Because most of the methods return an `IEnumerable<T>` instance, method chaining is a common pattern when writing LINQ queries.

Now that you know how LINQ enables method chaining, let's discuss how extension methods are evaluated by the compiler.

A.3.2　*Method evaluation*

When you design an extension method, you have to know how the compiler evaluates the calls to it. Let's start with an example.

> **Listing A.4　A set of extension methods that add methods to different classes**

C#

```
public static class Extensions
{
  public static string ExtMethod(this List<Order> orders)
  {
    return "Method on List<Order>";
  }

  public static string ExtMethod(this IEnumerable<Order> orders)
  {
    return "Method on IEnumerable<Order>";
  }

  public static string ExtMethod<T>(this List<T> orders)
  {
    return "Method on generic List";
  }
}
```

VB

```
Module Extensions
  <Extension()> _
  Public Function ExtMethod(ByVal orders As List(Of Order)) As String
    Return "Method on List<Of Order>"
  End Function

  <Extension()> _
  Public Function ExtMethod(ByVal orders As IEnumerable(
    Of Order)) As String
    Return "Method on IEnumerable<Of Order>"
  End Function

  <Extension()> _
  Public Function ExtMethod(Of T)(ByVal orders As List(Of T)) As String
    Return "Method on generic List"
  End Function
End Module
```

The class in listing A.4 contains three extension methods that extend three different classes. Let's see how the compiler resolves the calls, starting with the following code:

C#
```
List<Order> o1 = new List<Order>();
var x = o1.ExtMethod();
```

VB
```
Dim o1 as New List(Of Order)
Dim x = o1.ExtMethod()
```

All of the extension methods in listing A.4 are suitable for being executed by the call to the `o1.ExtMethod` in the preceding example, but only one is actually executed. To identify the method that must be executed, the compiler checks the object to be extended and uses the one closest to the variable definition of the object in the calling code, starting from the bottom of the inheritance hierarchy.

In this case, because the `o1` variable is of type `List<Order>` and the first extension method extends that type, it's the one that's attached.

Now let's see what method is invoked by the next snippet:

C#
```
IEnumerable<Order> o2 = new List<Order>();
var x2 = o2.Method();
```

VB
```
Dim o2 as IEnumerable(Of Order) = New List(Of Order)()
Dim x2 = o2.Method()
```

Here you have a situation where the real object is `List<Order>`, but it's put into an `IEnumerable<Order>` variable. As we've said, the compiler uses the variable declaration, so in this case the second extension method of listing A.4 is invoked even if the first would be more appropriate.

Here's one more example:

C#
```
List<Company> o3 = new List<Company>();
var x3 = o3.Method();
```

VB
```
Dim o1 as New List(Of Company)
Dim x3 = o3.Method()
```

Here, the second and the third methods of listing A.4 would be suitable; but because `List<T>` is lower in the inheritance hierarchy, the third method is used by the compiler.

> **NOTE** All of this method resolution is resolved at compile time. There's nothing dynamic at runtime.

As you learned in chapter 4, this resolution pattern turns out to be useful when writing LINQ to Entities queries that use other LINQ standard operators.

A.4   Lambda expressions

A lambda expression is the evolution of the anonymous method feature introduced in .NET 2.0. It's difficult to explain what a lambda expression is, so we'll discuss it using examples and comparisons with its predecessor.

A.4.1   Anonymous methods

Before digging into the lambda expression world, let's start with the beginning. In .NET 1.0, the only way to execute a piece of code was to create a method like the following one.

Listing A.5   A method that searches orders by date

C#
```
OrderCollection GetOrdersByDate(OrderCollection orders, DateTime date)
{
  OrderCollection result = new OrderCollection();
  foreach(Order order in orders)
  {
    if (order.OrderDate.Date == date.Date)
    {
      result.Add(order);
    }
  }
  return result;
}
```

VB
```
Private Function GetOrdersByDate(ByVal orders As OrderCollection, _
  ByVal theDate As DateTime) As OrderCollection
    Dim result As New OrderCollection()
    For Each order As Order In orders
        If order.OrderDate.Date = theDate.Date Then
            result.Add(order)
        End If
    Next
    Return result
End Function
```

Likely, you're quite comfortable with the code in listing A.5 and see no problems with it, and indeed there aren't any. But with the advent of .NET 2.0 and its anonymous methods, there is a lot that can be optimized in this code.

After refactoring to use the new features, the code from listing A.5 looks like this.

Listing A.6   Searching orders by date using anonymous methods

C#
```
DateTime date = DateTime.Today;
List<Order> result = orders.Find(delegate (Order order)
  {
    return order.OrderDate.Date == date.Date;
  }
```

```
);
```

VB

```
Dim theDate As DateTime = DateTime.Today;
Dim result As List(Of Order) = orders.Find(Function(ByVal order As Order) _
  order.OrderDate.Date = theDate.Date)
```

The amount of code you need to write is reduced a lot. The Find method handles most of the plumbing code in the previous version, as it iterates over the items and automatically passes each one to the code expressed in form of a *predicate.*

The predicate is the piece of code you put into the Find method. It decides whether the current object must be included in the result or not. The predicate lets you express the filter that must be applied; in the end, the filter is the only thing you should care about.

This syntax is far more concise than the original in listing A.5, but it still suffers from some verbosity because there was no type inference in the C# 2.0 compiler. For instance, because the list contains Order instances, there's no point in repeating this in the predicate. C# 3.0 adds type inference, but instead of improving anonymous methods, the team opted to include a brand-new feature called *lambda expressions.*

A.4.2   *From anonymous methods to lambda expressions*

Now that you've had a quick refresher on coding before .NET 3.5, you're ready to dive into lambda expressions and understand their logic. Let's start by refactoring the example in listing A.6 using lambda expressions like in figure A.4.

There's probably no way you can write less code than what you see in figure A.4. The syntax is different from what you were used to in previous versions of C# and VB. The left part of the statement (the part before the = sign) uses the type inference to understand the output of the right part of the statement (the part after the = sign). It's not mandatory to use type inference here because you know exactly what the type of the output is: IEnumerable<Order>. That means you can replace var with the concrete type.

Where is a LINQ extension method that filters the list on the basis of the statement that's passed as input. The statement that the method receives in input is the lambda expression.

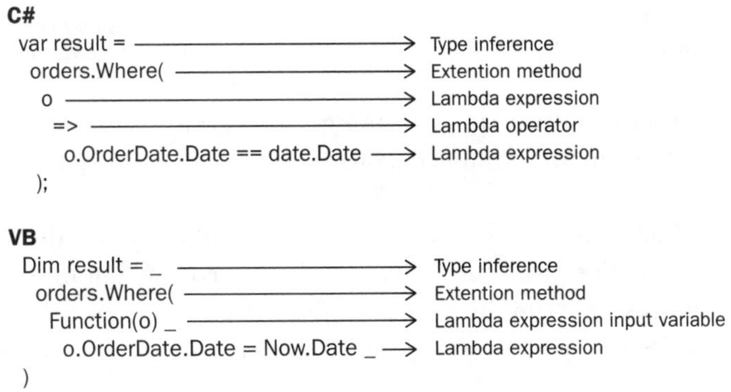

C#

```
var result = ──────────────────→  Type inference
orders.Where( ─────────────────→  Extention method
  o ───────────────────────────→  Lambda expression
    => ─────────────────────────→  Lambda operator
      o.OrderDate.Date == date.Date ──→  Lambda expression
);
```

VB

```
Dim result = _ ────────────────→  Type inference
orders.Where( ─────────────────→  Extention method
  Function(o) _ ────────────────→  Lambda expression input variable
    o.OrderDate.Date = Now.Date _ ─→  Lambda expression
)
```

Figure A.4   The structure of a LINQ query that uses a lambda expression

NOTE   Sometimes LINQ extensions methods are also referred to as *operators* or *clauses.*

In C#, a lambda expression is formed by two main blocks separated by the lambda operator. The left block declares the input parameters for the lambda expression. You don't have to explicitly set the type of the parameter because the compiler relies once again on type inference to correctly identify it. Because the list that must be filtered contains `Order` instances, in this case, the input variable type (`o`) is of type `Order`. If the lambda expression accepts more than one parameter, they must be separated using a comma, and the left part must be surrounded by brackets, as in the following snippet:

```
var result = orders.Where((o, i) => o.OrderDate.Date == date.Date && i
  > 10);
```

The block at the right of the lambda operator contains the lambda expression that's applied to each object to determine whether it should be included in the result. The difference between the lambda expression–based code and the anonymous method–based code is that the `return` keyword is omitted. The C# team has enabled you to omit the `return` keyword to further reduce code.

In VB, the lambda expression is introduced by the `Function` keyword and includes the parameters in parentheses. Furthermore, unlike in C#, the lambda operator doesn't exist. The rest of the syntax matches the C# syntax.

To fully understand lambda expressions, let's look at how a method that accepts a lambda expression is declared using the `Where` method as an example.

Listing A.7   Anatomy of an extension method

C#
```
public static IEnumerable<TSource>  Where<TSource> (
  this IEnumerable<TSource> source,
  Func<TSource, bool> predicate
)
```
❶ **Lambda expression declaration**

VB
```
<Extension> _
Public Shared Function _
  Where(Of TSource)(
    ByVal source As IEnumerable(Of TSource),
    ByVal predicate As Func(Of TSource, Boolean))
As IEnumerable(Of TSource)
```
❶ **Lambda expression declaration**

As you can see, `Where` is a function, so the first thing you need to do is declare the output type. Because the `Where` method filters data without modifying it, its return type is the same as its input.

The `Where` method accepts a generic parameter that is the type of the elements contained in the collection the `Where` method filters. The predicate parameter ❶ represents the lambda expression. `Func` is a class of the .NET Framework that lets you declare a delegate concisely. It accepts from 2 to 17 generic parameters. Regardless of how many parameters you use, the last parameter represents the output type and the others are input types. In this example, `TSource` is the input type (`Order`), and `bool` is the result of the expression.

Now that you have a clear understanding of lambda expressions, we can move on to another interesting feature: object initializers.

A.5 *Object initializers*

When you have to instantiate an object and initialize its properties, you have two methods at your disposal. If the class provides a constructor that accepts properties to initialize values, you can use that. Alternatively, you can use one of the other constructors and initialize the properties one by one, as shown here:

C#
```
Order o = new Order();
o.Id = 1;
o.Address = "5th Street, 234";
```

VB
```
Dim o as New Order()
o.Id = 1
o.Address = "5th Street, 234"
```

Writing code like this is tedious and redundant. In .NET Framework 3.5, the C# and VB teams introduced *object initializers*. An object initializer allows you to instantiate an object and set its properties in a single statement. With object initializers, you can drastically reduce the number of lines of code with a convenient syntax:

C#
```
Order o = new Order { Id = 1, Address = "5th Street, 234" };
```

VB
```
Dim o As New Order With { .Id = 1, .Address = "5th Street, 234" }
```

When the compiler intercepts the preceding statement, it generates the same code created by the previous snippet. Both approaches produce the same result with exactly the same performance.

> **NOTE** By using tools like Reflector, this matching performance can be easily verified. If you look, you'll see that both examples produce the same IL code. Because Reflector relies on IL to regenerate original code, if you switch to C# or VB view, you'll see that the code looks like the first snippet in this section.

By default, the compiler uses the constructor with no parameters to instantiate the class. If that constructor isn't available, you'll have to use one of the available constructors and then open the curly brackets to set the properties, as in the following code:

C#
```
Order o = new Order(1) { Address = "5th Street, 234" };
```

VB
```
Dim o As New Order(1) With { .Address = "5th Street, 234" }
```

The object initializers offer a practical syntax and are very useful. But the real reason for their introduction is that they lay the foundation for the anonymous types feature.

A.6   *Anonymous types*

The *anonymous types* feature enables you to create objects without declaring a class beforehand. Because the newly created object doesn't have a class, the var keyword is the only way to declare it, and the object initializers offer the syntax to create properties.

Here's an example:

C#

```
var x = new { Id = 1, Address = "5th Street" };
```

VB

```
Dim x = New With {.Id = 1, .Address = "5th Street"}
```

The x variable contains an instance of a class with two properties: Id and Address. The types of the properties are automatically inferred using type inference.

One point must be clear when dealing with anonymous types: anonymous types can't be used to generate types dynamically. The types are generated by the compiler during compilation, so nothing is dynamic at runtime.

Figure A.5 shows how the class created in the previous snippet is generated by the compiler.

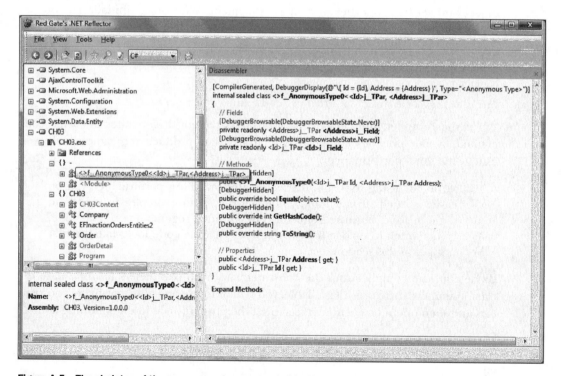

Figure A.5   The skeleton of the anonymous type generated by the compiler

Anonymous types suffer from some nasty limitations:

- *The object has the scope of the method where it's generated.* When you instantiate an anonymous object, it doesn't have an explicit type that can be specified as input or output for other methods. The name is generated only at compile time, so there's no way to use it outside the method that generated it.
- *In C#, the object is immutable.* The type in figure A.5 shows a peculiarity of anonymous types in C#. When the compiler generates the properties of an anonymous type, only their getter methods are created. As a result, any instance of this anonymous type can't be modified after it has been created.

Object initializers and anonymous types are part of the foundation of LINQ. Their combined use allows you to process a list with a defined source and return another list made of other objects generated with data from the input source. As a result, these features enable projections like the one in the following snippet:

C#
```
var x = orders.Select(o => new { o.OrderId, o.ShippingAddress });
```

VB
```
Dim x = orders.Select(Function(o) New With { .o.OrderId, _
    o.ShippingAddress })
```

Here the `Select` method is used to make a projection that creates a list containing anonymous objects with the ID and shipping address.

Writing LINQ queries is easy with the features we've looked at so far, but there's another way of doing it. Because almost all developers know the SQL language, LINQ has a set of statements that allows you to write queries using a SQL-like syntax.

A.7 Query syntax

The last LINQ-related improvement made to the C# and VB languages is the query syntax. This particular feature avoids using extension methods and lambda expressions and instead offers a syntax closer to SQL. Here's an example:

C#
```
var x = from o in orders
        where o.OrderDate.Date == DateTime.Now.Date
        select o;
```

VB
```
Dim x = From o In orders
        Where o.OrderDate.Date = DateTime.Now.Date
```

Although there are significant differences between this and the SQL language, this way of writing queries is far more readable than the combination of extension methods and lambdas.

> **NOTE** The most noticeable difference between SQL and this query syntax is the position of the `select` clause. It's at the end for autocompletion purposes. Specifying the `from` clause at the beginning allows Visual

Studio to provide autocompletion for all the following clauses. Except for a grouping query, the select clause is mandatory for query syntax in C#; for VB, it's optional and implicitly returns the type specified in the from clause.

The query syntax is pure *syntactic sugar* because at compile time the code is converted to use extension methods and lambda expressions.

You have to keep in mind that the query syntax doesn't cover all that the LINQ extension methods offer. If you need to use a method that isn't supported by the query syntax, you'll have to resort to extension methods and lambda expressions. Furthermore, VB and C# support different keywords, so there are many differences between the languages.

A.8   Deferred execution

LINQ is lazy by nature. If you start the debugger and execute a query block, you aren't really executing anything. Although this may seem strange, it's pretty obvious in a lazy environment. When you execute a query, you aren't using its result unless you invoke a method that forces result creation. The LINQ query gets executed only when you fetch the data it returns, such as when you use a foreach, use a for, refer to an object in a list by index, or invoke methods like ToList, ToArray, First, Single, and so on.

The following listing contains some examples of query execution.

Listing A.8   Deferred and immediate execution of a LINQ query

C#
```
var res = from o in orders
          where o.Customer.CompanyId == 1         Nothing happens
          select c;
...
foreach (var order in res){                       Query is
   ...                                             evaluated
}
var res2 = (from o in orders
          where o.Customer.CompanyId == 1          Query is
          select c).ToList();                      immediately evaluated
```

VB
```
Dim res = From o In orders
          Where o.Customer.CompanyId = 1           Nothing happens
...
For Each order in res                              Query is
   ...                                             evaluated
Next

Dim res2 = (From o In orders
          Where o.Customer.CompanyId = 1).ToList()  Query is
                                                     immediately evaluated
```

When using LINQ to objects, you may not spot the difference; but when you're using LINQ to Entities, knowing this behavior may spare lots of resources, as you learned in chapter 3 when we talked about inadvertent query execution.

A.8.1 Runtime query composition

Deferred execution is important because it enables scenarios where you compose a query in different steps. Often, queries aren't fixed but are created depending on runtime conditions.

Consider a search form that accepts many optional parameters. The search condition isn't fixed because the optional parameters aren't determined. This requires a set of conditional statements and the construction of a query based on data the user enters. The following listing shows an example of this.

> **Listing A.9 Composing a query at runtime**

C#

```
var result = orders.AsQueryable();

if (year.Text != String.Empty)
  result = result.Where(o => o.OrderDate.Year ==
    Convert.ToInt32(year.Text));

if (companyName.Text != String.Empty)
  result = result.Where(o => o.Company.Name.StartsWith(companyName.Text));

var data = result.ToList();
```

VB

```
Dim result = orders.AsQueryable()

If year.Text <> String.Empty Then
  result = result.Where(Function(o) o.OrderDate.Year = _
    Convert.ToInt32(year.Text))
End If

If companyName.Text <> String.Empty
  result = result.Where(Function(o) _
    o.Company.Name.StartsWith(companyName.Text))

Dim data = result.ToList()
```

This feature is another main piece of the LINQ architecture that you have to keep in mind while writing queries.

appendix B:
Entity Framework
tips and tricks

Mastering Entity Framework doesn't only mean knowing its set of APIs and their internal behavior. It also means finding the best ways to use it and to simplify development. This appendix is all about that.

We won't cover a specific subject here; we'll touch on various subjects, offering tips and tricks that couldn't be included in previous chapters. Here you'll find a set of classes and extension methods that let you write less code, making that code more readable and easier to maintain.

You'll read about an extension method for simplifying the process of attaching entities, you'll learn how to perform specific actions once an entity is persisted on the database, and you'll discover how to perform full-text searches. You'll also see how to transform some string-based methods to lambda-based methods (such as Include and SetModifiedProperty), and much more.

Let's start with a smarter way to attach entities to the context.

B.1   A smart way of attaching entities

In chapter 12, you created an extension method that, using EDM and a bit of reflection, adds or attaches an entity to the context depending on the value of the entity's key property. When the entity is attached, it goes to the Unchanged state, and you then need to modify a property or use context or state manager methods to mark it as Modified or Deleted.

If you know what the entity state should be after it's attached, wouldn't it be better to set it immediately in the same call?

B.1.1   *Attaching an entity as Modified or Deleted*

To mark the entity as Modified or Deleted, you need to call the ChangeState method immediately after attaching the entity to the context. You've seen this several times in the book.

But to specify whether you want the entity to be marked as Modified, you need to pass a new parameter to the SmartAttach method, whose signature is as follows:

C#
```
public static void SmartAttach<T>(this ObjectSet<T> os, T input,
    AttachState state)
```

VB
```
Public Shared Sub SmartAttach(Of T)(os As ObjectSet(Of T), input As T,
    state As AttachState)
```

The state parameter is of type AttachState. It's an enum that specifies what state the entity must be set to after it has been attached. These are its values:

- Unchanged—The entity remains unchanged
- Modified—The entity is changed to Modified state
- Deleted—The entity is changed to Deleted state

This way, you can set the state of the entity using the code in the following listing. (We haven't included the first part of the method here, but you can find it in chapter 12.)

> **Listing B.1   Marking the entity as Modified or Deleted after attaching it**

C#
```
if (id.Equals(Convert.ChangeType(value, idType)))
  os.AddObject(input);
else
{
  os.Attach(input);
  var entry = set.Context.ObjectStateManager.GetObjectStateEntry(input);
  if (state == AttachState.Modified)
    entry.ChangeState(EntityState.Modified);
  else if (state == AttachState.Deleted)
    entry.ChangeState(EntityState.Deleted);
}
```

VB
```
If id.Equals(Convert.ChangeType(value, idType)) Then
  os.AddObject(input)
Else
  os.Attach(input)
  Dim entry = os.Context.ObjectStateManager.GetObjectStateEntry(input)
  If state = AttachState.Modified Then
    entry.ChangeState(EntityState.Modified)
  ElseIf state = AttachState.Deleted Then
    entry.ChangeState(EntityState.Deleted)
  End If
End If
```

This method is pretty cool. Now you can attach an entity to the context and have it marked as Modified or Deleted in a single call. (The same method can be used to add an entity too, in which case the state parameter is ignored.) The following snippet marks the entity as Modified:

C#
```
ctx.Orders.SmartAttach(order, AttachState.Modified);
```

VB
```
ctx.Orders.SmartAttach(order, AttachState.Modified)
```

But that's not enough. You know that when you use the ChangeState method to mark an entity as Modified, not only does ChangeState mark the entity, but it also marks all the entity's properties as Modified. Sometimes you don't want to mark all the properties, just some of them. In that case, you need to use the SetModifiedProperty method of the state-manager entry.

B.1.2 *Modifying only selected properties after attaching*

The SetModifiedProperty method is as useful as it is badly designed, because it accepts the property name as a string. Thanks to lambda expressions, we're living in the strong-typing age. Why not create a new overload of the SetModifiedProperty method that accepts a lambda?

Take a look at this listing.

Listing B.2 Strongly typed extension method for marking a property as Modified

C#
```
public static ObjectStateEntry SetModifiedProperty<T>(
  this ObjectStateEntry entry, Expression<Func<T, object>> expression)
{
  var body = expression.Body as MemberExpression;
  if (body == null) throw new ArgumentException("expr must be a        ◁  Extracts
    memberexpression");                                                   property
                                                                      ❶ name
  entry.SetModifiedProperty(body.Member.Name);                     ◁
  return entry;
}                                                                      Sets property
                                                                   ❷ as modified
```

VB
```
<System.Runtime.CompilerServices.Extension> _
Public Shared Function SetModifiedProperty(Of T)(entry As ObjectStateEntry,
  expression As Expression(Of Func(Of T, Object))) As ObjectStateEntry
  Dim body = TryCast(expression.Body,
    MemberExpression)
                                                                      Extracts
  If body Is Nothing Then                                             property
    Throw New ArgumentException("expr must be a memberexpression")  ❶ name
  End If

  entry.SetModifiedProperty(body.Member.Name)                     ◁
  Return entry                                                         Sets property
End Function                                                        ❷ as modified
```

This extension method accepts a lambda expression that specifies the property name. It then extracts the property name as a string ❶ and passes it to the string-based Set-ModifiedProperty method ❷. Now you can use the following code to call the method:

C#
```
entry.SetModifiedProperty(o => o.ShippingAddress);
```

VB
```
entry.SetModifiedProperty(Function(o) o.ShippingAddress)
```

The code in the previous listing can't be included in the SmartAttach method because it's a generic method that must handle any type of entity. You must enable the caller of the SmartAttach method to specify which properties must be marked for update.

To do that, you need to add another parameter to the SmartAttach method so you can pass in a list of properties (in a typed manner). The new signature is shown in the following snippet:

C#
```
private static void SmartAttach<T>(this ObjectSet<T> os,
  T input, AttachState state,
  params Expression<Func<T, object>>[] modifiedProperties)
```

VB
```
Private Shared Sub SmartAttach(Of T)(os As ObjectSet(Of T),
  input As T, state As AttachState,
  ParamArray modifiedProperties As Expression(Of Func(Of T, Object))())
```

As you can see from the signature, SmartAttach now accepts an array of Expression objects. Each object specifies the property to be modified using the lambda expression. When the array isn't null or empty, the code iterates over it and passes the expression to the extension method in listing B.2. The following listing shows this code.

Listing B.3 Adding code to mark the selected properties

C#
```
if (id.Equals(Convert.ChangeType(value, idType)))
  os.AddObject(input);
else
{
  os.Attach(input);
  var entry = os.Context.ObjectStateManager.GetObjectStateEntry(input);
  if (state == AttachState.Modified)
  {
    if (modifiedProperties != null &&          ❶ If properties
      modifiedProperties.Any())                    are specified...
      foreach (var property in modifiedProperties)
        entry.SetModifiedProperty(property);   ❷ ...they're marked
    else                                           as modified
      entry.ChangeState(EntityState.Modified);
  }                                              Otherwise all
}                                                entities are
                                               ❸ modified
```

```
  else if (state == AttachState.Deleted)
    entry.ChangeState(EntityState.Deleted);
}
```

VB

```
If id.Equals(Convert.ChangeType(value, idType)) Then
  os.AddObject(input)
Else
  os.Attach(input)
  Dim entry = os.Context.ObjectStateManager.GetObjectStateEntry(input)
  If state = AttachState.Modified Then
    If modifiedProperties IsNot Nothing _
      AndAlso modifiedProperties.Any() Then
      For Each [property] As var In modifiedProperties
        entry.SetModifiedProperty([property])
      Next
    Else
      entry.ChangeState(EntityState.Modified)
    End If
  ElseIf state = AttachState.Deleted Then
    entry.ChangeState(EntityState.Deleted)
  End If
End If
```

❶ **If properties are specified...**

❷ **...they're marked as modified**

◁ **Otherwise all entities are**
❸ **modified**

The only part of this code that has been modified is that related to the modification of the entity. If some properties are passed ❶, they're marked as Modified ❷; otherwise, the classic ChangeState method is used ❸, and all properties are marked as Modified.

Now you can invoke SmartAttach method as in the following snippet:

C#

```
ctx.Orders.SmartAttach(order, AttachState.Modified,
  o => o.ShippingAddress
  o => o.ActualShippingDate);
```

VB

```
ctx.Orders.SmartAttach(order, AttachState.Modified,
  Function(o) o.ShippingAddress,
  Function(o) o.ActualShippingDate)
```

We have been using the SmartAttach extension method for the last couple of years and it works pretty well. It also helps in cutting down several lines of code. We strongly recommend you use it.

Now let's move on and see how you can inject some logic before and after persistence.

B.2   *Building an auditing system*

One of the questions that developers often ask on forums or at live events is: how can we build an auditing mechanism to know when an entity is persisted? In chapter 6, you saw a basic solution to this problem, but here we'll expand on that idea and make it more robust and reusable.

This will take several steps because it uses many features of Entity Framework:

1 Create an attribute to mark the auditable entities.

2 Customize the designer to let the user visually specify what entities must be audited.

3 Customize the template that generates entities to mark the auditable entities with an attribute.

4 Create a class that inherits from `ObjectContext` and that overrides `SaveChanges`, invoking a method to handle the entities to be persisted.

5 Modify the template that generates the context to let the generated context inherit from the context created in step 4.

There's a lot to do, but once we've finished, you'll understand how easy it is.

B.2.1 Creating an attribute to mark auditable entities

Most of the time, you don't want to audit all entities. For instance, you don't want to keep track of modifications made to the details, just to the orders. To do that, you can use an attribute to mark the entities you want audited.

> **NOTE** You may consider this to be plumbing code that should stay out of the entities. Although this is theoretically true, it's a little tweak that doesn't create any problems and simplifies things.

Creating the attribute class is simple, as you can see in the next snippet:

C#
```csharp
public class AuditableAttribute : Attribute { }
```

VB
```vb
Public Class AuditableAttribute
  Inherits Attribute
End Class
```

When you have the attribute, you just need to mark the auditable entities with it. Instead of creating partial classes or modifying the code generated by the template (remember that modifications will be lost when the code is regenerated), you can save this information in the EDM. But modifying the EDMX file is tedious, so why not create a designer extension?

B.2.2 Customizing the designer

Creating a designer extension is simple. Chapter 13 covered everything you need to know about this subject.

The only difference between that example and this one is that here the custom property applies to the entity and not to one of its key properties. This difference is expressed in the `EntityDesignerExtendedProperty` attribute of the designer extension's factory class, which you can see in the following listing.

Listing B.4   The factory for the custom property of the entity in the designer

C#
```
[Export(typeof(IEntityDesignerExtendedProperty))]
[EntityDesignerExtendedProperty(                                    Sets property
  EntityDesignerSelection.ConceptualModelEntityType)]               scope to entity
class AuditableFactory : IEntityDesignerExtendedProperty
{
  public object CreateProperty(XElement element,
    PropertyExtensionContext context)
  {
    return new AuditableValue(element, context);
  }
}
```

VB
```
<Export(GetType(IEntityDesignerExtendedProperty))> _
<EntityDesignerExtendedProperty(                                    Sets property
  EntityDesignerSelection.ConceptualModelEntityType)> _            scope to entity
Class AuditableFactory
  Implements IEntityDesignerExtendedProperty
  Public Function CreateProperty(element As XElement,
    context As PropertyExtensionContext) As Object
    Return New AuditableValue(element, context)
  End Function
End Class
```

The code is simple. It creates a custom property for each entity in the designer.

The AuditableValue class isn't complex either, as you see in the next listing.

Listing B.5   Class that manages the auditable custom annotation for the entity

C#
```
class AuditableValue
{
  internal static XName ELEMENTNAME =
    XName.Get("Auditable", "http://EFEX");

  private XElement _property;
  private PropertyExtensionContext _context;

  public AuditableValue(XElement property,              ❶ Stores CSDL
    PropertyExtensionContext context)                     EntityType
  {                                                        node
    _context = context;
    _property = property;
  }

  [DisplayName("Auditable")]
  [Description("Get or set the value indicating if the class is
  auditable")]
  [Category("Extensions")]
  [DefaultValue(false)]
  public bool Value
  {
    get
```

```
    {
      XElement child = _property.Element(ELEMENTNAME);
      return (child == null)
        ? false : bool.Parse(child.Value);
    }
    set
    {
      using (EntityDesignerChangeScope scope =
        _context. CreateChangeScope("Set Auditable"))
      {
        var element = _property.Element(ELEMENTNAME);
        if (element == null)
          _property.Add(
            new XElement(ELEMENTNAME, value));
        else
          element.SetValue(value);
        scope.Complete();
      }
    }
  }
}
```

② Reads custom annotation value

③ Writes custom annotation value

VB

```
Class AuditableValue
  Friend Shared ELEMENTNAME As XName = _
    XName.Get("Auditable", "http://EFEX")

  Private _property As XElement
  Private _context As PropertyExtensionContext

  Public Sub New(prop As XElement,
    context As PropertyExtensionContext)
    _context = context
    _property = prop
  End Sub

  <DisplayName("Auditable")> _
  <Description("Get or set the value indicating if the class is
➡ auditable")> _
  <Category("Extensions")> _
  <DefaultValue(False)> _
  Public Property Value() As Boolean
    Get
      Dim child As XElement =
        _property.Element(ELEMENTNAME)
      If child Is Nothing Then
        Return False
      Else
        Return Boolean.Parse(child.Value)
    End Get
    Set
      Using scope As EntityDesignerChangeScope =
        _context.CreateChangeScope("Set Auditable")
        Dim element = _property.Element(ELEMENTNAME)
        If element Is Nothing Then
          _property.Add(
```

① Stores CSDL EntityType node

② Reads custom annotation value

③ Writes custom annotation value

```
            New XElement(ELEMENTNAME, value))
        Else
          element.SetValue(value)
        End If
        scope.Complete()
      End Using
    End Set
  End Property
End Class
```

The `AuditableValue` class constructor receives and stores the `EntityType` node and the context from the factory ❶. The property getter retrieves the value of the custom annotation ❷ (if it exists), and the setter writes, in the scope of a transaction, the custom annotation ❸.

The result is that when you click an entity, the custom property is shown in the property window; and once you set it, the following XML code is written in the CSDL:

```
<EntityType Name="Order">
  ...
  <efex:Auditable>true</efex:Auditable>
</EntityType>
```

Now that you have the custom annotation in the CSDL, you need to modify the template that generates entities to let it read the custom annotation and generate the attribute.

B.2.3   *Customizing the template that generates entities*

Modifying the template that generates entities isn't hard. Before writing entity code, you need to check whether the custom annotation exists. If it exists and its value is true, you add the `Auditable` attribute. The following snippet shows the template code (C# only):

```
<#
var auditableElement = entity.MetadataProperties
  .FirstOrDefault(p => p.Name == "http://EFEX:Auditable");
if (auditableElement != null &&
  bool.Parse(((XElement)auditableElement.Value).Value)){
  #>
  [Auditable]
  <#
}#>
```

That's all you need to do. On the entity side, you're finished. Now you have to work on the context.

B.2.4   *Overriding the persistence process with a custom context*

Next, you need to create a class, `ExtendedObjectContext`, that inherits from `Object-Context` and that adds auditing behavior. This can be done by overriding the `SaveChanges` method and placing the code in there. You can then let the generated context inherit from `ExtendedObjectContext`, and you're done.

Not only does this design enable you to handle auditing, but it also lets you perform *any* operation before or after persistence. To perform any operation before or after persistence, you can create an IObjectPersistenceNotification interface that exposes two methods: one invoked before persistence and one invoked after. This interface is shown in the next snippet:

C#
```csharp
public interface IObjectPersistenceNotification
{
  void BeforePersistence(ObjectStateEntry entry, ObjectContext context);
  void AfterPersistence(ObjectStateEntry entry, ObjectContext context);
}
```

VB
```vb
Public Interface IObjectPersistenceNotification
 Sub BeforePersistence(entry As ObjectStateEntry, context As ObjectContext)
 Sub AfterPersistence(entry As ObjectStateEntry, context As ObjectContext)
End Interface
```

As you can see, the methods accept a single entry. This means they're invoked once for each entry in the Added, Modified, or Deleted state.

After that, you need to create the PersistenceNotification class, which implements the IObjectPersistenceNotification interface and writes to audit tables. This class is shown in the following listing.

Listing B.6   The class that writes auditing data

C#
```csharp
public class PersistenceNotification : IObjectPersistenceNotification
{
  string _username;
  public PersistenceNotification(string username)
  {
    _username = username;
  }

  public void BeforePersistence(ObjectStateEntry entry,
    ObjectContext context)
  {
  }

  public void AfterPersistence(ObjectStateEntry entry,
    ObjectContext context)
  {
    var type = entry.Entity.GetType();
    if (type.GetCustomAttributes(                        ❶ Searches
      typeof(AuditableAttribute), false).Any())            Auditable attribute
    {
      string properties = null;
      if (entry.State ==
    EntityState.Modified)                                ❷ Retrieves
        properties = String.Join(", ",                     modified
          entry.GetModifiedProperties());                  properties
```

```
      context.ExecuteStoreCommand(
        "Exec InsertAudit {0}, {1}, {2}, {3}, {4}",
        type.FullName, DateTime.Now, _username,
        entry.State.ToString().Substring(0,1),
        properties);
    }
  }
}
```

❸ **Persists modified properties information**

VB

```
Public Class PersistenceNotification
  Implements IObjectPersistenceNotification
  Private _username As String
  Public Sub New(username As String)
    _username = username
  End Sub

  Public Sub BeforePersistence(entry As ObjectStateEntry,
    context As ObjectContext)
  End Sub

  Public Sub AfterPersistence(entry As ObjectStateEntry,
    context As ObjectContext)
    Dim type = entry.Entity.GetType()
    If type.GetCustomAttributes(
      GetType(AuditableAttribute), False).Any() Then
      Dim properties As String = Nothing
      If entry.State = EntityState.Modified Then
        properties = String.Join(", ",
          entry.GetModifiedProperties())
      End If

      context.ExecuteStoreCommand(
        "Exec InsertAudit {0}, {1}, {2}, {3}, {4}",
        type.FullName, DateTime.Now, _username,
        entry.State.ToString().Substring(0, 1),
        properties)
    End If
  End Sub
End Class
```

❶ **Searches Auditable attribute**

❷ **Retrieves modified properties**

❸ **Persists modified properties information**

Again, the code is simple. The BeforePersistence method does nothing; the AfterPersistence method is where the auditing works. If the entity is marked with the Auditable attribute ❶, the code extracts the modified properties (only if the entity is in the Modified state) ❷ and invokes the auditing stored procedure, passing in the entity name, the timestamp, the username, the entity's state, and the modified properties ❸.

> **NOTE** As we said before, this technique can be used for other purposes than auditing. For example, you can enable logical deletes. You can mark an entity as Deleted in the code, but before persistence you mark it as Modified and set the logical cancellation flag to true. This way, the code is much easier to write (and read).

The next step is to create the `ExtendedObjectContext` class we mentioned at the beginning of this section. The first thing you have to create in the `ExtendedObject-Context` class are its constructors that accept an `IObjectPersistenceNotification` parameter. This way, whoever uses the context just needs to create an instance of the `PersistenceNotification` class, pass it to the context, and they're done.

The second thing you have to do to create the `ExtendedObjectContext` class is to override `SaveChanges` so it invokes the methods of the `IObjectPersistence-Notification` interface before and after the actual persistence of the objects. The code of the `ExtendedObjectContext` class is shown in the following listing.

Listing B.7 The new context class

C#
```
public class ExtendedObjectContext : ObjectContext
{
  protected IObjectPersistenceNotification PersistenceNotification
  {
    get;
    set;
  }

  public ExtendedObjectContext(string ConnectionString,
    string ContainerName, IObjectPersistenceNotification notification)
    : base(ConnectionString, ContainerName)
  {
    this.ContextOptions.LazyLoadingEnabled = true;
    PersistenceNotification = notification;
  }

  public ExtendedObjectContext(EntityConnection connection,
    string ContainerName, IObjectPersistenceNotification notification)
    : base(connection, ContainerName)
  {
    this.ContextOptions.LazyLoadingEnabled = true;
    PersistenceNotification = notification;
  }

  public override int SaveChanges(SaveOptions options)
  {
    DetectChanges();
    if (PersistenceNotification != null)
      ObjectStateManager.GetObjectStateEntries(
        EntityState.Added | EntityState.Modified |
        EntityState.Deleted)
        .ForEach(
          e => PersistenceNotification.
            BeforePersistence(e, this));

    var result = base.SaveChanges(SaveOptions.None);

    if (PersistenceNotification != null)
      ObjectStateManager.GetObjectStateEntries(
        EntityState.Added | EntityState.Modified |
        EntityState.Deleted)
```

1 Detects object modifications

2 Calls subscribers before persistence

3 Persists modifications

4 Calls subscribers after persistence

```
        .ForEach(
          e => PersistenceNotification.
            AfterPersistence(e, this));                    4

      if (options.HasFlag(SaveOptions.AcceptAllChangesAfterSave))
        AcceptAllChanges();                          Resets entity state
      return result;                              5  if required
    }
}
```

VB

```
Public Class ExtendedObjectContext
  Inherits ObjectContext
  Protected Property PersistenceNotification() _
    As IObjectPersistenceNotification

  Public Sub New(ConnectionString As String, ContainerName As String,
    notification As IObjectPersistenceNotification)
    MyBase.New(ConnectionString, ContainerName)
    ContextOptions.LazyLoadingEnabled = True
    PersistenceNotification = notification
  End Sub

  Public Sub New(connection As EntityConnection, ContainerName As String,
    notification As IObjectPersistenceNotification)
    MyBase.New(connection, ContainerName)
    ContextOptions.LazyLoadingEnabled = True
    PersistenceNotification = notification              Detects object  1
  End Sub                                             modifications

  Public Overrides Function SaveChanges(options As SaveOptions) As Integer
    DetectChanges()
    If PersistenceNotification IsNot Nothing Then
      ObjectStateManager.GetObjectStateEntries(              2  Calls
        EntityState.Added Or EntityState.Modified Or            subscribers
        EntityState.Deleted)                                   before
        .ForEach(Function(e)                                   persistence
          PersistenceNotification.
            BeforePersistence(e, Me))
    End If

    Dim result = MyBase.SaveChanges(SaveOptions.None)     3  Persists
                                                            modifications
    If PersistenceNotification IsNot Nothing Then
      ObjectStateManager.GetObjectStateEntries(              4  Calls
        EntityState.Added Or EntityState.Modified Or            subscribers
        EntityState.Deleted)                                   after
        .ForEach(Function(e)                                   persistence
          PersistenceNotification.
            AfterPersistence(e, Me))
    End If

    If options.HasFlag(SaveOptions.AcceptAllChangesAfterSave) Then
      AcceptAllChanges()
    End If                                          Resets entity state
    Return result                              5  if required
  End Function
End Class
```

Constructors are simple; they take as input an IObjectPersistenceNotification instance. What's interesting here is the SaveChanges method. First, you use the DetectChanges method to sync the state manager with the entities ❶. Then, you detect the entities that are ready to be persisted and invoke the BeforePersistence method for each of them ❷. You then invoke the base implementation of the SaveChanges method, passing in the SaveOptions.None parameter ❸. This ensures that the DetectChanges and AcceptAllChanges methods aren't invoked. Next, you call the AfterPersistence method for each persisted entity ❹. Finally, if the input parameter states that AcceptAllChanges must be invoked, you call that method ❺.

The last step needed to build the auditing system is to modify the context template to generate a class that inherits from ExtendedObjectContext and that calls the constructors correctly.

B.2.5 *Customizing the context template*

Modifying the context template is pretty simple. The first step is changing the name of the base class and adding its namespace to the using list, as follows (only the C# code is shown for brevity):

```
using OrderIT.Model.Notifications;

<#=Accessibility.ForType(container)#> partial class
  <#=code.Escape(container)#> : ExtendedObjectContext
```

When that's done, you need to modify the generation of the existing constructors to invoke the base constructors and pass a null value to the IObjectPersistence-Notification parameter. You also need to modify the template to create new constructors that accept the same parameters as the existing ones plus an IObjectPersistenceNotification parameter that's then passed to the base constructor. The following listing shows the template code for the default parameterless constructor, and the code for the constructor that accepts an IObjectPersistence-Notification parameter.

Listing B.8 Template code for generating correct constructors

```
public <#=code.Escape(container)#>()
  : base(ConnectionString, ContainerName, null)
{
  <#WriteLazyLoadingEnabled(container);#>
}
public <#=code.Escape(container)#>(
  IObjectPersistenceNotification notification)
  : base(ConnectionString, ContainerName, notification)
{
  <#WriteLazyLoadingEnabled(container);#>
}
```

For the sake of brevity, we haven't shown the code for all constructors. The preceding listing contains all you need to know to create them, and the complete code is available in the book's source code.

That's it for the auditing system. Now you just need to write code to use the classes you've created.

B.2.6   *Using the code*

Writing code that to use the classes we created in the previous section is simple. You just need to create an instance of the `PersistenceNotification` class and pass it to the context constructor, as you can see in this listing.

> **Listing B.9   The code that uses the new infrastructure**

C#
```
var c = new Customer() { ... };
var notification =
  new PersistenceNotification("username");          ❶ Creates
                                                        auditing class
using (var ctx = new OrderITEntities(notification))   Instantiates
{                                                       context with
  ctx.Companies.SmartAttach(c);                       ❷ auditing class
  ctx.SaveChanges();
}
```

VB
```
Dim c = New Customer() With { ... }
Dim notification =
  New PersistenceNotification("username")            ❶ Creates
                                                        auditing class
Using ctx = New OrderITEntities(notification)         Instantiates
  ctx.Companies.SmartAttach(c)                          context with
  ctx.SaveChanges()                                   ❷ auditing class
End Using
```

In this code, you create a `Customer` instance, create the auditing class ❶ and pass it to the context constructor ❷, attach the customer to the context (the ID is 0, so it will be in `Added` state), and persist it. Now, when you execute the code and open the `Audit` table in the database, you'll see a record saying that a new customer has been added.

Easy as pie, isn't it? The solution we presented in this section can be further extended. You could create a method that first creates a `PersistenceNotification` instance, then creates a context passing in the `PersistenceNotification` instance, and finally returns the context. This way, the code is even shorter than listing B.9 and you wouldn't even be aware of the auditing class.

That was a long trip, but the solution was worth the effort. Next, let's talk about two subjects related to querying: the `Include` method and full-text searches.

B.3   *Two tips for querying data*

In this section, we'll talk about two features that are important in many applications:

- The `Include` method, which enables eager loading in LINQ to Entities queries
- Full-text search capability, which enables fast searching in text columns

We'll improve the `Include` method, making it more usable, ;and we'll look at how to use the full-text search capabilities of the SQL Server database.

B.3.1 Improving the Include method

Let's face it: the `Include` method is as useful as it is badly designed. Its string-based nature makes it ugly, because using a string to specify which properties to load in the strong-typing age is horrible. We need to do something to improve this.

In section B.1.2, you saw how to pass a lambda expression to a method to specify what property should be marked `Modified`. Using the same idea, you can create an `Include` method that accepts a lambda expression to specify what navigation property you want loaded. Here's the code.

> **Listing B.10 The code that uses the new infrastructure**

C#
```csharp
public static ObjectQuery<T> Include<T, TProp>(
  this ObjectQuery<T> oq, Expression<Func<T, TProp>> expression)
{
  var body = expression.Body as MemberExpression;
  if (body == null)
    throw new ArgumentException("Parameter expression must be a
      memberexpression");

  return oq.Include(body.Member.Name);
}
```

VB
```vbnet
<System.Runtime.CompilerServices.Extension> _
Public Shared Function Include(Of T, TProp)(oq As ObjectQuery(Of T),
  expression As Expression(Of Func(Of T, TProp))) As ObjectQuery(Of T)
  Dim body = TryCast(expression.Body, MemberExpression)
  If body Is Nothing Then
    Throw New ArgumentException("Parameter expression must be a
      memberexpression")
  End If

  Return oq.Include(body.Member.Name)
End Function
```

The `Include` method shown in the previous code accepts a lambda expression, then takes the property name as a string, and invokes the real `Include` method of the `ObjectQuery` class.

Now you can write `Include` as in this snippet:

C#
```csharp
ctx.Orders.Include(o => o.OrderDetails);
```

VB
```vbnet
ctx.Orders.Include(Function(o) o.OrderDetails)
```

This is much better than passing the `OrderDetails` string. If you refactor your code, having a lambda expression helps a lot.

What's bad about this expression is that you can load only first-level properties. For instance, you can eager-load the details and the customer related to the order, but you can't go deeper, loading products related to the details. To do that, you need to create another extension method that applies to navigation properties and that lets you define a deeper hierarchy.

Writing such a method isn't that difficult, but it requires a deep knowledge of expression trees, which is one of the toughest subjects in the entire .NET Framework. The preceding code gives you the fundamentals, and you can use it as a base for writing a more clever method.

Now that you know how to improve the `Include` method, we can move on to full-text searches.

B.3.2 *Enabling full text search in Entity Framework*

Entity Framework doesn't provide any native way to integrate itself with the full-text search capabilities of SQL Server. This means you have to let stored procedures perform full-text queries, and then use these stored procedures from the code. Entity Framework doesn't even know that inside the stored procedure there's a full-text search query. Easy as pie!

Alternatively, you can also use a defining query that takes data from a table-valued function (as you did in chapter 11). But although this gives you more flexibility in the querying phase, it makes the code and the EDM harder to write and maintain. Stored procedures are generally much easier to use.

Now, let's look at how to handle database data types that aren't natively understood by Entity Framework.

B.4   *Working with special database types*

Entity Framework doesn't understand all the data types that some databases use. Try this experiment. Create a table with an `int` and a `Geometry` column, and import it into the designer. The designer will shows an entity with just *one* column: the `int` column. If you open the EDMX as XML, you'll see the following warning in the SSDL before the entity description:

```
<!--Errors Found During Generation:
   warning 6005: The data type 'geometry' is not supported; the column 'geom'
     in table 'OrderIT.dbo.GeometrySample' was excluded.
-->
```

This happens because Entity Framework can't translate the `Geometry` database type into a .NET type it understands. So the question is, how do you handle this type of data if Entity Framework itself doesn't know how to handle it? There are two easy solutions.

The first solution is to create a view where the `Geometry` data type is converted to a `varbinary(max)` column. You can then import the view instead of the table, and Entity Framework will map the binary column to an array of bytes that it knows how to handle. Here's the query for the view:

```
SELECT StateID, StateName, CONVERT([varbinary](MAX), geom, 0) SpatialData
FROM dbo.state
```

The second option is useful when you can't modify the database to create the view. In this case, you create a *defining query* using the same SQL code you would write for the view. You then use the designer to create a class that maps to the defining query, and you're done. The defining query is declared as follows:

```
<EntitySet Name="GeometrySample"
  EntityType="OrderITModel.Store.GeometrySample">
  <DefiningQuery>
    SELECT Id, CONVERT([varbinary](MAX), SpatialData, 0) SpatialData
    FROM dbo.GeometrySample
  </DefiningQuery>
</EntitySet>
```

In both cases, the entity (`GeometrySample`) that maps to the database is the one shown in figure B.1.

Querying with a view or a defining query is like querying a table, so nothing changes there. When it comes to persistence, some extra work is required because you have to use stored procedures or EDM embedded commands. It's not too difficult; you saw how to do this in chapter 10.

Figure B.1   The class that maps to the table. It exposes the `Id` as `Int32` and `SpatialData` as an array of bytes.

What's tedious is that instead of working with a property of `SqlGeometry` type (the `SqlGeometry` type is defined in the `Microsoft.SqlServer.Types` assembly), you have to work with the `byte[]` type. Let's improve things by reusing what you've learned throughout the book.

What you can do is extend the `GeometrySample` class (the one mapped to the table) through a partial class. In the partial class, you can define a property, say `Typed-SpatialData`, of `SqlGeometry` type. In its getter, you can take the `SpatialData` property, convert it to a `SqlGeometry` instance, and return it. In the setter, you go the opposite way: you create an array of bytes from the input value. Here's the code.

Listing B.11   The partial class that defines the `TypedSpatialData` property

C#
```
public partial class GeometrySample
{
  SqlGeometry _geometry = null;

  public SqlGeometry TypedSpatialData
  {
    get
    {
      if (_geometry == null)
      {
        _geometry = new SqlGeometry();
```

```
            using (var stream =
        MemoryStream(SpatialData))
              using (var rdr = new BinaryReader(stream))
                _geometry.Read(rdr);
        }

        return _geometry;
      }
      set
      {
        _geometry = value;
        using (var ms = new MemoryStream())
        {
          using (var bw = new BinaryWriter(ms))
            value.Write(bw);
          SpatialData = ms.ToArray();
        }
      }
    }
  }
}
```

❶ Converts array of bytes to SqlGeometry

❷ Converts SqlGeometry to array of bytes

VB

```
Private _geometry As SqlGeometry = Nothing

Public Property TypedSpatialData() As SqlGeometry
  Get
    If _geometry Is Nothing Then
      _geometry = New SqlGeometry()
      Using stream = New MemoryStream(SpatialData)
        Using rdr = New BinaryReader(stream)
          _geometry.Read(rdr)
        End Using
      End Using
    End If

    Return _geometry
  End Get
  Set
    _geometry = value
    Using ms = New MemoryStream()
      Using bw = New BinaryWriter(ms)
        value.Write(bw)
      End Using
      SpatialData = ms.ToArray()
    End Using
  End Set
End Property
```

❶ Converts array of bytes to SqlGeometry

❷ Converts SqlGeometry to array of bytes

To perform the conversion, you have to use streams. To convert an array of byes into a SqlGeometry type, you have to fill a memory stream with the bytes and then pass the stream to a binary reader, which is then used by SqlGeometry to populate itself ❶.

To convert a SqlGeometry instance to an array of bytes, you do the opposite. You create a stream and pass it to a writer that the SqlGeometry instance writes to. You then set the SpatialData property with the array of bytes of the stream ❷.

When you use the `GeometrySample` class, you can use the `TypedSpatialData` property without any problems, because it automatically synchronizes with the `Spatial-Data` property:

C#
```
var entity = ctx.GeometrySamples.First();
var geometries = entity.TypedSpatialData.STNumGeometries();
```

VB
```
Dim entity = ctx.GeometrySamples.First()
Dim geometries = entity.TypedSpatialData.STNumGeometries()
```

Always remember that because the `TypedSpatialData` isn't defined in the EDM, you can't use it in LINQ to Entities or EntitySQL queries.

We have used this technique for the `Geometry` data type, but you can use the same approach for any type you have. It's a pretty cool pattern, isn't it?

index